World Development Report 1985

Published for The World Bank
Oxford University Press

Oxford University Press
NEW YORK OXFORD LONDON GLASGOW
TORONTO MELBOURNE WELLINGTON HONG KONG
TOKYO KUALA LUMPUR SINGAPORE JAKARTA
DELHI BOMBAY CALCUTTA MADRAS KARACHI
NAIROBI DAR ES SALAAM CAPE TOWN

First printing July 1985

ISBN 0-19-520481-6 cloth bound
ISBN 0-19-520482-4 paperback
ISSN 0163-5085

The Library of Congress has cataloged this serial publication as follows:
World development report. 1978–
[New York] Oxford University Press.
v. 27 cm. annual.
Published for The World Bank.

1. Underdeveloped areas—Periodicals. 2. Economic development—
Periodicals I. International Bank for Reconstruction and Development.

HC59.7.W659   330.9'172'4   78–67086

Foreword

This is the eighth *World Development Report*. It focuses on the contribution that international capital makes to economic development—a topical issue in view of the international concern with external debt over the past several years. While this Report pays close attention to the events of the recent past, it also places the use of foreign capital in a broader and longer-term perspective.

Using such a perspective, the Report shows how countries at different stages of development have used external finance productively; how the institutional and policy environment affects the volume and composition of financial flows to developing countries; and how the international community has dealt with financial crises.

The financial links between industrial and developing countries have become as integral to the world economy as trade has hitherto been. This growing interdependence is a development of profound significance. Just as governments recognize that their trading policies have international consequences, so they are starting to see that the same is true of their financial policies. Their fiscal and monetary policies, rules on foreign borrowing and lending, and attitudes toward foreign investment are not only components of domestic policy, they also determine the efficiency with which world savings are used.

Nothing has better illustrated this new interdependence than the experience of the recent past. Expanded financial flows helped developing countries to sustain high levels of investment and to smooth structural adjustments. When difficulties arose, individual governments, central banks, international agencies, and commercial bankers have contributed to the task of stabilizing the world's financial system. Their approach has been pragmatic, devising remedies according to each country's difficulties. Their efforts have been complemented by the very painful adjustment measures implemented by the debtor countries themselves. More has been achieved than many observers thought possible when the recession was at its trough.

We are now in a period of transition—an essential and intermediate phase before returning to sustained growth and normal relationships between debtors and creditors. A successful transition will require continuing efforts by governments, international agencies, and commercial banks. All participants in the rescheduling exercises of the past three years will need continued patience and imagination to smooth out the hump of repayments in the next five years, when about two-thirds of the debt of developing countries falls due, and to place debt on a sounder longer-term footing.

Stable and noninflationary growth in industrial economies is an essential component of a successful transition. Policies that produce a softening of interest rates and an easing of protectionism would facilitate the developing countries' resumption of growth and the restoration of their creditworthiness, without which they cannot get the extra capital that they need from abroad to promote their development.

How much they obtain will depend largely on their success in restoring creditworthiness, which in turn hinges on the policies they pursue. A recurring theme of this Report is that the countries in debt-servicing difficulties are not necessarily those with the largest debts or those that have suffered the biggest external shocks. A country's ability to borrow and service its foreign debt is largely determined by the quality and flexibility of its policies, its ability to appraise and implement sound investment projects, and by good debt management. Foreign finance is a complement to, and not a substitute for, domestic efforts.

The same basic policy prescriptions apply to every country. However, this Report highlights the particular constraints on countries in sub-Saharan Africa. For the foreseeable future, most African countries will have to continue to rely on concessional aid for the bulk of their external finance. Their needs are great and increasing every year. Linked to policy reforms, additional aid could have a marked impact on halting the decline in living standards, particularly in the poorest countries.

This Report concludes that the developing countries will have a continuing need for external finance. It demonstrates that many of the policies required to attract external finance and promote economic growth are either being implemented or planned already. No government—either in an industrial or a developing country—is being asked to act against its own long-term interests. If each follows the route outlined, all can and will benefit from a more prosperous and stable world. That is the cautiously optimistic conclusion of this Report.

Like its predecessors, this year's *World Development Report* is a study by the staff of The World Bank, and the judgments in it do not necessarily reflect the view of our Board of Directors or the governments they represent.

A. W. Clausen
President
The World Bank

May 24, 1985

This Report was prepared by a team led by Francis Colaço and comprising Alexander Fleming, James Hanson, Chandra Hardy, Keith Jay, John Johnson, Andrew Steer, Sweder van Wijnbergen, and K. Tanju Yürükoğlu, assisted by Oliver Adler, Nadeem Burney, Sandra Gain, Shahrzad Gohari, Tina Jacobsen, Tani Maher, Hossein Ali Partoazam, Kesavan Pushpangadan, and James Rosen. The Economic Analysis and Projections Department, under the direction of Jean Baneth, supplied data for the Report. Enzo Grilli and Peter Miovic coordinated the work of the Economic Analysis and Projections Department on projections. Ramesh Chander, assisted by David Cieslikowski, supervised the preparation of the World Development Indicators; Shaida Badiee was responsible for systems design. The authors would also like to thank staff from various parts of the Bank, as well as other contributors and reviewers. Thanks are also due to the production staff, especially Joyce Eisen, who designed the cover, Pensri Kimpitak, and Carol Cole Rosen. Special thanks go to the support staff, headed by Rhoda Blade-Charest and including Banjonglak Duangrat, Jaunianne Fawkes, Pamela Holmes, Carlina Jones, and Patricia Smith. The work was carried out under the general direction of Anne O. Krueger and Costas Michalopoulos, with Rupert Pennant-Rea as principal editor.

Contents

Boxes

Definitions and data notes

Capital flows

• *Components of capital flows.* International movements of capital may come from either official or private sources. Official sources are (a) governments and governmental agencies (also called *bilateral lenders*) and (b) international organizations (called *multilateral lenders*). Private sources comprise (a) commercial suppliers and manufacturers, which provide export credits for the purchase of their goods, (b) commercial banks, which provide export credits or cash loans, (c) other private investors, who invest in foreign enterprises in which they seek a lasting interest (direct investment) or purchase stocks or bonds issued by foreign companies or governments (portfolio investment), and (d) charitable organizations, which provide financial aid, goods, and services as grants.

• *Concessional flows.* International lending on terms more favorable to the borrower than those obtainable through normal market transactions. In this text, concessional flows are defined as those having a grant element of 25 percent or more.

• *Direct foreign investment.* Investment made to acquire a lasting interest in an enterprise operating in an economy other than that of the investor, the investor's purpose being to have an effective voice in the management of the enterprise.

• *Equity financing.* Investment that confers whole or partial ownership in an enterprise and entitles the investor to share in the profits from its operation. International equity financing flows may be included in either foreign direct or portfolio investment.

• *Export credits.* Finance provided by lenders in a given country for exports of specific goods or services. Conventionally, one distinguishes between private and official export credits. *Private export credits* consist of (a) supplier credits, which are extended by the exporting company to the foreign buyer and (b) buyer credits, which are extended by commercial banks in the exporting country on behalf of the exporters. *Official export credits* are extended by an agency of the exporting country's government.

• *Grant.* A current transfer of capital, goods, or services to a foreign country that results in no current or future obligation to make a like transfer from the recipient country to the donor.

• *Grant element.* The extent to which a loan can be considered a grant is determined by its *grant element*—the difference between the original face value of the loan and the discounted present value of debt service, as a percentage of the original face value. Thus a true grant has a grant element of 100 percent. A discount rate of 10 percent is conventionally used in the calculation. The grant element is used to compare the concessionality of assistance provided under differing terms and conditions.

• *Net flows of lending.* Loan disbursements less amortization of principal.

• *Nonconcessional flows.* Lending on or near terms prevailing in private financial markets.

• *Official development assistance.* Loans and grants made on concessional financial terms from official sources, with the objective of promoting economic development and welfare. It includes the value of technical cooperation and assistance.

• *Private nonguaranteed debt.* Private nonguaranteed loans are external obligations of private debtors that are not guaranteed for repayment by a public entity of the debtor country.

• *Public and publicly guaranteed debt.* Public loans are external obligations of public debtors, including national governments, their agencies, and autonomous public bodies. Publicly guaranteed loans are external obligations of private debtors that are guaranteed for repayment by a public entity of the debtor country.

Trade and finance

• *Balance of payments.* A systematic record of the economic transactions between a nation's residents and nonresidents during a given period, usually one calendar or fiscal year. It covers the flows of real resources (including factor services, such as the services of labor and capital) across the boundaries of the domestic economy, changes in foreign assets and liabilities resulting from economic transactions, and transfer payments to and from the rest of the world. Balance of payments accounts comprise two broad categories: the current account, which measures merchandise trade, factor and nonfactor service income, and transfer receipts and payments, and the capital account, which measures changes in domestic and foreign capital assets and liabilities.

• *Current account balance.* A representation of the transactions that add to or subtract from an economy's stock of financial items. It is given as the sum of net exports of goods and nonfactor services, net factor income, and net transfers. Official capital grants are excluded.

• *Debt reorganization.* Any change in the payment arrangements associated with an existing stock of debt mutually agreed upon by the borrower and the lender. In *debt refinancing,* new loans are negotiated to meet debt service obligations on existing debt. In *debt rescheduling,* arrangements are agreed upon for postponing payments of principal or interest or otherwise changing the terms of repayment or of interest charges.

• *Debt service.* The sum of interest payments and repayments of principal on external debt. The *debt service ratio* is total debt service divided by exports of goods and services.

• *External debt.* Debt that is owed to nonresidents. World Bank data, unless otherwise specified, cover external debt that has an original or extended maturity of one year or more and that is repayable in foreign currency, goods, or services. Transactions with the International Monetary Fund are excluded (with the exception of Trust Fund loans). A distinction in medium- and long-term debt is made between *private nonguaranteed debt* and *public and publicly guaranteed debt.*

• *Interest rates.* The *nominal rate* on a given loan is the percentage stipulated in the loan contract and may be expressed as a *fixed rate,* that is, an interest rate that is constant over the duration of the loan, or as a *variable, or floating, rate,* an interest rate that is recalculated at fixed intervals (such as every six months). Variable interest rates consist of a base rate (such as the six-month London interbank offered rate) plus a margin, or spread. *Market, or world, rates* reflect the terms of borrowing at any given time in private capital markets; market rates

are usually differentiated as *long-term rates*—the current rates payable on financial instruments, such as bonds, having maturities of more than one year—and *short-term rates*—those on such instruments maturing in one year or less. The *real interest rate* is the nominal rate adjusted to account for changes in the price level.

• *Intermediation.* The process whereby a private or official financial agency accepts funds from investors and onlends them to borrowers.

• *Maturity.* For a loan, the date at which the final repayment of principal is to be made. *Short-term loans* are those with original maturity of a year or less; *medium- and long-term loans* are those with original or extended maturity of more than one year.

• *Reserves.* A country's international reserves comprise its holdings of monetary gold and special drawing rights; its reserve position in the International Monetary Fund; its holdings of foreign exchange under the control of monetary authorities; its use of IMF credit; and its existing claims on nonresidents that are available to the central authorities. Reserves are also expressed in terms of the number of months of imports of goods and services they could pay for.

• *Resource balance.* The difference between exports of goods and nonfactor services and imports of goods and nonfactor services.

• *Spread.* The difference between a reference rate used to price loans and the rate at which funds are lent to final borrowers. A widely used reference rate is the London interbank offered rate, or LIBOR—the rate at which banks participating in the London market are prepared to lend funds to the most creditworthy banks. Another is the U.S. prime rate.

• *Terms of trade.* A measure of the relative level of export prices compared with import prices. Calculated as the ratio of a country's index of export unit value to the import unit value, this indicator shows changes over a base year in the level of export prices as a percentage of import prices.

• *Trade balance.* The difference between merchandise exports f.o.b. and merchandise imports f.o.b.

National accounts

• *Gross domestic product.* The total final output of goods and services produced by an economy—that is, by residents and nonresidents, regardless of the allocation to domestic and foreign claims. It is calculated without making deductions for depreciation.

• *Gross national product.* The total domestic and foreign output claimed by residents. It comprises gross domestic product adjusted by net factor income from abroad. Factor income comprises receipts that residents receive from abroad for factor services (labor, investment, and interest) less similar payments made to nonresidents abroad. It is calculated without making deductions for depreciation.

• *Investment.* The sum of gross domestic fixed investment and the change in stocks (or inventories). Gross domestic investment covers all outlays of the private and public sectors for additions to the fixed assets of the economy, plus the value of change in stocks (or inventories).

• *Savings.* Gross domestic savings is defined as the difference between GDP and total consumption, and gross national savings are obtained by adding net factor income from abroad and net current transfers from abroad to gross domestic savings.

Country groupings

• *Developing countries* are divided into: *low-income economies,* with 1983 gross national product (GNP) per person of less than $400; and *middle-income economies,* with 1983 GNP per person of $400 or more. Middle-income countries are also divided into *oil exporters* and *oil importers,* identified below.

• *Middle-income oil exporters* comprise Algeria, Angola, Cameroon, People's Republic of the Congo, Ecuador, Arab Republic of Egypt, Gabon, Indonesia, Islamic Republic of Iran, Iraq, Malaysia, Mexico, Nigeria, Peru, Syrian Arab Republic, Trinidad and Tobago, Tunisia, and Venezuela.

• *Middle-income oil importers* comprise all other middle-income developing countries not classified as oil exporters. A subset, *major exporters of manufactures,* comprises Argentina, Brazil, Greece, Hong Kong, Israel, Republic of Korea, Philippines, Portugal, Singapore, South Africa, Thailand, and Yugoslavia.

• *High-income oil exporters* (not included in developing countries) comprise Bahrain, Brunei, Kuwait, Libya, Oman, Qatar, Saudi Arabia, and United Arab Emirates.

• *Industrial market economies* are the members of the Organisation of Economic Co-operation and Development, apart from Greece, Portugal, and

Turkey, which are included among the middle-income developing economies. This group is commonly referred to in the text as industrial economies or industrial countries.

• *East European nonmarket economies* include the following countries: Albania, Bulgaria, Czechoslovakia, German Democratic Republic, Hungary, Poland, Romania, and USSR. This group is sometimes referred to as *nonmarket economies.*

• *Sub-Saharan Africa* comprises all thirty-nine developing African countries south of the Sahara, excluding South Africa, as given in *Toward Sustained Development in Sub-Saharan Africa: A Joint Program of Action* (World Bank 1984).

• *Middle East and North Africa* includes Afghanistan, Algeria, Arab Republic of Egypt, Iran, Iraq, Israel, Jordan, Kuwait, Lebanon, Libya, Morocco, Oman, Saudi Arabia, Syrian Arab Republic, Tunisia, Turkey, Yemen Arab Republic, People's Democratic Republic of Yemen, and United Arab Emirates.

• *East Asia* comprises all low- and middle-income countries of East and Southeast Asia and the Pacific, east of, and including, Burma, China, and Mongolia.

• *South Asia* includes Bangladesh, Bhutan, India, Nepal, Pakistan, and Sri Lanka.

• *Latin America and the Caribbean* comprises all American and Caribbean countries south of the United States.

• *Major borrowers* are countries with disbursed and outstanding debt estimated at more than $15 billion at the end of 1983 and comprise Argentina, Brazil, Chile, Egypt, India, Indonesia, Israel, Republic of Korea, Mexico, Turkey, Venezuela, and Yugoslavia.

Acronyms and initials

BIS Bank for International Settlements.
DAC The Development Assistance Committee of the Organisation for Economic Co-operation and Development comprises Australia, Austria, Belgium, Canada, Denmark, Finland, France, Federal Republic of Germany, Italy, Japan, Netherlands, New Zealand, Norway, Sweden, Switzerland, United Kingdom, United States, and Commission of the European Communities.
EC The European Communities comprise Belgium, Denmark, France, Federal Republic of Germany, Greece, Ireland, Italy, Luxembourg, Netherlands, and United Kingdom.
FAO Food and Agriculture Organization.

GATT General Agreement on Tariffs and Trade.

GDI Gross domestic investment.

GDP Gross domestic product.

GDS Gross domestic savings.

GNP Gross national product.

GNS Gross national savings.

IBRD International Bank for Reconstruction and Development.

IDA International Development Association.

IFC International Finance Corporation.

ILO International Labour Office.

IMF International Monetary Fund.

LIBOR London interbank offered rate.

NGO Nongovernmental organization.

ODA Official development assistance.

OECD The Organisation for Economic Co-operation and Development members are Australia, Austria, Belgium, Canada, Denmark, Finland, France, Federal Republic of Germany, Greece, Iceland, Ireland, Italy, Japan, Luxembourg, Netherlands, New Zealand, Norway, Portugal, Spain, Sweden, Switzerland, Turkey, United Kingdom, and United States.

OPEC The Organization of Petroleum Exporting Countries comprises Algeria, Ecuador, Gabon, Indonesia, Islamic Republic of Iran, Iraq, Kuwait, Libya, Nigeria, Qatar, Saudi Arabia, United Arab Emirates, and Venezuela.

SDR Special drawing right.

UN United Nations.

UNCTAD United Nations Conference on Trade and Development.

UNDP United Nations Development Programme.

Unesco United Nations Educational, Scientific, and Cultural Organization.

UNICEF United Nations Children's Fund.

Data notes

Billion is 1,000 million.

Tons are metric tons (t), equal to 1,000 kilograms (kg) or 2,204.6 pounds.

Growth rates are in real terms unless otherwise stated. Growth rates for spans of years in tables cover the period from the beginning of the base year to the end of the last year given.

Dollars are current U.S. dollars unless otherwise specified.

The symbol . . in tables indicates data are not available.

All tables and figures are based on World Bank data unless otherwise specified. Throughout this volume, unless otherwise noted, World Bank data on debt cover medium- and long-term public and publicly guaranteed plus private nonguaranteed debt outstanding and disbursed. Data on short-term debt have been estimated by World Bank staff from the published semiannual series of the Bank for International Settlements on the maturity distributions of international lending; adjustments to the BIS data have been made to exclude known amounts that have been rolled over into long-term debt during reschedulings. The World Development Indicators at the back of this volume use the country groupings given above but include only countries with a population of 1 million or more.

Data from secondary sources are not always available through 1983. The numbers in this *World Development Report* shown for historical data may differ from those shown in previous Reports because of continuous updating as better data become available, and because of recompilation of certain data for a ninety-country sample. The recompilation was necessary to permit greater flexibility in regrouping countries for the purpose of making projections.

Part I Overview and Historical Perspective

1 Overview

The economic turbulence of the past few years has subsided. The recovery of industrial economies in 1983–84, policy adjustments by many developing countries, and flexibility by commercial banks in dealing with debt-servicing difficulties have all helped to calm the atmosphere of crisis. This does not mean, however, that the world economy has regained its momentum of the 1960s or that development is again making rapid progress. Growth has slowed in most developing countries that experienced debt-servicing difficulties and in many of those that did not. Average per capita real incomes in most of Africa are no higher than they were in 1970; in much of Latin America, they are back to the levels of the mid-1970s. Dozens of countries have lost a decade or more of development.

The experience of the past few years has raised many questions about the role of international capital in economic development. Only a few years ago, there was general agreement that the more advanced developing countries could and should borrow more commercial capital from abroad. That consensus has been broken. Some people believe that the case by case approach to addressing debt difficulties is creating a sustainable balance of growth and debt servicing that will in time encourage more lending, including bank lending. Others believe that new approaches are needed if developing countries are to service their debt and resume economic growth. As with so many changes in conventional wisdom, both new and old arguments are often stylized and exaggerated. It is important not to lose sight of the fundamentals of international finance.

Capital has long flowed from richer to poorer countries. It has done so because it is relatively scarcer in economies that are at earlier stages of development, and the expected rates of return tend to be correspondingly higher. What is at issue is the nature of capital flows, their terms, and their uses. These questions were relevant in the nineteenth century and remain so today.

This Report offers a broad and long-term perspective on the role of international capital in economic development. It emphasizes that international flows of capital can promote global economic efficiency and can allow deficit countries to strike the right balance between reducing their deficits and financing them. The availability of international capital also involves risks, however: first, that it may delay the policy reforms required for adjustment; and second, that countries may borrow too much if they misjudge the way in which external economic conditions are going to evolve.

Both benefits and costs can be illustrated by recent experience. On the benefits side, most developing countries have made substantial economic progress over the past twenty years. Their GDP growth averaged 6.0 percent a year in 1960–80. The life expectancy of their people rose from an average of forty-two years in 1960 to fifty-nine years in 1982, while infant mortality was halved and the primary school enrollment rate rose from 50 to 94 percent. These advances reflected principally the efforts of developing countries themselves. But there is considerable evidence that capital flows, often accompanied by technical know-how, have played a part.

Foreign capital has also helped individual countries to cushion shocks—either internal ones such as harvest failures or external ones such as big changes in commodity prices or recessions in industrial economies. External finance can act as a shock absorber, allowing countries to adjust their spending gradually and reallocate their resources for a new environment. In the 1970s many developing countries were able, in the first instance, to pay for more expensive oil by borrowing more. Those countries that accompanied borrowing with policy reforms restored rapid growth and avoided debt-servicing difficulties. Other countries used borrowing to avoid the policy actions required for adjustment. Many of them ran into debt-servicing problems and needed to take even more drastic and costly adjustments later.

This contrast emphasizes that foreign borrowing is not a painless or riskless alternative to adjustment. The accumulation of debt makes a country more susceptible to international financial fluctuations, as the swing from negative real interest rates to unprecedentedly high positive rates has made all too plain. The need for rapid adjustment increased. Borrowers and lenders often fail to take full account of the institutional, social, and political rigidities that restrict a country's capacity to adjust.

The historical context

The ten years 1973–82 saw a big increase in the foreign finance going to developing countries. As a result, both the gross and net debt of developing countries increased sharply. Between 1970 and 1984 the outstanding medium- and long-term debt of developing countries expanded almost tenfold, to $686 billion (see Figure 1.1), despite the decline

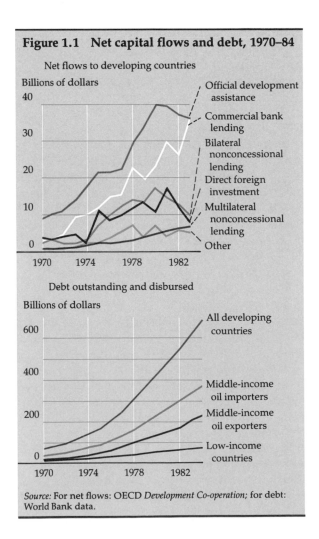

Figure 1.1 Net capital flows and debt, 1970–84

Net flows to developing countries

Source: For net flows: OECD *Development Co-operation;* for debt: World Bank data.

in capital flows since 1981. The most striking feature of this growth was the surge in lending by commercial banks. Their share of total new flows to developing countries increased from 15 percent in 1970 to 36 percent in 1983.

On every measure, the debt-servicing abilities of developing countries deteriorated, particularly after 1974, as their debt increased (see Figure 1.2). The ratio of debt to GNP more than doubled, from 14 percent in 1970 to almost 34 percent in 1984. The ratio of debt service to exports rose from 14.7 percent in 1970 to a peak of 20.5 percent in 1982, declining to 19.7 percent in 1984. Interest payments on debt increased from 0.5 percent of GNP in 1970 to 2.8 percent of GNP in 1984 and accounted for more than half of all debt service payments in that year. These averages conceal wide regional and country differences.

Dramatic though the recent growth of foreign borrowing has been, it is not unprecedented. As Chapter 2 makes clear:

• The volume of international capital flows has often been larger in relative terms than in the 1970s. Between 1870 and 1913, Great Britain invested an average of 5 percent of its GNP abroad, rising to almost 10 percent just before World War I. For France and Germany, the figure was 2 to 3 percent of GNP. As a proportion of the recipient country's GNP, capital inflows were also often larger in earlier periods. Inflows to Canada, for example, averaged 7.5 percent of its GNP between 1870 and 1910 and accounted for 30 to 50 percent of its domestic investment. During the investment booms in Argentina and Australia, foreign capital was roughly half of all gross domestic investment. By contrast, net capital inflows to all developing countries averaged 2 to 3 percent of their GNP between 1960 and 1973, while financing 10 to 12 percent of their gross investment; since then, net capital inflows have been between 3 and 6 percent of their GNP and have financed 10 to 20 percent of their gross investment.

• The structure of financial flows to developing countries has changed several times. In the years before World War I, private bond markets were the main source of capital. In the 1930s, following the Great Depression and widespread defaults by borrowers in both industrial and developing countries, commercial lending to developing countries virtually stopped. It was replaced after World War II by an expansion of official flows, mainly on concessional terms; the largest part was bilateral aid, but some was channeled through the new multilateral agencies such as the World Bank and later the

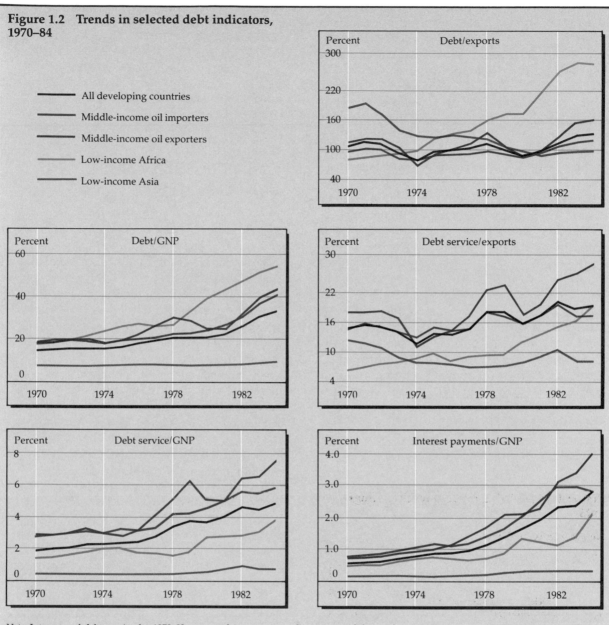

Figure 1.2 Trends in selected debt indicators, 1970–84

All developing countries
Middle-income oil importers
Middle-income oil exporters
Low-income Africa
Low-income Asia

Note: Interest and debt service for 1970–83 are actual (not contractual) service paid during the period. Interest and debt service for 1984 are projections of contractual obligations due based on commitments received through the end of 1983 and take into account reschedulings through the end of 1984.

Source: World Bank data.

International Development Association. Along with private direct investment and supplier credits, official finance provided the bulk of external capital for developing countries until the late 1960s, when commercial banks started to play a prominent role.

• Debt-servicing difficulties have been common and usually have been caused by a combination of poor domestic policies and a deteriorating world environment. The fifty years before World War I saw several debt repudiations, including the Peruvian and Turkish crises in the 1870s and the Argentinian and Brazilian crises of the 1880s and 1890s. Defaults, however, were not confined to developing countries: some borrowers in the United States, for example, defaulted on their debts in these years. In the 1930s defaults were widespread, starting with Germany in 1932. Argentina

3

was the only country in Latin America to service its debt on the terms contracted during these years. Except in the 1930s, countries were able to resume borrowing (albeit on more expensive terms) once they had reformed their policies.

By historical standards, debt-servicing difficulties in the 1960s and 1970s do not seem unduly serious. In 1955–70 seven developing countries (Argentina, Brazil, Chile, Ghana, Indonesia, Peru, and Turkey) were involved in seventeen debt reschedulings. There were also some debt reschedulings for low-income countries, including India, but these were designed to provide additional finance when official lenders could not increase new lending. In the 1970s, despite the sharp fall in their terms of trade in 1973–74, an average of three developing countries a year rescheduled their debts.

It is only in the 1980s that debt problems have multiplied. The number of reschedulings rose to thirteen in 1981 and to thirty-one (involving twenty-one countries) in 1983 and a similar number in 1984 (see Figure 1.3). Countries have restructured their repayment schedules, sometimes for several years at a time, in the context of agreed upon programs of policy reform. Low-income countries, however, particularly in Africa, have yet to benefit from the kind of multiyear

Table 1.1 Composition and terms of capital flows to developing countries in selected periods

Component and term	1960–65	1975–80	1980–83
Direct foreign investment as a percentage of net capital flows	19.8	15.5	12.9
Floating interest rate loans as a percentage of public debt	. .	26.5	37.9
Average years maturity on new public debt commitments	18.0	15.0	14.0

Source: For investment: OECD *Development Co-operation*; for terms: World Bank data.

rescheduling that some major debtors have negotiated.

The similarities with the past should not obscure some differences as well. Developing countries have become more vulnerable to debt-servicing difficulties for three related reasons. First, loans have far outstripped equity finance. Second, the proportion of debt at floating interest rates has risen dramatically, so borrowers are hit directly when interest rates rise. Third, maturities have shortened considerably, in large part because of the declining share of official flows and debt—and by even more than Table 1.1 suggests, if account is taken of the way in which higher inflation and interest rates have front-loaded repayments.

Another major and disturbing difference today is that many of the countries with debt-servicing difficulties are in the low-income group. This is partly because their aid receipts have been erratic. The dollar value of receipts of net official development assistance (ODA) by all developing countries in 1975 was two and a half times the level in 1970, stagnated between 1975 and 1977, almost doubled between 1977 and 1980, and has declined since then. In real terms the pattern is similar, but the fluctuations are less marked. This pattern is explained by variations in bilateral ODA, particularly flows from OPEC countries, since multilateral ODA increased steadily between 1973 and 1980 and has declined only slightly since then. Many low-income and lower-middle-income countries borrowed commercially and accumulated large amounts of debt. In earlier periods, the poorest countries had obtained virtually all their foreign capital in the form of direct investment, especially for export-earning activities, or official flows on concessional terms.

The historical perspective reveals certain broad characteristics of debt-servicing problems. The financial links between industrial and developing

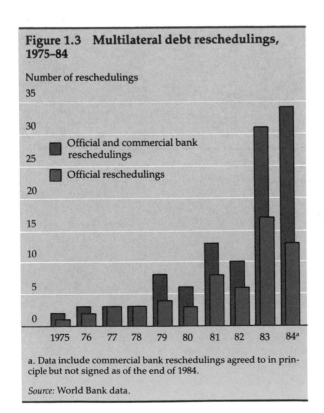

Figure 1.3 Multilateral debt reschedulings, 1975–84

Number of reschedulings

■ Official and commercial bank reschedulings

■ Official reschedulings

a. Data include commercial bank reschedulings agreed to in principle but not signed as of the end of 1984.

Source: World Bank data.

countries depend on three variables: (a) the policies of industrial countries; (b) the policies of developing countries; and (c) the financial mechanisms through which capital flows to developing countries. No analysis of international finance is complete unless it takes account of all of these variables. In doing so, it reveals a much wider range of country experience and why some countries have borrowed and encountered debt-servicing difficulties, while others have not. It also highlights the fact that the economic difficulties of the early 1980s were the product of individual economic decisions that seemed rational when they were made.

Policies of industrial countries

As Chapter 3 makes clear, the fiscal, monetary, and trade policies of industrial countries largely determine the external climate for developing countries. The connection is not simply that rapid growth in the industrial world pulls up the growth of developing economies, though it helps to do so. Nor is it just that prolonged recession and increased protectionism in the industrial countries cause difficulties for developing countries. Increasingly, the links are financial, through changes in the availability of finance and movements in interest rates and exchange rates.

This became clear in 1979–80, for example, when U.S. monetary policy switched from targeting interest rates to targeting monetary aggregates. Interest rates became more volatile. Latin America, with a higher proportion of floating rate debt, was more affected by this change than either East Asia or Africa. The result was abrupt increases in debt service payments. Developing countries find it difficult to make sudden and large changes in debt service payments. The strains felt by many developing countries were increased in the early 1980s by the recession in the industrial countries, which reduced export volumes and weakened commodity prices at a time when real interest rates were rising (see Figure 1.4 and Chapter 3, Figure 3.6). It is hardly surprising that the combination made it difficult for many countries to service their debts.

The recovery in the industrial countries has helped to ease some of the liquidity pressures on developing countries. World trade grew by about 8.5 percent in 1984, and world output increased by 4.2 percent. In developing countries GNP grew by 4.1 percent, and the volume of their exports increased by an estimated 8.9 percent, compared with less than 4 percent a year in 1981 and 1982. Real interest rates have softened a little but remain

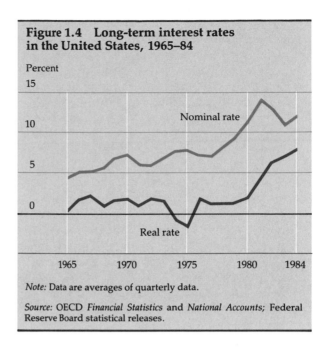

Figure 1.4 Long-term interest rates in the United States, 1965–84

Percent

Note: Data are averages of quarterly data.

Source: OECD *Financial Statistics* and *National Accounts*; Federal Reserve Board statistical releases.

at historically high levels. The world recovery in 1983–84 did not lead, however, to the normal cyclical rise in commodity prices in dollar terms. This was in part due to the U.S. dollar's further appreciation, as well as to technological and other factors affecting the demand for commodities. Thus net primary commodity exporters (including Brazil) benefited less than countries that are net commodity importers (such as the Republic of Korea). In addition, developing countries continue to be affected by protectionist measures in the industrial economies.

For the future, the effects that industrial countries have on developing countries will depend primarily on what happens in two areas of policy: real interest rates and protectionism. Interest rate developments are explored in detail in Chapter 3. The analysis there concludes that large budget deficits in industrial countries remain an obstacle to lower interest rates. As a proportion of national income, combined budget deficits of all levels of government rose substantially between 1979 and 1984 in nine of the principal industrial countries except the Federal Republic of Germany and Japan. In 1984 the combined deficits of these industrial economies, adjusted for inflation, were 2.3 percent of their national income. The U.S. deficit has grown the fastest over the past five years. Credible measures are needed in these countries to reduce public sector reliance on domestic and foreign savings; this could lower interest rates and foster growth. The United States has recently announced steps that, when implemented, would permit significant reduction in its fiscal deficits in the next few years. Avoiding a recessionary impact of such a policy change will require careful coordination with monetary policy in the United States and with monetary and fiscal policies in the other large industrial countries.

The second issue of vital concern to developing countries is protectionism. To service their foreign debts, the biggest debtors will need to run large trade surpluses in the next few years. Yet many import restrictions—on steel, sugar, and beef, for example—have affected primarily major debtors including Argentina, Brazil, Korea, and Mexico. Other restrictions, such as the Multifibre Arrangement, affect a broader range of countries. The harder the big debtors find it to service their debt, the greater the strains on the world's banking system.

When developing countries cannot earn the foreign exchange to expand their imports, exporters in the industrial countries are also damaged. To take one example, this was an important factor in explaining why U.S. exports of manufactures to major debtors fell by 40 percent between 1980–81 and 1983–84. Such harm is widespread, since industrial economies run a surplus on trade in manufactured goods with developing countries. And protectionism acts as a brake on the adjustment and growth that the industrial countries themselves so badly need.

Over the longer term, protectionist barriers in the industrial world can have a profound effect on development strategy. They suggest to governments in developing countries that a strategy based on export growth is highly risky, and thus encourage a return to the inward-looking policies of earlier years. Evidence is abundant that such policies are bad for growth and employment in the developing countries and also reduce the scope for industrial countries to promote improvements in productivity in their own economies.

Policies of developing countries

The past dozen years have underlined, as discussed in Chapter 4, the crucial role of domestic policies in determining the performance of developing countries—particularly in the use they make of foreign finance. Foreign finance can promote growth through higher investment and technology transfers. It can allow countries to adjust gradually to new circumstances in the world economy. But it can also be misused, so that countries end up with more debt but no corresponding increase in their ability to service it.

In the 1970s it was right for countries to borrow when real interest rates were low or negative—but only if they followed appropriate policies and invested in economically justified projects. Caution in defining borrowing limits was required. It was wrong to assume that low interest rates would continue, and it is always expensive to reverse investment decisions. These mistakes are quickly exposed when world conditions deteriorate, as they did in the early 1980s.

Developing countries suffered in 1979–84 from a combination of more expensive oil, historically high real interest rates, prolonged recession in industrial economies, and more trade barriers. Despite this, as many as 100 countries have continued to service their foreign debt without interruption. Some have experienced only small shocks (for example, some countries that are oil exporters) or have benefited from workers' remittances (for example, certain Asian and Middle Eastern countries). Some had borrowed only a little or mainly on concessional terms in the 1970s (for example, China, Colombia, and India). And some who borrowed undertook economic policy reforms that facilitated debt servicing (for example, Indonesia and Korea).

Countries that ran into debt-servicing difficulties, however, were not necessarily those that had suffered the biggest shocks. They were countries that had borrowed and failed to adjust or had not tackled the new problems with sufficient urgency. Among these were the low-income countries of Africa, in which development is a long-term process constrained by weak institutional structures, a shortage of skills, and often (as in the past ten years) natural disasters as well. These countries have traditionally used concessional capital from abroad to finance the bulk of their investment. In the 1970s they were faced with higher import bills. Many African countries that had commodity booms were able to borrow on commercial terms when interest rates were low. They used this foreign finance partly for consumption and also for investment in large public projects, many of which contributed little to economic growth and to increased exports needed to service the debt. Capital inflows enabled some countries to postpone policy reforms. Debt-servicing difficulties could have been expected and did occur. The net result has been a further setback to their economic development.

The second group of countries with debt difficulties includes many countries in Latin America and some major debtors. The reasons for their financing problems are more complex, but three common features are (a) fiscal and monetary policies that were too expansionary to achieve a sustainable external balance; (b) overvalued exchange rates that prevented exports from competing on world markets and encouraged capital flight; and (c) increased domestic savings efforts but investment increases that were even larger. Some countries, such as Chile and Uruguay, attempted comprehensive economic reforms, but parts of their policy package were defective and the timing of measures taken was inappropriate. Other countries borrowed heavily and undertook some policy changes (for example, Brazil, Ivory Coast, and the Philippines), but they underestimated the length and depth of the recession and the large rise in interest rates in the early 1980s. Many of these countries are now in the process of reforming their policies, with results that are thus far encouraging.

The diverse experiences of developing countries emphasize certain basic lessons for policy. One can be summarized as the need for flexibility. A characteristic of foreign finance is that it requires both borrowers and lenders to take account of uncertainty. The best way of doing so is to be able to respond flexibly to changes in the external environment. Countries as varied as India, Indonesia, Korea, and Turkey have adapted their economic policies to changed circumstances. The most critical changes in the short term are the ability to reduce fiscal deficits and adjust real exchange rates and real interest rates. When for political or other reasons countries cannot adjust their policies quickly, they should be conservative in resorting to foreign borrowing.

A second lesson is that the policies required to make best use of external finance are essentially the same as those that make best use of domestic resources. A country must earn a return on its investments which is higher than the cost of resources used. In the case of foreign finance, however, a country also has to generate enough foreign exchange to cover interest payments, plus remittances of dividends and profits. This depends on three groups of policies:

• Key economic prices must be aligned with opportunity costs. These encourage activities in which the country has a comparative advantage and increase the flexibility of productive structures. Subsidies, when used, should be carefully targeted, for example, to the poorest segments of society. When oil prices rose in 1973–74, many countries—including both oil importers and oil exporters—delayed raising their domestic energy prices, thus increasing pressures on their balance of payments; many other countries avoided these pressures by raising energy prices earlier. Furthermore, investment decisions are influenced by the appropriateness of pricing structures, including interest rates. Governments need to evaluate carefully their own investment programs and to create a framework of incentives to ensure that private investors allocate resources in the most efficient way. Countries such as Brazil, Ecuador, Ivory Coast, Nigeria, Peru, and Turkey combined negative real interest rates with overambitious or inefficient investment programs. By contrast, Colombia and Malaysia had more appropriate interest rate levels and investment incentives.

• Exchange rates and trade policies also play an important role. In the 1970s and early 1980s many countries—notably Argentina, Chile, Mexico, Nigeria, the Philippines, Turkey, and Uruguay—allowed their exchange rates to become overvalued and their trade policies to become distorted. This biased production toward the domestic market, stimulated imports, and provoked capital flight. Comprehensive trade and price reforms by Turkey, following difficulties it experienced in the late 1970s, produced good results.

• Efforts to raise domestic savings should be strengthened despite the availability of external capital. The correct role of foreign finance is to supplement domestic savings; it must not substitute for savings. The danger of poor savings performance was well understood by many governments. In fact, many developing countries managed a creditable performance on savings in the 1970s, with two-thirds of a sample of forty-four developing countries increasing their domestic savings ratios. They included such diverse economies as Cameroon, India, Korea, Malawi, Malaysia, and Tunisia. In other cases, including Morocco, Nigeria, and Portugal, inadequate domestic savings efforts contributed to overborrowing. Improvements in savings performance require measures by both public and private sectors. In the public sector, tax measures, realistic pricing of public goods and services, and cuts in spending are required to reduce deficits and increase public savings. If higher public spending is financed by borrowing more from abroad rather than by increasing fiscal revenues, cumulative strains are put on budgets (since governments have to pay debt interest) and the balance of payments. Mexico's experience in 1981–82, when the budget deficit more than doubled as a proportion of GNP to meet increased public consumption and was financed partly by external capital, sowed the seeds for its debt crisis in 1982. As for private savings, domestic interest rates that are kept low curtail savings, contribute to capital flight, lead to credit rationing, and increase the pressures for borrowing abroad. Government policies of adjusting exchange rates by less than the rate of inflation and of subsidizing foreign borrowing artificially lower the domestic currency cost of borrowing, thereby inducing capital inflows. This was the case in Argentina, Chile, and Uruguay.

Managing foreign borrowing and debt

Policies determining the level of domestic savings and investment also determine the need for foreign borrowing, so the management of capital flows should be an integral part of macroeconomic management. Certain aspects of debt management deserve special attention, and these are discussed in Chapter 5.

The first issue is whether and how governments should regulate foreign borrowing and lending by the private and public enterprise sectors. The answer depends fundamentally on a government's macroeconomic and incentive policies; in general, less government intervention is needed the more that prices, interest rates, and exchange rates reflect opportunity costs. Although some governments have constructed elaborate controls over capital inflows and outflows, experience strongly suggests that these are no substitute for sound macroeconomic policies. Nonetheless, some procedures for regulating capital movements—prior approval for borrowing, minimum maturity or deposit requirements, or withholding taxes—have sometimes proved a helpful complement to fiscal, monetary, and trade policies.

The second broad area of concern is the composition of capital flows and debt. This involves decisions about (a) the terms of foreign borrowing—interest, maturity, and cash flow profiles; (b) the currencies in which liabilities are denominated; (c) the balance between fixed rate and floating rate instruments; (d) ways of sharing risk between lenders and borrowers, including the balance between debt and equity; and (e) the level and composition of a country's reserves. It is not possible to formulate precise rules for external debt management that will apply to all countries. The experience of the past few years, however, argues for prudence by developing countries in deciding

on both the volume of foreign borrowing and its composition, and in maintaining enough reserves to give a country time to adjust to domestic or international pressures without unduly jeopardizing its economic growth. If the capacity to borrow abroad is not stretched to its limits, it will provide a cushion in times of particular need.

Many countries fail to manage capital flows effectively because of inadequate data, a lack of technical expertise about financing options, and an absence of institutional arrangements to integrate debt management with macroeconomic decision-making. In all these areas, institutional development is an important priority.

Financial mechanisms

Developing countries account for only a small proportion of international flows of capital, so their influence on the international financial system is limited. The system itself changes in response to three main factors. The first is the external environment. For example, changes in regulations, financial innovation, and high and volatile inflation in the 1970s led investors to lend on floating rate rather than fixed rate terms. The second factor is the demand for the services of financial markets and institutions, which is heavily affected by imbalances in global payments. For example, OPEC countries in the 1970s and early 1980s initially preferred to keep their surpluses in highly liquid form, so commercial bank deposits and lending increased. More recently, the large current account deficits run by the United States, which have their counterpart in surpluses in Japan and other industrial countries, have led to a much larger role for international asset markets. The third factor is the preferences of financial institutions. For example, in the 1970s commercial banks chose to lend abroad to satisfy their own portfolio and profitability objectives (see Chapter 8).

In the short term, developing countries have to make the most of the opportunities presented by the international financial system. From a longer-term point of view the critical policy questions are: how can the stability of external capital flows be enhanced and lending by banks be restored? what arrangements can be made for future capital flows, including enough concessional assistance to meet the needs of low-income countries?

The answers lie in five areas:

• *Longer maturities.* Developing countries can borrow long term, though seldom directly from the market; they rely almost exclusively on the intermediation of the World Bank and regional development banks. These institutions will remain the primary sources of longer-maturity capital for developing countries in the next few years. They need to have the capability to provide more financing to developing countries, since the prospects for expansion of private financing are not good. Financial innovation to expand the range of maturities available to developing countries would help them to manage their debt and reduce refinancing risks.

• *Hedging.* The nature of the financing instruments used in the 1970s meant that developing countries assumed the risks of adverse developments in the world economy. One of the central functions of a financial system—effective risk sharing—was not efficiently served. Instruments for hedging risks already exist in many financial markets: it would be desirable to make greater use of them in lending to developing countries.

• *Commercial risk sharing.* Whereas conventional bank loans do not involve sharing of commercial risks, foreign direct and portfolio investment does (see Chapter 9). The introduction of equity-based instruments in lending to developing countries is another area in which progress could be made.

• *Secondary markets.* As most commercial lending to developing countries in the 1970s was done by banks, it tended to increase risks by concentrating assets in a single group of creditors. The expansion of secondary markets for some kinds of liabilities of developing countries could widen the range of lenders and so increase the stability of lending. Such a development, although desirable, must be a phased process. In the long run, secondary markets could also provide an extra indicator of country creditworthiness, making it easier for lenders to diversify their risks.

• *Aid volume and effectiveness.* Low-income countries need a considerable quantity of aid, more than is available at present. They also need to use aid efficiently (see Chapter 7). Donors can improve their own efficiency by focusing their aid primarily on development objectives and by coordinating their efforts within programs agreed upon with the recipient.

Prospects and options

How much and what kind of foreign finance will developing countries need in the years ahead? That question can be answered only by analyzing the global outlook for growth, trade, interest rates, and so on. Traditionally, *World Development Report*s present alternative scenarios for the future. Such

scenarios, it must be emphasized, are not predictions; their outcome depends on the policies adopted in industrial and developing countries. Nor do they allow for exogenous shocks to the world economy. Last year's Report contained scenarios to 1995. The discussion in this year's Report, in Chapter 10, is in the context of last year's scenarios, but pays greater attention to the next five years.

The next five years are a period of transition. During that time, about two-thirds of the debt of the developing countries will have to be rolled over or amortized. The constructive and collaborative actions taken by debtors, creditors, and international agencies in recent years need to be continued. Their objective is to accelerate the return to creditworthiness of countries that are pursuing sound economic policies, but have sizable short- to medium-term debt-servicing requirements. They need in particular to be extended to countries—several middle-income exporters of primary commodities and many low-income African countries—in which debt-servicing difficulties and development problems are intertwined. Consideration needs to be given to the extent to which multiyear debt restructurings for official credits and other arrangements might be considered on a case by case basis, as part of the overall financing package supporting stabilization and adjustment, particularly in low-income sub-Saharan African countries committed to strong adjustment efforts. Beyond that, much will depend on whether industrial and developing countries successfully pursue policies for structural adjustment.

Over the past few years, many developing countries have made progress in dealing with their financial difficulties. The economic situation, however, continues to remain fragile in many countries. Growth of GDP in 1980–85 is currently estimated at slightly more than one-half that of 1973–80. Exports have grown at close to 6 percent a year, but the pressure of continued high interest payments has meant that imports could grow at only a little more than 1 percent a year. Substantial trade surpluses run by many developing countries have been used to meet greatly increased interest payments. The high level of real interest rates is thus one of the critical variables whose course will influence outcomes in the next five years. Developing countries need to keep the rate of growth of export earnings above the rate of interest—even if the current account net of interest payments remains in balance—if the principal debt ratios are to return to more sustainable levels. This will depend not only on their own policies, but also on the rate of growth of industrial economies and whether protectionist measures are rolled back.

Two simulations—a Low and a High—have been prepared for the period 1985–90 and are discussed in detail in Chapter 10. Both simulations assume that developing countries continue with their present course of policies, which in many cases (as in some low-income Asian economies) imply substantial policy reforms and adjustment efforts. Policy improvements are in three principal areas—key economic prices, exchange rates and trade policies, and domestic savings. These contribute to efficiency in the use of resources and to export competitiveness. As for industrial economies, the difference between the simulations is that the Low one assumes a set of policies that fail to address current problems and as a result lead to further problems, whereas the High one embodies policy changes that result in greater progress in adjustment. The Low simulation makes three basic assumptions: no progress in reducing budgetary deficits and in improving the monetary-fiscal balance so that real interest rates remain high; a failure to tackle labor market rigidities so that unemployment stays high and real labor costs continue to increase; and a substantial increase in protection. By contrast, the High simulation assumes reduced fiscal deficits compared with the Low simulation, thus permitting improvements in the monetary-fiscal balance and a resultant lowering of real interest rates; reductions in labor market rigidities such that unemployment declines and the increase in real labor costs slows down; and an increasing success in adjustment that results in a steady decline in protection.

For developing countries, the implications of these assumptions are far reaching. In the High simulation their output grows at a healthy 5.5 percent a year (or 3.7 percent a year per capita), and there is a major improvement in all the major debt indicators. The Low simulation produces a different and more problematic outcome: growth slows to 4.1 percent a year (or 2.3 percent a year per capita). If there is a sizable reduction in economic growth, however, the impact on debt servicing is even more striking. A combination of high real interest rates and protection makes debt servicing considerably more difficult. The main debt indicators deteriorate; for a large number of countries debt service ratios reach high levels. The volume of concessional aid declines as a result of slower growth in industrial economies, and "involuntary" lending, in the face of deteriorating cre-

ditworthiness, continues to be required.

The two simulations outline a continuing bleak outlook for many low-income African countries. In the High simulation, their average per capita income stagnates at present reduced levels; in the Low simulation, there is yet another period of falling per capita incomes. Special efforts are therefore needed to deal with these prospects. Additional external assistance is not, by itself, the solution to Africa's problems. It must be based on major changes in African programs and policies. Nonetheless, such reforms are unlikely to be sustained without additional external assistance, over and above that projected in the High simulation.

The challenge for the next five years is to ensure that the world reaches the High case. How it could do so will be implicit in many of the chapters in this Report and is made explicit in Chapter 10. It is quite clear that foreign capital will play a significant part in meeting the challenge of faster growth; it is also possible that its legacy from the past ten years will act to slow growth, unless creditors, debtors, and the international community continue to ease the pressure of debt.

In contributing to the resumption of growth and the restoration of creditworthiness of the developing countries, the World Bank is addressing investment and institutional development issues crucial to sustaining longer-term progress. Against the background of growing strength in domestic institutions in borrowing countries and much greater resource scarcity than in the 1960s and 1970s, Bank assistance is helping governments to strike an appropriate balance between additional investments and the maintenance of existing capacities, to achieve greater selectivity and efficiency in public sector investments, and to develop a framework of policy and institutional arrangements conducive to the growth of activities in the private sector.

The financial resources provided directly by the Bank make important contributions to restored growth and momentum in development, but they can never be more than a rather small proportion of the total resources required. The Bank is, therefore, strengthening its catalytic functions, particularly with respect to aid coordination in sub-Saharan Africa, cofinancing with commercial banks and export credit agencies, and the promotion of private investment. In addition to its direct lending, the tasks of complementing and—to the extent possible—exercising a constructive influence on capital flows from other sources are also important factors in shaping the future role of the Bank.

In dealing with all these issues, the Report starts with a historical perspective on the role of international finance in economic development (Chapter 2). It then assesses the policies of industrial economies from the perspective of developing countries (Chapter 3). The importance of developing countries' policies in deriving benefits from foreign capital is taken up in Chapter 4; and issues in managing capital flows are covered in Chapter 5. The Report then discusses the main mechanisms through which foreign capital flows to developing countries. Chapter 6 gives an overview of the international financial system and its relations with developing countries. Chapter 7 examines issues in official development finance. Chapter 8 outlines the evolving relationship between the developing countries and international capital markets; and Chapter 9 examines the possibilities for a bigger role for direct and portfolio investment in developing countries. The Report ends by looking at prospects for the future and the policies needed to promote faster growth.

2 A historical perspective

The history of international finance is full of examples of its productive contribution to economic development. It has also produced occasional financial crises and, more frequently, debt-servicing difficulties for a variety of countries. This chapter starts by examining the role of international capital since the late nineteenth century. The object is to highlight lessons that help to analyze the experience of the 1970s and 1980s, rather than to provide a detailed history. The chapter then pays closer attention to the postwar period and particularly to the past two decades.

The pre-1945 period

The years before 1945 an be conveniently divided into two parts, 1870–1914 and the interwar period, each of which had its own distinctive features.

From 1870 to 1914

This period was dominated by the London financial market as a source of capital for other countries. Europe's industrial revolution produced a strong demand for food and raw materials, which could be satisfied only by investment in many other parts of the world. Expansion of railroads and other infrastructure was externally financed, and foreign investors were repaid later from the resulting export earnings. Some of the countries where these investments were made—such as Argentina, Australia, Canada, and the United States—were able to buy imports of manufactures from the more industrialized countries in Europe. Then, as now, this growing economic interdependence was facilitated by international finance.

What was unique about the years 1870–1914 was the scale of international finance. Over the period as a whole, Great Britain invested 5 percent of its GNP abroad, reaching a peak of 10 percent just before World War I. Its net receipts of investment income from abroad were in the range of 5 to 8 percent of GNP, implying that new foreign invest-

ment did not keep up fully with inflows of interest and dividends. As a proportion of British savings, capital outflows ranged between 25 and 40 percent. France and Germany also invested heavily abroad, though not as much as Britain. By the late nineteenth century, French and German gross capital exports were averaging 2 to 3 percent of GNP.

The nature of the capital flows varied considerably in 1870–1914. The largest single group included the market-oriented investments, largely undertaken by Britain, in the resource-rich countries of North America, Latin America, and Oceania. In 1914, these accounted for 70 percent of Britain's total foreign investments and more than half of all gross foreign assets. A second group, accounting for a quarter of all foreign investment, involved investments in Russia and other Eastern European countries and in Scandinavia; France and Germany were the principal investors. A third group covered the primarily politically motivated investments in China, Egypt, India, Turkey, and some African colonies. These three groups received capital at different times, so new regions were financially linked with the world economy only gradually.

For the large debtors in the nineteenth century, capital inflows had only a small weight in their economies. For most decades, capital inflows to the United States were around 1 percent of its GNP and never exceeded 6 percent of its domestic investment. For the smaller debtors, however, capital inflows as a proportion of GNP were higher than they are for many developing countries today. Capital inflows to Canada averaged 7.5 percent of its GNP, accounting for between 30 percent and 50 percent of annual investment from 1870 to 1910. Ratios were similar in Australia and the Scandinavian countries. The most striking case was that of Argentina, where capital inflows annually ranged between 12 and 15 percent of GNP and financed about 40 percent of its total investment during the first two decades of the twentieth century. By contrast, net capital inflows to all developing countries averaged 2 to 3 percent of GDP between 1960 and 1973. Since 1973 they have not exceeded 6 percent of GDP and have financed between 12 and 20 percent of gross investment.

Differences do not stop with geography and the relative volume of external finance. In the years 1870–1914:

• Almost all lending came from private sources, in the form of stock and bond issues.

• Lending terms were long: maturities of up to ninety-nine years were not uncommon.

• Nearly two-thirds of foreign capital went to finance investment in railroads and utilities.

• A large proportion of the flows went to then relatively high-income countries; North America, Latin America, and Australia received more than half of the total. The international capital market in the nineteenth century did not, and was not designed to, provide poorer countries with access to capital. For example, even India—though favored in British capital markets—received very little investment. Capital was drawn to investments that yielded higher returns than were available in the domestic economy. Thus it operated selectively, to the advantage of high-income borrowers; although there were some politically motivated investments with marginal economic returns, they were not significant in terms of the volume of flows.

These differences compared with the recent past were also accompanied by some close parallels: periodic debt-servicing difficulties and an early version of what is now known as conditionality. Lenders and borrowers operated against a backdrop of large cyclical swings in international economic activity compounded by rebellions and wars. Sometimes borrowers failed to make their payments. They fell into two broad categories. First, countries such as Argentina and Brazil, where foreign capital was important in integrating their economies into an expanding world economy, experienced cyclical problems related to abrupt declines in foreign exchange earnings. Foreign loans were used, along with domestic policy changes, to alleviate liquidity crises until exports recovered. In some cases, foreign creditors got involved in domestic policy issues. In the Brazilian crisis of the 1890s, for example, the government pledged all its customs receipts and agreed to a moratorium on new (internal and external) debt issues.

The second kind of debt crisis was the result of stagnant domestic revenues and expanding fiscal deficits. Countries in this group included Egypt, Peru, and Turkey in the 1870s, and Greece in the 1890s. Capital inflows could not continually finance deficits and became increasingly expensive. These countries' export growth slowed considerably before they defaulted. In these cases, creditors intervened not only at the moment of default but sometimes much sooner. In the Turkish crisis, for example, a foreign loan (the first in a series) was issued in London with the encouragement of the British government. A condition of the loan was that commissioners should be sent to oversee the expenditure of the proceeds.

Notwithstanding all these difficulties, the record up to 1914 shows that investment abroad was profitable for investors in Great Britain and continental Europe. It earned returns that have been calculated to be between 1.6 and 3.9 percentage points higher than returns on domestic investment. Within that average, although there were a number of defaults on foreign loans, the most profitable investments were in railroads in the United States. Although they were untypically lucrative, they helped to foster a general climate in favor of foreign investment. Another influence working in the same direction was that loans were used to purchase British exports, so financial and real flows went together. When borrowers got into difficulty, they found that the London capital market was not an unyielding taskmaster.

The interwar period

Between the two world wars, the pattern of international investment shifted dramatically. The United States emerged not merely as a net creditor country, but as the main source of new capital flows. In certain respects, it played a role similar to Britain's earlier one. It financed many long-term bond issues: of the 1,700 foreign dollar issues offered in the United States in the 1920s, almost half had average maturities of twenty years. Some 4 percent had average maturities of forty years, and 1 percent of more than forty years. At least forty-three governments borrowed during the 1920s, and none defaulted. During the peak period of flotations, from 1924 to 1928, the interest rate differential in favor of new foreign issues was between 1.7 and 1.9 percentage points. The United States also financed a large amount of direct investment, mainly in Canada and Latin America. Its direct investment rose by almost $4 billion during the 1920s, two-thirds of it going to Western Hemisphere countries.

However, the 1920s were different from earlier decades in several vital respects. First, the volume of government lending and borrowing was far greater. Borrowings by governments accounted for nearly half of the foreign dollar issues in the United States. No less important, World War I had left a legacy of official debt. The United States was owed almost all the debts made between the Allies, totaling more than $16 billion. In addition, the Allies had heavy reparation claims against Germany.

The second difference was that foreign capital was no longer part of an integrated pattern of population and trade. By the mid-1920s, commodity prices were falling. Some countries borrowed to finance a growing stockpile of unsold commodities; one example was Brazil in the 1920s, to finance coffee stocks. In the mid-1920s, there was an increase of 75 percent in commodity stocks, financed indirectly by foreign capital.

The third difference with the pre–World War I period was the trade policy followed by the major global creditor. British free trade had served to guarantee debtors a market for their products. The United States was more protectionist and its external trade was a relatively small portion of its GDP. Following the recession of 1920–21, it raised tariffs back to where they had been before some liberalization in 1913. If debtors could not generate export surpluses, they needed capital inflows to service past debts. The process inevitably produced ever increasing debt.

The Great Depression of 1929–32 turned a potential threat into a disaster. Between 1929 and 1932, output in industrial countries fell 17 percent and the volume of world trade by more than a quarter. The international monetary system disintegrated. There was no lender of last resort to provide liquidity, a function that the United Kingdom had previously undertaken. And the liberal trading system of the prewar years virtually disappeared. Most countries raised tariffs and applied quotas and exchange controls. Lack of finance contributed to the decline of international trade, and vice versa.

Several industrial countries defaulted on their war debts and reparation. Germany, facing declining production, exports, and prices, first obtained a one-year moratorium in 1931 and then defaulted on all its external debts in 1932. Developing countries were also failing to service their debt. Bolivia defaulted on its dollar obligations in 1931 and was soon followed by most other Latin American countries. By the end of 1933 Argentina was the only

Latin American country that maintained full servicing on its external debts. Effectively, access by developing countries to commercial markets ceased until the 1960s.

Although the deterioration in the general economic climate was the proximate cause of defaults in the interwar period, it was not the only one. Other contributions came from excessive borrowing, particularly between 1925 and 1929; poor risk assessment on the part of lenders; panic; and an abrupt cessation of lending just before a default. In general, the financial penalties for defaulting were rather small in the 1930s. Defaulting governments had established a precedent, and the number of private defaulters was too large for sanctions to be enforced. However, the cost in domestic adjustment could be severe. Between 1929 and 1938, the maximum peak-to-trough declines in output for major Latin American countries ranged from 7 percent for Brazil to 26 percent for Peru.

Some historical lessons

Three broad lessons emerge from the experience of international finance between 1870 and 1939.

• Finance seeks out profit: in general, the highest returns were from investments that directly or indirectly exploited natural resources. Technological innovation—such as the expansion of railroads in the nineteenth century—was also a major absorber of capital, and international capital in particular. Repayments were more likely when investments led to increased exports (as was generally the case before 1914) than when the ability to export was constrained by protectionist measures in capital-exporting countries (as was the case in the interwar period). Political risk was minimized by investing in colonies or in countries that were integrated with capital exporters through trade and finance.

• The volume and composition of finance changes to reflect shifts in the world economy. Before World War I, private capital markets were dominant; in the interwar period, public borrowing and lending assumed a much larger role. Financial innovation is also influential: for example, the nineteenth century saw the establishment of mutual funds, which separated ownership from the management of portfolios and spread risk more widely.

• Reschedulings and defaults were the result of inadequate policy responses by borrowers to declining terms of trade. Defaults were typically settled in negotiations with bondholder committees on terms that seldom preserved more than a small fraction of the original capital value. Negotiators explicitly assessed the borrowers' ability to undertake policy reforms; this "capacity to repay" formed the basis for determining how much debt should be forgiven. In most cases, existing debt was consolidated and extended with a significant reduction in principal and interest due; interest arrears were often waived entirely. External intervention, including military force, was common

From 1945 to 1972*

From 1945 to 1972

After World War II, the United States continued as the major creditor country, and its dollar became the main reserve currency. In 1947 it announced the Economic Recovery Program (or Marshall Plan), designed for the reconstruction of the war-ravaged countries of Europe. Between 1948 and 1951, the program provided over $11 billion to Western Europe, with a further $2.6 billion

---

Box 2.1 The Bretton Woods conference and its twin institutions

The International Monetary and Financial Conference of the United and Associated Nations was convened in Bretton Woods, New Hampshire, on July 1, 1944. By the time the conference ended on July 22, 1944, based on substantial preparatory work, it had defined the outlines of the postwar international economic system. The conference also resulted in the creation of the International Monetary Fund (IMF) and the International Bank for Reconstruction and Development (IBRD, or the World Bank)—the Bretton Woods twins.

The World Bank was to assist in reconstruction and development by facilitating the flow and investment of capital for productive purposes. The International Monetary Fund was to facilitate the expansion and balanced growth of international trade and to contribute thereby to the promotion and maintenance of high levels of employment and real income. Also discussed at Bretton Woods were plans for an International Trade Organization (ITO). This institution did not materialize, but some of its proposed functions are performed by the General Agreement on Tariffs and Trade (GATT), which was established in 1947.

The discussions at Bretton Woods took place with the experience of the interwar period as background. In the 1930s every major country sought ways to defend itself against deflationary pressures from abroad—some by exchange depreciation, some by introducing flexible exchange rates or multiple rates, some by direct controls over imports and other international transactions. The disastrous consequences of such policies—economic depression with very high unemployment—are well known. The participants in the Bretton Woods conference were determined to design an international economic system where "beggar thy neighbor" policies, which characterized the international economic community when World War II began, did not recur. There was also a widespread fear that the end of World War II would be followed by a slump, as had the end of World War I.

Thus the central elements of the system outlined at Bretton Woods were the establishment of convertibility of currencies and of fixed but adjustable exchange rates, and the encouragement of international flows of capital for productive purpose. The IMF and the World Bank were to assist in the attainment of these objectives. The economic accomplishments of the postwar period are in part the result of the effectiveness of these institutions.

---

where lending had been determined by political factors. When countries ran into liquidity difficulties, they were able to borrow more if they revised their policies and while they waited for their export earnings to recover.

The post-1945 period

The Bretton Woods Conference (see Box 2.1) in July 1944 outlined the postwar international economic system and led to the creation of the International Monetary Fund and the International Bank for Reconstruction and Development. This discussion will divide the postwar era into two periods: 1945–72 and 1973–84.

between 1951 and mid-1953. The aid primarily took the form of grants of commodities. The counterpart funds were used to finance investment. This helped Europe to make a dramatic recovery: the countries participating in the Economic Recovery Program increased their industrial production by 39 percent between 1948 and 1952.

The ending of Marshall aid did not produce a big swing in the U.S. balance of payments. On the contrary, U.S. foreign investment expanded as a result of incentives to U.S. banks and corporations to invest abroad, plus a big devaluation of European currencies against the dollar in 1949 and the large U.S. military presence in Europe. The United States also increased its loans and grants to devel-

15

oping countries, and private direct investment increased sharply in Latin America. The overall U.S. balance of payments moved into deficit in 1950 and stayed there for many years. During the 1950s, this aroused little concern. It was a commonly held view that there was a "dollar shortage" and that such deficits were appropriate for the leading international creditor.

Europe's balance of payments improved considerably in 1958, boosting its foreign reserves. At the end of that year, most European governments declared their currencies convertible (Japan did the same only in 1964). Capital markets in Europe and the United States started to integrate, with private capital flows becoming responsive to movements in interest rates. In the late 1950s European banks, notably in London and Switzerland, began to deal in dollars. This marked the inception of what came to be known as Eurocurrency markets (described in Chapter 8, Box 8.3). The decade had begun with official capital flows contributing to economic growth and trade expansion; it ended with a growing volume of private capital flowing between industrial economies.

The postwar years also saw the progressive decolonization of the developing countries. The United States and later other industrial countries began their formal programs of foreign aid. In the early 1950s, the World Bank shifted its focus from reconstruction to development, though it continued lending to industrial countries, including Japan, during the 1950s and 1960s. In 1956 the International Finance Corporation (IFC) was created to assist the private sector in developing countries through loans and equity investments. In 1960 governments formed the International Development Association (IDA) to provide a multilateral source of concessional finance for low-income countries. These years also saw the establishment of several regional development banks, including the Inter-American Development Bank (1959), the African Development Bank (1964), and the Asian Development Bank (1966).

For most of the 1960s, the world economy enjoyed a period of largely untroubled progress. Industrial economies grew by an average of 5 percent a year, with little year to year variability in growth rates. World trade grew even faster, at an average of 8.4 percent a year, helped by the progressive trade liberalization policies pursued under the GATT. Inflation rates in industrial economies as a group varied between 2 and 4 percent a year, though individual countries had bouts of more rapid price increases. Nominal interest rates

adjusted for inflation (that is, real interest rates) were usually in the 2 to 3 percent range.

Developing countries benefited from these international conditions. As a group, their output increased by over 5 percent a year. Some developing countries grew much faster than others, accentuating the differences in average incomes. Current account deficits were financed chiefly by official flows (loans and grants), by private direct investment, and by trade finance. Official aid grew by about 3 percent a year in real terms in 1950–65. Direct foreign investment also increased rapidly, as multinational corporations sought new supplies of raw materials in developing countries. Export credits revived as a source of finance for developing countries—a mixed blessing, as their relatively short maturities contributed to debt-servicing problems for many countries.

Several developing countries ran into debt difficulties in the 1950s and 1960s. Between 1956 and 1970, there were seventeen debt reschedulings involving seven countries (Argentina, Brazil, Chile, Ghana, Indonesia, Peru, and Turkey), each of them more than once. The reasons for their difficulties varied. Argentina, Brazil, Chile, Peru, and Turkey shared certain problems: large budget deficits; rapid inflation and delayed adjustments of the exchange rate; deteriorating terms of trade; declining export earnings; the accumulation of short-term external debt. Ghana and Indonesia also had these problems—though more acutely, because they launched large, long-term projects that they financed with short-term credits and executed inefficiently. In a number of other cases, including India, debt rescheduling was used to provide increased capital flows to low-income countries when concessional flows from industrial economies were constrained.

Creditors rescheduled their loans through ad hoc multilateral groups, such as the Paris Club. The International Monetary Fund was also involved in providing extra finance to support policy reforms. In general, creditors did not incur capital losses; they extended maturities and received interest on schedule. Borrowers undertook policy reforms designed to bring their balance of payments into better equilibrium and to establish the basis for economic growth.

Although the 1960s saw a rapid expansion of world output and trade, some international monetary problems started to emerge. The United States made efforts to control capital outflows. Many countries experienced difficulty in maintaining their exchange rates, notably Britain in the mid-1960s and France a few years later. The need for reform of the international monetary system was formally recognized as early as 1963.

By the end of the 1960s, the rate of growth of industrial economies had begun to slow and inflationary pressures to build up (see Chapter 3). Continued deficits in the U.S. balance of payments found their counterpart in surpluses in Europe and Japan. The dollar's exchange rate started to come under pressure. In August 1971 the United States temporarily suspended the convertibility of the dollar into gold. In December 1971 it devalued the dollar as part of a general realignment of currencies. Further pressures on exchange markets led to generalized floating of exchange rates in 1973. In the same year, the first major increase in oil prices took place. The world had changed.

From 1973 to 1984

With the oil price increases, the financial system was faced with a major change in world current account imbalances. The industrial economies went into deficit in 1974 but reverted to a surplus in 1975. Oil-importing developing countries had run current account deficits that averaged slightly more than 2 percent of their GNP in the 1960s and were at a low of 0.8 percent of their GNP in 1973. In 1974 they reached 3.5 percent of GNP and climbed to 4.0 percent in 1975 (see Table 2.1, national accounts data). Current account deficits did not return to historical levels until 1976–78, when developing countries benefited from recovery in industrial economies and their own policy reforms.

The years between 1979 and 1983 saw a second series of major external shocks for developing countries. Oil prices rose sharply in 1979–80. Real interest rates increased dramatically in 1980–81 (see Figure 1.4), reaching historically high levels. There was a prolonged recession in industrial countries in 1981–83. There was a recovery in 1984. Industrial countries grew by 4.8 percent in 1984, and developing countries 4.1 percent. Fastest

Table 2.1 Current account balance as a percentage of GNP in selected country groups and years, 1960–84

Data source and country group	1960[a]	1965[a]	1970	1971	1972	1973	1974	1975	1976	1977	1978	1979	1980	1981	1982	1983	1984
Based on national accounts																	
Low-income countries	-1.6	-1.8	-1.1	-1.6	-1.0	-0.9	-1.7	-2.1	-0.9	-0.7	-1.2	-1.4	-2.2	-1.4	-0.9	-1.0	-1.3
Asia	-1.4	-1.6	-0.9	-1.0	-0.5	-0.6	-1.1	-1.2	-0.1	0.4	-0.1	-0.6	-1.4	-0.5	0.2	-0.2	-0.6
Africa	-3.3	-4.1	-3.4	-7.3	-5.6	-4.4	-7.8	-10.2	-7.3	-7.6	-8.3	-7.7	-9.8	-10.5	-12.0	-10.0	-9.4
Middle-income oil importers	-2.9	-2.0	-3.2	-3.6	-1.2	-0.8	-4.8	-5.3	-2.9	-2.3	-2.2	-3.2	-4.1	-5.2	-4.7	-4.4	-2.7
Exporters[b]	-2.7	-2.0	-3.2	-3.5	-0.9	-0.9	-5.7	-5.5	-2.8	-1.6	-1.7	-3.1	-3.6	-4.2	-4.0	-3.1	-1.3
Other	-3.5	-2.0	-3.0	-4.0	-2.2	-0.2	-1.8	-4.5	-3.4	-4.5	-3.9	-3.7	-5.9	-8.3	-7.3	-8.6	-7.4
Middle-income oil exporters	-1.6	-2.4	-3.0	-3.0	-2.4	-1.1	3.3	-3.4	-2.4	-3.6	-5.1	-0.2	0.8	-3.8	-4.4	-2.1	-0.7
All developing countries	-2.2	-2.0	-2.3	-2.7	-1.4	-0.9	-1.9	-3.9	-2.2	-2.2	-2.6	-2.0	-2.3	-3.9	-3.7	-2.8	-1.8
Oil-importing developing countries	-2.3	-1.9	-2.2	-2.7	-1.1	-0.8	-3.5	-4.0	-2.2	-1.7	-1.8	-2.6	-3.4	-3.9	-3.4	-3.1	-2.1
High-income oil exporters	9.7	20.9	15.7	26.2	22.5	21.2	51.5	40.2	35.0	26.3	15.5	21.2	31.4	32.2	20.1	-4.7	..
Industrial countries	1.0	0.9	0.8	1.0	0.9	0.7	-0.2	0.6	0.1	0.1	0.7	.0	-0.5	.0	.0	0.3	-0.4
Based on balance of payments[c]																	
All developing countries	..	..	-2.6	-3.0	-1.7	-1.3	-2.3	-4.2	-2.8	-2.6	-3.3	-2.9	-3.3	-4.9	-4.8	-2.8	-1.8
Oil-importing developing countries	..	..	-2.5	-3.0	-1.5	-1.1	-3.9	-4.3	-2.6	-2.1	-2.5	-3.4	-4.6	-5.1	-4.2	-3.1	-2.1

a. Data for 1960 and 1965 do not include net private transfers.
b. Major exporters of manufactures.
c. Excluding official transfers.
Source: World Bank data.

Table 2.2 Current account balance and its financing in selected years, 1970–84
(millions of dollars)

Country group and item	1970	1973	1980	1981	1982	1983[a]	1984[b]
Low-income Asia							
Net exports of goods and nonfactor services	−1,358	−879	−15,755	−11,498	−6,831	−7,246	−8,688
Net factor income	−390	−427	78	−212	−983	−522	−604
Interest payments on medium- and long-term loans	286	375	1,363	1,560	1,515	1,598	1,833
Current account balance	−1,551	−972	−9,685	−6,166	−1,363	−1,001	−3,083
Financing							
Official transfers	370	569	1,952	2,084	1,885	2,011	1,953
Medium- and long-term loans	987	1,145	4,878	3,227	3,957	4,199	6,541
Official	971	1,189	3,410	3,452	3,883	3,542	4,222
Private	16	−44	1,468	−225	74	657	2,319
Net direct investment	29	−16	159	422	488	546	643
Changes in reserves	−28	1	1,152	882	−4,127	−4,224	−3,184
Low-income Africa							
Net exports of goods and nonfactor services	−381	−607	−5,385	−5,901	−4,590	−4,359	−3,78
Net factor income	−161	−274	−901	−1,098	−1,004	−1,029	−1,291
Interest payments on medium- and long-term loans	80	143	698	643	567	662	1,000
Current account balance	−679	−998	−5,837	−6,419	−5,432	−4,900	−4,594
Financing							
Official transfers	377	649	2,109	1,813	1,515	2,008	1,925
Medium- and long-term loans	277	911	3,349	2,863	2,198	1,910	2,025
Official	247	412	2,366	2,249	1,858	1,922	2,231
Private	30	499	983	614	340	−12	−206
Net direct investment	173	164	236	221	223	211	86
Changes in reserves	−38	−381	781	555	945	171	607
Middle-income oil importers							
Net exports of goods and nonfactor services	−7,064	−6,572	−47,071	−50,500	−35,135	−12,234	9,972
Net factor income	−2,728	−4,364	−22,246	−31,510	−38,583	−42,035	−49,049
Interest payments on medium- and long-term loans	1,565	3,272	19,337	25,055	29,272	26,872	33,841
Current account balance	−7,423	−4,508	−53,823	−65,758	−57,894	−39,712	−24,367
Financing							
Official transfers	1,085	2,237	5,569	5,829	5,840	5,833	6,273
Medium- and long-term loans	5,337	8,882	33,190	42,027	36,917	24,535	28,272

(continued)

growing were the East and South Asian countries, in contrast to sub-Saharan Africa where output continued to decline in 1984. For oil-importing developing countries as a group, current account deficits reached a peak of $78 billion in 1981—more than 5 percent of their GNP, compared with $33 billion and 4.3 percent of GNP in 1975 (see Table 2.1, balance of payments data). The deficits of all developing countries were $105 billion or 4.9 percent of their GNP in 1981 (Table 2.2).

The finance for these large deficits was obtained without particular difficulty until 1982, when Mexico's debt-servicing problems caused an abrupt slowdown in bank lending. Developing countries then had to reduce their current account deficits and did so most commonly by cutting imports. In 1984, however, exports from developing countries

grew by 8.9 percent, and many countries produced trade surpluses. Current account deficits as a proportion of GNP have declined continuously since 1981. In 1984, the current account deficit of all developing countries was 1.8 percent of their GDP. But the interest payments of all developing countries in 1984 totaled $58 billion, exceeding their combined current account deficits of $36 billion (Table 2.2).

The changing nature of capital

Two major shifts in international capital have occurred in the past two decades: from equity to debt and from official to private finance (see Figure 2.1). The more advanced developing countries obviously obtained the bulk of commercial capital.

Table 2.2 *(continued)*

Country group and item	1970	1973	1980	1981	1982	1983ᵃ	1984ᵇ
Middle-income oil importers (continued)							
Official	1,667	2,939	10,996	11,258	10,732	11,685	12,959
Private	3,670	5,943	22,194	30,769	26,185	12,850	15,314
Net direct investment	1,225	2,976	6,009	7,981	7,244	5,868	5,732
Changes in reserves	−1,160	−7,547	488	126	13,547	7,372	−9,092
Middle-income oil exporters							
Net exports of goods and nonfactor services	−915	1,286	14,628	−10,713	−13,701	7,854	16,666
Net factor income	−2,207	−4,313	−16,186	−19,008	−23,982	−22,631	−24,692
Interest payments on medium- and long-term loans	693	1,296	11,454	13,903	16,660	17,463	21,252
Current account balance	−2,930	−2,652	1,501	−27,302	−35,683	−11,052	−3,543
Financing							
Official transfers	595	1,213	2,008	2,483	1,919	1,918	1,809
Medium- and long-term loans	1,643	5,396	16,998	23,559	20,503	18,133	13,323
Official	762	1,433	4,800	4,706	5,314	3,660	6,194
Private	881	3,963	12,198	18,853	15,190	14,473	7,129
Net direct investment	890	1,312	4,192	6,369	5,283	3,717	2,922
Changes in reserves	−309	−2,884	−15,602	4,730	17,542	3,549	−7,339
All developing countries							
Net exports of goods and nonfactor services	−9,717	−6,772	−53,582	−78,612	−60,256	−15,966	14,168
Net factor income	−5,486	−9,378	−39,255	−51,828	−64,553	−66,238	−75,640
Interest payments on medium- and long-term loans	2,624	5,086	32,851	41,161	48,014	46,596	57,925
Current account balance	−12,583	−9,130	−67,844	−105,645	−100,373	−56,665	−35,588
Financing							
Official transfers	2,427	4,668	11,638	12,208	11,159	11,768	11,960
Medium- and long-term loans	8,243	16,333	58,414	71,675	63,575	48,778	50,162
Official	3,646	5,972	21,572	21,665	21,786	20,810	25,606
Private	4,596	10,361	36,842	50,011	41,788	27,969	24,556
Net direct investment	2,317	4,426	10,595	14,992	13,237	10,342	9,383
Changes in reserves	−1,534	−10,811	−13,180	6,292	27,907	6,868	−19,008

Note: Data are based on a sample of ninety developing countries. Data for the current account balance exclude official transfers.
a. Estimated.
b. Projected.
Source: World Bank data.

However, even in low-income countries the share of private flows (including trade finance) increased. In low-income Africa, it did so in the mid-1970s; in low-income Asia, only after 1979.

Official supplies of foreign capital, concessional and nonconcessional, provided 50 percent of all the developing countries' inflows in 1970; for the low-income countries, their share was 78 percent. By 1983 these figures had fallen to 46 percent and 45 percent, respectively (see Table 2.3). Even in nominal terms, official development assistance has fallen since 1980; by contrast it rose sharply after the first rise in oil prices, by almost 80 percent (or 21 percent a year) between 1973 and 1976. Bilateral ODA declined in the 1970s as a proportion of total inflows for every group of developing countries— and fastest of all for the low-income countries. The falling share of bilateral aid was partly offset by more multilateral flows, particularly for low-income countries. In the 1980s retrenchment of expenditure programs by developing countries resulted in a decline in multilateral aid disbursements.

The weight of debt-creating foreign capital gained particular prominence during the 1970s. For all developing countries receipts of medium- and long-term loans averaged 4.4 percent of GNP over the decade, rising steadily from 3.1 percent in 1970 to 5.7 percent in 1979. These funds financed between 10 and 21 percent of gross domestic investment in that period. There were, however, great variations among country groups. Debt-creating flows averaged just over 1 percent of GNP and 4 percent of gross domestic investment in low-

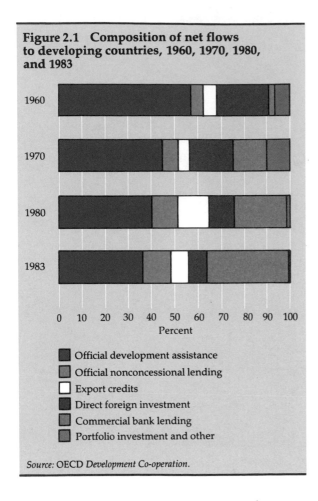

Figure 2.1 Composition of net flows to developing countries, 1960, 1970, 1980, and 1983

1960
1970
1980
1983

0 10 20 30 40 50 60 70 80 90 100
Percent

■ Official development assistance
■ Official nonconcessional lending
□ Export credits
■ Direct foreign investment
□ Commercial bank lending
■ Portfolio investment and other

Source: OECD *Development Co-operation.*

ing countries, as recorded in the World Bank's Debtor Reporting System (DRS), increased from $68 billion to $686 billion, an average increase of 16.7 percent a year. The 1984 figure includes an estimated $25 billion of short-term liabilities consolidated into long-term debt through reschedulings. Including countries not covered by the DRS, as well as short-term debt and borrowings from the International Monetary Fund, the total external liabilities of all developing countries reached almost $900 billion in 1984 (see Box 2.2).

Debt service payments increased from $9.3 billion in 1970 to $100 billion in 1984. Interest payments, which were about one-third of total debt service in 1970, had increased to over one-half in 1984. The rise reflects both the increased amount of debt and also the higher level of interest rates.

The terms that developing countries obtained on medium- and long-term finance changed significantly during the 1970s. The average maturity of their total public debt shortened from 20.4 years in 1970 to 14.2 years in 1982, because loans from private sources (the fastest growing component) carried shorter maturities—an average of 8.2 years in 1983. The reduction in average grace periods was less dramatic, from 5.5 years in the 1970s to 3.9 years in 1983. In 1983 the average maturity and grace periods for new lending were the shortest ever recorded for developing countries.

Among the important changes in the structure of developing countries' debt was the increasing use of floating rate loans and of debt denominated in dollars.

• The share of floating rate debt in total outstanding disbursed public debt rose from 16 percent in 1974 to 43 percent in 1983. The increase was concentrated among the middle-income countries, particularly in Latin America, which borrowed heavily from private sources. For low-income countries, the share of variable rate debt did not increase much (see Table 2.4). Interest rates on new long-term loans to public borrowers, which had averaged 7.0 percent in 1974–76, increased to an average of 10.5 percent in 1980–82 before falling to just under 10 percent in 1983 (see Figure 2.2).

• The share of long-term public and publicly guaranteed debt denominated in dollars rose from 65 percent in 1974 to 76 percent in 1983 (see Table 2.5). Again, there were regional differences: in 1983 the ratio was almost 90 percent for Latin America, 68 percent for East Asia, and only 54 percent for sub-Saharan Africa. For many countries, the rise in the dollar has increased the cost, in terms of domestic goods, of servicing the debt. The

income Asia. In low-income Africa—much more dependent on external capital—the ratios were 5 and 30 percent, respectively. Among the middle-income countries, the major exporters of manufactures financed less than 20 percent of investment with such funds. For other middle-income oil importers the share was 25 percent, rising to more than 35 percent in the early 1980s.

The increased lending by commercial banks was the main reason for the dramatic increase in external financing. Accordingly, although private direct investment continued to increase in nominal terms, its share in total external finance declined from 20 percent in 1970 to less than 9 percent in 1983. The increase in commercial bank lending was accompanied by a large increase in export credits, which maintained their share of total foreign financing between 1970 and 1980. In the early 1980s, however, export credits declined sharply.

The growth of borrowing during the past ten to fifteen years has produced a corresponding rise in external debt. Between 1970 and 1984, the outstanding medium- and long-term debt of develop-

Table 2.3 Net resource receipts of developing countries from all sources in selected years, 1970–83
(billions of dollars)

Type of receipt	1970	1975	1980	1981	1982	1983
Official development assistance	8.1	20.1	37.5	37.3	34.7	33.6
Bilateral	7.0	16.2	29.7	29.4	27.2	26.1
Multilateral	1.1	3.9	7.8	7.9	7.5	7.5
Grants by private voluntary agencies	0.9	1.3	2.3	2.0	2.3	2.2
Nonconcessional flows	10.9	34.3	59.4	70.5	60.4	63.9
Official or officially supported flows	3.9	10.5	24.5	22.2	22.0	19.6
Private export credits	2.1	4.4	11.1	11.3	7.1	5.5
Official export credits	0.6	1.2	2.5	2.0	2.7	2.1
Multilateral flows	0.7	2.5	4.9	5.7	6.6	7.0
Other official and private flows	0.2	0.8	2.2	2.0	2.6	3.0
Other donors	0.3	1.6	3.8	1.2	3.0	2.0
Private flows	7.0	23.8	34.9	48.3	38.4	44.3
Direct investment	3.7	11.4	10.5	17.2	11.9	7.8
Bank lending[a]	3.0	12.0	23.0	30.0	26.0	36.0
Bond lending	0.3	0.4	1.4	1.1	0.5	0.5
Total	19.9	55.7	99.2	109.8	97.4	99.7
Memo items						
Short-term bank lending	..	..	26.0	22.0	15.0	−2.0
IMF purchases (net)	0.3	3.2	2.6	6.2	6.4	12.4

a. Excluding bond lending and export credits extended by banks, which are included in private export credits.
Source: OECD 1984.

Table 2.4 Floating interest rate loans as a percentage of public debt in selected years, 1974–83

Country group	1974	1976	1978	1979	1980	1981	1982	1983
Low-income Asia	0.0	0.0	0.4	0.6	1.8	2.9	3.7	3.9
Low-income Africa	8.5	8.1	6.7	6.8	7.0	9.4	9.1	7.6
Middle-income countries								
Oil importers	18.5	26.6	30.3	35.2	36.5	40.2	41.4	43.7
Oil exporters	23.9	30.4	34.9	40.1	41.7	45.2	48.3	54.6
All developing countries	16.2	23.0	27.3	31.8	33.2	36.7	38.7	42.7
Memo item								
Major borrowers	18.4	26.8	32.5	39.0	40.5	45.0	46.7	51.2

Note: Data are for public debt outstanding and disbursed.
Source: World Bank data.

desirability of developing countries' diversifying the currency composition of their borrowings and debt is discussed in Chapter 5.

Trade and debt indicators

As a group, developing countries expanded their exports considerably in the 1970s, from about 13 percent of their GDP in 1970 to over 23 percent in 1983. In low-income Africa, however, the share of exports in GDP fell steeply. Then the world recession of 1981–82 reduced commodity prices and slowed the growth in the volume of developing countries' exports. The volume of oil exports fell, as did the oil price, hitting the middle-income oil exporters. The economic recovery since 1983 has raised the growth of exports, but the terms of trade of developing countries have deteriorated since 1980 (details of trade are in the Statistical Appendix, Tables A.8 and A.9).

Figure 2.2 Interest rates on new long-term commitments to public borrowers, 1975–83

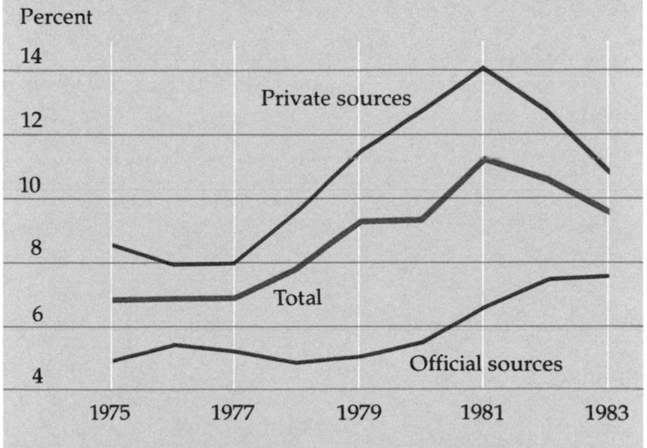

Note: Data are the weighted average interest rates on new loans at the time of commitment. For loans on variable interest rates, interest actually paid will vary with changes in market rates.

Source: World Bank data.

Box 2.2 External liabilities of developing countries

Both the quantity and quality of information on international finance have improved considerably in recent years. The main sources of information are:

• *The World Bank's Debtor Reporting System (DRS).* Comprehensive data are collected on debt with a maturity of more than one year, plus annual figures on commitments, disbursements, amortization, and interest payments. Publication: *World Debt Tables* (published annually).

Developing-country governments report public and publicly guaranteed debt on a loan by loan basis. Figures on private nonguaranteed debt are incomplete, so they are supplemented by staff estimates. By convention the DRS excludes the use of IMF credit, which is treated as a ''monetary movement'' rather than a medium-term loan. For some low-income countries, however, obligations to the IMF are a large part of their nonconcessional external debt.

• *IMF balance of payments statistics.* Comprehensive balance of payments data are compiled according to the standards of the IMF Balance of Payments Manual and reported periodically to the IMF. They include internationally comparable data on private and public sector grants and all capital flows, including direct investment, long-term borrowing, short-term borrowing, and reserve movements. Publication: *International Financial Statistics, Supplement on Balance of Payments* (formerly called *Balance of Payments Yearbook*; published annually).

Both the DRS and the IMF data are limited by the ability of developing countries to marshal primary statistics. However, both data sources have become more comprehensive in recent years, partly as a result of intensive technical assistance to member countries by both the IMF and the World Bank.

Information on debtors can usefully be supplemented by figures on creditors and bank lending. The main sources are:

• *OECD annual aid questionnaire and Creditor Reporting System.* Data from the annual aid questionnaire prepared by the seventeen countries that are members of the Development Assistance Committee (DAC) show annual disbursements and repayments of official grants and loans to each developing country. The Creditor Reporting System provides individual reports on all official long-term loans, plus summary information on export credits. The OECD estimates financial flows from OPEC and centrally planned economies, building on DRS data. It then prepares comprehensive estimates of developing-country debt. Publications: *Development Co-operation* and *External Debt of Developing Countries* (both published annually).

The OECD figures on long-term intergovernmental loans are a valuable cross-check on DRS data. However, its figures on officially guaranteed export credits contain, in some instances, future interest due, and it excludes export credits that are not guaranteed in the creditor country. A more general drawback is that the OECD's primary statistics are not global in their coverage, although DAC countries are the chief source of financial flows to developing countries.

• *BIS banking statistics.* The Bank for International Settlements compiles figures on lending by banks in fifteen countries. A quarterly series classifies banks on a residency basis, and a semiannual series on a nationality basis (that is, ''United States loans'' are those made by mainland U.S. banks plus their offshore branches). The six-monthly series classifies loans by maturity and thus provides the main estimates of developing countries' short-term debt. Unfortunately, the figures are compiled according to the time remaining to maturity, so they are not comparable with DRS and OECD data, which document loans by their original maturity. Publications: *International Banking Developments* (published quarterly); *Maturity Distribution of International Banking Lending* (published semiannually).

• *IMF banking statistics.* These collate international

Table 2.5 Shares of key currencies in public long-term debt, 1974–83

(percent)

Currency	1974	1975	1976	1977	1978	1979	1980	1981	1982	1983
U.S. dollars[a]	65.1	69.0	70.3	67.8	64.8	66.8	68.1	71.8	73.4	76.3
Deutsche mark	8.8	7.3	7.6	8.2	9.2	8.6	7.3	6.3	6.0	4.8
Japanese yen	3.8	3.8	4.1	5.4	7.2	5.9	6.9	6.2	6.0	6.0
French francs	4.3	4.3	4.1	4.4	4.8	4.9	4.6	3.8	3.6	2.9
Pounds sterling	5.6	4.3	3.3	3.1	2.7	2.5	2.3	1.9	1.6	1.5
Swiss francs	0.8	0.7	0.8	1.1	1.6	1.5	1.3	1.4	1.3	1.0
Canadian dollars	1.5	1.5	1.5	1.3	1.1	1.1	1.1	1.1	1.0	0.9
Others	10.1	8.9	8.4	8.6	8.7	8.8	8.4	7.6	7.2	6.5
Total	100	100	100	100	100	100	100	100	100	100

Note: Data are based on the currency of denomination, not the currency of repayment.
a. The share of U.S. dollars includes ''multiple currency'' lending, predominantly in dollars, at variable interest rates, and accounting for an 8–10 percent share of external debt during 1974–83. The share of U.S. dollars is therefore an upper bound, but the trend is unaltered, with the dollar's share rising by eleven percentage points in a decade.
Source: World Bank data.

banking assets and liabilities. They are comparable to those of the BIS, but ultimately come from a wider group of banking centers. The figures were first published in 1984, as the first stage of a project to integrate all data on the external debt of developing countries. Publication: *International Financial Statistics* (published monthly).

• *Joint OECD/BIS external debt project.* A project designed to integrate data on (a) officially guaranteed trade-related bank credits collected by the OECD and (b) developing-country debt to commercial banks. So far, the project has eliminated the duplication of figures on officially guaranteed export credits extended by banks, which had appeared in both sets of data. Publication: OECD, *Development Co-operation (1984 Review).*

When all these data sources are brought together, a reasonable estimate of external liabilities of developing countries emerges (Box table 2.2A).

Box table 2.2A   External liabilities of developing countries, 1980–84
(billions of dollars, unless otherwise noted)

Country group	1980	1981	1982	1983[a]	1984[b]
DRS reporting countries[c]	540	629	699	761[e]	810[f]
Medium- and long-term debt[d]	412	470	525	598[e]	655[f]
From official sources	160	174	191	209	225
From private sources	252	296	334	388[e]	430[f]
Short-term debt[g]	119	145	155	134[e]	122[f]
Use of IMF credit[h]	9	14	19	29	33
Other developing countries[i]	70	73	76	82	85
Medium- and long-term debt[d]	59	58	57	60	62
From official sources	17	18	19	20	20
From private sources	42	40	38	40	42
Short-term debt[g]	11	15	16	20	20
Use of IMF credit[h]	0	0	3	2	3
Total	610	702	775	843	895
Memo item					
Growth of total liabilities (percent)	. .	15.1	10.4	8.8	6.2

a. Preliminary.
b. Estimated.
c. Includes data for 104 developing countries for which standard and complete reporting is made through the World Bank's Debtor Reporting System (DRS).
d. Debt of original maturity of more than one year.
e. Reflects the rescheduling of $22 billion of short-term debt to banks into long-term debt during 1983.
f. Reflects the rescheduling of $25 billion of short-term debt to banks into long-term debt during 1984.
g. Debt of original maturity of no more than one year. Data are estimated from information on bank claims on developing countries as reported by the Bank for International Settlements and are amended to take account of information on short-term debt reported by individual developing countries.
h. Excludes loans from the IMF Trust Fund; they are included in medium- and long-term debt.
i. Includes data for developing countries that do not report through the DRS and for those that either have reported incomplete data through the DRS, or report in a form that does not permit publication in the standard tables. Excludes debt of the high-income oil-exporting countries and includes estimates for developing countries that are not World Bank members but are included in the global analysis underlying the *World Development Report*.

The composition of the developing countries' exports has also changed considerably over the past two decades. The share of manufactures rose from about 15 percent of the total in the early 1960s to nearly 50 percent in the early 1980s, while the relative importance of all primary products declined. Although this greater diversity of exports has reduced the vulnerability of developing countries to world recession, the increased share of manufactures has made them more vulnerable to protection in the industrial countries whose main focus is manufactured goods.

Despite this robust export performance, the rapid growth of borrowing combined with big increases in interest rates contributed to the deteri-

oration in the main debt indicators (see Table 2.6). For all developing countries, the ratio of debt service to exports for all developing countries rose from 15 percent in 1970 to 21 percent in 1982, then declined slightly to 20 percent in 1984; the ratio of debt to GNP increased from 14 percent in 1970 to 34 percent in 1984 (Box 2.3). The ratio of debt to exports also increased, from 109 percent (1970) to 135 percent (1984); and the ratio of interest payments to GNP more than quintupled, from 0.5 percent in 1970 to 2.8 percent in 1984.

There were, however, major differences among developing countries. With the exception of low-income Asia, the debt to GNP ratio increased significantly for all groups. The rise was sharpest for

Table 2.6 Debt indicators for developing countries in selected years, 1970–84
(ratios in percent; amounts in billions of dollars)

Country group and item	1970	1974	1976	1978	1980	1981	1982	1983	1984
Low-income Asia									
Ratio of debt to GNP	7.0	7.2	8.2	7.8	7.8	8.1	8.8	9.0	9.7
Ratio of debt to exports	183.6	128.4	131.6	123.1	96.7	89.5	95.1	98.9	100.0
Debt service ratio	12.4	7.8	7.7	7.2	8.0	9.3	10.9	8.3	8.4
Ratio of interest service to GNP	0.2	0.1	0.2	0.2	0.3	0.3	0.3	0.3	0.3
Total debt outstanding and disbursed	12	18	22	29	38	40	43	46	53
Private debt as percentage of total	6.9	5.4	4.1	5.6	17.3	14.7	13.6	13.9	16.7
Low-income Africa									
Ratio of debt to GNP	17.5	23.8	27.7	26.9	39.8	43.4	47.7	52.0	54.5
Ratio of debt to exports	75.2	99.5	135.3	162.3	175.8	216.5	260.6	279.5	278.1
Debt service ratio	6.1	8.6	8.5	9.6	12.5	13.8	15.7	16.5	19.9
Ratio of interest service to GNP	0.5	0.7	0.6	0.7	1.3	1.2	1.1	1.4	2.1
Total debt outstanding and disbursed	3	7	10	15	21	23	25	25	27
Private debt as percentage of total	33.5	39.3	36.6	38.9	29.8	29.3	26.9	22.4	18.4
Major exporters of manufactures									
Ratio of debt to GNP	16.2	18.0	20.1	22.1	22.8	24.7	27.9	34.4	37.6
Ratio of debt to exports	91.5	76.0	90.9	92.4	77.3	81.7	97.1	105.2	109.1
Debt service ratio	15.1	13.7	14.2	17.7	16.1	17.1	19.3	16.2	16.0
Ratio of interest service to GNP	0.7	1.1	1.1	1.4	2.0	2.5	2.9	2.9	3.6
Total debt outstanding and disbursed	24	57	82	124	167	191	216	242	267
Private debt as percentage of total	73.2	75.5	75.9	76.7	77.0	77.8	78.6	78.5	76.9
Other middle-income oil importers									
Ratio of debt to GNP	21.4	20.3	21.1	24.9	29.7	33.4	40.2	47.5	53.0
Ratio of debt to exports	111.0	88.7	98.3	122.7	120.7	136.4	155.4	175.5	183.9
Debt service ratio	13.6	11.4	14.8	20.9	17.2	20.8	22.7	23.1	24.9
Ratio of interest service to GNP	0.8	0.9	1.0	1.3	1.9	2.4	3.1	3.3	3.9
Total debt outstanding and disbursed	12	21	27	43	68	79	89	98	108
Private debt as percentage of total	42.9	42.1	43.8	47.8	51.0	51.6	51.5	49.6	49.3
Middle-income oil exporters									
Ratio of debt to GNP	18.4	18.0	22.4	30.1	24.7	24.9	32.0	39.9	43.8
Ratio of debt to exports	115.3	67.2	102.1	136.0	87.4	98.5	123.7	157.8	164.2
Debt service ratio	18.1	11.0	14.5	22.9	17.8	19.8	25.0	26.1	28.1
Ratio of interest service to GNP	0.7	0.9	1.1	1.6	2.1	2.2	3.1	3.3	4.0
Total debt outstanding and disbursed	18	38	63	103	136	155	174	208	232
Private debt as percentage of total	57.2	63.3	66.5	67.7	69.4	71.2	71.8	75.3	75.1
All developing countries									
Ratio of debt to GNP	14.1	15.4	18.1	21.0	20.9	22.4	26.3	31.3	33.8
Ratio of debt to exports	108.9	80.0	100.2	113.1	89.8	96.8	115.0	130.8	135.4
Debt service ratio	14.7	11.8	13.6	18.4	16.0	17.6	20.5	19.0	19.7
Ratio of interest service to GNP	0.5	0.8	0.8	1.1	1.6	1.9	2.3	2.3	2.8
Total debt outstanding and disbursed	68	141	204	313	430	488	546	620	686
Private debt as percentage of total	50.9	56.5	59.0	61.5	62.9	64.1	64.6	65.8	65.0

Note: Interest and debt service for 1970-83 are actual (not contractual) service paid during the period. Interest and debt service for 1984 are projections of contractual obligations due based on commitments received through the end of 1983 and take into account reschedulings through the end of 1984.
Source: World Bank data.

low-income Africa, from 18 percent in 1970 to 55 percent in 1984. Although the absolute size of Africa's debt is small—$27 billion in 1984—in relation to income and exports it is the highest among developing countries.

Reschedulings

Although about a hundred developing countries have avoided debt difficulties so far in the 1980s, the deterioration in debt indicators was reflected in a spate of debt reschedulings. The number of formal reschedulings for World Bank members rose from an average of five a year in 1975–80 to thirteen in 1981 and thirty-one (involving twenty-one countries) in 1983. At least that number of debt negotiations took place in 1984, but formal agreement was reached on only twenty-one, involving

Box 2.3 How inflation affects loan repayments

The last few years have seen substantial fluctuations in inflation and interest rates. Inflation and interest rates influence the debt indicators usually relied on to evaluate the creditworthiness of borrowers. First, the nominal value of debt must be deflated by some price indicator to obtain a realistic assessment of its real value. Second, to the extent that inflation either outstrips or lags behind the rise in nominal interest rates, a real transfer of resources will occur—to the debtor in the former case and to the creditor in the latter. Finally, the real debt burden will not be altered by inflation if nominal interest rates exactly keep pace with inflation. In that case, nevertheless, the loan will be amortized at a faster real rate than the original terms might indicate.

When inflation goes up and nominal interest rates rise in line, interest payments include a component to compensate the lender for the erosion in the *real* value of loans. Although this does not change the real value of all repayments, it does speed up the *real* amortization: the inflation component of nominal interest rates is added to the regularly scheduled nominal amortization payments. Thus, for a given loan maturity, higher inflation rates

produce larger *real* debt repayments in the near future and lower real debt repayments near the end of the loan repayment schedule. This forward tilt in the real amortization schedule (''front-loading'') is more pronounced the longer the original maturity of the loan.

Box table 2.3A shows how the different components of total debt service have moved over time. A variety of price indexes could be used in these calculations. Here the developing countries' export prices (merchandise, f.o.b., excluding fuel) are used. This implies measuring the value of the debt service in terms of the domestic goods that need to be exported to service the debt. The debt service ratio shows very little variation from year to year, but total amortization payments fluctuate widely as a result of the inflationary component of interest payments. The share of debt service in export earnings declined during the period 1971–73, but the inflation-adjusted amortization payments reached their highest level in 1973. Similarly, the debt service ratio increased during the period 1980–82, but in fact the share of inflation-adjusted amortization payments showed a sharp decline.

Box table 2.3A Inflationary effects on debt service
(percent)

Year	Debt service/exports	=	Inflation-adjusted amortization/exports				+	Inflation-adjusted interest payments/exports
			Scheduled amortization	+	Inflation-induced amortization	= Total amortization		
1970	14.7		10.6		3.0	13.6		1.2
1971	15.6		11.2		−4.2	7.0		8.6
1972	15.2		10.9		5.9	16.8		−1.6
1973	14.1		9.9		32.4	42.3		−28.1
1974	11.8		7.9		19.1	27.0		−15.1
1975	13.9		9.0		−8.6	0.4		13.5
1976	13.6		8.9		8.2	17.2		−3.5
1977	14.8		9.7		10.0	19.7		−5.0
1978	18.4		12.3		6.0	18.3		0.1
1979	18.4		11.7		13.5	25.2		−6.8
1980	16.0		9.2		12.5	21.7		−5.6
1981	17.6		9.4		−6.8	2.6		15.0
1982	20.5		10.4		−7.4	3.0		17.5
1983	19.0		9.1		0.5	9.6		9.3
1984	19.7		8.2		−0.4	7.8		11.9

Note: The decomposition of the debt service ratio into inflation adjusted interest payments and inflation adjusted amortization is based on the identities

$$DS = IN + AM$$
$$IN = (i - p)D + pD$$

where *DS* is debt service; *IN* is interest payments; *AM* is amortization; *i* is the nominal interest rate calculated as the ratio of interest payments in the current period *(IN)* to debt outstanding and disbursed in the previous period *(D)*; *p* is the annual inflation rate based on the merchandise *(F.O.B.)* deflator excluding fuel. Thus,

$$DS = (i - p)D + pD + AM$$

where $(i - p)D$ equals inflation adjusted interest payments, and $pD + AM$ equals inflation adjusted amortization. The various components may not add up to debt ratio due to rounding.
Source: World Bank data.

sixteen countries and just over $11 billion by the end of the year. Although more than $115 billion was under negotiation in 1984, three countries—Argentina, Mexico, and Venezuela—accounted for $93 billion, four-fifths of the total.

Creditors have rescheduled debt on a case by case basis, mostly through the adaptation of well-established channels (see Box 2.4). The terms of reschedulings were generally easier in 1984 than in 1982 and 1983. Maturities and grace periods were generally longer; spreads over the London interbank offered rate (LIBOR) on rescheduled debt ranged from one and seven-eighths to two and one-half percentage points in 1982 and 1983, but fell to one and one-eighths to two percentage points in 1984. Rescheduling fees are also known to have declined.

The approach to reschedulings has varied, mainly in response to the concerns of the commercial banks. They have wanted assurances of the soundness of countries' policies. Multilateral institutions—and particularly the IMF—have been involved in designing packages that included policy reforms, debt restructurings, and new money. Central banks have made important contributions, either indirectly through the Bank for International Settlements (BIS) or directly, as in the case of the Federal Reserve Board. Latin American debtors have been the main beneficiaries of this approach. A path-breaking multiyear rescheduling of $49 billion of Mexico's debt to commercial banks was agreed to in principle in 1984; this was followed by a multiyear rescheduling of almost $21 billion of Venezuela's debt. At the end of 1984 discussions were in progress on a multiyear rescheduling of about $50 billion of Brazil's debt. These and other negotiated agreements have relieved the debt constraints on growth of some major borrowers. Nonetheless, some observers have suggested that debt difficulties need to be treated more radically (see Box 2.5).

Aside from a few major borrowers, reschedulings have been on a year by year basis. In varying degrees they have involved official flows (including guaranteed export credits) from bilateral sources, as well as commercial flows. Official debt has been rescheduled under the aegis of the Paris Club, often with parallel exercises for commercial debt. This approach has ensured broadly equal treatment of creditors. It is also one that has been best suited to dealing with liquidity problems and restoring normal debt servicing in the expectation that a debtor's exports will recover.

However, year by year rescheduling has certain

shortcomings. In 1983–84 alone, twenty-five countries (including Cuba and Poland) have rescheduled—mainly their guaranteed and insured export credits, which were originally provided by private lenders. These reschedulings have put great strains on the resources and solvency of export credit and insurance agencies in creditor countries. In addition, a number of African countries have rescheduled. Their difficulties often arise from structural weakness compounded by a short-term lack of liquidity. For them, as well as for the middle-income countries that depend heavily on exports of primary commodities, rescheduling has not produced the benefits that some Latin American countries have obtained. Only in the case of Sudan did a country's creditors and donors consider its long-term financing needs, in a meeting organized by the World Bank and the IMF. In a later meeting, the Paris Club members provided debt relief over an extended period. But this was not successful because the size of rescheduling was not sufficient and the country was not able to pursue the required policies.

Conclusions

During periods of global economic stability, such as the 1950s and 1960s, international finance has contributed significantly to economic growth. In periods of volatile change, such as the past fifteen years, it has played a dual role. On the one hand, it helped countries adjust to external shocks, as happened during the 1974–75 recession. On the other hand, it was an additional channel for the transmission of external shocks, as in the 1981–83 recession.

Within the total flows of capital to developing countries, shifts from equity to debt financing and from official to private sources were perhaps to be expected. As developing economies grow and their structures change, their relations with the world economy increasingly resemble those of the industrial countries. As infrastructure projects require a smaller share of investment, as industry expands, as exports shift from primary to manufactured products, as the domestic financial system matures, so developing countries increase their ability to exploit opportunities in international financial markets.

However, the flow of private external capital to developing countries did not increase slowly, in line with their economic progress. It expanded suddenly in the 1970s and was accompanied by unprecedented imbalances in international pay-

Box 2.4   The changing nature of debt renegotiations

There are two main institutional arrangements for debt relief: the Paris Club for debts to or guaranteed by governments; and ad hoc consortia of commercial banks (sometimes called the London Club) for uninsured debts to financial institutions.

The Paris Club

The Paris Club was born in 1956 when a group of creditor countries met in Paris to renegotiate Argentine debt owed to export credit guarantee institutions, which had reimbursed private creditors following delays in Argentina's debt service to them. Although the club has no written rules, it has evolved a standard approach based on experience and precedent, one objective being equitable treatment of all creditors.

The scope of the club's debt relief covers service on all bilateral official loans, including concessional credits and officially guaranteed export credits. Consolidation periods are normally for one year, but successive agreements are common: debt relief has been extended more or less continuously during the past decade to Liberia, Senegal, Sudan, Togo, and Zaire. Previously rescheduled debt has been consolidated when circumstances required.

Debt relief is normally restricted to current maturities. The proportion typically rescheduled varies from 80 to 100 percent. This consolidated portion is repaid over eight to ten years, with a grace period of four to five years. For countries with severe balance of payments problems, the nonconsolidated portion may be repaid over the grace period; in such cases, debt relief approaches 100 percent of eligible maturities. Arrears are occasionally rescheduled, but they are normally repaid at a faster rate.

The Paris Club arrangements help restore normal trade and project finance to debtor countries. When the debtor countries experience severe international liquidity difficulties resulting in a breakdown in relationships with their creditors, a Paris Club agreement sets the framework for rescheduling arrears to official creditors and clears the way for direct or guaranteed new credits. It is followed by bilateral agreements with each of the participants in the Paris Club meeting within the agreed framework. After bilateral agreements are concluded (sometimes a lengthy process), each agency concerned restores export credit cover to the rescheduling countries. Indeed, debtor countries can approach the Paris Club even before encountering liquidity problems that would lead to the cessation of trade finance; ideally, they should do so. The Paris Club requires that debtor countries take prompt and effective measures to address their underlying economic problems; an IMF-supported adjustment program that will give a country access to the upper credit tranches is, typically, a prerequisite to a Paris Club agreement. The Paris Club, while still considering debt relief mainly in the context of short-term liquidity problems, has shown flexibility in its response to the debt-servicing problems of developing countries

that are willing to take steps to address their problems.

The Paris Club has worked best, however, for countries where temporary liquidity difficulties were due principally to a bunching of debt service payments. The Paris Club has been less successful in resolving the difficulties of countries, such as those in sub-Saharan Africa, where debt service difficulties are related to structural economic problems. When prospects for restoring normal debt service are dim for many years, successive annual reschedulings of payments for a decade often has served only to postpone the problem. The flexibility that the Paris Club has demonstrated provides the basis for expecting that it will adapt its practices to address these problems as well.

Commercial bank debt

By contrast to the Paris Club, arrangements for renegotiating debt owed to commercial banks have developed only since the late 1970s (see Box figure 2.4A). Since much of this debt consists of syndicated loans, as well as uninsured trade or project finance, and the number of creditor banks may be in the hundreds, the banks are represented by an "advisory" committee that negotiates with the government of the debtor country. An agreement, when reached, must be approved by each creditor bank. The process has become increasingly streamlined in the 1970s, with small advisory committees now the rule and with coordinated actions to seek rapid agreement from all participating banks.

Commercial banks reschedule mainly current maturities of long-term debts, and occasionally arrears of principal as well. They do not reschedule interest; any arrears of interest must be settled before rescheduling agreements become effective. Some agreements have consolidated short-term debts. In many recent reschedulings, fresh long-term loans and trade credit facilities have been extended as part of a debt relief package, in effect offsetting interest payments. The negotiations have been flexible; some have arranged year to year deferments of debt while comprehensive longer-term agreements were still being discussed. Repayment of consolidated debt typically ranges from six to nine years, including two to four years of grace. Interest charges vary from a margin of one and seven-eighths to two and one-half points over LIBOR. Debt rescheduling is normally accompanied by a commission charge of 1 1/4 to 1 1/2 percent.

Year to year rescheduling has effectively overcome immediate debt-servicing difficulties, but it leaves uncertainty over the debtor's future position, which can prevent its returning to normal market financing. In Mexico's case, the commercial banks signed an agreement in March 1985 to consolidate public sector debt falling due in 1985–90 and to accept repayment over fourteen years, with lower spreads for the early years of the repayment period and no restructuring fees. Recently a multiyear

(continued)

Box figure 2.4A Multilateral debt renegotiations, 1975–84
(millions of dollars)

Country	1975	1976	1977	1978	1979	1980	1981	1982	1983	1984
Argentina		970								23,241
Bolivia							444			536
Brazil									4,532	5,350
									3,478	
Central African Rep.							55		13	
Chile	216								3,400	
Costa Rica									97	
									1,240	
Dominican Rep.									497	
Ecuador									200	4,475
									1,835	590
Gabon				105[a]						
Guyana					29			14		24
Honduras										148
India	157	169	110							
Ivory Coast										153
										306
Jamaica					126		103			106
										148
Liberia						30	25	27	18	17
										71
Madagascar							142	103		195
										120
Malawi								24	30	
									59	
Mexico									1,550[b]	48,725[c]
									23,625	
Morocco									1,225	530
Mozambique										200
Nicaragua						582	188	102		
Niger									33	22
										28
Nigeria									1,920	
Pakistan							263			
Peru				478					450	1,000
					821				380	1,415
Philippines									4,904	
										685
Romania								234	195[d]	
								1,598	567	
Senegal							77	84	64	97
Sierra Leone			27			41				25
										88
Sudan					373		638	174	502	245
Togo					170		92		114	55
						68			74	
Turkey					2,640		3,100			
				1,223	873	2,600				
Uganda							56	22		
Uruguay									815	
Venezuela										20,750
Yugoslavia									988[b]	500[b]
									1,586	1,246
Zaire		211	236		1,147	402	574		1,317	
Zambia									285	150
										75
Total	373	1,350	373	1,806	6,179	3,723	5,757	2,382	51,089	116,220

Key: ■ Paris Club renegotiation
  ■ Commercial bank renegotiation
  ■ Aid consortia renegotiation
  □ Agreed in principle

Note: Data in italics are estimates. a. Denotes an agreement of a special task force. b. Agreement of a creditor group meeting, not a Paris Club. c. Includes debt of $23,625 million previously rescheduled in 1983. d. Proposed. *Source:* World Bank data.

agreement has been reached with Ecuador. A similar agreement in principle was reached with Venezuela in late 1984, and an agreement with Brazil is in the advanced stages of negotiation. These multiyear agreements have been implemented for countries that have made substantial progress in adjusting their balance of payments and have credible commitments to future policy directions.

Year to year reschedulings, whether of official or commercial bank debt, are expensive in the use they make of the time of senior officials in both developing countries and creditor institutions. They also tend to focus attention on financial problems to the detriment of policy reforms. Multiyear arrangements, on a case by case basis, in support of policy reforms are a preferred approach.

Box 2.5   Recent proposals for dealing with debt-servicing difficulties

Numerous solutions have been offered for the debt crisis. The proposals reflect a range of views about the nature of debt-servicing difficulties and appropriate responses to them. They include ad hoc financing arrangements; case by case debt reschedulings; interest capitalization schemes; formal insurance; stabilization funds; innovative instruments, including equity shares in public enterprises in borrowing countries as swaps with outstanding debt; and comprehensive restructurings, including write-downs or external claims. The objective of these solutions is to permit the resumption of growth and restoration of creditworthiness of developing countries and the restoration of ''spontaneous'' lending by commercial banks. It is not the purpose here to discuss the individual proposals. The proposed solutions can best be evaluated by considering four elements that go to the heart of the relationship between debtors and creditors.

• *The distinction between the collective interests of creditors and their individual interests.* If the creditors of debtor countries cannot be paid full debt service, it is in their collective interest to defer payment—perhaps even to forgive part of the payment—rather than provoke a moratorium or repudiation by debtors. Individual creditors, however, have an incentive to hold out for repayment, in effect by being bought out by other parties. Any debt reform scheme must provide an answer to this ''free rider'' problem. Some of the proposals advocate a once-and-for-all restructuring of developing countries' debt into long-term low-interest loans. Most proposals argue that debts should be taken over by a new international agency and raise questions about the availability of additional official capital for this purpose.

• *Limits to debt service.* Debtor countries have now shown their ability to run big trade surpluses to service their debt. For some countries, at their present levels of development, it may be difficult to keep running trade surpluses large enough to pay all interest, particularly if interest rates rise. So a feasible debt reform plan must not only reschedule all principal, in some cases it may also have to reduce the current interest burden.

In order to reschedule principal, most proposals suggest that bank loans should be converted into some other long-term asset, particularly long-term bonds. To reduce the burden of interest payments, some proposals argue for relending interest; others suggest an automatic process of relending interest by capitalizing interest payments. A few proposals advocate new instruments—such as replacing fixed claims on a country with shares in the country's foreign exchange earnings, or with equity in state-run enterprises.

• *Continuing uncertainty.* Any scheme that attempts to settle the debt problem at a stroke must either reduce the expected burdens on countries so much that a second rescue will not be needed or make some allowance for future contingencies, such as world recession or higher interest rates. It must also offer inducements for banks to keep lending in the future.

Several proposals contain measures to deal with uncertainty, ranging from stabilization funds for fluctuations in oil prices and interest rates to establishing a formal insurance scheme to avoid another crisis. It is less clear how these proposals ensure future lending by banks; which route is taken has important implications for the distribution of the burdens and for future access to international capital markets.

• *Maintaining the solvency of the banking system.* Major banks hold claims on developing countries equal to several times their capital. Any scheme that implies a large write-down of debt must therefore provide for the continued operation of these banks. Most proposals attempt to minimize write-downs, so that banks remain solvent. Others include the use of official capital to buy part of developing-country debt.

The current approach, which combines restructuring of debt service payments with adjustment policies by debtor countries, has an answer for each of these four issues. Abstracting from important details, it deals with the free rider problem through ad hoc pressure and suasion on banks; it relies on conventional reschedulings to reduce the interest burden by relending; it copes with uncertainty by keeping the banks involved, and therefore it preserves the ability to demand additional loans from existing creditors; and it copes with the solvency problem by avoiding write-downs. So far this approach has worked better than many had expected. However, wider use of multiyear debt restructurings on a case by case basis as a part of an overall financial package supporting stabilization and adjustment, particularly in sub-Saharan Africa, will help to alleviate debt-servicing difficulties.

ments. The potential for using foreign capital to expand investment was therefore limited by the immediate need to pay for dearer oil.

Despite the economic shocks of the past dozen years, some developing countries made enough progress to qualify for increased access to international financial markets under "normal" circumstances. Those that managed to avoid a debt crisis in the early 1980s had for the most part fulfilled the key prerequisites for commercial borrowing. They had a prolonged period of growth before entering the market, they had expanded their traded goods sector, and they had diversified exports. Although they borrowed heavily in the 1970s, they were able to withstand reasonably well the unprecedented rise in real interest rates, world recession, and volatile exchange rates in the early 1980s. At the center of the historical experience and the outlook for the future, therefore, are the policies of industrial countries and developing countries. These are taken up in the next two chapters.

Part II Role of Economic Policies

3 Macroeconomic and trade policy in industrial countries: a developing-country perspective

International trade and capital flows form the primary economic links between industrial and developing countries. The policies in industrial countries—fiscal, monetary, and trade—largely shape the international economic environment for developing countries. Most of the influences are well known. The pace of economic growth in industrial countries affects the exports of developing countries, as does the scale of protectionism; interest rates and exchange rates in industrial countries influence the cost of borrowing for many developing countries; and so on.

Less familiar is the extent to which industrial countries are affected by what happens in the developing world. Some 30 percent of all their exports in 1983 went there. The 48 percent decline in U.S. exports to the five major Latin American borrowers over 1981–83 was a major factor in the deterioration of the U.S. trade balance over that period. The past few years have also highlighted the risks for the banks in industrial countries when their developing-country borrowers run into debt-servicing difficulties. Like many cliches, the phrase "an interdependent world" is founded on solid facts.

Recent economic developments have again borne this out. The strong recovery in the United States has been the main cause of expanding world trade. The volume of world trade fell by 2.5 percent in 1982, in line with the slowdown in the U.S. economy, but recovered strongly to reach an estimated 8.5 percent growth rate in 1984. Developing countries benefited: their exports grew by an estimated 9 percent in 1984, up from 1.7 percent in 1982. Although most major borrowers increased their supply of exports by reducing domestic demand and reforming their trade regime, the expansion in foreign demand has also played an important role. This is shown by the fact that prices of developing countries' exports increased more than those of traded goods in general.

However, the economic recovery in industrial countries has been unusual in certain respects that

tend to limit its benefits to the rest of the world. Worrisome features are the unprecedented level of real interest rates, especially in the United States, and the large appreciation of the U.S. dollar. High real interest rates increase the debt-servicing burden for borrowing countries. The high real exchange value of the dollar has contributed to depressed primary commodity prices in terms of purchasing power over goods imported from the United States, so net exporters of primary commodities that import a great deal from the United States, like Brazil, have profited less from the recovery in industrial countries than they normally do at this stage of the business cycle (see Box 3.1). Nonetheless, the dollar exchange rate may be a factor behind the high U.S. trade deficits which have led to rapid growth in export volume for several developing countries.

This chapter first gives a broad description of macroeconomic developments in the industrial economies in the last fifteen years to illustrate the changing nature of capital flows between industrial and developing countries. It then analyzes policy issues, paying particular attention to the influence of macroeconomic policies on world interest and exchange rates and on the volume of credit available to developing countries, and to the impact of protectionism on trade and on the debt-servicing capacity of the major borrowers.

Macroeconomic constraints and capital flows

The upheavals of 1969–73 produced major current account imbalances across the world. Higher oil prices transferred income from moderate and low savers (industrial and developing countries) to (at that time) high-saving oil exporters. The resulting excess supply of world savings put downward pressure on world output and interest rates. In real terms, interest rates turned negative for several years, clearly a situation that led to misallocation of resources and that could not be sustained.

The current account developments during the

Box 3.1 Primary commodity prices, business cycles, and the real exchange rate of the dollar

Commodity prices have always been strongly influenced by the economic cycle in industrial countries. Some econometric evidence suggests that a one percentage point rise in the OECD unemployment rate leads to a 15 percent fall in real commodity prices. However, this relationship seems to have changed in the present cyclical upswing. In real terms, commodity prices fell 44 percent between 1979 and 1982—real in this case meaning the nominal prices deflated by the U.S. GDP deflator—but, after rising in 1983, prices have fallen steadily since mid-1984, despite the economic recovery.

Part of the explanation for the sharp fall in the period 1980-82 and for the unusual decline since mid-1984 lies in the large real appreciation of the dollar since 1980. A rise in the real value of the dollar with respect to other industrial countries makes American goods more expensive in terms of goods from those countries. For given commodity prices, demand for primary commodities in the United States will rise since their cost in terms of U.S. goods has fallen. This will divert some commodity exports from the other industrial countries to the United States and also bring forth some extra supply. The net effect will be a fall in commodity prices in terms of U.S. goods and a rise in terms of goods from other industrial countries. If the United States has a larger share in world trade than its commodity imports have in total OECD commodity imports, commodity prices will fall in terms of traded goods in general after an appreciation of the dollar. Empirical analysis shows that a 10 percent real appreciation of the dollar brings real commodity prices in terms of U.S. goods down by 6 percent.

This relationship has obvious implications for coun-

tries such as Brazil: Brazil is a net primary commodity exporter, but a large share of its imports come from the United States. For countries like Brazil many things went wrong simultaneously in 1981-82. Interest rates rose while the recession depressed commodity prices; the dollar appreciation also depressed primary commodity prices further and raised the cost of imports. Net primary commodity importers such as Korea at least got the benefit of cheaper commodity imports. Box figure 3.1A demonstrates this by plotting the real interest rate in terms of export prices—LIBOR minus the rise in dollar export prices—for Korea and Brazil.

Box figure 3.1A Real LIBOR for Brazil and the Republic of Korea, 1965–84

Source: IMF *International Financial Statistics*.

---

mid-1970s, although easy to explain with hindsight, were unexpected at the time. First, the OPEC surpluses were "recycled" with surprising ease, largely because of the growth of the Eurodollar market (see Chapter 6); the second surprise was the pattern of current account deficits that emerged.

Industrial countries—the main oil importers—were expected to run deficits to offset the OPEC surpluses, with developing countries playing a minor role in recycling. Most observers judged that the financial mechanisms needed for recycling surpluses to developing countries simply did not exist. Table 3.1 shows how things in fact developed. The seven largest industrial countries quickly reverted to pre-1973 patterns in their external accounts. They had a $2.8 billion deficit in 1974, then swung back into surpluses averaging $20 billion a year in 1975-78 compared with $9.7 billion in 1973. Although some smaller industrial countries

had deficits, industrial countries as a whole averaged surpluses of $12 billion a year during 1975-78. In contrast, oil-importing developing countries went into substantial deficit in 1974 and 1975. Deficits remained high in 1976-78, compared with the level in 1973, although they declined somewhat as a proportion of GNP in those countries.

OPEC surpluses were thus recycled largely to the developing countries, not to industrial countries. This was made possible by a major change in the structure of financial flows between industrial and developing countries, as commercial banks became much more prominent than they had been. Although official loans and grants from industrial countries increased considerably in 1974-75, the biggest change was the growth of commercial bank lending to developing countries. This established international capital markets as a major channel for transmitting the effects of macroeconomic policies in industrial countries to

Table 3.1 Current account balances of industrial and developing countries, 1970–84
(billions of dollars)

Country group	1970–72[a]	1973	1974	1975–78[a]	1979	1980	1981	1982	1983	1984
Industrial countries	7.0	10.3	−14.6	12.1	−5.6	−38.8	3.1	1.2	2.2	−34.2
United States	0.4	9.1	7.6	1.2	2.6	6.6	10.7	−3.8	−35.5	−93.4
Other six large industrial countries	9.3	0.6	−10.4	19.0	4.6	−18.7	8.8	17.7	39.0	53.2
Middle Eastern oil exporters	2.0	6.5	55.9	33.8	61.9	99.6	56.3	3.3	−11.1	−6.0
Developing countries[b]	−12.8	−9.1	−21.0	−39.5	−51.7	−68.0	−105.1	−99.2	−56.7	−35.6

Note: World total does not equal zero because of measurement errors and incomplete coverage.
a. Annual average.
b. Based on a sample of ninety developing countries.
Source: IMF and World Bank data.

developing countries.

Industrial countries reduced their savings and investment rates in the 1970s. As Chapter 4 makes clear, however, savings ratios rose in most developing countries—the exceptions being in sub-Saharan Africa. Therefore, much of the extra finance obtained by developing countries was used to increase investment. This allowed them to maintain or even raise their GDP growth rates. Without these expansionary policies in developing countries and the resulting increase in their import demand, the recession in industrial countries would have been even deeper. However, with their debt much increased and a higher proportion of it carrying floating interest rates, developing countries were more exposed to the fiscal and monetary policies of the industrial world. The significance of this exposure became clear in the early 1980s.

The beginning of 1980 saw industrial countries in a deepening recession. In many of them budget deficits were already so large that a fiscal stimulus to escape recession was thought to be infeasible. In the same period, governments in industrial countries turned to monetary restraint to tackle inflation. The change in monetary policy was sharpest in the United States. In 1979 the Federal Reserve Board switched from targeting interest rates to targeting the monetary aggregates. This change in operating procedures, coupled with tighter restraint, resulted in both higher and more volatile interest rates, with major implications for countries with substantial parts of their debt at floating rates or in need of refinancing. The increased use of floating interest loans effectively shifted interest rate risk to borrowing countries (see Box 3.2).

The second major increase in oil prices in 1979–80 failed to stop the increase in real interest rates: OPEC surpluses were short lived, and monetary restraint in the major industrial countries was much tighter. Developing countries were thus hav-ing to pay higher interest rates on their external debt at the same time as demand was falling in their main export markets.

Macroeconomic policies, interest rates, and exchange rates

Until the summer of 1982, policies in the industrial countries produced predictable results. Temporarily high real interest rates were the unavoidable by-products of monetary disinflation policies. Monetary restraint was most pronounced in the United States. This contributed to both the appreciation of the dollar and the fact that the downturn in the United States was more severe than in the other major industrial countries despite tighter fiscal policy in most European countries and Japan. Moreover, the expansionary fiscal policy that started taking shape in the United States in 1981 plainly laid the basis for economic recovery by raising both after-tax personal incomes and after-tax returns on corporate investment.

Since mid-1982 developments in industrial economies followed a less predictable path. In the United States changes in banking regulations caused large, erratic movements in the demand for money which were accommodated by the Federal Reserve. At the same time, its earlier restraint started to pay off: inflation came down in 1982 and has since remained at around 4 to 5 percent (see Figure 3.1). But nominal interest rates did not fall in line with inflation; in real terms (measured by nominal rates minus actual inflation), they therefore continued to rise (see Figure 1.4). Moreover, long-term interest rates rose more than short-term rates (see Figure 3.2). This upward tilt in the term structure is an issue of considerable importance to developing countries: since long-term rates reflect expectations about the future path of short-term rates, high long-term rates imply that developing country debtors should anticipate that their debt

Box 3.2 Interest rate variability, risk shifting, and floating rate debt

For developing-country borrowers, it may appear that a switch from fixed rate to floating rate loans passed all the risk on to them. That is not necessarily so. The switch does not have any consequence for real interest rates if changes in real interest rates are brought about by changes in inflation. However, if real interest rates fluctuate because nominal rates do, the lender takes all the risk under fixed rates while the borrower does so under floating rates.

Neither fixed nor floating rate loans provide complete protection from fluctuations in real interest rates. This protection can be obtained from loans whose interest rate is indexed to inflation. Such instruments have largely failed to materialize in international capital markets or in the domestic markets of most major industrial countries (an exception is the United Kingdom, where part of government debt is index linked). And even with indexed loans, a borrower will be more exposed to interest risk if the loan carries a short maturity since it will have to be refinanced frequently at potentially higher rates.

In assessing their financing options, borrowers also need to consider an obvious, though occasionally overlooked, point: their loan will be more expensive whenever the lender bears some or all of the interest rate risk. The analogy is with, say, house or automobile insurance:

to escape risk entirely, one must pay a premium.

Moreover, a country should be concerned not only about variability of interest payments on foreign debt, but also about variability of national income, of which interest payments are only one (negative) component. Sometimes these offset each other. Take the example of an exporter of primary commodities with a large foreign debt.

When aggregate demand shocks are the main source of global instability, interest rates will move up and down with primary commodity prices. In those circumstances, variable real rate debt may be attractive for a commodity exporter: when low primary commodity prices reduce export earnings, real rates are also likely to be low, thereby reducing the country's debt service burden and helping to shield national income from the fluctuations in export revenues.

This example demonstrates that reducing the variability of one component of national income (in this case real interest payments on foreign debt) may in fact increase variability of national income itself if the shocks to different components are correlated among each other. Whether indexed debt is attractive for a borrower will therefore depend on the source of shocks to the world economy and on the structure of trade of the country.

---

service obligation will remain high for some time to come.

At least four factors have been proposed as explanations of the higher real interest rates in the United States.

• *Monetary restraint.* Tight money helps to

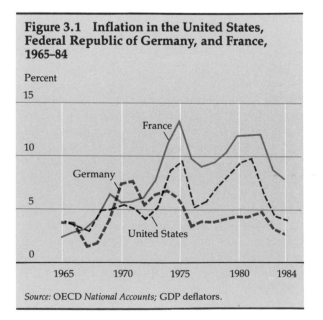

Figure 3.1 Inflation in the United States, Federal Republic of Germany, and France, 1965–84

Percent

Source: OECD National Accounts; GDP deflators.

explain developments through 1982. As is to be expected in periods of tight money, inflation and output fell, the stock market declined, and real interest rates went up. Monetary policy was tighter in the United States than abroad, contributing to the real appreciation of the dollar. However, such effects are temporary and should therefore raise short-term interest rates initially before fading away. Accordingly, after a tightening of monetary policy short-term rates should rise more than long-term rates. In fact, short-term rates rose less than long-term rates. Therefore, other factors must also be part of the explanation of why real interest rates stayed high after 1982.

• *Expectations of high future inflation.* If future inflation is expected to be much higher than the current rate, long-term interest rates are high in nominal terms but not in real terms. Such an argument is not consistent with the high real exchange value of the dollar; high expected future inflation should lead, other things being equal, to a dollar depreciation, not the appreciation that in fact took place. Thus, expectations alone cannot explain the rise in U.S. interest rates.

• *A tax-induced investment boom.* In 1981 the United States changed its tax system in ways that

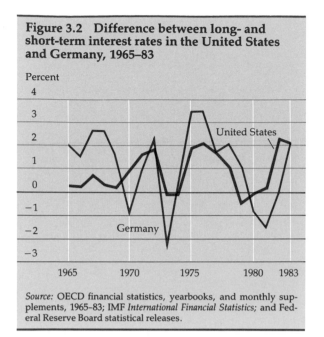

Figure 3.2 Difference between long- and short-term interest rates in the United States and Germany, 1965–83

Source: OECD financial statistics, yearbooks, and monthly supplements, 1965–83; IMF *International Financial Statistics;* and Federal Reserve Board statistical releases.

favored capital investment. The changes resulted in (a) the strong stock market recovery in the United States in 1983–84, and (b) the sharp rise in investment—more than usual at an early stage of the business cycle—high real interest rates notwithstanding. As Figure 3.3 shows, the average rate of profit taxation has indeed fallen considerably. However, the 7 percent decline in the effective rate of profit tax can, on current estimates of the marginal productivity of capital, explain less than a percentage point increase in long-run interest rates. Moreover, the effects of such a tax change on the return to capital might be expected to decline over time, because additional investment in response to the increased after-tax return should, over time, bring down the rate of return on capital. This would point to a flattening of the yield curve—that is, long rates rising less than short rates; the flattening did not take place. Furthermore, investment has not been particularly high by historical standards: 14.7 percent of U.S. GNP in 1983 compared with a 15.5 percent average for 1970–79. Therefore, tax changes are also likely to account for only part of the increases in real interest rates.

• *Budget deficits.* Controversy about the role of deficits starts with their definition (discussed in Box 3.3). But there is no dispute on the strong pressures to increase deficits; in every industrial country, public expenditure has been rising steadily (see Figure 3.4), while taxes and social security contributions have risen much less. In the United States, net government receipts (total government

receipts minus social security outlays) actually fell from 23.7 percent of national income in 1965 to 23 percent in 1984. But government expenditure on goods and services (including interest payments but not social security outlays) actually rose from 23.3 percent of national income in 1965, and 23.9 percent in 1979, to 27.4 percent in 1984.

Budget deficits have grown in the major industrial economies (see Table 3.2, which gives inflation-adjusted deficits of all levels of government). Only Germany and Japan managed to reduce their inflation-adjusted deficits between 1979 and 1984. The biggest change was in the United States, from an inflation-adjusted surplus of 3.6 percent of national income in 1979 to a deficit of 2.7 percent in 1984. Further large deficits are projected unless current policies are changed.

To judge whether the growth of budget deficits contributed to the rise in real interest rates, the analysis cannot stop with figures showing deficits as a proportion of national income. Since world savings equal world investments, an increase in government deficits can be matched in either of two ways: a decline in investment or an increase in domestic and foreign savings. One popular theory argues that reductions in tax revenues will be offset one for one by private savings, with no need for adjustment in investment, the current account of the balance of payments, or world interest rates. This hypothesis is not borne out by experience. Private savings in the United States has been on a steady decline since the mid-1960s with an upturn only since 1982 as the economy came out of the recession. A budget deficit of 2.7 percent of national income is more than half the net private

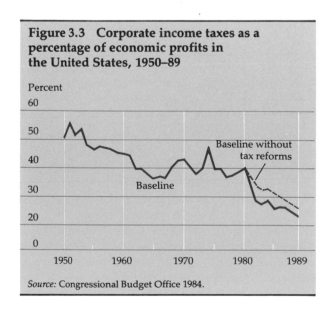

Figure 3.3 Corporate income taxes as a percentage of economic profits in the United States, 1950–89

Source: Congressional Budget Office 1984.

35

Box 3.3 Measurement of government deficits

Problems with the measurement of government deficits involve both accounting conventions and issues of economic analysis.

• *Accounting issues.* Most countries have several layers of government—national, state, and local. The relative importance of the national government varies by country and reflects differences in the scope of its activities. All their accounts should be included in computing the size of the public sector debt, since all have to be financed.

Definitional problems also arise over the treatment of inflation. If, for example, prices are rising at 10 percent a year, a debt of $100 will, after a year, have a real value of only $90. Inflation acts as a hidden capital levy on outstanding debt. Knowing this, lenders demand compensation in the form of higher interest rates. So some of a government's debt interest represents repayment of principal rather than the real cost of borrowing. However, standard measures of government deficits count total interest payments on public sector debt as part of public expenditure. They therefore overestimate the real cost of servicing government debt. The inflation-adjusted deficit (referred to in this chapter) treats only the real interest costs of public debt as being part of public expenditure.

Box figure 3.3A shows both concepts for the United Kingdom. The difference between uncorrected deficits and the inflation-adjusted balance narrows considerably in the 1980s, reflecting falling inflation. It is striking to see that the United Kingdom throughout most of the 1970s and early 1980s actually ran a budget surplus.

• *Analytical issues.* Any analysis of the effects of budget deficits needs to establish what it is that has produced the deficit. A cut in, say, employers' contributions to social security (basically a payroll tax) has different effects on the economy from an increase in defense spending, even though they may produce identical increases in deficits. No single measure will capture all relevant aspects of the complex spending and tax patterns that make up fiscal policy.

A second issue concerns the cyclical adjustment of deficits. A government's budget is affected by the state of the economic cycle: rising unemployment will produce a rising deficit, because tax revenues decline while spend-

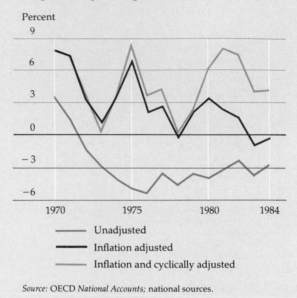

Box figure 3.3A   Public sector surplus in the United Kingdom as a percentage of national income, 1970–84

Unadjusted
Inflation adjusted
Inflation and cyclically adjusted

Source: OECD *National Accounts;* national sources.

ing on unemployment benefits increases. Some analyses of budgetary policy exclude these cyclical influences in order to establish the underlying fiscal stance. The figure shows that the gap between the United Kingdom's inflation-adjusted deficit with and without cyclical adjustment widened dramatically after 1979–80, when unemployment rose.

Cyclically adjusted deficit measures attempt to remove the part of the deficit related to changes in the economy other than changes in fiscal policy. However, deficits caused by other factors still need to be financed by offsetting changes in either private or foreign savings or investment. Where therefore the concern is with the effect of changes in public sector deficits on the balance between savings and investment, and through that on interest rates, rather than with the fiscal policy stance in itself, cyclically adjusted measures are less useful.

(corporate and household) savings rate, adjusted for inflation (see Box 3.3). And the change in the inflation-adjusted fiscal deficit—6.3 percentage points of national income between 1979 and 1984—has not nearly been matched by the two percentage point increase in the private savings rate since 1979. Also, the tax changes in 1981 have broadly offset the negative effects of high real interest rates on the user cost of capital, so investment has not fallen significantly since 1979. As a result, the United States has been absorbing savings from the

rest of the world on a considerable scale. In 1984 the U.S. current account deficit was more than twice that of all developing countries.

These trends can be expected to put upward pressure on world interest rates, to restore balance between global savings and investment. Higher interest rates drew foreign savings to the United States. The large deterioration in the external position of the United States and, to a lesser extent the Middle Eastern oil exporters, was matched by dramatic reductions in current account deficits of oil-

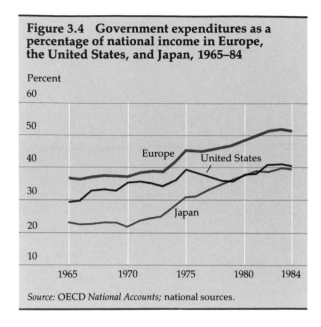

Figure 3.4 Government expenditures as a percentage of national income in Europe, the United States, and Japan, 1965–84

Source: OECD *National Accounts*; national sources.

importing developing countries and industrial countries other than the United States (see Figure 3.5).

Between 1979 and 1984, the U.S. inflation-adjusted budget deficit (see Box 3.3) deteriorated by $162 billion, a shift that was far greater than, for example, the $70 billion current account deterioration of oil-exporting countries over the same period. To put this in perspective, total gross world savings in 1979 is estimated at $2,060 billion. The $162 billion increase therefore represents 8 percent of world savings in 1979. Budget shifts of this size can explain a significant part of the increase in real interest rates. Fiscal deficits can also explain the upward tilt in the term structure of interest rates. Since the U.S. budget deficit is expected to remain high, future short-term interest rates are also

expected to be high—a view consistent with high long-term interest rates at the moment.

To bring real interest rates down for more than a short period, a credible change in fiscal policy in the United States therefore seems desirable. The high dollar exchange rate has stimulated exports to the United States and has therefore increased production in other countries. Avoiding any recessionary impact of such a policy change will require careful coordination with monetary policy in the United States and also with monetary and fiscal policies in other industrial countries. However, failing such a policy change, high real interest rates and a continued high exchange value of the dollar would eventually tend to reduce growth in industrial countries and continue to divert world savings away from developing countries. Moreover, sustained trade imbalances and exchange rate misalignments will lead to increased protectionist pressure in industrial countries. In those circumstances, developing countries would find it increasingly difficult to increase export earnings and service their debts.

Protectionism

Increased protectionism in industrial countries against developing countries' exports reduces the export earnings that developing countries would otherwise obtain. That is detrimental to their capacity to import and to service their debt. It therefore is a threat to efficient economic growth and to a satisfactory solution of the debt problems many developing countries face.

In aggregate, exports from oil-importing developing countries have in fact grown faster than world trade in general since 1974 (in volume terms). With less protectionism they would have

Table 3.2 Inflation-adjusted government budget balance as a percentage of national income in selected industrial countries, 1965–84

Year	United Kingdom	Germany	Italy	France	Japan	United States	Nine large industrial countries Including United States	Nine large industrial countries Excluding United States
1965–73	3.8	1.0	−3.6	1.8	1.8	1.6	1.5	1.4
1974–78	2.7	−2.4	0.3	0.5	2.4	1.0	0.1	−0.6
1979	2.1	−1.9	−0.7	0.8	−4.4	3.6	0.7	−1.3
1980	3.4	−2.1	4.5	2.2	−3.6	2.0	0.7	−0.2
1981	2.2	−2.5	2.0	0.5	−3.3	2.4	0.6	−0.8
1982	1.5	−1.9	−0.3	−0.4	−2.8	−2.0	−1.6	−1.3
1983	−1.1	−1.7	−0.4	−1.5	−3.4	−3.0	−2.7	−2.4
1984	−0.3	−0.4	−4.7	−1.9	−1.7	−2.7	−2.3	−1.9

Note: Negative sign indicates deficit.
Source: OECD *National Accounts*; national sources.

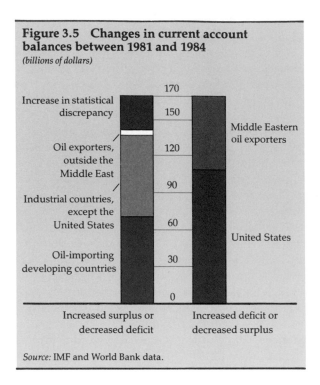

Figure 3.5   Changes in current account balances between 1981 and 1984
(billions of dollars)

Increase in statistical discrepancy

Oil exporters, outside the Middle East

Industrial countries, except the United States

Oil-importing developing countries

Middle Eastern oil exporters

United States

170
150
120
90
60
30
0

Increased surplus or decreased deficit

Increased deficit or decreased surplus

Source: IMF and World Bank data.

done that to a larger degree. Furthermore, their export prices have grown less (by nearly a percentage point a year) than the unit value of trade in general since 1974.

The harm done to industrial countries by their protectionist measures is well documented. The losses they inflict on developing countries can also be substantial. Increased protectionism in industrial countries would reduce the volume of exports from developing countries and adversely affect the latter's terms of trade. By way of illustration, an increase in protectionism big enough to produce a 10 percent deterioration in the terms of trade of Latin America would cost the region as much as the real interest cost of their entire debt.[1]

At the moment, the most severe trade interventions in industrial countries aimed at developing countries are almost all directed primarily against major debtor countries (the Multifibre Arrangement being an exception). Restrictions on steel imports in Japan, the United States, and the EC affect each others' exports, but also those of Korea,

Brazil, and to a lesser extent Mexico, three of the largest developing-country debtors. Restrictions on imported sugar in Europe, Japan, and the United States hit Latin America and the Philippines, another country with debt problems. Restrictions on beef imports in Japan and the EC damage Argentina's terms of trade. The list is long and getting longer.

In the next few years, without a significant increase in capital inflows, the major debtors will need to run substantial trade surpluses. That will require an increase in their domestic savings. These increased savings, however, also need to be translated into increased export earnings: in technical terms, the ex ante trade surplus needs to be brought in line with the ex ante excess of domestic production over expenditure. If industrial countries increase barriers to exports from developing countries, that will require a much larger real depreciation of the exchange rate—or much higher levels of unemployment. Lower levels of trade therefore imply higher social costs for the adjustment programs of developing countries. This in turn seriously threatens the continued implementation of such programs and, more generally, the creditworthiness of these countries and, by straining the ability of major debtors to repay their debts, the stability of the global financial system.

The roots of protectionism

Increased protectionist pressure during the past fifteen years is closely related to the change in the nature of the disturbances to the international economy that took place over the same period. One example is the change in cyclical behavior of inflation. The 1970–73–75 economic cycle (trough-peak-trough) is the only major business cycle in U.S. history in which inflation during the contraction exceeded inflation during the upswing, by some 8.4 percentage points. Until then, inflation was dominated by demand fluctuations: an increase in aggregate demand brought forth higher output, but also (in time) higher prices. But supply shocks, such as an increase in raw material prices, lead to low output and high inflation simultaneously. Demand management can cure one or the other, but not both at the same time. More rapid structural adjustment was necessary to restore growth, yet that was seldom forthcoming. As a result, economic growth slowed down.

Many commentators and governments have attributed this slowdown to the large increase in oil prices in 1973–74. But that is not the whole

1. The calculation is as follows: in 1983, the ratio of external debt (including short-term debt) to GDP was 54.8 percent in Latin America. Assuming that 3.5 percent is the expected real interest rate in the long run (see Chapter 10), such a debt to GDP ratio leads to real interest payments equal to 1.9 percent of GDP a year. Exports were 19 percent of GDP, so a permanent 10 percent terms of trade deterioration would also yield a permanent annual loss of 1.9 percent of GDP. An increase in protectionism in industrial countries that would permanently worsen Latin America's terms of trade by 10 percent would thus deprive the region of income equivalent (in discounted value terms) to its entire external debt.

story. Difficulties had started earlier. In the United States large fiscal deficits in the late 1960s triggered an economic boom and an acceleration in inflation. In European countries real wages began rising faster than labor productivity. Labor markets became increasingly rigid. Profits came under pressure, and investment became more sluggish.

The boom in commodity prices began in 1972, stimulated by near simultaneous expansion in the industrial countries (see Figure 3.6). Its final phase was the jump in oil prices in 1973–74. Since real wages did not adjust sufficiently, profitability declined steeply. Investment therefore slowed down just when higher oil prices were making much of the existing capital stock obsolete. As part of a process of structural adjustment, countries required more, not less, investment. Increasing obsolescence of the capital stock meant that supply side weaknesses were projected into the future as the structure of the capital stock got increasingly out of line with new factor prices.

The link between aggregate supply shocks, rising unemployment, and increasing capital obsolescence helps to explain the revival of protectionist sentiment. When economies were growing rapidly, they could accommodate increased exports from developing countries. Necessary changes in the allocation of the capital stock could be made on the margin out of gross investment; low unemployment meant limited resistance from labor unions to structural change; and so on. But with the need to effect long-term restructuring at a time when growth was slowing and inflation accelerating, rising imports were seen as an additional complication. They became a convenient excuse for policy failures, especially when accommodating them would require further structural adjustment (steel is a good example).

Moreover, there is abundant evidence to show that import restrictions do not save jobs, do not improve the trade balance, and add upward pressure on the real exchange rate. This highlights the perversity of protectionism. Not only do its roots lie in a failure to adjust, but its adoption simply compounds that failure.

Japan and the United States offer good illustrations of what might happen if protection increases. Both countries are currently projected to approach their natural rate of unemployment in 1985. There are, of course, serious difficulties in defining the natural rate of unemployment. In this context, it is defined as the rate of unemployment below which wage-price pressure cannot be contained because additional jobs cannot be created without bidding workers away from other parts of the economy. Therefore, when imports are restricted, every job gained in import-competing industries means a job lost in export industries. Protectionism might save jobs in, say, steel, but, by keeping wages higher than they would be otherwise, it will not save jobs in general. Capital that would have gone to high technology industries or into agriculture will instead be directed to protected sectors. This implies that protection accorded to import-competing industries is protection taken away from export industries. An import control therefore has effects similar to an export tax: it will bring down imports *and* exports, not just imports alone. For the same reason, trade intervention will not improve a country's trade balance, since exports will go down in line with imports. Developing countries, denied the access to markets in, say, the United States—access they need to earn the dollars that can then be used to buy U.S. goods—will cut back on such imports.

In Europe, of course, full employment is still far out of reach. However, this does not mean that increased protectionism there will save jobs. Real wages are rigid in relation to the prices of all consumer goods. Protectionism, by making foreign goods more expensive, will lower the real wage in terms of foreign goods. To maintain the real wage in terms of all goods consumed, it will therefore be necessary for wages to go up in terms of domestic goods. This may actually lead to a fall in employment. Moreover, to the extent that such employment losses are temporary until wages adjust, pro-

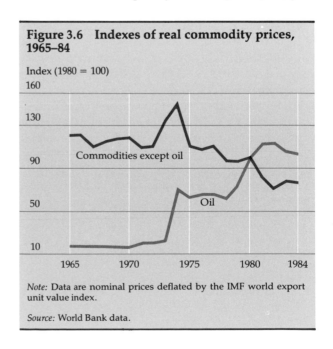

Figure 3.6 Indexes of real commodity prices, 1965–84

Index (1980 = 100)

Note: Data are nominal prices deflated by the IMF world export unit value index.

Source: World Bank data.

39

tectionism will cause a temporary decline in income. This could lead to a deterioration in the current account balance, as consumers will cut expenditure less than one for one with a temporary fall in income.

The new protectionism

Tariff reductions undertaken since World War II were continued in the Tokyo Round negotiations, which lowered tariffs to levels not seen before in this century. But while the reductions have been extended to the developing countries under the Most Favored Nation clause, tariffs have been lowered less than the average on products of interest to developing countries. Moreover, the fact that tariffs rise as raw materials go through progressive stages of processing means that the trading system discourages processing industries in the developing countries.

A more serious danger to developing countries' exports is the growing use of nontariff barriers (NTBs). On one measure—the proportion of imports subject to restriction—the extent of NTBs more than doubled in the United States between 1980 and 1983 and increased by 38 percent in the EC. A much larger share of industrial-country imports from developing countries is subject to NTBs than imports from other industrial countries (see Table 3.3). Such ratios do not reflect tightening of existing NTBs and may therefore underestimate their increased use. One example is the progressive tightening of the Multifibre Arrangement each time it is renegotiated.

Commodity by commodity, NTBs do considerable harm:

• *Agriculture.* Although much attention is paid to the trade barriers erected against the manufactured exports of developing countries, in fact they are less prevalent than those against agricultural exports. In 1983, 29 percent of developing countries' agricultural exports to industrial countries

Table 3.3 Share of imports subject to nontariff barriers in industrial-country markets, 1983

	Percentage of imports from:		
Market	Industrial countries	All developing countries	Major borrowers
EC	10.2	21.8	24.9
Japan	9.3	10.5	9.6
United States	7.7	12.9	14.5
All industrial countries	10.5	19.8	21.9

Note: Data are based on 1981 weighted averages for all world trade in all products except fuels.
Source: World Bank data.

were affected by NTBs; for manufactured exports, the ratio was 18 percent. The persistent protectionism of the main industrial countries has produced surpluses that are often dumped on world markets. This inhibits domestic production in developing countries, even though it would often be more efficient than production in the industrial countries. The tariffs and NTBs used to protect sugar growers in industrial countries inflict income losses on developing-country sugar exporters equal to nearly 10 percent of all the aid from industrial countries to *all* developing countries. The loss of export revenues is estimated to be almost 30 percent of the total aid bill (see Box 3.4).

• *Steel.* The volume of steel imported into the United States fell 3.3 percent a year in 1971–73 when quotas were imposed. It then grew at an annual rate of 8.3 percent in the mid-1970s after quotas were removed. But when the trigger price mechanism was introduced in 1977 it slowed down to 2.6 percent a year.

• *Footwear.* Korean exports of footwear to the United Kingdom increased by 57.5 percent a year in real terms in 1973–79 but fell 19.1 percent a year in 1979 and 1980 after nontariff barriers were imposed.

NTBs do much more damage to the competitive structure of a market than tariffs. Once the quotas have been fulfilled, marginal foreign competitors are excluded from the market—thereby increasing the monopoly power of domestic firms. Tariffs do not remove marginal foreign competitors but simply give them a cost disadvantage. From the exporter's point of view, voluntary export restraints (VERs) are preferable to quotas administered by importers; with VERs, exporters can at least sell their products at market prices prevailing in the importing country rather than at the lower world price. However, the long-term damage of VERs is likely to be higher than that caused by quotas administered by importers: they lock in the existing set of suppliers and keep out any lower-cost competitors that may emerge. Taking the Multifibre Arrangement on textiles as an example of a VER, Korea or Hong Kong may not lose too much—but newcomers like China or Sri Lanka certainly do.

Even more damaging than the direct costs of trade restrictions could be the signal they send to developing countries about the merits of export-oriented policies. Further proliferation of NTBs could very well revive (and justify) the export pessimism that prevailed in many developing countries in the 1930s and 1940s. Yet the empirical evi-

Box 3.4   The costs of protecting sugar and beef

Sugar and beef are the two agricultural commodities most affected by trade barriers in the industrial countries. They account for about half of all the export earnings lost by developing countries as a result of intervention in agricultural trade. Box tables 3.4A and 3.4B show one study's estimates of the costs involved.

Welfare costs are defined as the amount of money that exporters would need to receive to be as well off with protectionism against them in industrial countries as they would be without such measures. These costs are derived from a model of the world market in sugar (raw and refined) and a model of the world beef market. The research covered seventeen industrial countries and fifty-eight developing countries. It distinguished between different forms of trade controls and included the special arrangements on preferential access that the EC has with various groups of developing countries.

For developing-country exporters of sugar, the foreign exchange losses from these barriers amounted in 1983 to almost $7.4 billion (at 1980 prices and exchange rates).

Box table 3.4A   Estimated effects of trade barriers on sugar exporters
(millions of 1980 dollars)

Effect and exporter	Annual average, 1979–81	1983
Welfare costs		
Latin America	670.4	1,111.0
Africa	76.7	130.9
Other developing countries	507.3	886.2
Total	1,254.4	2,128.1
Loss of export revenues		
Latin America	2,224.2	3,391.0
Africa	269.2	421.9
Other developing countries	2,614.9	3,578.1
Total	5,108.3	7,391.0

Source: Zietz and Valdez (background paper).

Box table 3.4B   Estimated effects of trade barriers on beef and veal exporters
(millions of 1980 dollars)

Effect and exporter	Annual average, 1979–81
Welfare costs	
Latin America	506.4
Africa (sub-Saharan)	7.6
Other developing countries	21.7
Total	535.7
Loss in export revenues	
Latin America	4,692.6
Africa (sub-Saharan)	99.0
Other developing countries	303.5
Total	5,095.1

Source: Zietz and Valdez (background paper).

For comparison, the aid programs of all industrial countries in 1983 totaled $22.5 billion (again at 1980 prices and exchange rates).

Losses of welfare and of export revenues are heavily concentrated in Latin America (especially Argentina, Brazil, Dominican Republic, and Mexico) and in the Philippines and India. All are among the biggest debtors in the world. Sub-Saharan Africa, although also a net loser, is not affected as much as Latin America—partly because it has no big sugar producers and also because many African countries have preferential access to EC markets.

Trade barriers on beef and veal exporters also produced substantial welfare losses and export revenue shortfalls for developing countries (Box table 3.4B). Moreover, these losses are almost completely borne by Latin American beef producers, mostly Argentina and, to a lesser extent, Brazil. Again the main developing-country losers from industrial-country protectionism are countries that currently have external debt problems.

---

dence of the benefits of trade for growth is overwhelming. At a time when more and more governments in the developing world are accepting this link, increased protectionism in industrial countries is a major threat to economic growth.

Conclusions

The rapid growth in capital flows has cemented the links between industrial and developing countries that developed through the growth of trade over the past forty years. Protectionism and the level of economic activity rightly concern developing countries, since they affect those countries' exports and terms of trade. Those concerns still

exist, but increased financial links of developing countries with world capital markets have added important channels through which macroeconomic developments in industrial countries are transmitted to developing countries.

The significance of this has become clear in the past few years. Macroeconomic and trade policies in industrial countries directly affect the cost of debt servicing, the volume of capital flows, and the ability of developing countries to earn foreign exchange. High real interest rates have dramatically increased the debt service burden of developing countries, the appreciation of the dollar has depressed commodity prices, and so on. Structural adjustment, sound fiscal policies, and continued

Box 3.5 Implications for developing countries of changes in interest rates, terms of trade, and growth in industrial countries

The external accounts of developing countries are influenced by developments in the industrial countries. Box table 3.5A tries to quantify just what that influence is. It considers only "first-round" effects, ignoring any policy response by developing countries ("second-round" effects are examined in Chapter 10). This is a good measure of welfare costs because, if developing countries were to receive these amounts, they would in fact be able to pursue previous policies and would therefore be as well off as they would be in the absence of such adverse developments in the industrial countries.

• *Interest rates.* Higher interest rates lead immediately to higher interest costs on variable interest rate debt (37 percent of the total debt, including undisbursed debt, of developing countries at the beginning of 1984). Furthermore, as more and more fixed rate debt is repaid and needs to be refinanced, interest payments on it will increase. So will payments on new debt. Thus the extra cost to developing countries is initially only $2.3 billion but it increases to $8 billion in 1990.

• *The terms of trade.* An improvement of one percentage point in the developing countries' terms of trade with respect to industrial countries would have yielded

them $2.2 billion in 1984. As trade expands, so the benefits increase to $4.8 billion in 1990.

• *Growth.* Faster growth in industrial countries will increase the volume of exports from developing countries and improve their terms of trade. Terms of trade effects on economic welfare will dominate, unless increases in volume are produced with resources that would otherwise be idle. This has not been the case recently since increased exports have largely been at the expense of domestic expenditure. The focus therefore is on terms of trade effects, which depend on world demand and supply and also heavily on what happens to the exchange rate of the dollar. If it appreciates, then developing countries might gain little or no improvement in their terms of trade, since prices of their primary commodity exports would be depressed (see Box 3.1) while prices of their dollar-denominated imports would rise. The second set of estimates assumes a dollar appreciation large enough to prevent any real increase in commodity prices, which is what has happened during the 1983–85 recovery. Without the real increase in commodity prices, the current account gain in 1990 is reduced from $7.7 billion to only $2.9 billion.

Box table 3.5A Effects of macroeconomic changes on the current account balance of all developing countries
(billions of dollars)

Type of change	1984	1990
One percentage point increase in interest rates		
Existing variable rate debt	−2.3	−2.3
Existing fixed rate debt refinanced at new higher rate	0.0	−1.6
New debt	0.0	−4.1
Total	−2.3	−8.0
One percentage point improvement in terms of trade	2.2	4.8
One percentage point improvement in industrial countries' GNP growth		
A. *Without dollar appreciation*		
Through terms of trade effect of increased commodity prices	2.2	4.8
Direct terms of trade effect	1.3	2.9
Total	3.5	7.7
B. *With dollar appreciation*		
Through terms of trade effect of increased commodity prices	0.0	0.0
Direct terms of trade effect	1.3	2.9
Total	1.3	2.9

Source: van Wijnbergen (background paper).

and coordinated monetary restraint in industrial countries to bring down real interest rates and more properly align exchange rates are of utmost importance if adjustment policies in developing countries are to lead to renewed growth and restored creditworthiness (see Box 3.5).

There are, moreover, new reasons for concern about the protectionist trends emerging in industrial countries. The costs of such policies to industrial countries' consumers and developing countries' exporters are well documented. The recent debt service problems have added a new dimension to these concerns. Capital flows allow a more efficient use of world savings if borrowing coun-

tries follow rational policies. Servicing of the resulting foreign debt would be impeded seriously if increased protection in industrial countries were to deny developing countries access to industrial countries' markets. This is turn would jeopardize the effective functioning of the financial system.

The industrial countries' policies that have been singled out as beneficial for developing countries would also foster stable and noninflationary growth in industrial countries and would create a more liberal trading environment. They would therefore benefit industrial and developing countries alike.

4 Foreign borrowing and developing-country policies

Foreign borrowing has two potential benefits for a developing country. It can promote growth, and it can help an economy to adjust to internal and external shocks. However, recent experience has graphically illustrated that borrowing also has potential disadvantages. It can be wasted on inefficient investment. It can allow a government to delay essential economic reforms. And the accumulation of debt can make an economy more vulnerable to financial pressures from the world economy.

How can a developing country obtain the benefits of capital inflows while taking reasonable precautions to avoid debt-servicing difficulties? This chapter draws on the experience of the past two decades to identify the criteria for success in using international capital. It deals primarily with debt-creating capital; equity investment is discussed in Chapters 5 and 9. This chapter's main theme is that the economic policies of developing countries are the fundamental determinant of the level of capital inflows, the efficiency with which they are used, and a country's capacity to service its debts.

This is not to say that policy failings have been the only cause of recent debt-servicing problems. Nor is it to imply that sound macroeconomic policies and less borrowing would have avoided those difficulties. Chapter 3 has shown that the combination in the early 1980s of world recession and rising real interest rates was unusual and severe; it is not clear that developing countries should seek to protect themselves fully against all risks including those that have little chance of materializing with any frequency. But flexibility in policymaking and economic structures can cushion the impact of external shocks, however severe.

There is, of course, no single set of policies that is right for every country. The extent to which a country should borrow from abroad depends on the external environment that it faces in world trade and capital markets, its natural and human resources, and its economic and political structures. In view of this, the chapter begins with a brief description of the variety of country experiences with foreign capital over the past twenty years, based on a sample of forty-four developing countries. (For a listing of these countries, see Statistical Appendix, Table A.11.)

This is followed by a discussion of the two main uses of external finance. First, it may be used systematically to raise investment and growth to a higher level than could be financed by domestic savings. Second, it may be used to finance balance of payments disequilibria, caused either by inadequate domestic policies or by external or internal shocks. The discussion explores the questions of when borrowing for balance of payments purposes is appropriate and how governments can borrow to facilitate adjustment rather than to postpone it.

Country experience over two decades

The diversity of developing countries' experience with foreign capital is illustrated in Figure 4.1. Countries' rankings differ according to the indicators chosen. For example, countries with similar debt to GNP ratios may have very different debt to export or debt service ratios. These differences are explained by the degree of openness of an economy and the structure of its debt. In 1980–82, for instance, countries that were relatively "closed"—much of Latin America, but also others such as Yugoslavia and Pakistan—had relatively low debt to GNP ratios but high debt to export ratios. Those with a large export base—some East Asian countries (Korea, Malaysia, and Thailand), oil and gas exporters (such as Algeria, Indonesia, and Venezuela) and Africa's main commodity exporters (Ivory Coast)—tended to have relatively low debt to export ratios.

However, high ratios of debt to GNP or debt to exports do not necessarily imply high debt service ratios. Low-income countries such as India, Sri Lanka, Sudan, and Tanzania, as well as countries such as Egypt, tend to receive much of their capital inflows in low-interest, long-maturity loans (see

Figure 4.1 The debt ladder
(percent)

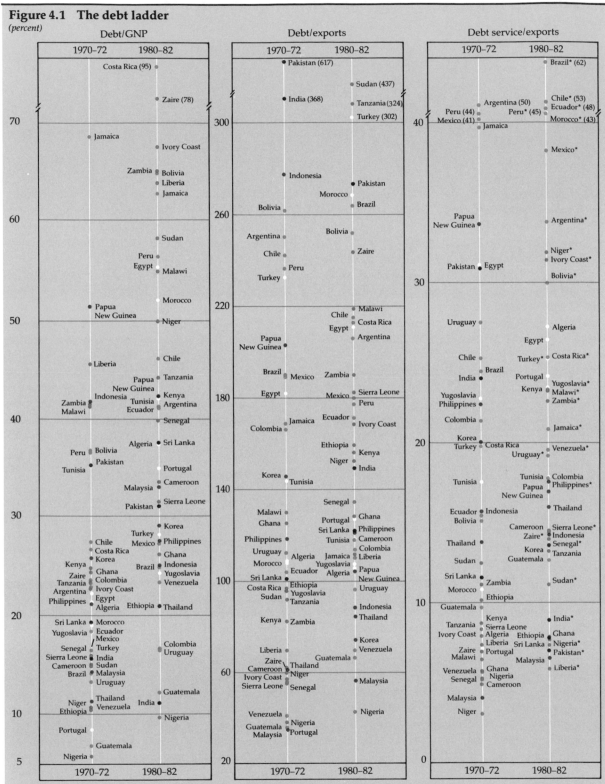

| Debt/GNP | Debt/exports | Debt service/exports |

- ● Latin America and Caribbean
- ● Sub-Saharan Africa
- ● South Asia
- ● East Asia and Pacific
- ○ Europe and North Africa

Note: Debt is defined as medium- and long-term public and publicly guaranteed plus private nonguaranteed debt outstanding and disbursed. Short-term debt is not included. For the major borrowers, the inclusion of short-term debt would raise the external debt registered during 1980–82 by about 30 percent. The debt service figures used are those for actual (not contractual) debt service paid during the period. Exports cover goods and total services. An asterisk indicates that the country rescheduled its debt between 1975 and 1984.

Source: World Bank data.

World Development Indicators, Table 17). By contrast, upper-middle-income countries—for example, Algeria, Portugal, and Venezuela—usually are less able to sustain high debt ratios because the servicing costs of their borrowing are high.

The debt service ratio has traditionally been regarded as a good guide to a country's debt problem. But, as the debt ladder in Figure 4.1 shows, there is no clear link between high debt service ratios and countries that have had to reschedule their debt. Experience has shown that the more economic policies and structures can react flexibly to changing demands, the less are high debt service ratios a cause for concern. An inflexible economy with a modest debt service ratio may be more prone to crisis than one with a higher ratio but with a government that takes rapid corrective action when growth and exports are threatened.

This point can be demonstrated by comparing the two main groups of reschedulers described in Chapters 1 and 2. In general, low-income Africa has had lower debt service ratios than middle-income Latin American countries. This might suggest that African countries are in less serious difficulties. In fact, the opposite is true. Although the policies of both groups were insufficiently flexible in the 1970s and early 1980s, Latin American countries would have found it easier to make the necessary adjustments to external pressures. Their higher incomes provide greater scope for increasing savings; their more developed economies can respond more quickly to changing prices and market opportunities. The low-income African countries, with weak institutional structures and limited human and natural resources, face much more daunting problems.

Three broad factors have determined the growth of debt in recent years. All of them are related to the economic policies of developing countries.

• *Borrowing strategy.* Some governments have chosen to borrow abroad to increase investment and promote domestic growth. Brazil and Korea, for example, increased their borrowing in the 1960s, and both initially had high debt ratios. Both countries also grew and borrowed rapidly in the 1970s, taking advantage of low or negative real interest rates. But their debt ratios moved in opposite directions, as Korea outstripped Brazil in expanding output and exports. Other countries have chosen to borrow relatively little, preferring to rely on domestic savings and other non-debt-creating inflows (such as workers' remittances). India in the 1970s was one example. Thailand also borrowed little from commercial sources during most of this period. Colombia, which had been a large recipient of aid in the 1960s and early 1970s, renounced further concessional assistance in 1974. It made only limited use of foreign credit during the 1970s, though it benefited from rapid growth in nontraditional export earnings.

• *Access to foreign funds.* Clearly not all developing countries have access to all types of foreign capital. This has influenced their borrowing experiences and the current size and composition of their debt. A country's opportunity to borrow commercially tends to grow as its economy progresses: higher per capita income tends to go hand in hand with "graduation" away from reliance on concessional funds and toward expanded access to private sources of finance (see Figure 4.2 and Statistical Appendix, Table A.12). But factors other than income are important determinants of a country's access to commercial finance. In the commodity boom of the 1970s, many middle-income countries—and even low-income countries such as Niger and Sudan—found it possible to borrow from foreign banks, though their loans were often only marginally related to the economic viability of the projects being financed. When these projects ran into difficulty and commodity prices fell, banks stopped lending.

• *Macroeconomic imbalances.* Foreign borrowing is often the unintended consequence of other economic policies. Large budget deficits, overvalued exchange rates, and measures that discourage domestic savings all bias an economy toward relying on foreign capital. They have been common in some of the countries near the top of the debt ladder—for example, Argentina, Peru, and Turkey. By contrast, Malaysia and several other East Asian countries have consciously avoided big fiscal deficits and distortions of prices and exchange rates; they are near the bottom of the debt ladder. Macroeconomic imbalances have also been caused by sharp changes in terms of trade. Many countries resorted to foreign borrowing in the 1970s to finance what they expected to be temporarily large external resource gaps.

Capital inflows and investment

Foreign capital allows a country to invest more than it could if it used only national savings. In the early stages of a country's development, when its capital stock is small, returns to investment are generally higher than in industrial countries. This is the basic economic justification for developing countries to obtain capital from abroad, and it

45

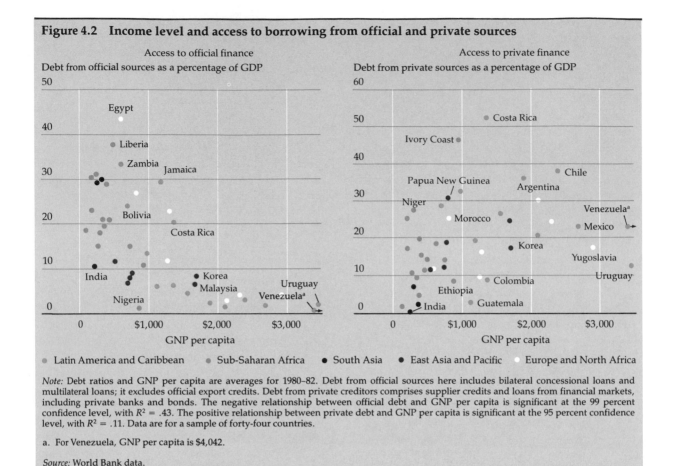

Figure 4.2 Income level and access to borrowing from official and private sources

Access to official finance
Debt from official sources as a percentage of GDP

Access to private finance
Debt from private sources as a percentage of GDP

● Latin America and Caribbean   ● Sub-Saharan Africa   ● South Asia   ● East Asia and Pacific   ○ Europe and North Africa

Note: Debt ratios and GNP per capita are averages for 1980–82. Debt from official sources here includes bilateral concessional loans and multilateral loans; it excludes official export credits. Debt from private creditors comprises supplier credits and loans from financial markets, including private banks and bonds. The negative relationship between official debt and GNP per capita is significant at the 99 percent confidence level, with R^2 = .43. The positive relationship between private debt and GNP per capita is significant at the 95 percent confidence level, with R^2 = .11. Data are for a sample of forty-four countries.

a. For Venezuela, GNP per capita is $4,042.

Source: World Bank data.

underlies the so-called debt cycle (see Box 4.1). In 1960–83, domestic savings financed about 90 percent of the investment in developing countries; in industrial countries, savings actually exceeded domestic investment requirements by about 3 percent.

However, patterns of saving and investment of groups of countries began to change perceptibly after 1973, as shown in Figure 4.3.

• The traditional surplus of savings generated by the industrial countries was reduced, with two brief periods of deficit in 1974 and 1979.

• This coincided with the increased reliance of oil-importing developing countries on foreign capital inflows, first to finance greater investment and later to replace declining domestic savings. Latin American countries demonstrate this pattern best.

• In Africa, the long-term decline in domestic savings was more significant.

• Middle-income oil exporters began raising investment in the early 1960s; the domestic savings effort began improving from the late 1960s.

These countries were net lenders to the rest of the world for brief periods following two rounds of oil price increases, but were otherwise substantial borrowers. Declines in oil-based incomes during 1981–82 depressed domestic savings and reduced inflows of foreign savings, forcing even larger corrections in investment.

• In contrast, the low-income countries of South Asia were able to increase domestic savings from the late 1960s to finance higher levels of investment, reducing in relative terms their use of foreign capital. (Statistical Appendix, Table A.11, gives details for forty-four developing countries.)

Figure 4.4 suggests that, until recently, countries that borrowed tended to raise their investment rates. The positive relationship between borrowing and investment is statistically significant in the 1965–72 and 1973–78 periods, but not in 1979–83. The link between borrowing and growth is more complex. As Figure 4.5 shows, the relationship between changes in the debt to GDP ratio and economic growth was positive but not significant in the 1965–72 and 1973–78 periods. In the latter

Box 4.1 The debt cycle hypothesis

As development proceeds, changes in domestic income, rates of saving, capital stock accumulation, and rates of return on investment can be expected to alter the rate and direction of international capital flows. This has led to the formulation of the debt cycle hypothesis: countries will move through stylized balance of payments and debt stages, as shown in Box figure 4.1A. Each stage is characterized as follows:

Stage I: Young debtor

- Trade deficit.
- Net outflow of interest payments.
- Net capital inflow.
- Rising debt.

Stage II: Mature debtor

- Decreasing trade deficit, beginning of a surplus.
- Net outflow of interest payments.
- Decreasing net capital inflow.
- Debt rising at diminishing rate.

Stage III: Debt reducer

- Rising trade surplus.
- Diminishing net outflow of interest payments.
- Net capital outflow.
- Falling net foreign debt.

Stage IV: Young creditor

- Decreasing trade surplus, then deficit.
- Net outflow of interest payments, then inflow.
- Outflow of capital at decreasing rate.
- Net accumulation of foreign assets.

Stage V: Mature creditor

- Trade deficit.
- Net inflow of interest payments.
- Diminishing net capital flows.
- Slow-growing or constant net foreign asset position.

In the aggregate, of course, the world cannot be in either a net debt or net asset position. Therefore, as more countries move toward the mature creditor stage, the relative size of their asset position should tend to diminish. The fact that industrial countries' collective net asset position is small relative to their GNP, although gross capital flows are very large, corresponds well with the debt cycle hypothesis. So does the pattern of structural balance of payment changes in the United Kingdom and the United States over the past 150 years. Until very recently the balance of payments of these two countries followed the five stages quite closely.

For developing countries, the evidence is mixed. In the colonial period, many countries, particularly primary product exporters, ran current account surpluses, becoming, in effect, capital exporters. A small group of advanced developing countries moved from the young debtor to the mature debtor stage between 1950 and

1975, but most oil-importing countries remained in the first stage until very recently. A few, such as China, remained net creditors throughout all or most of this period.

The debt cycle model does not predict reliably how long a country may remain in any given stage of the debt cycle. The hypothetical example in Box table 4.1A depicts a developing country passing from the first to the second stage of the cycle, where it remains for a prolonged period. The trade account and net interest payments continue in deficit throughout. The rate of return on investment (as approximated by the inverse of the incremental capital output ratio) is higher than in surplus countries, warranting a mutually beneficial transfer of savings to the developing country. In the first decade, the real growth rate of exports is lower than the real interest rate, leading to rapidly growing current account deficits and debt; the latter rises from zero in the first year to $100 million after ten years. When the debt service and debt to GDP ratios reach what are regarded as their maximally sustainable levels of 30 percent and 40 percent, respectively, a surge in exports is required to finance interest payments and amortization. In the fif-

Box figure 4.1A Balance of payments flows and debt stock during the debt cycle

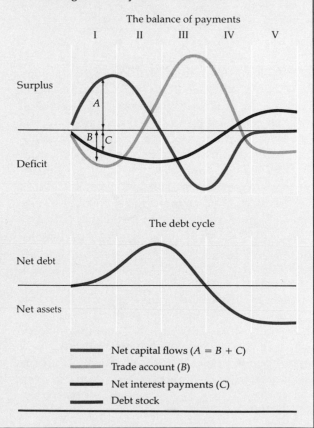

The balance of payments

I II III IV V

Surplus

A

B C

Deficit

The debt cycle

Net debt

Net assets

———— Net capital flows ($A = B + C$)
———— Trade account (B)
———— Net interest payments (C)
———— Debt stock

teenth year, growth rates of exports and GDP, as well as the debt ratios, settle down to their long-run sustainable levels. Export growth has risen to 6 percent, which is sufficient to sustain continued current account deficits and steadily growing debt.

Sudden shifts in major economic variables, as have occurred with particular force in the past decade, often lead to major departures from the predicted path. During the latter half of the 1970s, many developing countries thought to be mature debtors reverted to the early debtor stage, importing capital and running mounting trade deficits. In the 1980s, many of these same countries have been moved to the third, or early creditor, stage, reducing net debt by running huge trade surpluses. This development is, of course, the mirror image of what has occurred in some industrial countries. For example, in terms of the debt cycle hypothesis, the United States recently reentered the early debtor stage of the debt cycle, incurring debt at an accelerating rate while increasing its trade deficits. The reasons for these shifts are complex and are explored in the Report.

Box table 4.1A Sustainable growth of debt: a hypothetical case
(average annual percent, unless otherwise noted)

Variable	1st to 5th years	6th to 10th years	11th to 15th years	16th to 20th years	21st to 30th years
Interest rate	3.75	3.75	3.75	3.75	3.75
Growth of exports	3.0	3.0	14.1	6.0	6.0
Growth of GDP	6.2	7.4	6.4	6.0	6.0
Current account deficit/GDP	2.1	6.4	3.9	2.4	2.4
Debt service/ exports	2.1	17.5	32.0	31.0	31.0
Debt/GDP	4.6	24.0	42.0	42.0	42.0
Debt at end of period (millions of dollars)	16.5	103.0	210.0	280.0	530.0

Note: Calculations are based on a simulation model that makes the following assumptions: incremental capital output ratio = 3.5; consumption = 80 percent of GDP; import elasticity = 1.0; Maturity of debt = 12 years. Growth rates and interest rates are expressed in real terms.

period, some countries that borrowed heavily grew slowly or not at all. In some instances—such as Peru and Zambia—slow growth was associated with stagnant investment ratios; foreign capital was being used to cover balance of payments deficits caused by unsustainable macroeconomic policies and falling commodity prices. In other countries—mainly in Africa—substantial capital inflows helped to raise investment rates, but the investments themselves were often inefficient. Nonetheless, countries such as India (see Box 4.2), Indonesia, and Korea achieved moderate or even very high growth rates without raising their borrowing rates. Finally, in 1979–83, the relationship between changes in debt to GDP and growth of GDP was negative. In an environment of rising real interest rates and contracting world economic output, increased borrowing no longer translated into higher growth. Again, however, the experience is not uniform for all countries. Malaysia, for example, borrowed heavily, but also achieved impressive growth.

The range of country experiences with borrow-

ing, investment, and growth highlights the imperative of using all capital efficiently. Public sector investments require careful appraisal, taking reasonable precautions for downside risks. Private sector projects need a framework of incentives—rewards and penalties—which encourage efficient investment. Failure in these two areas has been a primary cause of slow growth in some countries in the past decade (see Box 4.3).

Where foreign capital is involved, countries can run into a "transformation problem"—that is, the projects fail to generate (or save) enough foreign exchange to service the foreign debt. This can happen for several reasons. Project gestation periods may be mismatched with the maturity profile of the loans—an issue of portfolio management that will be discussed in the next chapter. Alternatively, certain projects may never be able to generate or save sufficient foreign exchange over any time period. That would not matter in an economy undistorted by overvalued exchange rates, high protection, and consumption and investment subsidies. Whether investments produced traded goods (exportables or import substitutes) or goods that could not be internationally traded, such as education, electricity, or piped water, would be irrelevant: so long as rates of return were higher than the cost of the borrowed funds, output and savings would be raised, leaving an extra exportable surplus large enough to repay the debt.

However, where policy-induced price distortions occur, as in many developing countries, there is no

guarantee that enough foreign exchange will be generated. In Jamaica, Peru, and Turkey, vulnerability to debt-servicing difficulties was especially high in the 1970s because policy distortions led to export growth slower than in most other middle-income countries. Obviously, the best solution to this problem is to remove the distortions. Turkey reversed its policies in the early 1980s and export growth accelerated dramatically. Where it is not

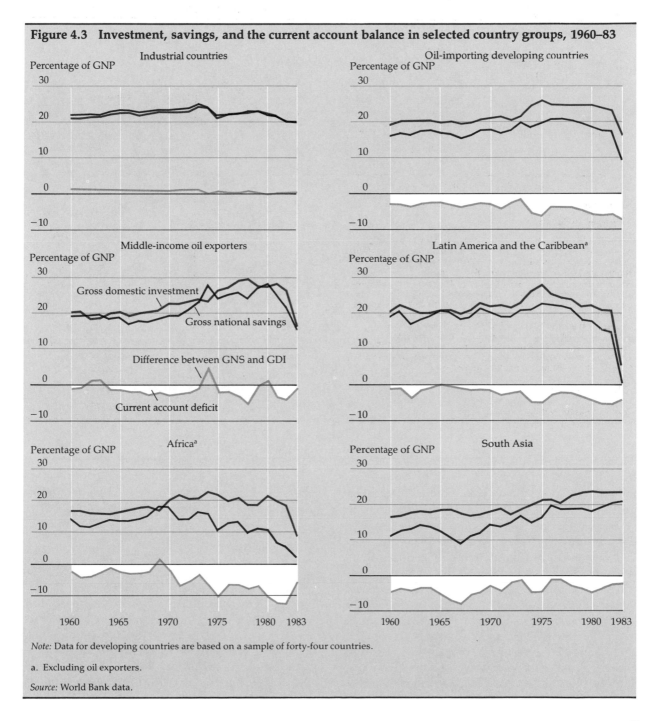

Figure 4.3 Investment, savings, and the current account balance in selected country groups, 1960–83

Note: Data for developing countries are based on a sample of forty-four countries.

a. Excluding oil exporters.

Source: World Bank data.

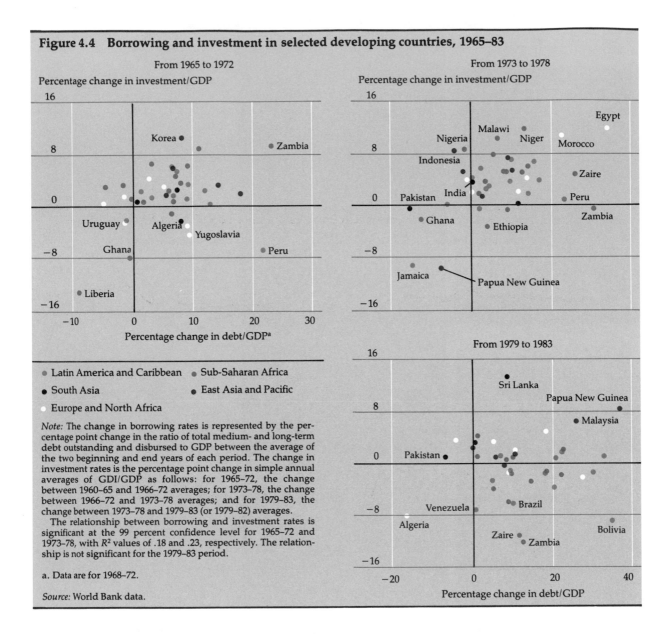

Figure 4.4 Borrowing and investment in selected developing countries, 1965–83

From 1965 to 1972

Percentage change in investment/GDP

From 1973 to 1978

Percentage change in investment/GDP

From 1979 to 1983

Percentage change in debt/GDP[a]

Percentage change in debt/GDP

- Latin America and Caribbean
- Sub-Saharan Africa
- South Asia
- East Asia and Pacific
- Europe and North Africa

Note: The change in borrowing rates is represented by the percentage point change in the ratio of total medium- and long-term debt outstanding and disbursed to GDP between the average of the two beginning and end years of each period. The change in investment rates is the percentage point change in simple annual averages of GDI/GDP as follows: for 1965–72, the change between 1960–65 and 1966–72 averages; for 1973–78, the change between 1966–72 and 1973–78 averages; and for 1979–83, the change between 1973–78 and 1979–83 (or 1979–82) averages.

The relationship between borrowing and investment rates is significant at the 99 percent confidence level for 1965–72 and 1973–78, with R^2 values of .18 and .23, respectively. The relationship is not significant for the 1979–83 period.

a. Data are for 1968–72.

Source: World Bank data.

feasible to remove distortions for political or other reasons, countries would be wise to reduce their reliance on foreign finance. Even where policy distortions are not significant, certain countries in the earliest stages of development may experience transformation problems because their capacity to increase their output of tradable goods may be severely limited. As discussed in Chapter 7, countries in that position will generally require concessional assistance.

While the sustainable level of debt will differ from country to country, borrowing can be successful only if the rate of return on all investment exceeds the cost of borrowed funds. Furthermore, sufficient foreign exchange needs to be generated to service existing debt. If current account deficits

are run for development purposes, the growth of output and exports must in the long run exceed the interest rate on debt to ensure that debt levels do not become unsustainable (see Box 4.4).

Appraising public investment

Efficiency in the public sector is crucial, because public sector investment accounts for a high proportion of total domestic investment in developing countries. In many countries in the mid to late 1970s, the rapid growth of public investment was the precursor to later debt-servicing difficulties.

In appraising public investments, many governments have not drawn a distinction between financial and economic returns. Investments by public

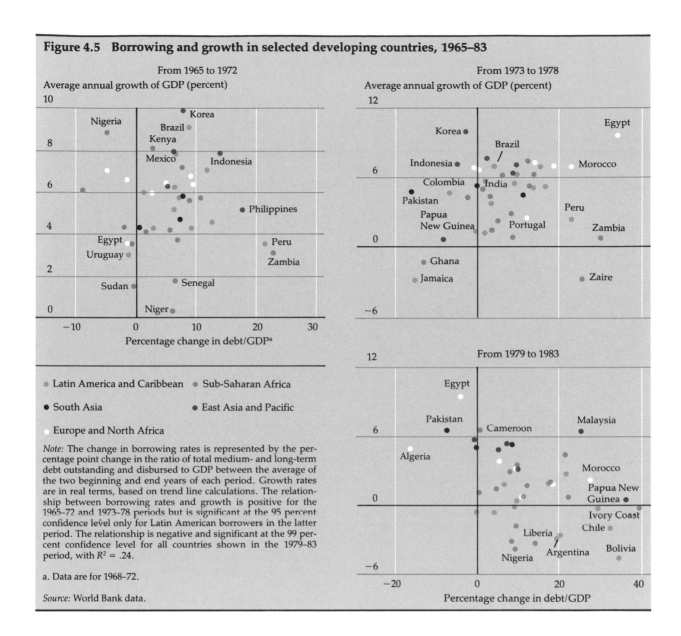

Figure 4.5 Borrowing and growth in selected developing countries, 1965–83

From 1965 to 1972

Average annual growth of GDP (percent)

Percentage change in debt/GDP[a]

From 1973 to 1978

Average annual growth of GDP (percent)

From 1979 to 1983

Percentage change in debt/GDP

- Latin America and Caribbean
- Sub-Saharan Africa
- South Asia
- East Asia and Pacific
- Europe and North Africa

Note: The change in borrowing rates is represented by the percentage point change in the ratio of total medium- and long-term debt outstanding and disbursed to GDP between the average of the two beginning and end years of each period. Growth rates are in real terms, based on trend line calculations. The relationship between borrowing rates and growth is positive for the 1965–72 and 1973–78 periods but is significant at the 95 percent confidence level only for Latin American borrowers in the latter period. The relationship is negative and significant at the 99 percent confidence level for all countries shown in the 1979–83 period, with $R^2 = .24$.

a. Data are for 1968–72.

Source: World Bank data.

enterprises that appear to be profitable in financial terms may be so because the industries are protected by tariffs and regulations or because they are subsidized by the government through low-interest loans or cash transfers. In economic terms, however, the project may be unprofitable and may contribute little or nothing to the economy's growth. The discrepancy between financial and economic evaluation can be overcome by making more use of techniques such as shadow pricing in project appraisal and, more importantly, by policy reforms—liberalizing imports, decontrolling prices, reducing subsidies—designed to narrow the gap between financial and economic returns.

The problem of inadequate appraisal is common in most developing countries, but is particularly severe in Africa. A recent World Bank report, *Toward Sustained Development in Sub-Saharan Africa,* in discussing the large inflows of commercial borrowings in the 1970s, concludes:

While part of these borrowings was used to maintain consumption when commodity prices fell (such as in Zambia), most of them went to finance large public investments, many of which contributed little to economic growth or to generating the foreign exchange to service the debt. These projects covered a wide spectrum of sectors and countries. Examples include projects such as large conference centers, administrative buildings, university centers, hotels, and highways, as well as projects in the industrial sector, such as oil and

Box 4.2 Careful borrowing and risk avoidance: the case of India

Throughout the 1960s and 1970s, India controlled inflows of foreign capital. Whenever balance of payments pressures became severe, the government reduced imports—in the short term through contractionary fiscal and monetary policies, investment licensing, and direct controls; over the long term through selective import substitution. What foreign borrowing did take place was mainly on concessional terms.

The first round of oil price increases in 1973–74 worsened India's already vulnerable external accounts and exacerbated inflation. Although the economy was already in recession, the government decided against borrowing abroad to absorb this new shock. Instead, domestic savings were boosted from 14 percent of GDP in 1965–72 to 19 percent in 1973–78 by raising taxes and interest rates, reducing public spending, and tightening monetary policy. Domestic energy prices were also raised quickly to the new international levels. The recession deepened, narrowing the trade deficit significantly. In addition, workers' remittances increased from $200 million in 1974 to almost $1 billion in 1977, as many Indians worked in the Middle East construction boom.

By 1978, India's external adjustment was complete. Indeed, the country had become a net lender to the rest of the world, with a small trade and current account surplus, a comparatively low debt to GDP ratio (around 15 percent), and large foreign reserves ($8.3 billion in 1978, equivalent to almost eleven months of imports). Stabilization and adjustment had been emphasized to the extent that the economy's growth had been held back.

In the early 1980s, to raise efficiency and speed up growth, India gradually liberalized import controls, increased incentives for investment, and borrowed more from abroad. Although most borrowing continued to be concessional, foreign loans from commercial sources increased modestly, from 3 percent of external public debt in 1979 to roughly 8 percent in 1983. Domestic savings also rose further and averaged 23 percent of GDP during 1976–83—well above earlier rates.

Despite another increase in oil prices and a severe drought, India's growth rate has picked up. In 1979–84, it averaged 5.1 percent a year, compared with 3.6 percent a year in 1950–79. Although the debt service ratio is expected to rise somewhat in the next few years, diminished dependence on imported food and energy, combined with good prospects for raising export growth, provide India with greater flexibility than before in managing its external debt and the balance of payments.

Box 4.3 Foreign borrowing and investment efficiency in the Philippines, Argentina, and Morocco

The damage done by inefficient investment is well illustrated by three otherwise dissimilar countries.

• *The Philippines.* In the 1960s and 1970s, the Philippines had an investment-led, high-growth strategy, based on import substitution. Its economy grew rapidly, but its investment was less productive than that of many neighboring developing countries. Much of it went into industries protected by high and uneven import barriers. The currency was overvalued, interest rates were held down by controls, and credit was often allocated on political rather than commercial criteria.

In the early 1970s public enterprises increased their investment considerably. Lacking internal finance, many became dependent on government support and foreign credit. The government's mechanisms for evaluating and supervising projects remained weak. Investments were concentrated in infrastructure projects with long gestation periods. Consequently, the large rise in foreign borrowing did not produce a matching increase in debt-servicing capacity. The incremental capital output ratio (ICOR—the measure of investment per unit of additional output) more than doubled during 1978–82. The government is now seeking to strengthen its investment programming and evaluation and is reforming some key incentives for efficient investment.

• *Argentina.* Until recently, Argentina had one of the highest investment ratios in Latin America, averaging around 22 percent of GDP. Nearly two-thirds of this investment was in the private sector. However, much of it was inefficient—the result of volatile and often inconsistent policies, import-substituting industrialization, and high and variable inflation. The economy-wide ICOR rose from 4.4 in 1963–72 to around 11 during 1973–81. This ratio was by far the highest among big Latin American economies. Of the $35 billion borrowed from abroad between 1976 and 1982, little, if any, was used to finance net additional investment. This was a critical factor in explaining the dimensions of Argentina's current debt difficulties.

• *Morocco.* Heavy foreign borrowing during the 1970s helped sustain investment of 25 percent of GDP in Morocco, nearly double the rate of the 1960s. Increasing domestic protectionism—coupled with inflationary macroeconomic policies, subsidies, and price controls—distorted investment incentives. The economy's ICOR rose from 2.6 in 1965–72 to 6.7 in 1979–82. The public sector, which undertook the bulk of new investment, achieved low, sometimes negative, rates of return on projects in irrigation, transport, and education. Public investment for each new job created was about thirty times higher than the national average, while the production costs of some state products, such as refined sugar, were as much as 2.6 times the world price.

Box 4.4 Guidelines for borrowing

Debt accumulates when loans are used to finance an excess of imports over exports as well as interest payments on existing debt. Countries running a resource gap need to be concerned with the behavior and relationship of a number of critical debt-related variables, including the growth rate of debt, the growth rate of exports and income, the size of the resource gap relative to income or debt, and the interest rate at which borrowing takes place. Specifically they will want to ensure that neither the interest rate nor the growth of debt persistently exceeds the growth of exports or income.

If these guidelines are not observed, debt and debt ratios may well grow at explosive rates.[1] Example 1 in Box figure 4.4A shows a hypothetical country that adheres to the guidelines. Both exports and GDP grow fast enough for the current account deficit eventually to decline—and, with it, debt and debt ratios. Example 2 shows a country that violates both guidelines. The growth of debt exceeds the growth of exports and income, and the interest rate exceeds the growth rate of both GDP and exports. Capital inflows accelerate; debt and debt ratios grow on an explosive, unsustainable path. Example 3 shows an intermediate case. While the debt ratios grow continuously, their rate of growth diminishes, and the ratios move toward a stable plateau. Such a country may, therefore, be able to maintain both liquidity and solvency. Apart from these guidelines that relate to macroeconomic variables, a borrower will, of course, want to ensure adherence to a simple rule of prudent borrowing: the cost of an additional loan should not exceed the rate of return on the additional investment.

---

1. The guidelines can be derived mathematically as follows:

$$\Delta D = T + iD$$
$$t = T/D$$
$$\Delta D/D = \dot{D} = t + i$$

where D is debt outstanding; T is the current account balance on goods and nonfactor services; t is the resource gap as a proportion of debt; and i is the interest rate on debt. Overdots indicate growth rates. Hence,

$$(\dot{D/Y}) = \dot{D} - \dot{Y} = t + (i - \dot{Y})$$
$$(\dot{D/X}) = \dot{D} - \dot{X} = t + (i - \dot{X})$$

where Y is GDP, and X is exports.

Box figure 4.4A Hypothetical borrowing experiences

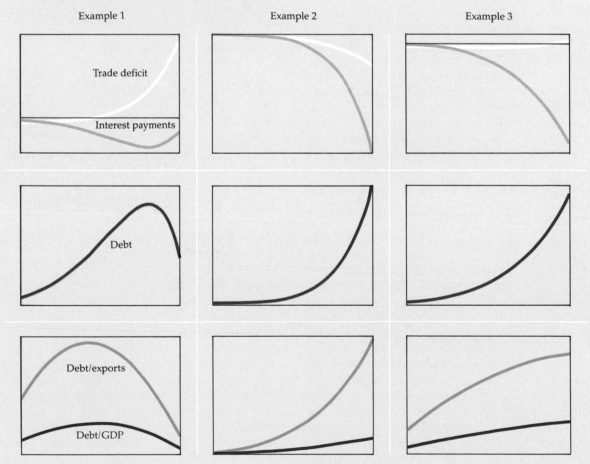

Example 1   Example 2   Example 3

Trade deficit

Interest payments

Debt

Debt/exports

Debt/GDP

sugar refineries, steel mills, and textile and cement factories. They occurred in low-income countries as well as in middle-income countries and most oil exporters. Clearly investment in social, economic, and political infrastructure is necessary, as is industrial investment and investment in service sectors (in hotels, for example). However, experience demonstrates that too much investment has gone into projects that have failed to generate significant increases in output. Genuine mistakes and misfortunes cannot explain the excessive number of "white elephants." Too many projects have been selected either on the basis of political prestige or on the basis of inadequate regard for their likely economic and financial rate of return. (World Bank 1984, p. 24.)

In contrast, most East Asian countries have invested public money fairly efficiently over the last decade. The state enterprise sector has remained relatively small and, in many instances, is largely confined to energy-related activities. Large investments in domestic energy production—geothermal, coal, and hydropower plants in the Philippines; nuclear power plants in Korea; and natural gas, lignite, and hydropower plants in Thailand—were generally combined with energy prices that encouraged conservation. However, mistakes have been made. In some instances, political rather than economic criteria have been employed in selecting investments; expectations about future price developments have sometimes been wrong. The development of a steel industry in Indonesia in the mid-1970s and extensive government-sponsored investment in heavy industry in Korea in the late 1970s are cases in which greater care and prudence could have been used in making economic appraisals.

Table 4.1 Price distortions, rescheduling, and export growth in selected developing countries

INCREASING DISTORTION (↓)

Country	*Debt rescheduling, 1975–84*	*Export growth, 1970–80*[a]	
		Country rate	*Group average*
Malawi	yes	4.8	
Thailand	no	8.1	
Cameroon	no	3.1	
Korea	no	23.0	
Malaysia	no	8.3	7.1
Philippines	yes	6.4	
Tunisia	no	7.3	
Kenya	no	0.9	
Yugoslavia	yes	3.8	
Colombia	no	5.6	
Ethiopia	no	−1.8	
Indonesia	no	9.3	
India	yes	8.4	
Sri Lanka	no	−1.8	
Brazil	yes	7.9	5.2
Mexico	yes	7.9	
Ivory Coast	yes	5.0	
Egypt	no	6.9	
Turkey	yes	4.3	
Senegal	yes	6.3	
Pakistan	yes	−0.9	
Jamaica	yes	−2.5	
Uruguay	yes	9.6	
Bolivia	yes	3.0	
Peru	yes	−0.4	
Argentina	yes	7.1	1.9
Chile	yes	11.6	
Tanzania	no	−4.8	
Bangladesh	no	2.7	
Nigeria	yes	3.3	
Ghana	no	−8.0	

Note: Analysis of price distortions is based on foreign exchange pricing, factor pricing, and product pricing and is averaged over the decade of the 1970s. Hence, rankings of some countries, based on their policy performance over a more recent period, might vary considerably from the order presented above.

a. Average annual trend rate of growth of real exports of goods and nonfactor services in constant U.S. dollars.

Source: For price distortions: World Bank *World Development Report 1983*, p. 62; for export growth: World Bank data; for rescheduling: World Bank *World Debt Tables*, 1984–85 ed., table 2, p. xvi.

Incentives for efficient investment

Government policies profoundly influence the type and volume of private investment in developing countries. Many governments, wanting to promote domestic manufacturing industries, protect them with import barriers and subsidize their costs through repressed interest rates and overvalued exchange rates. These policies are sometimes supplemented by price controls and subsidies that are designed to help the poor but that mainly benefit those who could afford to pay for more. The principal effect of such measures is to boost consumption, encouraging local producers to concentrate on the home market. They therefore neglect exports, further reducing the foreign exchange earnings needed to service debts.

ROLE OF PRICES. Earlier *World Development Reports* have noted the relationship between price distortions and economic growth. The 1983 Report contained price distortion indices for thirty-one countries, using measures of distortion of foreign exchange pricing, factor pricing, and product pricing. It showed that, in the 1970s, countries with higher government-induced distortions grew more slowly. Table 4.1, using the same ranking, shows that big distortions also lead to slower growth of exports and a greater likelihood of debt-servicing difficulties. Most countries with serious distortions have been forced to reschedule their debts. Those that have not, such as Bangladesh, Ghana, and Tanzania, have borrowed very little on commercial terms. By contrast, most countries with low distortions have avoided debt rescheduling. Malawi is a notable exception. Its debt-servicing difficulties stemmed not from pricing distortions, but largely from borrowing to postpone fiscal adjustment, as well as excessive reliance on commercial credits.

ROLE OF TRADE AND EXCHANGE RATE POLICIES. While most developing countries weathered the shocks of the mid-1970s surprisingly well, those that did not—such as Argentina, Peru, and Turkey—had generally favored inefficient import substitution and capital-intensive industrial growth. They had let their exchange rates become overvalued, had high barriers against imported finished products, and had low tariffs on capital goods. These policies stimulated highly capital-intensive production, leading to declining efficiency of investment. In all three countries, incremental capital output ratios rose sharply in the 1970s.

The difficulties encountered by many Latin American countries in the early 1980s contrast with the success of East Asian countries. Although outward-oriented policies did increase the Asian countries' exposure to external shocks, it also enabled them to capture the greater gains from international trade, so they grew faster. One study found that the annual growth rate for outward-oriented developing countries averaged 6.2 percent in 1976–79, compared with 2.4 percent for inward-oriented countries. In the years of recession, 1979–82, the respective annual figures were 1.0 percent and 0.2 percent.

The experience of the East Asian countries suggests that the surest way to discourage the financing of low-productivity investments with foreign capital is to maintain competitive exchange rates and avoid excessive import substitution. Such policies allow investors to gauge the true economic costs and benefits of alternative investments, particularly when foreign borrowing is involved.

Capital inflows and adjustment

Previous editions of the *World Development Report* have described how developing countries responded to the dramatic changes in the international economic environment in the 1970s. The world economy ran into difficulty once again in 1981–82. Nominal interest rates rose; real rates (measured against inflation in industrial countries)

rose even more. Interest obligations on foreign debt increased by as much as 5 percent of GDP for some of the major borrowers (the percentage depended on the proportion of concessional versus nonconcessional debt and the proportion of long-term, fixed interest rate debt versus short-term or floating rate debt). At the same time, the terms of trade for commodity exporters continued to decline, raising the effective real interest rate still higher. Export volumes also fell as a result of recession, and protectionism increased in both the industrial countries and the developing world.

The effect of these shocks was enormous, particularly for the biggest commercial borrowers. Brazil's net interest payments in 1981 were 60 percent larger than they would have been if real rates had remained constant, and in 1982, 80 percent larger. These increases were equivalent to 15 percent and 25 percent of actual exports in those years. At the same time, Brazil's terms of trade fell 25 percent below what might have prudently been expected in 1980. Moreover, Brazil's exports to its important markets in other developing countries suffered when they reduced their imports, and Brazil had to cut the amount of export credit it could offer. In general, the combination of high interest rates and recession in 1981 and 1982 damaged the capacity of developing countries to sustain growth and avoid debt-servicing difficulties much more than either of the two oil price shocks in the mid and late 1970s (see Table 4.2).

However, the countries with debt-servicing difficulties were not necessarily those that suffered the biggest shocks. Hardest hit were those that had failed to adjust their economies to earlier difficulties or that had failed to tackle the new problems with sufficient urgency. Oil-importing developing countries that had to reschedule their debt generally did not experience more severe shocks than countries that avoided rescheduling. And some oil exporters, beneficiaries from higher oil prices, found themselves in as much difficulty as the oil-importing countries. For example, Korea experienced large negative shocks in all periods shown in Table 4.2, while Nigeria had a cumulative benefit. But, unlike Nigeria, Korea did not have serious debt-servicing difficulties, and its GDP grew by an average of 8 percent a year in real terms in 1973–83.

It is possible, therefore, to exaggerate the role played by external disturbances in causing debt difficulties. In most instances, countries that ran into trouble had failed to adjust because of mistaken expectations in three important areas:

• Many oil importers that had weathered the

first rise in oil prices relatively comfortably, thanks to buoyant commodity prices and plentiful foreign finance, assumed that the second oil shock could be handled in the same way. They did not pay enough attention to serious policy reforms.

• Many countries underestimated the depth and

Table 4.2 Impact of external shocks on the balance of payments in selected developing countries
(average annual percentage of GNP)

Country	1974–75	1979–80	1981–82
Reschedulers[a]			
Argentina	−0.6	−1.9	−6.4
Brazil	−3.7	−2.8	−8.6
Chile	−4.7	−1.2	−13.3
India	−2.6	−1.6	−4.2
Ivory Coast	0.5	−5.6	−18.9
Jamaica	−9.6	−13.3	−29.4
Mexico	−1.0	−0.2	1.0
Peru	−4.5	−1.5	−5.6
Nigeria	16.7	5.8	3.8
Morocco	0.2	−4.0	−9.7
Philippines	−6.2	−2.4	−10.1
Yugoslavia	−6.7	−2.0	−10.0
Nonreschedulers			
Colombia	−1.4	−3.6	−8.3
Kenya	−8.1	−8.7	−19.0
Egypt	−8.7	−0.8	−1.2
Tunisia	−2.1	2.7	1.9
Korea	−9.5	−8.1	−21.7
Indonesia	12.0	5.6	5.4
Tanzania	−9.3	−6.0	−14.3
Thailand	−3.7	−2.3	−10.1

Note: External shocks are defined as the impact on the balance of payments of: (a) changes in the terms of trade; (b) a decline in the growth rate of world demand for a country's exports; and (c) increases in interest rates. Data for 1974–75 show the change from 1971–73; data for 1979–80 and 1981–82 show the change from 1976–78.
a. Countries that had rescheduled as of the end of 1984.
Source: Balassa 1981; Balassa and McCarthy 1984.

length of the 1980–83 recession. They borrowed heavily, hoping to ride out the recession and leave their economies well placed to take advantage of the expected recovery in 1982.

• Exporters of certain commodities—oil, uranium, coffee, cocoa—which had benefited from huge windfall gains in the 1970s, assumed that the subsequent price declines were temporary and borrowed to complete ambitious investment programs designed when foreign exchange was abundant (see Box 4.5).

When a country's current account deteriorates, as it did for many countries in 1981–82, it can react in three possible ways. First, it can slow down the rate of economic growth, and in turn the demand for imports. This is often essential for countries with low foreign exchange reserves. Second, it can keep up its growth rate, simply paying for its imports by borrowing abroad or running down its reserves. Or third, it can adopt policies that restructure the economy toward greater produc-

Box 4.5 Windfall gains and foreign borrowing

During the 1970s, many countries obtained big windfall gains from rising commodity prices. Many of them have since run into debt difficulties. The contrast has partly been due to the fall in commodity prices since the late 1970s, but it also reflects the way that windfall gains were used.

Typically, countries were at first unable to spend their windfalls, so they built up their foreign reserves. After a year or two, their governments increased public spending and then began borrowing abroad against future export earnings. Before their spending programs were completed, commodity prices fell. Thinking that the fall was temporary, governments borrowed even more to replace lost export and fiscal revenues. Within a few years, they had burdened themselves with crippling debts that required immediate and painful adjustment. This pattern can be illustrated by several examples (see Box figure 4.5A).

• Nigeria benefited from the quadrupling of oil prices in 1973–74. By 1976, it had expanded public investment almost threefold in real terms, and its external current account was back in deficit. Cost overruns on investment projects and burgeoning import demands coincided with falling oil revenues in 1977–78. The government slashed public spending, restricted credit, and tightened controls on imports. These deflationary measures led to a sharp fall in investment and output during 1978. Nigeria almost defaulted on its foreign trade credits, but its finances were restored when oil prices doubled in 1979. The government then delayed adjustment until the end of 1983, by which time the country had lost nearly all its reserves, experienced three years of declining GDP, and accumulated $6 billion of arrears on foreign trade credits.

• Niger, a low-income country, borrowed heavily in the late 1970s to invest in uranium production and infrastructure. At the time, international specialists were predicting that export prices for uranium would appreciate at least as fast as prices of oil and natural gas. Through 1980, most of the increase in public investment was still being financed by domestic revenues, and the public investment program was reasonably efficient. However, nonguaranteed debt owed by private banks and uranium mining companies had expanded from virtually nothing in 1975 to one and a half times the size of public debt in 1979. These unregistered debts were to play a key role in Niger's debt crisis.

When world uranium markets softened in 1980, the government borrowed more from abroad to maintain investment. This raised the public debt to GDP ratio to

tion of exports and import substitutes. This takes time. Its ultimate purpose is to restore the country's productive potential and allow it to improve the current account through higher output and increased exports. The difference between the second and third options explains much of what has

happened to different developing countries in the recent past.

Borrowing to postpone adjustment

A country that faces a shock (be it internal or external) that is considered to be temporary and revers-

49 percent in 1983. Uranium capacity was built in excess of demand, although some large projects were shelved after prices collapsed in 1981. The stock of private non-guaranteed debt declined after 1981, but the shorter maturities on this debt significantly worsened the country's debt service burden. Some 70 percent of the external debt accumulated after 1975 was commercial in origin. By 1983, total debt had reached the equivalent of 60 percent of GDP and 219 percent of exports, compared with 13 percent and 51 percent in 1973. Niger now has a stabilization program.

• The Ivory Coast enjoyed a coffee and cocoa boom in

1976–77. Between 1976 and 1978, public investment increased from 15 percent of GDP to 25 percent. Much of it was financed by foreign borrowing and went to large projects with high unit costs and low economic returns. The productivity of public investment declined by approximately 40 percent. In 1977–78, coffee prices fell by 31 percent and cocoa prices by 10 percent, while import prices rose. Thus the terms of trade fell by 29 percent between 1977 and 1980 and over 40 percent by 1983. The country is now struggling to adjust and has rescheduled its debt in 1984.

Box figure 4.5A   Change in debt and terms of trade in three countries, 1970–83

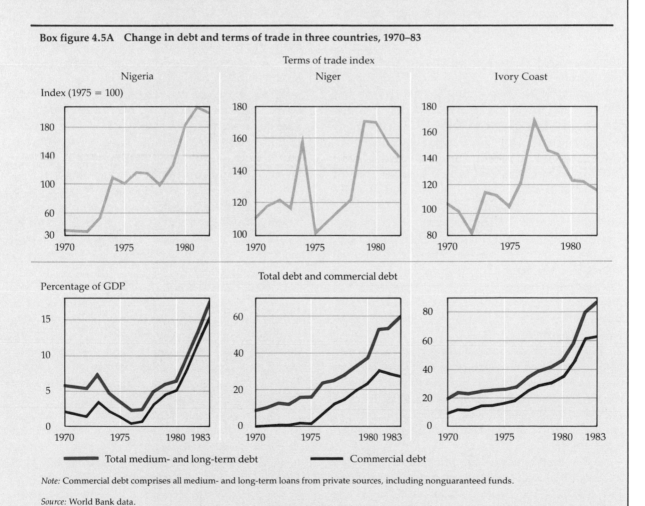

Note: Commercial debt comprises all medium- and long-term loans from private sources, including nonguaranteed funds.

Source: World Bank data.

ible is justified in borrowing abroad for balance of payments purposes. In these circumstances, it does not need to implement policies to restructure its economy. In practice, however, it is often difficult to distinguish beforehand between temporary and permanent shocks. Because of the obvious political and social costs of adjustment, policymakers may be inclined to err on the side of optimism. If they do, the price is a more painful adjustment later. Borrowing for balance of payments purposes is an inherently risky policy.

The nature of the eventual adjustment will depend on the uses to which borrowed money is put. If it is used to raise investment, it provides the potential for extra output with which to meet future debt service. If borrowing is used to maintain or increase consumption, however, the economy's productive potential has not increased while debt service obligations have.

What were the major symptoms of delayed adjustment in the 1970s and early 1980s? This section examines three connected issues: domestic saving, public sector deficits, and capital flight.

FOREIGN CAPITAL AND DOMESTIC SAVINGS. The correct role of foreign capital is to supplement domestic savings; it is essential that it does not substitute for them. In many countries over the past fifteen years, however, foreign borrowing has been an attractive alternative to increasing savings. As Figure 4.6 shows, three-quarters of a sample of forty-four developing countries raised the ratio of investment to GDP between 1965–72 and 1973–78, while two-thirds raised savings rates. But only about one-quarter of the sample raised savings rates more, or lowered them less, than investment rates. In view of the low—at times negative—real cost of foreign borrowing during the 1970s, this was understandable. But the strategy became a significant, though indirect, cause of the debt difficulties in the 1980s, forcing an even sharper reduction in investment.

A government can raise domestic savings in two main ways. The first is by promoting private savings, especially through improvements in the functioning of domestic financial markets. The second is by raising public savings through taxation, cost recovery, and reductions in government expenditure.

The decreased reliance on domestic savings during the 1970s coincided in many countries with slower growth of their financial markets. While credit grew faster than GDP in many developing countries, domestic financial markets were allowed to languish; additional foreign borrowing was the main source of extra credit. In the twenty-four countries in Table 4.3, foreign finance accounted for between 18 and 81 percent of total credit in 1972, with an average of 47 percent. By 1979, the share of foreign credit had risen by five percentage points or more in fourteen of the twenty-four countries, and the average share was 54 percent. By 1982, the share of foreign credits had increased even more, to an average of 56 percent. Among the major commercial borrowers, only Korea reduced its reliance on foreign credits. In eight of the ten major borrowers, foreign credits as a percentage of total credit have increased by five percentage points or more since 1979.

A large part of the cross-country differences can be explained by the public sector's reliance on foreign borrowing. Breaking down the figures on credit into sources and uses reveals five main patterns (examples are shown in Figure 4.7):

• A few countries, such as Indonesia, reduced their reliance on foreign credits after 1972 and restrained public borrowing, leaving a larger share to the private sector.

• Countries such as Korea and Thailand maintained all types of credit in roughly the same proportions during most of the period; this involved a large expansion of domestic financial resources to keep pace with the increased ratio of foreign debt to GDP. (However, some of these countries have recently increased their foreign short-term borrowings more rapidly than other forms of credit.)

• Countries such as Argentina, Portugal, and Turkey increased their dependence on foreign borrowing at different times between 1972 and 1978. By allowing private sector credit to fall as a percentage of GDP, they induced private borrowers to seek foreign loans.

• Most developing-country governments increased their reliance on public and publicly guaranteed foreign borrowings between 1972 and 1982, while decreasing the public sector's reliance on domestic financial markets. Brazil was one example of this approach, which permitted an expansion of public borrowing without an equivalent crowding-out of the private sector.

• Some governments, mainly the oil exporters, actually used their foreign borrowings to build up deposits in the domestic banking system in excess of their local borrowing. As a result, public borrowing from domestic markets was effectively negative, as in the case of Venezuela. This made possible a rapid expansion of credit to the private sector (in India, for example). But it also allowed these

Figure 4.6 Change in investment, savings, and terms of trade in selected countries, 1965–83

Change between 1965–72 and 1973–78 period averages

	GDS/GDP decreased or constant		GDS/GDP increased		
GDI/GDP decreased or constant	*Sri Lanka (0,0) *Chile (−1,−2) *Pakistan (−1,−3) *Sierra Leone (−1,−5)	*Zambia (−1,−11) Ghana (−2,0) Ethiopia (−4,−3) Jamaica (−9,−12)	Colombia (0,3) *Papua New Guinea (−10,16)		
GDI/GDP increased	Peru (1,−3) Portugal (2,−5) *Tanzania (2,−6) *Uruguay (2,−1) *Yugoslavia (2,−1)	Brazil (3,0) *Turkey (4,0) *Sudan (5,−1) *Zaire (5,−10) *Liberia (8,−8)	*GDI/GDP increased more than GDS/GDP*	*Costa Rica (4,2) *Kenya (4,1) *Senegal (5,2) *Guatemala (6,4) Venezuela (7,4)	Morocco (11,1) *Niger (12,6) Egypt (12,3) Algeria (19,13)
			GDI/GDP increased less than GDS/GDP	*Thailand (1,3) *India (3,6) *Korea (5,11) Malaysia (5,7)	*Educador (7,10) Indonesia (8,15) Nigeria (8,13)
			GDI/GDP and GDS/GDP increased approximately equally	Mexico (2,1) *Argentina (4,5) Bolivia (4,5) Tunisia (4,4)	Ivory Coast (5,5) Cameroon (6,6) *Philippines (7,6) Malawi (10,11)

Change between 1973–78 and 1979–81 period averages

	GDS/GDP decreased or constant			GDS/GDP increased		
GDI/GDP decreased or constant	*Ethiopia (0,−4) *Argentina (−1,−5) *Guatemala (−1,−3) *Nigeria (−1,−3) *Sudan (−1,−6) *Turkey (−1,−1)	*Liberia (−2,−7) *Malawi (−2,−4) *Morocco (−2,−4) *Senegal (−2,−11) *Jamaica (−3,−1) Bolivia (−6,−8)	*Brazil (−6,−5) Ghana (−6,−6) Venezuela (−7,−6) *Zambia (−11,−14)	Ecuador (0,2) Peru (−1,7)	Algeria (−7,2) Zaire (−11,3)	
GDI/GDP increased	*Colombia (1,−1) *Pakistan (1,−2) *Sierra Leone (1,3) *Tanzania (1,−1) *Thailand (2,0)	Ivory Coast (3,−3) *Kenya (3,−3) *Uruguay (3,0)	*Chile (5,0) *Papua New Guinea (6,−4) Sri Lanka (13,0)	*GDI/GDP increased more than GDS/GDP*	*India (3,1) *Korea (3,1) *Philippines (3,1) Cameroon (4,2)	Egypt (4,2) Malaysia (5,2) *Portugal (5,3)
				GDI/GDP increased less than GDS/GDP	Indonesia (2,5) *Niger (3,7)	*Yugoslavia (4,6)
				GDI/GDP and GDS/GDP increased equally	*Costa Rica (3,3) Tunisia (3,3)	Mexico (5,5)

Change between 1979–81 and 1982–83 period averages

	GDS/GDP decreased or constant			GDS/GDP increased	
GDI/GDP decreased or constant	*Ghana (0,−4) *Pakistan (0,0) *Portugal (0,−1) *Sri Lanka (0,0) *Sudan (0,−6) Algeria (−2,−2)	*Peru (−2,−6) *Philippines (−3,−3) *Zambia (−3,−7) *Guatemala (−4,−3) *Sierra Leone (−4,−2) *Ecuador (−5,−2)	*Kenya (−5,0) *Korea (−5,0) *Thailand (−5,−3) *Bolivia (−7,−7) *Chile (−11,−5)	*India (0,2) *Senegal (−1,4) *Costa Rica (−5,5)	Malawi (−5,2) Uruguay (−5,1) *Mexico (−8,2)
GDI/GDP increased	*Ethiopia (1,−2) Tunisia (1,−3) Indonesia (2,−7)	*Jamaica (3,−5) *Malaysia (4,−5) *Papua New Guinea (7,−5)			

Note: Figures in parentheses are absolute changes in percentage points between the two periods given: the first figure is the change in GDI/GDP, and the second is the change in GDS/GDP, measured in current dollars. An asterisk indicates that the country experienced a decline in its terms of trade index.
Source: World Bank data.

Table 4.3 Credit indicators in selected developing countries, 1972, 1979, and 1982
(percent)

Country	Total credit/GDP[a]			Foreign/total credit[a]		
	1972	1979	1982	1972	1979	1982
Argentina*	33.0	40.6	53.0[b]	32.6	41.7	51.7[b]
Bangladesh	43.8[c]	42.4	61.2	65.0[c]	60.5	68.7
Brazil*	34.9	43.7	38.5	43.5	66.9	76.9
Chile*	32.9	58.6	71.3[b]	43.8	69.6	73.0[b]
Colombia	36.4[d]	28.4	40.6	56.4[d]	67.6	64.8
Ecuador	54.7	57.9	63.1	65.5	72.7	68.3
India	44.2	49.9	57.8	36.7	22.7	22.4
Indonesia*	51.6	39.1	40.3	81.2	71.8	64.7
Ivory Coast	42.5	68.1	131.1	51.7	60.0	81.5
Kenya	20.3	54.6	84.4	..	53.8	66.4
Korea, Rep. of*	86.7	59.6	83.8	65.6	50.9	59.4
Mexico*	61.8[e]	53.6	93.7	..	51.8	70.0
Morocco	58.2	78.2	112.1	50.9	51.9	70.8
Nigeria	25.7	26.5	44.5[b]	39.9	22.5	22.7[b]
Pakistan	105.7	79.5	77.2	58.0	48.7	50.5
Peru	69.7	66.3	71.0	71.4	89.4	83.8
Philippines	50.6	56.7	79.7	64.3	72.3	77.9
Portugal	104.1[f]	115.7	145.2	21.2[f]	38.3	56.9
Sri Lanka	42.2	57.1	80.2	48.6	66.1	63.1
Thailand	40.4	55.9	73.7	32.2	38.9	41.1
Turkey	42.1	40.8	62.7	41.4	47.5	66.9
Venezuela*	27.8	67.0	81.3	39.9	69.7	60.3
Yugoslavia*	99.6[e]	99.5	86.3[b]	18.4[e]	20.5	36.4[b]
Zaire	44.8	91.5	106.3[b]	61.3	83.3	92.4[b]

Note: Asterisks indicate countries among the ten largest developing-country commercial borrowers from international financial markets, measured in U.S. dollars, as of the end of 1982.
a. Total credit consists of net domestic credit plus credit from foreign sources. Domestic credit can be subdivided into net claims on the public sector (the central governments) and the private sector held by the monetary authorities and resident commercial banks. Net domestic credit is defined as domestic credit less the foreign liabilities of the monetary authorities and resident commercial banks. These foreign liabilities, which include long-term foreign borrowing by the public and private sectors as well as short-term liabilities of the domestic banking system, were converted to local currency at end-of-year exchange rates and defined as credit from foreign sources.
b. Data for 1981.
c. Data for 1978.
d. Data for 1973.
e. Data for 1977.
f. Data for 1976.
Source: IMF International Financial Statistics; Morgan Guaranty Bank data; and World Bank data.

governments substantially to increase the amount of credit that they subsidized and directed. And it often increased the reliance on short-term foreign finance by both the public and private sectors. Recently, some of these countries have had balance of payments difficulties and have been forced to slow the growth of private sector credit.

To some extent, the rising share of foreign borrowing simply reflected its relative cheapness during the 1970s. But in many cases it was also the result of policies that repressed domestic financial markets. Some countries, such as Ecuador, Nigeria, Peru, and Turkey, kept local deposit rates generally negative in real terms. Domestic financial intermediaries often had little incentive to use domestic savings for lending because spreads on local currency loans were controlled, while those on foreign capital were not. As a result, potential depositors in many countries sent their money

abroad. Meanwhile, domestic companies and financial institutions often enjoyed subsidized access to central bank lending or subsidized guarantees for their foreign borrowings.

The failure to develop and deepen domestic financial markets in the 1970s had serious consequences when world interest rates rose in the early 1980s and capital inflows slumped. Many governments were unable to reduce their budget deficits quickly, but found domestic credit markets too small to absorb much additional debt. These governments had to resort to inflationary finance; to the extent that they did borrow from domestic lenders, they crowded out the private sector.

PUBLIC SECTOR DEFICITS AND OVERBORROWING. Experience has shown that countries following prudent fiscal policies rarely experience prolonged difficulties with their external payments. Virtually

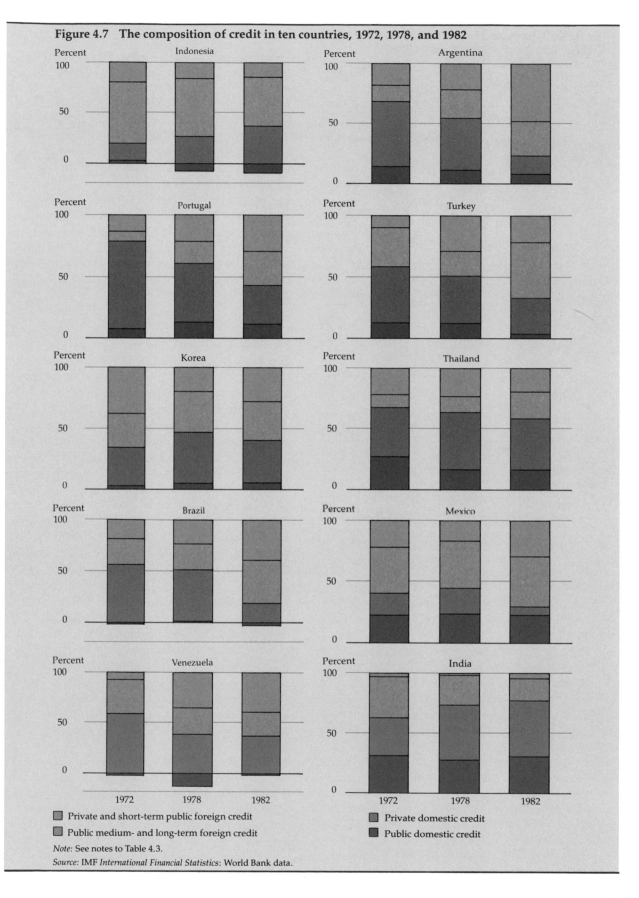

Figure 4.7   The composition of credit in ten countries, 1972, 1978, and 1982

Indonesia

Argentina

Portugal

Turkey

Korea

Thailand

Brazil

Mexico

Venezuela

India

1972   1978   1982

1972   1978   1982

■ Private and short-term public foreign credit

■ Private domestic credit

■ Public medium- and long-term foreign credit

■ Public domestic credit

Note: See notes to Table 4.3.

Source: IMF *International Financial Statistics*: World Bank data.

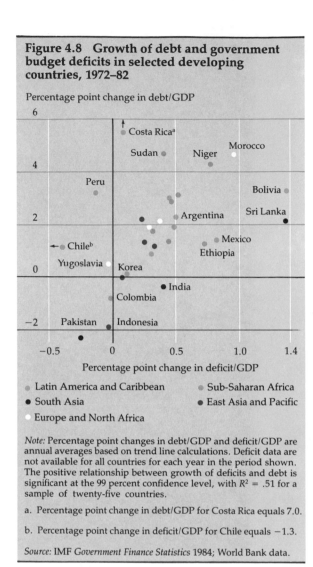

Figure 4.8 Growth of debt and government budget deficits in selected developing countries, 1972–82

Percentage point change in debt/GDP

Percentage point change in deficit/GDP

- Latin America and Caribbean
- South Asia
- Europe and North Africa
- Sub-Saharan Africa
- East Asia and Pacific

Note: Percentage point changes in debt/GDP and deficit/GDP are annual averages based on trend line calculations. Deficit data are not available for all countries for each year in the period shown. The positive relationship between growth of deficits and debt is significant at the 99 percent confidence level, with $R^2 = .51$ for a sample of twenty-five countries.

a. Percentage point change in debt/GDP for Costa Rica equals 7.0.

b. Percentage point change in deficit/GDP for Chile equals −1.3.

Source: IMF *Government Finance Statistics* 1984; World Bank data.

every major payments crisis in the 1970s and 1980s was preceded by large and growing budget deficits. In some instances, external shocks were the proximate factor in generating both the payments and fiscal crises. But in other cases, deficits arose from a deliberate policy to stimulate the economy out of recession or because the government lost control of its budgetary process. As Figure 4.8 shows, there is a significant positive relationship between growing government deficits and the accumulation of foreign debt.

Deficits are caused by any or all of the following: (a) excessive public sector investment; (b) growing government consumption, often in the form of subsidies to public enterprises to cover operating deficits resulting from lagged adjustments in prices; and (c) a reluctance to raise taxes as spending increases. Large public deficits are not only unsustainable, they also frequently produce an inefficient allocation of resources.

Furthermore, rapid increases in public spending are seldom implemented efficiently. In Turkey, for example, the number of public investment projects rose from 3,000 in 1976 to nearly 9,000 in 1980. In Peru, the government took over most of the country's large industrial and agricultural enterprises, invested heavily in import-substituting industries, and constructed an oil pipeline that was bigger than the capacity of Peru's oil fields. In the Ivory Coast, the share of public investment in GDP increased from 15 percent in 1976 to 25 percent in 1978. Much of the agricultural investment was in sugar complexes that had unit operating costs two to three times world market prices. The bulk of educational investment was in higher educational facilities, unsuited to the country's needs. The productivity of public investment in the mid-1970s declined by about 40 percent.

The experience of Argentina, Mexico, and Morocco illustrates the connection between fiscal deficits and inflows of foreign finance (see Figure 4.9). Note that the external debt figures cited below include short- and long-term obligations.

- *Argentina.* Public spending rose from 30 percent of GDP in 1969 to 49 percent in 1983, while the budget deficit of the public sector rose from 1 percent of GDP to 16 percent. It had started to grow in the early 1970s, largely because of lagging prices in state enterprises, the ending of certain temporary taxes, an amnesty for tax evasion, and the corrosive effects of mounting inflation on real tax collections. In 1973, a new government sought to redistribute income and raise basic living standards by massive increases in public sector transfers, subsidies, and real wages. Meanwhile, measures to raise taxes were transitory and inadequate. In three years, the deficit rose from 5 percent of GDP to 15 percent, and the economy reached the verge of hyperinflation and collapse. After declining in the mid-1970s, deficits began to rise once again after 1977, peaking at 16 percent of GDP in 1983.

State enterprises, public banks, and the government borrowed heavily from abroad. Public external debt increased by over 30 percent a year between 1975 and 1983—more than twice the average rate in any period in Argentina's postwar history. Between 1969 and 1983, public external debt (excluding the nonguaranteed debt consolidated with public debt in 1983) rose seventeenfold to about $30 billion, or from 7 percent of GDP to 45 percent.

- *Mexico.* Its government began the 1970s with modest budgetary deficits. Then a new administration started increasing consumer subsidies, transfers to state enterprises, and public investment. Public spending grew from 17.6 percent of GDP in 1968–70 to nearly 26 percent in 1974–76. The fiscal deficit of the public sector rose steadily from 3 percent of GDP to 10 percent. Its growth, alongside the limited domestic capital markets, was behind the surge in public foreign borrowing: debt nearly quintupled in six years, to $20 billion in 1976. This triggered a crisis of confidence in 1976, prompting the new government to cut the budget deficit sharply and devalue the peso. The balance of payments stabilized.

As Mexico increased its oil production enormously during the late 1970s, foreign lenders revised their lending limits. The government abandoned its austerity program. Public spending exploded—from 30 percent of GDP in 1978 to 35 percent in 1980 and 48 percent in 1982. Even the rapid growth in oil revenues failed to keep pace. The budget deficit rose to 8 percent of GDP in 1980, 15 percent in 1981, and 18 percent in 1982. Foreign borrowing went up in step. Between 1970 and 1982, public and publicly guaranteed debt rose 1400 percent to $59 billion, equivalent to 32 percent of GDP.

• *Morocco.* Starting with small fiscal deficits and little external debt in the early 1970s, Morocco raised government investment from 5 percent of GDP in 1973 to 20 percent in 1977, to finance large investments in agriculture, energy, transport, education, and heavy industry. Defense outlays also rose sharply. The country ran into severe balance of payments difficulties in 1978, and the government responded with some budget austerity. However, social unrest in 1979 persuaded it to abandon its public sector wage guidelines and approve higher consumer subsidies on imported food and oil. Government deficits grew, reaching 14 percent of GDP in 1982. The public sector's foreign debt rose from $1 billion in 1973 to over $12 billion in 1983. That was equivalent to 90 percent of GDP and 400 percent of exports—among the highest debt ratios in the world. At that point, Morocco exhausted its foreign reserves and could no longer obtain new credits. With the help of a recent rescheduling agreement and an IMF loan, Morocco has substantially reduced its budget deficits.

CAPITAL FLIGHT AND EXCHANGE RATES. Large-scale capital flight was a significant factor in the balance of payments pressures on several countries in the early 1980s. It occurs when the expected returns from holding money abroad are

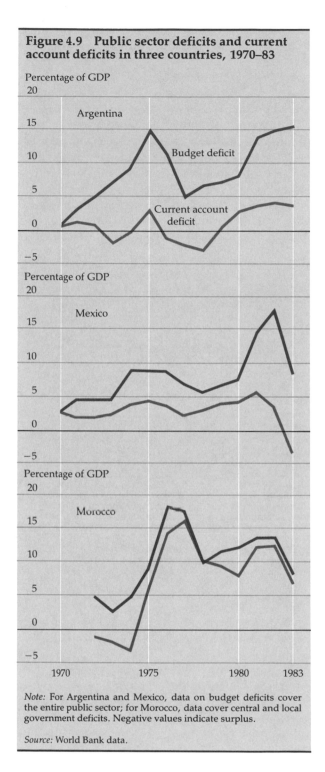

Figure 4.9 Public sector deficits and current account deficits in three countries, 1970–83

Note: For Argentina and Mexico, data on budget deficits cover the entire public sector; for Morocco, data cover central and local government deficits. Negative values indicate surplus.

Source: World Bank data.

higher or safer than at home. It is usually associated with several factors: an overvalued exchange rate, which makes foreign assets seem cheap but also causes fears of devaluation; high and variable inflation, which creates uncertainty and reduces real interest rates; repressive financial policies, which maintain real interest rates at negative levels during periods of rapid inflation; and high domestic protection, which makes foreign debt harder to service.

An overvalued exchange rate—and the anticipation of a sharp correction—is the most common and important cause. At some point, a real devaluation appears inevitable; this encourages speculative capital outflows, further increasing pressure on the exchange rate. Often foreign exchange controls are tightened to try to stanch the flow, usually to little effect. Leads and lags in commercial payments reverse the normal inward flow of trade and other credits, as foreign exporters press for immediate payment while domestic importers extend

Table 4.4 Capital flight and gross capital inflows in selected countries, 1979–82

Country	Capital flight (billions of dollars)[a]	Gross capital inflows (billions of dollars)[b]	Capital flight as a percentage of gross capital inflows
Venezuela	22.0	16.1	136.6
Argentina	19.2	29.5	65.1
Mexico	26.5	55.4	47.8
Uruguay	0.6	2.2	27.3
Portugal	1.8	8.6	20.9
Brazil	3.5	43.9	8.0
Turkey	0.4	7.9	5.1
Korea	0.9	18.7	4.8

a. Data are estimates. Capital flight is defined as the sum of gross capital inflows and the current account deficit, less increases in official foreign reserves. For some countries (notably Argentina and Venezuela), the estimate may overstate capital flight to the extent that unreported imports and normal portfolio investment abroad are included.
b. Defined as the sum of changes in gross foreign debt (public and private) and net foreign direct investment.
Source: World Bank data.

credit on foreign goods. By underinvoicing exports and overinvoicing imports, residents export capital illegally.

The attractions of foreign borrowing are increased whenever governments guarantee foreign borrowing or undertake to make good capital losses resulting from devaluation (as they usually did for public enterprises). In some cases, such as Mexico and Chile in 1980 and 1981, private companies were also encouraged to borrow abroad. Borrowers gambled (correctly, it turned out) that the government would continue to provide relatively cheap foreign exchange for debt service, even after a devaluation. In other cases, such as Argentina and Uruguay, governments offered cheap forward cover for exchange risk.

All these difficulties have been compounded by

the recent tendency in debt reschedulings to include even nonguaranteed debt as part of government obligations. The public sector shoulders the transfer risk associated with servicing foreign debt contracted by the private sector, even though the assets acquired with this debt are usually held outside the country, where they provide scant benefit to the local economy. Measures encouraging foreign borrowing usually make a country's eventual debt problem even worse: once the large capital inflows have increased the overvaluation of the exchange rate, an even greater adjustment is needed to service the extra debt.

Capital flight cannot be measured directly, but can be roughly estimated as a residual. As the estimates in Table 4.4 show, it was massive in Argentina, Mexico, and Venezuela. Effectively, much of the money being borrowed from abroad was funneled straight out again, thereby not earning returns that could be used to service debt. In such cases, foreign borrowing was a recipe for disaster.

In absolute terms, no country has suffered more from capital flight than Mexico. Mexico traditionally maintained a fixed exchange rate until a devaluation in 1976. In the late 1970s, the rapid growth in public spending and deficits fueled mounting inflation. Once it became clear the government would not reverse its expansionary policies quickly, the exchange rate came under strong pressure. The surge of official borrowing in 1980–81 helped to support the rate for a time, but it was running into waves of capital flight. In August 1982, Mexico was forced to suspend debt service payments, reschedule its debt, and devalue heavily. By somewhat different routes, several other Latin American countries encountered similar exchange rate difficulties (see Box 4.6).

Capital flight has not been confined to Latin America. In the Philippines, the government increased foreign borrowing sharply in 1981, anticipating that exports would soon recover and interest rates fall. The expected upturn in the world economy did not occur. Political uncertainty and lagging economic policy adjustment triggered capital flight. The government eventually had to devalue and reschedule. In Nigeria, official reluctance to devalue the exchange rate during 1981–83, when inflation was running at 20 percent a year, discouraged foreign direct investment, induced substantial capital flight, and encouraged firms to build up large inventories of imports. Having exhausted its official reserves and borrowing limits, Nigeria built up its arrears on trade credit to $6 billion by the end of 1983.

In the mid-1970s, the Southern Cone countries of Latin America—Argentina, Chile, and Uruguay—introduced major reforms aimed at breaking out of chronically slow growth, fast inflation, and frequent balance of payments crises. By 1978, all had turned around their external accounts and slowed inflation. Chile and Uruguay had also speeded up their growth.

Despite these achievements, inflation in all three countries was still well above its historical average. So in 1978–79, the three governments decided to launch a policy experiment of fixing the exchange rate, with a predetermined path of decreasing small devaluations. They hoped that this strategy, coupled with lower import protection and open financial markets, would quickly cut inflation, improve industrial efficiency, and lower interest rates.

In fact, inflation declined more slowly than anticipated, so real exchange rates appreciated substantially. Uncertainty about policy intentions continued, keeping domestic interest rates high. Attracted by the high yields available on dollar-denominated assets, large amounts of capital flowed into the three countries. These inflows were not regarded initially as a cause for concern because

of widespread expectations that foreign borrowing would remain cheap and its supply would be plentiful.

As exchange rates became more overvalued, doubts grew about the sustainability of the exchange rate policy. In Argentina and Uruguay, these doubts were reinforced by mounting fiscal deficits; in Chile by the rapid increase in real wages during a period of shrinking profit margins. In all three countries, many companies incurred losses, while lax lending practices led to the collapse of several large banks. Governments sought to allay fears of devaluation by offering exchange rate guarantees, but these only enhanced the windfalls to be gained from currency speculation. Imports grew at unprecedented rates, while export earnings lagged far behind.

The three countries were able to maintain their exchange rates only by increasing their foreign borrowing. When capital inflows slowed in 1981–82 because of tighter money in the industrial countries and increasing doubts about the three countries' policies, large outflows of capital soon forced large devaluations. The principal legacy of the exchange rate experiment was heavy foreign debt.

Borrowing to facilitate adjustment

While many governments have borrowed abroad to postpone adjustment at home, some have done so to adjust more effectively. Governments have used foreign capital to help implement policy reforms and to buy particular imports to restructure the economy.

POLICY REFORM.   By the end of the 1970s, many developing countries needed to change their policies in two broad areas. First, they had to curb their domestic spending and increase their foreign exchange earnings to service their growing foreign debt. Second, they needed to improve incentives for efficiency and expansion to strengthen their long-term growth prospects. Of course, both reforms are complementary. Measures to encourage long-term growth usually founder without balance of payments stability; yet stability brings only short-term benefits unless economic efficiency is also being improved (see Box 4.7).

Foreign capital has a valuable part to play in giving reforms time to take effect. Some of the measures needed to boost long-term growth may initially cause a country's current account to deteriorate. For example, trade liberalization is essential to encourage efficiency, increase supplies

of spare parts, and improve the competitiveness of exports, but imports will usually rise before exports do. Through borrowing, a government can avoid having to deflate the economy to offset these effects. It can therefore hope to secure broad support for its reforms, which might otherwise be lost if the whole economy had to go through a recession.

The speed of progress toward reform has varied greatly. Some countries have embarked on policy reforms only to abandon them prematurely; others have carried them through. The cases of Kenya and Turkey—the first two countries to obtain a structural adjustment loan (SAL) from the World Bank (see Box 4.8)—illustrate the variety of experience.

Kenya introduced a comprehensive program of reforms in 1975. But the huge increase in coffee prices in 1976 and 1977 produced a boom, making the program seem less urgent; only a few of the planned measures were carried out. In 1980, following the second oil shock, the government again adopted a reform program, supported by an IMF standby loan and an SAL. The measures included a more market-oriented pricing policy, reduced protection for domestic industries, more active use of exchange rate policy, more demanding goals for state enterprises, improved debt management,

Box 4.7 Stabilization and adjustment

Policies for short-run stabilization and for longer-term adjustment are often complementary. But short-term concerns are sometimes so urgent that policymakers give no thought to longer-term restructuring. In the case of Argentina, for example, the response to the 1982 crisis was a 40 percent reduction in the volume of imports—which quickly turned trade deficits into sizable surpluses. But with the annual inflation rate continuing to exceed 600 percent and the fiscal deficit still in excess of 10 percent of GDP, internal stabilization was barely started. Faster and more stable economic growth will require among other things several structural reforms, including significant improvement in public sector investment and other spending controls, rationalization of the tax structure, reform of the financial system, and reduction of trade restrictions.

In other countries, structural reforms have been interrupted or delayed by short-term disturbances. Between 1979 and 1981, Romania adopted measures designed to (a) increase the responsibility of the state enterprises for controlling costs and planning production and investment; (b) improve production incentives; and (c) restrain excess demand. The government eased price controls on energy and other products and unified the exchange rate. However, Romania's large external debt—coupled

with mounting concern over creditworthiness in Eastern Europe in general—prompted foreign lenders to cut off most lines of credit in late 1981. The government moved promptly to reschedule convertible currency debt and impose stringent import and investment controls. These measures produced a dramatic improvement in the convertible current account, and the government is well on its way to its goal of halving external debt by 1986. But the severity of its austerity program has also delayed technological innovation in key export sectors, harming the economy's long-term potential.

A third group of countries has successfully combined its response to balance of payments pressure with policies for longer-term adjustment and growth. Indonesia, a major exporter of oil and natural gas, delayed adjusting domestic oil prices, leading to greatly expanded oil subsidies between 1979 and 1981. It also embarked on a major new investment program. This had to be abandoned when the international recession, lower oil prices, and large-scale capital flight put pressure on the external balance. In early 1983, the government slashed subsidies, canceled or postponed nearly fifty import-intensive investment projects, devalued the *rupiah*, and put it on a managed float. In less than two years, the current account deficit was halved and the overall balance of

Box 4.8 The World Bank's lending for adjustment

To support economic restructuring, the World Bank has introduced several new lending mechanisms. The most important have been structural adjustment lending, introduced in 1980, and the Special Action Program, introduced in early 1983.

Structural adjustment loans (SALs) are intended to help countries with deep-rooted balance of payments difficulties to reform their policies. Unlike traditional World Bank loans, SALs do not fund specific projects. They provide foreign exchange to help meet the transitional costs of restructuring and policy reform. SALs can also act as a catalyst for other inflows of foreign capital. Since economic restructuring normally takes several years, SALs are designed to span five or more years, involving up to five separate loans.

The first SAL program was initiated in March 1980. By June 1984, twenty-nine loans totaling $4.5 billion had

been agreed upon in support of policy reforms in sixteen countries (see Box table 4.8A). Although the speed of progress has varied considerably, SALs are now making significant contributions to economic recovery in most of these countries. How many SALs a country receives depends both on its need and on the progress it makes in meeting policy objectives. Thus Turkey, for example, has already received five, whereas several countries have had only one.

Structural adjustment lending is only appropriate for countries that give high priority to comprehensive and sustained reform of policies and institutions and that have a reasonable chance of implementing their programs. In other countries, the World Bank promotes adjustment by concentrating its lending on particular sectors of the economy. Policy-oriented sector lending has also increased in volume and importance in recent

Box table 4.8A Structural adjustment lending by the World Bank, fiscal 1980–84

Item	1980	1981	1982	1983	1984
Number of SALs	3	7	6	7	6
Amount of SALs (millions of dollars)	305.0	717.0	1070.7	1,284.7	1,081.9
SALs as a percentage of total World Bank lending	2.7	5.8	6.2	8.9	7.0
Cumulative number of countries covered	3	8	13	15	16

Source: World Bank data.

payments position transformed from a deficit of $3.2 billion to a surplus of $2 billion. Indonesia's government followed this improvement by liberalizing interest rates and abolishing credit ceilings. In 1983–84, the economy recovered, growing by about 5 percent yearly.

In the late 1970s, Hungary resumed implementation of a program of economic liberalization initiated a decade earlier. Market-based production incentives were enhanced, subsidies reduced, and the autonomy of enterprises expanded. When the international economic environment deteriorated in 1979–82, Hungary did not halt liberalization, but did reverse the deterioration in the balance of payments through stabilization measures such as devaluations, reductions in investment, and sharp increases in domestic energy prices. The stabilization program led to a temporary slowing of economic growth from 5 percent in the 1970s to 2 percent in 1980–83, but prospects for restoring moderate, sustainable growth are now good. Meanwhile, Hungary has continued to extend the reach of its market-based, outward-oriented development strategy, which played a key role in steering the country clear of debt rescheduling difficulties in recent years.

years, particularly in the form of sector adjustment loans.

The Special Action Program comprises financial measures and policy advice to help countries implement adjustment measures needed to restore growth and creditworthiness. The principal elements of the program are (a) expanded lending for high-priority operations in support of policy changes, (b) measures to accelerate disbursements under existing and new high-priority projects, and (c) advice to governments on reordering investment priorities and improving external debt management.

Through December 1984, forty-four countries benefited from the program. Fourteen new loans were made under this program, including two SALs and twelve sector adjustment loans. Ongoing projects were modified to increase cost sharing, establish revolving funds, restructure design and implementation, add financing for working capital and recurrent costs, and make use of supplementary loans. By releasing the immediate financial constraint, these operations have permitted the continued implementation of 267 projects, representing an approximate value of about $13 billion. Overall, the Special Action Program will raise World Bank disbursements in fiscal 1984–86 by about $4.4 billion over what they would otherwise have been. The program has now been formally terminated, but the instruments introduced during its implementation will continue to be used, as needed, as part of the Bank's overall operations.

and tighter fiscal and monetary policy. In terms of stabilization, the results have been good; the budget and current account deficits have been reduced substantially. But progress toward longer-term efficiency has been slow. In particular, the government has failed to carry through most of its trade reforms, postponing the vitally needed expansion of exports.

Turkey, too, avoided adjustment in the 1970s. It financed its current account deficits by borrowing heavily and continued to protect domestic industry behind high import barriers. This promoted a high-cost, inefficient industrial structure; the incremental capital output ratio for manufacturing had tripled in a decade. In an effort to maintain growth, the government pursued expansionary monetary and fiscal policies. Nevertheless, GNP growth fell from about 6 percent a year in 1967–72 and 1973–76 to 2 percent a year in 1976–80. By the late 1970s, annual inflation had risen to 100 percent and debt service obligations (including short-term debt) were three times the value of exports. Between 1978 and 1980, Turkey rescheduled over $9 billion, or nearly 80 percent, of its external debts.

In January 1980 the government announced a shift toward an outward-oriented development strategy, with greater reliance on market forces. The early stages of the program involved a large devaluation of the exchange rate and the adoption of a crawling peg, tight monetary restraint; deregulation of interest rates; a phased reduction in consumption subsidies; rationalization of the public investment program; and higher prices for state enterprises. Within two years, the benefits were quite apparent. GNP grew by roughly 4 percent a year in 1980–83; inflation was cut by two-thirds; merchandise exports doubled despite a world recession; the current account deficit declined from over 5 percent of GDP to 3 percent; and the country's creditworthiness was restored.

With the easing of the immediate crisis, the Turkish government has been able to develop its reforms. It is gradually decreasing import quotas and reducing tariffs, reforming the management and financing of state enterprises, tightening its management of external debt and domestic banking, strengthening the tax system, and raising energy and agricultural prices closer to international levels. Although much has been achieved, more recently the adjustment process has weakened, as evidenced by the way that inflation and the budget deficit started to rise again during 1983–84. However, Turkey's overall performance since 1980 has been one of the most impressive turnarounds among developing countries for many years.

BORROWING AND RESTRUCTURING. Structural adjustment is seldom ensured merely by "getting prices right," essential though that is. Unless a country is able to expand imports, its farmers and businessmen may lack the basic ingredients—fuel, fertilizer, components, machinery—needed to expand exports and revive economic growth. They will not be able to take advantage of the right prices. In these circumstances, foreign borrowing makes an essential contribution, as Korea has demonstrated. Faced with the oil price increase in

1973–74, the Korean government decided not to slow economic growth. Instead, it devalued the currency and borrowed heavily to expand export capacity (see Box 4.9).

In recent years, the World Bank has increased its lending in support of trade liberalization and export expansion, though its role is largely catalytic. For example, Brazil has borrowed to finance the liberalization of its import duty drawback system, which will reduce the costs of producing for export. Mexico and Egypt have borrowed to increase the reserves available through their export development banks and other intermediaries to finance export-oriented industries. Ghana has an

---

Box 4.9 Borrowing for adjustment: the case of Korea

Until 1960, Korea emphasized import-substituting industrialization. It then switched to promoting exports. Since 1960, GDP growth has averaged more than 9 percent a year, per capita incomes have more than tripled, and the number of people with incomes below the poverty line has fallen from 40 percent of the population to 15 percent. Domestic saving has risen steadily since the mid-1960s to about 27 percent of GDP in 1984. Investment's share grew even faster, to 29 percent of GDP.

To achieve this rapid increase in investment, policymakers encouraged foreign borrowing. The country's external commercial debt (including short-term debt) grew from $22 million in 1960 (1 percent of GDP) to over $33 billion in 1983 (44 percent of GDP). Korean and foreign studies have estimated that inflows of foreign capital added about four percentage points to Korea's annual growth rate during the 1960s, and nearly two percentage points a year in 1972–82. These inflows, mainly in the form of commercial credits, were channeled almost entirely into productive investments. For the most part, capital was used efficiently. The incremental capital output ratio—which measures the extra investment needed to produce an extra unit of output—averaged about 3, one of the lowest in the developing world.

Korea was among the developing countries hardest hit by external shocks. When oil prices rose in 1973–74, the deterioration in its terms of trade generated a loss equivalent to about 10 percent of GDP. To cushion the shock, the country borrowed from abroad; it also devalued its currency by 22 percent. This devaluation, together with long-established policies of export promotion, helped set the stage for a spectacular increase in manufactured exports. Korean firms were also successful at winning overseas construction contracts totaling more than $15 billion by 1978. However, the investment boom did lead to overexpansion of heavy industry, high inflation, and a rising real exchange rate during the late 1970s, blunting the export drive.

The shocks of 1979–80 were similarly costly, resulting

in terms of trade and interest rate losses equivalent to 8 percent of GDP. But the world outlook was less accommodating than in the mid-1970s. External finance was no longer available on the easy terms of previous years. Exports were unlikely to grow as fast as they had in the mid-1970s because of rising international protectionism and the deepening world recession. Nor were Korea's internal conditions as favorable. The problems of inflation, exchange rate overvaluation, and investment misallocation were compounded in 1979 by a disastrous harvest and by political turmoil following the assassination of the country's president.

The government therefore opted for a different adjustment path. As in 1974–75, it increased its foreign borrowing (by 25 percent a year during 1978–81) and devalued the exchange rate. But, unlike the 1974–75 experience, investment and growth were sharply curtailed by tightening credit to nonexport sectors, reducing real wages, cutting public investment, and rapidly increasing domestic energy prices.

The medicine was strong. The economy stagnated in 1979–80. After rapid export growth resumed in 1981, credit policies were relaxed, but fiscal and wage restraint was continued. Korea's GDP grew by 6 percent in 1981–82, and then, with the help of economic recovery in the United States and Japan, by 9 percent in 1983–84. Inflation declined from nearly 40 percent in 1980 to 3 percent in 1983; real export growth accelerated to over 10 percent; the current account deficit was cut by two-thirds; and growth in external debt slowed from $5 billion to $2 billion yearly. The debt service ratio (including amortization of short-term debt) now stands at a modest 20 percent of export earnings, and access to foreign financial markets is normal. However, to reduce the growth of debt still further, the government is attempting to raise domestic savings by 4 percent of GDP over the next several years through financial reform and greater promotion of exports.

Export Rehabilitation Program to provide intensified technical assistance and management training in primary export industries.

In many countries, economic restructuring has involved heavy investment in energy production. These projects often require substantial foreign finance. However, much can be achieved by raising domestic prices to international levels. This has the dual effect of encouraging conservation and making domestic energy production more attractive. Furthermore, the energy producers benefit from higher prices, so they can often afford to invest in plant and equipment without having to borrow. However, foreign exchange savings accrue gradually, although some countries have made substantial progress in recent years. Thailand has successfully begun to substitute domestic gas for imported oil. Brazil also reduced its oil import dependence from 83 percent in 1977 to 50 percent in 1984 through enhanced conservation efforts, stepped up domestic oil production, accelerated hydropower development, and a fuel alcohol program.

Uses of foreign borrowing

Some broad generalizations about the uses of foreign borrowing can be inferred from the diverse country experiences. Four periods can be distinguished:

• From the mid-1960s to the early 1970s, financing was predominantly from official sources for specific investments. Economic growth was accelerated, and the capacity to service rising debt was maintained or improved. Borrowing for balance of payments purposes was limited because developing countries had limited access to commercial bank lending.

• Between 1973 and 1978, a high proportion of borrowed resources continued to flow into investment. Many economies grew rapidly. However, in order to adjust to higher energy prices and to maintain the momentum of growth, developing countries shifted the composition of their investment in favor of large-scale energy production and projects in heavy industry and infrastructure. Low international real interest rates and domestic policies led in many cases to investment with low returns, particularly in Africa and Latin America. The availability of cheap foreign funds also led to the rechanneling of some borrowing into the financing of balance of payments and fiscal deficits, although project-related finance remained predominant. The potential gains from borrowing were diminished in many cases, however, by a deterioration in the quality of economic policies and investment management.

• During 1979–82, there was a boost in the demand for balance of payments and fiscally related finance. In many developing countries outside of Asia, borrowing was used primarily to postpone, rather than buy time for, structural adjustment. Hence, its contribution to growth was small, if any.

• Since 1982, net capital flows have slowed considerably. Available financing has in many cases been linked with debt-servicing and balance of payments difficulties. It is more closely tied to programs of structural adjustment, and its contribution to establishing a basis for recovery in growth has been, by and large, positive, especially among the largest borrowing countries. Most new commercial finance is available only for trade and project-related purposes and only to a small number of developing countries that have maintained high standards of creditworthiness.

Conclusions

Participating in the world economy provides significant benefits. It also entails some risks. The more a developing country is linked with the rest of the world, the greater its potential benefits—but also, if policies are inappropriate, the more vulnerable it is to external shocks. Some people concentrate on the risks, arguing that the recent experience of massive shocks and slower worldwide growth proves that developing countries should avoid outward-oriented policies and also reduce their reliance on foreign capital.

The first part of the argument is excessively short-term, and even then misplaced. It is true that inward-oriented developing countries suffered a smaller absolute fall in their growth rate during the early 1980s. But they still grew less rapidly than outward-oriented economies; and, over a longer period, much less rapidly. As for the second part, it is wrong to specify the precise amount of foreign borrowing a country should do. This chapter has shown that many factors influence that decision.

Much depends on a country's ability to adjust rapidly in the face of external shocks. The greater its ability, the more it can afford to borrow. The key issues are the government's efficiency and its political strength to resist interest groups that oppose policy changes. Governments should assess how far they would be willing and able to implement austerity measures, or to move the economy in a new direction, should conditions change suddenly. Declining savings rates, chronic budget deficits, or overvalued exchange rates are clear warning signs that borrowed funds are being used to postpone rather than facilitate adjustment.

An economy's capacity to adjust is also affected by its structure. For example, a high dependence on the foreign exchange earned from a few key commodity exports reduces flexibility in adapting to a sudden decline of prices. In contrast, an economy producing a high proportion of diversified and internationally tradable goods and services, while also vulnerable to terms of trade shocks, can more easily avoid debt-servicing difficulties. This is because expenditure-switching adjustment policies, such as a devaluation, have a larger base on which to operate. Similarly, a well-trained, mobile workforce, an efficient financial system, and effective marketing channels all greatly improve an economy's ability to respond quickly to changing circumstances.

These lessons have been learned and relearned during the past few difficult years. Many developing countries are now reforming their policies. Those that began early and have persevered are already beginning to enjoy the benefits of faster and more durable economic growth. In others, however, reform is too slow. The price of failing to adjust to the harsh realities of the 1980s is high: for some, slow growth; for others, increasing poverty.

5 Managing foreign finance

The previous chapter showed that sound economic policies can raise the expected return from international borrowing. Furthermore, with adaptable policymaking and flexible economic structures, countries can also reduce the risks involved in foreign borrowing. This chapter switches the focus from the policies that determine the level and effectiveness of capital inflows to the management of the inflows themselves. By the management of capital flows we refer to the technical and institutional aspects of organizing the external liabilities and assets of the nation; its purpose is to pick the best possible combination of risk and return consistent with the supply conditions in capital surplus countries.

Effective management of foreign capital is not a substitute for sound macroeconomic management; it is an essential part of it. Lending and borrowing decisions cannot be made independently of macroeconomic policies. Debt managers need a clear understanding of expected macroeconomic developments, while policymakers must have a good grasp of expected new borrowing requirements and debt service payments. Although these principles seem obvious, many countries suffer from a lack of communication between debt managers (usually in the Ministry of Finance), reserves managers (usually in the central bank), and macroeconomic planners (often in the Ministry of Planning). Governments have often treated the level of capital inflows as a residual and have framed their fiscal and monetary policies independently of their effect on the level and structure of debt. A recent study of twenty countries by the IMF found that only one-fifth of developing countries were explicitly managing their debt systematically. Several countries are now arranging to bring debt management into the mainstream of economic decision-making.

This chapter discusses two sets of issues. First, to what extent should governments seek to regulate inflows of foreign capital, beyond ensuring that their economic policies are sound? Second, what is the appropriate composition of capital inflows and debt?

Managing the level of capital inflows

In a world where all decisions were made by market forces alone, governments would not be involved in deciding how much their countries should borrow from abroad. In reality, they are involved—for two main reasons. First, in most countries the public sector itself is the largest borrower. Second, the set of prices facing private companies may be distorted by government policies, so the private sector may be encouraged to borrow too much or too little. While private companies can be expected to try to ensure that their investments will generate enough domestic currency to repay a loan, the availability of enough foreign exchange is the responsibility of the monetary authorities.

How much borrowing?

Each individual loan must be justified on its own merits. But experience suggests that it is also necessary to pay attention to the aggregate level of inflows and debt. The sustainable rate of borrowing depends on the rate of growth of a nation's income and more particularly its exports. As long as income is growing faster than the rate of interest over the long run, the country is solvent. To minimize the likelihood of liquidity problems, it is necessary for the rate of growth of exports to exceed the rate of interest—that will ensure that the proportion of export revenues required to service the debt will not continually rise (see Box 4.4).

A number of rules of thumb have been suggested for managing the overall level of indebtedness—such as the need to limit the total debt service ratio to 20 percent—but caution must be exercised. No simple rule is adequate in all circumstances. A country's ability to sustain any particular debt ratio depends on a number of factors including the outlook for the country's exports, expectations about future terms of trade and interest rates, and the flexibility of the country to adjust rapidly if necessary. For example, a country with a proven ability to take necessary measures when difficulties arise may be able to sustain a debt service ratio of 30 percent, while a less flexible country may encounter difficulties with a ratio of less than 20 percent.

A few developing countries have statutory rules on how much borrowing can be done by the public sector and by the country as a whole; Korea is one such example. About a third of all developing countries—though the number is falling—have no clear borrowing guidelines; in effect, they judge each investment on its own economic, commercial, and political merits and on the availability of foreign funds. Most countries follow strategies between these two extremes—usually overall guidelines are announced either in the form of the absolute value of new commitments in any year or in terms of some debt or debt service ratio. Often, target levels of public debt are approved by the government or by parliament at the beginning of the year, but on many occasions these targets are not observed. Usually nonguaranteed debt is not included in the guidelines.

Formal borrowing rules do not guarantee that debt-servicing difficulties will be avoided. The Philippines has one of the most systematic approaches, relying primarily on a statutory ceiling of 20 percent for the public debt service ratio (see Box 5.1). Although its controls were useful during much of the 1970s, they did not prevent a debt service moratorium in 1983. This was partly because the rules were not comprehensive and partly because, faced with a steep fall in the terms of trade, the government adopted fiscal and monetary policies that were inconsistent with a sustainable current account balance.

However, some countries have found that borrowing limits can be a useful complement to macroeconomic decisionmaking. Thailand, for example, has an official debt committee charged with ensuring that guidelines are met (see Box 5.2). Guidelines require that amortization and interest payments on government and government-guaranteed debt should not exceed 9 percent of export earnings over a five-year rolling period. When this guideline was exceeded in 1983 and again in 1984, the debt committee was requested to plan future borrowing so as to reduce the public debt service ratio to below 9 percent by 1987, the beginning of the next Five Year Plan period. This ceiling is supplemented by a rule limiting new commitments of government and government-guaranteed debt to 20 percent of budget appropriations.

Box 5.1   Borrowing rules: the case of the Philippines

The government of the Philippines aims to limit foreign borrowing by stipulating that debt service payments in a given year may not exceed 20 percent of the foreign exchange receipts (including capital inflows) of the preceding year. This rule is part of a framework for debt management that has operated since the balance of payments crisis of 1969–70.

Enforcing the 20 percent limit requires comprehensive figures on debt. The central bank's Management of External Debt and Investment Accounts Department (MEDIAD) has a monthly reporting system that requires all borrowers to report in detail on their debts. MEDIAD also sets guidelines on the uses and terms of foreign borrowing. Its other responsibilities include informing the central bank about demands for foreign loans by the public and private sectors and ensuring that borrowers queue up for medium- and long-term loans.

Two other features of the Philippines' debt management system are the Consolidated Foreign Borrowing Program (CFBP) and the Investment Coordination Committee (ICC). The CFBP borrows large sums from abroad and then onlends the money to banking institutions to finance development projects or to refinance existing debt. The ICC, which was established in 1978, is responsible for approving projects and setting priorities within the context of the national development plans.

This institutional framework for debt management worked well throughout most of the 1970s, but the past five years have illustrated three weaknesses: (a) inadequate monitoring of short-term debt and banking debt; (b) a failure to integrate debt management fully with economic management; and (c) too much attention on the current year at the expense of future years. In addition, the definition of the 20 percent limit was changed several times so as to maintain debt service payments within legal limits. It can even be argued that the statutory ratio gave a false sense of security and so failed to warn of the crisis in time for preventive actions to be taken.

Aware of these drawbacks, the government has over the past two years sought to complement the statutory debt service ratio with other controls. For example, short-term debt is being monitored more closely, and an approval system for short-term borrowing has been established.

Box 5.2 Integrated debt management: the case of Thailand

The Thai government has traditionally taken a prudent approach to international borrowing. Thailand's debt service ratio has been one of the lowest among middle-income countries. Its guidelines on public external borrowing have been administered by an External Debt Committee chaired by the minister of finance.

In 1984, in part prompted by debt-servicing difficulties in the Philippines, the Thai government decided to upgrade the role of the External Debt Committee and to bring debt management into the mainstream of macroeconomic policymaking. In particular, it decided that public external debt should no longer be considered independently of private borrowing and public domestic borrowing. Reflecting this change, the committee's name was changed to the Committee for National Debt Policy. It is chaired by the minister of finance and consists of senior representatives from the Bank of Thailand, the National Economic and Social Development Board, and the Bureau of the Budget. Its secretariat is based in the Ministry of Finance. It will benefit from an improved data management system currently being installed there,

especially if staff training is stepped up.

The committee's responsibilities include vetting all requests for loans (including military loans) from government agencies and public enterprises, within the context of the country's debt service capacity. It is also considering possible guidelines for foreign borrowing: (a) operating deficits may not be financed by foreign borrowing; (b) any subsidies to public enterprises must be made explicit in the central government budget; and (c) pricing policies of public enterprises should be analyzed for their effect on the financial viability of the enterprises and their ability to service foreign debts. However, a final determination on guidelines has not yet been made.

The committee is also responsible for monitoring and reporting disbursement performance under foreign-financed projects, for managing the composition of external debt, and for reporting to the Economic Cabinet every four months. It suggests limits on public borrowing for the year ahead and points out any inconsistency between government budgetary policy and these limits.

In general, a formal ceiling on borrowing is useful. It encourages discipline and helps to focus official attention on central macroeconomic questions. Official borrowing rules can be particularly helpful if they cover military expenditures and projects that, for political reasons, are not always easy to control. But formal rules also carry dangers. They can create a sense of security that may not be justified. They rarely cover all types of borrowing: for example, short-term debt is usually uncontrolled and may rise dangerously, as happened in Mexico in early 1982. Sometimes the overall debt structure can be biased by partial controls. In Thailand, for example, the public sector's foreign borrowing has been subject to clear ceilings but its domestic borrowing has not. As a result, the public sector may borrow heavily from the domestic market, crowd out the private sector, and so force it to borrow abroad—often at higher interest rates and shorter maturities than the government could have obtained.

How much control?

The level of control over capital inflows has, on average, increased in the 1980s. Increased control has been required mainly because of the inadequacy of economic policies. To the extent that governments adhere to fiscal and monetary policies that are consistent with a sustainable balance of payments position and to the extent that governments set prices—including interest rates and exchange rates—to reflect opportunity costs, the need to actively control the level of capital flows is diminished. However it may still be desirable to control the structure or composition of borrowing.

The extent to which the central government controls foreign borrowing as a whole varies greatly from country to country (see Table 5.1). Even its procedures for approving and monitoring its own borrowing differ. Generally, the Ministry of Finance is the official borrower on behalf of the government. However, if the loan is to support the exchange rate or to build up reserves, the central bank may well be the borrower. In a few cases, other government departments have independently borrowed from abroad, usually short term.

In most developing countries, public enterprises are allowed to borrow on their own account. Usually they must register their loans with the central government; in a growing number of countries, they now need its prior approval. Sudan recently introduced this requirement, and Costa Rica, Turkey, and Zambia have strengthened the screening process. Mexico introduced a foreign borrowing law in 1977, requiring all borrowing by public bodies to be authorized in writing—though some (notably PEMEX) have occasionally borrowed without explicit permission. In a few countries, the central government borrows on behalf of public

Table 5.1 A taxonomy of external borrowing controls

Borrowers	Range of controls	Country examples
Central government	Tight control within overall statutory ceilings.	Thailand, Philippines, Brazil.
	Government departments permitted reasonable freedom within loose overall borrowing controls.	Most countries.
Public enterprises and local governments	All borrowing must be initiated by and undertaken by the central government.	Indonesia.
	Borrowing must be authorized by the central government.	Mexico, Ecuador, Korea, Portugal, Brazil.
	No controls unless government guarantee requested.	Sudan.
	Local authorities permitted to borrow freely.	Yugoslavia (pre-1982), Nigeria (pre-1982).
Commercial banks	Selective restrictions on foreign borrowing.	Brazil, Korea.
	Freedom to borrow and lend in any currency and to incur exchange risks.	Chile, Ecuador, Argentina (pre-1982).
Private (nonbank) borrowers	Borrowing must be approved; minimum maturity and maximum interest rate stipulated.	Turkey, Costa Rica, Philippines, Brazil, Korea.
	Borrowing must be approved and is often required for capital goods imports over a certain level.	Portugal.
	Borrowing must be registered, but is almost always approved.	Thailand, Mexico, Ecuador.
	No controls or accurate measurement.	Indonesia.

Source: World Bank informal survey.

enterprises. For example, following the PER-TAMINA crisis in the mid-1970s, the Indonesian government prohibited most public enterprises from borrowing abroad; public enterprise debt is now generally indistinguishable from central government debt.

It is common practice for governments to guarantee foreign loans made to public enterprises and even to the private sector (sometimes for a fee, as in Pakistan). The potential advantages of a guarantee include better borrowing terms and greater control over the investment programs of public enterprises. But guarantees place an extra financial burden, potentially a large one, on the central government. They also transfer part of the responsibility for project appraisal to the government, further stretching its scarce administrative capacity. And by ensuring a dependence on the government, a guarantee policy may unintentionally stop public enterprises from becoming more financially sophisticated and more accountable for their actions.

In most developing countries, local or regional authorities are not permitted to borrow abroad independently of the central government. There have been a few exceptions, in federal states such as Nigeria and Yugoslavia. But autonomous borrowing by local government can seriously compli-

cate the management of overall public debt. Following recent difficulties, the government of Yugoslavia has coordinated all the foreign debts of the regions.

Control over foreign borrowing by the private sector varies greatly (see Table 5.2). Until recently, some developing countries sought to encourage private companies to borrow abroad. In Argentina and Mexico in 1981 and 1982, governments urged large corporations to get foreign loans so as to make room in domestic financial markets for increased public borrowing. Exchange rate guarantees have also been a fairly common means of encouraging private borrowing, particularly in Latin America. Asian governments have generally not provided formal guarantees, though central banks have sometimes offered a "swap" facility, which effectively achieves the same goal.

With the debt-servicing difficulties of the past few years, governments have tightened their controls on foreign borrowing by the private sector. In about half of the developing countries, private borrowers need permission from the government. A few governments—including those in Brazil, Korea, and the Philippines—have used their powers actively to control the level and composition of total debt. Costa Rica and Turkey are two countries that have recently begun to control private borrowing more carefully. In Mexico, private foreign debt was neither controlled nor even registered until exchange controls were introduced in 1982; now private debtors must register their borrowings and report any changes every six months.

Part of the reason for closer government involvement in private borrowing is that, in a crisis, the central government may be obliged to take responsibility for private sector debt, even if it had not initially guaranteed it. This has happened in several cases, notably Mexico and the Philippines. In principle, the government has been required to ensure the availability of foreign exchange to service the debts (transfer risk) while the commercial risk remained the province of the private companies. In practice, however, the distinction between transfer and commercial risk has been blurred. Mexico's rescheduling agreement has produced legal disputes between the government and foreign banks on this very issue.

Some governments have used indirect measures to control private foreign borrowing. These include withholding taxes on interest payments (for example, Indonesia, Malaysia, and Thailand) and requirements that borrowers should deposit a proportion of their loan with the central bank at zero or low interest rates (for example, Brazil and Chile). Other governments have set limits on the interest rates on new private debt, trying to protect private borrowers who may be inexperienced in dealing with foreign lenders. This runs the risks of limiting foreign borrowing opportunities to well-established local borrowers and discriminating against smaller innovative companies. Other measures are designed to influence the maturity structure of a country's debt, such as the prohibition of short-term borrowing. Finally, monetary policy may be used to vary the attractions of foreign borrowing. Many governments have at times raised domestic interest rates in order to encourage capital inflows or discourage outflows, and in some instances interest rates have been lowered in order to discourage inflows.

Managing market access

Not all financial markets are open to all developing countries. A country may be able to obtain Eurodollar loans but not bond finance or loans in non-dollar currencies. Some countries may be able to do swap transactions at low cost; for others, they may be expensive or impossible. It is important that debt managers think strategically about how to increase access to markets at low cost.

Managing market access involves two elements. First, coordination is required because borrowing can be much more expensive if several borrowers from the same country approach the same market simultaneously. Some governments require public bodies to queue up, with only one borrower at a

Table 5.2 Instruments affecting private foreign borrowing in selected developing countries

Country	Prior approval	Minimum maturity	Deposit requirement	Ceiling on interest rate or spread	Withholding tax on interest payments abroad	Import restriction based on financing	Exchange rate guarantee
Argentina	○	○	○	○	○	●	●a
Brazil	●	●	●	●	○	●	●
Chile	●	●b	●	●	○	○	○
Costa Rica	●	●	○	●	○	○	○
Ecuador	○	○	○	○	○	●	○
Indonesia	○	○	○	○	●	○	○
Korea	●	○	○	○	○	●	○
Mexico	○	○	○	○	○	○	●a
Morocco	●	○	○	○	○	○	○
Philippines	●	●	○	●	○	●	○
Sudan	●	○	○	○	○	○	○
Thailandc	○	○	○	○	●	○	○
Turkey	●	●	○	●	○	○	○
Yugoslaviad	●	○	○	○	○	●	●
Zambia	●	○	○	○	○	○	○

Note: ● = instruments used at present or in the recent past; ○ = instruments not used at present or in the recent past.
a. No new guarantees are provided at present.
b. Not in place at present.
c. Contracting of supplier credit requires Bank of Thailand approval.
d. Refers to borrowing by self-managed social sector enterprises.
Source: World Bank data.

time being allowed to approach the market. The Korean government includes Korean commercial banks (the main private borrowers) in this system, so as to avoid competing for loans. And Portugal is one example of a country in which the central bank can refuse to authorize borrowing if the spread over the London interbank offered rate (LIBOR) or the U.S. prime rate is above a specified level.

Second, countries must establish a good name for themselves. Reputation depends partly on economic performance and a willingness to change policies. Indonesia, for example, can borrow at lower cost than most countries at similar income levels because, in times of difficulty during the past decade, its government has consistently shown a willingness to cut spending, raise revenues, or devalue the currency.

It is also important for lenders to get to know borrowers. International capital markets are segmented, so a welcome in one does not guarantee a welcome elsewhere. In the late 1970s, Mexico could borrow in the syndicated loan market at spreads as low as Sweden's, but it failed to borrow from the dollar bond market, because it was not familiar there. Bond investors—usually individuals and nonbank financial institutions—may have perceptions of a country's creditworthiness quite different from those of commercial bankers. Countries can gradually gain access to markets by borrowing on a small scale when money is not urgently needed.

Although this discussion relates primarily to borrowing from commercial markets, it is also necessary for policymakers to make strategic decisions concerning borrowing from official sources. Countries can often borrow more nonconcessional official money if they want to. But building up a pipeline of good projects takes time. Bilateral and multilateral agencies usually operate within the framework of rolling three- or five-year lending programs. It is generally not possible to increase lending quickly. Debt managers must therefore focus on foreign exchange needs over the medium term, as well as for the current year.

Lessons from recent experience

The following conclusions emerge from the experience of the past few years:
• Close control of government borrowing and careful coordination and monitoring of all borrowing by public enterprises are essential.
• Whether it is desirable or necessary to control private borrowing depends on a government's economic policies. Less control is needed the more that prices, interest, and exchange rates are aligned with world market levels; if they are not, a country runs the risks of large capital inflows or outflows, probably regardless of controls.
• Where governments have actively encouraged private borrowing, the encouragement has almost always been in the context of policies (such as an overvalued exchange rate or an excessive government deficit) that are unsustainable over the long run. The resulting borrowings have delayed needed policy reforms and have contributed to the magnitude of future debt-servicing difficulties.
• Where the costs and risks of foreign borrowing to the nation as a whole exceed those to the private borrowers—where a government may have to take over private debts, for example—there is a good case for a modest tax on private foreign borrowing.

Managing the composition of capital inflows

Debt servicing in future years is largely determined by the composition of external borrowing. The total volume of borrowing that can be undertaken from one year to the next is not independent of the source and terms on which it is undertaken. Among the issues on which decisions need to be made are (a) the appropriate balance between debt and equity capital flows, (b) the relative roles of official and commercial sources of funds, (c) the proportion of debt at floating rates and fixed rates, (d) the appropriate maturity structure of the debt, and (e) the appropriate currency composition of borrowing. Of course, these are not totally self-contained issues, nor may a borrowing country have adequate options. If the desired composition of capital inflows is not possible, it may be necessary to cut back on the level.

The appropriate structure of foreign liabilities differs among countries and varies over time. It depends on external conditions (such as the outlook and uncertainty concerning interest rates, exchange rates, and access to international markets) and internal conditions (such as the growth of domestic savings and exports and the capacity to adjust rapidly in a time of crisis). The more flexible are policies and the more diversified is an economy's structure, the more risk the country is able to bear.

Debt managers have two primary tasks. First, they must continually assess the extent to which the structure of *existing* net liabilities is optimal within the constraints of the financial instruments available to the country. Some techniques suggested below for modifying the structure of existing debt—such as interest rate and currency swaps—are not available to all developing countries, but others—such as adjusting the currency composition of the nation's official reserves in light of the composition of its debt—are available to all. Second, careful management of the composition of *new* capital inflows is necessary.

The balance between debt and equity

Equity finance—direct foreign investment and portfolio investment—declined in importance during the 1970s, largely because of the ready availability of bank loans carrying low or negative real interest rates. Nonetheless, equity funds have two advantages over debt. First, the foreign investor bears both the commercial and the exchange rate risk. This lowers the overall risk to the recipient country, so it can sustain larger capital inflows and a higher level of investment. Second, direct foreign investment is generally accompanied by management and technology, which often benefits the recipient country and raises the rate of return on the project. But equity finance may cost the recipient more. Although measuring the rate of return on foreign investment is extremely difficult, most studies show that, over long periods of time, the average return required by direct foreign investors is several percentage points higher than the interest rate on commercial debt.

Direct foreign investment is generally not a substitute but a complement for borrowed money. It usually is part of a package in which there is some equity financing, some commercial bank credit, and some export credit. But in some cases countries have a choice between debt and equity. A particular investment can be made by a domestic company that borrows from foreign banks, or by a foreign company bringing in finance, or as a joint venture. Although political considerations may suggest that ownership should be retained in domestic hands, on economic grounds there is a strong case for increasing the share of foreign equity in total capital inflows, particularly in the present climate of high real interest rates. The scope for enlarging the role of equity finance is discussed in detail in Chapter 9.

The balance between official and commercial sources

The proportion of developing-country debt financed from commercial sources has risen rapidly over the last decade. In the aggregate, the supply of official funds to developing countries—both concessional and nonconcessional—increased only slowly, while there was an explosive increase in commercial financing. But there may be more flexibility for individual countries than is often assumed. Obviously a country will generally maximize its use of any highly concessional funds before resorting to commercial markets, but for less concessional official flows and for "mixed" credits—where concessional and nonconcessional loans are linked—a careful strategy is required, based upon the following considerations.

First, the true costs and benefits of official lending vary according to the supplier and the terms on which it is offered. Official finance is usually accompanied by technical assistance, usually of longer maturity than commercial loans, and often at fixed interest rates. But even grants can be expensive if the donor wants them to finance low-priority projects. And official lenders may also misdirect a country's investment pattern if their loans come through export credit agencies that are biased toward certain types of capital goods.

Second, there may be a tradeoff between the volume of ODA and its grant element. Some donors may be willing to give more ODA than others, but on less concessional terms. Japan, for example, provides a volume of ODA that is about average for OECD countries, but the proportion it gives as grants and the grant element of its loans are below the OECD average. The opposite is true of countries such as Australia, New Zealand, and Norway. Methods of estimating the grant element of a loan or of a mixture of grants and loans are described in Box 5.3.

Managing interest rate risk

As fixed interest rates on medium- and long-term loans are generally available only from official bilateral sources, borrowers may have no option but to obtain floating rate debt. Even multilateral institutions such as the World Bank have found it necessary to lend at rates that vary over the life of the loan (although the variability is generally much lower than on most commercial loans). This makes it essential to explore future debt service payments on various assumptions about interest rates. The ratio of future interest payments to projected export earnings—the interest to export ratio—is a particularly useful indicator of vulnerability, since interest payments generally cannot be rescheduled. Table 5.3 gives some indication of the vul-

Box 5.3 Estimating the grant element

The grant element in a loan is defined as the difference between the original face value of the loan and the discounted present value of debt service, as a percentage of the original face value. As Box table 5.3A shows, the grant element is greater the lower the interest rate on the loan and the longer its maturity or grace period.

Box table 5.3A Grant element of selected loan terms

Loan terms			
Interest rate	Maturity	Grace period	Grant element[a]
			10 percent discount rate
0	30	5	77 percent
6	20	0	23 percent
6	10	0	15 percent
6	10	5	21 percent
			15 percent discount rate
6	10	5	40 percent

a. Assumes immediate disbursement of loan and equal annual repayments.

In theory, the discount rate should be carefully chosen to reflect the cost of capital. In practice, a 10 percent rate is usually assumed for all currencies and time periods—the convention used in the grant element tables published by the OECD. However, using any single inflexible rate has obvious drawbacks, as it does not take account of changes in market interest rates or of big differences in rates for different currencies.

A better alternative is to set the discount rate equal to the rate of interest at which commercial finance with the same maturity could be borrowed in international markets at the time and in the particular currency of the loan in question. In many instances, of course, commercial funds would not be available for such long maturities, so a premium should be added to the discount rate to make allowance for this. The effect of a discount rate that varies according to currency and over time is to lower the grant element for official loans from countries in which interest rates are low and to raise it for loans from countries in which rates are high and during periods of high international rates in general.

Box 5.4 Three innovative financial instruments and their use by developing countries

Three financial instruments that are increasingly used in domestic financial markets (notably the mortgage market) have not yet been used by developing countries, but may have certain merits for them.

• *Flexible maturity loans.* Instead of variable interest rates, loans carry a variable maturity. Debt service payments are held constant in absolute terms (or, perhaps, in relation to a borrower's income). When interest rates rise, the amortization part of debt service declines and the loan's maturity increases accordingly. With a large rise in interest rates, negative amortization will occur; lenders will effectively be providing new money to borrowers. Flexible maturity loans offer advantages to both borrowers and lenders. Borrowers are certain of their debt-servicing obligations. Lenders are able to manage their assets with less worry about debt rescheduling and possible write-offs. For developing countries, this would be doubly attractive if debt service payments could be tied to export receipts, as it would reduce the uncertainty over volatile commodity prices.

• *Graduated payment loans.* Debt service payments are initially low and gradually build up. In the early years of a loan, amortization may even be negative. This instrument could be particularly suitable for project finance, where earnings and debt-servicing capacity rise as the project matures. By matching the stream of debt service obligations with the expected foreign exchange earnings of a project, debt managers would avoid tying up foreign reserves for debt servicing.

• *Shared equity loans.* Lenders would accept below-market interest rates in return for a share in the equity of projects. For the borrower, the risk involved in a project is shared with the lender. However, since a project's earnings depend on what price is charged for its output, a loan agreement would have to contain some pricing formula. This would give lenders some influence over the management of the project (though it would also raise their administrative costs). Lenders might also want to stipulate some compensation procedure or insurance against political risks.

nerability of borrowing countries to rising interest rates. For those developing countries that have recently rescheduled their debts, the proportion of debt at floating rates (34 percent at the end of 1983) was nearly twice that of nonrescheduling countries. Similarly, the interest to exports ratio of reschedulers was more than twice that of nonreschedulers and rose much faster between 1980 and 1982.

Debt managers may sometimes be able to raise the proportion of debt at fixed terms. For example, official export credits can often substitute for commercial borrowing (see Chapter 7). New financial instruments, such as flexible maturity and shared equity loans, are becoming available to developing countries (see Box 5.4). And some middle-income countries are already using interest rate swaps to exchange floating rate for fixed rate loans (see Box 5.5).

The maturity structure of debt

Recent debt-servicing difficulties have often been caused or exacerbated by a shortening of the maturity structure of foreign debt. The average maturity of total medium- and long-term debt of the major borrowing countries fell from 17.9 years in 1972 to 12.7 years in 1981. The average maturity was even lower for the largest borrowers: Brazil, 9.7 years in 1981; and Mexico, only 8.7 years. In part this occurred because commercial bank debt rose much faster than ODA and other official financing. The sharp increase in short-term debt, especially after 1979, has further shortened the debt structure. By early 1983, short-term debt of developing countries had increased to an estimated $130 billion, roughly one-quarter of all developing-country debt.

For many countries, the shortening of maturities was not a deliberate policy that then led to difficulties. Often they faced a choice between borrowing short term or not borrowing at all, since commercial creditors were no longer willing to lend longer term. Heavy short-term debts were therefore at least as much a symptom as a cause of difficulties. But in many instances they should have signaled the need to change economic policies before those changes were forced upon policymakers by creditors during rescheduling negotiations.

Table 5.3 Indicators of vulnerability to rising interest rates
(percent)

Country and indicator	1973	1975	1977	1979	1980	1981	1982	1983
Argentina*								
Interest/exports	12.3	13.7	8.2	9.6	12.9	17.2	25.0	23.3*
Debt at floating rates	6.8	17.5	39.4	48.0	57.1	59.4	70.0	75.0
Brazil*								
Interest/exports	10.6	20.6	14.9	26.4	27.1	29.4	39.8	31.5*
Debt at floating rates	34.8	51.8	54.3	59.6	61.2	67.3	69.6	76.5
Costa Rica*								
Interest/exports	5.6	6.1	5.3	10.5	14.0	11.2	9.7	45.0*
Debt at floating rates	19.3	29.2	32.0	46.6	46.5	52.1	51.9	57.0
Indonesia								
Interest/exports	3.6	4.6	5.6	6.8	5.3	5.7	7.4	8.2
Debt at floating rates	4.5	19.4	18.7	14.5	16.8	17.8	20.0	22.7
Kenya								
Interest/exports	4.0	4.5	3.8	7.2	8.3	9.2	11.6	10.9
Debt at floating rates	3.8	2.9	5.1	8.3	11.4	13.0	11.0	9.1
Korea								
Interest/exports	5.9	5.3	3.8	4.7	6.0	6.4	7.2	6.2
Debt at floating rates	8.7	21.0	23.0	27.8	29.0	37.5	40.9	42.1
Mexico*								
Interest/exports	10.4	16.9	18.7	20.5	18.3	19.6	26.7	30.1*
Debt at floating rates	40.0	51.2	53.3	69.7	71.1	74.8	76.0	82.4
Philippines*								
Interest/exports	3.6	3.6	5.0	7.5	6.9	9.1	10.5	10.3
Debt at floating rates	8.0	21.0	21.9	24.9	29.5	30.8	36.2	36.0
Turkey*								
Interest/exports	4.5	5.8	8.0	8.3*	17.2*	13.9*	12.0	15.0
Debt at floating rates	0.5	0.8	7.8	29.2	22.7	22.1	23.3	25.0
Developing countries[a]								
Interest/exports	4.3	5.0	5.0	6.7	6.9	8.2	10.1	9.8
Debt at floating rates	6.4	9.4	11.8	15.5	17.3	19.0	20.2	21.6
Reschedulers[b]								
Interest/exports	7.0	7.4	7.0	9.9	10.5	12.4	16.5	17.0[c]
Debt at floating rates	11.9	17.2	23.1	29.9	31.2	33.2	34.9	38.3
LIBOR (3 months)	9.2	11.0	5.6	8.7	14.4	16.5	13.1	9.6

Note: Asterisk denotes rescheduler and time of rescheduling. (The Philippines rescheduled in 1984.) The interest to exports ratio reflects interest actually paid on medium- and long-term debt. Exports include goods and services. Debt at floating rates refers to public medium- and long-term debt.
a. Arithmetic average for ninety developing countries. Because of the averaging method used, data differ from those in other chapters.
b. Average for twenty-seven countries rescheduling between 1975 and 1984, as indicated in Figure 4.1. For details, see Box 2.4.
c. Estimate.
Source: World Bank data.

Loan maturities should, to the extent possible, be matched with the payoff period of investments that are financed. Many countries have run into problems by borrowing too short. For example, in the late 1950s and early 1960s debt-servicing difficulties of Argentina, Brazil, Chile, Ghana, and Indonesia were largely due to the mismatch of five- to seven-year supplier credits with investment programs having a much longer gestation.

Two further lessons can be derived from recent experience. First, "bunching" of debt service obligations must be avoided. This was one cause of recent problems in Argentina, for example, where the introduction of the exchange rate guarantee system in 1981 encouraged the extension of existing loans by eighteen months, and where the elimination of deposit requirements encouraged large-scale short-term borrowing in 1980–81; all of these obligations fell due at about the same time in 1982. Second, it is dangerous to assume that short-term borrowing will be continually rolled over. Many countries—including Ecuador, the Philippines, Portugal, and Romania—have found that the withdrawal of roll-over privileges because of poor economic performance has contributed to debt-servicing difficulties.

The use of short-term borrowing for general balance of payments support can jeopardize a country's access to these funds for valid trade-related purposes. Occasionally countries have successfully borrowed short term to prevent reserves from falling (for example, Korea in 1980), and on rare occasions some countries have successfully borrowed short-term funds to buy time to bargain for lower rates on medium- and long-term loans (for example, Brazil in 1980). But generally, heavy short-term borrowing for other than trade-related purposes has proved costly.

What therefore is an appropriate level of short-term debt? Although there are no hard and fast rules, some general guidelines are useful, based on the level of a country's noncapital goods imports and needs for pre-export finance. (Capital goods imports, accounting for about 25–35 percent of total imports, are generally financed by longer-term funds.) Since trade finance is generally for 90–120 days, this implies that short-term debt generally should not exceed three months of imports, and in most normal situations should probably be less. (An exception must be made for countries that act as international money centers, where short-term banking liabilities may be higher.) Figures 5.1 and 5.2 bear out this simple rule of thumb.

To reduce their short-term borrowing, some developing countries now impose a minimum maturity or a deposit requirement on foreign borrowing by private enterprises. Some countries—including Brazil, Korea, and the Philippines—control access to trade credit by specifying acceptable terms and the items for which credits are permit-

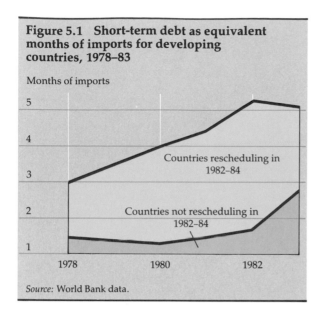

Figure 5.1 Short-term debt as equivalent months of imports for developing countries, 1978–83

Months of imports

Countries rescheduling in 1982–84

Countries not rescheduling in 1982–84

Source: World Bank data.

ted. Other countries—for example, Costa Rica and Turkey—control all short-term borrowing. In Chile, the proportion of loan proceeds that has to be deposited with the central bank is higher for shorter maturities.

Managing exchange risk

Some countries have informal rules on the currency composition of their debt. For example, Portugal in 1978–80 insisted on dollar-denominated loans, despite much lower interest rates on other currencies, on the grounds that over time the dollar was likely to depreciate. Some industrial countries have adopted more explicit guidelines. Some, such as Sweden, have diversified their debt portfolios by increasing the number of currencies in which they borrow. Others have sought to minimize exchange risk by borrowing in currencies with which their own currencies are linked; Ireland, for example, has incurred almost half of its debt in deutsche marks—the dominant currency in the European Monetary System, to which Ireland belongs.

In recent years over three-quarters of foreign borrowing of developing countries has been denominated in dollars (see Table 2.5). This was partly due to the ready availability of dollar loans in comparison with other currencies. But in many instances dollar-denominated loans were actively chosen by debt managers. In retrospect, this has often harmed borrowing countries, because of the large appreciation of the dollar. Loans denominated in nondollar currencies have benefited some

developing countries greatly. For example, some loans made by the World Bank between 1978 and 1982 will have effective interest rates of less than 1 percent a year when expressed in dollars, if exchange rates remain unchanged between now and the loans' maturity. But hindsight always produces successful strategies. More important is whether there are lessons that will assist portfolio managers in the future.

In simple terms, borrowers have two objectives: (a) to minimize the variability of their debt service obligations and (b) to minimize the cost of borrowing. These objectives correspond to two components of a borrowing decision, the hedging and the speculative.

• The hedging component reflects the choice of a borrower concerned solely with minimizing risk. Under this strategy, currencies are chosen that will help to insulate the economy from currency volatility and changes in terms of trade. The object is to choose currencies whose real values rise and fall with the borrower's real income.

• The speculative component reflects the borrower's expectations of changes in exchange rates and interest rates. For any particular loan the borrower should choose the currency that will minimize the expected cost of borrowing, adjusted for the expected exchange rate changes. To the extent that (a) interest parity holds (that is, the premium

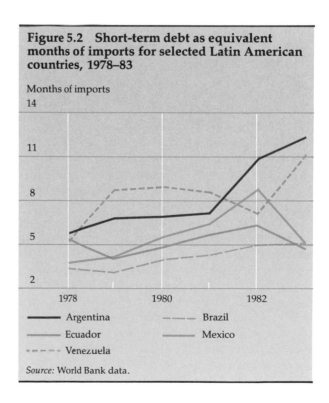

Figure 5.2 Short-term debt as equivalent months of imports for selected Latin American countries, 1978–83

Months of imports

——— Argentina   - - - - - Brazil

——— Ecuador   ——— Mexico

- - - - Venezuela

Source: World Bank data.

Some twenty-eight developing countries are now using computerized systems for debt analysis and management. Some, such as Brazil, have created their own without outside assistance. Others have hired international firms to design a system for their particular needs or have bought ready-made designs.

Peru has recently installed one of the most sophisticated systems in the developing world. It was created by a private firm under a technical assistance loan provided by the World Bank in conjunction with an analysis and planned reorganization of the bodies that manage Peru's debt. It cost over $1 million (including hardware), and a Peruvian technical team has been trained to maintain it. The new system can track future requirements for foreign exchange and manage daily requirements; produce letters authorizing debt payments; incorporate all kinds of debt—public and private, short- or medium- or long-term, external and internal; and handle fixed and variable rate loans. The system is not yet being used efficiently because of difficulties in making the legal and administrative changes needed to ensure the required flow of information among agencies. Another system, costing about the same as Peru's, evolved from an advisory group's experience in helping countries in debt rescheduling negotiations; thus the system is good at analyzing alternative debt strategies. Mozambique uses this system, and Indonesia is installing it.

A more modest system has recently been developed by UNCTAD. It is designed for countries that have well-organized and centralized control of their external debt. The system classifies each loan; monitors foreign exchange liabilities on a daily basis; evaluates fixed and variable rate loans; and generates standard reports. The system is designed to run on a microcomputer, and UNCTAD provides the software free. The UNCTAD package is now being installed in Bolivia, Liberia, Madagascar, and Togo. Another system that will be free to developing countries is being developed by the Commonwealth Secretariat.

Whichever system is used, all basic data on debt must be reported promptly to the debt office. Specifically, this means centralization of loan agreements, prompt reporting of disbursements by implementing agencies, and prompt reporting of debt service payments by banks. As for the systems themselves, sometimes they are too sophisticated. By attempting to include both accounting and analytical functions, it may do neither efficiently. Focusing separately on these two areas may be more appropriate, especially because data in many countries are still unreliable.

or discount between forward and spot exchange rates reflects only nominal interest rate differentials) and (b) the forward rate is an unbiased predictor of the future rate, there will be no speculative decision to make. "Perfect market" conditions will ensure that expected borrowing costs in all currencies are identical.

Both these principles present practical difficulties. Predicting movements in exchange rates and interest rates is notoriously difficult. In addition, some of the relationships required—such as the positive correlation between the borrower's real income and another currency's exchange rate—may not be very stable, and the past may be a poor guide to the future.

In the light of these difficulties, one favored strategy is to base the currency composition of a country's debt on the pattern of its trade. This would mean that countries borrow in the currencies they earn from exporting and hold their reserves in the currencies in which their imports are denominated. If the currency of an export market appreciates, the borrower's terms of trade are likely to improve, thus partially offsetting the higher costs of servicing debt in that currency.

This strategy is attractively simple and practical.

With hindsight, it would have been superior to the dollar-borrowing strategy of most borrowers in recent years, which was based on the belief that the dollar would fall. However, it is not necessarily consistent with the hedging and speculative strategies, and in some instances would lead to inappropriate borrowing. There may be no alternative but to make pragmatic judgments about changes in trade, interest rates, and exchange rates.

Technical assistance

Managing a country's foreign debt and borrowing requires two particular kinds of technical expertise. First is the capacity to assess the costs and benefits of external borrowing and reserve-management strategies on various assumptions about interest rates, export growth, and so on. Second is familiarity with the international financial markets and the ability to use them to the best advantage.

Governments in many developing countries are using technical assistance in both these areas. The World Bank and the IMF, as part of their support for member countries, provide analysis of macroeconomic policies and their implications for external portfolio management. They and others also help to develop debt management systems (see Box 5.6). As for the practical details of borrowing from commercial markets, most developing countries now retain financial advisors to assist them. The advisors are concerned with what financial instruments to use and for how much, when to approach the markets, and so on. On such issues, it may not be cost effective for some developing countries to build up in-house expertise. But on debt management systems and macroeconomic analysis, a main function of technical assistance must be to strengthen each country's capacity to undertake these tasks for itself.

Managing international reserves

International reserves form an integral part of a nation's overall portfolio of foreign assets and liabilities. At least two questions face the portfolio manager: what is an appropriate level of reserves? and when should a government borrow in order to support or increase the level of reserves? Neither question has a clear-cut answer. In general, however, a country should maintain higher reserves the more variable are its export earnings, the higher its debt exposure, the less flexible its economic policies and structures, and the less likely it is to have access to a steady flow of external capital. It is therefore sensible for most developing countries to have higher reserve coverage levels than do industrial countries. The experience of the past few years argues for prudence by developing countries in maintaining enough reserves to allow a country to adjust to domestic or international pressures without unduly jeopardizing its economic growth. A reserve level equivalent to three months of imports is sometimes suggested as a desirable norm for developing countries, but this should not be regarded as a hard and fast rule.

Looking back over the last decade, four points are worthy of note. These are illustrated in Figure 5.3. First, in developing countries as a whole, reserves as a proportion of imports have risen and fallen with the commodity price booms of 1973–74 and 1978–79. Second, reserve levels in low-income African countries have fallen to particularly low levels—from 2.7 months of imports in 1970–73 to 1.5 months in 1980–82. Third, reserve levels in oil-exporting countries rose sharply (from 3.4 months of imports in 1970 to over 8.1 months in 1974) and thereafter fell back almost as dramatically, as development programs rapidly absorbed the foreign exchange holdings. Finally, considerable variation has been evident among countries in reserve

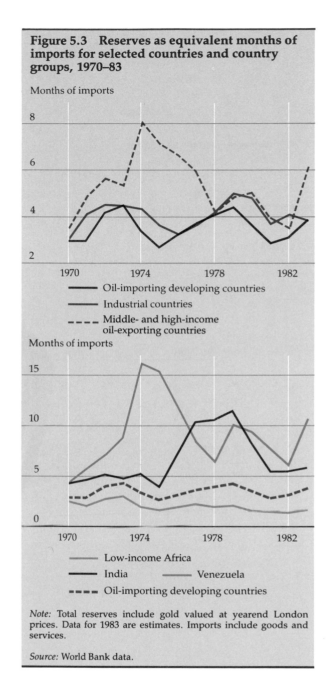

Figure 5.3 Reserves as equivalent months of imports for selected countries and country groups, 1970–83

Note: Total reserves include gold valued at yearend London prices. Data for 1983 are estimates. Imports include goods and services.

Source: World Bank data.

management strategies. For example, some countries, such as India (1975–80) and China, have deliberately maintained high reserves, while others have sailed closer to the wind, allowing reserves to remain at low levels for long periods.

Low reserves can sometimes be augmented by borrowed funds or lines of credit. There are obviously costs to such a strategy since at the margin costs of borrowing exceed earnings on reserves, usually by one or two percentage points, and unused lines of credit involve commitment fees. Furthermore, borrowing also increases future debt service payments and is subject to the roll-over problems discussed earlier. With these caveats, borrowing for reserve accumulation can sometimes be desirable in limited amounts. First, borrowing is usually easier and cheaper when funds are not needed urgently. Second, the level of reserves is itself an important indicator to financial markets that a country is financially sound; thus it could lead to lower borrowing costs. Finally, by borrowing when funds are not urgently needed, the government may be able to tap new sources of finance—for example, the bond market.

The need for information

In many developing countries, economic managers suffer from a dearth of information on external finance. Debt-servicing difficulties are often seriously exacerbated by the absence of information. In the 1950s and 1960s, crises in Ghana and Indonesia were brought on by an almost complete lack of facts on the size of debt and debt service obligations. More recently, Romania, Sudan, and Zaire are examples of countries that have run into costly and disruptive debt problems due partly to data inadequacies.

Most developing countries have good information on public long-term debt, although several (including Costa Rica, Turkey, and Yugoslavia) have recently found that their data on public enterprise and local government debt were inadequate, and many still fail to include military debt in reported statistics. As for private long-term debt, data are poor in more than half of the developing countries and a few industrial countries, such as Denmark and Ireland. Many governments are now trying to correct these weaknesses, tightening up monitoring procedures and using more staff.

Recording short-term debt presents even greater difficulties. Only a minority of developing countries have accurate data, even though the rapid growth of short-term debt has often been central to recent debt-servicing difficulties. Only about a quarter of developing countries maintain systematic information on trade credits, although the data are usually available from commercial banking accounts.

Information must not only be accurate, it must also be timely. Delays in data gathering and processing have caused serious difficulties for managers. In Mexico, for example, the law requires that borrowing need not be reported until forty-five days after the end of the quarter. In 1981–82 this delay allowed $15 billion to be borrowed in one quarter, essentially to finance capital flight, despite an annual authorization of only $4.5 billion. In some countries, the stock of foreign assets and liabilities may be accurately measured at one time, perhaps by outside consultants, but the data are not updated. This static picture may then become the basis for borrowing and lending decisions, even though it becomes steadily less relevant.

A growing number of developing countries are introducing computerized systems for debt management; some of these systems are described in Box 5.6. Similarly, many countries are now making use of centralized data sources—including data from the BIS, the IMF, the OECD, and the World Bank's Debtor Reporting System—to supplement their own sources and to check for consistency.

Part III   Mechanisms for International Financial Flows

6   The international financial system and the developing countries

The international financial system has evolved in response to the changing requirements of borrowers and lenders, most of them in the industrial countries. It has also responded to changes in the objectives, constraints, and behavior of the financial institutions operating in the system. It is therefore a dynamic system constantly adapting to the global economic and financial environment. The speed of adaptation has been faster in some parts of the system—particularly among banks in recent years—than it has in others.

This chapter, which serves as an introduction to Part III, examines the international financial system from the perspective of developing countries. It describes how the system has evolved and the factors that have driven its evolution. Against this background, it suggests some criteria for assessing whether the arrangements have provided sufficient opportunities for developing countries to manage their external borrowing and debt successfully.

Functions and use of the system

In many ways the international financial system performs on a global basis what a national financial system does domestically. It provides a payments mechanism and offers facilities for borrowing and disposing of surplus funds. It creates different types of financial assets and liabilities, which aim to satisfy the portfolio preferences of lenders, investors, and borrowers. To the extent that it is not hindered by national policies, such as controls on capital movements, it helps to allocate funds to their most efficient use around the world. It also determines the ease with which capital can be moved between countries, which has a significant influence on the choices open to governments in adjusting to shocks. The efficiency with which the international financial system performs its various functions can influence the volume of savings and investment generated in the world economy. The functioning of the system therefore has an impor-

tant impact on economic activity in developing countries.

The term international financial system normally covers the institutional arrangements for ensuring that the world's surplus funds flow to countries or entities in deficit, the rules governing the international exchange rate regime, and the mechanisms for creating and distributing liquidity. In Part III of the Report, the focus is on the institutional arrangements—the institutions, instruments, and markets—for channeling finance specifically to developing countries. These arrangements involve a wide range of participating entities—international financial institutions, governments, commercial banks, and industrial companies—that provide or channel funds to developing countries. Sometimes the funds flow directly to developing countries, but other times they flow through various intermediaries and markets. Roughly 40 percent of net flows to developing countries went through intermediaries and markets in 1970, but this figure had risen to more than 60 percent by 1983.

The institutional arrangements relevant for developing countries can be divided into two parts. The official sector contains direct channels for capital flow—for example, bilateral aid—and a number of intermediaries, such as the World Bank and the other multilateral development banks. The private sector, too, has direct mechanisms—direct foreign investment, for instance—as well as intermediaries, such as commercial banks and markets for international bonds and other securities.

Because intermediaries of all kinds have become increasingly important in channeling finance to developing countries, the range of maturities, currencies, and financial instruments offered to developing countries has grown. The economies of scale achieved by financial intermediaries—in terms of information, transaction costs, research, credit assessment, and portfolio diversification—yield efficiencies that reduce costs and risks for savers and borrowers. Ultimately, improvements in

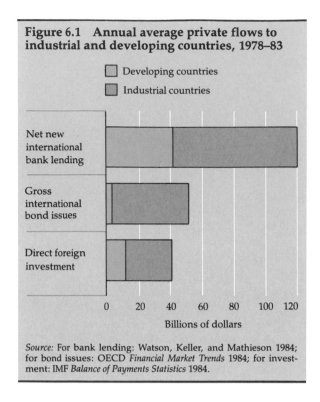

Figure 6.1 Annual average private flows to industrial and developing countries, 1978–83

Developing countries
Industrial countries

Net new international bank lending

Gross international bond issues

Direct foreign investment

0 20 40 60 80 100 120

Billions of dollars

Source: For bank lending: Watson, Keller, and Mathieson 1984; for bond issues: OECD *Financial Market Trends* 1984; for investment: IMF *Balance of Payments Statistics* 1984.

financial efficiency can mean increased flows to developing countries at lower costs.

Most global capital flows are associated with economic and financial relationships between industrial countries. Developing countries have greatly expanded their use of external capital over the last decade, but industrial countries still account for the bulk of the main types of private flows (see Figure 6.1). Between 1978 and 1983, the share of developing countries in net new international bank lending was 36 percent; in gross international bond issuance, 7 percent; and in direct foreign investment, 27 percent. Most official flows, of course, go to developing countries.

The evolving institutional arrangements

The evolution of the institutional arrangements for channeling finance to developing countries has mirrored changes in the world economy. In the postwar period, they have passed through three broad phases. The first phase lasted from the end of World War II to the late 1960s, when official flows, direct foreign investment, and trade finance were the main forms of external capital for developing countries. The financing of current account deficits was done largely through governmental arrangements and international organizations. Financial intermediaries were mainly involved in

domestic business and in financing international trade for their domestic clients. The overseas operations of commercial banks in the industrial countries were limited by exchange and other controls.

The second phase covered the period from the late 1960s to 1982. It was characterized by considerable volatility in exchange rates and interest rates and by much larger current account imbalances. In this environment, the structure of the institutional arrangements changed, and several new mechanisms were introduced. Institutions operating in the international banking and bond markets proved very innovative. International banking developed rapidly, shifting from trade financing to more direct balance of payments financing. Encouraged by the reduction or abolition of controls on international flows of capital, banks participating in international lending grew in number and broadened the range of their countries of origin. As a share of net flows to developing countries, direct foreign investment fell from 19 to 12 percent between 1970 and 1982. The international bond markets—especially the Eurobond market—grew quickly, although developing countries tapped them to a limited extent. Official flows kept pace with the growth in private flows during this

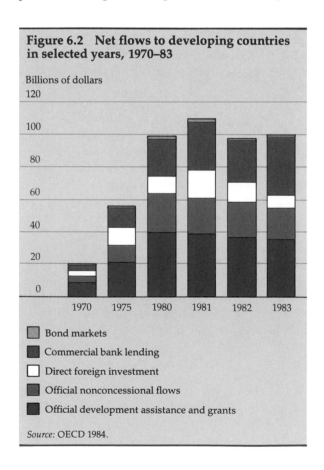

Figure 6.2 Net flows to developing countries in selected years, 1970–83

Billions of dollars

120

100

80

60

40

20

0

1970 1975 1980 1981 1982 1983

Bond markets
Commercial bank lending
Direct foreign investment
Official nonconcessional flows
Official development assistance and grants

Source: OECD 1984.

Box 6.1 The growth and distribution of World Bank lending

The World Bank has increased its lending to developing countries substantially, especially since 1970. By the end of the World Bank's 1984 financial year cumulative IBRD lending totaled $94.2 billion and IDA credits reached $33.6 billion.

There have been some distinct changes in the sectoral distribution of World Bank lending over time (see Box figure 6.1A). During the 1950s and 1960s the main thrust of World Bank lending was for the development of basic infrastructure; lending for power and transportation was predominant. There was a reorientation of lending during the 1970s toward agricultural projects in recognition of the potential high rates of return associated with such projects. Furthermore, given that a large proportion of the poor were engaged in agriculture, this shift in emphasis also directly increased their standard of living.

For similar reasons social sector lending was also raised. The sharp increase in oil prices in the 1970s led to a growth in projects aimed at increasing oil and gas capacity. Since 1980 the financing requirements of the major structural adjustments being made in developing countries have been met in part by the introduction of structural adjustment lending (see Box 4.8 in Chapter 4).

The regional composition of lending has changed more slowly than the sectoral composition. In the 1980s, however, taking the IBRD and IDA together, there has been a shift toward greater lending to Asia—mainly related to the development financing needs of a new member, China. The acute developmental problems of sub-Saharan Africa have also led to an increase in lending to that region.

Box figure 6.1A World Bank average annual lending, 1950–84

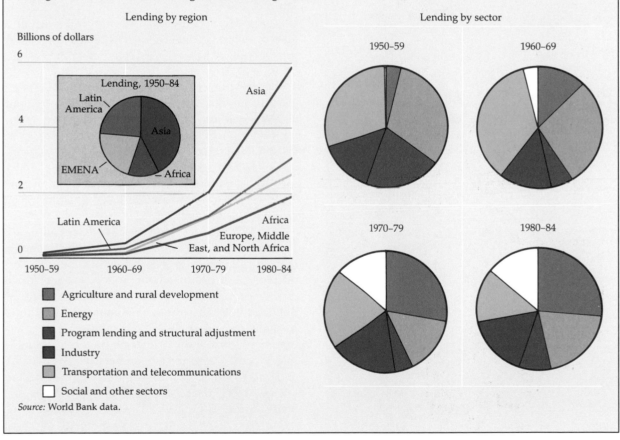

Source: World Bank data.

phase. Within the official sector concessional official flows (or official development assistance, ODA) expanded quickly, but the fastest growth was in the activity of the World Bank (see Box 6.1) and other multilateral institutions. These institutions became increasingly active as borrowers in the bond markets and lent the proceeds to developing countries.

As illustrated in Figure 6.2, these developments led to a major increase in the flow of capital to developing countries. Of particular significance was the shift from equity financing (mainly direct foreign investment) to debt-creating flows. That development increased the vulnerability of devel-

Figure 6.3 Gross disbursements of medium- and long-term loans from official and private sources to country groups, selected years, 1970–83

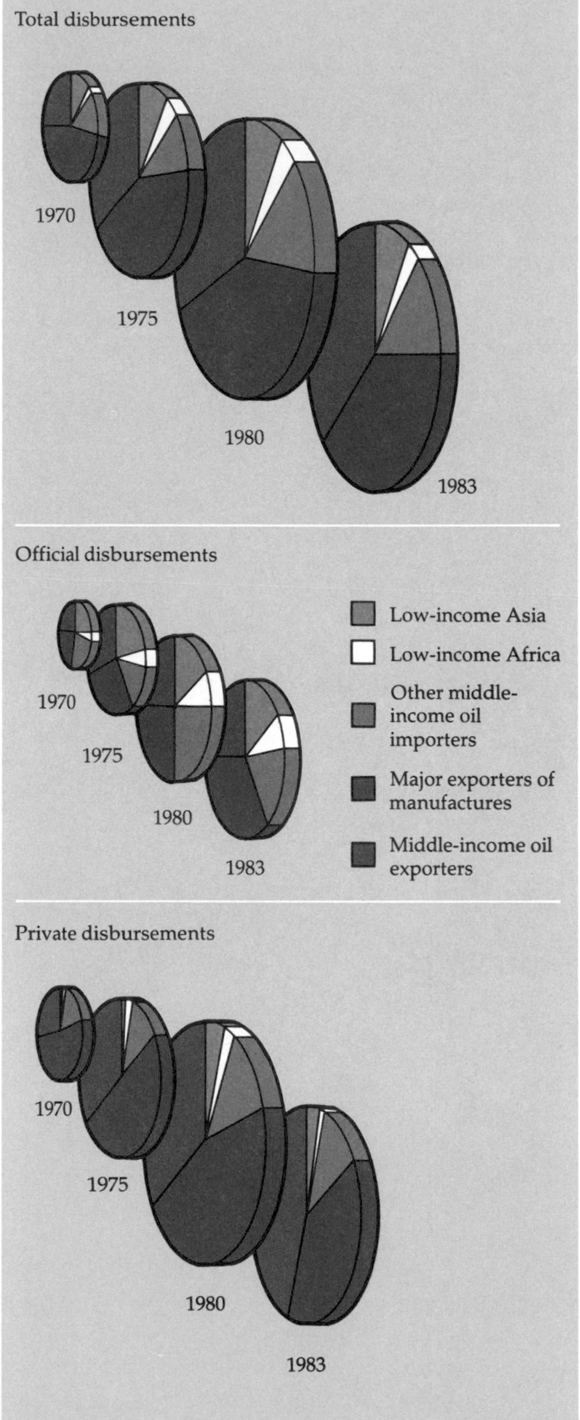

Total disbursements

Official disbursements

Low-income Asia

Low-income Africa

Other middle-income oil importers

Major exporters of manufactures

Middle-income oil exporters

Private disbursements

Note: The size of the pie charts shown for each year is proportional to the amount of disbursements in that year.

Source: World Bank data.

oping countries to changes in the international financial environment.

The third phase began in 1982, when commercial banks started to reassess their exposure to developing countries, and budgetary pressures in several industrial countries worked against aid. A fall in OPEC's current account surplus also led to a reduction in its aid. As Figure 6.2 shows, ODA has fallen in nominal terms since 1981. Other official flows, notably from some of the multilateral institutions, have leveled off. Direct foreign investment registered a nominal decline. A significant portion of commercial bank lending reflected concerted loans raised as part of debt rescheduling agreements. A more cautious attitude toward private lending to developing countries evolved against a background of further significant structural changes in the banking and bond markets. And the pace of innovation quickened markedly in this third phase.

The scale and growth of the flows of medium- and long-term capital, both official and private, to the various categories of developing countries can be gleaned from Figure 6.3. Disbursements of official credit to developing countries in 1970 totaled $5.2 billion, but by 1983 had grown to $31.9 billion. Disbursements of private credit grew more quickly, from $9.7 billion in 1970 to $73.8 billion in 1980, before falling in the wake of the debt difficulties to $60.2 billion in 1983. As a result, the share of private credit in total credit increased from 65 percent in 1970 to 72 percent in 1980, declining to 65 percent again in 1983.

The low-income countries have been highly dependent on official financing. In 1983 some 74 percent of disbursements to low-income Asia and 84 percent of disbursements to low-income Africa were from official sources. It is only in years of high liquidity in private markets that the low-income countries have been able to raise any appreciable amounts of private finance. The middle-income countries, especially the major exporters of manufactures and the middle-income oil exporters, have borrowed primarily from private sources since 1970. These two categories of countries received up to 80 percent of their medium- and long-term finance from private sources.

Throughout its postwar evolution, the international financial system has been responding to pressures for change in ways that have affected the institutional arrangements for capital flows to developing countries. Changes in the financial climate have often acted as a spur to innovation. In

Box 6.2 The deployment of the OPEC surplus

The big increases in oil prices in 1973–74 and 1979–80 produced substantial current account surpluses for all OPEC members, "low absorbers" and "high absorbers" alike.[1] Between 1973 and 1982 the net foreign assets of low-absorbing countries increased from $12 billion to $32 billion, while high absorbers swung from net liabilities of $5 billion to net assets of $23 billion. Placements by OPEC have fluctuated significantly. From a total of $57 billion in 1974 they fell to $20 billion in 1978 before rising to a peak of $100 billion in 1980. With the subsequent fall in oil prices, placements have been substantially lower.

Roughly 40 percent of the cumulative OPEC surplus went to the United States and the United Kingdom, countries with deep and efficient financial markets. Considerable sums were also placed in France, Germany, Japan, and Switzerland. There have been significant

changes in the type of instrument or market in which funds have been placed (see Box table 6.2A). After the first oil price rise about 50 percent of placements took the form of bank deposits, mainly in the Eurocurrency markets. After the second oil price rise, this figure was 61 percent. In each instance OPEC members thereafter gradually deployed their surplus in higher yielding, less liquid assets. Their initial preference for highly liquid assets reflected both a lag in recognition of the potential size of the surplus and a possible inability to gather information quickly on suitable long-term investments.

Apart from bank deposits, OPEC members favored placements in Treasury securities, other bonds, and stocks in the United States. Outside the United States and the Eurocurrency markets OPEC members purchased equity and property and provided increased private credits and ODA to developing countries (see Box 7.4 in Chapter 7). Loans were also made to international organizations.

1. Low-absorbing OPEC members comprise Kuwait, Libya, Qatar, Saudi Arabia, and United Arab Emirates. These countries possess a relatively low propensity to turn revenues into domestic expenditures.

Box table 6.2A OPEC international placements, 1974–83
(billions of dollars)

Type of placement	1974	1975	1976	1977	1978	1979	1980	1981	1982	1983
Placements in the United States										
Bank deposits	4.2	0.6	1.9	0.4	0.8	5.1	−1.3	−2.0	4.6	0.9
Other	7.3	7.3	9.2	6.9	−0.4	1.9	18.4	19.8	8.1	−10.4
Eurocurrency bank deposits	22.0	8.7	11.2	16.4	6.6	33.4	43.0	3.9	−16.5	−11.9
Other bank deposits	2.4	0.6	−0.9	1.2	0	2.0	2.6	0.5	−0.4	0
Other placements[a]	20.3	26.0	21.0	20.9	18.6	19.7	37.5	40.7	18.2	11.6
Total	56.2	43.2	42.4	45.8	25.6	62.1	100.2	62.9	14.0	−9.8
Bank deposits as a percentage of total	50.9	22.9	28.8	39.3	28.9	65.2	44.2	3.8	..	..

a. Other placements include those in OECD countries, international organizations, and developing countries. The last include net flows of concessional assistance, syndicated Eurocurrency credits, bond issues, and direct investment.
Source: For U.S. placements and other bank deposits: Bank of England *Quarterly Bulletin* March 1985; for Eurocurrency placements: U.S. Department of the Treasury, Office of International Banking and Portfolio Investments, and Bank of England *Quarterly Bulletin* March 1985; for other placements: Sherbiny (background paper).

the past ten years, for example, the most obvious pressure for innovation came from changes in financial regulations and from the high and volatile inflation experienced over that period. The latter contributed to big fluctuations in interest rates and exchange rates. Lenders and depositors sought to cover themselves against interest rate movements, with the result that lending increasingly switched from fixed rate to floating rate terms. The rapid development of technology that reduced the costs of getting information and dealing internationally also contributed to the process.

The financial system has also been influenced by the size and distribution of current account imbalances; it has responded to the portfolio pref-

erences of investors and depositors in different parts of the world. One example was the OPEC members in the mid-1970s and early 1980s that wanted to keep their surpluses initially in highly liquid form (see Box 6.2), primarily in bank deposits. Another important factor in the 1970s was that leading banks were choosing to lend abroad to satisfy their own portfolio and profitability objectives. The result was a greater willingness of commercial banks to finance the growing current account deficits of developing countries. More recently, the large current account deficits run by the United States have had their counterpart in the surpluses of Japan and some other industrial countries. In this instance the surplus countries have had a preference for U.S. government securities and paper issued in the international bond and note markets.

These pressures for change operate within a regulatory framework for domestic and international financing. Exchange controls, for example, were used extensively before the 1970s. Their abolition in many industrial countries during the 1970s significantly increased the ability of banks to lend abroad. Moreover, monetary controls, though aimed primarily at containing money supply growth or influencing interest rates, can have major international side effects: such controls in the United States and some other industrial countries were one reason for the growth of the offshore Eurocurrency markets (see Box 8.3 in Chapter 8). Similarly, access to the foreign bond markets has been subject to controls: the markets operate formal or informal entry requirements and queuing systems. The role of taxation in influencing the pattern of capital flows can also be illustrated with reference to the bond markets. Some governments, for instance, have imposed interest equalization taxes, blunting demand for foreign issues of bonds, or have removed withholding taxes in order to encourage capital inflows for the purchase of bonds. In general, however, the 1970s were an era of financial liberalization, and this had a decisive impact on the pace at which financial institutions internationalized their business.

Prudential controls on commercial banks have probably had some effect on international lending (see Box 8.4 in Chapter 8), although the effect is difficult to measure. Most industrial countries have recently urged banks to be more prudent in dealing with the added risks faced in international lending. Banking supervisors have encouraged banks to raise their capital ratios and strengthen their balance sheets. They have also sought to ensure that the banks have adequate means of assessing country risk. The increasingly global nature of banking has led the supervisors to cooperate to strengthen the international banking system.

Finally, political factors have combined with economic pressures to limit certain types of capital flows. The limited constituency for aid, combined with budget stringencies in several industrial countries, has reduced the amount or slowed the growth of their aid in recent years. And some developing countries have restricted inflows of equity investment to prevent their domestic resources from passing into foreign control or ownership.

Several broad trends can be discerned in the financial system, which may have implications for the future pattern of external financing for developing countries:

• A gradual increase in world wealth has led to a greater demand for financial assets and a diversification of asset holding across markets and currencies worldwide. One measure of this trend is the share of external claims of banks in their total claims, which has increased from 8.5 percent in 1973 to 18.4 percent in 1983. Deregulation in domestic banking markets and the changing portfolio objectives of the banks may slow this process or reverse it in the future. It is possible, however, that other forms of wealth holding may be internationalized; increased institutional purchase of foreign stocks and bonds might eventually lead to enhanced flows to developing countries.

• There has been movement toward lending at floating rates both in the banking markets and in bond markets. In the latter the floating rate note (35 percent of total bond issues in 1984) has recently found favor, especially with banks seeking greater marketability in their portfolios. In the banking markets floating rates seem here to stay even if inflation and interest rate volatility subside. In the bond markets the issuance of fixed rate bonds will remain subject to periodic fluctuations depending on inflation and interest rate expectations. About 43 percent of developing countries' long-term external debt was in floating rate form in 1983, compared with 16 percent in 1974.

• A trend has emerged toward greater use of bonds and other types of securities in international lending; a so-called process of securitization may be under way. Given the debt service difficulties of many developing countries and the high creditworthiness required in these markets, there is a question as to the extent to which these countries can benefit from the trend.

• Major advances in information technology and the widening of the range of business transacted by individual financial institutions have led to an integration of financial markets. The various national banking markets have been drawn together by the workings of the international interbank market (see Box 6.3) because banks are able to switch funds quickly between markets. Close links also exist between conditions in the banking markets and those in the bond markets. The advent of currency and interest rate swaps (see Box 5.5 in Chapter 5) has helped integrate financial markets, as has the growth of hybrid instruments that blend features of the banking and bond markets. The trend toward integration is important for

Box 6.3 The international interbank market

National banking markets are closely linked through the workings of the international interbank market. In the mid-1970s only a few hundred banks participated in the interbank market. By the early 1980s, their number had grown to well over a thousand banks from more than fifty countries. The size of the interbank market, that is, total cross-border interbank claims, amounted to some $1,950 billion in mid-1984. The only entry criterion for a bank is that it must be creditworthy in the eyes of other participating banks; banks of different creditworthiness command different credit limits and terms on their business.

The interbank market is informal, is conducted by telephone or telex, and trades mainly in dollars. It is not independent of other markets. Interbank interest rates move closely in line with those in domestic money markets, with funds flowing—where exchange controls permit—between them. This is because most banks are active in domestic as well as international markets.

The interbank market performs two main functions:

• Some banks attract more deposits than they immediately want to use, while others are unable to exploit lending opportunities because of a shortage of funds. The interbank market acts as a clearinghouse, increasing the efficiency of banking services.

• It permits banks to manage the exchange and interest rate risk that arises from their customer business, because they can match precisely their assets and liabilities.

Both of these functions serve to increase the stability of the international banking system. In recent years, the market itself has been tested by debt difficulties and bank failures. This has forced banks to reevaluate the credit quality of their interbank transactions, and those from Latin America and Eastern Europe have had to pay stiffer terms for their interbank borrowing. Inasmuch as banks are becoming more discriminating, the international interbank market is becoming a higher quality market and hence a more stable one.

developing countries' debt management in that shifts in sentiment in one market rebound increasingly on fund availability in another.

• There has recently been a stagnation of official flows and direct foreign investment at a time when banks want to lend less to developing countries. This is a matter of particular concern. Greater cooperation between official and private lenders has been one response to the problem. Banks have increasingly lent in conjunction with IMF adjustment programs. The World Bank has also sought to increase the financing available to developing countries through the expansion of its cofinancing program. The official sector is in some instances playing the role of catalyst for the private sector; an example is the IFC through its encouragement of equity investment. There are also several initiatives, including a proposal for a multilateral investment guarantee agency (see Box 9.5 in Chapter 9), to increase direct foreign investment through the provision of more extensive investment insurance.

Assessing the institutional arrangements

Developing countries have to match their external financing needs to the type of capital that is available. For example, most low-income countries have only limited access to commercial finance. They are almost totally dependent on concessional flows from official sources and on official or officially guaranteed trade credits. The middle-income countries have a potentially wider range of borrowing opportunities because of their greater creditworthiness. But the existence of sovereign risk, as Box 6.4 explains, limits this range, particularly in comparison with sovereign borrowers from industrial countries. Commercial banks, because of their widely ranging business relationships with developing countries, have a comparative advantage in sovereign lending. Governments have in some instances a degree of political leverage in the provision of official finance, and so have a similar advantage. Direct investors are at a distinct disadvantage in coping with sovereign risk. This is one reason why national schemes for investment insurance and, more recently, a private insurance market have sprung up. Bond investors are also disadvantaged, and so bond finance has not been a significant form of capital for developing countries.

As Chapter 5 made clear, for a developing country to obtain external finance carrying a suitable combination of cost and risk, it may need a mixed portfolio of liabilities. The broader the mix of liabilities, the less exposed are developing countries to interruptions in the supply or increases in the cost of any one element. The desired mix may contain the following.

• Equity and debt to reduce commercial risks and ensure that interest or dividends correlate with the borrower's ability to service the external capital.

• Different currency denominations of loans to

Box 6.4 Sovereign risk and its implications for international lending

When a government borrows from abroad or guarantees a loan, the legal status of the contract is unlike that between two private companies. It is much harder to enforce, since a sovereign borrower may reject a claim against it within its own territory. The problems arising from this limited enforceability are complicated by the fact that governments have considerable discretion over policy choices that affect their own ability to fulfill a contract. Many of these policies—shifts in monetary policy, limits on exchange remittances, changes in competition policy, changes in taxes—could not be deemed a breach of contract, even though their effect might be to negate the substance of the loan.

The ability of governments to influence economic outcomes, coupled with a lender's limited scope for imposing legal sanctions, means that contracts between developing countries and the private market have little economic value unless both parties feel it is in their long-term interest to honor their obligations. This means that the (present discounted) economic value to a borrower of meeting its obligations must be equal to or greater than the present value of not meeting them. In short, the countries that are most likely to service their debts are those that would suffer most if they did not do so.

To a borrower, the cost of possible sanctions depends on the importance of its future trade and finance with the lender (and its sponsoring government). Countries that are heavily involved in international trade depend on a continual flow of finance, the use of transport facilities, smooth customs clearance, and so on. They are therefore very open to sequestration orders and to a cutoff of trade credits. Their past success has been made possible by the network of trade and finance. They are unlikely to choose to jeopardize the chances of future success by excluding themselves from that network.

The major international banks have a comparative advantage in dealing with sovereign risk because they are closely involved in a number of facets of a developing country's international business. This helps explain the growth in importance of banking intermediation during the 1970s.

reduce exchange rate risks for the borrower.

• Fixed and floating rate finance to mitigate the borrower's interest rate risk.

• Long-maturity borrowing (for projects) and short-term borrowing (to finance trade) to smooth out debt service payments and reduce the borrower's refinancing risks.

• Concessional and nonconcessional lending to ease the debt-servicing burden, especially for low-income countries.

A key question for developing countries is whether the financing opportunities available to them can produce the appropriate liability portfolio. Any answer must distinguish between (a) policy deficiencies in lending and borrowing countries, to which the institutional arrangements respond; and (b) the problems inherent in the functioning and evolution of the institutional arrangements themselves. The financial system cannot be blamed for high and volatile interest rates, for instance; they stem from policies followed in the major industrial countries. Similarly, sluggishness in direct investment cannot be attributed to a systemic failure; it may have more to do with the policies and procedures of home and host countries. And a dearth of commercial finance for low-income countries and some middle-income countries in many instances reflects appropriate market judgments rather than a failure of the system. What creates an additional difficulty

for these countries, however, is that the level of official finance, and especially ODA, is in large part a matter of donor budget priorities often unrelated to the development policies of either donor or recipients.

With these caveats in mind, institutional arrangements that provide for efficient liability management and contribute to steady growth in developing countries would have three qualities.

• *Flexibility.* This refers to the capacity to respond to changes in the economic and financial environment and, specifically, the changing funding requirements of developing countries. Financial innovation is not an arbitrary process. It has been particularly marked among private financial institutions where competitive pressures have been intense. Multilateral development institutions have also adapted to the changing needs of developing countries, particularly in the 1970s and early 1980s.

• *Stability.* This refers to the ability to maintain a steady flow of finance to developing countries, within limits determined by creditworthiness considerations. Maintaining a stable flow of financing is important in facilitating a smooth net absorption of real resources, in avoiding unduly severe balance of payments adjustment, and in sustaining the debt-servicing capacity of borrowers. Stability implies an absence of "herd instincts" among lenders and investors. Official flows and direct investment grew steadily for much of the past decade, providing a foundation for other flows. Banks, while contributing to the system's flexibility, have nonetheless been inclined to lend excessively to a few developing countries; some have then suddenly withdrawn altogether from lending to specific countries, as happened in 1982 with the largest Latin American debtors.

• *Balance.* This refers to the range of instruments and facilities offered, so that borrowers can spread their risks and diversify the currency composition of their debt at minimum cost. A high degree of dependence on a single kind of institution or instrument makes borrowers vulnerable to abrupt changes in supply or cost. Taken as a whole, the sources of capital became more diversified in the 1970s, even though not all developing countries were eligible for all of them all the time. However, there was a concentration of risks in a small number of large banks in meeting the financing requirements of major borrowers.

Judged by these three yardsticks that contribute to efficient liability management and steady growth in developing countries, the system responded quickly and effectively to the pressures of the 1970s. However, the early 1980s exposed some serious weaknesses that were inherent in bank lending. The rapid growth of lending in the 1970s was unstable. If the growth in such lending during the 1980s is construed as a one-time stock adjustment by banks, then moderation in this growth might have happened even without the deterioration in the world economy that began in 1979. A system in which one type of lender grows increasingly exposed to relatively few borrowers may be inherently unstable. Furthermore, the banks' main form of lending, the syndicated credit, carried a medium-term maturity whose cost was linked to a short-term interest rate. The risks of rising interest rates were thus transferred to borrowers.

Another weakness was the behavior of ODA. It increased substantially in the aftermath of the first oil price increase in the early 1970s, but it stagnated in the 1980s at the very time when the banks were seeking to reduce their lending.

Any assessment of the present institutional arrangements must therefore consider how the stability of external capital flows can be increased and lending by commercial banks be restored. In particular, it must address the question of how future capital flows, including the provision of enough concessional finance to meet the needs of low-income countries, can be made available. There is a need for solutions that will avoid a recurrence of the difficulties of the early 1980s. Remedies lie in five main areas:

• The provision of longer-maturity capital.
• Commercial risk sharing through the development of secondary markets for developing-country debts.
• An increase in equity investment.
• Increased levels and better coordination of aid programs to improve their effectiveness.
• Greater availability of mechanisms for hedging interest rate and exchange rate risks.

The first four of these are explored in greater detail in the Chapters 7, 8, and 9; the last was noted in Chapter 5. None of these changes will come about quickly. But even slow progress on every front would do much to reduce the weaknesses and increase the strengths of the present institutional arrangements.

7 Official development flows

Since the end of World War II, a variety of ways to provide economic assistance to developing countries have evolved; these range from grants and highly concessional loans to loans on nearly commercial terms. The number of donors has also increased: most industrial countries, OPEC members, and centrally planned economies have become bilateral donors, while multilateral institutions include the World Bank, the regional development banks, the OPEC and European Community development funds, and some UN agencies. The evolution of these development-oriented official economic assistance flows—generally referred to here simply as official flows—is described in Box 7.1. These changes suggest an increasing recognition of the complexity of development and the desire to structure assistance accordingly.

The motives for these official flows range from the humanitarian desire to reduce poverty to the political, security, and commercial interests of suppliers. Underlying the general effort of donors to promote and accelerate the development process and alleviate poverty has been the recognition that many countries cannot get from private sources the external capital and other services they need. Development, particularly in the low-income countries, is a long-term process that requires investment in basic human, physical, and institutional infrastructure. Used to good effect, official flows—both concessional and nonconcessional—can enhance investment and growth in developing countries, increase global output and efficiency, and improve the long-term ability of poor people to increase their own incomes. In this process, developing countries' demand for imports from industrial countries also increases. Thus, if used effectively, the process benefits both donor and recipient.

Official flows, particularly concessional flows or official development assistance (ODA), have been especially important for low-income countries. During 1981–82 they represented 82 percent of the total net capital receipts of such countries.

With the growth of commercial lending and the

Box 7.1 A brief chronology of official development flows

The years between World War II and the early 1970s saw:
- The creation of the International Monetary Fund and the World Bank, first agreed to at the Bretton Woods conference in 1944; the establishment in 1945 of the United Nations and its various specialized agencies which provide technical assistance to the developing countries; and the enactment in 1947 by the United States of the Marshall Plan which provided grants for the reconstruction of Europe. Between 1947 and 1951, the United States provided aid to Europe equivalent to 2.5 percent of the U.S. GDP.
- The gradual establishment and expansion of ongoing bilateral aid programs for developing countries. In 1951 the United States established the Point Four program which provided technical assistance to developing countries—initially capital funding was left largely to the private sector and the Export-Import Bank. In 1957 the United States set up the Development Loan Fund (the predecessor to the current U.S. Agency for International Development program) to provide concessional long-term project and nonproject loans. By the late 1950s the larger European countries also had in place ongoing aid programs. In 1961 the main donors set up the Development Assistance Committee (DAC) of the OECD as a forum for aid coordination and for discussion of development issues. The continued expansion in the number and size of bilateral donors can be seen in the fact that, while the United States in the early 1960s provided over 60 percent of total DAC bilateral development assistance and with three other countries (France, Germany, and the United Kingdom) accounted for over 90 percent, by the early 1970s the United States accounted for less than 30 percent of the total, and these four countries combined constituted less than 70 percent.
- In the late 1960s, the establishment by the United Nations of an aid target for donors of 0.7 percent of their GNP. Some donors strongly supported this target, some accepted it more as a statement of intent, but others specifically rejected it.
- The formation in 1958 of the aid consortium for India, the first of the country aid consultative groups.
- The creation of a concessional affiliate of the World Bank, the International Development Association (IDA), in 1960, reflecting an increasing recognition of the needs of the low-income countries.

"graduation" of some developing countries away from aid, the relative importance of these official flows to the developing world as a whole has shrunk. Nonetheless, they remain a large and relatively stable source of capital. In 1983 official flows still accounted for 40 percent of the total net capital receipts of all developing countries. Some $26.1 billion came in bilateral ODA; $7.5 billion in multilateral ODA; and $7.0 billion in nonconcessional flows from multilateral institutions. Not included in these official flow figures, and only briefly treated in this chapter, are (a) drawings from the IMF, which, although official, are generally treated as monetary transactions (see Box 7.6), and (b) export credits, which are viewed primarily as commercial transactions, although they receive official support (see Box 7.2). Another significant source of assistance for the developing world not

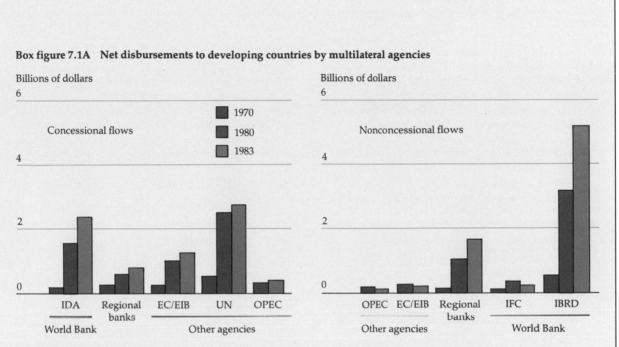

Box figure 7.1A Net disbursements to developing countries by multilateral agencies

Note: Data for regional banks comprise disbursements by the African Development Bank, the Asian Development Bank, and the Inter-American Development Bank. EC/EIB indicates the European Investment Bank of the European Communities.

Source: OECD 1984.

• The establishment of the regional development banks: the Inter-American Development Bank (1959), the African Development Bank (1964), and the Asian Development Bank (1966).

The 1970s witnessed:

• A rapid growth in official flows, from $11 billion in 1972 to over $42 billion in 1980. Even in constant 1982 prices and exchange rates, the increase was substantial—from $24 billion to $40 billion.

• The spectacular growth of OPEC aid, with developing-country receipts of OPEC bilateral ODA jumping from only $450 million in 1972 to $4.2 billion in 1974 to a peak of over $8.7 billion in 1980.

• A substantial growth of multilateral aid (see Box figure 7.1A), which increased its share of DAC donors' total ODA from less than 6 percent in 1965 to 15 percent in 1970–71 to 32 percent in 1977–78. The European Community's multilateral assistance programs became a significant source of finance. UN agencies also expanded their

work, notably the UN Development Programme and the World Food Program.

• The continued growth in DAC bilateral ODA, with developing-country receipts increasing from less than $6 billion in 1970 to over $18 billion in 1980.

The early 1980s have seen:

• A fall in official flows of $2 billion to $41 billion, reflecting a decline of over 40 percent in the level of OPEC ODA. DAC countries' bilateral ODA stagnated.

• An apparent shift in emphasis by donors toward bilateral assistance. Between 1980 and 1983, DAC contributions to multilateral financial institutions (including the EC) remained virtually unchanged in nominal terms. The proportion of total DAC ODA accounted for by multilateral agencies fell from a high of 32 percent in 1977–78 to 28 percent in 1982–83. Correspondingly, multilateral concessional flows, which are dependent upon donor contributions, have stagnated.

Box 7.2 Export credits

There are two basic forms of export credit: (a) supplier credits, which are extended by an exporter to his customer, and (b) buyer credits, which are credits extended to the buyer by somebody other than the exporter—usually a bank. Export credits become ''official'' when the exporter's government participates in the credit, either as a lender or as insurer or guarantor to the lender.

In 1980, gross disbursements of medium- and long-term official and officially supported export credits from DAC countries to developing countries totaled $35 billion (see Box table 7.2A). Net disbursements were $14 billion, or 14 percent of the net financial receipts of developing countries. Export credits currently represent a little over 20 percent of developing countries' long-term debt, and almost one-third of their annual debt service payments. For the low-income countries, they account for some 18 percent of long-term debt (the share of commercial debt is less than 10 percent) and nearly 40 percent of their debt service requirements.

Since 1981 the flow of export credits to developing countries has fallen sharply. In 1983, net export credits totaled about $8 billion—less than 8 percent of developing countries' net receipts. This decline reflected cuts in the investment programs of developing countries, as well as retrenchment by the export credit agencies themselves in response to operating losses. The falloff was particularly sharp for the low-income African countries, where disbursements of new medium- and long-term credits fell from over $1.25 billion in 1980 to only $250 million in 1983. Middle-income countries with debt-servicing problems have also found it harder to obtain export credits.

Although export credits tend to be concentrated on the main developing-country markets, they are more widely distributed among countries than bank lending has been. Approximately 25 percent go to low-income countries, 15 percent to lower-middle-income countries, and 60 percent to upper-middle-income countries. The credits have been a significant source of project finance for many developing countries, with interest and repay-

Box table 7.2A Export credits to developing countries, 1970–72 and 1977–83
(billions of dollars, unless otherwise noted)

Item	1970–72 average	1977	1978	1979	1980	1981	1982	1983
Net disbursements from DAC countries								
Official export credits	0.8	1.4	2.2	1.7	2.5	2.0	2.7	2.1
Private export credits	1.9	8.8	9.7	8.9	11.1	11.3	7.1	5.5
Total	2.8	10.3	11.9	10.6	13.6	13.3	9.8	7.6
Total export credits as a percentage of developing-country total receipts	15	15	14	12	14	12	10	8
Gross disbursements from DAC countries	7.7	22.9	27.7	28.7	34.9	36.2	32.9	29.9

Note: Data are for official or officially supported medium- and long-term export credits.
Source: OECD *Development Co-operation.*

Box 7.3 Nongovernmental organizations

Nongovernmental organizations (NGOs) have a long tradition of relief and development assistance. Such NGOs as Oxfam, Red Cross and Crescent, Misereor, World Vision, Caritas, and CARE are particularly active in supporting education, health and population services, rural and urban development, and small-scale enterprise development.

In 1983, NGOs from industrial countries provided about $3.6 billion in concessional aid. They raised about $2.3 billion from their own members and private supporters and received almost $1.3 billion in cash, services, and commodities from official aid donors. The largest NGO aid was from the United States ($1.9 billion), Germany ($547 million), Canada ($257 million), and the Netherlands ($128 million). These figures underestimate the real contribution of the NGOs, since they do not include the value of the services provided by volunteers—often a major element of the NGOs' efforts.

In the past few years, NGOs have put greater emphasis on development programs and less on relief assistance. They are trying to reach marginal groups, tackle widespread poverty at the grassroots, and strengthen popular participation in development. As a corollary, NGOs pay increasing attention to cost effectiveness, cost recovery, and evaluation of projects. They also recognize the need to coordinate their activities with other donors. Support for closer government-NGO cooperation in development is provided by bilateral aid agencies, international NGOs, and multilateral institutions such as the EC, the UNDP, UNICEF, and the World Bank.

ment profiles that often match the nature and characteristics of projects more closely than most bank loans do.

However, there have been many cases of export credits' supporting inappropriate and poorly designed projects, promoting an excessive amount of borrowing, leading to overpricing of goods, or being an instrument of corruption. In recent years several developing countries have used short-term export credits to finance their longer-term investments, thus exacerbating their external debt position. Such problems arise because the basic purpose of export credits is the promotion of exports, not development; and some developing countries do not have any machinery for reviewing and controlling the use of export credits.

In order to promote their exports, industrial countries have often provided credits on concessional terms. In the late 1970s, they sought to reduce the rapidly expanding use of subsidized loans. Under the OECD Consensus, they adopted guidelines on the terms and conditions of export credits, including minimum interest rates and maximum maturities. Many developing countries, however, view this agreement not as an effort to improve the quality of export credits, but rather as a cartel that reduces interest rate competition and increases the cost of export credits.

To increase the contribution that export credits can make to longer-term programs of structural reform and faster economic growth in developing countries, all governments need to address two issues: first, how to encourage export credit agencies to resume guarantees and insurance to developing countries that are implementing adjustment programs; and second, recognizing that the basic objective of export credit agencies is to promote exports, what steps to take to enhance the developmental impact of export credits. One key to both objectives may be to increase the availability and use of information on adjustment and investment programs of individual developing countries.

included are the private and religious relief agencies such as CARE, the Red Cross, and Catholic Relief Services; their role is discussed in Box 7.3.

Since 1980 the dollar value of the various types of ODA has stagnated or fallen (see Figure 7.1). On present prospects little or no real increase is likely for the foreseeable future. The recent decline has occurred in the face of a continuing need for substantial external capital flows and a slowdown in the growth of commercial lending. It highlights the need to ensure that external capital is put to the best possible use by the recipients. For that, the developing countries' own economic policies have an important role to play—an issue discussed in Chapter 4.

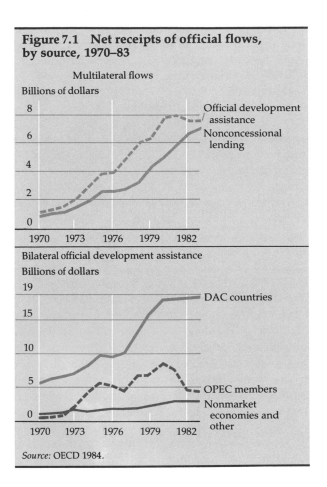

Figure 7.1   Net receipts of official flows, by source, 1970–83

Multilateral flows

Billions of dollars

Official development assistance

Nonconcessional lending

Bilateral official development assistance

Billions of dollars

DAC countries

OPEC members

Nonmarket economies and other

Source: OECD 1984.

This chapter focuses on four issues.

• The basic arguments for official assistance and the way that the motives and objectives of donors can influence the effectiveness of their assistance programs.

• The criticisms that have been leveled against aid.

• The attempts that have been made to measure the impact of these official flows on development.

• Recent efforts to make aid more effective.

Changing perceptions of development

The nature of official flows is strongly influenced by the way that donors and recipients perceive development. The success of the Marshall Plan in the 1940s and 1950s led many to believe that a similar transfer of capital to developing countries would, despite their physical, human, and institutional limitations, achieve similar results. The early model of development therefore placed nearly total emphasis on increasing physical capital to raise production and income and to alleviate poverty. This strategy meant investing not only in machinery and equipment, but also in physical infrastructure such as roads and ports. The World Bank, for example, devoted almost 50 percent of its lending in its first fifteen years to power projects and railroads; less than 10 percent went to agriculture, and none went directly to the social sectors.

In the 1950s and 1960s overall growth was the objective, and industrialization was regarded as its prime instrument. For political as well as economic reasons, many developing countries were convinced that a modern society meant an industrialized one. To achieve industrial growth, many governments opted for import substitution, using high tariffs and quantitative controls against imports. These policies distorted domestic prices and made the exchange rate increasingly overvalued. This in turn discouraged exports and encouraged the growth of inefficient industries. Agriculture was largely neglected. Some governments tacitly or explicitly relied on the ready availability of food aid, assuming that agriculture could be improved once industrial strength was ensured.

The longer these inward-looking development strategies persisted, the more evidence accumulated on the costs of these policies not only to the economy but also particularly to the poor. An increasing number of countries also started to show that the possibilities for expanding agricultural output and exports were larger than had been assumed. As a result, a more outward-looking, market-oriented approach to development increasingly became the standard. It also became increasingly recognized that the development of human capital was a critical factor in the promotion of development.

In the early 1970s some observers began to question the appropriateness of the conventional emphasis on overall growth. A number of economic studies of the relationship of economic growth and income distribution, as well as more casual observations of the incidence of poverty in individual countries, led some economists and aid supporters to conclude that the major beneficiaries of development efforts had often been the middle- and upper-income groups; growth had not "trickled down" to the poor. These observations were an important element in the development of the so-called basic human needs approach. Some supporters of the approach saw a conflict between programs that sought to promote growth and those that sought to help the poor and therefore argued that development efforts needed to be directly targeted to the poor and to addressing basic needs—education, health, and nutrition.

For others, however, this was an artificial dichotomy: economic growth and improving the lot of the poor were not mutually exclusive goals; indeed, they were largely interdependent. Long-term economic growth was critically dependent upon increasing the productive capacity of the poor, including improving their health and education. At the same time, the ability of the poor to achieve a sustainable increase in income necessary to meet their basic needs depended on the economy's ability to both grow and generate additional employment opportunities: redistribution was not enough. From this perspective, the issue was not one of equity versus growth, but rather the nature of growth. Supporters of this "growth with equity" approach have emphasized the need for a mixture of efforts, some aimed directly at the problems and constraints faced by the poor, others aimed at increasing growth and output and improving economic policies, which directly or indirectly benefit the poor. As a result of this debate, poverty alleviation has gained greater attention in the design and evaluation of development programs. For most donors, the demonstration that aid funds do in fact seek to address the basic long-term problems faced by the poor and do not primarily benefit the higher-income groups in recipient countries has been an important element in public and legislative support for aid programs.

The economic pressures of the past dozen years have highlighted the complexity of development. The differing achievements of developing countries have emphasized the critical role of their own economic policies, including (a) the cost of inefficient import substitution, price distortions, and consumer subsidies and the major contribution to growth and employment that can be made through open trade policies and realistic exchange rates and domestic prices, (b) the part that agriculture can play not only in boosting economic growth and strengthening the balance of payments, but also in raising the incomes and nutritional standards of the poor, and (c) the importance of developing a country's institutional as well as its physical infrastructure.

The recent past has also raised questions about the flexibility of official institutions and flows in meeting the specific needs of developing countries. Such questions cover the ability and willingness of official institutions to support policy reform efforts, to finance local costs, to fund the maintenance and rehabilitation of existing capital, to help develop the institutional capacity of developing countries, or to finance critical imports. Also at issue is the right balance between short-term and longer-term assistance and between different forms of assistance, including general balance of payments support and sector and project assistance.

Rationale for official flows

The economic case for official flows has two basic strands: efficiency and equity. These are often reinforced by a recognition of what is realistically possible given the economic, political, and social structure of the country.

The efficiency argument is based on the view that private markets for capital, technology, and other services do not provide the amount and type of resources most suited to the specific economic conditions and potentials of individual developing countries and to the efficient allocation of world savings. Official action and assistance, by complementing the flows from these markets, can improve the worldwide allocation of resources. Rates of return on investment are often higher in developing countries, so providing these resources (concessionally and nonconcessionally) to them can yield higher future income not only for the recipients but also for the world as a whole.

Although private capital markets supplied large amounts of finance to middle-income countries in the 1970s, many countries, including those in the low-income category, had limited access to private capital. This limited access to private capital stems from several factors: (a) the existence of sovereign risk, which constrains the volume of lending; (b) industrial countries' regulations on their capital markets, which discriminate against overseas lending by certain financial institutions; (c) the nature of many investments in developing countries (particularly those in basic infrastructure), which yield high social returns, but may yield benefits that are not readily capturable or in the short run earn little or no foreign exchange with which to service foreign commercial loans; (d) inadequate information for lenders about investment opportunities and the capacity of developing countries to repay loans; and (e) the traditional objections of private banks to long-term funding.

This last point is particularly important. Many of the investments needed to ease the basic constraints on development—health, education, agricultural research, and some types of infrastructure—yield high returns. For example, the real rate of return on primary education in Africa has been estimated to be as high as 30 percent, and for sec-ondary education over 15 percent. Numerous studies of agricultural research have indicated real returns well above the 10–15 percent range. However, these yields may be realized over a period of thirty to forty years, with no returns at all in the early years. This makes them unsuitable for private markets, so official help is needed at least during the initial stages of development.

Furthermore, economic development depends on more than just accumulating physical capital and improving human resources. It also requires institutional development, technology transfers and adaptation, and an appropriate framework for economic policy. Foreign private investment can provide a package that may include financial and physical capital, technology transfer, and managerial services. But, as discussed in Chapter 9, foreign investment not only has tended to be highly selective in its choice of sectors and countries, but also has been in limited supply. In addition, the types of technical services and resources needed are often not easily obtainable in private financial markets. Low-income countries, in particular, may also lack the technical skills to identify, evaluate, and acquire them. Official flows can be a vehicle for providing the combination of capital, technical assistance, and policy advice that developing countries need. Donors can help to build up institutions that can then make more effective technical and policy choices. By assisting in the creation of basic infrastructure, the development of institutions, and the promotion of market-oriented policies, official flows often encourage, directly or indirectly, inflows of private capital.

The efficiency argument provides the rationale for official action but says little about whether such flows should be on concessional or nonconcessional terms. One argument for providing official flows on concessional terms rests on equity considerations. Although concessional assistance is voluntary, in economic terms the line of reasoning can be viewed as a simple extension of the progressive taxation argument, whereby income transfers are made between rich and poor countries rather than between higher- and lower-income groups within a donor country. In this view, higher-income industrial countries can use part of their domestic tax revenues to fund transfers to the lower-income developing countries in order to improve directly the welfare of citizens in the latter and—through expansion of economic activity and trade—also indirectly increase world welfare. Concessional aid, compared with a similar initial financial flow on market terms, more effectively serves this objective because it provides a larger net flow of capital over the long run.

There can also be a practical rationale for concessional assistance. In low-income countries many of the direct beneficiaries of public investments and services (health and education are examples) are too poor to pay their full cost—yet the economy as a whole benefits. Since the benefits occur somewhere in the economy, it might be argued that governments should be able to capture a portion of them, through fees and taxes, in order to service borrowing on market terms. However, the time period over which the returns accrue can be very long, thus producing a debt-servicing mismatch for commercial loans. In addition, it is often difficult for a government, for social, political, or administrative reasons, to capture the benefits of such investments, particularly those designed to increase the earning capacity and well-being of the poor. It has also been argued that in certain cases—for example, clean water supplies and immunization programs—attempts to charge fully for the services can substantially reduce their use by the poor, thereby harming the economy and society as a whole.

Another practical argument for concessional assistance relates to the fact that to service external debt not only do domestic resources have to be increased, but they also have to be converted into foreign exchange. Countries at early stages of development—where there is great need to undertake investments in social services and infrastructure—often face institutional and other constraints that can reduce their capacity to increase export earnings rapidly. Since concessional flows do not generate as large a debt-servicing and foreign exchange burden as flows at market rates, they increase the ability of these countries to make such needed investments.

The arguments for concessional assistance apply primarily to the low-income countries. Although middle- and upper-income developing countries also need to invest in basic social infrastructure, which has long gestation periods and externalities, their more developed economies provide a basis to obtain increased levels of private capital and also to generate the foreign exchange needed to service commercial loans. However, even in many middle-income countries, official assistance can play a valuable role by providing not only long-term nonconcessional capital, but also technical assistance and policy advice. It can also be a catalyst to private flows, stimulating increased levels and improved terms.

Given that the economic objective of official assistance is ultimately to improve the allocation of resources and to increase the rate of economic development, the form of assistance that will most effectively promote this objective can vary significantly among countries depending on the country's specific economic situation. It will also be influenced by the capabilities and strengths of the individual donor—of course, as the next section discusses, other donor motivations also influence the nature of assistance. From a development perspective the basic question is, What are the basic constraints to economic growth and how can official assistance help reduce or remove them? In many countries in order for existing and future investment to contribute effectively to increased economic growth, policy reforms are needed to remove economic distortions that prevent the efficient allocation of resources. Such policy reforms, however, generally take time to produce positive results while additional costs may arise very quickly. In such circumstances, nonproject assistance can both encourage the undertaking of the needed reform and provide rapidly disbursing resources needed during the transition process. Similarly, when countries face severe balance of payments and domestic budget constraints, efforts that help stabilize the economy and lay the foundation for future growth and investment can be a critical component of a package of actions and programs designed to assist the country. Such efforts can include: the financing of the importation of intermediate inputs, which will permit the use of existing private and public sector idle capacity, thereby quickly increasing domestic supplies and exports; and the financing of the maintenance and rehabilitation of existing investment. These types of assistance have been particularly important in many of the middle- and low-income countries, where the flow of private capital has typically declined with the onset of debt-servicing difficulties.

Donors' objectives

Donors supply official assistance for many different reasons: to assist the economic development of the recipient; to further their own strategic, political, and commercial interests; to maintain historical and cultural ties; and to express their humanitarian concern. This combination of objectives can affect the nature of official flows—and can seriously reduce the effectiveness of such flows in promoting development. The level, growth, and relative performance of different countries in the provision of concessional assistance, ODA, is illustrated in Figure 7.2 and Box 7.4.

Recent studies have demonstrated the role of nondevelopmental considerations in determining the distribution of ODA. Political interests undoubtedly played an important role in the allocation during 1981–82 of 39 percent of U.S. bilateral ODA to Egypt and Israel; of 38 percent of French ODA to four overseas departments and territories; and of 42 percent of OPEC members' bilateral and multilateral ODA to two countries, Jordan and Syria. Similarly, the mineral resources of Zaire and Zambia are often cited as a significant commercial reason for U.S. aid to these countries.

The influence of nondevelopmental motives for aid is also highlighted by a comparison of bilateral and multilateral programs. During 1980–82 only 40 percent of the bilateral aid from the DAC countries and less than 20 percent of OPEC bilateral aid went to low-income countries, whereas two-thirds of all multilateral aid went to them.

In addition, DAC donors usually require the recipient to purchase goods and services in the donor country; this is not true for OPEC donors. This "tying" of aid covered some 43 percent of bilateral ODA from DAC donors in 1982–83, while another 11 percent was classified as partially tied. These figures probably understate the volume of tied aid, since informal arrangements often exist to place orders with donors. The result can be a lower quality of goods and services, often more expensive and less appropriate to the needs of the recipient. Studies on the costs of aid tying suggest that it reduces the value of development loans by about 15 to 20 percent, and in individual cases by much more.

In recent years, donors have increasingly used mixed credits (combining aid with export credits) to promote their commercial interests. Use of this financing mechanism can distort trade flows and reduce the effectiveness of aid (see Box 7.5).

In contrast, most procurement resulting from multilateral assistance is subject to international competitive bidding procedures. Indeed, one of the often-cited advantages of multilateral assistance is that it is generally far less influenced by nondevelopmental interests than is bilateral aid.

Does aid help development?

Foreign aid has always been controversial. Its critics believe either that it is often badly administered, severely reducing its ability to promote

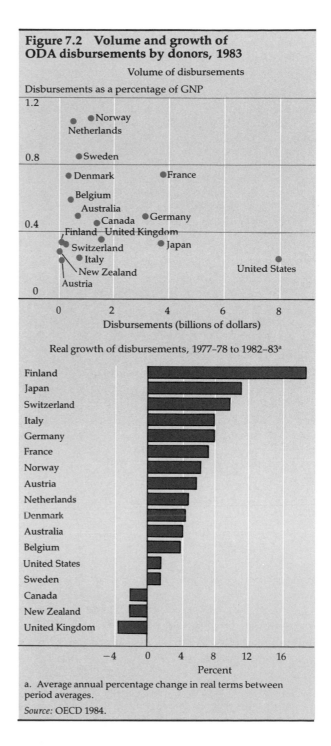

Figure 7.2 Volume and growth of ODA disbursements by donors, 1983

a. Average annual percentage change in real terms between period averages.

Source: OECD 1984.

development and tackle poverty, or that it is harmful in principle. Those who object to aid on principle do so from two distinct viewpoints:

• One school derives from dependency theory, arguing that underdevelopment is not merely the absence of progress; it reflects active exploitation of the "periphery" by the developed market economies of the "center." Aid is therefore a tool to

101

Box 7.4   OPEC economic assistance

Until 1973, only three OPEC members (Kuwait, Libya, and Saudi Arabia) were significant aid donors. Most of their assistance took the form of grants for budgetary support for Egypt, Jordan, and Syria; it averaged a little over $400 million a year in 1970–72. OPEC members' aid for long-term development averaged between $40 million and $60 million a year before 1973 when it had two sources only: the Kuwait Fund and the Abu Dhabi Fund.

After the rise in oil prices in 1973–74, OPEC assistance increased dramatically. During 1974–77 net disbursements averaged more than $5 billion a year, almost 30 percent of total ODA from all sources. They also represented a much larger proportion of the GNP of OPEC donors than the aid from DAC donors, which was between 0.3 and 0.4 percent of GNP throughout the 1970s. In 1975 ODA as a proportion of GNP reached 7

percent for Kuwait, 8 percent for Saudi Arabia, 12 percent for the United Arab Emirates, and 16 percent for Qatar.

OPEC's disbursements of ODA reached a peak in 1980 and have since declined by over 40 percent in nominal terms and in 1983 accounted for 15 percent of world ODA flows (see Box table 7.4A). This decline reflects in part the declining oil revenues and balance of payments position of these countries as well as the political conflict in the Gulf region. The sharpest falls have been from Iran, Iraq, and the United Arab Emirates. Kuwait and Saudi Arabia provided 90 percent of total OPEC aid in 1983.

OPEC donors kept more than 80 percent of their ODA in 1981–83 in bilateral programs. Over 85 percent of their geographically identified bilateral disbursements went to

Box table 7.4A   Concessional aid flows from OPEC members, selected years, 1970–83
(net disbursements in millions of dollars)

Source	1970	1975	1980	1981	1982	1983[a]
Arab states						
Kuwait	148	946	1,140	1,154	1,168	995
Qatar	..	338	270	250	50	22
Saudi Arabia	173	2,756	5,943	5,664	4,028	3,916
United Arab Emirates	..	1,046	909	811	402	100
Other OPEC donors	77	1153	1328	645	243	444
Total	398	6,239	9,589	8,525	5,891	5,476
Total as a percentage of GNP	1.18	2.92	1.80	1.51	1.06	1.05
Total as a percentage of world ODA	4.8	28.3	24.0	22.7	15.9	15.1
Arab states total as a percentage of their GNP	4.04[b]	8.50	4.48	3.45	2.65	2.98

a. Preliminary.
b. Average of the aid-giving countries.
Source: OECD *Development Co-operation.*

perpetuate the dominance of donors. If aid provides any benefits, these merely prevent unrest and keep developing countries in a submissive state.

• The other school claims that aid inevitably expands the role of government, distorts market signals, and finances some investments that the private sector would undertake if it were given the chance. Indeed, these critics would also argue that a liberalized private sector could provide all the resources needed for development, so aid is not justified.

Neither of these extreme views is convincing. The critics of aid offer little analytical evidence for their view, relying instead on anecdotal accounts of cases in which aid was used for nondevelopmental reasons or aid projects were badly

designed. In essence, such criticism is about the way aid is implemented rather than its basic rationale.

The effectiveness of aid can also be analyzed as an empirical question. At the most general level, it should be noted that the progress made by many developing countries over the past thirty years is inconsistent with the charge that aid hinders development. Nor do the facts support the claim that aid fosters government control and undermines incentives. A number of early aid recipients such as Brazil, Colombia, Korea, and Thailand have grown rapidly and have thriving private sectors. Contrary to the expectations of dependency theorists, these and other countries that have adopted outward-looking policies have had the most success in raising income and improving gen-

Arab countries and 10 percent to non-Arab African countries. More than half of all OPEC bilateral aid goes for general budgetary support, and less than one-fifth for project assistance.

Within their bilateral programs, four of the OPEC donors (Abu Dhabi, Iraq, Kuwait, and Saudi Arabia) have established National Funds that administer a significant part of their project assistance. These National Funds have an authorized capital of $16 billion. They disbursed slightly less than $600 million in 1983, down from nearly $900 million in 1980.

Of the 15 to 20 percent of total OPEC aid that is channeled through multilateral organizations, 40 percent goes to multilateral institutions with a broad membership; IDA and IFAD are the main recipients. The remaining 60 percent goes to multilateral agencies established by OPEC members. The largest is the OPEC Fund, which received 30 percent of OPEC multilateral contributions. Other significant agencies are the Arab Fund for Economic and Social Development, the Islamic Development Bank, and the Arab Bank for Economic Development in Africa (BADEA). These four institutions have an authorized capital of close to $10 billion. They disbursed an average $360 million a year in net ODA between 1981 and 1983.

The assistance offered by OPEC to the developing countries in the future will continue to be influenced by its liquidity position. Given present prospects for oil prices, the volume of OPEC aid commitments may not register significant growth in the next few years. However, the level of aid disbursements by OPEC members is likely to decline less rapidly than their commitments for some time, reflecting the lag in the former. Moreover, the lending levels of the development institutions created by OPEC members, because they have their own capital endowments, may not experience as sharp a decline in lending as OPEC government-to-government programs.

eral economic welfare.

It is also true that governments have a central role to play in developing countries in building the basic infrastructure, administration, and human skills needed for long-term growth and in creating an environment in which the private sector can expand—a fact generally ignored by the ardent antigovernment critics. As noted earlier, a significant quantity of official assistance has been directed to developing basic infrastructure, which is an essential precondition for a modern private sector. Assistance has also been used to finance imports that have permitted the liberalization of the country's trade regime and to promote other critical economic policy reforms aimed at improved efficiency and increased reliance on market forces and private initiative. Furthermore, a large propor-

tion of aid directly supports private sector activity: for example, aid to agriculture generally benefits private farmers, and much of the money put into development finance institutions is channeled into private industrial investment. Official donors, particularly the MDBs, have also directly encouraged private sector flows through their cofinancing with the private sector.

The role played by official assistance in support of the private sector is substantiated by the analysis and conclusions of the 1982 study by the U.S. Treasury Department of the multilateral development banks (MDBs). The study identified only 8 percent of MDB loans supporting public sector activities that would clearly have been supplied by the private sector in an economy like that of the United States. The study noted that even this 8 percent may be an overestimate, since such activities might not have been undertaken at all without MDB financing, given the small size of the private sector in most developing countries. The study also concluded that overall the MDBs' policy approach and advice have taken a fairly conventional market orientation.

Over the years many studies have tried to identify more precisely, and if possible to quantify, the impact of aid on development. The biggest and most systematic attempts have been those that evaluate individual projects. In the case of the World Bank, for the past ten years each of its completed loans and credits has been covered by a Project Performance Audit Report or Project Completion Report. The results are largely favorable. For 504 projects where it was feasible to reestimate economic rates of return, returns of 10 percent or better were expected from 79 percent of the projects. The average return, weighted by project cost, was almost 18 percent. By sector, returns averaged more than 20 percent in agriculture, 18 percent in transport, and a little less than 13 percent in industry. For 459 projects for which rates of return were not estimated at the time of project appraisal, 93 percent were judged substantially to have achieved their main objectives. Overall, only 14 percent of the projects, accounting for 9 percent of total investment, were judged at the time of audit to be unsatisfactory or uncertain in outcome. Although rates of return have not differed much between the loans to the low-income countries made by IDA and those from the IBRD to the less poor countries, the number of projects with inadequate rates of return has recently been growing. These have been mainly in agriculture and in Africa.

Box 7.5 Mixed credits

The term mixed credit usually refers to loans that are a combination of aid and government (or government-guaranteed) trade credits that are given to finance specific exports from the lending country. Until the late 1970s, mixed credits were only a small fraction of total aid budgets and export credits; the main exception was in France, which used mixed credits as a standard part of its aid program. However, with recession and balance of payments difficulties in the late 1970s and early 1980s, all industrial countries came under increasing domestic pressure to use mixed credits to promote exports and to match the mixed credit offers of other donors.

Data on mixed credits are sketchy. The DAC is seeking to increase the availability and quality of data on the use of "associated financing" credits, a concept that covers all trade financing in which some ODA is included but which is composed primarily of mixed credits. Although mixed credits have been estimated to have totaled less than a quarter of a billion dollars in 1975, some $10.5 billion of associated financing was reported by fifteen DAC countries for 1981–83. The amount of ODA involved in these associated financing transactions totaled $3.1 billion. France accounted for 45 percent of the total, followed by the United Kingdom with 23 percent, and Italy and Japan each with 9 percent.

Since mixed credits are largely based on commercial considerations, they could easily dilute the development impact of a donor's program. Mixed credits can divert funds to capital-intensive and import-intensive projects—such as transportation, telecommunications, and power generation. They have a built-in bias against projects and programs with a low import content, such as rural development or primary health care, and in particular against local cost financing. In 1981–83, energy accounted for 30 percent of associated financing transactions; industry and transport for 20 percent each; food and agriculture for 10 percent; but health and social infrastructure for only 2 percent. Similarly, exporters are keen to extend mixed credits to middle- and high-income countries where trade competition is greatest, which would shift aid away from the low-income countries.

Supporters of mixed credits have argued that mixed credits can promote development by "stretching" ODA; increase the total flow of finance to the developing world; improve the quality of export credits by bringing the judgment and monitoring of aid agencies to bear; reduce the cost of finance for countries with limited debt-servicing capacity; and provide more appropriate, less concessional financing terms for middle-income countries. The merits of these points, however, remain in dispute. Not only is there little evidence that aid stretching actually occurs, but also opponents have argued that such effects could be attained more effectively through other mechanisms, such as the direct allocation of a limited volume of aid to a country. Reflecting the concern over the potential distortion of aid and trade that can result from mixed credits, the DAC in June 1983 adopted "Guiding Principles on the Use of Aid in Association with Export Credits and Other Market Funds." The objective of these guidelines was to avoid aid and trade distortions by increasing the transparency of such transactions and strengthening the deterrent to the possible diversion of aid resources to purposes that are primarily commercial. In 1984 the DAC adopted measures to improve the reporting by members of associated financing transactions, and in April 1985 the ministers of the OECD agreed on reinforced notification and consultation procedures and an increase in the minimum permissible grant element for such transactions. Supportive of DAC objectives, the World Bank has recently established a cofinancing "framework" agreement with one member country, which involves, among other flows, mixed credits.

The Inter-American Development Bank (IDB) and the Asian Development Bank (ADB) have also evaluated samples of their loans. Their results are broadly similar: 60 percent or more of their projects met their objectives fully; about 30 percent partially did so; well under 10 percent were unsatisfactory or marginal. Several bilateral donors have also developed evaluation programs. These generally do not place as much emphasis on the quantification of project results. However, those studies that have looked at the impact of particular projects have usually found a substantial measure of success.

Even where failures do occur it is important that they be placed in perspective. A significant propor-

tion of aid has been provided to countries at low levels of development with weak institutional and managerial structures. Investments, whether undertaken by private or official sources, are therefore more risky than those in more advanced countries. Furthermore, the innovative or experimental nature of some activities adds to their risks, but the lessons derived from these efforts, both successes and failures, can be critical to the design and implementation of future projects.

To judge the cumulative impact of individual projects, and donors' contributions to policy, studies of countries would obviously provide a better guide. They too involve problems, the most fundamental being the question of what would have happened in the absence of aid. Two recent studies—one supported by the U.S. Department of State (Krueger and Ruttan 1983) and the other carried out for the Development Committee of the World Bank and the IMF—analyzed the role of aid in promoting economic growth in, together, close to a dozen developing countries. They note that the impact of aid has varied considerably from country to country and over time. They identify areas in which results could have been improved. But both conclude that aid has generally brought long-term benefits to recipient countries.

Another inescapable conclusion of these studies is that much depends on the recipient's policy framework and institutional strength, both areas where official assistance is actively involved. To take some well-known examples, growth in Korea accelerated sharply when the government adopted more liberal trade and industrial policies; the performance of Ghana until recently has been as different from neighboring Ivory Coast as its policy regime; India's faster growth in recent years results in part from its policy reforms in 1980; and the general lack of progress in sub-Saharan Africa has its roots in part in institutional and policy failings that governments there increasingly recognize.

Another factor that shows up repeatedly in country studies and project evaluations is the time it takes for investments to produce results, and hence the importance of perseverance. In Korea, secondary education programs undertaken in the 1940s and 1950s seemed to yield relatively low returns at first; the same was true of overseas training programs in the 1960s and transport and power investments in the 1950s and early 1960s. Yet they all clearly contributed to the country's rapid growth from the mid-1960s onward. The extensive assistance to India's agriculture began as early as 1950, and for years did not seem to be producing beneficial results. But it developed the necessary institutional framework for adopting the high-yielding grains of the green revolution.

Both the detailed assessments of individual projects and the broader studies of particular countries provide strong support for the view that aid can and often does contribute effectively to development. Where they have demonstrated the shortcomings of aid, they have been a valuable spur to making it more effective—the aid process indeed has involved a large component of learning from experience. One of the major objectives of donor evaluation programs is in fact to identify and disseminate the lessons from successes and failures.

The effectiveness of dissemination not only among donors, but also within aid institutions is, however, considered by many to be inadequate. Lessons learned from aid assessments need to be exchanged among donors and transmitted to aid project managers to a much greater extent than currently occurs.

Much remains to be done to ensure the best use of aid flows, particularly in low-income African countries. One important aspect of Africa's economic crisis is the low rate of return on its capital investments, which have been extensively financed by external assistance. Many donor-financed projects have taken much longer to complete than anticipated and have been much more expensive. These startup problems have frequently been followed by disappointing operational performance due to a lack of staff, equipment, and materials and to poor maintenance and administrative weaknesses. In the worst cases, new aid has been needed to rehabilitate projects completely. It is from this perspective that donors are seeking to structure their assistance to more effectively address the problems faced by the low-income countries.

Improving the effectiveness of aid

Economic difficulties in developing countries and the budgetary constraints of donors have focused attention on increasing the effectiveness of official aid. Donors have responded in three related ways: (a) by putting greater emphasis on policy reform in recipient countries; (b) by developing flexible instruments to meet the specific needs of recipients; and (c) by coordinating their assistance programs more closely.

Emphasizing policy reforms

The need for policy reforms, highlighted by the external shocks that have affected many developing countries in the past dozen years, is now common ground between donors and recipients. The recent World Bank report entitled *Toward Sustained Development in Sub-Saharan Africa* observed that: ''Neither the essential objectives of Africa's development nor the policy issues that must be addressed to achieve them are in dispute, . . . the emerging consensus on policy issues dwarfs any remaining areas of dissent'' (pp. 2–3). There remain, of course, questions about the timing and detail of these reforms as well as the finance that donors will provide for support.

The IMF has often played a key role in promoting policy reform in countries facing severe balance of payments problems (see Box 7.6). The scale of its financial assistance has increased enormously in the past five years. Between 1981 and October 1984, developing-country net drawings from the IMF totaled almost $26 billion. At the end of October 1984, thirty-one developing countries had programs with the IMF, involving a total of SDR 13 billion. Many developing countries, however, face large and growing repayments obligations to the IMF. For example, sub-Saharan African countries will have to repay to the IMF about $1 billion a year over the next few years.

Given that IMF financing is relatively short term, it needs to be complemented by longer-term concessional and nonconcessional finance from private and official sources. To provide longer-term support for policy reforms, the World Bank in 1981 launched its structural adjustment loan (SAL) pro-

---

Box 7.6 IMF lending, its role, and its size

The International Monetary Fund's first financial operation was in 1947. Since the early 1960s, its main instrument for assisting member countries has been the standby arrangement. Under a standby arrangement, the IMF agrees to make available during a certain period (usually a year, but it can be up to three years) a specified amount of its resources, which the member may use in support of an agreed upon program of economic adjustment designed to reestablish a viable balance of payments position. Drawings are phased over the life of the arrangement and are contingent on the country's fulfillment of its program. Since the first standby arrangement in 1952, the IMF has approved 548 standby arrangements for a total of SDR 50 billion (one SDR currently equals about one dollar).

During the 1960s, governments believed that the supply of international reserves was likely to become inadequate. They therefore agreed to create a facility in the IMF for a new international reserve asset, the special drawing right (SDR), which is allocated to IMF members in proportion to their quotas. Since 1969 the IMF has allocated SDR 21.4 billion in SDRs.

After the adoption of floating exchange rates by most major countries in the early 1970s, and the amendment of the IMF Articles of Agreement in 1978 to permit arrangements of a member's choice, the IMF was given new responsibilities with regard to the firm surveillance of the exchange rate policies of members and the domestic policies impinging on exchange rates. The IMF carries out its surveillance mainly through annual consultations with most members, assessing all aspects of members' economic and financial policies that might have an impact on exchange rates.

In addition to the standby arrangement, the IMF has established other facilities in response to members' specific needs. In 1963 the Compensatory Financing Facility (CFF) was set up, allowing members to make drawings on the IMF to support their balance of payments when they faced temporary shortfalls in their exports. This facility has been liberalized several times, both in the access to resources that it provides and in the range of compensable shortfalls, which now include exports of services and cereal imports. Drawings under the CFF grew dramatically during the late 1970s and early 1980s, reaching SDR 2.6 billion in 1982 and SDR 2.8 billion in 1983. In 1969 the IMF established the Buffer Stock Financing Facility, which allows members in balance of payments difficulties to draw on the IMF to finance their contributions to international buffer stocks that meet certain criteria. The use of this facility has been very limited.

The IMF has also recognized that a short-term standby arrangement is not always the most appropriate form of assistance for members having deep-seated balance of payments problems. In 1974 it created the Extended Fund Facility (EFF) to provide larger loans in support of three-year adjustment programs for members whose balance of payments problems were occasioned by a distorted structure of production and trade, with widespread cost and price distortions. To date, the IMF has approved thirty-three extended arrangements for a total amount of SDR 24.5 billion.

The IMF has also temporarily adapted its policies in response to specific problems arising in the international economy, as in the case of the IMF oil facilities of 1974 and 1975. Similarly, in response to the particularly difficult balance of payments and adjustment problems of many of its members in the past five years, members' quotas in the IMF were again increased both in 1980 and 1983. They now total over SDR 89 billion.

Access to the IMF's resources has been expanded, first under the Supplementary Financing Facility (SFF) and more recently under the enlarged access policy. Members' access to IMF resources under standby and extended arrangements was traditionally a maximum of 25 percent of quota a year, with a cumulative maximum of 100 percent of quota. It can now go as high as 95 or 115 percent of quota a year, with cumulative net limits of 408 or 450 percent of quota, depending on the seriousness of the balance of payments need and the strength of the adjustment effort. In addition, for a number of heavily indebted countries under severe balance of payments pressures, the IMF has also recently helped mobilize additional assistance from official and commercial sources.

gram. This involves close collaboration with the borrower in developing policies and programs for restructuring the economy. To date, SAL programs have been negotiated in sixteen countries, including six in Africa. Other donors have encouraged the Bank to work with developing countries on such programs, sometimes reinforcing the Bank's efforts through their own bilateral programs. In principle, donors recognize that nonproject aid can sometimes be the most effective way to support policy reforms and to finance the imports an economy needs for completion, rehabilitation, and maintenance of existing projects. On one estimate, up to a third of total ODA is for nonproject assistance. A large part of this aid is special-purpose assistance, such as disaster relief, food aid, and debt relief.

However, most donors still prefer to finance specific projects. Project lending is a highly effective form of assistance. Apart from finance, it provides countries with institutional support and other technical assistance that many badly need. However, the preference for project lending, coupled with a lack of aid coordination, can produce an inordinate proliferation of projects, straining the financial and manpower capacity of recipient countries to implement, monitor, and maintain them. For example, Kenya in the early 1980s was trying to cope with 600 projects from sixty donors. Similarly, the UNDP has estimated that there were 188 projects from fifty donors in Malawi; 321 projects from sixty-one donors in Lesotho; and 614 projects from sixty-nine donors in Zambia. In such numbers, the effectiveness of aid can be severely reduced; in sub-Saharan Africa, the proliferation of projects may actually have undermined the development effort of individual countries. The keys to dealing with this problem are the formulation of well-articulated investment programs by recipient countries and coordination by donors of their activities (discussed below).

Meeting the needs of recipients

The distinction between project and nonproject lending should not be exaggerated. Indeed, they can be viewed as part of a spectrum of assistance. Several donors, including the World Bank, have created a variety of flexible forms of assistance, tailored to the specific needs of the recipient. The World Bank adopted a Special Action Program in 1983, which concentrated on accelerating disbursements to rehabilitate existing capacity and complete priority projects in response to the urgent needs of developing countries. Bilateral donors have also funded the local and recurrent cost component of projects in individual cases. In 1979 DAC adopted its "Guidelines on Local and Recurrent Cost Financing" and in 1982 supplemented these with "Guidelines for Maintenance and Strengthening of Existing Services and Facilities." Direct financing of local costs by DAC members, however, still averages only about 8 percent of their ODA.

One challenge for all donors is to increase the proportion of concessional assistance going to low-income countries. There has been some progress in increasing the level and share of concessional assistance going to low-income Africa. Its share of total ODA has increased by roughly five percentage points since the mid-1970s, to approximately one-fifth of the total today. This increase, however, seems to have come largely from a shift of aid away from other low-income countries, such as India, not from middle-income countries. India and China, which account for 50 percent of the developing world's population, now together receive only 10 percent of the total net flow of ODA. The reduction in the level of IDA resources provided by the current replenishment represents a further serious constraint to expanding concessional flows to the low-income countries (Box 7.7).

The need for more aid for Africa was highlighted in the recent World Bank report on sub-Saharan Africa mentioned earlier. The report recommended additional assistance to support policy reforms, structural adjustment, and rehabilitation, and donors have responded by recently committing some $750 million in direct contributions and about $500 million in special joint financing for the World Bank's Special Facility for Africa. Several bilateral donors have also increased their African programs. The United States "economic policy reform program" would provide additional aid up to $500 million over five years to African countries that undertake to reform their price structures and other policies. Commitments to the African Development Fund of the African Development Bank for 1985–87 are up by 50 percent ($500 million) over the previous replenishment. But the resources provided by these initiatives will still fall short of requirements, and projections still indicate a decline in the net concessional capital flows to these countries over the next several years.

Coordinating assistance

Effective coordination among donors, and

between donors and recipients, is needed to avoid duplication and proliferation of projects, to share information and experience, and to increase the overall impact of aid efforts. Yet coordination has often been superficial at best, and many low-income countries have not developed their own machinery to coordinate aid flows and programs. Donors and recipients have increasingly recognized this need and have started to act on it. The World Bank is now taking action to increase the number of consultative groups in sub-Saharan Africa from the current eleven to possibly as many as eighteen. Existing consultative groups are paying special attention to sectoral problems and to improving their coordination within the countries concerned (see Box 7.8).

Despite these efforts to improve the effectiveness of aid there remain significant barriers. Nondevelopmental motives still play a major role in aid programs. They can sometimes stand in the way of multilateral institutions' efforts to promote a policy dialogue with aid recipients. A high proportion of aid remains tied; if anything, its share is increasing, particularly through the use of mixed credits. Although donors have recently tried to negotiate a framework for reducing mixed credits, the results of their efforts are unclear.

Finally, the overall level of aid is a major cause of concern. The low- and middle-income oil-importing countries now face serious debt and balance of

---

Box 7.7 IDA

The International Development Association (IDA) is currently the largest single multilateral source of concessional assistance for low-income countries. While the terms of IDA are highly concessional, its projects are generally identical in scope and rigor to IBRD projects. Since its inception, twenty-seven countries have graduated from IDA to IBRD lending, and thirteen countries, including India, receive a blend of IBRD and IDA financing.

Following its establishment in 1960 with an initial subscription of $750 million, IDA's resources have been augmented through seven replenishments totaling $40 billion. The association provided 5 percent of net ODA flows during 1979–83 to eligible countries, namely, those with 1983 GNP per capita of $790 or less. Within the eligible group, IDA has concentrated its lending in the poorest countries. Over 80 percent of total commitments since 1960 have been made to countries with 1983 per capita incomes below $400. In 1981–83, this share of IDA commitments increased to 89 percent.

Since the beginning of the 1980s, IDA's resources have become increasingly constrained, because of slower than anticipated contributions to the sixth replenishment (IDA 6) and, more recently, because of the reduced size of the seventh replenishment (IDA 7)—$9 billion compared with $12 billion for IDA 6. These reductions have caused a decline in IDA lending, in current dollars, from an annual level of $3.8 billion in 1980 to $3.2 billion on average over the subsequent three years. A further decline in real annual lending is in prospect over the next several years.

In 1980 China joined IDA and became eligible for IDA credits. This addition, coupled with the overall decline in IDA lending, produced a sharp fall in per capita lending levels from an average of $2.24 between 1978 and 1980 to an average of $1.47 in 1984. Under the IDA 7 replenishment per capita lending is expected to decline further, to an average of $1.15.

In order for IDA to concentrate its resources on the poorest countries, it has been necessary to put a ceiling on its lending to those recipients economically capable of servicing funds on harder terms. These countries, which receive a blend of IDA and IBRD loans, include India and China and would on a strict application of IDA's allocation criteria receive three-quarters of its resources. The ceiling has reduced their share substantially below that, and it will fall further during the IDA 7 period, with India's share being reduced and China's share being increased.

The 1980–83 period was also characterized by increased external financing requirements on the part of a number of IDA recipients, particularly those in sub-Saharan Africa. The plight of sub-Saharan African countries has been recognized by IDA in its shift in allocation toward these countries in recent years. Lending to this region has increased to an average of 32 percent of IDA commitments between 1981 and 1984 from 24 percent in the previous three years. Further increases are planned. On a per capita basis, IDA lending to sub-Saharan African countries increased from an average of $2.10 over the 1978–80 period to an average of $2.79 over the 1981–84 period. Because of the sharply reduced resources of the seventh replenishment, per capita lending to sub-Saharan African countries is expected to remain about the same as during the early 1980s.

In recognition of the resource needs of low-income African countries, a meeting of donor countries in January 1985 agreed to establish a Special Facility for the region. This facility, which will be administered by IDA, is important to maintaining adequate levels of concessional assistance to some of IDA's poorest recipients. These funds along with IDA credits will support policy dialogue with governments on sectoral and institutional adjustments that are critical for their economic development.

Box 7.8   Aid coordination

Aid coordination has been the subject of discussion and at times controversy since the early years of the international aid effort. The term coordination encompasses a broad range of activities: from general discussions in an international forum; to periodic meetings of donors and recipients, which address the recipients' development constraints and policies and the donors' assistance plans; to very narrow and concrete actions by several donors and a recipient concerning specific project or sector assistance activities.

At the international level the major aid donors in 1961 established the Development Assistance Committee (DAC) of the Organisation for Economic Co-operation and Development. The DAC has played a central role in (a) the collection, analysis, and dissemination of information on assistance programs and policies, and (b) the analysis and discussion of development issues among its members and the formulation of general principles of donor assistance. It has not, however, generally dealt with the analysis of the development constraints of individual countries or sought to coordinate donor programs in specific countries.

The World Bank has taken the lead in sponsoring aid groups, often called consultative groups or consortia, which are one of the main mechanisms for coordinating aid to particular countries. The first aid group was established in 1958 for India. Since then, some thirty countries have had one or more of these aid group meetings; twenty of these groups are still active.

Aid groups typically meet at one- to two-year intervals, for some countries less frequently. These meetings generally review the World Bank's economic analysis of the country, the recipient's development plan, and the donors' current and prospective assistance programs. These meetings are often the only real opportunity to bring donors and recipients together to explore the coun-try's development problems and the programs of the donors.

Another forum for aid coordination is the Round Tables of the United Nations Development Programme (UNDP). The Round Tables, although not new, have assumed increased importance since the 1981 UN Conference on the Least Developed Countries. Many of the poorest countries did not at that time have formal aid coordination groups and saw the Round Tables as one means of focusing donor attention on their individual development problems; most of these countries have now had a Round Table or World Bank lead aid group meeting.

Other coordinating groups operate at the international, regional, and sectoral levels. They include the Club du Sahel, the Central America Consultative Group, a coordination group for Arab funds, and the Consultative Group on International Agricultural Research (CGIAR). Ad hoc conferences, such as the UN Conference on Renewable Energy and the UN Conference on Population, have also provided opportunities to discuss development issues and improve coordination.

All these efforts need to be complemented by closer on-the-spot coordination. At several recent aid group meetings, donors and recipients agreed to establish or strengthen parallel groups that would meet more frequently in the recipient countries and deal mainly with operational issues. The World Bank plans to develop models of on-the-spot coordination in some African countries, in association with the recipients, the UNDP, the African Development Bank, and interested bilateral donors. In sub-Saharan Africa it is establishing a number of new resident missions, strengthening existing missions, and organizing new consultative groups. In most cases, subgroups concentrating on specific sectors are also being formed.

payments problems, a result in part of their reliance on commercial borrowing, particularly short-term trade credits, to finance long-term development requirements during the 1970s. For low-income Africa debt service has reached about 20 percent of export earnings, and for middle-income oil-importing countries 25 percent. This necessitates difficult stabilization and adjustment programs. These countries will need substantial flows of official assistance to undertake, maintain, and extend these policy reforms and support the efforts to restructure their development and investment programs. Current trends, however, point to (a) a substantial drop in net capital flows to low-income countries because of a stagnation of gross flows in nominal terms and the substantial growth in debt service, and (b) a continuing overall stagnation in assistance levels or at best a small increase. As a result, many developing countries may face an undesirable choice: either they try to borrow more from commercial sources, running the risk that their debt-servicing burden will become unsustainable, or they retrench even more, creating further economic dislocation, losing the opportunity to make better use of their existing resources, and by cutting investment harming their long-term economic potential. For many of these countries this could translate into little if any increase in per capita incomes over the remainder of the decade. Both courses imply increased hardship for people living in the developing countries. They also threaten an unnecessary loss in efficiency and global economic growth.

8 International bank lending and the securities markets

The relationship between commercial banks and developing countries has been transformed in the past fifteen years. Before 1970 banks lent developing countries relatively small amounts to finance trade and to meet the requirements of subsidiaries of multinational companies located there. After 1970, banks went on to become the fastest-growing and most flexible source of foreign finance for developing countries—primarily to cover balance of payments deficits—only to run into the debt problems of the early 1980s. The past three years have been traumatic for many banks and their borrowers in the developing world. There has been a retrenchment of bank lending that has emphasized the instability of the relationship with developing countries. All parties have learned some valuable lessons, which will help to redefine their relationship for the years ahead. The securities markets, in contrast, have not had such strong ties with developing countries. Given that the markets for bonds and a number of innovative securities have grown recently while traditional bank lending has fallen, there is a question as to whether the securities markets could play a bigger role in financing developing countries.

The banking relationship

The commercial links between banks and developing countries are complex and extensive. They run from simple deposit taking to short-term lending, trade financing (both with and without official guarantees), and medium-term lending (often in syndicated form). All of these types of business appear on banks' balance sheets. But off-balance-sheet operations have also been important; they include advice on managing debt and reserves, and business such as letters of credit for financing trade.

These ties often started when developing countries placed their liquid reserves with the banks. As Figure 8.1 shows, the low-income countries have consistently been net depositors with the banks, while the middle-income groups have become net borrowers. This contrast reflects the fact that low-income countries are seldom creditworthy enough to borrow from the banks.

Developing countries have dealt both with the head offices of international banks and with offices operating in the Eurocurrency markets. However, many banks have set up offices in developing countries, both to channel external finance and to undertake domestic banking business. Altogether the various banks located within developing countries have received about 36 percent of the funds channeled by outside banks to these countries over the past four years. Developing countries' own banks are playing an increasing role in raising external funds for domestic users as well as in performing a broad range of business services (see Box 8.1).

Lending has been the main form of international banks' business with developing countries (see Figure 8.2), and it grew very rapidly between 1973 and 1981. Bank claims on developing countries increased at an average annual rate of 28 percent over this period. In 1973 total new international lending amounted to $33 billion, of which 29 percent went to developing countries. By 1981 new lending was $165 billion, of which developing countries composed 32 percent. Much of the lending was syndicated Eurocurrency loans carrying five- to ten-year maturities and floating interest rates. Lending to developing countries in this form increased from $7 billion in 1973 to $45 billion in 1981. Most syndicated loans were arranged by a core of twenty-five to fifty large commercial banks (hereafter called first-tier banks) based in the industrial countries. Up to 3,000 others (second-tier banks) joined in from time to time. They included regional banks from industrial countries, banks from developing and centrally planned economies, and consortium banks.

Initially in the 1970s it was the large U.S. banks that increased their international lending, with much going to developing countries. By 1977 the

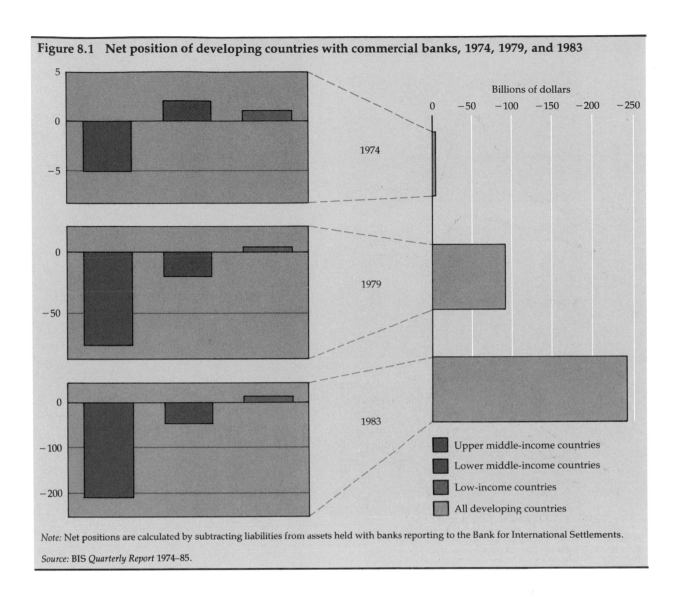

Figure 8.1 Net position of developing countries with commercial banks, 1974, 1979, and 1983

Billions of dollars

Upper middle-income countries
Lower middle-income countries
Low-income countries
All developing countries

Note: Net positions are calculated by subtracting liabilities from assets held with banks reporting to the Bank for International Settlements.

Source: BIS *Quarterly Report* 1974–85.

Box 8.1 Developing-country banks

In many developing countries, the growing presence of industrial-country banks has provided significant competition for local banks. They in turn have expanded their international operations to include:

• *More branches and representative offices in the major international financial centers.* Banks from the newly industrializing countries have often followed domestic companies abroad, financing their trade and other activities. Other banks have set up branches where migrant workers have settled, serving as a channel for repatriating their savings.

• *Lending in the Eurocurrency markets.* One example is the State Bank of India, which has arranged a large share of India's syndicated loans and played a role in managing loans to a number of other countries. Mexican and

Brazilian banks have also been active managers, while some Arab banks have become major international lenders (see Box 8.2).

• *Borrowing in the international interbank markets.* Some developing-country banks won the confidence of the interbank market and have been able at certain junctures to use it for funding some domestic lending. They have therefore enjoyed cheaper financing than that offered by more traditional types of loans.

The international experience gained by developing-country banks has benefited their domestic operations as well. Not only have they been able to identify new business and develop markets, they have also introduced new techniques and ideas into the financial systems of developing countries.

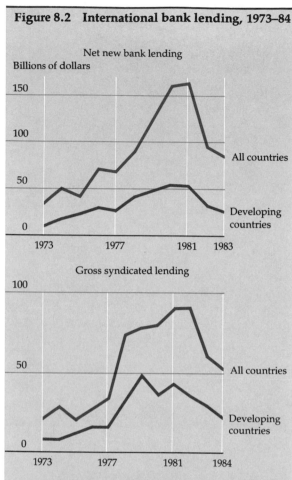

Figure 8.2 International bank lending, 1973–84

Net new bank lending
Billions of dollars

All countries

Developing countries

1973   1977   1981   1983

Gross syndicated lending

All countries

Developing countries

1973   1977   1981   1984

Note: International bank lending is measured here in two ways. First, total international lending is measured net of loan repayments for a defined set of reporting banks (in this instance, banks reporting to the Bank for International Settlements). These data, after 1976, are adjusted for the valuation effects of exchange rate movements. Second, a major element of international lending—syndicated loans—is measured on a gross basis, no allowance being made for repayments. Only published syndicated lending is covered by the data, however.

Source: For net bank lending: Watson, Keller, and Mathieson 1984; for syndicated lending: OECD *Financial Market Trends*.

8.2), but banks from other developing countries have also been increasingly active in international lending. The ability of non-American banks to participate in what was primarily a dollar-based market was enhanced by the growth of the international interbank market (see Box 6.3 in Chapter 6). This market permitted the distribution of dollar liquidity around the international banking system.

The relationship between banks and developing countries expanded rapidly in the 1970s for two main reasons: changes in the pattern of global current account balances and changes in the willingness and ability of banks to act as intermediaries.

Global imbalance and portfolio choice

On one theory, changes in the distribution of current surpluses and deficits around the world should not change the role of banks; they would still act as intermediaries between lenders and borrowers. But that theory holds good only if (a) the portfolio preferences of all lenders are the same; (b) banks have the same perception of creditworthiness for all potential borrowers; and (c) the interbank market operates without friction to redistribute liquidity. Without these conditions, the pattern of surpluses and deficits does indeed have a powerful effect on the banks.

During the 1970s both the volume and geographical structure of current account balances changed dramatically (see Table 3.1 in Chapter 3). The members of OPEC ran large surpluses for much of the 1970s and initially had a strong preference for bank deposits (see Box 6.2 in Chapter 6). They favored the Eurocurrency market rather than domestic banking systems, in part because of the higher returns available in the former. Over the decade, sizable amounts of funds were transferred by oil importers from domestic banks in industrial countries to OPEC members and ultimately to the Eurocurrency markets. Such a switch of funds increased the lending capacity of the Eurocurrency markets.

The expansion of liquidity in the banking markets coincided with a positive shift in the attitude of the banks toward international lending. After the first major increase in oil prices, when there was a need to recycle large amounts of funds, banks were lauded for the success with which they performed this function. Confidence in the banking system was maintained by central banks and deposit insurance agencies, which gradually increased their protection for depositors at the major banks. The behavior of regulators—or, more

twelve largest U.S. banks derived almost half of their total earnings from international lending, the bulk of which came from developing-country loans. Groups of banks from several different countries next increased their international exposure—particularly those from the Federal Republic of Germany, France, and the United Kingdom. Japanese banks also assumed an important role in international lending, but they were sometimes held back by adverse developments in Japan's balance of payments position. The second-tier banks from the United States also gradually increased their participation. The most notable recent entrants, however, were the Arab banks (see Box

Box 8.2 Arab banks and international business

Many of the well-established Arab banks became involved in international lending during the 1970s, some linking up with Western partners to form consortium banks. Further impetus came from wholly owned Arab international banks and the establishment of Islamic banks (offering an alternative to *riba*, the charging and paying of interest). Some banks set up in the new regional centers—Bahrain, Dubai, and Kuwait—and many expanded abroad. London hosts the largest number of Arab banks (sixty), followed by Paris (thirty-nine), New York and Singapore (nineteen each), and Switzerland and Hong Kong (fifteen each). Arab banks have also been expanding into developing countries.

The volume of syndicated Eurocurrency loans led by

Arab banks increased gradually during 1978–80, but sharply during 1981 (see Box table 8.2A). Their lending volume fell in 1983 and 1984, amid generally more subdued activity in the market as a whole. Arab-led syndicates channeled about one-quarter of their lending to the industrial countries and the rest to developing countries. Arab developing countries received the bulk of Arab bank lending in 1978–80, but others then took an increasing share. The main source of finance for Arab banks has been the international interbank market, though some OPEC money may have been channeled through them as well. Some specialized Arab banks have become heavily involved in arranging international bond issues and in undertaking direct investment.

Box table 8.2A   Arab-led syndicated lending, 1977–84
(billions of dollars, unless otherwise noted)

Type of lending	1977	1978	1979	1980	1981	1982	1983	1984
Total market lending	34	74	79	81	91	91	60	52
Arab-led syndications[a]	1.0	2.3	2.5	3.6	9.1	9.8	6.9	5.3
To industrial countries	0.1	0.3	0.7	1.1	2.6	1.9	1.6	..
To developing countries	0.9	2.0	1.8	2.5	6.5	7.9	4.6	..
Arab-led syndications as a percentage of total lending	2.9	3.1	3.2	4.4	10.0	10.8	11.5	10.2

Note: Data are for Eurocurrency credits with a maturity of one year or more, publicly announced in the year given.
a. Syndications in which one or more Arab banks acted as lead or colead managers.
Source: For total market lending: OECD *Financial Market Trends;* for Arab-led syndications: *Middle East Economic Survey.*

precisely, expectations of their behavior—gave comfort to depositors and helped attract money to banks. This may have led banks, in turn, to take larger lending risks than would otherwise have been the case.

The preferences of developing countries also encouraged the growth of bank lending in the 1970s. Developing countries were attracted by the general purpose nature of bank finance and by the large volumes and flexibility of instruments available at a time when alternative sources of finance were growing very slowly. Developing countries naturally favored the low or negative real interest rates charged by banks in preference to the conditionality attached to some official finance and the strict creditworthiness standards of bond markets.

The supply of banking services

In addition to the macroeconomic forces working to increase bank lending in the 1970s, several factors specific to the behavior of banks were pushing in the same direction.

• *The increased efficiency of international banking.*

As in many other industries, banking benefited from innovations that increased its efficiency. The growth of the Eurocurrency market (described in Box 8.3) was especially significant, because banks operating there were free of reserve requirements. They were therefore able simultaneously to offer higher interest rates for depositors and lower rates for borrowers than other banks could. The market was also efficient in that it could quickly mobilize very large loans.

• *Changes in the portfolio objectives and preferences of banks.* Banks radically changed their portfolio objectives in the 1970s, placing greater emphasis on balance sheet growth rather than the immediate rate of return on assets or other measures of profitability. International lending was a means of satisfying this aim when domestic loan demand was weak and when banking liquidity, induced by easy monetary policy, was high. Foreign lending also offered a means of diversifying portfolios, which was seen as a way of reducing risks because domestic lending often had an inferior loan-loss record. Banks saw the rapid growth achieved by many developing countries as an indication that

Box 8.3 The origins of the Eurocurrency markets

The origins of the Eurocurrency markets—that is, the markets in currencies traded outside their respective domestic economies—go back to the late 1950s and early 1960s. Several factors were behind their birth.

• The centrally planned economies were reluctant to hold bank deposits in the United States, so they put their dollar earnings on deposit in London. Gradually other European dollar holders did the same, a tendency that was particularly marked when the United States ran large balance of payments deficits.

• Balance of payments pressures made the United Kingdom government limit British banks' external use of sterling, so they had a strong incentive to develop business in foreign currencies.

• By the end of 1958 the main industrial countries had restored full convertibility of their currencies. The new freedom produced a surge of international banking business.

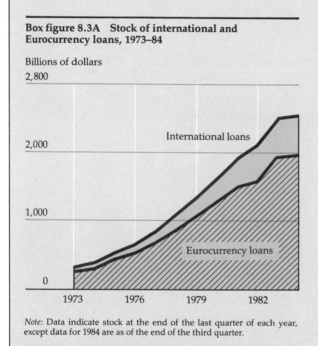

Box figure 8.3A Stock of international and Eurocurrency loans, 1973–84

Billions of dollars

Note: Data indicate stock at the end of the last quarter of each year, except data for 1984 are as of the end of the third quarter.

Source: BIS *Quarterly Report* 1974–85.

The growth of the Eurocurrency market was also stimulated by certain monetary regulations in the United States. For instance, Regulation Q put a ceiling on the interest rates that banks operating in the United States could offer to domestic depositors. Since market rates often went above the ceiling, depositors were naturally attracted to Eurobanks that were not bound by Regulation Q. In addition, banks in the United States were required to hold non-interest-bearing reserves. By diverting dollar deposits to their offshore branches or subsidiaries, U.S. banks were able to avoid tying up so much of their funds in reserve requirements at a zero rate.

General controls on the movement of capital also helped to boost the Eurocurrency markets. One example was the introduction, in 1965, of the Voluntary Foreign Credit Restraint Program (VFCR) in the United States. The specific goal of the VFCR was to limit the growth of foreign lending by U.S. banks. Instead, their foreign branches—which were not subject to the VFCR—took deposits and onlent them outside the ceiling. Between 1964 and 1973 the number of U.S. banks with overseas branches increased from 11 to 125. The number of branches increased from 181 to 699 over the same period.

At the end of the 1960s and during the early 1970s the Eurocurrency markets, which had been located in Western Europe (and centered in London), expanded to a number of other "offshore" banking centers. These were typically small territories that had tax, exchange control, and banking laws favorable to international banks. The business was entrepôt in nature, with foreign currency funds deposited by one foreign source and then onlent to another. Offshore centers have been set up in the Caribbean area, Latin America, the Middle East, and Southeast Asia. A recent development has been the establishment of international banking facilities (IBFs) in the United States designed to bring the locus of American banking business back "onshore."

With the recent strong growth of domestic currency lending abroad, total international lending is now the most meaningful lending aggregate, and it encompasses Eurocurrency market activity. Box figure 8.3A shows the growing stock of total bank lending alongside that of the Eurocurrency market.

---

the returns on lending to these countries would be high compared with the risks involved. Aside from the direct returns they expected on loans, banks wanted to develop a wider and more profitable business relationship with developing countries.

• *The development of mechanisms for dealing with sovereign risk.* One important development that helped banks overcome their concern about sovereign risk was the introduction of a cross-default clause covering publicly guaranteed debt. A cross-

default clause specifies that the loan will be considered to be in default if the borrower defaults on any other loan. It strengthened the guarantee on sovereign loans and blurred the differences in risk between individual borrowers or projects within a developing country. Hence, bankers paid less attention to the viability of the particular projects they financed, and more to macroeconomic conditions in borrowing countries. Furthermore, if a developing-country borrower defaulted, cross-default clauses would ensure that all bank lenders would be affected. As a result, a borrower confronted with debt-servicing difficulties had a strong incentive to reschedule its lending rather than default on a loan. This type of lending therefore appeared less risky to banks. Furthermore, the view that sovereign lending was less risky than domestic commercial lending because the sovereign states could not go bankrupt was widely held among banks. These perceptions contributed to the growth of lending and the fine terms (spread and fees) carried on many loans.

• *Innovations in banking.* Banks proved adept at designing instruments—like the syndicated loan—that would match their portfolio requirements (for country risk diversification and interest risk minimization) with the requirements of borrowers (longer-maturity, high-volume loans). This particular innovation enabled banks to make long-term loans on the basis of short-term deposits—a process of maturity transformation—without having to absorb the interest rate risk themselves, since lending rates were tied to a short-term rate (LIBOR). But this proved to be a volatile element in debt service for borrowers. Other key innovations included the certificate of deposit (and variations on it), which allowed banks to offer a marketable and high-yielding asset to depositors while providing the banks themselves with flexibility in the management of their liabilities.

• *Changes in the regulatory environment.* Most changes in the regulatory environment were conducive to bank lending to developing countries. The industrial countries eased or abolished their exchange controls, thus encouraging banks to also lend abroad off their base of domestic deposits. The growth of largely unregulated offshore banking centers (as noted in Box 8.3) also gave a significant stimulus to overseas lending. Regulations such as the requirement to maintain certain capital ratios, which had the effect of limiting the growth of banks' total assets, did not disproportionately affect developing countries.

All of these factors produced a strong momentum for lending to developing countries. Although some banks may have come up against their lending limits for certain developing countries, overall lending grew rapidly in part because unconstrained banks new to international lending entered the market. Indeed, banks competed vigorously, exhibiting, in some instances, ''herdlike'' behavior in their quest for new business.

Problems in the banking relationship

In the late 1970s and early 1980s banks were becoming increasingly concerned about their exposure to both lending and funding risks in their international business. Much of their developing-country lending, for instance, had been concentrated in a narrow range of countries (see Figure 8.3). On average, 72 percent of it went to the upper-middle-income countries over the 1978–81 period. The five largest borrowers alone accounted for 53 percent of developing-country borrowing. Having shifted the interest rate risk onto the borrowers, banks were becoming increasingly aware that in practice they had simply traded off one risk (see Box 3.2 in Chapter 3) for greater potential transfer and commercial risk. On the liabilities side, many banks had come to depend on interbank markets for a large part of their funding. This had made them susceptible to sudden funding

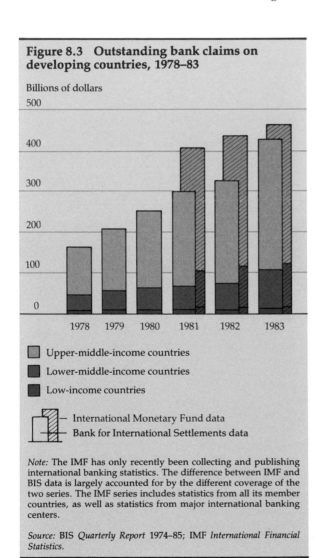

Figure 8.3 Outstanding bank claims on developing countries, 1978–83

Billions of dollars

- Upper-middle-income countries
- Lower-middle-income countries
- Low-income countries

— International Monetary Fund data
— Bank for International Settlements data

Note: The IMF has only recently been collecting and publishing international banking statistics. The difference between IMF and BIS data is largely accounted for by the different coverage of the two series. The IMF series includes statistics from all its member countries, as well as statistics from major international banking centers.

Source: BIS *Quarterly Report* 1974–85; IMF *International Financial Statistics.*

Box 8.4 Bank supervision and its impact on lending to developing countries

Banking supervisors in industrial countries seek in a variety of ways to ensure that commercial banks are prudent in their lending and balance sheet management.

• *The assessment of capital adequacy.* To ensure that banks have enough capital to meet potential losses, supervisors typically prescribe a ratio of capital to total assets. The ratio varies in its makeup and desired level from country to country, but the normal range is 4 to 6 percent—that is, $4 million to $6 million of capital can support $100 million of lending. In determining this ratio, some supervisors weight assets according to their riskiness: the riskier the loan, the more capital a bank must have to back it.

• *Exposure limits.* Supervisors pay close attention to how bank assets are diversified, aiming to avoid any undue concentration of risk. In recent years some of the adverse risks attached to international lending materialized simultaneously, which underlined the need to bolster banks' capital bases. Supervisors normally require that lending to a single borrower be limited to a fraction of the bank's capital, or a group of large exposures to a multiple of capital. In some countries, borrowers may be consolidated for the purpose of determining exposure

limits, and lending to two or more subsidiaries owned by a single holding company may count as a single exposure. Typically borrowers within a country are not consolidated, so that banks can lend to a variety of enterprises within a country without meeting exposure limits. Tighter exposure limits have not generally been introduced. Increasingly, however, as developing-country debt is rolled over in new financing packages for the government and, as sometimes occurs, the government takes over private sector debt, these loans are accrued to a single borrower, and exposure limits may be reached.

• *Loan-loss provisioning.* Supervisors have been concerned in recent years that the quality of assets on banks' books are properly reflected in their balance sheets and so have encouraged banks to provision against losses. Policies regarding provisioning—that is, the setting aside of funds to cover potential general or specific losses—vary significantly among countries. The accounting and tax treatment of loan losses can have important implications for the profitability of banks' loans to some countries and therefore for their willingness to lend. The accounting issue revolves around whether provisions can be counted as part of a bank's capital base or not;

Box 8.5 Financial deregulation in Japan: some implications for developing countries

Developing countries and international development banks have been active in raising funds from Japan (see Box tables 8.5A and B). As of the end of 1983, developing countries accounted for 24 percent of total yen-denominated foreign bonds issued in Japan, with international development banks accounting for another 24 percent. In 1983, Japanese banks made total medium- and long-term loan commitments of some $16.8 billion, 49 percent of which were for oil-importing developing countries. Along with other foreign borrowers, developing countries could perhaps benefit from the gradual liberalization of the world's second-largest capital market.

The deregulation of the Japanese financial system has been prompted by a marked change in the domestic flow of funds resulting from the slowdown in economic growth since the mid-1970s. Industrial investment grew less rapidly; corporate demand for credit fell; and house-

Box table 8.5A External loans by Japanese banks denominated in foreign currency, 1980–83

Year	Amount (billions of dollars)	Share of oil-importing developing countries (percent)
1980	6.7	41
1981	12.7	44
1982	18.0	33
1983	16.8	49

Source: Japanese Ministry of Finance *International Finance Bureau Annual Reports.*

Box table 8.5B Foreign bond issues denominated in yen, 1980–83

Year	Amount (billions of dollars)	Share of developing countries (percent)[a]
1980	261.0	35
1981	612.5	16
1982	856.0	11
1983	899.0	16

a. Developing countries as defined by the DAC.
Source: Japanese Ministry of Finance *International Finance Bureau Annual Report* 1984.

hold savings, which had once gone largely into companies, either were used to finance the public sector deficits or found profitable investment opportunities overseas. Exchange controls were liberalized, while many Japanese corporations raised money abroad to strengthen their overseas operations. At the same time, the government liberalized some domestic interest rates to be able to finance its own deficits.

These moves have recently been extended. External lending by Japanese banks is now free of any restrictions except those dictated by prudential guidelines. The government has made it easier for foreigners to issue yen-denominated bonds in Japan through both public issues and private placements. It has also eased restrictions on Euroyen bond issues and Euroyen lending. As a result, the Euroyen market could become as accessible to nonresidents as the Eurodollar market already is.

this can affect a bank's capacity to lend. The tax treatment is a matter of whether banks can write off their provisions as a tax loss against income. In some European countries banks benefit from relatively favorable tax treatment, but in the United States and Japan banks have had more limited possibilities for tax deductibility.

As supervisory rules and practices vary from country to country, central bankers have been trying to harmonize them through the Cooke Committee,[1] which meets under the auspices of the Bank for International Settlements. At present supervisors are seeking to consolidate branches and subsidiaries into the accounts of parent banks. The need to ensure adequacy of capital and diversification of lending on a global basis could slow lending to developing countries as the adjustment in reporting is being made. However, by strengthening the fabric of the international banking system, effective supervision can ensure a more stable flow of funds to developing countries in the long run.

1. The committee has drafted a revised concordat that sets out the principles that should govern the allocation of supervisory responsibilities for banks operating in different international centers.

pressure if concerns about the quality of their assets developed.

In addition, the capital to assets ratios of many banks in the industrial countries had been falling for much of the period between 1977 and the early 1980s (see Figure 8.4), partly reflecting the growth in their international lending, which outstripped the growth of their capital. This trend was exacerbated for non-U.S. banks by the strength of the U.S. dollar after 1980. Capital to assets ratios were weakened because a dollar appreciation increased the domestic currency equivalent of a bank's outstanding dollar lending, inflating the denominator of the ratio.

Given these pressures alone, the banks' relationship with developing countries may well have run into difficulties. In any case the large growth in bank lending registered in the 1970s could perhaps be attributed to a one-time stock adjustment toward international assets, which was nearing completion at the turn of the decade. A natural moderation in the pace of lending growth might have been expected.

The banking relationship was modified more abruptly, however, by three factors. First, the onset of debt difficulties in a number of developing countries led to a need to reschedule significant volumes of debt. The sudden deterioration in the

perceived creditworthiness of developing countries led to a reduced willingness by banks to increase their exposure further. Bank regulators responded to the same concerns by seeking to monitor liquidity and solvency ratios more closely. Furthermore, banks were urged to diversify their lending and also encouraged or required to set more funds aside in loan-loss reserves (see Box 8.4). The need to strengthen capital ratios led to the banks' placing greater emphasis on profitability; the growth of assets became less important.

Second, these changed attitudes to international lending were reinforced by the emergence of profitable opportunities for lending within some industrial countries, particularly as economic growth revived. In addition, financial markets in several industrial countries—especially the United States and the United Kingdom—began a process of deregulation, so banks faced competition from other financial institutions and concentrated on consolidating their domestic position. In the case of Japan, however, financial deregulation has led to the opening up of domestic capital markets to foreign borrowers, including developing countries, and Japanese banks will now be freer to lend overseas (see Box 8.5). One casualty of the trend toward domestic lending has been the syndicated loan market, which has become much less active than it once was (see Box 8.6).

Third, the era of OPEC surpluses and large bank

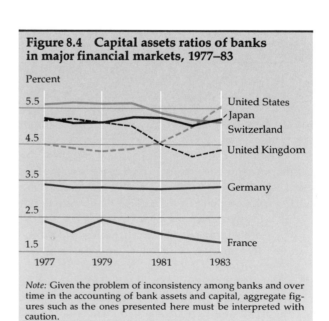

Figure 8.4   Capital assets ratios of banks in major financial markets, 1977–83

Percent

United States
Japan
Switzerland
United Kingdom
Germany
France

1977   1979   1981   1983

Note: Given the problem of inconsistency among banks and over time in the accounting of bank assets and capital, aggregate figures such as the ones presented here must be interpreted with caution.

Source: Watson, Keller, and Mathieson 1984.

Box 8.6   The rise and fall of syndicated lending

The syndicated Eurocurrency credit is a relatively new invention. Although some small private syndications were arranged in 1968 and 1969, the market did not take off until 1972 (see Box table 8.6A). From then on, it grew rapidly—and particularly for developing countries in 1976–79. With the world economy moving into recession in the early 1980s, banks' perceptions of risk—especially in regard to developing countries—increased. Bankers increasingly felt that the spreads on their loans did not adequately reflect the risks. Lending spreads rose in the early 1980s and the average maturities of loans fell (see Box figure 8.6A). With the onset of debt-servicing problems in many developing countries in 1982, new lending commitments fell sharply. Only the most creditworthy borrowers—including some developing countries from East Asia—were able to borrow on the same terms as before.

Developing countries now face a two-tier market. East Asian countries can still attract "spontaneous" lending from banks on competitive terms. But countries with

debt difficulties have had to rely on "concerted" lending arranged in conjunction with debt restructuring. The data in Box table 8.6A contain $14.3 billion in 1983 and $11.3 billion in 1984 of new money provided under the umbrella of rescheduling packages. Most of these amounts went to Latin American countries. These countries were able to secure very litle spontaneous lending in 1983 and 1984. During 1984 there was a more general easing of terms (in conjunction with multiyear rescheduling) reflecting what were perceived to be favorable policy adjustments in those developing countries that had earlier experienced debt-servicing difficulties.

The stock of syndicated loans outstanding was estimated at about $125 billion at the end of 1982. By the end of 1984, however, this figure had fallen to close to $100 billion. When the present difficulties subside, traditional syndicated lending may well revive—but it is unlikely to regain its earlier momentum. As illustrated in Boxes 8.7 and 8.8 there are an increasing number of substitutes for the syndicated loan. For many highly creditworthy bor-

Box table 8.6A   Syndicated Eurocurrency lending to developing countries, by region, 1972–84
(billions of dollars, unless otherwise noted)

Region	1972	1973	1974	1975	1976	1977	1978	1979	1980	1981	1982	1983	1984
East Asia and Pacific	0.40	0.5	2.0	3.3	2.9	2.4	7.5	7.6	8.8	10.7	10.3	7.7	7.4
Percentage of total	11	7	24	28	20	15	22	16	24	24	27	25	33
Europe and Mediterranean	0.60	0.8	1.2	0.5	0.6	0.9	2.3	6.6	3.9	3.5	3.2	2.9	2.2
Percentage of total	16	11	14	4	4	5	7	13	11	8	8	10	10
Latin America and Caribbean	2.00	3.4	4.5	6.0	8.7	9.0	17.4	26.0	19.9	24.9	22.2	15.0	11.4
Percentage of total	53	47	53	51	60	55	51	53	55	55	58	50	50
Other regions[a]	0.80	2.6	0.8	1.9	2.4	4.1	6.9	8.8	3.6	5.8	2.6	4.6	1.7
Percentage of total	20	35	9	16	16	25	20	18	10	13	7	15	7
Total	3.80	7.3	8.5	11.7	14.6	16.4	34.1	49.0	36.2	44.9	38.3	30.2	22.7

a. Includes sub-Saharan Africa, China, India, the Middle East, North Africa, and South Asia.
Source: OECD *Financial Market Trends*.

deposits has given way to an entirely different mixture of surpluses and deficits, with different financial implications. OPEC members are now net borrowers from the international banks, and the industrial countries, which had also been significant net depositors until recently, are placing less with banks (see Figure 8.5). The major imbalance in the world economy is now between the United States, with a large current account deficit, and the Federal Republic of Germany and Japan, with large surpluses. Given the nature of the U.S. financial system, the deficit has been financed rather more by trading in financial assets than through the intermediation of banks. The United States has both the assets and the markets to make this feasible. The option might also be open to sev-

eral other industrial countries, but not available to developing countries. As a result the process of intermediation has been shifting from banking to asset markets even while many developing countries remained dependent on bank finance.

In principle, had the interbank market worked without friction, their demand for banking funds could have been satisfied. Even though the surplus countries chose not to hold bank deposits, international banks could have bid in money markets to fund the continuing demand for credit by deficit developing countries. International banks were, however, increasingly constrained by both capital and sovereign risk considerations, so were reluctant to increase their exposure to developing countries or their banks. In fact, many developing

rowers the syndicated loan is now a relatively expensive borrowing option. Indeed, some banks have reportedly disbanded their syndicated credit departments in favor of a more broadly based lending operation.

Box figure 8.6A Spreads and maturities on syndicated lending, 1972–84

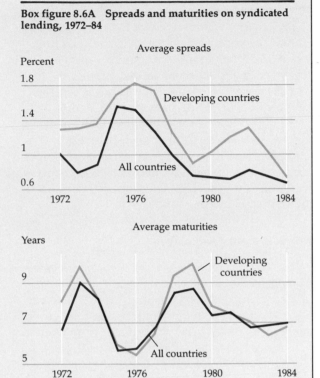

Note: Data are for new publicized syndicated loans.

Source: Bond 1985.

---

countries, even some that did not experience debt-servicing difficulties, reduced their demand for bank lending.

As a result of these factors, banks' net lending to developing countries fell significantly after 1981 (see Figure 8.2). Spontaneous lending fell most and concerted lending (in conjunction with IMF programs) became an increasingly important source of funds for developing countries (see Box 8.6). Most of the spontaneous lending went to developing countries in East Asia and Europe. Evidence provided by the latest BIS data for end-December 1984 suggests that banks' outstanding claims on developing countries have remained virtually unchanged, at $433 billion, compared with a year earlier (see Figure 8.3).

Debt rescheduling and the banks

Banks have had to temper their desire to contain the growth of exposure to some developing countries with their need to safeguard existing loans. Accordingly they have adopted a flexible approach to dealing with countries with debt-servicing difficulties. Banks quickly realized that rescheduling only principal payments due or in arrears was not adequate. Debtors needed more relief, and banks rescheduled debt and provided new loans in the context of IMF programs. Each bank's share of the new loan was based on its share of all the bank debt owed by the rescheduling country. While not without difficulties, this burden-sharing approach has been generally successful.

In some of the early reschedulings, short-term bank debt was included along with one or two years of maturities of long-term bank debt. However, all the participants soon recognized the spe-

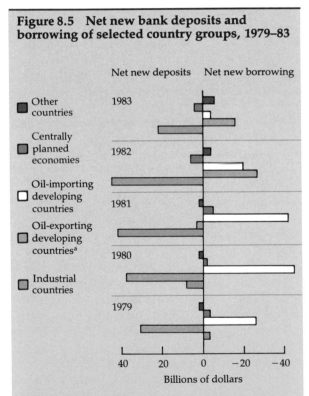

Figure 8.5 Net new bank deposits and borrowing of selected country groups, 1979–83

Note: Data are for banks reporting to the Bank for International Settlements. Net deposits with the banks take place when new deposits by a country group exceed new borrowing; a repayment of past borrowing would also serve to increase net deposits. Net borrowing takes place when new borrowing exceeds new deposits by a country group; it might also reflect a reduction in outstanding deposits with banks.

a. Mainly OPEC members.

Source: IMF 1981, no. 7; Watson, Keller, and Mathieson 1984; BIS data.

cial nature of short-term debt and its importance for maintaining the debtor's foreign trade. More recently, banks have been handling short-term credits separately or creating short-term credit facilities. Bankers have also realized that high spreads and large fees may be self-defeating. In 1983, when they signed major rescheduling agreements with (among others) Brazil, Chile, Ecuador, Mexico, Uruguay, and Yugoslavia, their interest spreads on rescheduled loans ranged from one and seven-eighths to two and a half percentage points. However, during the second half of 1984 spreads on rescheduled loans under agreements in principle with Argentina, Mexico, and Venezuela were reduced to a range of seven-eighths to one and one-quarter percentage points. Bankers have reduced or eliminated their fees and sometimes dropped the expensive pricing option of using the U.S. prime rate. Lenders are also being given the option of shifting the denomination of some of their dollar loans to their home currencies, which could reduce some interest costs for debtor countries.

Perhaps the most significant development in debt reschedulings is the movement toward multi-year agreements for some countries that have made significant progress in adjusting their economies. A bunching of loan maturities poses an obstacle to the restoration of a normal market relationship between a rescheduling country and its creditors. The Mexican agreement covers public sector maturities through 1990 and stretches out payments over fourteen years. The Venezuelan agreement covers public sector maturities through 1988 and spreads payments over twelve and a half years. In both these schemes, a combination of long repayment periods and shorter grace periods smooths out principal payments. Both agreements provide for the monitoring of the debtor's economic performance; banks wanted to be assured of the strong commitment of rescheduling countries to policy adjustment and reform. In the cases of Mexico and Venezuela, the banks will receive the semiannual reports on consultations between these countries' authorities and the International Monetary Fund.

The first-tier banks have therefore adopted a pragmatic approach to the debt-servicing problems of major debtors. The second-tier banks, however, with smaller exposures to the big debtors, have been less willing to join in debt rescheduling arrangements because there was a strong incentive for an individual bank to withdraw from lending to countries in difficulty.

Despite the progress made in tackling debt-servicing difficulties, problems remain. Banks and other creditors have, for instance, sometimes reduced trade financing when a developing country has run into difficulty. They have insisted on guarantees and have preferred sovereign borrowers. They have also been reluctant to lend for fear that foreign exchange will be reserved for servicing long-term public debt and that short-term commercial credits will be rescheduled into long-term claims. The decline in commercial credit has therefore harmed borrowers and inhibited developing countries' ability to secure needed imports.

In summary, new lending by banks is an essential part of a financing package designed to support policy reforms for structural adjustment by developing countries. On a case by case basis, consideration needs to be given to multiyear debt restructurings to smooth out debt service streams for those countries that are implementing structural adjustment programs.

Access to securities markets

At the same time as banks are reappraising their relationship with developing countries a significant structural change is taking place. The securities markets—and the institutions that operate in them—have increased in importance. A number of new instruments have been developed—such as the note issuance facility (see Box 8.7)—which blend some of the features of bank loans and bonds. These innovations increase the marketability and hence the liquidity of international assets. From the banks' standpoint such innovations have served to reduce some of the risks associated with more traditional lending. Those banks that wish to maintain a significant presence in international lending are switching the focus of their operations toward these new instrumentalities. A trend toward the securitization of international lending may be under way, which could have significant implications for the nature of private lending to developing countries in the future.

Despite the development of hybrid instruments, the traditional international bond markets have flourished in recent years. International bond markets have two components: the Eurobond and the foreign bond markets. Eurobonds are underwritten by an international group of banks and are issued in several different national markets simultaneously; they are not subject to formal controls. Foreign bond markets are simply domestic bond markets to which foreign borrowers are permitted

Box 8.7 Increasing the flexibility of bank lending

Two new market instruments are examples of financial innovation that help increase the liquidity of banks' portfolios and encourage banks (especially in the second tier) to maintain a lending relationship with developing countries.

• *Transferable loan instrument (TLI).* The TLI provides a standardized means by which a transfer of lending commitments can take place from a primary lender to a secondary market. In effect, TLIs create a secondary market for bank loans. When a bank makes a loan commitment, it can sell one or more TLIs to another bank or financial institution. The TLI entitles its holder to receive interest and other benefits of the original loan agreement, just as though the holder had itself been the primary lender. The TLI would be sold in various denominations, subject to some minimum size. It would typically be repaid in one lump sum on a date determined by the scheduled repayment dates on the original loan. From the borrower's standpoint, the amount, terms, and conditions of the original loan remain intact. From the lender's stanpoint, TLIs offer international banks scope for managing their assets more flexibly. And because TLIs can be sold in packages of varying maturities and denominations, they are potentially attractive to second-tier banks.

Although TLIs have thus far been used for industrial-country loans, they could be extended to developing-country finance as well. However, borrowers and lenders will have to move gradually, so that the market value of developing-country debt is not abruptly reduced when TLIs are traded.

• *Note issuance facility (NIF).* The NIF combines the characteristics of a traditional syndicated credit and a bond. The NIF is one of a set of hybrid instruments which have recently been launched in the market. A NIF is a medium-term loan which is funded by selling short-term paper, typically of three or six months' maturity. A group of underwriting banks guarantees the availability of funds to the borrower by purchasing any unsold notes at each roll-over date or by providing a standby credit. As funds are drawn, the underwriter either sells the securities or holds them for its own account. The borrower has guaranteed access to long-term funds; the underwriter holds a liquid, marketable security, potentially attractive to a wide range of investors. The facility has the added attraction to the borrower that it can be substantially cheaper than a standard Eurocurrency loan. The Korean Exchange Bank and the Republic of Portugal have, for instance, recently arranged Euronote facilities.

The fast pace of growth of NIFs and similar hybrid instruments—which totaled $9.5 billion in 1983 and increased to about $20 billion in 1984—has raised concerns among banking regulators. Banks could have to take on their books high-risk loans if a borrowing entity (faced with, say, a fall in its creditworthiness) were not able to refinance its Euronotes in the market.

---

access. Foreign bonds are denominated in the currency of the host country, which often subjects borrowers to tight entry requirements.

Developing countries have been attracted to the international bond markets primarily because they offer long-term money, at either fixed or floating rates of interest. As a group, developing countries have indirect access to the bond markets, since the World Bank and regional development banks are major borrowers there and onlend the proceeds to their member governments. However, few developing countries have managed to borrow in those markets directly, and then only in small amounts. One important reason is the existence of sovereign risk (described in Chapter 6, Box 6.4). Bondholders enjoy none of the advantages that banks have in coping with sovereign risk. Their relationship with developing countries is extremely remote, so they have virtually no leverage to enforce repayments in the event of debt difficulties. It is noteworthy, however, that those developing countries in difficulty have continued to service outstanding bonds held by nonbanks so as not to damage their reputation in the bond markets.

In the 1960s and early 1970s bonds issued by developing countries averaged little more than 3 percent of total issues (see Table 8.1). By 1978 developing countries had increased the volume of their borrowing to $5.2 billion and their market share to 15 percent. In 1979 and 1980, however, their borrowing and market share declined sharply, reviving only slightly in 1981. Since then, only developing countries that have avoided debt problems have been able to tap the markets. In 1984 they raised $3.8 billion in bond issues, with ten countries accounting for the bulk of the total.

The most promising conditions in which developing countries might issue bonds are when the markets as a whole are buoyant and competition from more creditworthy borrowers is light. Fixed rate markets are most buoyant when inflation is relatively low and stable. The shape of the yield curve also influences the chances of issuing fixed rate bonds: if short-term interest rates exceed long-term rates, it is difficult to launch new issues. As for competition from other borrowers, that can be affected by the actions of the host government. If it is borrowing heavily to finance its own budget deficit, it is likely to crowd out others. However, if the host country has a strong current account and wishes to encourage a capital outflow, it will often allow its domestic bond market to be tapped by foreign borrowers.

Another type of security that is already established and may become more important for developing countries is the floating rate note (FRN). These instruments have flourished in recent years in the Eurobond market and some foreign bond markets (see Table 8.1 and Box 8.8). They have provided much of the buoyancy in bond markets.

As FRNs can be more marketable than fixed rate bonds, they offer a means by which some developing countries might graduate to the fixed rate markets.

Assessment

The growth in international bank lending during the past fifteen years has on balance been beneficial to developing countries, despite the difficult economic adjustments they have had to make recently. In the 1970s, the banks' recycling of the

Table 8.1   International bond issues and placements, 1965, 1970, and 1975–84
(billions of dollars, unless otherwise noted)

Type of issue or placement	1965	1970	1975	1976	1977	1978	1979	1980	1981	1982	1983	1984
Issues or placements in foreign markets	2.4	2.4	12.3	18.9	16.6	20.7	20.3	17.9	20.5	25.2	27.1	27.8
Amount by developing countries	0.1	0.1	0.5	0.9	1.6	2.2	1.2	0.6	1.1	0.6	0.6	1.2
Percent by developing countries	4.2	4.2	4.1	4.8	9.6	10.6	5.9	3.4	5.4	2.4	2.2	4.3
Issues in the Eurobond market	0.9	3.5	10.5	15.4	19.5	14.9	18.6	20.4	31.3	50.3	50.1	81.7
Amount by developing countries	0	0.1	0.2	1.1	2.5	3.0	1.9	1.2	3.1	3.7	2.1	2.6
Percent by developing countries	0	2.9	1.9	7.1	12.8	20.1	10.2	5.9	9.9	7.4	4.2	3.2
Total international bond issues	3.3	5.9	22.8	34.3	36.1	35.6	33.9	38.3	51.8	75.5	77.2	109.5
Amount by developing countries	0.1	0.2	0.7	2.0	4.1	5.2	3.1	1.8	4.2	4.3	2.7	3.8
Percent by developing countries	3.0	3.4	3.1	5.8	11.4	14.6	8.0	4.7	8.1	5.7	3.5	3.5
Issues of floating rate notes												
Amount by all entities	..	..	0.3	1.4	2.2	2.9	4.2	4.8	11.3	15.3	19.5	38.2
Percent of total bond issues	..	..	1.3	4.1	6.1	8.1	10.8	12.5	21.8	20.3	25.2	34.9

Note: Details may not add to totals because of rounding.
Source: OECD *Financial Statistics* 1971; OECD *Financial Market Trends* 1984.

Box 8.8   Floating rate notes

The first floating rate note (FRN) was launched in the Eurodollar market in 1970. As Box figure 8.8A shows, issues grew quite slowly until the late 1970s, but have expanded dramatically in the past four years.

Private corporations, commercial banks, and government bodies all issue FRNs. Only a few developing countries have done so: Mexico and Brazil before their debt-servicing difficulties in 1982, and since then mainly those East Asian countries that have avoided debt problems. For some developing countries—such as Malaysia and Thailand recently—the FRN market has became less expensive than syndicated loans. Institutional investors and individuals have bought FRNs, but the biggest buyers are commercial banks. They have taken about 70 percent of all FRNs, either holding them on their books as investments (to match their floating rate liabilities) or using them as a substitute for syndicated lending.

There may be scope for developing countries to tap this market further as their creditworthiness improves. These instruments, however, require the borrower to bear the interest rate risk.

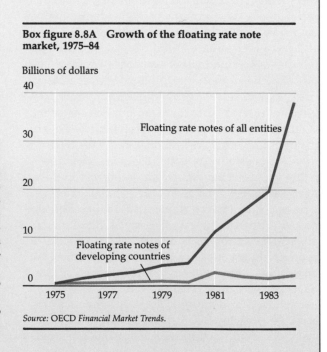

Box figure 8.8A   Growth of the floating rate note market, 1975–84

Billions of dollars

Floating rate notes of all entities

Floating rate notes of developing countries

Source: OECD *Financial Market Trends*.

Box 8.9 World Bank cofinancing

The World Bank has long encouraged other lenders—bilateral aid agencies and official export credit and banking institutions—to link their financing with the Bank's. The number of cofinanced projects almost doubled between 1975 and 1984, and cofinancing averaged $3.6 billion a year over this period (see Box table 8.9A).

The type of partners involved in cofinancing depends largely on the borrowers. For the poorest countries, lenders that can offer concessional terms are the main cofinancing sources, whereas for creditworthy developing countries the World Bank seeks commercial banks and official export credit agencies as cofinanciers. The volume of export credits used in cofinancing World Bank projects has grown in recent years, but is still a small part of the long-term export credits annually committed by industrial lenders to developing countries. Given the constraints on official aid and the cautious approach of commercial banks to increasing their international exposure, export credit cofinancing may play a bigger role in the future. The Bank is pursuing a more systematic approach that would help borrowers secure export credits in larger volumes and possibly on better terms.

Cofinancing with commercial banks has evolved more recently. In the mid-1970s, banks lent in parallel with standard World Bank loans (known as A loans in this context), with or without an optional cross-default clause or a memorandum of agreement with the World Bank. In 1983, however, the Bank introduced its B loans, which have terms and conditions that are more closely aligned with the loans of the cofinanciers.

These B loans offer three options designed to extend the range of cofinancing instruments and to benefit all three parties—the borrowers, the colenders, and the Bank. These options are (a) direct Bank participation in the late maturities of the B loan, with an option to sell all or part of its share; (b) a Bank guarantee of the late maturities, with an option to release all or part of its guarantee; and (c) Bank acceptance of a contingent obligation to finance part of the deferred principal at final maturity of a loan, with level debt service payments of floating rate interest and variable amounts of principal repayments. Despite the financial difficulties of the past few years, the new instruments have been broadly welcomed in the market. They have produced cofinancing worth more than $1 billion so far.

Box table 8.9A World Bank cofinancing operations, 1975–84
(billions of dollars, unless otherwise noted)

Fiscal year	Number of projects with cofinancing	Cofinanciers' contribution				Bank contribution		Total project costs
		Commercial banks	Export credit agencies	Other official sources	Total	IBRD	IDA	
1975	51	0.1	1.0	0.9	1.9	1.0	0.3	8.8
1976	67	0.3	0.9	1.1	2.2	1.6	0.4	9.6
1977	70	0.7	0.2	1.5	2.4	1.9	0.7	10.0
1978	79	0.2	0.5	1.8	2.5	1.7	0.8	11.4
1979	105	0.5	0.3	2.0	2.8	3.0	1.1	13.3
1980	86	1.7	1.6	2.6	5.9	3.0	1.6	20.3
1981	72	1.1	0.5	1.5	3.1	2.6	1.5	15.1
1982	98	1.2	1.8	2.2	5.3	4.1	1.2	20.0
1983	84	1.1	3.0	1.8	5.7	3.3	1.1	20.8
1984	98	1.1	0.9	2.0	4.0	4.6	1.3	21.7

Note: Components may not add to totals because of rounding. These amounts represent private cofinancing as reflected in the financing plans at the time of Board approval of A loans. They do not represent private cofinancing loans actually signed in the fiscal year. An analysis of cofinancing operations can also be found in World Bank *Annual Reports*.
Source: World Bank data.

OPEC surpluses prevented what might otherwise have been an even deeper world recession. Furthermore, the banks contributed to the substantial expansion of world trade through the provision of trade-related finance. Banking innovations also increased the flexibility of the international financial system's response to the borrowing requirements of developing countries in the 1970s. However, the "herd instinct" of banks periodically undermined the stability of finance for developing countries. More recently, banks have agreed to provide new money in conjunction with IMF programs. And the fact that bank lending was dominated by floating rate loans meant that developing countries were vulnerable to the vagaries of policy in the industrial countries.

Several factors are likely to shape the development of the international capital markets over the rest of this decade. International banks are currently redefining their strategies, after a decade of unprecedented growth in a highly competitive market. It is not clear whether their current caution signals a permanent shift toward slower growth in their international lending, or whether they are merely consolidating before starting a new phase of expansion. However, it is clear that international banks are having to learn new ways of collaborating—with each other, with the International Monetary Fund, with their own central banks, and with their largest borrowers in the developing world. They are also showing a renewed interest in project-related lending, so they are also cooperating with the World Bank on cofinancing (see Box 8.9). Furthermore, the banks are seeking ways to cope with some of the risks involved in international lending.

Despite the many problems they have had recently, developing countries need a continuing flow of bank lending to regain their growth momentum. For this to happen, however, developing countries must restore their creditworthiness—and that depends on their own policies and on the strength and stability of world economic growth. Because banks examine closely the returns relative to the risks involved on each loan, an increase in creditworthiness would reduce the risk and increase the attractiveness of developing-country loans. Beyond that, the revival of bank lending depends upon:

• *The ability of banks to rebuild their capital bases.* There is evidence that such a trend is already under way among U.S. banks. This is significant because these banks have been major lenders to developing countries in the past. Their capital grew by approximately 12 percent a year during 1982–84, and their capital ratios have risen sharply. U.S. banks' exposure to developing countries declined substantially relative to their capital in 1982–84. Whether this development will presage an increase in lending to developing countries will depend on the relative attraction of domestic lending during the present phase of financial deregulation in the United States. The capital position of non-U.S. banks would also improve if the dollar weakened appreciably on the foreign exchange markets.

• *The degree to which developing countries can embrace new instruments.* These instruments now evolving in the international markets may encourage second-tier banks and nonbanking institutions to maintain or increase their presence in international lending.

• *The evolution of a viable secondary market for bank loans.* Banks making loans are typically locked in for the duration, albeit at a variable interest rate, so are less able to adjust their exposure to changing circumstances. This makes them more reluctant to increase their lending. A secondary market might add depth to the lending market by encouraging a wider range of investors to take up developing-country paper. Without a mature secondary market, there is no adequate mechanism for pricing assets and revealing the market's collective judgment about risk. As a result, bank lending is more likely to be volatile. Secondary markets for loans to developing countries are controversial, however. Bankers, for instance, do not want to publicize the fluctuating value of their assets, and borrowers are concerned about the difficulty of managing their debt in the secondary market. Moreover, secondary markets offer a guide to creditworthiness that could signal the need to modify policies if borrowing difficulties were emerging. The expansion of secondary markets is desirable, but it must be a phased process in which creditors and debtors, as well as banking regulators, are given time to delineate and then adapt to their functions. Without a phased introduction of secondary markets, the banks, for instance, might be forced to write down the value of large amounts of lending, which could reduce their ability to provide new resources.

The international bond markets may continue to flourish, as they have done for the past three years. For the fixed rate markets to remain buoyant will require a continuation of low inflation. Floating rate notes, meanwhile, are likely to remain a feature of these markets. It is possible that the locus of lending to developing countries may shift to the innovative shorter-term segment of the securities markets. The restoration of the creditworthiness of developing countries will be the key to their access to the securities markets.

9 Direct and portfolio investment

Throughout most of the twentieth century, direct investment has been an important source of capital, technology, and expertise for countries in the process of development. In the early years of the century, foreign investors built railroads and electric power systems and invested in plantations and mines to produce for export markets. Later, direct investment in manufacturing industries and services became more common. Portfolio investment, in contrast, is a relatively new phenomenon that has only assumed significance with the growth of large public companies in developing countries and the emergence of local stock markets. Direct investment normally involves an ownership interest and an effective voice in the management of an enterprise, while portfolio investment entails a share in ownership but no significant influence over the enterprise's operations.

Many developing countries have recently made policy reforms that, among other things, give more scope for private sector activities. They have also become more receptive to foreign direct investment as lending by banks has declined. In the light of these changes, this chapter examines whether equity forms of investment can expand to provide a larger amount of capital to developing countries. It concludes that equity investment is beneficial to developing countries and can be increased, but that it is largely a complement to commercial bank lending, not a substitute for it. Because it is narrowly concentrated in countries and sectors, its potential for expansion is limited. To maximize that potential, developing countries need policies that promote trade, plus a stable economic and political environment that does not discriminate against foreign investment. For their part, industrial countries can support direct investment in developing countries by liberalizing their own trade and investment policies.

The nature and role of direct investment

Unlike commercial bank lending, direct investment provides finance as part of a package of tech-nology and management, both of which can increase the productivity of the capital. In addition, like portfolio investment, direct investment shares in both the risks and rewards of each particular project. The financial value of direct investment therefore normally understates its overall benefits to the recipient country.

Direct investment and other types of foreign capital are not necessarily substitutes; indeed, they often complement each other. For example, only about 60 percent of the external finance for the Latin American subsidiaries of American companies has come from their parent firms. The rest has come from commercial banks (both local and foreign) and trade credit. Roughly three-quarters of all the borrowing done by those subsidiaries has been in the form of trade credit. Other forms of international capital—such as bilateral and multilateral aid—have also facilitated direct investment by helping to create investment opportunities and by financing essential infrastructure.

The bulk of direct investment is done by a relatively small number of large firms. The 380 largest transnational corporations had foreign sales of about $1,000 billion in 1980, almost $3 billion a firm. They are usually attracted to invest abroad by a country's natural resources or its favorable economic environment; occasionally they are also attracted by the special inducements offered by host countries.

One common motive for a company to undertake foreign investment is a threat to an existing export market. The threat might come either from the actions of a competitor or from measures restricting the market to local producers. The only way to avoid the trade barriers is to be inside them. Companies are also keen to invest abroad when there are clear cost advantages from doing so. Direct investments in manufacturing and services are often made by firms with some kind of special advantage that is best utilized by maintaining management control of operations in foreign countries. Such advantages may be a superior product or production process, or a product that the for-

Table 9.1 Direct foreign investment in selected country groups, 1965–83

Country group	Average annual value of flows (billions of dollars)[a]				Share of flows (percent)			
	1965–69	1970–74	1975–79	1980–83	1965–69	1970–74	1975–79	1980–83
Industrial countries	5.2	11.0	18.4	31.3	79	86	72	63
Developing countries	1.2	2.8	6.6	13.4	18	22	26	27
Latin America and Caribbean	0.8	1.4	3.4	6.7	12	11	13	14
Africa	0.2	0.6	1.0	1.4	3	5	4	3
Asia, including Middle East	0.2	0.8	2.2	5.2	3	6	9	11
Other countries and estimated unreported flows	0.2	−1.0	0.6	4.8	3	−8	2	10
Total[b]	6.6	12.8	25.6	49.4	100	100	100	100

a. Figures converted from billions of SDR to billions of U.S. dollars based on average IMF-IFS exchange rates.
b. Total includes IMF estimates for unreported flows.
Source: For 1965–79: U.S. Department of Commerce 1984, Table 4; for 1980–83: IMF *Balance of Payments Statistics Yearbook* 1984.

eign company can differentiate from those of competitors.

Growth and concentration

While the nominal value of direct investment in developing countries grew by 10 percent a year between 1967 and 1982, its real value hardly increased at all. By contrast, the amount of medium- and long-term finance for developing countries from private lenders increased by about 9.5 percent a year in real terms. More than half of the measured flow of direct investment now takes the form of reinvested earnings from existing subsidiaries.

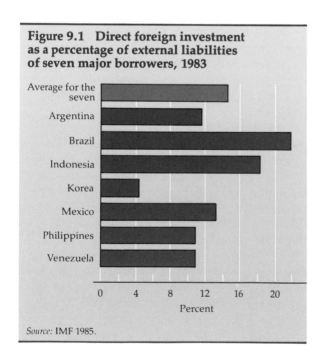

Figure 9.1 Direct foreign investment as a percentage of external liabilities of seven major borrowers, 1983

Source: IMF 1985.

Table 9.1 shows that about three-quarters of foreign direct investment has gone to industrial countries on average since 1965. The remainder has been concentrated for the most part in a few developing countries, predominantly the higher-income countries of Asia and Latin America. In particular, Brazil (see Box 9.1) and Mexico have received large volumes of direct investment. Within Asia, Hong Kong, Malaysia, the Philippines, and Singapore have been the largest recipients; Singapore alone has accounted for nearly one-half of total Asian receipts of foreign direct investment in recent years. Among those developing countries that have accumulated a large volume of external liabilities there are marked differences in the share of direct investment in the total (see Figure 9.1).

Direct investment has provided very little capital for the low-income countries. This often reflects the small size of their domestic markets and their lack of skilled manpower; in India's case, it has reflected in part the strong public sector bias of its industrial policies and in part a search for economic self-reliance (see Box 9.2).

Direct investment in developing countries comes almost entirely from industrial countries. Although companies from the United States and the United Kingdom are the largest foreign investors in developing countries, their relative status has declined. Companies from the Federal Republic of Germany and, until recently, Japan (see Box 9.3) have substantially increased their investment in developing countries. Together, these four countries have supplied more than three-quarters of direct investment in developing countries, with the United States alone accounting for nearly one-half of the total.

Almost all investing countries have a regional bias in their investment in developing countries.

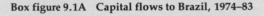
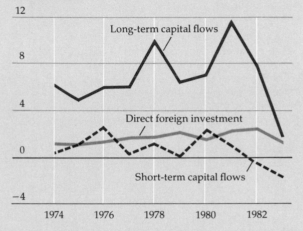
The United States' investment is largely in Latin America, while Japan's investment goes mainly to its Asian neighbors. Similarly, much of the United Kingdom's investment goes to Commonwealth nations, and France has focused on countries with past colonial ties, mainly in Africa.

Direct investment is also concentrated in a few economic sectors. Figure 9.2 shows that investment by U.K. and German firms in particular has been mainly in manufacturing; while U.S. and Japanese investment, although more evenly spread over the major economic sectors, has a bias toward manufacturing and the primary industries. And within manufacturing, direct investment has been mainly in transportation equipment, chemicals, and machinery (which includes electronics).

Causes of stagnation

The near stagnation of direct investment in the 1970s reflected the increased availability of bank lending and the low real interest rates on bank

loans. Returns required by private investors are estimated to have been much higher than those on bank loans.

At the same time, many developing countries increased restrictions on direct investment, reducing the range of industries in which foreigners could invest and raising local ownership requirements. Some policymakers in developing countries questioned the contribution that direct investment could make to economic development.

The reasons for their skepticism have always started with political opposition to letting national resources be controlled from abroad. In addition, critics charge that multinational companies use inappropriate technologies and that their centralized management structures prevent the development of local initiative. They also say that multinationals often fund themselves in the local capital market, crowding out potential domestic borrowers. Finally, they suggest that direct investors use transfer prices, royalty and interest payments, management fees, and other means to avoid price

Box 9.2 Direct foreign investment in India

The Indian government has traditionally been cautious about foreign investment. However, it has recently recognized that joint ventures—or collaborations—can be useful in bringing in new technologies, increasing exports, and creating domestic employment (see Box figure 9.2A). Regulations have therefore begun to be eased.

• While direct foreign investment still constitutes a small proportion of India's foreign capital flows, the number of collaborations and the amount of foreign investment approved by the government have risen significantly in recent years. Procedural simplification, improved industrial policy environment, and favorable reassessment of India's economic management and prospects have been major factors in this upsurge.

• Several industries are reserved to the public sector and therefore are closed to private domestic and foreign investment. Elsewhere, foreign ownership is normally restricted to 40 percent of a company's equity, though a higher percentage may be allowed if the venture is largely export oriented or brings with it a highly desired kind of technology. Companies exporting all their output can be wholly foreign owned.

• Corporate income taxes are high, and tax laws are complex. However, new companies can obtain various incentives that tend to reduce their potential tax liability in the first five years of their operations.

• Procedures governing inward investment and repatriation are elaborate and time consuming, though the government is now trying to streamline them. All applications for industrial approvals, including the granting of industrial licenses, the approval of foreign collaborations, and the import of capital goods, can now be made to one agency—the Secretariat for Industrial Approvals. The Indian Investment Centre meanwhile acts as a separate promotional agency operating alongside the existing regulatory structures.

Once the government approves a foreign investment, remittance of royalties and dividends are unrestricted. Repatriation of capital invested by foreigners is allowed subject to the provisions of the Foreign Exchange Regulation Act of 1973. This act, enforced by the Reserve Bank of India, governs the entry of foreign investment, the activities of resident foreigners, and the holding of and payments in foreign exchange.

Because of restrictions on foreign ownership and expansion, many multinational firms prefer to license their products in India. However, royalties and fees paid by Indian licensees are also subject to close scrutiny by the authorities. The royalty allowed in a technical collaboration will depend on the nature of the technology, but will normally not exceed 8 percent of the ex-factory value of production.

Box figure 9.2A Direct foreign investment in India, 1978–83

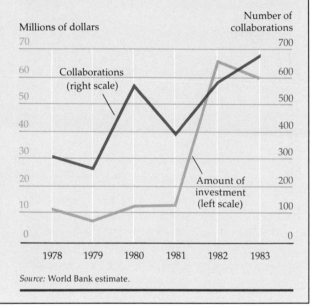

Source: World Bank estimate.

---

controls, foreign exchange regulations, local taxes, and limits on profit remittances.

These charges have been particularly common in countries where governments have used import restrictions to encourage local production. Inappropriate trade regimes sometimes provide foreign investors with financial rates of return that are markedly higher than the economic returns to the country. When governments attempt to control such profits, the controls provide incentives for firms to try to evade them. Open trade regimes increase the benefits to developing countries of foreign direct investment and reduce the problems associated with it.

The skepticism of developing countries was often echoed by potential investors. Faced with unreceptive host countries, volatile economic policies, and confusing combinations of incentives and restrictions, investors were wary of committing capital to developing countries. During the 1970s, multinational companies and developing-country governments put increased emphasis on unbundling the management, technology, and financial components of direct investment. Licensing and other contractual arrangements permitted developing countries to obtain some of the benefits of direct investment without incurring some of the perceived costs of foreign ownership. Recently, however, there has been a positive shift in the receptivity of some countries to direct investment.

Improving the environment for direct investment

Countries with large internal markets and import-substituting strategies are among those that have received the largest amount of direct investment. They are also the countries where prices have been most distorted and where complaints about the development contribution of direct investment have been most common. Countries that have followed a more open development strategy have had fewer problems with direct investment. Their strategy makes production for domestic and export markets equally attractive and generally requires market prices to reflect relative scarcities. In these countries, governments have tended to lower tariffs and to allow real interest rates to be positive. As a result, the direct investment that has taken place has been geared more closely to the country's comparative advantage. The contribution that direct investment makes to development therefore depends significantly on the policy framework in which it takes place.

The policies of host countries

All developing countries have policies and institutions for dealing with direct investment. These include investment incentives and the services and

Figure 9.2   Sectoral composition of direct foreign investment in developing countries by four source countries, 1980

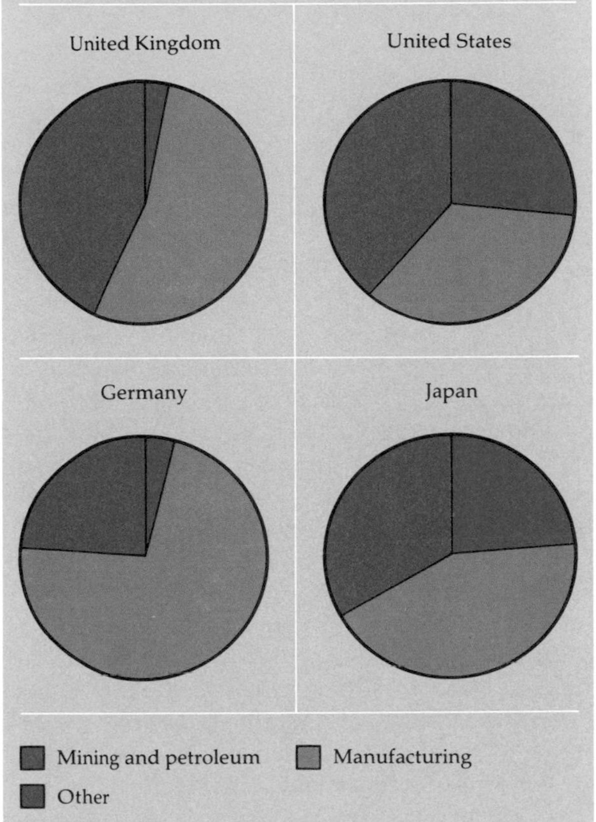

■ Mining and petroleum   ■ Manufacturing
■ Other

Source: IMF 1985.

Box 9.3   Japanese direct investment in manufacturing

Japan's overseas investment in manufacturing industries only became sizable in the late 1960s and early 1970s. Between 1971 and 1982 Japan's cumulative investment in manufacturing was about $16 billion, compared with its total cumulative direct investment abroad of some $50 billion. Japanese investment in manufacturing has differed in several ways from that of the other OECD countries. For example, most American foreign investment was done by sizable multinational firms usually in a large industrial country, for the purpose of supplying the local market. Their investments were normally in capital-intensive industries and often involved sophisticated technology.

By contrast, Japanese foreign investment in manufacturing was made by a large number of small and medium-sized firms in labor-intensive and low-technology industries, initially in such countries as Korea and Hong Kong, and much of it was aimed at export markets. These characteristics can be attributed in part to labor shortages in Japan and a rapid rise in real wages

that reduced the competitiveness of labor-intensive manufacturing. At the same time, large current account surpluses led the Japanese government to liberalize controls on overseas investment.

The pattern of Japanese direct investment is changing. Manufacturing investments are going more into industrial countries—especially North America—than developing countries. Between 1971 and 1980 Japanese direct investment in manufacturing in developing countries—the bulk of which was in Asia—represented 68 percent of cumulative investment in manufacturing worldwide. During 1981–82 this figure fell to 46 percent. This change is partly a reaction to the protectionist measures that some industrial countries have adopted to restrict Japanese imports; Japanese companies have sought to establish themselves inside the protectionist barriers. But it also reflects the view of many Japanese companies that the investment climate in developing countries has deteriorated as growth has slowed and some countries have run into debt-servicing difficulties.

infrastructure provided for foreign investors. They also include various restrictions on the way foreign companies can operate.

• *Incentives*. They are typically designed either to enhance the revenues of foreign firms or to reduce their costs. Revenue-enhancing incentives include import tariffs or quotas on the product concerned, tax breaks, and preferential treatments of various kinds. Among these none has been more influential than tariffs and other forms of protection covering products to be sold on the local market. Cost-reducing incentives include reduced tariffs on imports and exemptions from taxes on inputs. The nature of the incentives that a country offers will depend on the kind of investment it wishes to obtain and on competition from other countries to attract that type of investment. There are indications that incentives become less effective the greater their complexity and the more frequently they are altered. The impact of specific incentives for direct investment is uncertain. Numerous studies have suggested that business executives tend to ignore or downplay incentives in making decisions on where to invest. However, a study by the IFC suggests that incentives can influence the investment decision: other things being equal, companies might choose one country rather than another on the basis of the relative attractiveness of incentives.

• *Regulations*. These can take many forms. Some countries—including Brazil, Egypt, India, and Mexico—reserve key industries for local (and often state-owned) enterprises. Some countries allow foreign investors to hold only a minority stake in a company, unless the industry is defined as "high priority" or the production is mainly for export. In other countries—especially in Latin America—foreign companies are required to dilute ownership and control gradually through the sale of shares to residents.

Many developing countries restrict remittances of interest and dividends. This can be a major disincentive to foreign companies and has encouraged such practices as the manipulation of transfer pricing. Some governments in developing countries (Latin America, for instance) also stipulate performance requirements, so a company has to export a minimum proportion of its output or use a certain amount of local components, labor, and so on. Countries such as Argentina, Kenya, Peru, and Turkey have limited the amount of local borrowing that foreign investors can do. The IFC study showed that companies tend to take these requirements into consideration in choosing where to locate.

The specific incentives and regulations governing direct investment have had less effect on how much investment a country receives than has its general economic and political climate, and its financial and exchange rate policies. This conclusion can be illustrated by the varying experience of many different countries. Despite offering substantial incentives to potential investors, countries in Africa and the Caribbean—with small domestic markets and limited natural resources—have not attracted much direct investment. India, Nigeria, and several Latin American countries have had the potential to obtain direct investment for import-substitution purposes. They, too, have had only modest success because they have chosen to impose restrictions and performance requirements on foreign companies.

Box 9.4 Turkish seed production

When the World Bank was reviewing its lending plans for Turkey's agriculture in 1981, it concluded that farmers would benefit considerably if the quality of seed was improved. The Bank judged that the most effective way of doing this would be to promote a private sector seed industry, with the participation of foreign companies.

However, government policies toward the seed industry had discouraged direct investment by foreign firms and limited the supply and range of seeds that farmers could buy. These policies included price controls on seeds; restrictions on importing seeds for testing and market development; a government monopoly on testing; and lengthy and complicated certification proce-

dures before a new seed could be sold.

Partly as a result of initiatives by the Bank and the IFC, the government has changed many of these policies. Price controls have been abolished. Seed may be imported more freely into Turkey, and testing and certification procedures have been liberalized.

Eleven foreign seed companies have begun working in Turkey, importing seeds and testing them in local conditions. They then plan to develop distribution channels, importing the best varieties and selling them to test the market. Once a market is established, the companies intend to set up local growing and processing operations. Ultimately, they may establish local research facilities to develop new varieties.

By contrast, some of the newly industrializing countries in East Asia—Malaysia and Singapore, for instance—have obtained considerable inflows without offering significant incentives. Their export-oriented development policies have been the attraction. They prove a general rule: what is good policy for domestic investors is also good for foreign investors.

Although the macroeconomic climate is of prime importance, policies for specific sectors and industries can determine whether investments are actually made. Box 9.4 describes one case, the seed industry in Turkey, where sector-specific policies were crucial. Once policy failings were identified and acted upon, substantial new foreign investment took place in the industry.

The policies of industrial countries

As with the policies of host countries, it is the general economic policies of the industrial countries that have the most effect on the amount of direct investment going to developing countries. Lower rates of economic growth and high production costs at home will increase the attraction of foreign investment.

At the same time, the efforts of industrial countries to encourage and protect production at home have sometimes discouraged investment in developing countries. Some industrial countries provide generous concessions to attract investment from abroad. Although many of these incentives are directed toward specific industries, usually high technology ones, they can be directly competitive with the incentives offered by developing countries. Direct and indirect subsidies to ailing industries have also reduced the incentives for firms in these industries to consider investing in developing countries. Restrictions on trade flows have had similar effects. The 1982–85 restrictions on Japanese automobile exports to the United States, for instance, reduced the incentive for U.S. producers to seek lower-cost manufacturing bases in developing countries to produce parts and components. To increase investment in developing countries, it would clearly be desirable to remove the subsidies and tariffs that protect domestic industry in the industrial economies.

Some policy initiatives in industrial countries have had positive effects on investment in developing countries. Governments and trade bodies have spread information about investment opportunities. They have negotiated procedures for settling disputes over investment with governments of developing countries. They have tax laws that make it attractive for individuals to work abroad in a multinational company. Such measures are valuable. But the most powerful stimulus to invest in developing countries comes from liberal trade policies, since companies can then manufacture abroad to produce for industrial-country markets. As pointed out in Box 9.3, Japanese textile firms made direct investments in Asian developing countries in order to remain competitive in export markets.

Investment protection and insurance

As direct investment is long term and usually takes the form of plant and machinery, it is exposed to political risk—the threat of expropriation, blocked currency, war, revolution, or insurrection. To reassure actual and potential investors, many developing countries have passed laws protecting them against expropriation; some have embodied the protection in their constitutions. Governments in industrial and developing countries have concluded some 200 bilateral treaties on investment protection, which cover, among other things, transfer and expropriation risks. In addition, twenty-two countries—almost all industrial countries, as well as India and the Republic of Korea—have set up investment guarantee schemes.

These schemes offer guarantees to companies and individuals from each guaranteeing country against political risks abroad. National schemes differ appreciably in their terms and conditions, scope of coverage, and administrative practices. As a result, their coverage of direct foreign investment to developing countries ranges from less than 5 percent to more than 50 percent. In all, some 10 to 15 percent of direct foreign investment to developing countries from countries with national schemes was guaranteed in 1977–81. By the end of 1981, about 9 percent of the stock of direct foreign investment was covered by national guarantees.

Another approach to mitigating political risk has been through private insurance. In the early 1970s, underwriters and brokers of Lloyd's of London pioneered political risk insurance for overseas investments and export contracts. Since then, the practice has grown substantially. In 1973, private insurers received premiums of $2 million to $3 million from underwriting political risk, and their underwriting capacity did not exceed $8 million for each project. In 1982, total premiums were worth an estimated $95 million, the underwriting capacity for a single project had soared to $450 million, and the sum insured was estimated to be around $8 billion.

The role of the World Bank Group

Besides building up domestic infrastructures and providing complementary financing, the World Bank and its affiliate, the International Finance Corporation, try to promote policies in developing countries that will increase all investment, domestic and foreign. The focus of the Bank's structural adjustment lending, for example, is to encourage governments to reduce economic distortions by cutting subsidies, sharpening incentives, and phasing out protection for inefficient producers.

The Bank and the IFC are able to help in the design of policies to stimulate productive private investment. The IFC in particular is well placed to give such advice because it sees firsthand, as a participant, how policies affect investment decisions. Sometimes in collaboration with the Bank, it responds to requests from its member countries for policy advice on topics such as:

• The drafting or revision of investment codes, laws, and regulations that govern private direct or foreign investment.

• Measures to help private companies through the difficulties that occur when austerity or economywide restructuring programs reduce demand, make credit scarce, and change the relative prices that determine profits.

• Privatization of state-owned enterprises that the government no longer wishes to hold. The IFC may advise on strategic aspects of privatization: whether to sell, lease, or offer a management contract; the sequence in which enterprises should be privatized; the kinds of buyers to seek and how to seek them; and how to evaluate the enterprises. The IFC may also participate in the financing when particular enterprises are sold to private buyers.

Acting directly as an investor, but always as a minority participant, the IFC promotes the flow of foreign investment to developing countries and seeks to stimulate the domestic private sector. The 773 projects in eighty-four developing countries that the IFC has financed through June 1984 represent a total investment cost of almost $27 billion; the IFC has complemented its own investments of $3.7 billion by $2.5 billion that has been syndicated to other lenders. The IFC has also helped to attract to these projects direct foreign private investment amounting to roughly $1 billion.

The IFC provides services that help to bring domestic and foreign investors together. Its presence often serves to raise the confidence of foreign investors, and as a neutral partner it helps to structure projects so that the benefits are shared equitably among local public and private investors and foreign interests. Three recent examples of IFC

subscriptions would be paid in; the rest would be callable in case of need. MIGA's underwriting capacity would be subject to ceilings that would maintain a sound ratio between its capital and its liabilities under issued guarantees. In addition to its own guarantees, MIGA would be authorized to issue guarantees on behalf of "sponsoring members," which would recommend such guarantees and share in the risks on a pro rata basis. Under this additional window, guarantees of sponsored investments would have no ceiling.

In accordance with the proposed draft Convention, MIGA would be subrogated to the relevant rights of indemnified investors against host countries. Disputes between the agency and host countries concerning such rights would be settled by negotiation and, ultimately, international arbitration. Host countries' sovereignty would be safeguarded by the principle that both the investment and the agency's guarantee must be approved by the host country concerned.

assistance show the range of the services that go with its financing:

• It has arranged project technology agreements so that the foreign suppliers of technology bear a larger share of the risk when their technologies are unproven.

• In helping to draw up management agreements between foreign companies and developing-country companies, it has insisted that management fees be related to performance-related indexes, such as profitability, rather than to the value of sales or similar less relevant yardsticks.

• It has discouraged some developing-country governments from putting uneconomic performance criteria or other restrictions on foreign companies, where such measures might reduce the benefits from the projects.

The World Bank has also taken some international initiatives over foreign investment. The establishment of the International Center for the Settlement of Investment Disputes (ICSID) in 1965 has helped to improve the framework for direct investment by providing acceptable procedures for the settlement of disputes between foreign investors and their host countries. It has thereby built a greater measure of confidence in the relationship between these two parties. The increasing membership of ICSID, now totaling seventy-eight countries, with four other signatories expected to become members soon, is evidence of the growing recognition of the relevance of this institution to the investors and the countries that wish to attract them. The Bank's management has also proposed a multilateral investment guarantee agency (see Box 9.5).

Foreign portfolio investment

Portfolio investment has not yet provided much finance for developing countries, though its contribution is growing. An attractive feature is that it can provide equity finance for developing countries with fewer of the difficulties about foreign control that are associated with direct investment. However, many developing countries have been skeptical of the benefits of portfolio investment and so have restricted and regulated it. For their part, investors in the industrial countries have known little about the securities markets in developing countries and have been concerned about the perceived risks involved.

The experience of host countries

In many developing countries, companies have outgrown their domestic capital markets and would benefit from an injection of foreign equity. By the same token, more foreign investors would increase the demand for stocks in domestic capital markets. Greater market activity could ultimately lead to new stock issues and perhaps new investment. The secondary market would gain some much needed stability if purchases and sales by foreign investors helped to offset the cyclical behavior of domestic investors.

If developing countries are to obtain portfolio capital, they must take steps to attract it. At present, many have barriers against it, including:

• Capital gains taxes and unduly high withholding taxes on dividend income.

• Minimum periods during which foreign funds must remain invested.

• Foreign exchange restrictions on foreign portfolios.

• Restrictions on the types of shares that can be bought or held by foreign investors.

• Discriminatory treatment of foreign investors compared with domestic investors.

The removal of these barriers could facilitate a growth in portfolio investment.

The perspective of international investors

Portfolio investment offers the investor long-term returns and diversified risk without the responsibility of management and control. Thus far, almost all portfolio investment has been in the markets of the major industrial economies or in a few developing countries (such as Malaysia and Mexico). During the past five years, however, a number of developing countries have emerged as potential markets for portfolio investment. For example, equity funds of Brazilian, Indian, Korean, and Mexican shares have been organized.

The total capitalization of the developing countries' equity markets amounted to $133 billion in 1983. This was more than one-quarter of the European market capitalization, and 10 percent of all the stocks quoted outside the United States. Excluding Hong Kong and Singapore, the capitalization of developing-country markets totaled $75 billion.

The IFC has supported the development of local markets by helping to establish specialized equity funds for individual countries. One example is the Korea Fund (see Box 9.6). The IFC has also proposed the formation of investment trusts through which commercial banks would be able to sell some of their loans to developing countries for shares. The trusts would then swap the loans bought from the banks for equity stakes in the borrowing entities.

In general, developing countries have a reputation as high-risk options for portfolio investors from industrial countries. However, such invest-ment would allow investors to hold a broader range of international assets. Significantly, the returns from investing in the stock markets of the United States and other big industrial countries have not been synchronized with the returns from developing-country markets, so the widest spread of assets has also been the least risky. Furthermore, the returns obtainable from the emerging developing-country markets (excluding Hong Kong and Singapore) have recently been higher—in dollar terms on a cumulative basis—over the past eight years, more than double that of the world's major equity markets (see Table 9.2). However, devaluations and major economic changes in the developing countries mean that returns have been volatile.

Assessment

The following principal conclusions emerge from the preceding review.

• Equity forms of investment can clearly be beneficial to developing countries, and it is desirable that they be increased. Developing countries can reduce the level of risk attached to external capital inflows and secure the benefits of technology and expertise transfers by expanding the amount of direct investment in total external financing.

• Given that equity investment is desirable, there is a question of how developing countries

---

Box 9.6 The IFC and foreign portfolio investment: the Korean case

The Korea Fund is one example of the IFC's work in trying to stimulate foreign portfolio investment in developing countries. In the early 1980s the Korean authorities decided to open their securities market gradually to foreign investors. As a first step, two semi-open-end mutual funds (Korea Trust and Korea International Trust) were offered in the Euroequity market at the end of 1981. These offerings totaled $30 million (later doubled through a second tranche) and were underwritten by leading international securities houses. The minimum denominations of $10,000 were aimed at institutions and individuals with sizable portfolios. The funds are managed by two established Korean investment management companies.

As a second step, the Korea Fund was offered to the general public as well as institutional investors in mid-1984. This fund is a closed-end investment company, registered with the U.S. Securities and Exchange Commission and listed on the New York Stock Exchange. It is expected that normally at least 80 percent of the fund's assets will be invested in Korean listed stocks. The fund is managed by Scudder, Stevens & Clark, an American investment counseling firm, with the help of Daewoo Research Institute, an investment advisory firm in Korea. The IFC was involved from the beginning and acted as one of the colead managers of the underwriting.

In future years, foreign investment in Korean listed securities is likely to be liberalized further. As presently envisaged, the guidelines will say that total foreign investment should not exceed 10 percent of total market capitalization and that foreign holdings should not exceed 10 percent of the voting rights of any company, with a 5 percent restriction on any single foreign shareholder. As part of this development, leading Korean companies are expected to list their stocks on major international stock exchanges and offer their shares for public subscription in the Euroequity market. In addition, Korean securities firms are expected to allow international investment banks to take their shares.

Table 9.2   Return on investment in emerging markets, 1976–83

(percent)

Country group	1976	1977	1978	1979	1980	1981	1982	1983[a]	Average annual change, 1976–83[a]
Emerging markets									
Argentina	147.0	−43.6	79.9	233.6	−72.2	−54.5	66.2	124.5	18.7
Brazil	1.3	11.9	−6.0	−12.5	4.1	9.0	−19.9	97.4[b]	6.6[b]
Chile	103.4	146.3	56.3	131.6	92.7	−48.3	−52.1	−18.4	27.7
Hong Kong	40.0	−11.0	18.0	80.0	71.0	−16.0	−42.0	−8.6	9.2
India	34.1	13.7	51.2	21.1	42.3	23.8	−5.9	6.0	22.0
Jordan[c]			53.4	27.7	21.5	35.0	8.0	−7.0	19.9
Korea	72.4	114.2	23.7	−13.0	−26.5	40.2	7.9	7.4	21.5
Mexico	19.1	22.3	127.8	96.3	17.7	−46.8[d]	−79.8[d]	170.2[d]	−0.6[d]
Singapore	14.0	6.0	52.0	−12.0	29.0	15.0	−1.0	29.2	15.0
Thailand	0.4	187.7	43.2	−40.7	−12.9	−19.2	21.1	9.7	12.3
Zimbabwe	13.2	3.1	−6.9	178.7	30.4	−56.7	−32.4	−7.9	0.8
Industrial countries									
United States	23	−8	6	14	29	−4	21	20	13.5
Japan	25	15	52	−12	29	15	−1	23	16.8
Cumulative return									
Capital International world index[e]	114	116	136	152	192	184	205	250	12.1
IFC emerging market index[f]	134	196	304	514	645	593	412	617	25.5

Note: The returns depicted are calculated as follows. Assume a U.S. investor has $100 to invest in an emerging market. After conversion to domestic currency, the proceeds are placed in a basket of actively traded stocks. Dividends may be paid on the investment during the year, and capital gains may also be secured if the market price of the stock rises. These two sources of income are converted back to U.S. dollars at yearend exchange rates to yield a return denominated in U.S. dollars. This return is expressed as a percentage of the original $100 investment.
a. Returns for 1983 are up to the end of November for Argentina and to the end of December for Brazil, Hong Kong, India, Jordan, Mexico, Singapore, Thailand, and Zimbabwe.
b. Based on preliminary data for 1983.
c. Jordan's stock market opened in January 1978, hence data are not available for earlier years.
d. Based on *Capital International* data for 1981–83, including net dividends.
e. Based on *Capital International* data; January 1, 1976 = 100.
f. Returns in emerging markets included in this table, except for Hong Kong and Singapore, on a market-weighted basis (1980 for 1975–80; individual years for 1981–83); January 1, 1976 = 100.
Source: van Agtmael 1984; for emerging markets: IFC data; for industrial countries: *Capital International*.

might attract it and use it efficiently. Experience over the last decade suggests that countries with stable economic and political environments are the most successful in this regard. Some countries have succeeded in attracting direct investment by offering inducements of various kinds to compensate for inappropriate macroeconomic policies, but these normally encourage inefficient investment and malpractices in investing firms. Special incentives can be costly for individual developing countries and offsetting within developing countries as a group. In general, developing countries benefit most from equity forms of investment when the overall policy environment is favorable for investment and when the policies adopted toward foreign investors are the same as those under which domestic investors operate.

• Policies in industrial countries are also important for encouraging equity flows; liberal trade and industrial policies are most conducive to direct investment in developing countries. Bilateral understandings and insurance schemes have also proved useful in mitigating some of the risks inherent in direct investment. The World Bank has played an important catalytic role in fostering both direct and portfolio investment and in some instances has provided needed complementary financing to direct investment projects. While all of these factors could encourage a greater flow, direct investment, which is undertaken by relatively few companies in a narrow range of countries and industries, is likely to be relatively slow to respond.

• Foreign portfolio investment might be stimulated by the removal of restrictions, regulations, and tax barriers that impede international investors' access to domestic stock markets. Furthermore, major indigenous corporations might also be permitted to list their shares on international stock exchanges. A more favorable climate for foreign portfolio investment might stimulate interest among investors and facilitate the establishment of emerging equity market funds. Pension funds in the industrial countries have assets worth $1.5 trillion, and they are increasingly seeking investment opportunities worldwide. A small shift in investment toward emerging markets could increase the volume of capital flowing to developing countries.

• Both direct and portfolio investment have the potential for covering a higher proportion of the funding needs of developing countries than they have hitherto. To realize this potential, however, requires a wholesale reassessment of the benefits of those types of investment in host and investing countries alike. It is necessary, however, to be realistic about its potential for providing large amounts of finance to a broad range of developing countries.

Part IV Perspectives and Policies for the Future

10 Perspectives and policy agenda

The financial difficulties of the past few years have been effectively handled by a combination of economic recovery, very tough adjustment measures by debtors, and actions by creditors and international agencies. But the deep-seated problems of both industrial and developing countries continue to need fundamental treatment if sustainable growth and normal relationships between debtors and creditors are to be restored. Only when this happens will developing countries really be able to resume the encouraging progress they made in the 1960s and 1970s.

To examine the prospects for development, this chapter starts by presenting two broad scenarios—High and Low cases—for the years up to 1995. In essence, these are the same as those included in last year's *World Development Report*. However, the chapter then pays much closer attention to the period 1985–90. That is the time during which the transition to resumed sustained growth would occur, if all goes well. Such a successful transition will require continued policy reforms in developing countries, sustained growth in industrial countries, and a rollback of protectionism so that developing countries can access industrial countries' markets.

The next ten years

The two scenarios presented in last year's *World Development Report* and summarized here are not, it needs stressing, predictions or forecasts. What happens in the next ten years will depend critically on the policies adopted by industrial and developing countries, and their broad outlines can only be assumed. Nor do the projections include any cyclical volatility that in practice will probably occur, nor any major exogenous shocks caused by disruptions in the supplies or sharp rises in prices of critical commodities.

The Low case indicates what might happen if industrial countries fail to overcome the causes of their erratic performance in the past ten years.

Budgetary deficits, inflation, unemployment, and interest rates would remain high. GDP growth in industrial economies would average 2.5 percent a year. In developing countries, GDP would grow at 4.7 percent a year (or well below the 5.5 percent growth rate of 1973–80), and with increased protectionism in industrial economies GDP growth would be reduced to only 4.3 percent a year in 1985–95. All forms of foreign capital for developing countries would grow slowly, with only a small increase in aid. In such circumstances, most groups of developing countries would grow more slowly than they did in 1973–80, and all would grow much more slowly than in the 1960s (see Table 10.1). Including the difficult 1980–85 period, the Low case would mean fifteen years of very slow economic progress for many countries.

The High case, by contrast, assumes a path of sustained noninflationary growth in industrial economies. The long-term determinants of productivity growth in industrial economies were discussed in detail in last year's Report. The projected growth rate of industrial economies of 4.3 percent a year in 1985–95 assumes that industrial economies would be successful in putting into place policies that would permit output growth close to long-term potential rates. Unemployment, inflation, and interest rates would all fall, almost back to their levels in the 1960s. Governments would reduce trade barriers, allowing exports from developing countries to grow more rapidly. Capital flows to developing countries could be expected to expand, and the prospects for more aid for low-income countries would be considerably improved. Developing countries would restore their growth rates to somewhere near their average in the 1970s.

The contrast between the Low and High cases is even more pronounced when growth in developing countries is expressed in per capita terms (see Table 10.2). One striking feature is the bleak outlook for the low-income countries of Africa. Even in the High case, their per capita incomes decline—

Table 10.1 Average performance of industrial and developing countries, 1960–95
(average annual percentage change)

Country group	1960–73	1973–80	1980–85	1985–95 High	1985–95 Low
Industrial countries					
GDP growth	4.9	2.8	2.3	4.3	2.5
Developing countries					
GDP growth	6.1	5.5	3.0	5.5	4.7
Low-income countries					
Asia	6.0	5.2	6.4	5.3	4.6
Africa	3.7	2.7	1.4	3.2	2.8
Middle-income oil importers					
Major exporters of manufactures	6.8	5.9	2.1	6.3	5.2
Other countries	5.2	4.6	1.5	4.3	3.8
Middle-income oil exporters	6.1	5.8	1.8	5.4	4.7
Export growth	5.2[a]	4.1	5.7	6.4	4.7
Manufactures	13.8[a]	11.0	9.7	9.7	7.5
Primary goods	3.6[a]	1.3	2.8	3.4	2.1
Import growth	5.9[a]	5.9	1.2	7.2	5.1

Note: Projected growth rates, which are based on a sample of ninety developing countries, are from *World Development Report 1984*. Historical growth rates have been revised since last year's Report.
a. Historical growth rates are for the period 1965–73.
Source: World Bank data.

Table 10.2 Growth of GDP per capita, 1960–95
(average annual percentage change)

Country group	1960–73	1973–80	1980–85	1985–95 High	1985–95 Low
Industrial countries	3.9	2.1	1.8	3.7	2.0
Developing countries	3.6	3.4	0.9	3.5	2.7
Low-income countries	3.3	3.0	4.0	3.4	2.7
Asia	3.6	3.4	4.5	3.7	3.0
Africa	1.2	−0.1	−1.7	−0.1	−0.5
Middle-income oil importers	3.8	3.3	−0.2	3.6	2.6
Major exporters of manufactures	4.3	3.7	0.1	4.4	3.3
Other countries	2.5	2.1	−1.0	1.5	1.0
Middle-income oil exporters	3.5	3.1	−0.8	2.7	2.0

Note: Projections are from *World Development Report 1984*. Historical growth rates have been revised since last year's Report.
Source: World Bank data.

and that comes after ten years in which they have fallen steeply. Nothing could prove more clearly the urgent need for domestic policy reforms in Africa and for matching assistance from the world at large.

The second trend highlighted in Table 10.2 is the differing capacities of countries to benefit from improvements in the international environment and to resist any deterioration. Just as they have in the past, some of the major exporters of manufactures—such as Korea—could adjust rapidly to the vagaries of the world economy and maintain or increase their GDP growth rates. But the incipient economic recovery in some major debtor countries, particularly in Latin America, would be seriously set back by the Low case. Their difficulties in servicing their debt would increase enormously; the extra economic adjustments they would need

to make would strain the fabric of their societies.

The High and Low cases obviously produce very different outcomes for the current accounts and creditworthiness of developing countries. Last year's Report indicated that there were considerable uncertainties about the prospects for financing. Outcomes in the long term will depend on developments in the next five years. Accordingly, this Report examines that period in greater detail.

A period of transition, 1985–90

Many developing countries have made progress over the past few years in dealing with their financial difficulties. Despite this progress, the economic situation remains fragile in individual developing countries. As can be seen in Table 10.1, GDP growth in developing countries in 1980–85 is currently estimated at slightly more than one-half that of 1973–80. Despite export growth of close to 6 percent, imports have increased at a little more than 1 percent a year in recent years. The share of interest in total debt service has increased from 36 percent in 1979 to 52 percent in 1983. Many developing countries have run substantial trade surpluses in order to meet greatly increased interest payments. Current account deficits of developing countries declined sharply (in current prices) from $57 billion in 1983 to $36 billion in 1984. The high level of interest rates is thus one of the critical variables whose course will influence outcomes in the next five years. Developing countries need a rate of growth in export earnings in excess of the rate of interest to bring down the principal debt ratios to more sustainable levels, even if the current account net of interest payments remains in balance.

Over the next five years, policies in industrial and developing countries will determine whether developing countries can make a smooth transition back to creditworthiness and steady growth. In order to highlight the policy options and their consequences for developing countries in 1985–90, two simulations have been prepared: a High simulation which embodies policies that result in progress in adjustment, and a Low simulation which essentially assumes no particular further progress in adjustment.

Three aspects of industrial-country policy are particularly relevant.

• *Monetary-fiscal balance.* The High simulation assumes a sustained reduction in budget deficits in major industrial countries, particularly in the United States. By the end of the decade, deficits are assumed to be about one-third less than the levels that governments are currently projecting for that year. This permits steps to be taken to redress the monetary-fiscal balance and to accentuate international cooperation required for noninflationary growth in industrial countries. In these circumstances, real interest rates could be expected to come down by 1990 to the levels that prevailed in the 1960s and exchange rate relationships to become more reasonable. The Low simulation, on the other hand, assumes that fiscal deficits in 1990 will be no lower than officially projected. Real interest rates could thus be expected to rise and the exchange value of the U.S. dollar to continue to be strong.

• *Labor markets.* The High simulation assumes that industrial economies will have increased success in reducing rigidities in labor markets—an

indication of success in addressing adjustment problems—in the next few years. As a result, there is a reduction in unemployment rates, and the annual increase in real labor costs in industrial economies is assumed to slow by two percentage points. The Low simulation assumes that a failure to tackle labor market rigidities would contribute to some increases in real labor costs and to keeping unemployment, particularly in Europe, at high levels.

• *Protectionism.* Rapid and noninflationary growth in industrial economies in the High simulation would permit governments to reduce protection over the next few years. This would help to stimulate a more rapid growth of international trade from which both industrial and developing countries would draw benefits. By contrast, the Low simulation assumes that difficulties in adjustment and low rates of economic growth contribute to substantially increased protection against exports from developing countries.

The implications of these assumptions are summarized in Table 10.3. The average annual growth rate in industrial countries is nearly a percentage point higher (3.5 versus 2.7 percent) in the High simulation than in the Low. It should be noted that

Table 10.3 Average performance of industrial and developing countries, 1980–90
(average annual percentage change)

Country group	1980–85	1985–90 High	Low
Industrial countries			
GDP growth	2.3	3.5	2.7
Inflation rate[a]	0.5	7.5	5.0
Real interest rate[b,c]	6.8	2.5	6.5
Nominal lending rate[c]	12.6	6.1	11.8
Developing countries			
GDP growth	3.0	5.5	4.1
Low-income countries	5.9	5.6	5.2
Asia	6.4	5.8	5.4
Africa	1.4	3.4	2.5
Middle-income oil importers	1.9	5.9	3.6
Major exporters of manufactures	2.1	6.4	3.8
Other countries	1.5	4.2	2.8
Middle-income oil exporters	1.8	4.7	3.6
Export growth	5.7	6.7	3.5
Manufactures	9.7	10.4	5.4
Primary goods	2.8	3.1	1.7
Import growth	1.2	8.8	2.4

Note: Projected growth rates are based on a sample of ninety developing countries.
a. Industrial countries' U.S. dollar GDP deflator. Inflation in the United States is 3.5 percent a year in the High and 5 percent a year in the Low simulation.
b. Average of six-month U.S. dollar Eurocurrency rates, deflated by the rate of change in the GDP deflator of the United States.
c. End of period rate.
Source: World Bank data.

part of the reason for the faster growth in industrial countries is that they expand their exports to developing countries by 7.7 percent a year on average—whereas, in the Low simulation, those exports fall by an average of 1 percent a year. The difference is primarily due to increased protection in the industrial countries themselves—a vivid demonstration of how protection will reduce both imports and exports of the countries that raise the trade barriers. Higher protection in the Low simulation implies that developing countries have their export growth reduced to only 3.5 percent a year, compared with 6.7 percent a year in the High simulation. As a result, they have to cut back on their imports as well.

The difference in real interest rates between the High and Low simulations is also very striking. It is caused by a combination of three factors:

• The continued growth in fiscal deficits in the Low simulation keeps up the demand for credit.

• The deteriorating current accounts of the developing countries also have the same effect. Both of these run up against:

• Lower private savings in industrial economies, the result of slower GDP growth and larger increases in real labor costs.

Implications for developing countries

The simulations show a range of possibilities for developing countries over the next five years. It is assumed in both simulations that developing countries continue to implement policies required for structural adjustment. The specific policies differ by country, but generally involve improvements in three principal areas—key economic prices, exchange rates and trade policies, and domestic savings. These measures are designed to improve the efficiency of utilization of domestic and external resources and to ensure that external capital complements and does not substitute for domestic resources. Economic policies of individual developing countries thus are assumed to continue to play a central role in determining future outcomes. In the High simulation, investment in developing countries is more than 25 percent higher in 1990 than it is in the Low simulation. GDP growth is sustained at a healthy 5.5 percent a year in the High, but would be only 4.1 percent a year in the Low simulation. As the population of developing countries grows by about 2 percent a year, GDP per capita would rise more than half again as fast in the High simulation as in the Low—3.7 percent a year against 2.3 percent a year.

These aggregate numbers hide substantial regional variations. The average annual growth rate of GDP in low-income countries is reduced by 0.4 percentage points between the High and Low simulations; for African countries, it is 0.9 percentage points. For the middle-income oil importers, the difference is much greater—2.3 percentage points a year—because they are more affected by higher interest rates (on their debt) and increased protectionism (on their manufactured exports).

Under the High simulation, major exporters of manufactures would expand their manufactured exports at 10.5 percent a year (see Table 10.4), somewhat faster growth than they achieved in 1980–85. As a group, the middle-income oil importers would raise their GDP growth from the doldrums of the early 1980s to 5.9 percent a year in 1985–90—almost back to what they achieved in the 1960s and 1970s. Even among these countries, however, differences in economic performance could be expected. Under both the High and Low simulations, the more flexible East Asian econo-

Table 10.4 Change in trade in developing countries, 1980–90
(average annual percentage change)

Country group	Exports of goods and nonfactor services			Exports of manufactures			Exports of primary goods			Imports of goods and nonfactor services		
		1985–90			1985–90			1985–90			1985–90	
	1980–85	High	Low	1980–85	High	Low	1980–85	High	Low	1980–85	High	Low
Developing countries	5.4	6.8	3.6	9.7	10.4	5.4	2.8	3.1	1.7	1.1	9.3	2.5
Low-income countries	7.1	5.5	2.6	8.6	9.5	4.5	5.4	2.6	1.3	4.2	7.2	1.6
Asia	9.2	6.0	2.8	9.6	9.5	4.6	8.0	2.5	1.2	5.9	8.1	2.1
Africa	−1.6	2.5	1.5	−12.6	8.6	3.7	−1.2	3.1	1.8	−2.1	2.6	−0.8
Middle-income oil importers	7.2	8.2	4.3	9.3	10.4	5.5	5.7	3.4	2.1	1.5	10.9	2.9
Major exporters of manufactures	7.5	8.9	4.7	9.1	10.5	5.5	6.4	3.6	2.3	1.8	12.1	3.7
Other countries	6.3	4.8	2.6	12.1	9.6	4.7	4.4	3.1	1.7	0.6	5.9	−0.1
Middle-income oil exporters	1.0	4.1	2.1	17.0	11.0	6.0	0.0	2.8	1.5	−1.6	6.4	1.9

Source: World Bank data.

mies would continue to grow faster than Latin American countries. On average, the East Asian countries are less indebted, and their resilience to external shocks is greater. The large group of middle-income oil importers (other than major exporters of manufactures) would, in the High simulation, see their exports grow rapidly enough to permit them not only to meet required interest payments, but also to resume import growth (5.9 percent a year) and improve capacity utilization and economic growth. In the Low simulation, to the contrary, middle-income countries would be required to continue the compression of imports and cuts in investment that have characterized recent years. This would put in severe jeopardy efforts to achieve structural adjustments and establish the base for resumed growth in the 1990s. No doubt there is room for increasing allocative efficiency of economic resources, especially energy, in many middle-income countries. But the economic outcomes portrayed for them raise questions about the ability of sociopolitical fabrics in many countries to withstand such continuing pressures. The development crisis in many middle-income countries would become more pronounced.

For many low-income African countries, the economic outlook is bleak. The Low simulation would mean another five-year period of falling per capita incomes. Incipient economic reforms in many of these countries would surely fall victim to an international environment in which primary commodity prices would not improve from present very depressed levels, imports would need to be compressed further, and additional aid flows would not be available. Unfortunately, the High simulation holds out hopes only for a maintenance of average per capita incomes at the low levels to which they had declined by 1984. Additional external assistance, by itself, is not the key to dealing with the problems of low-income African countries. Reforms of domestic economic policies to improve the utilization of domestic and external resources are essential. Without them, no amount of external assistance can improve the economic conditions of African countries. Nonetheless, such reforms are unlikely to be effectively sustained unless there are parallel reforms in donor programs. Donors must, in particular, be willing to make adequate financial assistance, over and above that projected in the High simulation, available to support those low-income African countries that are implementing substantial policy reforms.

The Low simulation would also be a setback for

low-income Asia; although growing more rapidly than Africa, low-income Asian countries would be faced with a deteriorating external environment for trade and finance just when they are making progress in liberalizing their economies. They would hardly be encouraged to liberalize any further. But if the High simulation prevails, they could grow at 5.8 percent a year (or somewhat below the 6.4 percent growth rate of recent years). In the process, they would restructure their economies for stable and sustained growth in the 1990s.

Capital flows and debt

The financial implications of the two scenarios show profound differences (see Table 10.5 and Figure 10.1). In the High simulation, the developing countries' interest payments on medium- and long-term debt (in 1980 dollars) decline from $59 billion in 1984 to $45 billion in 1990. Interest payments in 1990 would be far outweighed by exports. The most significant outcome of the High simulation is that the creditworthiness of developing countries improves, partly because they persist with the policy reforms that are under way in many countries. As a result, developing countries would obtain more external capital (see Table 10.5)—enough to finance a rise in their current account deficits (in 1980 dollars) from $36 billion in 1984 to $61 billion in 1990. The bulk of that increase is accounted for by low-income Asian countries, which with their limited debt and low debt service ratios are also projected to attract more capital inflows, and by major exporters of manufactures and the oil exporters.

In the High simulation, total net financing flows (see Table 10.6) would increase in current prices from $72 billion in 1984 to $121 billion in 1990, or at an average annual rate of 11.6 percent. In 1980 prices, the growth rate would be only 3.8 percent a year, and total net financing flows would be only slightly larger in 1990 than they were in 1980. Net ODA flows are projected to be 0.37 percent of GNP of industrial countries and to increase by 10.3 percent a year in current prices and 2.7 percent a year in 1980 dollars. This would provide some limited scope for meeting the financing needs of low-income African countries without continuing the current process of diverting concessional financing from other low-income countries. An adequate response to the financing needs of low-income African countries would require aid flows larger than those projected in the High simulation. The share of net private capital flows (nonconcessional

Table 10.5 Current account balance and its financing in developing countries, 1984 and 1990
(billions of 1980 dollars)

Item	Developing countries			Low-income Asia			Low-income Africa		
	1984[a]	High 1990	Low 1990	1984[a]	High 1990	Low 1990	1984[a]	High 1990	Low 1990
Net exports of goods and nonfactor services	14.5	−38.6	6.3	−8.9	−19.9	−12.8	−3.9	−3.7	−3.0
Interest on medium- and long-term debt	−59.3	−44.9	−76.3	−1.9	−3.5	−4.2	−1.0	−1.0	−1.5
Official	−10.8	−12.8	−18.4	−1.1	−1.4	−1.8	−0.4	−0.9	−1.3
Private	−48.5	−32.1	−57.9	−0.8	−2.1	−2.3	−0.6	−0.1	−0.2
Current account balance[b]	−36.4	−60.7	−48.6	−3.2	−15.7	−9.4	−4.7	−4.3	−4.2
Net official transfers	12.2	15.2	14.5	2.0	1.9	1.8	2.0	2.4	2.3
Medium- and long-term loans[c]	51.3	55.1	36.6	6.7	15.7	7.4	2.1	1.9	1.8
Official	26.2	20.4	20.2	4.3	5.1	5.0	2.3	2.3	2.2
Private	25.1	34.7	16.4	2.4	10.6	2.4	−0.2	−0.4	−0.4
Debt outstanding and disbursed	702.5	716.2	741.4	54.1	93.2	78.8	27.2	27.1	29.6
As percentage of GNP	33.8	24.7	27.8	9.7	11.9	10.3	54.6	44.6	51.5
As percentage of exports	135.4	98.2	133.1	100.0	131.0	148.4	278.1	250.3	328.1
Debt service as percentage of exports	19.7	16.0	28.0	8.4	10.6	15.6	19.9	25.2	37.5

Note: The table is based on a sample of ninety developing countries. The GDP deflator for industrial countries was used to deflate all items. Details may not add to totals because of rounding. Net exports in this table exclude factor services and thus differ from those in Table 10.6. Net exports plus interest does not equal the current account balance because of the omission of net workers' remittances, private transfers, and investment income. The current account balance not financed by official transfers and loans is covered by direct foreign investment, other capital (including short-term credit and errors and omissions), and changes in reserves. Ratios are calculated using current price data.

private capital and direct investment) in total flows is projected to be in 1990 similar to that in 1980. Nonconcessional private lending (mainly by commercial banks) is projected to increase by 13.0 percent a year in current prices (5.1 percent a year in 1980 dollars). Private direct investment is projected to increase by 12 percent a year in current prices (4.2 percent in 1980 dollars).

Despite the increase in external finance in the High simulation, the main debt indicators all improve over the period. For developing countries as a group, debt outstanding as a percentage of exports declines from 135 percent in 1984 to 98 percent in 1990, and their debt service ratio falls from 20 to 16 percent. The prizes for achieving the High simulation are therefore substantial—a faster growth of output and exports, along with an improvement in creditworthiness and a reduction in the debt-servicing burden. The improvements in creditworthiness lead to increases in private financial flows in excess of interest payments by 1990 in most regions.

By contrast, the prospects offered by the Low simulation are very disturbing. Although developing countries are assumed to continue the policy reforms that are already in train, the less favorable external conditions produce slower growth and less external finance (see Table 10.6 and Figure 10.2). Total net financing flows would increase from $72 billion in 1984 to $82 billion in 1990; in 1980 prices, however, they would decline by 1.7 percent a year in the period 1985–90. This would be the result of very slow growth of official flows and a sharp contraction in lending by commercial banks. In the Low simulation, as in the High, ODA from industrial countries is assumed to be 0.37 percent of their GNP. However, since their GNP is lower in the Low simulation, ODA in 1990 is 15 percent less in current dollars (or 3.7 percent less in 1980 dollars). This would have major consequences for low-income countries, particularly those in Africa. Redistributing concessional capital among low-income countries would not be an adequate answer to their increased needs. Nonconcessional private lending (mainly by commercial banks) is projected to increase by 13.0 percent a year in current prices (5.1 percent in 1980 dollars) in the High simulation and decline by 5.0 percent a year in current prices (9.5 percent in 1980 dollars) in the Low, reflecting changes in creditworthiness and the differences in real interest rates. The rate of growth in private direct investment is projected to be 8.4 percent in current prices (3.2 percent in 1980 dollars) in the Low. Overall, net financing flows grow more than three times faster in current prices in the High simulation than the Low; in 1980

Middle-income countries								
Major exporters of manufacturers			Other oil-importing countries			Oil-exporting countries		
1984[a]	High 1990	Low 1990	1984[a]	High 1990	Low 1990	1984[a]	High 1990	Low 1990
20.0	−4.9	14.6	−9.8	−8.2	−2.2	17.1	−1.8	9.8
−26.4	−19.3	−33.7	−8.2	−6.3	−10.9	−21.7	−14.8	−26.2
−3.9	−4.4	−6.3	−2.5	−2.9	−4.2	−2.9	−3.3	−4.9
−22.5	−14.9	−27.4	−5.7	−3.5	−6.7	−18.9	−11.5	−21.3
−9.6	−19.7	−15.0	−15.4	−10.8	−10.7	−3.6	−10.2	−9.2
3.8	6.0	5.7	2.6	2.9	2.8	1.9	2.0	1.9
17.9	21.2	12.9	11.1	6.2	5.3	13.6	10.2	9.3
7.8	3.7	3.7	5.5	4.6	4.5	6.3	4.8	4.8
10.1	17.5	9.2	5.6	1.6	0.8	7.3	5.4	4.5
273.1	274.1	280.6	110.6	107.4	116.8	237.6	214.4	235.6
37.6	25.9	30.6	53.0	39.9	47.6	43.8	29.5	34.7
109.1	67.8	97.0	183.9	139.5	189.5	164.3	129.1	163.5
16.0	12.9	24.2	24.9	22.0	36.9	28.1	22.7	35.9

a. Estimated.
b. Excludes official transfers.
c. Net disbursements.
Source: World Bank data.

dollars, they increase by 3.8 percent a year in the High simulation and decline by 1.7 percent a year in the Low. In addition, interest rates increase significantly in the Low simulation, so that interest payments on medium- and long-term debt would increase from $58 billion in 1984 to $100 billion in current prices (and $76 billion in 1980 dollars) in 1990. Given the small amount of new capital they would obtain, developing countries would virtually have to double their trade surpluses just to satisfy their interest obligations. It is generally doubtful whether they could do that—or whether an increasingly protectionist trading regime would even allow them to try.

The full extent of the difficulties of the Low simulation are apparent from the indicators of developing countries' indebtedness. If current account deficits should increase as projected, in 1980 dollars, from $36 billion in 1984 to $49 billion in 1990, the outstanding debt of all developing countries would fall only slightly from the high present level of about 135 percent of exports, and the debt service ratio would rise to 28 percent, from 20 percent in 1984. Three groups of countries—low-income Africa, middle-income oil importers (aside from the main exporters of manufactures), and the oil exporters—would have debt service ratios of about 36 percent. The need for reschedulings and the

pressures for "involuntary" lending would be greatly increased.

Policies and priorities

The projections made in this chapter underline the essential message of the Report: the world has made progress in overcoming the financial difficulties of the early 1980s, but it still has much to do. Debt cannot be seen in isolation, as something that occasionally becomes a "crisis," needing urgent attention. On the contrary, international finance is an essential part of economic development in an interdependent world. If it reaches the proportions of a crisis, that is because countries have mishandled their policies over many years.

The constructive and collaborative actions by debtors, creditors, and international institutions to smooth out debt service payments in the context of countries' adjustment efforts needs to be continued. The objective is to accelerate the return to creditworthiness of countries that are pursuing sound economic policies and have sizable short- to medium-term debt-servicing requirements. Consideration needs to be given to the extent to which multiyear debt restructurings for official credits and other arrangements might be considered on a case by case basis as part of the overall financial

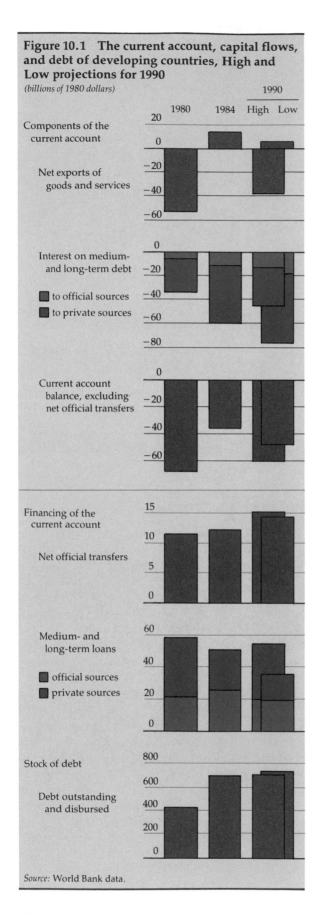

Figure 10.1   The current account, capital flows, and debt of developing countries, High and Low projections for 1990

(billions of 1980 dollars)

Components of the current account

Net exports of goods and services

Interest on medium- and long-term debt

■ to official sources
■ to private sources

Current account balance, excluding net official transfers

Financing of the current account

Net official transfers

Medium- and long-term loans

■ official sources
■ private sources

Stock of debt

Debt outstanding and disbursed

Source: World Bank data.

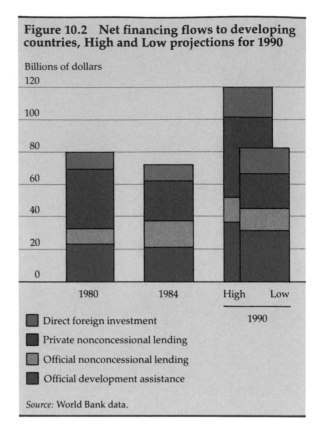

Figure 10.2   Net financing flows to developing countries, High and Low projections for 1990

Billions of dollars

□ Direct foreign investment
■ Private nonconcessional lending
▨ Official nonconcessional lending
■ Official development assistance

Source: World Bank data.

package supporting stabilization and adjustment, particularly in low-income sub-Saharan African countries committed to strong adjustment efforts.

The prospects for the next ten years do not exclude the possibility of further debt-servicing difficulty for many developing countries. The Low scenarios in this chapter show how it could happen. The world economy does not need to slump, as it did in 1981–82, for debt problems to recur. If industrial economies grow at 2.7 percent a year for the next five years, as in the Low simulation, and this growth is accompanied by high real interest rates and increased protectionism, several groups of developing countries could find themselves with heavier debt-servicing burdens at the end of this decade than they had at the beginning.

The financial outcomes of the Low scenarios are, of course, just one aspect of a much wider failure. Slow economic growth in the industrial countries would increase their unemployment, adding to the protectionist pressures that would, if conceded to, hamper growth still further. The attainment of long-term potential growth by industrial economies in the next ten years would become more remote. The developing countries would find it hard to liberalize their economic policies if their export efforts were frustrated by trade barriers and

Table 10.6 Net financing flows to developing countries in selected years, 1980–90
(billions of dollars, unless otherwise noted)

| | | | | 1990 | | Growth rate (percent)[a] | 1985–90 | |
| | | | | | | 1970–80 | | |
Type of flow	1980	1983	1984	High	Low	1970–80	High	Low
Official development assistance[b]								
Current dollars	23.4	19.9	21.3	36.8	31.7	16.8	10.3	7.1
1980 dollars	23.4	20.2	21.8	25.1	24.2	6.1	2.7	2.0
Noncessional loans								
Current dollars	46.7	40.6	40.8	66.3	35.1	23.6	12.3	−1.2
1980 dollars	46.7	41.2	41.8	45.2	26.9	12.3	4.4	−5.9
Official								
Current dollars	9.8	12.7	16.3	15.4	13.7	25.3	9.9	7.4
1980 dollars	9.8	12.8	16.6	10.5	10.5	13.9	2.3	2.3
Private								
Current dollars	36.8	28.0	24.6	51.0	21.4	23.1	13.0	−5.0
1980 dollars	36.8	28.4	25.1	34.7	16.4	11.9	5.1	−9.5
Direct investment								
Current dollars	10.6	10.3	9.4	18.1	15.4	16.4	12.0	8.4
1980 dollars	10.6	10.5	9.6	12.3	11.8	5.8	4.2	3.2
Total								
Current dollars	80.6	70.9	71.5	121.3	82.1	20.1	11.6	3.2
1980 dollars	80.6	71.9	73.2	82.6	62.9	9.1	3.8	−1.7
Memo items								
Net exports of goods and services[d]								
Current dollars	−92.8	−82.2	−61.5	−132.4	−101.0	..	..	..
1980 dollars	−92.8	−83.4	−62.9	−90.2	−77.3	..	..	..
Current account balance[e]								
Current dollars	−67.8	−56.7	−35.6	−89.2	−63.4	..	..	..
1980 dollars	−67.8	−57.5	−36.4	−60.7	−48.6	..	..	..
ODA from DAC countries as a percentage of their GNP	0.38	0.38	0.38	0.37	0.37	..	..	..

Note: All items net of repayments. Data are for a sample of ninety countries.
a. Average annual percentage change.
b. Includes ODA grants (official transfers). DAC reporting includes, and the World Bank Debtor Reporting System excludes, ODA flows from nonmarket economies and the technical assistance component of grants. There are also differences in coverage of recipient countries in the two data sources.
c. Excludes short-term capital and reserve changes.
d. Net exports of goods and nonfactor services plus net investment receipts minus interest on medium- and long-term debt.
e. Excludes official transfers.
Source: World Bank data.

by limited availability of official finance, including ODA. Yet a retreat from liberalization would slow down their economic growth and compound their debt-servicing difficulties. For many countries, development in its widest sense—people leading longer, healthier, fuller lives—would have to take second place to sheer economic survival.

However, such outcomes are avoidable. The High scenarios offer an entirely different prospect, of faster and more stable growth for both industrial and developing countries and improving credit-worthiness for every group of developing countries. This is not just a hope for the 1990s; it could be achieved during the transition of the next five years. And, it needs emphasizing, the High scenarios do not describe some idealized set of outcomes. They start from the less than ideal circumstances of 1985, with all its awkward legacies, and

proceed through a realistic set of assumptions about the future.

Those assumptions chiefly concern the policy choices of governments. For the industrial countries, the assumptions reflect the proclaimed goals of government leaders: smaller budget deficits, more flexible labor markets, freer trade. These policies would produce the results that governments say they want: faster growth, less unemployment, lower real interest rates, and low inflation. The means and the ends of the High scenarios are the same as those being discussed and strived for in the industrial countries. There is no gap between economic model and political reality.

The same is true for the developing countries. The High scenarios assume that the policy reforms already under way in many countries will be continued. The objectives of those policies—to restructure economies, ease debt-servicing burdens, and restore economic growth—are the results projected in the High scenarios. However difficult the policy reforms may have been to adopt, in due course they will create much easier conditions for developing countries than would prevail if the reforms are diluted or abandoned.

The High scenarios therefore convey a strong sense of encouragement. Policies and policy aspirations are on the right lines; governments are trying to steer their economies in directions that will indeed bear fruit. The achievements of the 1950s and 1960s—strong growth, low inflation, financial stability—can be recaptured. Under these circumstances, provided institutional innovations take place, normal relationships between private creditors and debtor countries can be resumed, and concessional aid can be expected to increase. International capital can then resume its productive role in economic development.

The role of the World Bank

The role of the Bank as a provider of finance and other services must be seen in the context of the increased importance of international finance in economic development. The Bank is playing an increasingly active role in assisting developing countries with needed policy reforms. It has been flexible in adapting its operations and instruments to the changing needs of its member countries. It complements and—to the extent possible—exercises a constructive influence on capital flows from other sources. In order to carry out these functions, the Bank's own financing must be on a scale that is meaningful both to borrowing countries and to other sources of finance.

The Bank is the major channel by which developing countries access the international bond market and other financial markets. This function is critical particularly for countries that rely mainly on commercial capital and are most sensitive to the impact of fluctuations in the world economy. Bank lending is an important component in the acceptable balance between official and private sources, between short- and long-term maturities, and between fixed and variable rate instruments.

Although the worldwide recession has meant temporary slowdowns in many investment projects in developing countries and reductions in private and public investment, resumed growth will involve increased ability to use external resources productively. The resumption of growth of private capital flows will be more likely if private

investors have confidence in the policies and programs of the recipient countries. Here, the Bank plays a dual role. In its own lending, the Bank has a unique perspective from which to analyze a country's prospects and needed policy reforms and to provide this analysis to policymakers. In its cofinancing efforts, the Bank provides instruments to increase the assurance of investors in projects and countries' development prospects. In order to carry out these functions, the Bank's ability to increase its own lending is crucial.

Low-income countries that must depend on concessional capital have experienced relative stagnation in new commitments in recent years. Attention has focused on sub-Saharan Africa, where the prospect for a dramatic decrease in concessional flows has been highlighted as an overriding obstacle to achieving sustainable development. This underscores the need for a substantial increase in IDA resources in the medium term to meet the needs of this region and to provide uninterrupted support to IDA borrowers in Asia.

In its proposals to respond to the potential decline in funds for sub-Saharan Africa, the Bank has stressed that increases in the volume of aid to the region must go hand in hand with improvements in aid effectiveness. It has also been recognized that ODA flows to Africa could be better utilized with new forms of aid coordination that emphasize targeted support by lenders for reform efforts by borrowers. The potential Bank contribution to achieving these dual objectives through enhanced aid coordination has received strong support from the aid community. In exercising this function, the Bank is prepared to assist borrowing governments in strengthening existing mechanisms for investment review to help ensure that proposed projects are consistent with explicit development priorities and with the capacity to effectively implement and operate projects.

The Bank also has a long history of collaboration with export credit agencies and commercial banks. Various cofinancing instruments have been developed and will continue to evolve in the future as the demand increases for resources from the Bank and other sources of finance. The Bank could, through its assessments of investment programs and individual projects, support the efforts of both export credit agencies and commercial banks to improve the quality of lending, thereby increasing the development benefits of such flows while strengthening the portfolios of the lending institutions. Beyond specific cofinancing arrangements, the Bank's role in regularly reviewing country policies and performance against the medium-term growth objectives should provide a basis for encouraging the flow of new lending into high-priority sectors and investments.

To ensure that the resumption of growth is sustainable, the continuing adjustment efforts must be based on a stable economy and a sound medium-term policy framework. This requires that the Bank's relations with the International Monetary Fund enable both institutions to provide consistent, effective support to their members. This objective is critical in resolving stabilization problems and in supporting the transition to sustainable growth in major middle-income debtor countries whose economies have recently begun to recover. This implies the need for a coherent approach to policy issues and coordinated efforts to mobilize support for policy reform.

Finally, foreign direct investment is an important aspect of the Bank's catalytic role and its function in international capital flows. In the past, the Bank Group has sought to encourage private investment both directly, through the activities of the IFC and certain specific Bank projects, and indirectly, by financing investments in physical and human infrastructure and by helping governments revise their foreign investment codes. Much of the work the Bank does in support of structural adjustment is also directly related to the prospects for private investment. An important new initiative is the proposed Multilateral Investment Guarantee Agency, which would provide various forms of guarantees to foreign investments, including multinationally financed investments, and reinsure guarantees written by national insurance agencies.

Statistical appendix

The tables in this Statistical Appendix present data for a sample panel of developing countries, along with information available for developed countries and high-income oil exporters. The tables show data on population, national accounts, trade, and external debt. The data shown have been used extensively for the analysis in this Report. Readers are urged to refer to the Technical Notes to the World Development Indicators for definitions and concepts used in these tables.

Table A.1 Population growth, 1965–84 and projected to 2000

Country group	1984 population (millions)	Average annual growth (percent)				
		1965–73	1973–80	1980–84	1984–90	1990–2000
Developing countries	3,386	2.4	2.0	2.0	1.8	1.8
Low-income countries	2,263	2.4	1.8	1.8	1.8	1.7
Asia	2,040	2.4	1.7	1.7	1.6	1.4
India	749	2.3	2.3	2.2	2.0	1.7
China	1,032	2.4	1.2	1.3	1.0	0.9
Africa	223	2.6	2.8	3.1	3.3	3.4
Middle-income countries	1,123	2.4	2.4	2.4	2.2	2.1
Oil exporters	491	2.5	2.6	2.6	2.5	2.4
Oil importers	632	2.4	2.2	2.2	2.1	1.9
Major exporters of manufactures	413	2.3	2.1	2.0	1.9	1.7
High-income oil exporters	19	4.5	5.3	4.4	3.9	3.4
Industrial market economies	729	0.9	0.7	0.5	0.5	0.4
World, excluding nonmarket industrial economies	4,134	2.1	1.8	1.8	1.6	1.6
Nonmarket industrial economies	390	0.8	0.8	0.8	0.7	0.6

Table A.2 Population and GNP per capita, 1980, and growth rates, 1965–84

Country group	1980 GNP (billions of dollars)	1980 population (millions)	1980 GNP per capita (dollars)	Average annual growth of GNP per capita (percent)					
				1965–73	1973–80	1981	1982	1983[a]	1984[b]
Developing countries	2,059	3,119	660	4.1	3.3	0.8	−0.7	−0.1	2.1
Low-income countries	547	2,098	260	3.0	3.1	2.0	2.8	5.2	4.7
Asia	495	1,901	260	3.2	3.5	2.5	3.4	6.0	5.3
China	284	980	290	4.9	4.5	1.6	5.8	7.6	7.7
India	162	687	240	1.7	1.9	3.5	0.4	4.2	2.0
Africa	52	197	270	1.3	0.0	−1.7	−2.6	−2.6	−1.5
Middle-income oil importers	962	579	1,660	4.6	3.1	−0.8	−2.0	−1.6	1.1
East Asia and Pacific	212	162	1,310	5.6	5.7	3.7	1.9	4.5	3.4
Middle East and North Africa	25	31	830	3.5	4.3	−2.5	2.6	0.5	−1.3
Sub-Saharan Africa	26	33	780	2.0	0.5	4.1	−4.8	−5.4	−5.4
Southern Europe	214	91	2,350	5.4	2.9	0.2	0.3	−0.5	0.2
Latin America and Caribbean	409	234	1,750	4.5	2.9	−4.1	−4.8	−4.5	1.1
Middle-income oil exporters	550	442	1,240	4.6	3.1	1.5	−2.3	−3.6	0.1
High-income oil exporters	229	16	14,050	4.1	6.2	−1.1	−7.8	−14.1	−6.4
Industrial market economies	7,477	714	10,480	3.7	2.1	0.7	−1.0	1.5	4.3

a. Estimated.
b. Projected.

Table A.3   GDP, 1980, and growth rates, 1965–84

Country group	1980 GDP (billions of dollars)	Average annual growth of GDP (percent)					
		1965–73	1973–80	1981	1982	1983[a]	1984[b]
Developing countries	2,085	6.6	5.5	3.3	1.9	2.0	4.1
Low-income countries	546	5.5	4.9	4.0	5.0	7.2	6.6
Asia	493	5.7	5.2	4.3	5.4	7.8	7.1
China	284	7.4	5.8	2.9	7.4	9.0	9.0
India	162	4.0	4.1	5.8	2.6	6.5	4.2
Africa	53	3.9	2.7	1.7	0.7	0.7	1.6
Middle-income oil importers	978	7.0	5.6	2.0	0.8	0.7	3.3
East Asia and Pacific	214	8.6	8.1	6.5	3.9	6.3	5.4
Middle East and North Africa	24	5.6	7.1	0.7	6.2	1.5	1.2
Sub-Saharan Africa	27	5.1	3.6	6.9	−1.0	−1.8	−2.1
Southern Europe	213	7.0	4.8	2.0	2.4	0.8	1.5
Latin America and Caribbean	420	7.1	5.4	−1.0	−1.5	−1.8	3.4
Middle-income oil exporters	561	7.1	5.8	4.6	0.9	−1.0	2.7
High-income oil exporters	230	9.2	7.7	0.1	−1.7	−7.0	0.6
Industrial market economies	7,440	4.7	2.8	1.4	−0.3	2.6	4.8

a. Estimated.   b. Projected.

Table A.4   Population and composition of GDP, selected years, 1965–84

(billions of dollars, unless otherwise specified)

Country group and indicator	1965	1973	1980	1981	1982	1983[a]	1984[b]
Developing countries							
GDP	327	736	2,085	2,210	2,126	2,046	2,111
Domestic absorption[c]	331	743	2,132	2,282	2,179	2,063	2,099
Net exports[d]	−4	−7	−47	−72	−53	−17	12
Population (millions)	2,239	2,710	3,119	3,183	3,251	3,319	3,386
Low-income countries							
GDP	141	248	546	537	539	561	593
Domestic absorption[c]	143	250	565	553	551	573	606
Net exports[d]	−2	−2	−19	−16	−12	−12	−13
Population (millions)	1,525	1,845	2,098	2,137	2,180	2,223	2,263
Middle-income oil importers							
GDP	128	333	978	1,034	1,027	940	963
Domestic absorption[c]	130	340	1,018	1,079	1,059	953	954
Net exports[d]	−2	−7	−40	−45	−32	−13	9
Population (millions)	412	496	579	592	605	618	632
Middle-income oil exporters							
GDP	58	155	561	639	560	545	555
Domestic absorption[c]	58	153	549	650	569	537	571
Net exports[d]	0	2	12	−11	−9	8	16
Population (millions)	302	369	442	454	466	478	491
High-income oil exporters							
GDP	7	28	230	266	255	219	. .
Domestic absorption[c]	5	16	148	174	193	. .	. .
Net exports[d]	2	12	82	92	62	. .	. .
Population (millions)	8	11	16	17	18	19	19
Industrial market economies							
GDP	1,369	3,240	7,440	7,498	7,418	7,672	8,417
Domestic absorption[c]	1,363	3,231	7,505	7,526	7,433	7,671	8,417
Net exports[d]	6	9	−65	−28	−15	1	0
Population (millions)	632	680	714	719	723	726	729

a. Estimated.   b. Projected.   c. Private consumption plus government consumption plus gross domestic investment.
d. Includes goods and nonfactor services.

Table A.5 GDP structure of production, selected years, 1965–82

(percent of GDP)

Country group	1965 Agriculture	1965 Industry	1973 Agriculture	1973 Industry	1980 Agriculture	1980 Industry	1981 Agriculture	1981 Industry	1982 Agriculture	1982 Industry
Developing countries	31	29	26	33	20	38	19	37	19	36
Low-income countries	44	27	42	31	36	36	36	34	36	34
Asia	44	28	42	32	35	38	35	36	36	35
India	47	22	50	20	37	25	35	26	33	26
China	43	36	37	41	33	48	35	46	37	45
Africa	47	15	42	19	41	18	41	17	41	17
Middle-income countries	22	31	17	35	14	39	14	38	14	37
Oil exporters	22	26	18	33	14	42	13	40	14	40
Oil importers	21	33	17	35	14	37	14	36	13	36
Major exporters of manufactures	20	35	15	37	12	39	12	38	12	38
High-income oil exporters	5	65	2	72	1	77	1	76	1	74
Industrial market economies	5	40	5	39	4	38	3	37	3	36
World, excluding nonmarket industrial economies	10	38	9	38	7	39	7	38	7	37

Table A.6 Sector growth rates, 1965–82

Country group	Agriculture 1965–73	Agriculture 1973–80	Agriculture 1980–82	Industry 1965–73	Industry 1973–80	Industry 1980–82	Service 1965–73	Service 1973–80	Service 1980–82
Developing countries	3.4	2.0	3.2	7.9	6.5	0.7	7.7	6.4	4.0
Low-income countries	3.5	1.3	4.2	7.0	8.1	4.8	7.7	6.7	4.5
Asia	3.7	1.2	4.6	6.9	8.5	5.3	8.5	7.2	4.6
India	3.7	2.0	−0.4	3.7	5.0	4.6	4.5	5.7	8.3
China	3.8	0.2	7.7	9.0	10.0	5.3	21.4	8.9	0.3
Africa	2.2	2.2	1.4	7.8	1.0	−4.1	4.3	4.0	3.4
Middle-income countries	3.4	2.7	2.3	8.2	6.0	−0.6	7.7	6.4	3.8
Oil exporters	3.9	2.0	1.8	8.3	5.2	−0.2	7.4	7.9	5.8
Oil importers	3.1	3.1	2.5	8.2	6.5	−0.9	7.8	5.6	2.8
Major exporters of manufactures	3.0	2.9	3.1	8.8	7.2	−1.0	8.5	5.7	3.0
High-income oil exporters	..	..	..	..	2.3	−16.4	..	..	..
Industrial market economies	1.7	0.9	1.2	5.1	2.3	−1.0	4.6	3.3	1.5

Table A.7 Consumption, savings, and investment indicators, selected years, 1965–83
(percent of GDP)

Country group and indicator	1965	1973	1980	1981	1982	1983[a]
Developing countries						
Consumption	79.8	76.7	75.6	77.2	77.9	76.0
Investment	21.1	24.3	26.7	26.0	24.6	24.7
Savings	20.2	23.3	24.4	22.8	22.1	24.0
Low-income Asia						
Consumption	79.8	75.1	75.5	76.3	75.8	74.7
Investment	21.5	25.4	27.6	25.7	25.7	26.5
Savings	20.2	24.9	24.5	23.7	24.2	25.3
Low-income Africa						
Consumption	88.6	85.7	90.4	92.7	94.1	94.6
Investment	14.2	16.8	18.7	17.3	16.2	14.7
Savings	11.4	14.3	9.6	7.3	5.9	5.4
Middle-income oil importers						
Consumption	79.1	77.0	77.5	78.7	79.1	77.0
Investment	22.0	24.9	26.6	25.7	24.0	24.0
Savings	20.9	23.0	22.5	21.3	20.9	23.0
Middle-income oil exporters						
Consumption	79.9	76.8	71.0	74.2	76.0	71.2
Investment	19.8	22.3	26.7	27.6	25.7	26.2
Savings	20.1	23.2	29.0	25.8	24.0	28.8
Industrial market economies						
Consumption	76.7	75.0	78.4	78.4	80.1	80.0
Investment	22.9	24.7	22.5	21.9	20.1	20.0
Savings	23.3	25.0	21.6	21.6	19.9	20.0

a. Estimated.

Table A.8 Growth of exports, 1965–84

Country group and commodity	Average annual change in export volume (percent)					
	1965–73	1973–80	1981	1982	1983[a]	1984[b]
Export volume, by commodities						
Developing countries						
Manufactures	13.8	11.0	14.1	1.0	11.5	15.0
Food	2.2	5.4	12.4	11.8	4.6	4.8
Nonfood	3.6	1.6	0.7	−3.9	1.3	−1.8
Metals and minerals	5.7	5.5	−2.4	5.9	−5.2	3.9
Fuels	3.9	−1.0	−12.9	1.6	1.6	5.1
World, excluding nonmarket industrial economies						
Manufactures	10.7	5.8	6.0	−2.1	4.4	11.7
Food	4.5	9.0	7.2	9.9	6.0	7.0
Nonfood	3.2	3.6	3.1	−0.9	−9.7	0.2
Metals and minerals	6.8	7.2	−15.7	−4.0	−5.7	0.5
Fuels	9.5	0.7	−7.9	−11.2	−5.7	2.5
Export volume, by country group						
Developing countries	5.2	4.1	3.3	3.2	5.8	8.9
Manufactures	13.8	11.0	14.1	1.0	11.5	15.0
Primary goods	3.6	1.3	−3.4	4.8	1.8	4.2
Low-income countries	3.1	5.2	7.0	6.6	3.6	11.4
Manufactures	5.3	6.5	17.0	−4.8	6.2	23.5
Primary goods	2.0	4.4	−0.1	16.1	2.3	2.9
Asia	2.3	7.2	13.0	8.1	5.6	12.8
Manufactures	5.2	6.7	20.7	−3.8	6.5	24.0
Primary goods	−0.1	7.8	5.6	21.4	4.8	2.8
Africa	5.1	−0.5	−14.8	−0.7	−5.3	3.2
Manufactures	5.6	3.1	−33.4	−30.5	−7.3	2.5
Primary goods	5.0	−0.9	−12.1	2.7	−5.1	3.2
Middle-income oil importers	7.3	8.3	12.5	4.5	7.3	9.1
Manufactures	17.0	12.2	13.8	1.6	11.1	13.2
Primary goods	3.1	4.3	10.8	8.7	2.0	3.1
Major manufacturing exporters	10.0	9.7	13.7	4.0	8.0	9.6
Manufactures	17.4	12.6	13.8	1.4	10.9	12.9
Primary goods	5.1	5.5	13.6	9.2	2.6	2.8
Other middle-income oil importers	1.6	3.4	7.2	7.0	3.9	6.9
Manufactures	13.5	7.6	13.9	5.2	14.5	17.1
Primary goods	0.3	2.4	5.3	7.6	0.7	3.5
Middle-income oil exporters	4.2	−0.4	−11.6	−0.5	3.6	7.4
Manufactures	11.5	6.9	13.5	5.0	27.5	24.5
Primary goods	4.1	−0.7	−13.2	−0.9	1.6	5.5
High-income oil exporters	15.9	1.1	−7.3	−25.5	−15.8	−7.6
Industrial market economies	9.5	5.6	2.9	−1.1	2.5	10.0
World, excluding nonmarket industrial economies	9.1	4.7	2.0	−2.5	1.9	8.7

a. Estimated.
b. Projected.

Table A.9 Change in export prices and in terms of trade, 1965–84

(average annual percentage change)

Country group	1965–73	1973–80	1981	1982	1983[a]	1984[b]
Change in export prices						
Developing countries	6.0	14.7	−2.5	−6.1	−3.7	−1.0
Manufactures	5.1	10.9	−5.0	−1.9	−4.2	−2.8
Food	5.8	8.0	−12.1	−17.4	10.2	7.3
Nonfood	4.0	10.3	−13.5	−8.1	4.8	−3.4
Metals and minerals	1.8	5.8	−10.5	−9.5	0.5	−4.9
Fuels	7.9	27.2	12.5	−3.2	−12.4	−2.4
High-income oil exporters	7.4	24.8	8.3	−2.7	−11.3	−1.6
Industrial countries						
Total	4.7	10.1	−4.6	−4.0	−3.2	−1.5
Manufactures	4.7	10.9	−6.0	−2.1	−4.3	−2.3
Change in terms of trade						
Developing countries	0.5	2.0	0.5	−1.1	−0.6	1.0
Low-income countries	0.4	−1.5	−0.2	−1.5	0.9	4.1
Asia	0.8	−1.6	1.3	−2.2	0.4	3.5
Africa	−0.7	−1.0	−7.2	1.1	4.2	7.8
Middle-income oil importers	−0.2	−2.3	−5.0	−2.2	3.7	0.4
Middle-income oil exporters	−0.4	9.0	11.7	1.7	−8.5	0.9
High-income oil exporters	2.9	12.3	14.6	2.3	−8.6	−1.0
Industrial countries	−0.5	−3.5	−2.1	2.0	2.1	−0.2

a. Estimated. b. Projected.

Table A.10 Growth of long-term debt of developing countries, 1970–84

(average annual percentage change)

Country group	1970–73	1973–80	1981	1982	1983[a]	1984[a]
Developing countries						
Debt outstanding and disbursed	18.3	21.3	13.5	11.9	13.5	10.8
Official	15.3	17.6	9.7	10.4	9.8	13.2
Private	21.1	24.0	15.7	12.8	15.6	9.5
Low-income countries						
Debt outstanding and disbursed	12.9	16.0	5.5	8.0	6.3	10.8
Official	12.5	14.1	7.7	10.2	8.2	10.5
Private	16.0	24.9	−2.3	−1.0	−2.2	12.3
Asia						
Debt outstanding and disbursed	11.1	13.2	2.9	8.6	7.8	14.1
Official	11.6	11.2	6.2	10.1	7.4	10.6
Private	4.3	33.2	−12.4	0.1	10.5	36.0
Africa						
Debt outstanding and disbursed	19.7	22.6	10.2	6.9	3.7	4.7
Official	17.3	24.2	10.9	10.6	10.1	10.2
Private	24.4	19.7	8.5	−2.0	−13.5	−14.6
Middle-income oil importers						
Debt outstanding and disbursed	19.7	21.0	14.9	12.9	11.5	10.3
Official	17.8	18.5	12.1	11.0	13.4	15.0
Private	20.8	22.2	16.1	13.7	10.7	8.3
Major exporters of manufactures						
Debt outstanding and disbursed	22.6	20.8	14.7	13.0	12.1	10.2
Official	21.0	18.9	10.5	9.1	12.6	18.8
Private	23.2	21.4	15.9	14.1	12.0	7.9
Other middle-income oil importers						
Debt outstanding and disbursed	13.4	21.5	15.4	12.8	9.9	10.5
Official	14.6	18.0	13.9	13.0	14.3	11.0
Private	11.9	25.8	16.8	12.5	5.8	10.0
Middle-income oil exporters						
Debt outstanding and disbursed	19.6	24.9	14.6	11.8	19.9	11.5
Official	15.5	20.6	7.9	9.4	4.9	12.8
Private	22.6	27.1	17.5	12.7	25.8	11.1

a. The increase in debt outstanding and disbursed and the shift from private to official sources is in part due to the impact of rescheduling.

Table A.11 Savings, investment, and the current account balance, 1965–83
(percent)

Country	Gross domestic investment/GNP			Gross national savings/GNP			Current account balance/GNP[a]		
	1965–72	1973–78	1979–83	1965–72	1973–78	1979–83	1965–72	1973–78	1979–83
Latin America and Caribbean									
*Argentina	20.4	24.6	20.5	20.3	26.2	17.9	−0.1	1.6	−2.6
Bolivia	17.5	21.1	9.0	12.9	16.1	−7.2	−4.6	−5.0	−16.2
*Brazil	25.8	28.1	22.5	24.0	24.0	17.6	−0.8	−4.1	−4.9
*Chile	15.3	15.3	17.2	13.0	11.9	7.0	−2.3	−3.4	−10.2
Colombia	19.0	18.8	20.0	15.4	19.1	17.2	−3.6	−0.3	−2.8
Costa Rica	21.2	24.5	27.1	11.9	17.7	11.5	−9.3	−6.8	−15.6
Ecuador	18.6	26.4	24.2	11.3	20.4	20.5	−7.3	−6.0	−3.7
Guatemala	13.2	19.3	15.6	10.2	14.8	11.7	−3.0	−4.5	−3.9
Jamaica	32.2	20.3	21.6	22.3	12.8	6.5	−9.9	−7.5	−15.1
*Mexico	21.3	23.4	26.1	19.2	20.2	24.2	−2.1	−3.2	−1.9
Peru	16.7	18.0	17.0	15.2	11.4	13.5	−1.5	−6.6	−3.5
Uruguay	11.9	14.4	15.2	11.8	10.6	10.3	− 0.1	−3.8	−4.9
*Venezuela	29.1	35.4	26.2	29.8	36.1	29.3	0.7	0.7	3.1
Africa									
Cameroon	15.6	21.6	26.0	12.3	17.6	19.4	−3.3	−4.0	−6.6
Ethiopia	13.1	9.5	10.1	10.7	7.6	3.4	−2.4	−1.9	−6.7
Ghana	12.4	10.0	4.2	8.8	9.5	3.9	−4.3	−0.6	−0.3
Ivory Coast	21.1	25.9	29.3	15.9	23.1	17.4	−5.2	−2.8	−11.9
Kenya	21.7	25.4	26.1	17.0	17.3	15.5	−4.7	−8.1	−10.6
Liberia	24.7	32.6	27.7	27.6	17.0	11.9	2.9	−15.6	−15.8
Malawi	19.8	29.8	25.0	4.8	17.4	11.2	−15.0	−12.4	−13.8
Niger	15.9	29.3	30.7	6.5	12.3	15.0	−9.4	−17.1	−15.7
Nigeria	20.0	28.0	25.2	15.2	28.8	23.8	−4.8	0.8	1.4
Senegal	13.7	18.9	17.3	6.4	7.7	−3.1	−7.3	−11.2	−20.4
Sierra Leone	14.0	13.2	14.5	8.0	3.1	−2.0	−6.0	−10.1	−16.5
Sudan	11.9	17.3	16.0	11.0	9.1	0.9	−0.9	−8.2	−15.1
Tanzania	19.7	20.5	21.6	17.7	11.3	9.8	−2.0	−9.2	−11.8
Zaire	27.7	29.3	18.9	20.9	9.1	11.2	−6.8	−20.2	−7.7
Zambia	32.5	31.8	19.1	38.1	24.6	6.7	5.6	−7.2	−12.4
South Asia									
*India	18.3	21.7	24.6	13.4	19.2	21.0	−4.9	−2.5	−3.6
Pakistan	16.3	15.9	15.8	10.2	10.0	12.1	−6.1	−5.9	−3.7
Sri Lanka	16.1	16.2	29.9	11.3	11.9	10.9	−4.8	−4.3	−19.0
East Asia									
*Indonesia	12.6	20.6	23.0	6.9	18.8	20.1	−5.7	−1.8	−2.9
*Korea	24.1	29.0	30.0	14.9	24.9	23.7	−9.2	−4.1	−6.3
Malaysia	19.6	25.7	33.4	20.8	27.2	26.3	1.2	1.5	−7.1
Papua New Guinea	31.0	20.1	28.8	1.8	16.3	10.2	−29.2	−3.8	−18.6
Philippines	20.9	28.6	29.6	17.1	23.9	23.3	−3.8	−4.7	−6.3
Thailand	23.8	25.4	25.3	21.3	23.6	20.5	−2.5	−1.8	−4.8
Europe and North Africa									
Algeria	28.8	46.8	40.2	27.3	39.2	38.2	−1.5	−7.6	−2.0
*Egypt	14.1	26.1	29.0	8.8	17.4	18.1	−5.3	−8.7	−10.9
Morocco	14.5	24.9	22.7	12.5	16.5	11.6	−2.0	−8.4	−11.1
Portugal	25.9	28.2	34.7	20.3	13.8	13.9	−5.6	−14.4	−20.8
Tunisia	22.9	28.2	30.5	15.6	21.0	23.1	−7.3	−7.2	−7.4
*Turkey	18.0	21.9	20.3	17.1	17.9	17.0	−0.9	−4.0	−3.3
*Yugoslavia	30.2	33.1	36.5	27.6	27.3	31.7	−2.6	−5.8	−4.8

Note: Asterisk indicates a major borrower.
a. Excluding net unrequited transfers.

Table A.12 Composition of debt outstanding, 1970–83

(percent of total debt)

Country	Debt from official sources			Debt from private sources			Debt at floating rates		
	1970–72	1980–82	1983	1970–72	1980–82	1983	1973–75	1980–82	1983
Latin America and Caribbean									
*Argentina	12.6	8.8	5.7	87.4	91.2	94.3	13.9	53.6	34.0
Bolivia	57.9	51.1	62.4	42.1	48.9	37.6	7.6	36.9	32.5
*Brazil	29.7	11.8	12.6	70.3	88.2	87.4	43.5	66.0	76.5
*Chile	47.1	11.8	9.9	52.9	88.2	90.1	9.6	58.2	72.0
Colombia	67.1	44.9	42.8	32.9	55.1	57.2	6.2	39.2	42.1
Costa Rica	39.9	37.6	39.4	60.1	62.4	60.6	24.6	50.2	57.0
Ecuador	54.8	31.5	24.4	45.2	68.5	75.6	11.9	50.5	71.1
Guatemala	47.6	74.8	76.0	52.4	25.2	24.0	5.2	8.6	19.0
Jamaica	7.4	67.2	77.2	92.6	32.8	22.8	35.7	22.7	19.7
*Mexico	19.8	11.2	8.2	80.2	88.8	91.8	46.8	74.0	82.4
Peru	15.7	40.5	36.3	84.3	59.5	63.7	31.0	28.0	37.4
Uruguay	48.7	20.8	14.3	51.3	79.2	85.7	11.6	33.5	65.0
*Venezuela	28.5	2.4	1.3	71.5	97.6	98.7	20.6	81.4	87.9
Africa									
Cameroon	81.6	56.9	59.0	18.4	43.1	41.0	3.0	12.8	6.6
Ethiopia	87.8	92.4	92.6	12.2	7.6	7.4	1.5	2.1	1.5
Ghana	56.3	82.5	87.4	43.7	17.5	12.6	0.0	0.7	0.0
Ivory Coast	51.3	24.0	27.3	48.7	76.0	72.7	23.3	43.2	47.0
Kenya	58.4	52.6	62.7	41.6	47.4	37.3	3.3	11.8	9.1
Liberia	80.8	74.8	76.0	19.2	25.2	24.0	0.0	16.0	18.1
Malawi	77.5	67.8	76.1	22.5	32.2	23.9	2.3	21.2	17.0
Niger	96.5	42.3	55.7	3.5	57.7	44.3	0.0	20.3	19.4
Nigeria	69.9	14.2	14.9	30.1	85.8	85.1	0.7	67.2	62.0
Senegal	59.0	70.6	78.6	41.0	29.4	21.4	26.1	9.8	8.1
Sierra Leone	61.0	70.4	75.6	39.0	29.6	24.4	3.8	0.1	0.1
Sudan	86.3	73.4	74.2	13.7	26.6	25.8	2.2	10.1	14.2
Tanzania	63.6	76.6	79.4	36.4	23.4	20.6	0.4	1.1	1.3
Zaire	24.5	65.7	78.2	75.5	34.3	21.8	32.8	11.8	10.5
Zambia	22.0	70.1	76.2	78.0	29.9	23.8	22.6	10.4	12.3
South Asia									
*India	95.2	94.9	91.6	4.8	5.1	8.4	0.0	3.1	5.0
Pakistan	90.9	92.2	91.1	9.1	7.8	8.9	0.0	1.5	1.2
Sri Lanka	81.8	79.4	73.2	18.2	20.6	26.8	0.0	11.9	14.5
East Asia									
*Indonesia	71.5	51.7	48.0	28.5	48.3	52.0	10.2	18.2	22.7
*Korea	38.8	38.6	40.4	61.2	61.4	59.6	15.1	35.8	42.1
Malaysia	49.1	21.7	16.3	50.9	78.3	83.7	23.0	47.2	62.9
Papua New Guinea	7.2	23.9	19.5	92.8	76.1	80.5	0.0	37.4	48.4
Philippines	21.3	32.4	35.3	78.7	67.6	64.7	15.7	32.2	36.0
Thailand	40.1	40.1	44.3	59.9	59.9	55.7	0.9	30.9	27.5
Europe and North Africa									
Algeria	45.0	16.6	20.8	55.0	83.4	79.2	34.0	24.2	21.3
*Egypt	66.0	82.2	79.2	34.0	17.8	20.8	4.8	3.1	1.2
Morocco	79.2	52.0	60.9	20.8	48.0	39.1	2.7	31.9	28.2
Portugal	39.1	25.7	23.1	60.9	74.3	76.9	0.0	23.5	31.7
Tunisia	72.4	60.8	65.7	27.6	39.2	34.3	0.0	14.1	8.7
*Turkey	92.1	65.9	67.5	7.9	34.1	32.5	0.8	22.7	25.0
*Yugoslavia	37.3	24.7	23.8	62.7	75.3	76.2	7.6	32.2	59.4

Note: Asterisk indicates a major borrower.

Bibliographical note

This Report has drawn on a wide range of World Bank work, as well as on numerous outside sources. World Bank sources include ongoing economic analysis and research, as well as project, sector, and economic work on individual countries. Outside sources include research publications and the unpublished reports of other organizations working on global economic and development issues. Selected sources are noted briefly by chapter, listed in three groups. The first two are background papers and country studies commissioned for this Report; they synthesize relevant literature and Bank work. Most include extensive bibliographies; the sources cited in these papers are not listed separately. Those issued as Staff Working Papers in the months following publication of this Report will be available from the Bank's Publications Sales Unit. The views they express are not necessarily those of the World Bank or of this Report. The third group consists of other selected sources used in the preparation of this Report.

Selected sources, by chapter

Chapter 1

The bibliographical and data sources in this overview chapter are discussed in detail in the notes to subsequent chapters.

Chapter 2

Historical capital flows data and analysis are based on a background paper by Fishlow and on Maddison 1982. Data on net flows to developing countries are from the OECD Development Assistance Committee (OECD 1984). Boxes 2.1 and 2.2 draw on the World Bank *World Debt Tables*, 1984–85 edition. Box 2.3 is based on Melton and Kincaid. Box 2.4 is based on a paper by Krugman. All other data on national accounts, balance of payments, and external debt come from the World Bank.

Chapter 3

Data used in this chapter draw on GATT, IMF, and OECD publications, as well as on World Bank data. The discussion of the links between macroeconomic developments in industrial countries and capital flows and trade intervention draws on a background paper by Dornbusch and on Bruno and Bruno and Sachs. The discussion of fiscal policies and interest rates is mostly based on the paper by Layard and others and on the background papers by Blanchard and Summers and van Wijnbergen. The analysis of macroeconomic effects of protectionism follows van Wijnbergen 1984, while the link between protectionism in industrial countries and the debt problem is stressed in Dornbusch and Fischer and quantified in a background paper by van Wijnbergen. Data on the extent of nontariff barriers are drawn from Nogues, Olechowsky, and Winters. Boxes draw on background papers prepared for this Report, as follows. Box 3.1 is based on Fleisig and van Wijnbergen. Boxes 3.2 and 3.3 draw on van Wijnbergen. Box 3.4 is based on Zietz and Valdez, while Box 3.5 draws on Fleisig and van Wijnbergen, van Wijnbergen, and Dornbusch.

Chapter 4

This chapter draws heavily on Bank operational experience and country economic work. The country group data draw from GATT, IMF, OECD, BIS, and UN publications, as well as World Bank sources. For an analysis of the origins and dimensions of external shocks in the 1970s and 1980s, see Balassa and McCarthy, Enders and Mattione, and Mitra. The discussion of country policy responses and economic structures draws mainly upon internal Bank documents. Other views on debt problems and shocks can be found in Cline, Donovan, Ffrench-Davis, and Hasan. Ardito-Barletta, Blejer, and Landau and Corbo and de Melo provide extensive analyses of the debt and adjustment problems in the Latin American countries of the Southern Cone. Box 4.1 on the debt cycle hypothesis draws on a background paper by Genberg and Swoboda and on Kindleberger, Crowther, and Halevi. Box 4.9 on World Bank lending for adjustment draws from the 1980–84 editions of the World Bank *Annual Report*.

Chapter 5

Most of the information in this chapter concerning the management of capital flows in various developing countries derives from recent World Bank and IMF missions to the countries cited. Data on the composition of capital flows comes from the World Bank's Debtor Reporting System, the OECD, the BIS, and the IFS. Estimates of short-term debt were derived from BIS data on the maturity structure of commercial banks' assets, adjusted by World Bank staff. Reserves data are from the IFS.

Chapter 6

Chapter 6 is an introductory chapter that draws out from the ensuing three chapters the main trends in the international financial system and how they have impinged on the developing countries. Some of the factors shaping the system are discussed in background papers by Llewellyn and Rybczynski. The evolution of World Bank lending the subject of Box 6.1—is from Bank data. Box 6.2, which analyzes the deployment of the OPEC surplus, is based on a background paper by Sherbiny and on Mattione. The discussion of the functioning of the international interbank market has drawn on a BIS study and on Johnston's book. The influence of sovereign risk on capital flows—Box 6.4—is covered in Lessard's background paper.

Chapter 7

This chapter draws heavily on the data and analysis prepared over the years by the OECD Development Assistance Committee, particularly its annual report, *Development Co-operation*. Additional information on Arab aid programs is contained in the background paper by Sherbiny. The contribution made by official flows to the development process is analyzed in the study of aid effectiveness by Krueger and Ruttan, which reviews the aid experience in a number of sectors, including infrastructure, population, and agriculture, and for five principal aid recipients. Mikesell and

others discusses the role aid can play in promoting development. Basic philosophical criticisms of aid are presented in Bauer, Krauss, and Hayter. The influence of donors' commercial interests on the nature of aid programs, including aid tying and the use of mixed credits, is discussed in Jay. Morss explores the impact that project proliferation has had on sub-Saharan African countries.

Chapter 8

The evolving relationship between banks and developing countries has been explored extensively in the financial press and journals. Some of the stages of this evolution are covered in the background paper by O'Brien and Calverley. Llewellyn's background paper highlights the separate forces working on the relationship through changes in the macroeconomic environment and changes in the willingness of banks to supply their services. Analysis contained in the IMF's series of occasional papers, collectively entitled "International Capital Markets: Recent Developments and Future Prospects," OECD's *Financial Market Trends*, the Bank of England's *Quarterly Bulletin*, and the World Bank's *World Debt Tables* are also employed in this chapter. The discussion of access to securities markets is based on the background paper by Fleming and Partoazam. In Box 8.2 the operations of Arab banks are discussed with reference to Sherbiny's background paper. The origins of the Eurocurrency markets (Box 8.3), which have been much discussed in academic literature, have benefited from the analysis contained in Johnston's book. A background paper by Wallich is the main source for gauging the impact of banking supervision on developing countries in Box 8.4. Further discussion of the trend toward financial deregulation in Japan—see Box 8.5—is contained in the background paper by Atsumi and Ishiyama. Box 8.6 draws on Bond. The new instrumentalities explored in Box 8.7 are covered in greater detail in Saini's background paper. This chapter also draws extensively on additional World Bank staff work.

Chapter 9

A number of papers and books have been written on equity investment recently. The key reference for Chapter 9 is a background paper by Weigel and Miller, which examines the role of direct foreign investment in economic development. Similar surveys in this area have been prepared by the U.S. Department of Commerce and by the IMF.

Another important source of material is Guisinger's book, which focuses on investment incentives and performance requirements. Portfolio investment has been the subject of studies by the IFC; many of these findings are contained in van Agtmael's book. All of the boxes in Chapter 9 are based upon internal World Bank analyses; Box 9.3 uses data from the Japanese Ministry of Finance.

Chapter 10

Data used in this chapter draw on GATT, IMF, OECD, and UNCTAD publications, as well as on World Bank data. Quantitative analysis of the implications of industrial-country policies for developing countries is in the two background papers by van Wijnbergen.

Background papers

Aliber, Robert. "Banks, Financial Intermediation, and the External Debt Crisis."

Atsumi, Keiko, and Yoshihide Ishiyama. "Capital Outflows from Japan to Developing Countries."

Blanchard, Oliver J., and Lawrence H. Summers. "Perspectives on High World Real Interest Rates."

Dornbusch, Rudiger. "The Effects of OECD Macroeconomic Policies on Non-Oil Developing Countries: A Review."

Fishlow, Albert. "Lessons from the Past: Capital Markets during the Nineteenth Century and the Inter-War Period."

Fleisig, Heywood, and Sweder van Wijnbergen. "Primary Commodity Prices, the Business Cycle, and the Real Exchange Rate of the Dollar."

Fleming, Alex, and Hossein Ali Partoazam. "Developing Country Access to the Securities Markets."

Genberg, Hans, and Alexander Swoboda. "The 'Stages in the Balance of Payments Hypothesis' Revisited."

Hooper, Peter. "International Repercussions of the U.S. Budget Deficit."

Lessard, Donald. "International Finance for Less Developed Countries: The Unfulfilled Promise."

Llewellyn, David. "International Financial Intermediation and the Role of Banks in Balance of Payments Financing."

Muller, Patrice, and Robert Price. "Public Sector Indebtedness and Long-Term Interest Rates."

O'Brien, Richard, and John Calverley. "Private Banks and Developing Countries."

Pushpangadan, Kesavan. "Effects of Interest Rates and Terms of Trade on LDC Borrowing: A Cross Country Analysis."

Rybczynski, T. M. "The Internationalization of the Financial System and the Developing Countries—The Evolving Relationship."

Sachs, Jeffrey D., and Warwick McKibbin. "Macroeconomic Policies in the OECD and Developing Countries' External Adjustment."

Saini, Krishan G. "Capital Market Innovations and Financial Flows to Developing Countries."

Sherbiny, Naiem A. "Arab Finance and Developing Countries."

van Wijnbergen, Sweder. "Global Interdependence via Trade and Capital Markets: An Empirical Analysis."

van Wijnbergen, Sweder. "International Repercussions of Trade Intervention and Macroeconomic Policies in the OECD: A Developing Country Perspective."

Wallich, Christine. "The Regulatory Environment for Capital Flows to Developing Countries: A Survey of Seven OECD Countries."

Weigel, Dale, and Robert Miller. "Foreign Direct Investment in Economic Development."

Zietz, Jochan, and Alberto Valdez. "The Costs of Protectionism to Less-Developed Countries: An Analysis for Selected Agricultural Products."

Country papers

Argentina: Johnson, John. "Role of International Finance in Argentine Development."

Brazil: Batista, Paulo Nogueira. "International Financial Flows to Brazil since the Late 1960s: An Analysis of Debt Expansion and Current Payments Problems."

Brazil: Knight, Peter, and C. Martone. "International Financial Flows to Development in Brazil, 1965–84."

Ethiopia: Codippily, Hilarian. "International Financial Flows, 1965–84."

Ivory Coast: Noel, Michel. "Adjustment Policies in the Ivory Coast."

Kenya: Ibrahim, Tigani. "Use of External Resources, 1965–84."

Korea: Iqbal, Farukh. "External Finance and Korean Development."

Morocco: Mateus, Abel M. "External Debt Management and Macroeconomic Policies."

Philippines: Khan, Sarshar. "The Philippine External Debt."

Turkey: Roy, Jayanta. "External Capital and Economic Development, 1963–84."

Yugoslavia: Pant, Chandraskekar. "External Shocks and Adjustment in the 1970s and 1980s."

Selected bibliography

Ardito-Barletta, Nicholas, Mario I. Blejer, and Luis Landau. 1984. *Economic Liberalization and Stabilization Policies in Argentina, Chile, and Uruguay.* Washington, D.C.: World Bank.

Avramovic, Dragoslav, and others. 1964. *Economic Growth and External Debt.* Baltimore, Md.: Johns Hopkins University Press for the World Bank.

Ayres, R. L. 1983. *Banking on the Poor.* Cambridge, Mass. MIT Press.

Balassa, Bela. 1981. *The Newly Industrializing Developing Countries after the Oil Crisis.* Reprint Series 190. Washington, D.C.: World Bank.

Balassa, Bela, and C. Balassa. 1984. "Industrial Protection in the Developed Countries." *World Economy* 7: 179–96.

Balassa, Bela, and F. Desmond McCarthy. 1984. *Adjustment Policies in Developing Countries: 1979–83.* Washington, D.C.: World Bank.

Bank for International Settlements. 1983. *The International*

Interbank Market: A Descriptive Study. Economic Papers 8. Basle.

Bauer, P. T. 1972. *Dissent on Development: Studies and Debates in Development Economics.* Cambridge, Mass.: Harvard University Press,

Bauer, P. T. 1981. *Equality, the Third World, and Economic Delusion.* London: Weidenfeld and Nicholson.

Bernanke, Ben S. 1983. ''Non-Monetary Effects of the Financial Crisis in the Propagation of the Great Depression.'' *American Economic Review* 73, 3: 257–76.

Blanchard, Olivier, and Rudiger Dornbusch. 1984. ''U.S. Deficits, the Dollar and Europe.'' *Banca Nazionale del Lavoro Quarterly Review* 148: 89–113.

Blanchard, Olivier, and L. Summers. 1984. ''Perspectives on High World Real Interest Rates.'' *Brookings Papers on Economic Activity* 2: 273–324.

Bond, I. D. 1985. *The Syndicated Credits Market.* Discussion Paper 22. London: Bank of England.

Bruno, Michael. 1983. ''The Age of Supply Shocks.'' In George von Furstenberg, ed. *International Money and Credit: The Policy Roles.* Washington, D.C.: International Monetary Fund.

Bruno, Michael, and Jeffrey D. Sachs. 1984. *The Economics of Worldwide Stagflation.* Cambridge, Mass.: Harvard University Press.

Casson, Mark. 1982. ''The Theory of Foreign Direct Investment.'' In John Black and John Dunning, eds. *Capital Movements.* Surrey, England: Macmillan.

Caves, Richard. 1982. *Multinational Enterprise and Economic Analysis.* Cambridge: Cambridge University Press.

Cline, William R. 1983. *International Debt and the Stability of the World Economy.* Policy Analyses in International Economics 4. Washington, D.C: Institute for International Economics.

Cline, William R. 1984. *International Debt: Systemic Risk and Policy Response.* Washington, D.C.: Institute for International Economics.

Colaço, Francis X. 1981. ''Capital Requirements in Economic Development: The Decade Ahead.'' Paper prepared for the International Economic Association Conference on Financing Problems of Developing Countries. Buenos Aires, October 26–30.

Colaço, Francis X., and Mia A. M. de Kuijper. 1981. *Market Borrowings, Reserves Accumulations and Borrowing Costs.* International Trade and Capital Flows Division Working Paper 1981-5. Washington, D.C.: World Bank.

Commonwealth Secretariat. 1984. *The Debt Crisis and the World Economy.* Report by a Commonwealth Group of Experts. London.

Congressional Budget Office. 1984. *A Report to the Senate and House Committee on the Budget.* Part 1: *The Economic Outlook.* Part 2: *Baseline Budget Projections for Fiscal Years 1985–1990.* Washington, D.C.: Government Printing Office.

Congressional Budget Office. 1984. *The Economic and Budget Outlook: An Update.* Washington, D.C.: Government Printing Office.

Corbo, Vittorio, and J. de Melo. 1985. ''Symposium on Liberalization and Stabilization in the Southern Cone.'' *World Development* forthcoming (August).

Crowther, G. 1957. *Balances and Imbalances of Payments.* Boston: Harvard Graduate School of Business Administration.

de Melo, Martha. 1984. ''Portugal's Use of External Resources, 1965–83.'' World Development Report country note. Washington, D.C.: World Bank.

de Vries, Barend A. 1983. *International Ramifications of the External Debt Situation.* World Bank Reprint 294. Reprinted from AMEX Bank Review Special Papers 8, November 1983, pp. 1–23.

Diaz-Alejandro, Carlos F. 1970. *Essays on the Economic History of the Argentine Republic.* New Haven, Conn.: Yale University Press.

Diaz-Alejandro, Carlos F. 1984. ''Some Aspects of the 1982–83 Brazilian Payments Crisis.'' *Brookings Papers on Economic Activity* 2: 515–52.

Donovan, D. J. 1984. ''Nature and Origins of Debt-Servicing Difficulties: Some Empirical Evidence.'' *Finance and Development* 21, 4: 22–25.

Dornbusch, Rudiger, and S. Fischer. 1984. ''The World Debt Problem.'' Cambridge, Mass.: MIT.

Dunning, John. 1973. ''Determinants of International Production.'' *Oxford Economic Papers,* 289–336.

Edelstein, Michael. 1982. *Overseas Investment in the Age of High Imperialism: The United Kingdom, 1850–1914.* New York: Columbia University Press.

Enders, Thomas O., and Richard P. Mattione. 1984. *Latin America: The Crisis of Debt and Growth.* Washington, D.C.: Brookings Institution.

Ffrench-Davis, R. 1983. *Las Relaciones Financieras Extranas.* Mexico City: Corporacion de Investigaciones Economicas Para Latinoamerica.

Frank, Andre G. 1979. *Dependent Accumulation and Underdevelopment.* New York: Monthly Review Press.

Garay, Luis Jorge. 1984. ''El Proceso de Endeudamiento Externo de Colombia.'' World Development Report country note. Washington, D.C.: World Bank.

Guisinger, Stephen, and others. 1985. *Investment Incentives and Performance Requirements.* New York: Praeger.

Halevi, N. 1971. ''An Empirical Test of the 'Balance of Payments Stages' Hypothesis.'' *Journal of International Economics,* 103–17.

Hasan, Parvez. 1984. ''Adjustment to External Shocks: Why East Asian Countries Have Fared Better than other LDCs.'' *Finance and Development* 21, 4: 14–17.

Hayter, Teresa. 1971. *Aid as Imperialism.* Harmondsworth, England: Penguin Books.

Hicks, John. 1969. *A Theory of Economic History.* Oxford: Clarendon Press.

Hung, Tran Q. 1983. *The Deceleration and Domestication of International Bank Lending and Funding.* New York: Salomon.

Independent Commission on International Development Issues. 1980. *North-South: A Program for Survival.* London: Pan Books.

Independent Commission on International Development Issues. 1983. *Common Crisis, North-South: Cooperation for World Recovery.* London: Pan Books.

International Monetary Fund. 1969. *The International Monetary Fund 1945–1965: Twenty Years of International Monetary Cooperation.* Vol. 1: *Chronicle,* by J. Keith Horsefield. Vol. 2: *Analysis,* ed. by J. Keith Horsefield. Vol. 3: *Documents,* ed. by J. Keith Horsefield. Washington, D.C.

International Monetary Fund. 1976. *The International Monetary Fund 1966–1971: The System under Stress.* Vol. 1: *Narrative,* by Margaret Garritsen de Vries. Vol. 2: *Documents,* ed. by Margaret Garritsen de Vries. Washington, D.C.

International Monetary Fund. 1985. *Foreign Private Investment in Developing Countries: A Study by the Research Department of the International Monetary Fund.* Occasional Paper 33. Washington, D.C.

Jay, Keith. 1985. *The Use of Foreign Assistance to Promote Commercial Interests.* Development Policy Issues Series 3. Washington, D.C.: World Bank.

Johnston, R. B. 1983. *The Economics of the Euro-Market: History, Theory, and Policy.* London: Macmillan.

Kessides, C. 1984. "Romania and Hungary: Comparative Case Studies of Domestic Policy and Debt Management." World Development Report country note. Washington, D.C.: World Bank.

Kincaid, G. Russell. 1981. "Inflation and the external debt of developing countries." *Finance and Development* 18, 4: 45–48.

Kindleberger, Charles P. 1978. "Debt Situation of the Developing Countries in Historical Perspective." In Stephen H. Goodman, ed. *Financing and Risk in Developing Countries.* New York: Praeger.

Kindleberger, Charles P. 1980. *Manias, Phobias, and Crashes: A History of Financial Crises.* New York: Basic Books.

Kindleberger, Charles P. 1981. *International Money: A Collection of Essays.* London: Allen and Unwin.

Kindleberger, Charles P. 1984. *A Financial History of Western Europe.* London: Allen and Unwin.

Kotte, Detlef J. 1984. "Mexico: A Case Study on External Debt Accumulation." Geneva: United Nations Conference on Trade and Development.

Krauss, M. B. 1983. *Development without Aid: Growth, Poverty and Government.* New York: McGraw-Hill.

Krueger, Anne O. 1984. "Aspects of Capital Flows between Developed and Developing Countries." Paper presented at the Pinnas Sapir Conference on Development, Tel Aviv, Israel, May 28–31.

Krueger, Anne O., and Vernon W. Ruttan. 1983. *The Development Impact of Economic Assistance to LDCs.* 2 vols. Washington, D.C.: Agency for International Development.

Krugman, Paul R. 1984. "Proposals for International Debt Reform." World Development Report background note. Washington, D.C.: World Bank.

Lal, Deepak. 1983. *The Poverty of Development Economics.* London: Institute of Economic Affairs.

Layard, R., and others. 1984. *Europe: The Case for Unsustainable Growth.* Brussels: Centre for European Policy Studies.

Leipziger, Danny M. 1983. *Lending versus Giving: The Economics of Foreign Assistance.* World Bank Reprint 291. Reprinted from *World Development* 2, 4: 329–35.

Maddison, Angus. 1982. *Phases of Capitalist Development.* Oxford: Oxford University Press.

Marsden, Keith, and Alan Roe. 1983. "The Political Economy of Foreign Aid." *Labor and Society* 8: 3–12.

Mason, Edward S., and Robert E. Asher. 1973. *The World Bank since Bretton Woods.* Washington, D.C.; Brookings Institution.

Mattione, Richard P. 1985. *OPEC's Investments and the International Financial System.* Washington, D.C.: Brookings Institution.

McClintock, Cynthia, and Abraham F. Lowenthal, eds. 1983. *The Peruvian Experiment Reconsidered.* Princeton, N.J.: Princeton University Press.

McDonald, Donough C. 1982. *Debt Capacity and Developing Country Borrowing: A Survey of the Literature.* Reprinted from *International Monetary Fund Staff Papers* 29, 4.

Meier, Gerald M., and Dudley Seers, eds. 1984. *Pioneers in Development.* New York: Oxford University Press for the World Bank.

Mellor, J. W. 1976. *The New Economics of Growth.* Ithaca, N.Y.: Cornell University Press.

Melton, William C. 1980. "Graduate Payment Mortgages." Federal Reserve Bank of New York *Quarterly Review* 5, 1: 21–28.

Mentre, Paul. 1984. *The Fund, Commercial Banks, and Member Countries.* Occasional Paper 26. Washington, D.C.: International Monetary Fund.

Mikesell, R. F., and others. 1982. *The Economics of Foreign Aid and Self-Sustaining Development.* Washington, D.C.: U.S. Department of State.

Mitra, P. K. 1983. "Accounting for Adjustment in Selected Semi-industrial Countries." Report DRD70. Washington, D.C.: World Bank.

Mitra, P. K. 1984. "Adjustment to External Shocks in Selected Semi-Industrial Countries, 1974–83." Report DRD114. Washington, D.C.: World Bank.

Moore, Geoffrey H., and Victor Zarnowitz. 1984. *The Development and Role of the National Bureau's Business Cycle Chronologies.* Working Paper 1394. Washington, D.C.: National Bureau of Economic Research.

Morss, Elliott R. 1981. *Crisis in the Third World.* New York: Holmes and Maier.

Morss, Elliott R. 1984. "Institutional Destruction Resulting from Donor and Project Proliferation in Sub-Saharan African Countries." *World Development* 12: 465–70.

Nogues, Julio, A. Olechowski, and L. Alan Winters. 1985. "The Extent of Non-Tariff Barriers to Industrial Countries' Imports." World Bank Report DRD115. Washington, D.C.: World Bank.

Noël, Michel. 1984. "Adjustment Policies in the Ivory Coast." World Development Report country note. Washington, D.C.: World Bank.

Noman, Akbar. 1984. "Uranium and the Debt Explosion in Niger." World Development Report country note. Washington, D.C.: World Bank.

Organisation for Economic Co-operation and Development. 1984. *Development Co-operation: Efforts and Policies of the Members of the Development Assistance Committee. 1984 Review.* Report by Rutherford M. Poats, chairman of the Development Assistance Committee. Paris.

Pecchiolo, R. M. 1983. *Internationalisation Banking: Policy Issues.* Paris: Organisation for Economic Co-operation and Development.

Pfeffermann, Guy. 1985. "Overvalued Exchange Rates and Development." *Finance and Development* 22, 1: 17–19.

Pilvin, H. 1984. "Sri Lanka: Economic Policies and Borrowing Strategies." World Development Report country note. Washington, D.C.: World Bank.

Sachs, Jeffrey D. 1981. "The Current Account and Macroeconomic Adjustment in the 1970s." *Brookings Papers on Economic Activity* 1: 201–68.

Sachs, Jeffrey D. 1983. "Real Wages and Unemployment in the OECD Countries." *Brookings Papers on Economic Activity* 1: 255–89.

Schultz, T. W. 1981. *Economic Distortions by the International Donor Community.* Agricultural Economics Paper 81: 8. Chicago: University of Chicago.

Smith, Gordon W., and John T. Cuddington, eds. 1985. *International Debt and the Developing Countries.* Washington, D.C.: World Bank.

Solomon, Robert. 1977. *The International Monetary System, 1945–1976: An Insider's View.* New York: Harper and Row.

Stanyer, Peter, and Mrs. J. A. Whitley. 1981. "Financing World Payments Balances." Bank of England *Quarterly Bulletin* 21, 2: 187–99.

Tapley, Mark, and Marc Simmonds. 1982. "International

Diversification in the Nineteenth Century." *Columbia Journal of World Business* 17, 2: 64–70.

United Nations Center on Transnational Corporations. 1983. *Transnational Corporations in World Development* New York: United Nations.

United Nations Conference on Trade and Development. 1983. *Handbook of International Trade and Development Statistics, 1983.* New York: United Nations.

U.S. Department of Commerce. 1984. *International Direct Investment.* Washington, D.C.: Government Printing Office.

U.S. Department of the Treasury. 1982. *United States Participation in the Multilateral Development Bank in the 1980s.* Washington, D.C.: Government Printing Office.

van Agtmael, Antoine W. 1984. *Emerging Securities Markets—Investment Banking Opportunities in the Developing World.* London: Euromoney Publications.

van Wijnbergen, Sweder. 1984. *Tariffs, Employment and the Current Account: the Macroeconomics of Protectionism.* Discussion Paper 30. London: Centre for Economic Policy Research.

van Wijnbergen, Sweder. 1985. "Oil Price Shocks, Investment, Employment and the Current Account: An Intertemporal Disequilibrium Analysis." *Review of Economic Studies,* forthcoming.

Wachtel, Paul, ed. 1982. *Crises in the Economic and Financial Structure.* Lexington, Mass.: Lexington Books.

Walstedt, Bertil. 1980. *State Manufacturing Enterprise in a Mixed Economy: The Turkish Case.* Baltimore, Md.: Johns Hopkins University Press for the World Bank.

Watson, Maxwell, Peter Keller, and Donald Mathieson. 1984. *International Capital Markets: Developments and Prospects, 1984.* Occasional Paper 31. Washington, D.C.: International Monetary Fund.

Wiesner, Eduardo. 1985. "Domestic and External Causes of the Latin American Debt Crisis." *Finance and Development* 22, 1: 24–26.

Williamson, John. 1984. *A New SDR Allocation?* Policy Analyses in International Economies 7. Washington, D.C.: Institute for International Economics.

World Bank. 1981. *Accelerated Development in Sub-Saharan Africa: An Agenda for Action.* Washington, D.C.

World Bank. 1982. *IDA in Retrospect.* New York: Oxford University Press.

World Bank. 1983. *The Energy Transition in Developing Countries.* Washington, D.C.

World Bank. 1984. *Toward Sustained Development in Sub-Saharan Africa: A Joint Program of Action.* Washington, D.C.

Zarnowitz, Victor, and Geoffrey H. Moore. 1984. *Major Changes in Cyclical Behavior.* Working Paper 1395. Washington, D.C.: National Bureau of Economic Research.

Annex

World
Development
Indicators

Contents

Key

In each table, economies are listed in their group in ascending order of GNP per capita except for those for which no GNP per capita can be calculated. These are listed in alphabetical order, in italics, at the end of their group. The reference numbers below reflect the order in the tables.

Figures in the colored bands are summary measures for groups of economies. The letter *w* after a summary measure indicates that it is a weighted average; the letter *m*, that it is a median value; the letter *t*, that it is a total.

.. Not available.

(.) Less than half the unit shown.

All growth rates are in real terms.

Figures in italics are for years or periods other than those specified.

Afghanistan	29	Honduras	45	Panama	80
Albania	120	Hong Kong	90	Papua New Guinea	51
Algeria	83	Hungary	119	Paraguay	65
Angola	68	India	14	Peru	58
Argentina	79	Indonesia	43	Philippines	52
Australia	112	*Iran, Islamic Republic of*	93	*Poland*	124
Austria	106	*Iraq*	94	Portugal	81
Bangladesh	2	Ireland	101	*Romania*	125
Belgium	104	Israel	89	Rwanda	15
Benin	18	Italy	102	Saudi Arabia	97
Bhutan	30	Ivory Coast	48	Senegal	36
Bolivia	40	Jamaica	63	Sierra Leone	24
Brazil	77	Japan	108	Singapore	91
Bulgaria	121	Jordan	73	Somalia	13
Burkina	6	*Kampuchea, Democratic*	32	South Africa	84
Burma	7	Kenya	26	Spain	100
Burundi	10	*Korea, Democratic People's Republic of*	70	Sri Lanka	25
Cameroon	54	Korea, Republic of	78	Sudan	28
Canada	114	Kuwait	98	Sweden	115
Central African Republic	16			Switzerland	118
Chad	31	*Lao People's Democratic Republic*	33	Syrian Arab Republic	74
Chile	76	*Lebanon*	71	Tanzania	12
China	19	Lesotho	37	Thailand	55
Colombia	67	Liberia	38	Togo	17
Congo, People's Republic of the	60	Libya	96	Trinidad and Tobago	92
Costa Rica	57	Madagascar	23	Tunisia	62
Cuba	69	Malawi	8	Turkey	61
Czechoslovakia	122	Malaysia	75	Uganda	9
Denmark	113	Mali	3	*Union of Soviet Socialist Republics*	126
Dominican Republic	64	Mauritania	39		
Ecuador	66	Mexico	82	United Arab Emirates	99
Egypt, Arab Republic of	46	*Mongolia*	72	United Kingdom	105
El Salvador	47	Morocco	50	United States	117
Ethiopia	1	*Mozambique*	34	Uruguay	85
Finland	110	Nepal	4	Venezuela	87
France	109	Netherlands	107	*Viet Nam*	35
German Democratic Republic	123	New Zealand	103	Yemen Arab Republic	42
Germany, Federal Republic of	111	Nicaragua	56	Yemen, People's Democratic Republic of	41
Ghana	22	Niger	11	Yugoslavia	86
Greece	88	Nigeria	53		
Guatemala	59	Norway	116	Zaire	5
Guinea	20	Oman	95	Zambia	44
Haiti	21	Pakistan	27	Zimbabwe	49

Introduction

The World Development Indicators provide information on the main features of social and economic development. Most of the data collected by the World Bank are on its developing member countries. Because comparable data for developed market economies are readily available, these are also included in the indicators. Data for nonmarket economies, a few of which are members of the World Bank, are included if available in a comparable form.

Every effort has been made to standardize the data. However, full comparability cannot be ensured and care must be taken in interpreting the indicators. The statistics are drawn from sources thought to be most authoritative but many of them are subject to considerable margins of error. Variations in national statistical practices also reduce the comparability of data which should thus be construed only as indicating trends and characterizing major differences among economies, rather than taken as precise quantitative indications of those differences.

The indicators in Table 1 give a summary profile of economies. Data in the other tables fall into the following broad areas: national accounts, agriculture, industry, energy, external trade, external debt, aid flows, other external transactions, demography, labor force, urbanization, social indicators, central government finances and income distribution. The table on central government expenditure is an expanded version of an earlier table, and is complemented by a table on central government current revenue.

The national accounts data are obtained from member governments by Bank missions and are, in some instances, adjusted to conform with international definitions and concepts and to ensure consistency. Data on external debt are reported to the Bank by member countries through the Debtor Reporting System. Other data sets are drawn from the International Monetary Fund, the United Nations and specialized agencies.

For ease of reference, ratios and rates of growth are shown; absolute values are reported only in a few instances. This year's edition presents new periods for the ratios and rates in growth. Most growth rates were calculated for two periods: 1965–73 and 1973–83, or 1965–82 if data for 1983 were not available. All growth rates are in constant prices and were computed, unless noted otherwise, by using the least-squares method. Because this method takes all observations in a period into account, the resulting growth rates reflect general trends that are not unduly influenced by exceptional values. Table entries in italics indicate that they are for years or periods other than those specified. All dollar figures are US dollars. The various methods used for converting from national currency figures are described, where appropriate, in the technical notes.

Some of the differences between figures shown in this year's and last year's editions reflect not only updating but also revisions to historical series.

As in the *World Development Report* itself, the economies included in the World Development Indicators are grouped into several major categories. These groupings are analytically useful in distinguishing economies at different stages of development. Many of the economies included are further classified by dominant characteristics to distinguish oil importers and exporters and to distinguish industrial market from industrial nonmarket economies. The major groups used in the tables are 35 low-income developing economies with a per capita income of less than $400 in 1983, 59 middle-income developing economies with a per capita income of $400 or more, 5 high-income oil exporters, 19 industrial market economies, and 8 East European nonmarket economies. Note that because of the paucity of data and differences in the method for computing national income, as well as difficulties of conversion, estimates of GNP per capita are not generally available for nonmarket economies.

The format of this edition generally follows that used in previous years. In each group, economies are listed in ascending order of income per capita except for economies for which no GNP per capita figure can be calculated. These economies are listed in italics in alphabetical order at the end of the appropriate income groups. This order is used in all tables. The alphabetical list in the key shows the reference number of each economy; italics indicate those economies placed at the end of a group due to unavailability of GNP per capita figures. Countries with populations of less than a million are not reported in the tables. The technical note to Table 1 shows some basic indicators for 35 small countries that are members of the United Nations, the World Bank, or both.

In the colored bands are summary measures—totals or weighted averages—that were calculated for the economy groups if data were adequate and meaningful statistics could be obtained. Because China and India heavily influence the overall summary measures for the low-income economies, summary measures are shown separately for several subgroups. These are: China and India, all other low-income economies and, in this year's edition, an additional subgroup for low-income sub-Saharan Africa. Because trade in oil affects the economic characteristics and performance of middle-income economies, summary measures are shown for oil importers and for oil exporters. Moreover, the group of middle-income economies is divided into lower and upper categories to provide more meaningful summary measures. Note that this year's edition also includes separate summary measures for middle-income sub-Saharan Africa. Note also that the term "sub-Saharan" applies to all countries south of the Sahara—excluding South Africa.

The methodology used in computing the summary measures is described in the technical notes. The letter *w* after a summary measure indicates

Groups of economies

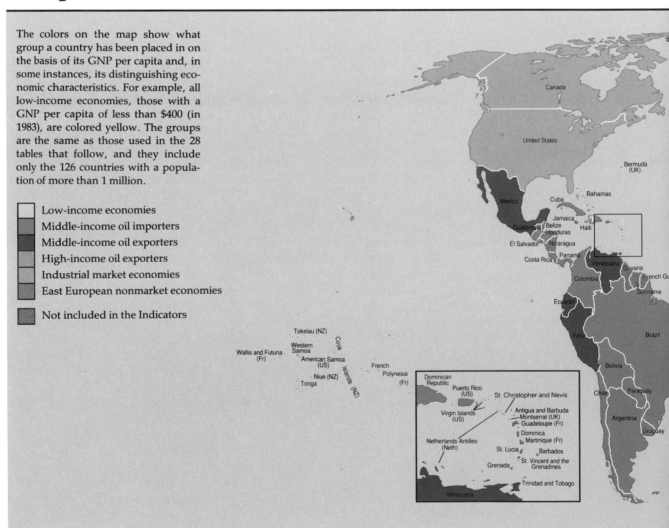

The colors on the map show what group a country has been placed in on the basis of its GNP per capita and, in some instances, its distinguishing economic characteristics. For example, all low-income economies, those with a GNP per capita of less than $400 (in 1983), are colored yellow. The groups are the same as those used in the 28 tables that follow, and they include only the 126 countries with a population of more than 1 million.

- Low-income economies
- Middle-income oil importers
- Middle-income oil exporters
- High-income oil exporters
- Industrial market economies
- East European nonmarket economies

- Not included in the Indicators

that it is a weighted average; the letter *m*, that it is a median value; and the letter *t*, that it is a total. Because the coverage of economies is not uniform for all indicators and because the variation around central tendencies can be large, readers should exercise caution in comparing the summary measures for different indicators, groups, and years or periods.

The technical notes should be referred to in any use of the data. These notes outline the methods, concepts, definitions, and data sources. The bibliography gives details of the data sources, which contain comprehensive definitions and descriptions of concepts used.

This year's edition includes four world maps. The first map, below, shows country names and the groups in which economies have been placed. The maps on the following pages show population, life expectancy at birth, and the share of agriculture in gross domestic product (GDP). The Eckert IV projection has been used for these maps because it maintains correct areas for all countries, though at the cost of some distortions in shape, distance, and direction. The maps have been prepared exclusively for the convenience of the readers of this Report; the denominations used, and the boundaries shown, do not imply on the part of the World Bank and its affiliates any judgment on the legal status of any territory or any endorsement or acceptance of such boundaries.

The World Development Indicators are prepared under the supervision of Ramesh Chander.

Population

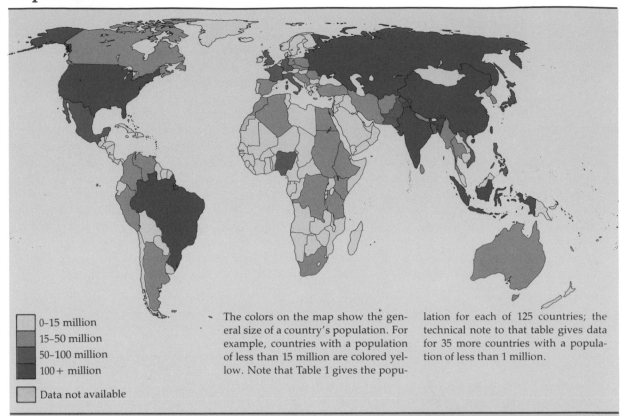

The colors on the map show the general size of a country's population. For example, countries with a population of less than 15 million are colored yellow. Note that Table 1 gives the population for each of 125 countries; the technical note to that table gives data for 35 more countries with a population of less than 1 million.

The bar chart at right shows population by country group for the years 1965 and 1983 as well as projected population for the year 2000. The country groups are those used in the map on the preceding pages and in the tables that follow.

The pie chart at right shows the proportion of total population, excluding countries with populations of less than 1 million, accounted for by each country group. "Other" refers to high-income oil producers.

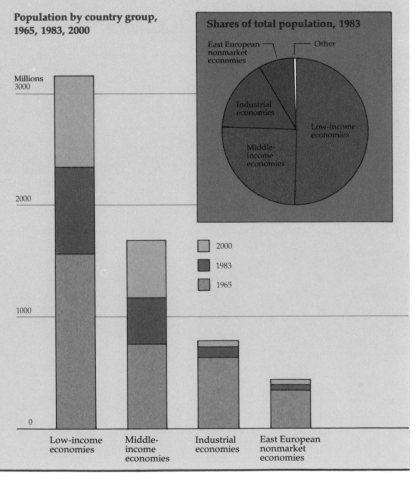

Population by country group, 1965, 1983, 2000

Shares of total population, 1983

Life expectancy

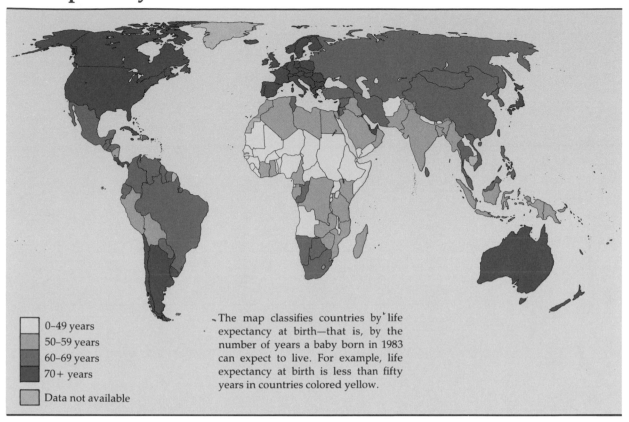

0–49 years
50–59 years
60–69 years
70+ years

Data not available

The map classifies countries by life expectancy at birth—that is, by the number of years a baby born in 1983 can expect to live. For example, life expectancy at birth is less than fifty years in countries colored yellow.

Share of agriculture in GDP

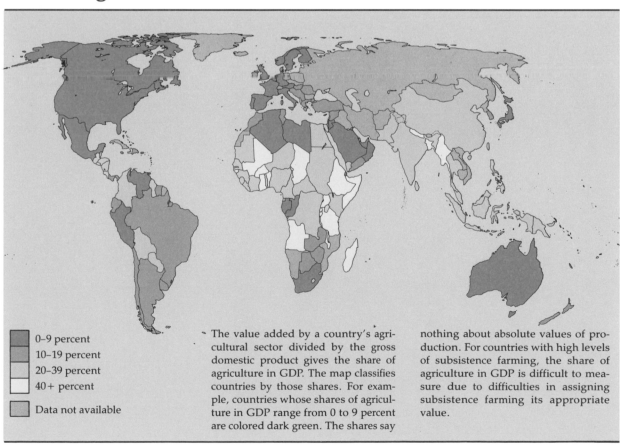

0–9 percent
10–19 percent
20–39 percent
40+ percent

Data not available

The value added by a country's agricultural sector divided by the gross domestic product gives the share of agriculture in GDP. The map classifies countries by those shares. For example, countries whose shares of agriculture in GDP range from 0 to 9 percent are colored dark green. The shares say nothing about absolute values of production. For countries with high levels of subsistence farming, the share of agriculture in GDP is difficult to measure due to difficulties in assigning subsistence farming its appropriate value.

Table 1. Basic indicators

	Population (millions) mid-1983	Area (thousands of square kilometers)	GNP per capita[a] Dollars 1983	GNP per capita[a] Average annual growth rate (percent) 1965–83[b]	Average annual rate of inflation[a] (percent) 1965–73	Average annual rate of inflation[a] (percent) 1973–83[c]	Life expectancy at birth (years) 1983
Low-income economies	2,335.4 *t*	31,603 *t*	260 *w*	2.7 *w*	1.4 *w*	5.4 *w*	59 *w*
China and India	1,752.3 *t*	12,849 *t*	280 *w*	3.2 *w*	0.9 *w*	3.7 *w*	62 *w*
Other low-income	583.0 *t*	18,754 *t*	200 *w*	0.7 *w*	4.8 *w*	13.8 *w*	51 *w*
Sub-Saharan Africa	245.2 *t*	15,451 *t*	220 *w*	−0.2 *w*	3.9 *w*	17.5 *w*	48 *w*
1 Ethiopia	40.9	1,222	120	0.5	1.8	4.4	43
2 Bangladesh	95.5	144	130	0.5	7.3	9.6	50
3 Mali	7.2	1,240	160	1.2	7.6	10.3	45
4 Nepal	15.7	141	160	0.1	5.8	8.1	46
5 Zaire	29.7	2,345	170	−1.3	18.7	48.2	51
6 Burkina	6.5	274	180	1.4	2.6	10.8	44
7 Burma	35.5	677	180	2.2	2.8	6.5	55
8 Malawi	6.6	118	210	2.2	4.5	9.8	44
9 Uganda	13.9	236	220	−4.4	5.6	62.7	49
10 Burundi	4.5	28	240	2.1	2.9	12.4	47
11 Niger	6.1	1,267	240	−1.2	4.0	11.8	45
12 Tanzania	20.8	945	240	0.9	3.2	11.5	51
13 Somalia	5.1	638	250	−0.8	3.8	20.1	45
14 India	733.2	3,288	260	1.5	6.3	7.7	55
15 Rwanda	5.7	26	270	2.3	7.7	11.2	47
16 Central African Rep.	2.5	623	280	0.1	3.0	14.4	48
17 Togo	2.8	57	280	1.1	3.1	8.3	49
18 Benin	3.8	113	290	1.0	3.6	10.8	48
19 China	1,019.1	9,561	300	4.4	−1.0	1.7	67
20 Guinea	5.8	246	300	1.1	3.0	4.0	37
21 Haiti	5.3	28	300	1.1	4.0	7.8	54
22 Ghana	12.8	239	310	−2.1	8.1	51.6	59
23 Madagascar	9.5	587	310	−1.2	4.1	13.9	49
24 Sierra Leone	3.6	72	330	1.1	1.9	14.7	38
25 Sri Lanka	15.4	66	330	2.9	5.1	14.5	69
26 Kenya	18.9	583	340	2.3	2.3	10.8	57
27 Pakistan	89.7	804	390	2.5	4.8	11.1	50
28 Sudan	20.8	2,506	400	1.3	7.2	18.0	48
29 *Afghanistan*	17.2	648	. .	0.5	3.8	. .	36
30 *Bhutan*	1.2	47	. .	. .	. .	. .	43
31 *Chad*	4.8	1,284	. .	. .	4.5	8.3	43
32 *Kampuchea, Dem.*	. .	181	. .	. .	. .	. .	. .
33 *Lao PDR*	3.7	237	. .	. .	. .	. .	44
34 *Mozambique*	13.1	802	. .	. .	. .	. .	46
35 *Viet Nam*	58.5	330	. .	. .	. .	. .	64
Middle-income economies	1,165.2 *t*	40,525 *t*	1,310 *w*	3.4 *w*	5.2 *w*	29.3 *w*	61 *w*
Oil exporters	542.6 *t*	15,511 *t*	1,060 *w*	3.3 *w*	4.4 *w*	19.6 *w*	57 *w*
Oil importers	622.6 *t*	25,014 *t*	1,530 *w*	3.5 *w*	5.7 *w*	34.4 *w*	64 *w*
Sub-Saharan Africa	148.2 *t*	5,822 *t*	700 *w*	1.9 *w*	4.8 *w*	12.4 *w*	50 *w*
Lower middle-income	665.1 *t*	18,446 *t*	750 *w*	2.9 *w*	5.6 *w*	17.9 *w*	57 *w*
36 Senegal	6.2	196	440	−0.5	3.0	8.9	46
37 Lesotho	1.5	30	460	6.3	4.4	11.9	53
38 Liberia	2.1	111	480	0.8	1.5	7.2	49
39 Mauritania	1.6	1,031	480	0.3	3.9	7.8	46
40 Bolivia	6.0	1,099	510	0.6	7.5	35.2	51
41 Yemen, PDR	2.0	333	520	. .	. .	. .	46
42 Yemen Arab Rep.	7.6	195	550	5.7	. .	13.9	44
43 Indonesia	155.7	1,919	560	5.0	63.0	18.0	54
44 Zambia	6.3	753	580	−1.3	5.2	10.3	51
45 Honduras	4.1	112	670	0.6	2.9	8.6	60
46 Egypt, Arab Rep.	45.2	1,001	700	4.2	2.6	13.2	58
47 El Salvador	5.2	21	710	−0.2	1.6	11.7	64
48 Ivory Coast	9.5	322	710	1.0	4.1	11.9	52
49 Zimbabwe	7.9	391	740	1.5	3.0	9.7	56
50 Morocco	20.8	447	760	2.9	2.0	8.4	52
51 Papua New Guinea	3.2	462	760	0.9	6.6	6.9	54
52 Philippines	52.1	300	760	2.9	8.8	11.7	64
53 Nigeria	93.6	924	770	3.2	10.3	13.3	49
54 Cameroon	9.6	475	820	2.7	5.8	12.6	54
55 Thailand	49.2	514	820	4.3	2.5	8.7	63
56 Nicaragua	3.0	130	880	−1.8	3.4	16.5	58
57 Costa Rica	2.4	51	1,020	2.1	4.7	23.2	74
58 Peru	17.9	1,285	1,040	0.1	10.1	52.3	58
59 Guatemala	7.9	109	1,120	2.1	1.9	9.9	60
60 Congo, People's Rep.	1.8	342	1,230	3.5	4.6	12.4	63
61 Turkey	47.3	781	1,240	3.0	10.5	42.0	63
62 Tunisia	6.9	164	1,290	5.0	3.4	9.4	62
63 Jamaica	2.3	11	1,300	−0.5	5.9	16.0	70
64 Dominican Rep.	6.0	49	1,370	3.9	2.7	8.5	63

Note: For data comparability and coverage see the technical notes.

	Population (millions) mid-1983	Area (thousands of square kilometers)	GNP per capita Dollars 1983	GNP per capita Average annual growth rate (percent) 1965-83[b]	Average annual rate of inflation (percent) 1965-73	Average annual rate of inflation (percent) 1973-83[c]	Life expectancy at birth (years) 1983
65 Paraguay	3.2	407	1,410	4.5	4.3	12.6	65
66 Ecuador	8.2	284	1,420	4.6	6.2	16.6	63
67 Colombia	27.5	1,139	1,430	3.2	10.8	24.0	64
68 *Angola*	8.2	1,247	..	..	..	..	43
69 *Cuba*	9.8	115	..	..	..	..	75
70 *Korea, Dem. Rep.*	19.2	121	..	..	..	..	65
71 *Lebanon*	2.6	10	..	..	2.5	..	65
72 *Mongolia*	1.8	1,565	..	..	..	..	65
Upper middle-income	500.1 *t*	22,079 *t*	2,050 *w*	3.8 *w*	5.3 *w*	34.0 *w*	65 *w*
73 Jordan	3.2	98	1,640	6.9	..	10.0	64
74 Syrian Arab Rep.	9.6	185	1,760	4.9	3.1	12.7	67
75 Malaysia	14.9	330	1,860	4.5	1.2	6.5	67
76 Chile	11.7	757	1,870	−0.1	50.3	86.2	70
77 Brazil	129.7	8,512	1,880	5.0	23.2	63.9	64
78 Korea, Rep. of	40.0	98	2,010	6.7	15.5	19.0	67
79 Argentina	29.6	2,767	2,070	0.5	24.1	167.8	70
80 Panama	2.0	77	2,120	2.9	2.4	7.1	71
81 Portugal	10.1	92	2,230	3.7	4.9	20.1	71
82 Mexico	75.0	1,973	2,240	3.2	4.8	28.2	66
83 Algeria	20.6	2,382	2,320	3.6	3.8	12.8	57
84 South Africa	31.5	1,221	2,490	1.6	5.8	13.3	64
85 Uruguay	3.0	176	2,490	2.0	51.7	51.0	73
86 Yugoslavia	22.8	256	2,570	4.7	10.9	22.8	69
87 Venezuela	17.3	912	3,840	*1.5*	3.3	11.7	68
88 Greece	9.8	132	3,920	4.0	4.4	16.8	75
89 Israel	4.1	21	5,370	2.9	8.2	73.0	74
90 Hong Kong	5.3	1	6,000	6.2	6.4	9.9	76
91 Singapore	2.5	1	6,620	7.8	3.1	4.5	73
92 Trinidad and Tobago	1.1	5	6,850	3.4	5.7	15.6	68
93 *Iran, Islamic Rep.*	42.5	1,648	..	..	5.5	..	60
94 *Iraq*	14.7	435	..	..	3.2	..	59
High-income oil exporters	17.9 *t*	4,312 *t*	12,370 *w*	3.8 *w*	6.1 *w*	13.5 *w*	59 *w*
95 Oman	1.1	300	6,250	6.5	7.1	17.9	53
96 Libya	3.4	1,760	8,480	−0.9	9.4	11.6	58
97 Saudi Arabia	10.4	2,150	12,230	6.7	5.1	16.5	56
98 Kuwait	1.7	18	17,880	0.2	4.6	10.2	71
00 United Arab Emirates	1.2	84	22,870	..	..	12.7	71
Industrial market economies	728.9 *t*	30,935 *t*	11,060 *w*	2.5 *w*	5.2 *w*	8.0 *w*	76 *w*
100 Spain	38.2	505	4,780	3.0	7.0	16.7	75
101 Ireland	3.5	70	5,000	2.3	8.5	14.5	73
102 Italy	56.8	301	6,400	2.8	5.1	17.4	76
103 New Zealand	3.2	269	7,730	1.2	7.2	14.2	74
104 Belgium	9.9	31	9,150	3.1	4.4	6.4	73
105 United Kingdom	56.3	245	9,200	1.7	6.2	14.3	74
106 Austria	7.5	84	9,250	3.7	4.5	5.4	73
107 Netherlands	14.4	41	9,890	2.3	6.4	6.2	76
108 Japan	119.3	372	10,120	4.8	6.0	4.7	77
109 France	54.7	547	10,500	3.1	5.3	10.8	75
110 Finland	4.9	337	10,740	3.3	7.2	10.6	73
111 Germany, Fed. Rep.	61.4	249	11,430	2.8	4.7	4.3	75
112 Australia	15.4	7,687	11,490	1.7	5.7	10.5	76
113 Denmark	5.1	43	11,570	1.9	7.6	9.5	74
114 Canada	24.9	9,976	12,310	2.5	4.4	9.4	76
115 Sweden	8.3	450	12,470	1.9	5.3	10.3	78
116 Norway	4.1	324	14,020	3.3	6.3	9.7	77
117 United States	234.5	9,363	14,110	1.7	4.7	7.5	75
118 Switzerland	6.5	41	16,290	1.4	5.5	3.9	79
East European nonmarket economies	386.1 *t*	23,422 *t*	..	..	..	..	70 *w*
119 Hungary	10.7	93	2,150	6.4	2.6	4.1	70
120 *Albania*	2.8	29	..	..	..	..	71
121 *Bulgaria*	8.9	111	..	..	..	..	70
122 *Czechoslovakia*	15.4	128	..	..	..	..	70
123 *German Dem. Rep.*	16.7	108	..	..	..	..	71
124 *Poland*	36.6	313	..	..	..	..	71
125 *Romania*	22.6	238	..	..	..	..	71
126 *USSR*	272.5	22,402	..	..	..	..	69

a. See the technical notes.   b. Because data for the entire period are not always available, figures in italics are for periods other than that specified.   c. Figures in italics are for 1973–82, not 1973–83.

Table 2. Growth of production

	GDP		Agriculture		Industry		(Manufacturing)[a]		Services	
	1965–73[b]	1973–83[c]	1965–73[b]	1973–83[c]	1965–73[b]	1973–83[c]	1965–73[b]	1973–83[c]	1965–73[b]	1973–83[c]
Low-income economies	**5.5** w	**5.0** w	**2.6** w	**2.9** w	**7.2** w	**7.1** w	..	..	**4.2** w	**5.0** w
China and India	**6.0** w	**5.4** w	**2.5** w	**3.0** w	**7.4** w	**7.5** w	..	..	..	**5.3** w
Other low-income	**3.7** w	**3.3** w	**2.8** w	**2.2** w	**5.6** w	**3.5** w	..	..	**4.2** w	**4.4** w
Sub-Saharan Africa	**4.2** w	**1.7** w	**3.1** w	**1.2** w	**6.9** w	**0.6** w	..	..	**4.6** w	**2.9** w
1 Ethiopia	4.1	2.3	2.1	1.2	6.1	2.6	8.8	3.5	6.7	3.6
2 Bangladesh	(.)	5.2	0.4	3.2	−6.1	8.1	..	..	1.5	7.4
3 Mali	3.1	4.1	0.9	5.0	5.2	0.6	..	..	4.7	4.5
4 Nepal	1.7	3.0	1.5	1.0	..	..	..	..	2.1	6.9
5 Zaire	3.9	−1.0	..	1.4	..	−2.0	..	..	..	−1.1
6 Burkina	2.4	3.5	..	1.3	..	5.1	..	..	..	4.5
7 Burma	2.9	6.0	2.8	6.6	3.6	7.7	3.2	6.1	2.8	5.1
8 Malawi	5.7	4.2	..	4.1	..	4.2	..	..	..	4.2
9 Uganda	3.6	−2.1	3.6	−1.6	3.0	−10.1	..	..	3.8	−1.0
10 Burundi	4.8	3.6	4.7	2.3	10.4	8.3	..	..	3.0	5.3
11 Niger	−0.8	5.2	−2.9	1.6	13.2	10.9	..	..	−1.5	5.9
12 Tanzania	5.0	3.6	3.1	2.6	6.9	0.2	..	..	6.2	5.4
13 Somalia	..	2.8	..	3.5	..	1.1	..	..	..	2.6
14 India	3.9	4.0	3.7	2.2	3.7	4.3	4.0	4.2	4.2	6.1
15 Rwanda	6.3	5.6	..	..	..	..	..	..	..	..
16 Central African Rep.	2.7	1.0	2.1	2.4	7.1	1.0	..	..	1.6	−0.7
17 Togo	5.3	2.3	2.6	1.1	6.2	2.6	..	..	7.3	3.0
18 Benin	2.2	4.8	..	2.7	..	6.9	..	..	..	6.0
19 China	7.4	6.0	1.9	3.5	9.1	8.4	..	..	..	4.5
20 Guinea	3.0	3.1	..	2.4	..	6.7	..	..	..	1.9
21 Haiti	1.7	3.0	−0.3	0.7	4.8	5.3	3.0	6.1	2.5	3.8
22 Ghana	3.4	−1.3	4.5	(.)	4.3	−7.0	6.5	−6.2	1.1	−0.3
23 Madagascar	3.5	0.3	..	−0.2	..	−1.8	..	..	..	1.2
24 Sierra Leone	3.7	1.9	1.5	2.2	1.9	−2.9	3.3	2.5	7.1	4.1
25 Sri Lanka	4.2	5.2	2.7	4.1	7.3	4.8	5.5	3.4	3.8	6.0
26 Kenya	7.9	4.6	6.2	3.4	12.4	5.3	12.4	6.3	7.8	5.3
27 Pakistan	5.4	5.6	4.7	3.4	6.6	7.2	6.2	7.0	5.4	6.3
28 Sudan	0.2	6.3	0.3	3.5	1.0	6.7	..	..	0.5	8.6
29 Afghanistan	1.0	2.4	−1.5	..	4.0	..	..	..	5.1	..
30 Bhutan	..	..	..	..	..	..	..	..	..	..
31 Chad	0.5	−5.8	..	..	..	..	..	..	..	..
32 Kampuchea, Dem.	−2.7	..	..	..	..	..	..	..	..	..
33 Lao PDR	..	..	..	..	..	..	..	..	..	..
34 Mozambique	..	..	..	..	..	..	..	..	..	..
35 Viet Nam	..	..	..	..	..	..	..	..	..	..
Middle-income economies	**7.1** w	**4.7** w	**3.3** w	**2.5** w	**9.1** w	**4.9** w	**9.3** w	**4.9** w	**7.5** w	**5.3** w
Oil exporters	**7.2** w	**4.9** w	**3.5** w	**1.8** w	**10.0** w	**5.2** w	**9.1** w	**6.4** w	**7.1** w	**5.9** w
Oil importers	**7.0** w	**4.5** w	**3.2** w	**3.1** w	**8.5** w	**4.7** w	**9.4** w	**4.2** w	**7.8** w	**4.9** w
Sub-Saharan Africa	**7.7** w	**1.4** w	**2.4** w	**−1.3** w	**17.7** w	**1.0** w	..	..	**7.1** w	**3.5** w
Lower middle-income	**6.6** w	**4.1** w	**3.4** w	**1.9** w	**10.6** w	**4.4** w	**8.5** w	**5.4** w	**6.8** w	**5.3** w
36 Senegal	1.5	2.6	0.2	0.3	3.5	6.1	..	..	1.5	2.2
37 Lesotho	3.9	5.5	..	..	..	..	..	..	..	..
38 Liberia	5.5	0.2	6.5	2.0	6.2	−1.5	13.2	0.5	3.8	0.8
39 Mauritania	2.6	2.5	−2.1	2.6	3.5	(.)	..	..	8.7	3.9
40 Bolivia	4.4	1.5	3.5	1.5	5.1	−0.6	4.2	1.7	4.3	2.6
41 Yemen, PDR	..	..	..	..	..	..	..	..	..	..
42 Yemen Arab Rep.	..	8.2	..	2.1	..	13.2	..	..	..	11.3
43 Indonesia	8.1	7.0	4.8	3.7	13.4	8.6	9.0	12.6	9.6	9.0
44 Zambia	3.0	0.2	..	1.4	..	−0.3	..	..	..	0.6
45 Honduras	4.4	4.0	2.4	3.3	5.8	5.1	6.5	5.5	5.5	4.0
46 Egypt, Arab Rep.	3.8	8.8	2.6	2.5	3.8	10.6	..	..	4.7	11.1
47 El Salvador	4.4	−0.1	3.6	0.7	5.2	−1.4	5.1	−2.4	4.4	0.0
48 Ivory Coast	7.1	4.7	3.7	4.0	8.8	7.4	8.9	4.5	8.5	4.1
49 Zimbabwe	7.3	1.8	..	1.2	..	(.)	..	..	..	3.3
50 Morocco	5.7	4.7	4.8	0.7	5.4	4.0	6.1	4.0	6.1	6.1
51 Papua New Guinea	6.7	1.0	..	2.6	..	3.7	..	..	..	−0.1
52 Philippines	5.4	5.4	4.1	4.3	7.4	6.4	8.5	5.0	4.8	5.2
53 Nigeria	9.7	1.2	2.8	−1.9	19.7	0.3	15.0	10.7	8.8	4.1
54 Cameroon	4.2	6.8	4.7	1.8	4.7	13.7	7.5	9.9	3.6	7.3
55 Thailand	7.8	6.9	5.2	3.8	9.0	9.0	11.4	8.9	9.1	7.6
56 Nicaragua	3.9	−1.3	2.8	1.4	5.5	−0.9	7.2	0.8	3.6	−2.9
57 Costa Rica	7.1	2.7	7.0	1.7	9.3	3.0	..	..	6.1	2.9
58 Peru	3.5	1.8	2.0	0.9	4.1	1.6	4.4	0.4	3.6	2.2
59 Guatemala	6.0	3.7	5.8	2.3	7.2	5.1	7.4	4.0	5.8	3.8
60 Congo, People's Rep.	6.8	7.9	4.1	0.4	9.3	12.7	..	..	6.7	6.8
61 Turkey	6.5	4.1	2.5	3.4	7.9	4.2	9.5	3.7	8.4	4.3
62 Tunisia	7.3	6.0	6.9	1.6	8.6	8.1	10.3	11.1	6.7	6.3
63 Jamaica	5.4	−1.7	0.6	−0.2	4.5	−4.3	4.0	−3.6	6.8	−0.3
64 Dominican Rep.	8.5	4.4	5.9	3.2	14.4	3.9	12.0	4.4	6.9	5.2

Average annual growth rate (percent)

Note: For data comparability and coverage see the technical notes.

	Average annual growth rate (percent)									
	GDP		Agriculture		Industry		(Manufacturing)[a]		Services	
	1965–73[b]	1973–83[c]	1965–73[b]	1973–83[c]	1965–73[b]	1973–83[c]	1965–73[b]	1973–83[c]	1965–73[b]	1973–83[c]
65 Paraguay	5.1	8.2	2.7	6.0	6.8	10.6	6.1	7.4	6.5	8.5
66 Ecuador	7.2	5.2	3.9	1.9	13.9	5.0	11.4	8.9	5.1	6.5
67 Colombia	6.4	3.9	4.0	3.7	8.2	2.2	8.8	1.9	6.9	4.8
68 *Angola*	..	..	..	..	..	..	..	..	..	..
69 *Cuba*	..	..	..	..	..	..	..	..	..	..
70 *Korea, Dem. Rep.*	..	..	..	..	..	..	..	..	..	..
71 *Lebanon*	6.2	..	1.4	..	5.5	..	..	..	7.1	..
72 *Mongolia*	..	..	..	..	..	..	..	..	..	..
Upper middle-income	**7.4** *w*	**4.9** *w*	**3.2** *w*	**3.2** *w*	**8.4** *w*	**5.0** *w*	..	..	**7.8** *w*	**5.2** *w*
73 Jordan	..	11.1	..	4.3	..	14.7	..	..	..	10.5
74 Syrian Arab Rep.	6.2	8.0	−0.7	8.2	14.7	5.9	..	..	6.1	8.9
75 Malaysia	6.7	7.3	..	4.4	..	8.7	..	..	..	8.2
76 Chile	3.4	2.9	−1.1	3.7	3.0	1.7	4.1	0.5	4.4	3.6
77 Brazil	9.8	4.8	3.8	4.2	11.0	4.7	11.2	4.2	10.5	5.0
78 Korea, Rep. of	10.0	7.3	2.9	1.5	18.4	11.2	21.1	11.8	11.3	6.9
79 Argentina	4.3	0.4	−0.1	1.5	5.1	−0.7	4.6	−1.8	5.5	1.1
80 Panama	7.4	5.3	3.4	*1.4*	9.3	4.2	..	..	7.8	6.4
81 Portugal	7.0	..	..	..	..	..	..	..	..	..
82 Mexico	7.9	5.6	5.4	3.5	8.6	6.2	9.9	5.5	8.0	5.7
83 Algeria	7.0	6.5	2.4	4.3	9.1	6.4	10.9	12.6	5.3	7.1
84 South Africa	5.2	3.1	..	..	..	..	..	..	..	..
85 Uruguay	1.3	2.5	0.4	1.5	2.0	2.4	..	..	1.1	2.7
86 Yugoslavia	6.1	5.3	3.2	2.2	7.1	6.3	..	..	6.4	5.4
87 Venezuela	5.1	2.5	4.5	2.6	4.1	1.5	5.7	3.7	6.0	3.1
88 Greece	7.5	3.0	2.5	1.3	11.1	2.3	12.0	2.7	7.3	3.8
89 Israel	9.6	3.2	..	..	..	..	..	..	..	..
90 Hong Kong	7.9	9.3	−0.6	1.1	8.4	8.2	..	..	8.1	9.8
91 Singapore	13.0	8.2	5.7	1.5	17.6	8.5	19.5	7.9	11.5	8.1
92 Trinidad and Tobago	3.5	5.2	*1.6*	..	2.3	..	..	..	4.5	..
93 *Iran, Islamic Rep.*	10.4	..	5.2	..	10.5	..	..	..	12.7	..
94 *Iraq*	4.4	..	1.7	..	4.8	..	..	..	5.1	..
High-income oil exporters	**9.0** *w*	**5.2** *w*	..	**6.7** *w*	..	**0.8** *w*	..	..	..	**12.3** *w*
95 Oman	21.9	6.5	..	..	..	..	..	..	..	..
96 Libya	7.7	3.0	11.5	6.5	6.6	−4.3	12.4	11.4	13.4	14.7
97 Saudi Arabia	11.2	6.9	2.6	6.6	13.3	3.9	10.6	8.0	8.3	12.9
98 Kuwait	5.1	1.4	..	9.1	..	−4.3	..	..	..	7.8
99 United Arab Emirates	..	10.8	..	..	..	..	..	..	..	..
Industrial market economies	**4.7** *w*	**2.4** *w*	**1.8** *w*	**1.0** *w*	**5.1** *w*	**1.9** *w*	**5.0** *w*	**1.1** *w*	**4.0** *w*	**2.1** *w*
100 Spain	6.4	1.8	2.8	..	8.6	..	..	..	5.6	..
101 Ireland	5.0	3.2	..	..	..	..	..	..	..	..
102 Italy	5.2	2.2	0.5	1.5	6.2	1.9	..	..	5.2	2.6
103 New Zealand	3.7	0.8	..	..	..	..	..	..	..	..
104 Belgium	5.2	1.8	2.2	1.9	6.4	0.7	7.4	1.0	4.4	2.6
105 United Kingdom	2.8	1.1	2.6	2.4	2.1	−0.3	2.6	−1.9	3.3	1.9
106 Austria	5.5	2.8	1.7	*1.3*	6.4	*2.3*	6.9	2.7	5.2	*3.5*
107 Netherlands	5.5	1.5	5.0	..	6.5	..	..	..	5.0	..
108 Japan	9.8	4.3	2.1	−1.6	13.5	5.5	..	..	8.3	*3.8*
109 France	5.5	2.5	1.7	..	6.7	..	..	..	5.2	..
110 Finland	5.3	2.7	1.0	1.1	6.4	2.9	7.5	3.6	5.6	2.8
111 Germany, Fed. Rep.	4.6	2.1	2.5	2.1	4.9	1.6	5.3	1.8	4.4	2.6
112 Australia	5.6	2.4	1.6	..	5.7	..	..	..	5.4	..
113 Denmark	3.9	1.8	−1.5	3.4	4.0	0.5	4.7	2.3	4.3	2.2
114 Canada	5.2	2.3	1.2	2.2	5.2	0.9	5.4	0.8	5.5	3.0
115 Sweden	3.6	1.3	1.1	−0.1	3.9	0.2	4.1	−0.1	3.6	2.1
116 Norway	4.0	3.7	−0.5	1.2	4.8	4.4	4.6	(.)	4.0	3.5
117 United States	3.2	2.3	1.8	1.4	2.8	1.2	2.9	1.4	3.5	3.0
118 Switzerland	4.2	0.7	..	..	..	..	..	..	..	..
East European nonmarket economies	..	..	..	..	..	..	..	..	..	..
119 Hungary[d]	6.1	3.7	3.1	3.1	6.5	4.4	..	..	7.5	3.3
120 *Albania*	..	..	..	..	..	..	..	..	..	..
121 *Bulgaria*	..	..	..	..	..	..	..	..	..	..
122 *Czechoslovakia*	..	..	..	..	..	..	..	..	..	..
123 *German Dem. Rep.*	..	..	..	..	..	..	..	..	..	..
124 *Poland*	..	..	..	..	..	..	..	..	..	..
125 *Romania*	..	..	..	..	..	..	..	..	..	..
126 *USSR*	..	..	..	..	..	..	..	..	..	..

a. Manufacturing is a part of the industrial sector, but its share of GDP is shown separately because it typically is the most dynamic part of the industrial sector.
b. Figures in italics are for 1966–73, not 1965–73.   c. Figures in italics are for 1973–82, not 1973–83.   d. Services include the unallocated share of GDP.

Table 3. Structure of production

	GDP[a] (millions of dollars)		Distribution of gross domestic product (percent)							
			Agriculture		Industry		(Manufacturing)[b]		Services	
	1965[c]	1983[d]	1965[c]	1983[d]	1965[c]	1983[d]	1965[c]	1983[d]	1965[c]	1983[d]
Low-income economies			43 *w*	37 *w*	29 *w*	34 *w*	14 *w*	14 *w*	28 *w*	29 *w*
China and India			42 *w*	37 *w*	32 *w*	38 *w*	15 *w*	15 *w*	26 *w*	25 *w*
Other low-income			44 *w*	38 *w*	16 *w*	19 *w*	11 *w*	12 *w*	40 *w*	43 *w*
Sub-Saharan Africa			44 *w*	41 *w*	16 *w*	17 *w*	9 *w*	7 *w*	40 *w*	42 *w*
1 Ethiopia	1,180	4,270	58	48	14	16	7	11	28	36
2 Bangladesh	4,380	10,640	53	47	11	13	..	..	36	40
3 Mali	370	980	49	46	13	11	..	..	38	43
4 Nepal	730	*2,180*	65	*59*	11	*14*	3	*4*	23	*27*
5 Zaire	1,640	*5,440*	22	*36*	27	*20*	17	*2*	51	*44*
6 Burkina	250	900	52	41	15	19	..	..	32	40
7 Burma	1,600	6,190	35	48	13	13	9	9	52	39
8 Malawi	220	1,330	50	..	13	13	..	..	37	..
9 Uganda	1,080	*3,360*	52	..	13	..	8	..	35	..
10 Burundi	160	1,020	..	58	..	16	..	..	..	26
11 Niger	370	1,340	63	33	9	31	..	..	28	37
12 Tanzania	790	*4,550*	46	*52*	14	*15*	8	*9*	40	*33*
13 Somalia	220	*1,540*	71	*50*	6	*11*	3	*6*	24	*39*
14 India	46,260	168,170	47	36	22	26	15	15	31	38
15 Rwanda	150	1,560	75	..	7	..	2	..	18	..
16 Central African Rep.	140	600	46	37	16	21	4	8	38	42
17 Togo	190	720	45	22	21	28	10	6	34	50
18 Benin	210	930	53	40	9	14	..	..	38	47
19 China	65,360	274,630	40[e]	37	38[e]	45	..	..	22[e]	18
20 Guinea	520	1,910	..	38	..	23	..	2	..	39
21 Haiti	350	1,630	..	..	..	..	..	..	..	..
22 Ghana	1,330	3,720	41	53	19	7	10	4	41	40
23 Madagascar	*730*	*2,850*	*31*	*41*	*16*	*15*	..	..	*53*	*44*
24 Sierra Leone	320	950	34	32	28	20	6	5	38	48
25 Sri Lanka	1,770	4,770	28	27	21	26	17	14	51	47
26 Kenya	920	4,940	35	33	18	20	11	12	47	46
27 Pakistan	5,450	25,880	40	27	20	27	14	19	40	46
28 Sudan	1,330	6,850	54	34	9	15	4	8	37	51
29 *Afghanistan*	620	..	..	..	..	..	..	..	..	..
30 *Bhutan*	..	..	..	..	..	..	..	..	..	..
31 *Chad*	240	*320*	47	..	12	..	..	..	41	..
32 *Kampuchea, Dem.*	870	..	..	..	..	..	..	..	..	..
33 *Lao PDR*	..	..	..	..	..	..	..	..	..	..
34 *Mozambique*	..	..	..	..	..	..	..	..	..	..
35 *Viet Nam*	..	..	..	..	..	..	..	..	..	..
Middle-income economies			21 *w*	15 *w*	31 *w*	36 *w*	20 *w*	21 *w*	47 *w*	49 *w*
Oil exporters			22 *w*	16 *w*	28 *w*	39 *w*	15 *w*	16 *w*	50 *w*	45 *w*
Oil importers			21 *w*	14 *w*	33 *w*	34 *w*	22 *w*	24 *w*	46 *w*	52 *w*
Sub-Saharan Africa			39 *w*	26 *w*	23 *w*	33 *w*	8 *w*	8 *w*	38 *w*	42 *w*
Lower middle-income			31 *w*	22 *w*	24 *w*	33 *w*	15 *w*	16 *w*	45 *w*	45 *w*
36 Senegal	810	2,570	25	21	18	26	..	17	56	54
37 Lesotho	50	*300*	65	*23*	5	*22*	1	*6*	30	*55*
38 Liberia	270	980	27	36	40	26	3	7	34	38
39 Mauritania	160	700	32	34	36	21	4	..	32	45
40 Bolivia	920	3,340	21	23	30	26	16	16	49	52
41 Yemen, PDR	..	850	..	..	..	..	..	..	..	..
42 Yemen Arab Rep.	..	3,710	..	21	..	17	..	7	..	62
43 Indonesia	3,630	78,320	59	26	12	39	8	13	29	35
44 Zambia	1,040	3,350	14	14	54	38	7	19	32	48
45 Honduras	460	2,640	40	27	19	26	12	15	41	47
46 Egypt, Arab Rep.	4,550	27,920	29	20	27	33	..	..	45	47
47 El Salvador	800	3,700	29	20	22	21	18	15	49	59
48 Ivory Coast	960	7,090	36	27	17	24	10	13	47	50
49 Zimbabwe	960	4,730	18	11	34	32	20	21	48	57
50 Morocco	2,950	13,300	23	17	28	32	16	17	49	51
51 Papua New Guinea	340	2,360	42	..	18	..	..	..	41	..
52 Philippines	6,010	34,640	26	22	28	36	20	25	46	42
53 Nigeria	4,190	64,570	53	26	19	34	7	5	29	40
54 Cameroon	750	7,220	32	24	17	32	10	11	50	45
55 Thailand	4,050	40,430	35	23	23	27	14	19	42	50
56 Nicaragua	710	2,700	25	22	24	32	18	26	51	47
57 Costa Rica	590	3,060	24	23	23	27	..	..	53	50
58 Peru	4,900	17,630	15	8	30	41	20	26	55	51
59 Guatemala	1,330	9,030	..	..	..	..	..	..	..	..
60 Congo, People's Rep.	200	2,110	19	7	19	55	..	6	62	38
61 Turkey	7,660	47,840	34	19	25	33	16	24	41	48
62 Tunisia	880	7,020	22	14	24	36	9	14	54	50
63 Jamaica	870	3,140	10	7	37	34	17	19	53	60
64 Dominican Rep.	960	8,530	26	17	20	29	14	18	53	55

Note: For data comparability and coverage see the technical notes.

		GDP[a] (millions of dollars)		Distribution of gross domestic product (percent)							
				Agriculture		Industry		(Manufacturing)[b]		Services	
		1965[c]	1983[d]	1965[c]	1983[d]	1965[c]	1983[d]	1965[c]	1983[d]	1965[c]	1983[d]
65	Paraguay	550	4,610	37	26	19	26	16	16	45	48
66	Ecuador	1,150	10,700	27	14	22	40	18	18	50	46
67	Colombia	5,570	35,310	30	20	25	28	18	17	46	51
68	Angola	..	..	..	..	..	..	..	..	..	..
69	Cuba	..	..	..	..	..	..	..	..	..	..
70	Korea, Dem. Rep.	..	..	..	..	..	..	..	..	..	..
71	Lebanon	1,150	..	12	..	21	..	..	..	67	..
72	Mongolia	..	..	..	..	..	..	..	..	..	..
Upper middle-income				17 w	11 w	35 w	37 w	22 w	24 w	49 w	52 w
73	Jordan	..	3,630	..	8	..	31	..	15	..	61
74	Syrian Arab Rep.	1,470	16,850	29	19	22	25	..	..	49	55
75	Malaysia	3,000	29,280	30	21	24	35	10	19	45	44
76	Chile	5,940	19,290	9	10	40	36	24	20	52	55
77	Brazil	19,260	254,660	19	12	33	35	26	27	48	53
78	Korea, Rep. of	3,000	76,640	38	14	25	39	18	27	37	47
79	Argentina	14,430	71,550	17	12	42	39	33	28	42	49
80	Panama	660	4,370	18	..	19	..	12	..	63	..
81	Portugal	3,740	20,340	..	8	..	40	..	..	..	51
82	Mexico	20,160	145,130	14	8	31	40	21	22	54	52
83	Algeria	3,170	47,200	15	6	34	54	11	13	51	40
84	South Africa	10,540	80,850	10	..	42	..	23	..	48	..
85	Uruguay	930	4,750	15	12	32	28	..	..	53	60
86	Yugoslavia	11,190	46,890	23	..	42	..	..	..	35	..
87	Venezuela	8,290	8,170	7	7	23	40	..	17	71	53
88	Greece	5,270	30,770	24	17	26	29	16	18	49	53
89	Israel	3,590	20,660	8	6	37	27	..	..	55	67
90	Hong Kong	2,150	27,500	2	1	40	30	24	22	58	69
91	Singapore	970	16,640	3	1	24	37	15	24	73	62
92	Trinidad and Tobago	660	8,620	5	..	38	..	19	..	57	..
93	Iran, Islamic Rep.	6,170	..	26	..	36	..	12	..	38	..
94	Iraq	2,430	..	18	..	46	..	8	..	36	..
High-income oil exporters				5 w	2 w	65 w	65 w	5 w	6 w	30 w	33 w
95	Oman	60	7,460	61	..	23	..	..	..	16	..
96	Libya	1,500	31,360	5	2	63	64	3	4	33	34
97	Saudi Arabia	2,300	120,560	8	2	60	66	9	6	31	32
98	Kuwait	2,100	21,330	(.)	1	73	61	3	6	27	38
99	United Arab Emirates	..	27,520	..	1	..	65	..	10	..	34
Industrial market economies				5 w	3 w	39 w	35 w	29 w	24 w	56 w	62 w
100	Spain	23,320	157,880	15	..	36	..	25	..	49	..
101	Ireland	2,690	18,040	..	..	..	..	..	..	..	..
102	Italy	62,600	352,840	11	6	41	40	..	..	48	54
103	New Zealand	5,580	23,820	..	8	..	33	..	23	..	59
104	Belgium	16,840	80,090	5	2	41	35	30	25	53	63
105	United Kingdom	99,530	455,100	3	2	41	32	30	18	56	66
106	Austria	9,470	66,640	9	4	46	39	33	27	45	58
107	Netherlands	19,700	136,520	..	4	..	33	..	24	..	63
108	Japan	90,970	1,062,870	9	4	43	42	32	30	48	55
109	France	97,930	519,200	..	..	..	..	..	..	..	..
110	Finland	8,190	49,390	15	7	33	33	21	23	52	60
111	Germany, Fed. Rep.	114,830	653,080	..	2	..	46	..	36	..	52
112	Australia	23,260	167,110	10	..	41	..	28	..	50	..
113	Denmark	10,180	56,360	8	4	32	23	20	16	60	72
114	Canada	51,840	324,000	5	3	34	29	23	16	61	68
115	Sweden	21,670	91,880	6	3	40	31	28	22	53	66
116	Norway	7,080	55,060	8	4	33	42	21	14	59	55
117	United States	688,600	3,275,701	3	2	38	32	29	21	59	66
118	Switzerland	13,920	97,120	..	..	..	..	..	..	..	..
East European nonmarket economies				..	..	..	..	..	..	..	..
119	Hungary[f]	..	21,020	24	19	37	42	31	35	39	39
120	Albania	..	..	..	..	..	..	..	..	..	..
121	Bulgaria	..	..	..	..	..	..	..	..	..	..
122	Czechoslovakia	..	..	..	..	..	..	..	..	..	..
123	German Dem. Rep.	..	..	..	..	..	..	..	..	..	..
124	Poland	..	..	..	..	..	..	..	..	..	..
125	Romania	..	..	..	..	..	..	..	..	..	..
126	USSR	..	..	..	..	..	..	..	..	..	..

a. See the technical notes.   b. Manufacturing is a part of the industrial sector, but its share of GDP is shown separately because it typically is the most dynamic part of the industrial sector.   c. Figures in italics are for 1966, not 1965.   d. Figures in italics are for 1982, not 1983.   e. Based on net material product.   f. Based on constant price series. Services include the unallocated share of GDP.

Table 4. Growth of consumption and investment

| | Average annual growth rate (percent) | | | | | |
| | Public consumption | | Private consumption | | Gross domestic investment | |
	1965–73[a]	1973–83[b]	1965–73[a]	1973–83[b]	1965–73[a]	1973–83[b]
Low-income economies	5.9 *w*	6.8 *w*	3.5 *w*	4.5 *w*	6.4 *w*	5.7 *w*
China and India	. .	. .	3.5 *w*	4.8 *w*	7.0 *w*	5.9 *w*
Other low-income	4.9 *w*	3.3 *w*	3.1 *w*	3.2 *w*	3.0 *w*	4.4 *w*
Sub-Saharan Africa	4.7 *w*	2.7 *w*	2.8 *w*	0.9 *w*	6.3 *w*	2.2 *w*
1 Ethiopia	3.7	7.1	4.2	2.6	1.5	2.6
2 Bangladesh	c	c	0.9	5.4	−6.4	4.2
3 Mali	(.)	7.5	3.9	2.8	1.0	4.2
4 Nepal	. .	. .	. .	. .	. .	. .
5 Zaire	5.8	2.2	2.2	−7.7	10.2	4.9
6 Burkina	10.7	3.6	0.4	4.9	13.7	−3.7
7 Burma	c	c	2.9	5.4	2.5	14.1
8 Malawi	3.0	. .	4.0	. .	16.0	. .
9 Uganda	c	c	3.8	−6.4	2.1	−5.2
10 Burundi	12.3	5.4	4.7	2.8	−1.4	15.7
11 Niger	2.1	2.3	−3.3	6.6	4.6	3.5
12 Tanzania	c	c	5.0	3.0	9.6	4.4
13 Somalia	. .	1.5	. .	7.9	. .	−8.2
14 India	6.8	8.8	3.3	3.3	3.9	4.2
15 Rwanda	2.8	. .	7.7	. .	6.3	. .
16 Central African Rep.	1.7	−1.5	3.6	3.2	2.3	−6.7
17 Togo	7.9	8.4	6.0	3.3	3.3	−0.2
18 Benin	3.6	3.7	1.1	3.1	3.9	10.3
19 China	c	c	3.7	5.5	8.9	6.6
20 Guinea	. .	6.4	. .	2.0	. .	−0.7
21 Haiti	3.1	5.1	0.8	2.9	14.4	8.4
22 Ghana	1.1	4.8	2.3	−1.3	−3.5	−8.1
23 Madagascar	3.3	3.9	4.0	−0.5	3.9	−1.0
24 Sierra Leone	5.3	−2.1	3.8	3.2	−1.4	1.1
25 Sri Lanka	2.3	1.6	3.5	4.3	7.9	15.7
26 Kenya	13.1	6.3	5.8	3.6	15.9	3.4
27 Pakistan	6.2	4.7	5.9	6.1	0.4	4.9
28 Sudan	1.4	4.5	−1.7	7.6	0.2	5.6
29 *Afghanistan*	c	. .	1.1	. .	−2.2	. .
30 *Bhutan*	. .	. .	. .	. .	. .	. .
31 *Chad*	6.0	. .	0.7	. .	4.5	. .
32 *Kampuchea, Dem.*	. .	. .	. .	. .	. .	. .
33 *Lao PDR*	. .	. .	. .	. .	. .	. .
34 *Mozambique*	. .	. .	. .	. .	. .	. .
35 *Viet Nam*	. .	. .	. .	. .	. .	. .
Middle-income economies	7.0 *w*	4.9 *w*	6.8 *w*	4.8 *w*	8.8 *w*	4.2 *w*
Oil exporters	8.8 *w*	6.4 *w*	6.3 *w*	5.8 *w*	9.4 *w*	6.0 *w*
Oil importers	6.3 *w*	4.0 *w*	7.1 *w*	4.2 *w*	8.5 *w*	3.1 *w*
Sub-Saharan Africa	12.0 *w*	4.3 *w*	4.3 *w*	2.8 *w*	12.3 *w*	3.2 *w*
Lower middle-income	8.5 *w*	6.1 *w*	5.4 *w*	4.4 *w*	8.4 *w*	5.1 *w*
36 Senegal	−1.2	6.6	0.1	3.3	8.1	−0.7
37 Lesotho	5.4	. .	5.9	. .	11.0	. .
38 Liberia	4.5	4.1	0.3	−0.1	5.6	1.5
39 Mauritania	6.1	1.4	2.7	3.0	12.5	7.0
40 Bolivia	8.4	2.3	3.1	2.9	6.9	−11.4
41 Yemen, PDR	. .	. .	. .	. .	. .	. .
42 Yemen Arab Rep.	. .	20.6	. .	5.8	. .	18.2
43 Indonesia	9.8	11.4	7.1	9.3	17.5	12.3
44 Zambia	10.4	−0.8	−1.2	3.9	6.2	−12.5
45 Honduras	7.0	6.3	3.8	4.3	4.3	0.7
46 Egypt, Arab Rep.	c	c	5.3	8.1	−1.5	12.0
47 El Salvador	8.3	3.3	3.0	0.6	3.7	−5.7
48 Ivory Coast	15.2	9.6	5.1	3.7	10.2	6.0
49 Zimbabwe	6.9	10.8	7.3	2.9	9.2	1.9
50 Morocco	5.5	c	5.1	5.5	11.0	2.4
51 Papua New Guinea	2.4	−2.2	5.2	3.1	10.9	4.2
52 Philippines	8.4	3.7	4.0	4.6	4.4	7.3
53 Nigeria	16.1	3.3	4.9	2.5	15.2	3.5
54 Cameroon	4.6	5.9	3.4	5.4	8.6	10.6
55 Thailand	9.8	9.4	6.9	5.9	7.6	6.2
56 Nicaragua	3.2	13.4	2.7	−4.3	3.3	−2.7
57 Costa Rica	6.8	3.7	5.1	1.9	9.3	−3.4
58 Peru	5.4	3.2	5.6	1.9	−2.6	−2.7
59 Guatemala	5.7	6.7	5.4	3.7	5.3	1.2
60 Congo, People's Rep.	7.4	5.0	3.9	10.8	9.3	10.2
61 Turkey	5.7	5.8	6.0	2.2	9.7	2.3
62 Tunisia	5.7	8.1	7.0	7.2	3.6	9.5
63 Jamaica	13.6	2.6	4.5	−2.0	7.5	−6.5
64 Dominican Rep.	−3.6	6.5	8.6	4.5	19.2	2.5

Note: For data comparability and coverage see the technical notes.

	Average annual growth rate (percent)					
	Public consumption		Private consumption		Gross domestic investment	
	1965–73[a]	1973–83[b]	1965–73[a]	1973–83[b]	1965–73[a]	1973–83[b]
65 Paraguay	6.2	10.3	5.0	7.0	8.4	14.0
66 Ecuador	7.0	8.5	5.2	6.4	6.0	3.2
67 Colombia	8.8	6.5	6.5	4.5	6.7	6.0
68 *Angola*	..	..	..	..	..	..
69 *Cuba*	..	..	..	..	..	..
70 *Korea, Dem. Rep.*	..	..	..	..	..	..
71 *Lebanon*	3.7	..	5.4	..	5.1	..
72 *Mongolia*	..	..	..	..	..	..
Upper middle-income	**6.5** *w*	**4.4** *w*	**7.6** *w*	**5.0** *w*	**8.9** *w*	**3.8** *w*
73 Jordan	..	9.5	..	11.5	..	19.9
74 Syrian Arab Rep.	12.5	10.7	6.5	9.2	7.2	11.3
75 Malaysia	6.9	10.2	4.6	7.2	9.1	11.9
76 Chile	6.3	0.4	4.8	2.6	(.)	−0.3
77 Brazil	7.3	*4.4*	10.2	*6.0*	11.3	2.5
78 Korea, Rep. of	7.3	5.8	8.7	6.0	19.7	9.1
79 Argentina	2.4	2.9	4.3	0.3	6.7	−2.0
80 Panama	9.7	..	5.2	..	15.4	..
81 Portugal	7.1	6.6	8.4	1.7	8.0	4.0
82 Mexico	8.7	6.9	7.7	5.4	8.4	4.5
83 Algeria	5.8	10.8	6.4	9.5	17.4	7.2
84 South Africa	5.2	..	6.1	..	6.1	..
85 Uruguay	2.1	3.7	4.1	1.1	3.9	7.0
86 Yugoslavia	2.2	2.4	9.7	3.9	4.8	5.2
87 Venezuela	6.8	*5.2*	5.5	*7.1*	9.0	2.5
88 Greece	5.7	5.2	6.9	3.0	11.1	−1.4
89 Israel	15.8	−1.1	6.9	5.4	13.3	−1.7
90 Hong Kong	6.9	9.4	9.5	10.2	3.7	10.8
91 Singapore	16.3	6.4	9.9	6.1	22.7	9.2
92 Trinidad and Tobago	c	c	4.9	7.7	2.4	*13.0*
93 *Iran, Islamic Rep.*	17.3	..	7.9	..	11.2	..
94 *Iraq*	c	..	3.3	..	7.2	..
High-income oil exporters	..	..	**8.7** *w*	..	**4.3** *w*	..
95 Oman	c	..	..	..	..	..
96 Libya	19.8	7.3	22.1	9.0	2.7	3.7
97 Saudi Arabia	c	c	8.8	21.2	9.4	27.1
98 Kuwait	c		4.3	..	0.8	..
99 United Arab Emirates	..	..	..	..	..	..
Industrial market economies	**3.2** *w*	**2.6** *w*	**4.8** *w*	**2.6** *w*	**5.4** *w*	**0.8** *w*
100 Spain	4.0	4.4	6.1	1.8	6.7	−2.3
101 Ireland	6.4	4.3	4.8	1.5	8.5	2.6
102 Italy	4.1	2.3	5.7	2.4	5.9	−1.0
103 New Zealand	2.9	1.8	3.2	0.5	2.6	−2.7
104 Belgium	4.9	2.9	5.0	2.2	4.1	−1.9
105 United Kingdom	2.1	1.5	2.9	1.5	3.1	(.)
106 Austria	3.8	3.1	4.7	2.5	6.9	0.4
107 Netherlands	3.2	2.5	5.1	2.0	5.9	−2.1
108 Japan	5.3	4.1	8.4	3.2	14.1	3.1
109 France	3.0	3.0	5.3	3.3	6.9	0.3
110 Finland	5.5	4.4	4.8	2.3	4.9	−0.4
111 Germany, Fed. Rep.	4.0	2.3	4.9	2.0	4.4	1.9
112 Australia	4.8	4.3	4.9	3.0	3.7	0.7
113 Denmark	6.0	3.8	2.9	1.2	4.9	−3.3
114 Canada	6.2	1.5	5.3	2.7	3.8	0.8
115 Sweden	4.9	3.0	2.9	1.0	2.1	−1.7
116 Norway	5.6	3.8	3.7	4.5	4.5	−2.7
117 United States	1.8	2.4	4.0	2.9	2.7	1.0
118 Switzerland	3.9	1.5	4.5	1.1	5.3	0.9
East European nonmarket economies	..	..	..	..	..	..
119 Hungary	..	3.9	..	3.2	..	*3.1*
120 *Albania*	..	..	..	..	..	..
121 *Bulgaria*	..	..	..	..	..	..
122 *Czechoslovakia*	..	..	..	..	..	..
123 *German Dem. Rep.*	..	..	..	..	..	..
124 *Poland*	..	..	..	..	..	..
125 *Romania*	..	..	..	..	..	..
126 *USSR*	..	..	..	..	..	..

a. Figures in italics are for 1966–73, not 1965–73. b. Figures in italics are for 1973–82, not 1973–83. c. Public consumption figures are not available separately; they are therefore included in private consumption.

Table 5. Structure of demand

	Distribution of gross domestic product (percent)											
	Public consumption		Private consumption		Gross domestic investment		Gross domestic savings		Exports of goods and nonfactor services		Resource balance	
	1965[a]	1983[b]	1965[a]	1983[b]	1965[a]	1983[b]	1965[a]	1983[b]	1965[a]	1983[b]	1965[a]	1983[b]
Low-income economies	10 *w*	12 *w*	75 *w*	70 *w*	21 *w*	26 *w*	19 *w*	24 *w*	6 *w*	9 *w*	−2 *w*	−2 *w*
China and India	..	..	75 *w*	68 *w*	22 *w*	28 *w*	21 *w*	28 *w*	4 *w*	8 *w*	−1 *w*	(.) *w*
Other low-income	12 *w*	13 *w*	78 *w*	80 *w*	16 *w*	18 *w*	11 *w*	7 *w*	18 *w*	15 *w*	−5 *w*	−11 *w*
Sub-Saharan Africa	13 *w*	16 *w*	74 *w*	78 *w*	15 *w*	16 *w*	13 *w*	7 *w*	24 *w*	18 *w*	−2 *w*	−8 *w*
1 Ethiopia	11	17	77	81	13	11	12	2	12	12	−1	−9
2 Bangladesh	9	8	83	91	11	17	8	2	10	8	−4	−15
3 Mali	17	27	72	75	23	17	11	−2	13	23	−11	−19
4 Nepal	c	c	100	91	6	20	(.)	9	8	10	−6	−11
5 Zaire	18	*19*	44	*55*	28	*24*	38	*26*	70	*33*	10	*2*
6 Burkina	7	14	91	100	10	12	2	−15	9	17	−8	−27
7 Burma	c	14	87	69	19	22	13	17	14	8	−6	−5
8 Malawi	16	16	82	70	14	23	2	14	16	19	−12	−9
9 Uganda	10	c	78	*95*	11	*8*	12	*5*	26	*5*	1	*−3*
10 Burundi	7	14	89	79	6	21	4	7	10	9	−2	−14
11 Niger	8	10	84	79	15	25	9	11	12	22	−7	−14
12 Tanzania	10	*22*	74	*70*	15	*20*	16	*8*	26	*11*	1	*−12*
13 Somalia	8	*24*	84	*78*	11	*20*	8	*−2*	17	*10*	−3	*−22*
14 India	10	*11*	74	*67*	18	*25*	16	*22*	4	*6*	−2	*−3*
15 Rwanda	14	..	81	..	10	..	5	..	12	..	−5	..
16 Central African Rep.	22	13	67	89	21	11	11	−1	27	23	−11	−13
17 Togo	8	17	76	79	22	23	17	4	20	31	−6	−19
18 Benin	14	12	83	91	12	12	3	−3	14	20	−9	−14
19 China	c	c	75	69	25	31	25	31	3	9	(.)	1
20 Guinea	..	19	..	65	..	14	..	16	..	29	..	2
21 Haiti	8	12	90	85	7	16	2	3	13	27	−5	−13
22 Ghana	14	6	77	90	18	8	8	5	17	5	−10	−3
23 Madagascar	23	*15*	74	*81*	10	*14*	4	*4*	16	*13*	−6	*−10*
24 Sierra Leone	8	7	83	91	12	9	9	2	30	12	−3	−7
25 Sri Lanka	13	8	74	78	12	29	13	14	38	26	1	−15
26 Kenya	15	20	70	61	14	21	15	19	31	25	1	−2
27 Pakistan	11	11	76	82	21	17	13	7	8	13	−8	−11
28 Sudan	12	13	79	88	10	15	9	−1	15	11	−1	−16
29 *Afghanistan*	c	..	99	..	11	..	1	..	11	..	−10	..
30 *Bhutan*	..	..	..	..	..	..	..	..	..	..	..	..
31 *Chad*	14	..	84	..	9	..	2	..	23	..	−7	..
32 *Kampuchea, Dem.*	16	..	71	..	13	..	12	..	12	..	−1	..
33 *Lao PDR*	..	..	..	..	..	..	..	..	..	..	..	..
34 *Mozambique*	..	..	..	..	..	..	..	..	..	..	..	..
35 *Viet Nam*	..	..	..	..	..	..	..	..	..	..	..	..
Middle-income economies	11 *w*	13 *w*	68 *w*	66 *w*	21 *w*	22 *w*	21 *w*	21 *w*	18 *w*	24 *w*	(.) *w*	−1 *w*
Oil exporters	11 *w*	14 *w*	68 *w*	62 *w*	19 *w*	22 *w*	21 *w*	24 *w*	19 *w*	25 *w*	2 *w*	2 *w*
Oil importers	11 *w*	13 *w*	67 *w*	68 *w*	22 *w*	23 *w*	21 *w*	20 *w*	18 *w*	23 *w*	−1 *w*	−3 *w*
Sub-Saharan Africa	11 *w*	13 *w*	70 *w*	68 *w*	18 *w*	20 *w*	19 *w*	19 *w*	27 *w*	21 *w*	1 *w*	−1 *w*
Lower middle-income	11 *w*	13 *w*	73 *w*	70 *w*	17 *w*	22 *w*	16 *w*	17 *w*	17 *w*	21 *w*	−1 *w*	−5 *w*
36 Senegal	17	19	75	78	12	17	8	3	24	28	−4	−13
37 Lesotho	18	*31*	109	*146*	11	*29*	−26	*−77*	16	*14*	−38	*−106*
38 Liberia	12	23	61	62	17	20	27	14	50	40	10	−5
39 Mauritania	19	23	54	88	14	18	27	−11	42	47	13	−29
40 Bolivia	10	9	80	94	16	7	11	−3	17	19	−5	−10
41 Yemen, PDR	..	..	..	..	..	..	..	..	..	..	..	..
42 Yemen Arab Rep.	..	41	..	79	..	29	..	−20	..	7	..	−50
43 Indonesia	6	11	88	69	7	24	6	20	5	25	(.)	−4
44 Zambia	15	26	44	60	26	15	41	15	50	31	15	−1
45 Honduras	10	15	75	72	15	17	15	13	27	27	(.)	−4
46 Egypt, Arab Rep.	19	25	67	63	18	28	14	12	18	29	−4	−16
47 El Salvador	9	13	79	81	15	12	12	6	27	21	−2	−7
48 Ivory Coast	11	17	69	67	19	18	20	16	35	34	1	−2
49 Zimbabwe	12	20	65	61	15	22	23	19	..	..	8	−3
50 Morocco	12	20	76	69	10	21	12	11	18	23	1	−9
51 Papua New Guinea	34	25	64	63	22	31	2	12	18	39	−20	−18
52 Philippines	9	8	70	71	21	27	21	21	17	20	(.)	−7
53 Nigeria	7	11	76	70	19	19	17	19	18	16	−2	0
54 Cameroon	14	10	73	54	13	27	13	37	25	32	−1	10
55 Thailand	10	13	71	67	20	25	19	20	18	22	−1	−5
56 Nicaragua	8	31	74	61	21	20	18	8	29	21	−3	−13
57 Costa Rica	13	16	78	64	20	21	9	20	23	35	−10	−1
58 Peru	12	15	69	72	21	13	19	14	16	21	−1	1
59 Guatemala	7	8	82	83	13	11	10	9	17	13	−3	−2
60 Congo, People's Rep.	14	13	80	51	22	46	5	35	36	55	−17	−11
61 Turkey	12	10	74	73	15	21	13	16	6	16	−1	−4
62 Tunisia	15	17	71	63	28	29	14	20	19	35	−13	−9
63 Jamaica	8	21	69	69	27	22	23	9	33	40	−4	−13
64 Dominican Rep.	18	9	75	73	9	22	7	18	15	15	−2	−4

Note: For data comparability and coverage see the technical notes.

	Distribution of gross domestic product (percent)											
	Public consumption		Private consumption		Gross domestic investment		Gross domestic savings		Exports of goods and nonfactor services		Resource balance	
	1965[a]	1983[b]	1965[a]	1983[b]	1965[a]	1983[b]	1965[a]	1983[b]	1965[a]	1983[b]	1965[a]	1983[b]
65 Paraguay	7	7	79	78	15	26	14	15	15	8	−1	−11
66 Ecuador	9	12	80	65	14	17	11	24	16	25	−3	7
67 Colombia	8	12	75	73	16	19	17	15	11	10	1	−4
68 Angola	. .	. .	. .	. .	. .	. .	. .	. .	. .	. .	. .	. .
69 Cuba	. .	. .	. .	. .	. .	. .	. .	. .	. .	. .	. .	. .
70 Korea, Dem. Rep.	. .	. .	. .	. .	. .	. .	. .	. .	. .	. .	. .	. .
71 Lebanon	10	. .	81	. .	22	. .	9	. .	36	. .	−13	. .
72 Mongolia	. .	. .	. .	. .	. .	. .	. .	. .	. .	. .	. .	. .
Upper middle-income	**11** w	**13** w	**65** w	**64** w	**23** w	**22** w	**24** w	**23** w	**19** w	**25** w	**1** w	**1** w
73 Jordan	. .	26	. .	91	. .	40	. .	−16	. .	43	. .	−56
74 Syrian Arab Rep.	14	21	76	66	10	23	10	13	17	12	(.)	−11
75 Malaysia	15	18	63	53	18	34	23	29	44	54	4	−5
76 Chile	11	15	73	75	15	8	16	11	14	24	1	2
77 Brazil	11	10	62	69	25	21	27	21	8	8	2	−1
78 Korea, Rep. of	9	11	83	62	15	27	8	26	9	37	−7	−1
79 Argentina	8	12	69	70	19	13	22	18	8	13	3	5
80 Panama	11	23	73	53	18	29	16	24	36	39	−2	−5
81 Portugal	12	15	68	69	25	29	20	16	27	32	−5	−13
82 Mexico	7	11	72	61	22	17	21	28	9	20	−1	11
83 Algeria	15	16	66	46	22	37	19	38	22	28	−3	1
84 South Africa	11	. .	62	. .	28	. .	27	. .	26	. .	(.)	
85 Uruguay	15	12	68	73	11	10	18	14	19	24	7	4
86 Yugoslavia	18	15	52	49	30	35	30	37	22	30	(.)	1
87 Venezuela	12	14	54	63	24	12	34	23	31	26	10	10
88 Greece	12	19	73	70	26	22	15	12	9	19	−11	−10
89 Israel	20	30	65	61	29	22	15	9	19	33	−13	−13
90 Hong Kong	7	8	64	67	36	27	29	25	71	95	−7	−2
91 Singapore	10	11	80	47	22	45	10	42	123	176	−12	−3
92 Trinidad and Tobago	11	c	66	69	23	34	23	31	39	36	(.)	−3
93 Iran, Islamic Rep.	13	. .	63	. .	17	. .	24	. .	20	. .	6	. .
94 Iraq	20	. .	50	. .	16	. .	31	. .	38	. .	15	. .
High-income oil exporters	**15** w	**26** w	**32** w	**35** w	**19** w	**29** w	**53** w	**39** w	**61** w	**53** w	**34** w	**10** w
95 Oman	. .	c	. .	54	. .	29	. .	46	. .	61	. .	18
96 Libya	14	34	36	31	29	23	50	35	53	43	21	12
97 Saudi Arabia	18	27	34	33	14	31	48	40	60	54	34	8
98 Kuwait	13	19	26	51	16	23	60	29	68	56	45	7
99 United Arab Emirates	. .	22		29	. .	32	. .	50	. .	57	. .	17
Industrial market economies	**15** w	**18** w	**61** w	**63** w	**23** w	**20** w	**23** w	**20** w	**12** w	**18** w	**(.)** w	**(.)** w
100 Spain	7	12	71	70	25	20	21	18	11	18	−3	−2
101 Ireland	14	20	72	59	24	23	15	21	35	53	−9	−2
102 Italy	15	19	62	63	20	17	23	18	16	26	3	1
103 New Zealand	12	17	63	58	27	25	25	25	22	31	−2	−1
104 Belgium	13	18	64	65	23	16	23	17	36	74	(.)	1
105 United Kingdom	17	22	64	60	20	17	19	18	20	27	−1	1
106 Austria	13	19	59	58	28	22	27	23	26	43	−1	1
107 Netherlands	15	18	59	60	27	18	26	22	43	58	−1	4
108 Japan	8	10	58	59	32	28	33	30	11	14	1	2
109 France	13	16	61	64	26	20	26	20	14	23	(.)	−1
110 Finland	14	19	60	55	28	25	26	25	21	31	−2	(.)
111 Germany, Fed. Rep.	15	20	56	57	28	21	29	23	18	30	(.)	2
112 Australia	11	17	63	63	28	21	26	20	15	15	−2	−1
113 Denmark	16	27	59	54	26	16	25	18	29	36	−2	2
114 Canada	15	21	60	57	26	19	25	22	19	26	(.)	3
115 Sweden	18	28	56	52	27	17	26	20	22	35	−1	2
116 Norway	15	19	56	48	30	24	29	33	41	46	−1	8
117 United States	17	19	62	66	20	17	21	15	5	8	1	−2
118 Switzerland	10	13	60	63	30	24	30	24	29	35	−1	(.)
East European nonmarket economies	. .	. .	. .	. .	. .	. .	. .	. .	. .	. .	. .	. .
119 Hungary	c	10	75	61	26	27	25	29	. .	40	. .	2
120 Albania	. .	. .	. .	. .	. .	. .	. .	. .	. .	. .	. .	. .
121 Bulgaria	. .	. .	. .	. .	. .	. .	. .	. .	. .	. .	. .	. .
122 Czechoslovakia	. .	. .	. .	. .	. .	. .	. .	. .	. .	. .	. .	. .
123 German Dem. Rep.	. .	. .	. .	. .	. .	. .	. .	. .	. .	. .	. .	. .
124 Poland	. .	. .	. .	. .	. .	. .	. .	. .	. .	. .	. .	. .
125 Romania	. .	. .	. .	. .	. .	. .	. .	. .	. .	. .	. .	. .
126 USSR	. .	. .	. .	. .	. .	. .	. .	. .	. .	. .	. .	. .

a. Figures in italics are for 1966, not 1965.   b. Figures in italics are for 1982, not 1983.   c. Public consumption figures are not available separately; they are therefore included in private consumption.

Table 6. Agriculture and food

		Value added in agriculture (millions of 1980 dollars)		Cereal imports (thousands of metric tons)		Food aid in cereals (thousands of metric tons)		Fertilizer consumption (hundreds of grams of plant nutrient per hectare of arable land)		Average index of food production per capita (1974–76=100)
		1970	1983[a]	1974	1983	1974/75[b]	1982/83[b]	1970[c]	1982	1981–83
Low-income economies				22,899 t	30,553 t	5,661 t	4,572 t	179 w	592 w	111 w
China and India				14,437 t	23,447 t	. .	327 t	230 w	804 w	115 w
Other low-income				8,462 t	7,106 t	4,079 t	4,245 t	148 w	387 w	102 w
Sub-Saharan Africa				2,232 t	3,277 t	765 t	1,969 t	23 w	42 w	94 w
1	Ethiopia	1,663	1,971	118	325	59	344	4	26	106
2	Bangladesh	5,427	6,545	1,719	1,844	2,130	1,252	142	512	101
3	Mali	403	606	281	183	114	88	29	30	106
4	Nepal	1,102	1,255	19	72	0	44	30	138	91
5	Zaire	1,503	1,866	343	273	(.)	110	8	8	93
6	Burkina	444	517	99	59	0	45	3	42	100
7	Burma	1,705	3,256	26	7	14	10	34	167	121
8	Malawi	. .	. .	17	21	(.)	3	52	138	101
9	Uganda	2,579	2,614	37	19	16	14	13		91
10	Burundi	468	585	7	20	6	7	5	10	97
11	Niger	851	649	155	45	75	12	1	8	122
12	Tanzania	1,583	1,886	431	214	148	171	30	44	103
13	Somalia	434	570	42	246	110	189	31	9	72
14	India	45,793	58,981	5,261	4,280	1,582	282	114	346	108
15	Rwanda	. .	. .	3	23	19	12	3	10	114
16	Central African Rep.	241	325	7	29	1	5	11	4	94
17	Togo	212	238	6	61	0	5	3	19	99
18	Benin	. .	415	8	67	9	14	33	17	95
19	China	73,170	116,986	9,176	19,167	. .	45	418	1,575	119
20	Guinea	. .	755	63	112	49	25	18	17	85
21	Haiti	. .	. .	83	209	25	90	4	51	90
22	Ghana	2,323	2,265	177	285	43	58	9	98	65
23	Madagascar	1,111	1,171	114	240	7	141	56	52	90
24	Sierra Leone	261	312	72	119	10	29	13	6	98
25	Sri Lanka	812	1,199	951	775	271	369	496	713	127
26	Kenya	1,223	2,253	15	160	2	165	224	289	86
27	Pakistan	5,005	7,061	1,274	396	619	369	168	616	105
28	Sudan	1,610	2,318	125	435	50	330	31	44	94
29	Afghanistan	. .	. .	5	156	10	66	24	56	105
30	Bhutan	. .	. .	23	13	0	3	(.)	10	104
31	Chad	339	. .	50	54	13	36	7	17	101
32	Kampuchea, Dem.	. .	. .	223	83	226	46	13	36	98
33	Lao PDR	. .	. .	53	35	13	(.)	4	6	125
34	Mozambique	. .	. .	62	287	34	166	27	130	68
35	Viet Nam	. .	. .	1,854	239	6	27	512	506	111
Middle-income economies				41,293 t	78,552 t	2,340 t	4,127 t	211 w	445 w	105 w
Oil exporters				18,022 t	43,580 t	1,078 t	2,355 t	139 w	468 w	105 w
Oil importers				23,271 t	34,972 t	1,262 t	1,772 t	254 w	432 w	105 w
Sub-Saharan Africa				1,521 t	4,859 t	111 t	411 t	40 w	91 w	93 w
Lower middle-income				16,776 t	29,831 t	1,491 t	3,999 t	176 w	398 w	105 w
36	Senegal	603	702	341	591	28	91	20	35	71
37	Lesotho	94	. .	49	91	14	28	17	151	76
38	Liberia	235	334	42	126	3	57	55	35	92
39	Mauritania	259	258	115	227	48	71	6	5	102
40	Bolivia	540	643	207	415	22	164	13	8	87
41	Yemen, PDR	. .	. .	149	205	38	9	(.)	109	84
42	Yemen Arab Rep.	451	761	158	556	0	28	1	51	80
43	Indonesia	12,097	20,225	1,919	2,992	301	155	119	750	121
44	Zambia	444	562	93	247	1	83	71	185	74
45	Honduras	477	664	52	83	31	95	160	137	107
46	Egypt, Arab Rep.	3,282	4,728	3,877	8,154	610	1,816	1,282	3,346	92
47	El Salvador	736	871	75	171	4	211	1,048	830	91
48	Ivory Coast	1,733	2,670	172	562	4	0	71	85	108
49	Zimbabwe	557	673	56	124	. .	6	466	532	79
50	Morocco	2,783	2,848	891	1,896	75	142	130	253	89
51	Papua New Guinea	655	926	71	155	. .	0	76	151	95
52	Philippines	5,115	8,609	817	1,343	89	49	214	288	113
53	Nigeria	17,186	16,001	389	2,336	7	0	3	65	98
54	Cameroon	1,492	1,955	81	178	4	6	28	57	84
55	Thailand	5,631	9,444	97	225	0	9	76	183	112
56	Nicaragua	410	608	44	109	3	51	184	186	74
57	Costa Rica	666	898	110	201	1	194	1,086	1,134	88
58	Peru	1,716	1,649	637	1,772	37	111	297	266	82
59	Guatemala	. .	. .	138	129	9	19	224	498	102
60	Congo, People's Rep.	147	164	34	90	2	9	112	19	99
61	Turkey	8,701	12,890	1,276	177	70	0	166	535	104
62	Tunisia	697	1,191	307	1,131	1	160	82	168	87
63	Jamaica	204	209	340	394	1	127	886	571	95
64	Dominican Rep.	993	1,577	252	392	16	167	354	353	95

Note: For data comparability and coverage see the technical notes.

		Value added in agriculture (millions of 1980 dollars)		Cereal imports (thousands of metric tons)		Food aid in cereals (thousands of metric tons)		Fertilizer consumption (hundreds of grams of plant nutrient per hectare of arable land)		Average index of food production per capita (1974–76=100)
		1970	1983[a]	1974	1983	1974/75[b]	1982/83[b]	1970[c]	1982	1981–83
65	Paraguay	640	1,193	71	94	10	1	58	39	109
66	Ecuador	1,054	1,343	152	400	13	8	123	277	92
67	Colombia	4,247	6,660	503	1,017	28	1	310	538	106
68	*Angola*	..	..	149	287	0	60	45	14	82
69	*Cuba*	..	..	1,622	2,105	..	2	1,539	1,726	127
70	*Korea, Dem. Rep.*	..	..	1,108	350	..	..	1,484	3,382	111
71	*Lebanon*	..	..	354	407	21	69	1,279	1,487	124
72	*Mongolia*	..	..	28	99	..	..	18	109	88
	Upper middle-income			24,517 *t*	48,721 *t*	849 *t*	128 *t*	242 *w*	486 *w*	106 *w*
73	Jordan	185	264	171	572	63	40	20	346	107
74	Syrian Arab Rep.	1,057	2,751	339	1,487	47	28	67	270	129
75	Malaysia	3,511	6,401	1,017	1,785	1	0	436	1,021	113
76	Chile	1,597	2,024	1,737	1,370	331	2	317	189	102
77	Brazil	18,425	33,202	2,485	4,925	31	0	169	365	113
78	Korea, Rep. of	8,176	12,250	2,679	6,354	234	53	2,466	2,817	109
79	Argentina	3,947	5,332	0	0			24	31	112
80	Panama	292	*344*	63	90	3	3	391	469	102
81	Portugal	..	2,194	1,860	3,031	0	0	411	720	82
82	Mexico	11,125	16,968	2,881	8,483			246	778	106
83	Algeria	1,731	2,693	1,816	3,667	54	2	174	211	83
84	South Africa	..	..	127	1,517			425	831	93
85	Uruguay	897	893	70	114	31	0	392	376	106
86	Yugoslavia	5,486	8,310	992	409			766	1,199	108
87	Venezuela	1,168	1,616	1,270	2,555			165	408	91
88	Greece	4,929	6,049	1,341	242			858	1,606	102
89	*Israel*	..	..	1,176	1,495	53	0	1,394	1,783	93
90	Hong Kong	321	244	657	907			..	..	101
91	Singapore	118	143	682	1,455	(.)	(.)	2,667	7,833	107
92	Trinidad and Tobago	160	..	208	295	..	(.)	640	304	70
93	*Iran, Islamic Rep.*	..	..	2,076	4,456	..	0	76	656	103
94	*Iraq*	..	..	870	3,512	1	(.)	35	145	110
	High-income oil exporters			1,379 *t*	5,250 *t*			58 *w*	55 *w*	..
95	Oman	..	..	52	173			(.)	272	..
96	Libya	168	572	612	808			64	385	84
97	Saudi Arabia	833	1,713	482	3,482			44	832	34
98	Kuwait	42	108	101	459			(.)	7,320	..
99	United Arab Emirates	..	..	132	328			(.)	3,324	..
	Industrial market economies			65,494 *t*	61,752 *t*			985 *w*	1,115 *w*	107 *w*
100	Spain	10,888	..	4,675	6,445			595	725	101
101	Ireland	..	..	631	514			3,573	6,438	97
102	Italy	22,099	25,577	8,100	6,128			962	1,614	112
103	New Zealand	..	..	92	89			8,875	9,468	110
104	Belgium[d]	2,212	2,798	4,585	6,043			5,686	5,206	103
105	United Kingdom	7,913	10,269	7,541	3,416			2,521	3,647	119
106	Austria	2,903	3,004	165	59			2,517	2,159	111
107	Netherlands	3,986	6,675	7,199	4,254			7,165	7,381	112
108	Japan	38,299	*39,554*	19,557	25,296			3,849	4,121	91
109	France	24,282	29,090	654	1,889			2,424	2,993	112
110	Finland	4,014	3,923	222	62			1,931	2,242	101
111	Germany, Fed. Rep.	15,442	19,586	7,164	4,209			4,208	4,350	113
112	Australia	7,102	8,337	2	32			246	237	103
113	Denmark	2,316	3,381	462	510			2,254	2,462	117
114	Canada	8,625	11,507	1,513	449			192	437	121
115	Sweden	3,983	4,252	301	122			1,639	1,612	108
116	Norway	2,048	2,380	713	404			2,471	3,185	114
117	United States	62,108	66,669	460	594			800	867	108
118	Switzerland	..	..	1,458	1,237			3,842	4,139	112
	East European nonmarket economies			18,543 *t*	41,006 *t*			635 *w*	1,128 *w*	100 *w*
119	Hungary	2,782	4,290	408	87			1,485	2,885	119
120	*Albania*	..	..	48	3			745	1,550	105
121	*Bulgaria*	..	..	649	204			1,446	2,501	117
122	*Czechoslovakia*	..	..	1,296	778			2,402	3,369	110
123	*German Dem. Rep.*	..	..	2,821	3,221			3,202	2,815	108
124	*Poland*	..	..	4,185	3,389		83	1,715	2,134	91
125	*Romania*	..	..	1,381	1,192			559	1,591	114
126	*USSR*	..	..	7,755	32,132			437	867	98

a. Figures in italics are for 1982, not 1983.   b. Figures are for the crop years 1974/75 and 1982/83.   c. Average for 1969–71.   d. Includes Luxembourg.

Table 7. Industry

		Distribution of manufacturing value added (percent; 1975 prices)					Value added in manufacturing (millions of 1975 dollars)	
		Food and agriculture 1982[a]	Textiles and clothing 1982[a]	Machinery and transport equipment 1982[a]	Chemicals 1982[a]	Other manufacturing 1982[a]	1970	1982[a]
Low-income economies								
China and India								
Other low-income								
Sub-Saharan Africa								
1	Ethiopia	27	27	. .	2	44	236	361
2	Bangladesh	30	37	4	17	12	647	1,294
3	Mali	30	53	5	1	11	44	57
4	Nepal	. .	. .	. .	. .	. .		
5	Zaire	. .	. .	. .	. .	. .	322	253
6	Burkina	74	7	. .	11	8	67	137
7	Burma	31	14	1	4	50	287	486
8	Malawi	54	10	. .	. .	36	44	76
9	Uganda	54	25	. .	. .	21	183	81
10	Burundi	. .	. .	. .	. .	. .	32	53
11	Niger	. .	. .	. .	. .	. .	54	158
12	Tanzania	. .	. .	. .	. .	. .	190	151
13	Somalia	. .	. .	. .	. .	. .	42	53
14	India	15	16	20	14	35	10,232	16,210
15	Rwanda	. .	. .	. .	. .	. .		107
16	Central African Rep.	57	28	0	2	13	68	29
17	Togo	. .	. .	. .	. .	. .	30	13
18	Benin	. .	. .	. .	. .	. .		59
19	China	. .	. .	. .	. .	. .		
20	Guinea	. .	. .	. .	. .	. .		26
21	Haiti	. .	. .	. .	. .	. .		
22	Ghana	. .	. .	. .	. .	. .	364	198
23	Madagascar	. .	. .	. .	. .	. .	295	233
24	Sierra Leone	. .	. .	. .	. .	. .	25	38
25	Sri Lanka	45	13	. .	. .	42	556	748
26	Kenya	26	10	31	8	25	167	536
27	Pakistan	46	14	7	16	17	1,492	2,967
28	Sudan	. .	. .	. .	. .	. .	253	433
29	*Afghanistan*	. .	. .	. .	. .	. .	. .	. .
30	*Bhutan*	. .	. .	. .	. .	. .	. .	. .
31	*Chad*	. .	. .	. .	. .	. .	37	21
32	*Kampuchea, Dem.*	. .	. .	. .	. .	. .	. .	. .
33	*Lao PDR*	. .	. .	. .	. .	. .	. .	. .
34	*Mozambique*	. .	. .	. .	. .	. .	. .	. .
35	*Viet Nam*	. .	. .	. .	. .	. .	. .	. .
Middle-income economies								
Oil exporters								
Oil importers								
Sub-Saharan Africa								
Lower middle-income								
36	Senegal	39	22	. .	. .	39	276	443
37	Lesotho	. .	. .	. .	. .	. .	3	10
38	Liberia	. .	. .	. .	. .	. .	25	39
39	Mauritania	. .	. .	. .	. .	. .	18	26
40	Bolivia	. .	. .	. .	. .	. .	241	344
41	Yemen, PDR	. .	. .	. .	. .	. .		
42	Yemen Arab Rep.	. .	. .	. .	. .	. .	25	118
43	Indonesia	29	7	7	12	45	1,517	6,072
44	Zambia	16	24	10	12	38	319	427
45	Honduras	. .	. .	. .	. .	. .	138	246
46	Egypt, Arab Rep.	. .	. .	. .	. .	. .	1,835	4,847
47	El Salvador	. .	. .	. .	. .	. .	252	255
48	Ivory Coast	. .	. .	. .	. .	. .	398	705
49	Zimbabwe	21	19	10	11	39	552	925
50	Morocco	31	12	9	10	38	1,138	1,960
51	Papua New Guinea	. .	. .	. .	. .	. .	59	138
52	Philippines	39	13	9	9	30	2,659	5,510
53	Nigeria	33	18	12	11	26	1,191	4,049
54	Cameroon	. .	. .	. .	. .	. .	199	533
55	Thailand	. .	. .	. .	. .	. .	1,675	4,837
56	Nicaragua	. .	. .	. .	. .	. .	282	382
57	Costa Rica	. .	. .	. .	. .	. .	261	452
58	Peru	26	13	11	12	38	2,929	3,963
59	Guatemala	. .	. .	. .	. .	. .		
60	Congo, People's Rep.	37	5	. .	7	51	73	121
61	Turkey	24	11	14	12	38	3,678	6,898
62	Tunisia	22	12	13	16	37	222	841
63	Jamaica	. .	. .	. .	. .	. .	328	284
64	Dominican Rep.	69	4	1	6	20	483	1,005

Note: For data comparability and coverage see the technical notes.

		Distribution of manufacturing value added (percent; 1975 prices)					Value added in manufacturing (millions of 1975 dollars)	
		Food and agriculture 1982[a]	Textiles and clothing 1982[a]	Machinery and transport equipment 1982[a]	Chemicals 1982[a]	Other manufacturing 1982[a]	1970	1982[a]
65	Paraguay	36	12	14	4	34	203	455
66	Ecuador	26	15	11	7	41	432	1,247
67	Colombia	32	15	11	12	30	1,625	2,686
68	Angola	..	..	..	..	..	..	..
69	Cuba	38	13	1	16	32	..	..
70	Korea, Dem. Rep.	..	..	..	..	..	..	..
71	Lebanon	..	..	..	..	..	..	..
72	Mongolia	21	29	..	5	45	..	..
Upper middle-income								
73	Jordan	..	..	..	..	..	55	300
74	Syrian Arab Rep.	27	32	4	4	33	706	1,510
75	Malaysia	20	7	22	5	46	1,022	3,287
76	Chile	19	4	11	12	54	1,881	1,694
77	Brazil	15	10	23	13	39	19,235	43,300
78	Korea, Rep. of	15	22	20	11	32	2,368	11,492
79	Argentina	14	11	21	14	40	9,554	8,980
80	Panama	51	11	2	6	30	204	288
81	Portugal	11	18	22	15	34	..	..
82	Mexico	19	8	20	12	41	14,592	30,217
83	Algeria	16	20	8	3	53	1,068	3,643
84	South Africa	15	12	18	11	44	..	..
85	Uruguay	37	18	9	9	27	723	787
86	Yugoslavia	15	14	20	8	43	4,844	12,605
87	Venezuela	27	6	8	8	51	3,419	5,709
88	Greece	21	25	9	9	36	2,558	4,381
89	Israel	15	12	25	8	40	..	..
90	Hong Kong	..	..	..	..	..	1,914	3,679
91	Singapore	5	3	53	5	34	827	2,431
92	Trinidad and Tobago	..	..	..	..	..	404	434
93	Iran, Islamic Rep.	14	21	10	5	50	2,601	..
94	Iraq	..	..	..	..	..	522	..
High-income oil exporters								
95	Oman	..	..	..	..	..	..	..
96	Libya	..	..	..	..	..	154	638
97	Saudi Arabia	4	..	..	..	96	1,726	3,817
98	Kuwait	..	..	..	..	..	368	894
99	United Arab Emirates	..	..	..	..	..	..	..
Industrial market economies								
100	Spain	13	15	16	10	46	18,331	28,734
101	Ireland	24	10	13	15	38	..	..
102	Italy	10	15	30	7	38	..	..
103	New Zealand	24	11	16	4	45	..	..
104	Belgium	19	8	28	13	32	14,386	19,192
105	United Kingdom	13	7	35	10	35	58,677	52,963
106	Austria	15	8	24	7	46	9,112	13,363
107	Netherlands	19	4	28	13	36	18,684	23,525
108	Japan	7	5	39	8	41	118,403	252,581
109	France	17	7	33	8	35	75,800	106,356
110	Finland	12	7	25	7	49	5,636	9,067
111	Germany, Fed. Rep.	10	5	38	10	37	149,113	187,404
112	Australia	19	8	21	9	43	20,206	23,604
113	Denmark	24	6	25	8	37	5,858	8,138
114	Canada	15	7	22	7	49	25,748	32,315
115	Sweden	10	3	35	7	45	16,743	18,046
116	Norway	14	3	30	8	45	5,322	6,181
117	United States	12	6	32	12	38	328,200	414,600
118	Switzerland	21	8	21	14	36	..	..
East European nonmarket economies								
119	Hungary	11	9	30	10	40	3,244	6,267
120	Albania	..	..	..	..	..	..	..
121	Bulgaria	24	16	16	6	38	..	..
122	Czechoslovakia	7	9	38	8	38	..	..
123	German Dem. Rep.	17	10	35	9	29	..	..
124	Poland	5	18	33	9	35	..	..
125	Romania	11	15	31	12	31	..	..
126	USSR	12	11	29	6	42	..	..

a. Figures in italics are for 1981, not 1982.

Table 8. Commercial energy

	Average annual energy growth rate (percent)				Energy consumption per capita (kilograms of oil equivalent)		Energy imports as a percentage of merchandise exports	
	Energy production		Energy consumption					
	1965–73[a]	1973–83	1965–73	1973–83	1965	1983	1965	1983[b]
Low-income economies	10.0 w	6.1 w	9.7 w	5.5 w	128 w	276 w	8 w	..
China and India	10.1 w	6.0 w	10.2 w	5.6 w	143 w	341 w	..	..
Other low-income	8.0 w	7.1 w	6.1 w	3.4 w	67 w	80 w	7 w	..
Sub-Saharan Africa	10.4 w	8.4 w	9.5 w	1.1 w	45 w	56 w	8 w	..
1 Ethiopia	11.1	6.2	11.4	4.4	10	19	8	
2 Bangladesh	..	12.6	..	7.4	..	36	..	20
3 Mali	80.5	5.0	4.6	4.8	15	22	16	..
4 Nepal	27.2	7.3	8.8	7.3	6	13	..	..
5 Zaire	4.8	9.1	6.0	1.5	67	77	6	..
6 Burkina	..	..	8.0	10.7	8	22	11	50
7 Burma	9.6	7.2	5.9	5.7	39	65	4	..
8 Malawi	31.1	8.3	8.3	4.3	25	45	7	..
9 Uganda	3.7	−2.6	8.4	−5.8	36	23	..	..
10 Burundi	..	30.2	5.6	12.5	5	17	11	..
11 Niger	..	..	14.7	11.7	8	43	9	17
12 Tanzania	6.8	5.9	10.5	−2.6	37	38	..	..
13 Somalia	..	..	9.3	16.8	15	84	9	..
14 India	3.7	7.7	5.1	6.6	100	182	8	..
15 Rwanda	15.7	2.0	11.4	13.0	8	35	10	..
16 Central African Rep.	10.6	3.9	9.8	4.7	22	35	7	..
17 Togo	−6.1	27.4	12.9	13.9	25	88	6	18
18 Benin	..	..	19.7	0.3	21	39	14	..
19 China	11.8	5.7	11.9	5.4	170	455	..	..
20 Guinea	17.1	2.2	2.3	1.5	56	54	..	..
21 Haiti	..	9.7	6.2	6.9	25	55	..	..
22 Ghana	43.4	1.0	15.0	−0.4	76	111	6	..
23 Madagascar	8.6	2.3	13.6	1.4	33	59	8	32
24 Sierra Leone	..	..	5.1	6.9	90	102	11	..
25 Sri Lanka	12.0	6.0	5.3	3.4	107	143	6	40
26 Kenya	9.9	15.0	7.1	1.4	114	109	..	..
27 Pakistan	5.8	8.6	1.7	7.8	136	197	7	49
28 Sudan	14.7	9.0	12.4	−3.3	67	66	5	57
29 Afghanistan	46.5	−0.3	5.5	2.4	30	46	8	..
30 Bhutan	..	..	..	..	106	..	..	..
31 Chad	..	..	..	..	..	..	23	..
32 Kampuchea, Dem.	..	..	19.8	0.8	19	..	7	..
33 Lao PDR	..	20.2	16.6	7.0	22	76	..	..
34 Mozambique	4.6	18.6	9.3	1.5	93	95	13	..
35 Viet Nam	−3.4	5.6	6.7	−2.1	..	90	..	..
Middle-income economies	8.5 w	(.) w	7.9 w	5.2 w	380 w	745 w	8 w	29 w
Oil exporters	9.1 w	−1.5 w	7.2 w	7.1 w	295 w	606 w	5 w	..
Oil importers	6.0 w	5.4 w	8.2 w	4.2 w	448 w	866 w	10 w	35 w
Sub-Saharan Africa	30.8 w	−2.5 w	8.9 w	7.0 w	90 w	189 w	5 w	..
Lower middle-income	15.9 w	2.2 w	7.4 w	5.5 w	183 w	382 w	8 w	..
36 Senegal	..	..	14.3	−2.8	169	151	8	58
37 Lesotho	..	..	..	..	..	..	..	..
38 Liberia	37.0	−0.4	16.1	1.9	181	357	6	..
39 Mauritania	..	..	16.0	3.6	48	130	2	..
40 Bolivia	17.8	−0.2	5.2	6.1	156	292	1	..
41 Yemen, PDR	..	..	−21.7	7.1	..	934	63	..
42 Yemen Arab Rep.	..	..	16.5	22.4	7	116	..	..
43 Indonesia	12.7	2.7	6.4	7.8	91	204	3	20
44 Zambia	26.3	6.4	1.6	1.9	464	432	5	..
45 Honduras	15.6	10.9	10.4	3.9	111	204	5	28
46 Egypt, Arab Rep	10.0	16.4	1.9	11.5	211	532	11	12
47 El Salvador	2.1	14.8	5.7	3.3	140	190	5	57
48 Ivory Coast	0.5	45.8	10.9	5.1	109	186	5	16
49 Zimbabwe	1.8	−2.6	9.9	0.5	441	491	(.)	..
50 Morocco	2.6	(.)	8.9	5.4	124	258	5	57
51 Papua New Guinea	16.5	7.8	20.3	3.6	56	223	7	..
52 Philippines	4.6	20.8	9.1	2.3	160	252	12	44
53 Nigeria	33.4	−4.4	9.6	15.4	33	150	7	..
54 Cameroon	1.2	45.6	6.5	8.0	67	128	6	4
55 Thailand	10.5	13.7	14.6	5.4	80	269	11	39
56 Nicaragua	4.8	6.4	9.8	0.7	187	262	6	46
57 Costa Rica	10.2	8.9	12.2	4.9	267	609	8	22
58 Peru	1.9	11.2	5.1	3.6	406	550	3	2
59 Guatemala	18.3	25.1	7.1	2.8	148	178	9	68
60 Congo, People's Rep.	33.4	10.5	7.5	11.9	90	216	8	..
61 Turkey	5.7	3.8	10.0	4.6	258	599	12	66
62 Tunisia	58.7	4.3	8.7	8.2	170	473	12	31
63 Jamaica	−1.8	2.2	10.2	−1.5	707	980	12	..
64 Dominican Rep.	4.9	40.0	18.6	1.8	130	407	7	71

Note: For data comparability and coverage see the technical notes.

	Average annual energy growth rate (percent)				Energy consumption per capita (kilograms of oil equivalent)		Energy imports as a percentage of merchandise exports	
	Energy production		Energy consumption					
	1965–73[a]	1973–83	1965–73	1973–83	1965	1983	1965	1983[b]
65 Paraguay	..	6.3	9.3	7.5	86	187	14	*1*
66 Ecuador	36.6	2.5	9.3	13.6	163	675	11	..
67 Colombia	2.2	3.6	6.5	5.6	416	786	1	21
68 *Angola*	47.1	−1.0	10.6	4.1	111	226	2	..
69 *Cuba*	7.2	11.8	5.6	3.8	604	1,042	12	..
70 *Korea, Dem. Rep.*	9.3	3.1	9.5	3.6	504	2,093	..	..
71 *Lebanon*	2.4	0.2	6.1	−4.2	713	610	5	..
72 *Mongolia*	11.2	8.5	9.1	9.0	471	1,137	..	..
Upper middle-income	**6.8** *w*	**−0.8** *w*	**8.1** *w*	**5.1** *w*	**646** *w*	**1,225** *w*	**8** *w*	**29** *w*
73 Jordan	..	..	4.3	15.3	226	790	33	101
74 Syrian Arab Rep.	164.4	3.6	9.7	13.3	212	847	13	..
75 Malaysia	60.8	15.9	8.5	7.1	312	702	10	*16*
76 Chile	4.1	1.5	7.2	0.6	657	755	5	*24*
77 Brazil	8.7	9.0	11.5	4.9	287	745	14	56
78 Korea, Rep. of	2.6	4.6	15.8	8.8	237	1,168	18	28
79 Argentina	6.4	4.5	5.9	2.7	977	1,460	8	9
80 Panama	2.7	17.0	7.6	−6.3	3,203	2,082	54	82
81 Portugal	3.9	(.)	8.7	3.7	506	1,194	13	48
82 Mexico	4.5	17.0	7.2	8.7	622	1,332	4	..
83 Algeria	7.2	3.3	11.2	12.5	226	982	(.)	2
84 South Africa	3.5	8.2	5.2	4.2	1,695	2,278	..	..
85 Uruguay	5.2	18.2	1.7	0.7	767	776	13	28
86 Yugoslavia	3.5	4.1	6.8	4.3	898	1,903	7	33
87 Venezuela	0.1	−3.5	4.3	4.5	2,269	2,295	(.)	*1*
88 Greece	12.7	9.0	11.7	3.8	615	1,790	29	59
89 Israel	53.4	−35.6	6.1	2.2	1,574	1,932	13	29
90 Hong Kong	..	..	11.0	5.8	599	1,647	4	7
91 Singapore	..	..	11.4	4.9	2,002	4,757	17	40
92 Trinidad and Tobago	0.6	0.8	2.7	3.9	4,132	5,191	59	4
93 *Iran, Islamic Rep.*	16.3	−12.9	13.3	1.0	537	976	(.)	..
94 *Iraq*	4.5	−7.0	6.2	8.3	399	763	(.)	..
High-income oil exporters	**11.7** *w*	**−2.8** *w*	**8.6** *w*	**7.9** *w*	**1,344** *w*	**3,858** *w*	**(.)** *w*	**..**
95 Oman	57.2	0.9	89.7	−4.1	..	764	..	*1*
96 Libya	8.6	−4.4	14.8	19.6	222	2,769	2	*1*
97 Saudi Arabia	15.7	−1.2	12.4	6.8	1,759	3,536	(.)	..
98 Kuwait	4.3	−9.8	0.5	0.4	..	5,443	(.)	..
99 United Arab Emirates	24.1	−1.7	65.3	25.4	108	7,554	..	..
Industrial market economies	**3.2** *w*	**1.6** *w*	**5.2** *w*	**0.1** *w*	**3,764** *w*	**4,733** *w*	**11** *w*	**25** *w*
100 Spain	3.2	3.6	8.6	2.3	901	1,858	31	59
101 Ireland	−1.4	12.1	5.8	2.7	1,504	2,354	14	14
102 Italy	2.3	0.5	7.1	(.)	1,568	2,458	16	34
103 New Zealand	4.5	4.3	4.7	1.5	2,622	3,808	7	18
104 Belgium	−9.0	4.0	6.0	−0.7	3,402	4,401	9	18
105 United Kingdom	−0.7	8.9	2.6	−1.4	3,481	3,461	13	12
106 Austria	−0.2	0.4	6.6	0.5	2,060	3,083	10	17
107 Netherlands	25.7	0.9	9.0	0.6	3,134	5,397	12	23
108 Japan	−3.1	5.0	11.9	0.4	1,496	2,929	19	40
109 France	−3.1	5.5	6.0	0.5	2,468	3,429	16	28
110 Finland	0.3	12.3	8.4	2.1	2,233	4,649	11	28
111 Germany, Fed. Rep.	(.)	0.3	4.9	(.)	3,197	4,156	8	19
112 Australia	16.1	4.5	6.4	2.5	3,287	4,811	10	*16*
113 Denmark	−32.5	36.1	4.8	−1.2	2,911	3,062	13	20
114 Canada	9.5	1.4	6.1	2.0	6,007	8,847	7	6
115 Sweden	2.8	5.6	4.5	0.4	4,162	5,821	12	22
116 Norway	6.0	16.2	5.4	2.6	4,650	8,087	11	8
117 United States	3.0	0.1	4.1	−0.4	6,586	7,030	8	30
118 Switzerland	3.1	4.3	6.2	0.8	2,501	3,794	8	13
East European nonmarket economies	**4.3** *w*	**3.5** *w*	**4.6** *w*	**3.2** *w*	**2,523** *w*	**4,279** *w*	**..**	**..**
119 Hungary	0.4	1.5	3.3	3.1	1,825	2,968	12	22
120 *Albania*	14.2	6.6	7.2	6.5	415	982	..	..
121 *Bulgaria*	0.8	4.7	7.7	4.3	1,788	4,390	..	..
122 *Czechoslovakia*	1.1	0.9	3.6	1.8	3,374	4,691	..	30
123 *German Dem. Rep.*	0.6	1.8	2.5	2.0	3,762	5,370	..	..
124 *Poland*	4.5	1.0	4.8	2.5	2,027	3,133	..	24
125 *Romania*	5.6	2.0	7.8	3.8	1,536	3,305	..	..
126 *USSR*	4.7	4.0	4.7	3.4	2,603	4,505	..	..

a. Figures in italics are for 1966–73, not 1965–73.   b. Figures in italics are for 1981 or 1982, not 1983.

Table 9. Growth of merchandise trade

	Merchandise trade (millions of dollars)		Average annual growth rate[a] (percent)				Terms of trade (1980=100)	
	Exports 1983	Imports 1983[b]	Exports 1965–73	Exports 1973–83[c]	Imports 1965–73	Imports 1973–83[c]	1981	1983
Low-income economies	45,991 *t*	57,333 *t*	1.5 *w*	0.9 *w*	−2.0 *w*	1.4 *w*	95 *m*	96 *m*
China and India	31,931 *t*	34,952 *t*	..	..	..	..	..	..
Other low-income	14,060 *t*	22,381 *t*	1.3 *w*	−0.8 *w*	0.2 *w*	0.6 *w*	95 *m*	96 *m*
Sub-Saharan Africa	7,827 *t*	11,501 *t*	2.4 *w*	−4.0 *w*	2.3 *w*	−2.2 *w*	88 *m*	94 *m*
1 Ethiopia	422	875	3.0	1.4	−0.2	2.7	68	86
2 Bangladesh	789	1,502	−6.5	1.7	−8.2	4.1	102	102
3 Mali	106	344	13.1	5.1	8.5	3.9	110	118
4 Nepal	94	464	..	..	..	..	..	..
5 Zaire	1,459	953	6.5	−8.7	9.6	−13.7	87	92
6 Burkina	99	288	−1.0	1.7	7.2	4.2	109	114
7 Burma	382	270	−4.8	4.9	−6.7	−0.6	111	84
8 Malawi	220	312	3.8	2.8	6.4	−0.6	106	126
9 Uganda	354	340	0.2	−8.0	−2.5	1.9	75	79
10 Burundi	76	194	..	..	..	..	..	..
11 Niger	301	443	6.1	19.0	4.4	11.5	84	112
12 Tanzania	480	1,134	0.9	−4.6	7.1	−2.7	88	91
13 Somalia	163	422	6.7	7.3	1.4	0.0	109	118
14 India	9,705	13,562	2.3	4.9	−5.7	2.8	91	96
15 Rwanda	80	279	6.3	2.6	4.6	12.9	65	66
16 Central African Rep.	106	132	−0.4	3.8	−0.5	2.5	73	97
17 Togo	242	284	4.4	3.5	6.6	7.4	103	107
18 Benin	85	523	12.4	−1.4	13.2	4.5	95	89
19 China	22,226	21,390	..	..	..	..	..	..
20 Guinea	390	279	..	..	..	..	..	..
21 Haiti	412	620	..	..	..	..	..	..
22 Ghana	895	719	3.5	−6.4	−3.3	−8.0	69	63
23 Madagascar	329	439	5.4	−4.3	1.5	−2.5	79	93
24 Sierra Leone	202	171	2.2	−5.3	0.9	−5.0	84	94
25 Sri Lanka	1,066	1,788	−4.7	2.6	−3.2	4.7	95	104
26 Kenya	876	1,274	3.8	−4.8	5.9	−4.6	87	89
27 Pakistan	3,075	5,341	3.7	8.1	−2.9	5.7	99	101
28 Sudan	624	1,354	3.8	−1.5	4.9	1.3	103	88
29 Afghanistan	391	798	5.9	6.8	−0.6	4.7	102	105
30 Bhutan	..	..	..	..	..	..	..	..
31 Chad	58	109	−3.5	−3.1	18.7	−8.6	105	112
32 Kampuchea, Dem.	..	..	..	..	..	..	..	..
33 Lao PDR	26	96	..	..	..	..	..	..
34 Mozambique	260	635	−7.9	−8.3	−8.9	−4.2	96	96
35 Viet Nam	..	..	..	..	..	..	..	..
Middle-income economies	333,532 *t*	350,734 *t*	5.9 *w*	−0.4 *w*	8.3 *w*	4.1 *w*	95 *m*	94 *m*
Oil exporters	146,833 *t*	132,305 *t*	5.8 *w*	−5.1 *w*	5.9 *w*	7.6 *w*	110 *m*	102 *m*
Oil importers	186,699 *t*	218,430 *t*	6.3 *w*	7.3 *w*	9.3 *w*	1.9 *w*	92 *m*	90 *m*
Sub-Saharan Africa	27,201 *t*	25,961 *t*	6.9 *w*	−5.8 *w*	6.5 *w*	8.2 *w*	95 *m*	99 *m*
Lower middle-income	91,138 *t*	110,575 *t*	4.8 *w*	0.1 *w*	4.5 *w*	1.4 *w*	94 *m*	94 *m*
36 Senegal	585	984	−1.3	−0.9	5.4	−1.2	104	88
37 Lesotho[d]	..	..	..	..	..	..	..	..
38 Liberia	841	415	8.9	−2.3	3.6	−4.3	93	104
39 Mauritania	246	227	9.7	0.5	15.4	−0.8	95	102
40 Bolivia	766	424	5.1	−2.4	0.9	−0.9	84	84
41 Yemen, PDR	449	1,010	..	..	..	..	..	..
42 Yemen, Arab Rep.	204	1,521	..	..	..	..	..	..
43 Indonesia	21,145	16,346	11.1	1.4	13.9	9.8	110	102
44 Zambia	866	690	−0.3	−0.8	3.0	−7.3	81	82
45 Honduras	660	823	4.2	0.6	3.1	−1.3	83	87
46 Egypt, Arab Rep.	4,531	10,274	3.8	2.3	−3.9	10.1	113	103
47 El Salvador	735	891	2.7	1.4	1.8	−2.2	73	72
48 Ivory coast	2,068	1,814	7.1	−1.4	7.8	0.1	92	102
49 Zimbabwe	1,273	1,432	..	..	..	..	..	..
50 Morocco	2,062	3,599	6.0	0.5	6.2	0.8	108	100
51 Papua New Guinea	822	1,071	..	..	..	..	..	..
52 Philippines	4,932	7,980	4.2	7.5	3.1	1.3	88	92
53 Nigeria	17,509	17,600	8.9	−6.2	8.9	13.6	112	94
54 Cameroon	1,067	1,226	4.2	3.9	6.3	5.1	77	76
55 Thailand	6,368	10,279	6.9	9.0	4.4	3.3	96	89
56 Nicaragua	411	799	2.6	−0.4	2.0	−3.7	70	67
57 Costa Rica	1,071	993	10.3	2.7	8.6	−2.4	90	95
58 Peru	3,015	2,688	−2.1	8.5	−2.0	−0.6	94	109
59 Guatemala	1,220	1,126	5.1	4.6	3.6	−0.1	76	83
60 Congo, People's Rep.	887	806	−2.2	4.4	−2.3	12.0	117	104
61 Turkey	5,671	8,548	..	6.3	..	−0.2	67	..
62 Tunisia	1,851	3,117	8.6	0.2	7.7	5.3	100	98
63 Jamaica	726	1,518	3.9	−3.0	6.6	−4.7	89	90
64 Dominican Rep.	648	1,279	11.0	2.2	13.3	−0.9	125	85

Note: For data comparability and coverage see the technical notes.

		Merchandise trade (millions of dollars)		Average annual growth rate[a] (percent)				Terms of trade (1980 = 100)	
		Exports 1983	Imports 1983[b]	Exports		Imports		1981	1983
				1965–73	1973–83[c]	1965–73	1973–83[c]		
65	Paraguay	252	506	5.2	2.2	3.1	5.1	100	103
66	Ecuador	2,550	1,465	3.4	−3.4	8.5	4.0	97	114
67	Colombia	3,081	4,967	5.4	2.8	5.5	10.5	87	90
68	Angola	1,859	768	5.4	−13.3	8.3	3.3	110	99
69	Cuba	..	..	1.3	3.3	3.6	−0.6	..	..
70	Korea, Dem. Rep.	..	..	..	..	..	..	..	..
71	Lebanon	767	3,390	14.3	−3.4	6.5	3.2	98	93
72	Mongolia	..	..	..	..	..	..	..	..
	Upper middle-income	**242,394** t	**240,159** t	**5.7** w	**0.5** w	**9.7** w	**4.0** w	**98** m	**97** m
73	Jordan	739	3,217	5.0	17.8	3.8	13.3	109	101
74	Syrian Arab Rep.	1,875	4,180	1.0	−3.3	8.8	9.1	112	105
75	Malaysia	14,130	13,234	8.0	4.9	4.4	7.3	91	87
76	Chile	3,836	2,754	−1.4	9.7	2.3	1.2	79	90
77	Brazil	25,127	16,844	10.1	8.2	18.4	−4.6	85	92
78	Korea, Rep. of	24,445	26,192	31.7	14.8	22.4	7.5	93	100
79	Argentina	7,910	4,666	2.4	8.6	5.4	−0.3	102	91
80	Panama	480	1,412	1.1	−6.6	6.5	−4.4	95	84
81	Portugal	4,602	8,257	2.8	..	15.1	..	..	..
82	Mexico	21,168	8,201	1.0	14.4	5.7	5.5	110	105
83	Algeria	11,158	10,332	1.4	−1.1	12.1	6.5	116	102
84	South Africa[d]	18,608	15,693	1.6	5.6	6.6	−0.3	71	..
85	Uruguay	1,008	787	−2.9	9.2	2.9	−1.5	91	81
86	Yugoslavia	9,914	12,154	7.7	..	12.3	..	101	..
87	Venezuela	15,040	6,667	0.2	−6.8	4.8	4.7	119	103
88	Greece	4,412	9,500	13.4	9.7	9.6	2.8	88	..
89	Israel	5,112	8,500	12.2	9.0	12.9	−0.2	93	100
90	Hong Kong	21,951	24,009	11.7	10.3	10.5	12.0	97	..
91	Singapore	21,833	28,158	11.0	..	9.8	..	..	..
92	Trinidad and Tobago	2,353	2,582	−1.0	−7.7	2.1	−5.1	99	93
93	Iran, Islamic Rep.	16,445	11,539	12.4	−17.2	12.6	3.6	113	91
94	Iraq	10,250	21,280	1.1	−8.5	4.6	21.2	125	110
	High-income oil exporters	**120,832** t	**68,868** t	**11.4** w	**−5.8** w	**10.1** w	**18.7** w	**119** m	**105** m
95	Oman	4,058	2,492	..	..	..	..	..	..
96	Libya	13,252	9,500	10.1	−8.7	14.2	7.2	117	98
97	Saudi Arabia	79,125	40,473	15.0	−4.5	10.4	27.6	120	115
98	Kuwait	10,447	8,283	5.5	−11.5	6.3	13.3	125	106
99	United Arab Emirates	13,950	8,120	19.6	−2.1	8.5	14.3	117	105
	Industrial market economies	**1,128,132** t	**1,183,257** t	**9.4** w	**4.2** w	**10.0** w	**3.0** w	**99** m	**100** m
100	Spain	19,711	28,926	15.8	..	7.0	..	92	..
101	Ireland	8,609	9,169	8.4	8.1	7.8	5.2	97	139
102	Italy	72,670	78,323	10.2	4.7	10.7	2.4	91	97
103	New Zealand	5,270	5,327	6.0	4.4	4.0	0.1	99	96
104	Belgium[e]	51,676	53,654	10.3	3.1	10.9	2.5	95	94
105	United Kingdom	91,419	99,240	5.0	4.7	6.5	3.8	101	98
106	Austria	15,423	19,322	11.2	6.2	10.6	4.7	96	102
107	Netherlands	65,676	61,585	12.7	2.8	10.3	1.9	100	101
108	Japan	146,804	125,017	14.7	7.4	14.9	1.3	103	106
109	France	91,145	105,272	11.4	4.6	11.8	4.7	96	99
110	Finland	12,510	12,846	7.6	5.1	7.6	1.5	99	102
111	Germany, Fed. Rep.	168,748	152,011	10.7	4.4	11.3	4.1	93	98
112	Australia	20,651	19,420	9.3	2.7	6.8	..	100	97
113	Denmark	15,601	16,179	6.6	4.7	7.1	0.8	97	100
114	Canada	72,420	60,477	9.5	3.6	9.4	1.5	95	97
115	Sweden	27,377	26,090	7.9	0.7	5.4	0.9	98	96
116	Norway	17,972	13,494	8.3	6.3	8.2	3.0	111	110
117	United States	199,144	267,971	6.8	2.8	9.4	3.1	103	112
118	Switzerland	25,307	28,934	6.7	3.6	11.8	4.2	106	111
	East European nonmarket economies	**176,222** t	**160,545** t	**8.3** w	**5.9** w	**7.0** w	**2.4** w	..	..
119	Hungary	8,722	8,481	10.4	6.2	9.8	3.8	99	95
120	Albania	..	..	..	..	..	..	..	..
121	Bulgaria	12,690	13,380	11.4	12.1	9.3	5.7	..	..
122	Czechoslovakia	16,477	16,324	6.8	5.7	6.7	2.5	96	..
123	German Dem. Rep.	23,793	21,524	9.5	6.5	10.1	3.8	..	..
124	Poland	11,572	10,590	−0.3	6.3	−1.6	−1.1	97	92
125	Romania	11,633	9,836	..	..	..	..	..	..
126	USSR	91,336	80,410	9.7	..	9.6	..	..	..

a. See the technical notes. b. Figures in italics are for 1982, not 1983. c. Figures in italics are for 1973–82, not 1973–83. d. Figures are for the South African Customs Union comprising South Africa, Namibia, Lesotho, Botswana, and Swaziland. Trade between the component territories is excluded. e. Includes Luxembourg.

Table 10. Structure of merchandise exports

	Percentage share of merchandise exports									
	Fuels, minerals, and metals		Other primary commodities		Textiles and clothing		Machinery and transport equipment		Other manufactures	
	1965	1982[a]	1965	1982[a]	1965	1982[a]	1965	1982[a]	1965	1982[a]
Low-income economies	11 w	20 w	65 w	30 w	16 w	18 w	1 w	5 w	7 w	28 w
China and India	..	21 w	..	23 w	..	17 w	..	6 w	..	33 w
Other low-income	12 w	15 w	78 w	55 w	5 w	20 w	(.) w	2 w	4 w	8 w
Sub-Saharan Africa	20 w	22 w	75 w	69 w	(.) w	1 w	(.) w	2 w	4 w	5 w
1 Ethiopia	(.)	8	99	91	(.)	(.)	(.)	(.)	(.)	1
2 Bangladesh	..	2	..	36	..	47	..	4	..	11
3 Mali	1	..	96	..	1	..	1	..	1	..
4 Nepal	..	(.)	..	72	..	10	..	(.)	..	17
5 Zaire	72	..	20	..	(.)	..	(.)	..	8	..
6 Burkina	1	(.)	94	85	2	2	1	6	1	7
7 Burma	5	..	94	..	(.)	..	(.)	..	(.)	..
8 Malawi	(.)	(.)	99	88	(.)	6	(.)	3	1	3
9 Uganda	13	..	86	..	(.)	..	(.)	..	1	..
10 Burundi	(.)	..	94	..	(.)	..	(.)	..	5	..
11 Niger	(.)	81	95	17	1	1	1	1	3	1
12 Tanzania	1	5	86	82	(.)	3	(.)	2	13	7
13 Somalia	(.)	(.)	86	99	(.)	(.)	4	(.)	10	(.)
14 India	10	7	41	33	36	24	1	7	12	29
15 Rwanda	40	..	60	..	(.)	..	(.)	..	1	..
16 Central African Rep.	..	..	..	..	..	..	..	..	..	..
17 Togo	33	52	62	33	(.)	1	1	1	4	13
18 Benin	1	..	94	..	(.)	..	2	..	3	..
19 China	..	26	..	20	..	15	..	6	..	34
20 Guinea	..	..	..	..	..	..	..	..	..	..
21 Haiti	..	..	..	..	..	..	..	..	..	..
22 Ghana	13	..	85	..	(.)	..	1	..	2	..
23 Madagascar	4	12	90	81	1	4	1	1	4	2
24 Sierra Leone	..	..	..	..	..	..	..	..	..	..
25 Sri Lanka	2	14	97	59	(.)	17	(.)	2	1	8
26 Kenya	13	29	77	57	(.)	(.)	(.)	2	9	12
27 Pakistan	2	6	62	34	29	46	1	2	6	12
28 Sudan	1	5	98	93	(.)	1	1	1	(.)	(.)
29 Afghanistan	(.)	..	87	..	13	..	0	..	(.)	..
30 Bhutan	..	..	..	..	..	..	..	..	..	..
31 Chad	5	..	92	..	(.)	..	(.)	..	3	..
32 Kampuchea, Dem.	(.)	..	99	..	(.)	..	(.)	..	(.)	..
33 Lao PDR	62	..	32	..	(.)	..	(.)	..	6	..
34 Mozambique	14	..	84	..	1	..	(.)	..	1	..
35 Viet Nam	..	..	..	..	..	..	..	..	..	..
Middle-income economies	36 w	37 w	48 w	21 w	4 w	8 w	3 w	11 w	10 w	23 w
Oil exporters	60 w	79 w	34 w	12 w	2 w	1 w	1 w	3 w	3 w	4 w
Oil importers	19 w	13 w	57 w	27 w	6 w	12 w	4 w	15 w	4 w	33 w
Sub-Saharan Africa	40 w	..	52 w	..	1 w	..	1 w	..	5 w	..
Lower middle-income	26 w	47 w	66 w	34 w	2 w	6 w	1 w	2 w	5 w	11 w
36 Senegal	9	52	88	29	1	5	1	4	2	11
37 Lesotho[b]	..	..	..	..	..	..	..	..	..	..
38 Liberia	72	67	25	31	(.)	(.)	1	1	2	1
39 Mauritania	94	..	5	..	(.)	..	1	..	(.)	..
40 Bolivia	93	..	3	..	(.)	..	(.)	..	4	..
41 Yemen, PDR	79	..	15	..	2	..	2	..	2	..
42 Yemen Arab Rep.	..	..	..	..	..	..	..	..	..	..
43 Indonesia	43	85	53	11	(.)	1	3	1	1	2
44 Zambia	97	..	3	..	(.)	..	(.)	..	(.)	..
45 Honduras	6	4	90	87	1	2	(.)	(.)	3	7
46 Egypt, Arab Rep.	8	70	71	22	15	6	(.)	(.)	5	2
47 El Salvador	2	1	81	55	6	15	1	3	10	22
48 Ivory Coast	2	13	93	76	1	2	1	3	3	6
49 Zimbabwe	24	..	47	..	6	..	6	..	17	..
50 Morocco	40	39	55	26	1	12	(.)	1	4	21
51 Papua New Guinea	(.)	51	90	40	(.)	(.)	(.)	2	10	7
52 Philippines	11	12	84	38	1	7	(.)	3	5	39
53 Nigeria	32	..	65	..	(.)	..	0	..	2	..
54 Cameroon	17	49	77	44	(.)	2	3	1	2	4
55 Thailand	11	7	84	64	(.)	10	(.)	6	4	13
56 Nicaragua	4	1	90	91	(.)	(.)	(.)	(.)	5	7
57 Costa Rica	(.)	1	84	71	2	3	1	4	13	21
58 Peru	45	69	54	17	(.)	8	(.)	1	1	5
59 Guatemala	(.)	2	86	69	4	5	1	2	9	22
60 Congo, People's Rep.	..	..	..	..	..	..	..	..	..	..
61 Turkey	9	10	89	47	1	20	(.)	5	1	18
62 Tunisia	31	57	51	10	2	15	(.)	2	16	16
63 Jamaica	28	22	41	18	4	3	(.)	4	27	54
64 Dominican Rep.	10	1	88	82	(.)	(.)	(.)	3	2	13

Note: For data comparability and coverage see the technical notes.

192

| | Percentage share of merchandise exports | | | | | | | | | |
| | Fuels, minerals, and metals | | Other primary commodities | | Textiles and clothing | | Machinery and transport equipment | | Other manufactures | |
	1965	1982[a]	1965	1982[a]	1965	1982[a]	1965	1982[a]	1965	1982[a]
65 Paraguay	(.)	..	92	..	(.)	..	(.)	..	8	..
66 Ecuador	2	64	96	33	1	(.)	(.)	1	2	2
67 Colombia	18	8	75	68	2	7	(.)	3	4	15
68 Angola	6	..	76	..	(.)	..	1	..	17	..
69 Cuba	4	..	92	..	(.)	..	(.)	..	4	..
70 Korea, Dem. Rep.	..	..	..	..	..	..	..	..	..	..
71 Lebanon	14	..	52	..	2	..	14	..	18	..
72 Mongolia	..	..	..	..	..	..	..	..	..	..
Upper middle-income	**41** w	**34** w	**38** w	**17** w	**5** w	**9** w	**3** w	**14** w	**12** w	**26** w
73 Jordan	27	23	54	27	1	4	11	17	6	29
74 Syrian Arab Rep.	1	..	89	..	7	..	1	..	2	..
75 Malaysia	35	35	59	42	(.)	3	2	15	4	5
76 Chile	89	65	7	27	(.)	(.)	1	3	4	5
77 Brazil	9	18	83	43	1	3	2	17	6	19
78 Korea, Rep. of	15	1	25	7	27	21	3	28	29	43
79 Argentina	1	9	93	67	(.)	1	1	7	4	16
80 Panama	..	23	..	64	..	6	..	(.)	..	7
81 Portugal	4	5	34	20	24	29	3	14	34	32
82 Mexico	22	78	62	10	3	1	1	4	13	7
83 Algeria	57	99	39	1	(.)	(.)	2	(.)	2	1
84 South Africa[b]	24	14	44	12	1	1	3	3	28	70
85 Uruguay	(.)	(.)	95	67	2	13	(.)	1	3	18
86 Yugoslavia	10	6	33	16	8	10	24	31	25	37
87 Venezuela	97	97	1	(.)	(.)	(.)	(.)	1	2	2
88 Greece	8	18	78	31	3	21	2	5	8	25
89 Israel	6	2	28	17	9	6	2	18	54	56
90 Hong Kong	2	2	11	6	43	34	6	19	37	39
91 Singapore	21	30	44	13	6	4	10	26	18	28
92 Trinidad and Tobago	84	87	9	2	(.)	(.)	(.)	3	7	8
93 Iran, Islamic Rep.	88	..	8	..	4	..	(.)	..	1	..
94 Iraq	95	..	4	..	(.)	..	(.)	..	1	..
High-income oil exporters	**98** w	**96** w	**1** w	**(.)** w	**(.)** w	**(.)** w	**1** w	**1** w	**(.)** w	**2** w
95 Oman	..	92	..	1	..	(.)	..	6	..	1
96 Libya	98	99	1	(.)	(.)	(.)	1	(.)	(.)	(.)
97 Saudi Arabia	98	99	(.)	(.)	(.)	(.)	1	1	1	(.)
98 Kuwait	98	84	1	1	(.)	1	1	5	(.)	9
99 United Arab Emirates	99	94	1	1	(.)	1	(.)	2	(.)	2
Industrial market economies	**9** w	**12** w	**21** w	**14** w	**7** w	**4** w	**31** w	**37** w	**32** w	**32** w
100 Spain	9	11	51	18	6	4	10	27	24	40
101 Ireland	3	3	63	32	7	7	5	25	22	34
102 Italy	8	8	14	8	15	11	30	31	33	41
103 New Zealand	1	5	94	71	(.)	2	(.)	8	5	14
104 Belgium[c]	13	13	11	13	12	7	20	23	44	45
105 United Kingdom	7	24	10	9	7	4	41	33	35	31
106 Austria	8	5	17	10	12	10	20	28	43	47
107 Netherlands	12	26	32	24	9	4	21	16	26	29
108 Japan	2	1	7	2	17	4	31	56	43	36
109 France	8	7	21	19	10	5	26	35	35	35
110 Finland	3	7	40	16	2	6	12	26	43	45
111 Germany, Fed. Rep.	7	6	5	7	5	5	46	47	37	35
112 Australia	13	37	73	41	1	1	5	5	9	16
113 Denmark	2	4	55	40	4	5	22	24	17	27
114 Canada	28	24	35	22	1	1	15	32	21	21
115 Sweden	9	9	23	12	2	2	35	43	30	35
116 Norway	21	60	28	9	2	1	17	15	32	16
117 United States	8	9	27	21	3	2	37	44	26	24
118 Switzerland	3	3	7	4	10	7	30	35	50	52
East European nonmarket economies	**..**	**..**	**..**	**..**	**..**	**..**	**..**	**..**	**..**	**..**
119 Hungary	5	9	25	27	9	6	32	32	28	26
120 Albania	..	..	..	..	..	..	..	..	..	..
121 Bulgaria	..	..	..	..	..	..	..	..	..	..
122 Czechoslovakia	..	6	..	7	..	6	..	50	..	32
123 German Dem. Rep.	..	..	..	..	..	..	..	..	..	..
124 Poland	..	17	..	8	..	7	..	47	..	22
125 Romania	..	..	..	..	..	..	..	..	..	..
126 USSR	..	..	..	..	..	..	..	..	..	..

a. Figures in italics are for 1981, not 1982.   b. Figures are for the South African Customs Union comprising South Africa, Namibia, Lesotho, Botswana, and Swaziland. Trade between the component countries is excluded.   c. Includes Luxembourg.

Table 11. Structure of merchandise imports

<table>
<tr><td colspan="11" align="center">Percentage share of merchandise imports</td></tr>
<tr>
<td rowspan="2"></td>
<td colspan="2" align="center">Food</td>
<td colspan="2" align="center">Fuels</td>
<td colspan="2" align="center">Other
primary
commodities</td>
<td colspan="2" align="center">Machinery
and transport
equipment</td>
<td colspan="2" align="center">Other
manufactures</td>
</tr>
<tr>
<td>1965</td><td>1982[a]</td>
<td>1965</td><td>1982[a]</td>
<td>1965</td><td>1982[a]</td>
<td>1965</td><td>1982[a]</td>
<td>1965</td><td>1982[a]</td>
</tr>
<tr><td>**Low-income economies**</td><td>21 w</td><td>17 w</td><td>5 w</td><td>18 w</td><td>8 w</td><td>11 w</td><td>32 w</td><td>20 w</td><td>34 w</td><td>34 w</td></tr>
<tr><td>**China and India**</td><td>..</td><td>17 w</td><td>..</td><td>15 w</td><td>..</td><td>15 w</td><td>..</td><td>17 w</td><td>..</td><td>36 w</td></tr>
<tr><td>**Other low-income**</td><td>20 w</td><td>16 w</td><td>5 w</td><td>24 w</td><td>4 w</td><td>4 w</td><td>28 w</td><td>25 w</td><td>43 w</td><td>30 w</td></tr>
<tr><td>**Sub-Saharan Africa**</td><td>17 w</td><td>15 w</td><td>6 w</td><td>23 w</td><td>4 w</td><td>3 w</td><td>28 w</td><td>28 w</td><td>45 w</td><td>31 w</td></tr>
<tr><td>1 Ethiopia</td><td>7</td><td>10</td><td>6</td><td>25</td><td>5</td><td>3</td><td>37</td><td>31</td><td>44</td><td>31</td></tr>
<tr><td>2 Bangladesh</td><td>..</td><td>26</td><td>..</td><td>12</td><td>..</td><td>8</td><td>..</td><td>22</td><td>..</td><td>32</td></tr>
<tr><td>3 Mali</td><td>21</td><td>..</td><td>6</td><td>..</td><td>3</td><td>..</td><td>23</td><td>..</td><td>47</td><td>..</td></tr>
<tr><td>4 Nepal</td><td>..</td><td>16</td><td>..</td><td>13</td><td>..</td><td>3</td><td>..</td><td>18</td><td>..</td><td>50</td></tr>
<tr><td>5 Zaire</td><td>19</td><td>..</td><td>7</td><td>..</td><td>4</td><td>..</td><td>33</td><td>..</td><td>37</td><td>..</td></tr>
<tr><td>6 Burkina</td><td>25</td><td>25</td><td>4</td><td>16</td><td>12</td><td>3</td><td>19</td><td>24</td><td>40</td><td>32</td></tr>
<tr><td>7 Burma</td><td>15</td><td>..</td><td>4</td><td>..</td><td>5</td><td>..</td><td>18</td><td>..</td><td>58</td><td>..</td></tr>
<tr><td>8 Malawi</td><td>16</td><td>11</td><td>5</td><td>17</td><td>2</td><td>2</td><td>21</td><td>24</td><td>57</td><td>46</td></tr>
<tr><td>9 Uganda</td><td>..</td><td>5</td><td>..</td><td>23</td><td>..</td><td>1</td><td>..</td><td>42</td><td>..</td><td>29</td></tr>
<tr><td>10 Burundi</td><td>18</td><td>..</td><td>6</td><td>..</td><td>7</td><td>..</td><td>15</td><td>..</td><td>55</td><td>..</td></tr>
<tr><td>11 Niger</td><td>13</td><td>24</td><td>6</td><td>15</td><td>4</td><td>4</td><td>21</td><td>26</td><td>55</td><td>32</td></tr>
<tr><td>12 Tanzania</td><td>..</td><td>7</td><td>..</td><td>31</td><td>..</td><td>2</td><td>..</td><td>35</td><td>..</td><td>25</td></tr>
<tr><td>13 Somalia</td><td>33</td><td>20</td><td>5</td><td>2</td><td>5</td><td>6</td><td>24</td><td>50</td><td>33</td><td>21</td></tr>
<tr><td>14 India</td><td>22</td><td>9</td><td>5</td><td>35</td><td>14</td><td>10</td><td>37</td><td>18</td><td>22</td><td>28</td></tr>
<tr><td>15 Rwanda</td><td>12</td><td>..</td><td>7</td><td>..</td><td>4</td><td>..</td><td>28</td><td>..</td><td>50</td><td>..</td></tr>
<tr><td>16 Central African Rep.</td><td>13</td><td>..</td><td>7</td><td>..</td><td>2</td><td>..</td><td>29</td><td>..</td><td>49</td><td>..</td></tr>
<tr><td>17 Togo</td><td>18</td><td>26</td><td>4</td><td>8</td><td>2</td><td>3</td><td>32</td><td>21</td><td>45</td><td>42</td></tr>
<tr><td>18 Benin</td><td>23</td><td>..</td><td>6</td><td>..</td><td>2</td><td>..</td><td>17</td><td>..</td><td>53</td><td>..</td></tr>
<tr><td>19 China</td><td>..</td><td>23</td><td>..</td><td>1</td><td>..</td><td>18</td><td>..</td><td>17</td><td>..</td><td>41</td></tr>
<tr><td>20 Guinea</td><td>..</td><td>..</td><td>..</td><td>..</td><td>..</td><td>..</td><td>..</td><td>..</td><td>..</td><td>..</td></tr>
<tr><td>21 Haiti</td><td>..</td><td>26</td><td>..</td><td>12</td><td>..</td><td>4</td><td>..</td><td>21</td><td>..</td><td>37</td></tr>
<tr><td>22 Ghana</td><td>13</td><td>..</td><td>4</td><td>..</td><td>2</td><td>..</td><td>33</td><td>..</td><td>48</td><td>..</td></tr>
<tr><td>23 Madagascar</td><td>20</td><td>16</td><td>5</td><td>24</td><td>2</td><td>3</td><td>25</td><td>30</td><td>48</td><td>27</td></tr>
<tr><td>24 Sierra Leone</td><td>19</td><td>24</td><td>9</td><td>14</td><td>1</td><td>1</td><td>29</td><td>18</td><td>41</td><td>42</td></tr>
<tr><td>25 Sri Lanka</td><td>41</td><td>13</td><td>8</td><td>31</td><td>4</td><td>3</td><td>12</td><td>24</td><td>34</td><td>30</td></tr>
<tr><td>26 Kenya</td><td>..</td><td>8</td><td>..</td><td>37</td><td>..</td><td>3</td><td>..</td><td>27</td><td>..</td><td>25</td></tr>
<tr><td>27 Pakistan</td><td>20</td><td>14</td><td>3</td><td>31</td><td>5</td><td>7</td><td>38</td><td>23</td><td>34</td><td>26</td></tr>
<tr><td>28 Sudan</td><td>24</td><td>19</td><td>5</td><td>19</td><td>3</td><td>3</td><td>21</td><td>22</td><td>47</td><td>37</td></tr>
<tr><td>29 Afghanistan</td><td>17</td><td>..</td><td>4</td><td>..</td><td>1</td><td>..</td><td>8</td><td>..</td><td>69</td><td>..</td></tr>
<tr><td>30 Bhutan</td><td>..</td><td>..</td><td>..</td><td>..</td><td>..</td><td>..</td><td>..</td><td>..</td><td>..</td><td>..</td></tr>
<tr><td>31 Chad</td><td>13</td><td>..</td><td>20</td><td>..</td><td>3</td><td>..</td><td>21</td><td>..</td><td>42</td><td>..</td></tr>
<tr><td>32 Kampuchea, Dem.</td><td>6</td><td>..</td><td>7</td><td>..</td><td>2</td><td>..</td><td>26</td><td>..</td><td>58</td><td>..</td></tr>
<tr><td>33 Lao PDR</td><td>32</td><td>..</td><td>14</td><td>..</td><td>1</td><td>..</td><td>19</td><td>..</td><td>34</td><td>..</td></tr>
<tr><td>34 Mozambique</td><td>17</td><td>..</td><td>8</td><td>..</td><td>7</td><td>..</td><td>24</td><td>..</td><td>45</td><td>..</td></tr>
<tr><td>35 Viet Nam</td><td>..</td><td>..</td><td>..</td><td>..</td><td>..</td><td>..</td><td>..</td><td>..</td><td>..</td><td>..</td></tr>
<tr><td>**Middle-income economies**</td><td>16 w</td><td>12 w</td><td>8 w</td><td>21 w</td><td>9 w</td><td>6 w</td><td>29 w</td><td>30 w</td><td>38 w</td><td>31 w</td></tr>
<tr><td>**Oil exporters**</td><td>16 w</td><td>15 w</td><td>6 w</td><td>10 w</td><td>6 w</td><td>4 w</td><td>33 w</td><td>39 w</td><td>39 w</td><td>32 w</td></tr>
<tr><td>**Oil importers**</td><td>17 w</td><td>10 w</td><td>8 w</td><td>26 w</td><td>11 w</td><td>6 w</td><td>27 w</td><td>26 w</td><td>37 w</td><td>31 w</td></tr>
<tr><td>**Sub-Saharan Africa**</td><td>13 w</td><td>20 w</td><td>5 w</td><td>7 w</td><td>3 w</td><td>3 w</td><td>32 w</td><td>35 w</td><td>47 w</td><td>35 w</td></tr>
<tr><td>**Lower middle-income**</td><td>17 w</td><td>14 w</td><td>7 w</td><td>19 w</td><td>5 w</td><td>5 w</td><td>29 w</td><td>31 w</td><td>41 w</td><td>32 w</td></tr>
<tr><td>36 Senegal</td><td>37</td><td>27</td><td>6</td><td>30</td><td>4</td><td>1</td><td>15</td><td>18</td><td>38</td><td>23</td></tr>
<tr><td>37 Lesotho[b]</td><td>..</td><td>..</td><td>..</td><td>..</td><td>..</td><td>..</td><td>..</td><td>..</td><td>..</td><td>..</td></tr>
<tr><td>38 Liberia</td><td>18</td><td>22</td><td>8</td><td>27</td><td>1</td><td>2</td><td>33</td><td>25</td><td>39</td><td>24</td></tr>
<tr><td>39 Mauritania</td><td>9</td><td>..</td><td>4</td><td>..</td><td>1</td><td>..</td><td>56</td><td>..</td><td>30</td><td>..</td></tr>
<tr><td>40 Bolivia</td><td>20</td><td>12</td><td>1</td><td>2</td><td>2</td><td>1</td><td>34</td><td>45</td><td>42</td><td>40</td></tr>
<tr><td>41 Yemen, PDR</td><td>21</td><td>..</td><td>39</td><td>..</td><td>3</td><td>..</td><td>10</td><td>..</td><td>26</td><td>..</td></tr>
<tr><td>42 Yemen Arab Rep.</td><td>..</td><td>32</td><td>..</td><td>8</td><td>..</td><td>1</td><td>..</td><td>25</td><td>..</td><td>34</td></tr>
<tr><td>43 Indonesia</td><td>6</td><td>7</td><td>3</td><td>21</td><td>2</td><td>5</td><td>39</td><td>38</td><td>50</td><td>29</td></tr>
<tr><td>44 Zambia</td><td>10</td><td>9</td><td>10</td><td>19</td><td>2</td><td>1</td><td>33</td><td>34</td><td>45</td><td>37</td></tr>
<tr><td>45 Honduras</td><td>12</td><td>10</td><td>6</td><td>22</td><td>1</td><td>2</td><td>26</td><td>20</td><td>56</td><td>46</td></tr>
<tr><td>46 Egypt, Arab Rep.</td><td>28</td><td>31</td><td>7</td><td>4</td><td>10</td><td>5</td><td>23</td><td>29</td><td>31</td><td>30</td></tr>
<tr><td>47 El Salvador</td><td>16</td><td>18</td><td>5</td><td>25</td><td>3</td><td>3</td><td>28</td><td>12</td><td>48</td><td>42</td></tr>
<tr><td>48 Ivory Coast</td><td>18</td><td>19</td><td>6</td><td>21</td><td>2</td><td>2</td><td>28</td><td>23</td><td>46</td><td>34</td></tr>
<tr><td>49 Zimbabwe</td><td>7</td><td>..</td><td>(.)</td><td>..</td><td>4</td><td>..</td><td>41</td><td>..</td><td>47</td><td>..</td></tr>
<tr><td>50 Morocco</td><td>36</td><td>16</td><td>5</td><td>27</td><td>9</td><td>10</td><td>18</td><td>24</td><td>31</td><td>23</td></tr>
<tr><td>51 Papua New Guinea</td><td>25</td><td>20</td><td>4</td><td>19</td><td>1</td><td>1</td><td>25</td><td>30</td><td>45</td><td>30</td></tr>
<tr><td>52 Philippines</td><td>20</td><td>10</td><td>10</td><td>26</td><td>7</td><td>4</td><td>33</td><td>22</td><td>30</td><td>38</td></tr>
<tr><td>53 Nigeria</td><td>9</td><td>21</td><td>6</td><td>3</td><td>3</td><td>3</td><td>34</td><td>38</td><td>48</td><td>35</td></tr>
<tr><td>54 Cameroon</td><td>12</td><td>10</td><td>5</td><td>4</td><td>3</td><td>2</td><td>28</td><td>35</td><td>51</td><td>49</td></tr>
<tr><td>55 Thailand</td><td>7</td><td>5</td><td>9</td><td>31</td><td>5</td><td>7</td><td>31</td><td>24</td><td>49</td><td>33</td></tr>
<tr><td>56 Nicaragua</td><td>13</td><td>12</td><td>5</td><td>23</td><td>1</td><td>1</td><td>30</td><td>23</td><td>51</td><td>40</td></tr>
<tr><td>57 Costa Rica</td><td>9</td><td>9</td><td>5</td><td>20</td><td>2</td><td>3</td><td>29</td><td>15</td><td>54</td><td>53</td></tr>
<tr><td>58 Peru</td><td>17</td><td>18</td><td>3</td><td>2</td><td>5</td><td>3</td><td>41</td><td>44</td><td>34</td><td>34</td></tr>
<tr><td>59 Guatemala</td><td>11</td><td>6</td><td>7</td><td>38</td><td>2</td><td>3</td><td>29</td><td>16</td><td>50</td><td>37</td></tr>
<tr><td>60 Congo, People's Rep.</td><td>15</td><td>17</td><td>6</td><td>15</td><td>1</td><td>1</td><td>34</td><td>25</td><td>44</td><td>42</td></tr>
<tr><td>61 Turkey</td><td>6</td><td>3</td><td>10</td><td>44</td><td>10</td><td>6</td><td>37</td><td>26</td><td>37</td><td>22</td></tr>
<tr><td>62 Tunisia</td><td>16</td><td>14</td><td>6</td><td>21</td><td>6</td><td>8</td><td>31</td><td>27</td><td>41</td><td>30</td></tr>
<tr><td>63 Jamaica</td><td>22</td><td>19</td><td>9</td><td>29</td><td>4</td><td>4</td><td>23</td><td>18</td><td>42</td><td>30</td></tr>
<tr><td>64 Dominican Rep.</td><td>25</td><td>16</td><td>10</td><td>34</td><td>2</td><td>3</td><td>23</td><td>19</td><td>40</td><td>29</td></tr>
</table>

Note: For data comparability and coverage see the technical notes.

		Percentage share of merchandise imports								
		Food		Fuels		Other primary commodities		Machinery and transport equipment		Other manufactures	
		1965	1982[a]	1965	1982[a]	1965	1982[a]	1965	1982[a]	1965	1982[a]
65	Paraguay	14	13	14	24	2	(.)	37	37	33	26
66	Ecuador	10	5	9	2	4	5	33	43	44	45
67	Colombia	8	11	1	12	10	5	45	39	35	33
68	*Angola*	18	..	2	..	2	..	24	..	54	..
69	*Cuba*	29	..	10	..	3	..	15	..	43	..
70	*Korea, Dem. Rep.*	..	..	..	..	..	..	..	..	..	..
71	*Lebanon*	29	..	9	..	9	..	17	..	36	..
72	*Mongolia*	..	..	..	..	..	..	..	..	..	..
Upper middle-income		**16** w	**11** w	**8** w	**22** w	**11** w	**6** w	**29** w	**30** w	**36** w	**31** w
73	Jordan	30	18	6	21	5	2	18	28	42	30
74	Syrian Arab Rep.	22	..	10	..	8	..	16	..	43	..
75	Malaysia	27	12	12	15	7	5	22	40	32	29
76	Chile	20	*12*	6	*15*	9	*3*	35	*37*	30	*33*
77	Brazil	20	8	21	54	9	4	22	17	28	17
78	Korea, Rep. of	15	*12*	7	*30*	26	*15*	13	*23*	38	*20*
79	Argentina	7	4	10	13	21	9	25	35	38	38
80	Panama	..	9	..	27	..	1	..	26	..	37
81	Portugal	16	14	8	27	18	8	27	27	30	24
82	Mexico	5	10	2	12	10	2	50	45	33	31
83	Algeria	27	21	(.)	2	5	4	15	40	52	34
84	South Africa[b]	5	3	5	(.)	10	4	42	43	37	50
85	Uruguay	10	7	17	*32*	14	5	24	*32*	36	*25*
86	Yugoslavia	16	6	6	26	19	12	28	28	32	28
87	Venezuela	12	17	1	*1*	5	*4*	44	*43*	39	35
88	Greece	16	13	8	29	11	6	35	26	30	27
89	Israel	16	11	6	23	11	5	28	27	38	33
90	Hong Kong	26	14	3	8	11	5	13	22	46	52
91	Singapore	24	8	13	34	18	4	14	28	30	26
92	Trinidad and Tobago	12	12	49	25	2	3	16	32	21	27
93	*Iran, Islamic Rep.*	16	..	(.)	..	6	..	36	..	42	..
94	*Iraq*	24	..	(.)	..	7	..	25	..	44	..
High-income oil exporters		**24** w	**13** w	**2** w	**2** w	**3** w	**2** w	**32** w	**42** w	**40** w	**41** w
95	Oman	..	13	..	10	..	2	..	42	..	33
96	Libya	14	18	4	*1*	3	2	36	38	43	*41*
97	Saudi Arabia	31	13	1	(.)	4	2	27	43	37	42
98	Kuwait	26	*15*	1	*1*	2	2	32	*41*	39	42
99	United Arab Emirates	..	10	..	6	..	2	..	41	..	42
Industrial market economies		**20** w	**11** w	**11** w	**26** w	**19** w	**8** w	**19** w	**24** w	**31** w	**31** w
100	Spain	20	12	10	40	14	9	27	19	28	20
101	Ireland	19	13	8	15	9	4	25	27	39	41
102	Italy	24	14	16	32	24	11	15	20	21	24
103	New Zealand	8	7	7	17	9	5	33	33	43	39
104	Belgium[c]	14	12	9	21	21	9	24	22	32	36
105	United Kingdom	32	14	11	13	24	9	11	29	23	36
106	Austria	15	7	7	16	12	9	31	28	35	40
107	Netherlands	16	16	10	26	12	6	25	19	37	34
108	Japan	23	13	20	50	38	16	9	6	11	15
109	France	20	11	15	27	18	7	20	24	27	32
110	Finland	10	7	10	27	11	7	35	28	34	30
111	Germany, Fed. Rep.	24	13	8	24	20	9	13	20	35	35
112	Australia	6	5	8	14	9	3	37	39	41	38
113	Denmark	15	12	11	23	10	6	25	21	39	38
114	Canada	10	8	7	10	9	5	40	48	34	29
115	Sweden	12	7	11	24	11	6	30	28	36	35
116	Norway	11	6	7	13	12	6	38	37	32	38
117	United States	20	8	10	27	20	6	14	29	36	31
118	Switzerland	17	9	6	12	9	5	24	26	43	47
East European nonmarket economies		**..**	**..**	**..**	**..**	**..**	**..**	**..**	**..**	**..**	**..**
119	Hungary	12	7	11	21	21	10	27	29	28	34
120	*Albania*	..	..	..	..	..	..	..	..	..	..
121	*Bulgaria*	..	..	..	..	..	..	..	..	..	..
122	*Czechoslovakia*	..	9	..	28	..	13	..	31	..	19
123	*German Dem. Rep.*	..	..	..	..	..	..	..	..	..	..
124	*Poland*	..	*18*	..	*20*	..	*10*	..	*31*	..	*21*
125	*Romania*	..	..	..	..	..	..	..	..	..	..
126	*USSR*	..	..	..	..	..	..	..	..	..	..

a. Figures in italics are for 1981, not 1982.   b. Figures are for the South African Customs Union comprising South Africa, Namibia, Lesotho, Botswana, and Swaziland. Trade between the component territories is excluded.   c. Includes Luxembourg.

Table 12. Origin and destination of merchandise exports

	Destination of merchandise exports (percentage of total)							
	Industrial market economies		East European nonmarket economies		High-income oil exporters		Developing economies	
Origin	1965	1983[a]	1965	1983[a]	1965	1983[a]	1965	1983[a]
Low-income economies	56 *w*	48 *w*	10 *w*	7 *w*	2 *w*	5 *w*	32 *w*	40 *w*
China and India	51 *w*	46 *w*	14 *w*	7 *w*	2 *w*	3 *w*	33 *w*	44 *w*
Other low-income	61 *w*	54 *w*	6 *w*	6 *w*	2 *w*	8 *w*	31 *w*	32 *w*
Sub-Saharan Africa	71 *w*	63 *w*	5 *w*	5 *w*	1 *w*	4 *w*	23 *w*	27 *w*
1 Ethiopia	78	66	3	1	6	6	14	28
2 Bangladesh	..	43	..	8	..	1	..	47
3 Mali	7	72	4	2	0	(.)	89	26
4 Nepal	..	42	..	(.)	..	(.)	..	58
5 Zaire	93	89	(.)	(.)	(.)	(.)	7	10
6 Burkina	17	48	0	(.)	0	(.)	83	51
7 Burma	29	34	8	3	1	2	62	61
8 Malawi	69	68	0	(.)	(.)	3	30	31
9 Uganda	69	84	2	(.)	1	(.)	28	15
10 Burundi	..	78	..	4	..	0	..	19
11 Niger	61	..	(.)	..	(.)	..	39	..
12 Tanzania	66	59	1	4	1	1	32	37
13 Somalia	40	16	(.)	(.)	3	66	57	18
14 India	58	55	17	12	2	7	23	26
15 Rwanda	96	92	0	(.)	0	0	4	8
16 Central African Rep.	71	82	0	1	0	(.)	29	16
17 Togo	92	52	2	1	0	0	6	46
18 Benin	88	79	(.)	(.)	0	0	12	20
19 China	47	42	12	5	2	2	40	52
20 Guinea	..	89	..	(.)	..	(.)	..	11
21 Haiti	97	98	(.)	(.)	(.)	(.)	3	2
22 Ghana	74	47	18	34	(.)	(.)	9	20
23 Madagascar	85	72	1	3	(.)	(.)	14	25
24 Sierra Leone	92	66	(.)	(.)	(.)	(.)	8	34
25 Sri Lanka	56	46	9	5	3	6	33	44
26 Kenya	69	47	2	1	1	1	28	51
27 Pakistan	48	35	3	4	4	22	45	39
28 Sudan	56	36	13	7	4	28	27	29
29 *Afghanistan*	47	33	27	55	0	1	25	10
30 *Bhutan*	..	..	..	..	..	..	..	..
31 Chad	64	72	0	0	2	(.)	34	28
32 *Kampuchea, Dem.*	36	..	6	..	0	..	58	..
33 *Lao PDR*	9	..	0	..	0	..	91	..
34 *Mozambique*	24	37	(.)	..	(.)	1	76	62
35 *Viet Nam*	..	..	..	..	..	..	..	..
Middle-income economies	69 *w*	62 *w*	7 *w*	3 *w*	1 *w*	3 *w*	23 *w*	32 *w*
Oil exporters	70 *w*	69 *w*	5 *w*	1 *w*	1 *w*	(.) *w*	24 *w*	30 *w*
Oil importers	68 *w*	57 *w*	8 *w*	5 *w*	1 *w*	4 *w*	23 *w*	33 *w*
Sub-Saharan Africa	81 *w*	73 *w*	2 *w*	1 *w*	(.) *w*	(.) *w*	17 *w*	26 *w*
Lower middle-income	70 *w*	69 *w*	9 *w*	2 *w*	1 *w*	2 *w*	20 *w*	27 *w*
36 Senegal	92	54	(.)	1	0	(.)	7	45
37 Lesotho[b]	..	..	..	..	..	..	..	..
38 Liberia	98	94	0	(.)	0	1	2	5
39 Mauritania	96	94	(.)	(.)	0	..	4	6
40 Bolivia	97	41	0	1	0	0	3	58
41 Yemen, PDR	38	56	(.)	(.)	1	1	61	43
42 Yemen Arab Rep.	..	26	..	6	..	17	..	50
43 Indonesia	72	73	5	1	(.)	1	23	26
44 Zambia	87	65	2	1	0	(.)	11	34
45 Honduras	80	81	0	2	0	2	20	15
46 Egypt, Arab Rep.	28	73	44	9	1	2	27	16
47 El Salvador	73	53	1	0	0	(.)	26	47
48 Ivory Coast	84	70	2	3	1	(.)	13	27
49 Zimbabwe	50	53	1	1	(.)	(.)	48	46
50 Morocco	80	65	7	5	(.)	3	12	28
51 Papua New Guinea	98	85	0	1	0	(.)	2	14
52 Philippines	95	77	0	2	(.)	1	5	20
53 Nigeria	91	74	3	(.)	(.)	(.)	6	26
54 Cameroon	93	85	(.)	(.)	(.)	(.)	7	15
55 Thailand	44	56	1	2	2	5	53	37
56 Nicaragua	81	74	(.)	2	0	(.)	19	24
57 Costa Rica	79	72	(.)	2	0	1	20	25
58 Peru	86	76	3	3	(.)	(.)	12	21
59 Guatemala	75	53	0	2	(.)	4	25	41
60 Congo, People's Rep.	86	98	1	(.)	0	0	13	2
61 Turkey	71	47	15	4	(.)	12	14	37
62 Tunisia	61	80	5	1	3	3	31	16
63 Jamaica	93	78	1	1	(.)	(.)	6	21
64 Dominican Rep.	99	84	0	7	0	(.)	1	9

Note: For data comparability and coverage see the technical notes.

	Destination of merchandise exports (percentage of total)							
	Industrial market economies		East European nonmarket economies		High-income oil exporters		Developing economies	
Origin	1965	1983[a]	1965	1983[a]	1965	1983[a]	1965	1983[a]
65 Paraguay	58	51	0	14	0	0	42	35
66 Ecuador	89	61	(.)	1	0	(.)	11	38
67 Colombia	86	78	2	4	(.)	(.)	12	18
68 Angola	55	66	1	2	(.)	(.)	45	32
69 Cuba	14	..	62	..	(.)	..	24	..
70 Korea, Dem. Rep.	..	..	..	..	..	..	..	..
71 Lebanon	43	12	4	(.)	35	47	18	41
72 Mongolia	..	..	..	..	..	..	..	..
Upper middle-income	**68** w	**60** w	**6** w	**4** w	**1** w	**3** w	**25** w	**33** w
73 Jordan	20	6	4	3	22	23	54	68
74 Syrian Arab Rep.	26	37	24	16	8	5	42	42
75 Malaysia	56	50	7	3	(.)	1	36	47
76 Chile	90	75	(.)	1	0	2	10	22
77 Brazil	77	66	6	7	(.)	2	18	26
78 Korea, Rep. of	75	65	0	(.)	(.)	10	25	25
79 Argentina	67	40	8	23	(.)	8	26	30
80 Panama	..	69	..	(.)	..	(.)	..	31
81 Portugal	65	82	1	2	(.)	1	34	16
82 Mexico	82	86	6	1	(.)	(.)	13	14
83 Algeria	90	92	1	(.)	(.)	(.)	8	8
84 South Africa[b]	96	45	0	(.)	(.)	0	4	55
85 Uruguay	76	34	5	8	0	3	19	55
86 Yugoslavia	40	32	42	46	(.)	3	17	18
87 Venezuela	63	60	(.)	(.)	(.)	(.)	37	39
88 Greece	64	63	23	7	2	11	12	18
89 Israel	72	71	4	1	0	0	24	28
90 Hong Kong	67	61	(.)	(.)	1	3	32	35
91 Singapore	28	42	6	1	2	5	64	52
92 Trinidad and Tobago	92	74	0	0	0	(.)	8	26
93 Iran, Islamic Rep.	67	66	3	1	2	(.)	28	34
94 Iraq	83	31	1	(.)	(.)	(.)	16	68
High-income oil exporters	**70** w	**66** w	**(.)** w	**1** w	**3** w	**4** w	**27** w	**30** w
95 Oman	..	69	..	(.)	..	0	..	31
96 Libya	97	74	(.)	3	(.)	(.)	3	23
97 Saudi Arabia	71	66	0	(.)	8	5	21	30
98 Kuwait	56	40	(.)	1	1	6	44	53
99 United Arab Emirates	69	80	0	(.)	5	2	26	18
Industrial market economies	**71** w	**69** w	**3** w	**3** w	**1** w	**4** w	**26** w	**24** w
100 Spain	73	61	3	3	(.)	5	24	31
101 Ireland	91	88	1	1	(.)	2	8	10
102 Italy	71	65	5	4	2	9	23	22
103 New Zealand	88	64	1	5	(.)	2	11	30
104 Belgium[c]	86	83	1	2	(.)	2	12	13
105 United Kingdom	63	73	2	2	2	6	33	19
106 Austria	71	70	15	12	(.)	3	13	15
107 Netherlands	83	84	2	2	1	2	14	13
108 Japan	49	50	3	2	2	8	47	39
109 France	68	68	3	4	(.)	4	28	25
110 Finland	71	61	21	28	(.)	1	9	10
111 Germany, Fed. Rep.	77	74	3	5	1	3	19	18
112 Australia	69	60	4	3	1	3	26	34
113 Denmark	85	80	4	1	1	3	11	16
114 Canada	87	86	3	2	(.)	1	10	11
115 Sweden	85	81	4	3	(.)	3	11	13
116 Norway	82	90	4	1	(.)	(.)	13	8
117 United States	61	58	1	1	1	4	37	36
118 Switzerland	76	72	3	3	1	5	20	20
East European nonmarket economies	**..**	**31** w	**..**	**51** w	**..**	**3** w	**..**	**14** w
119 Hungary	22	25	66	49	(.)	2	12	23
120 Albania	..	..	..	..	..	..	..	..
121 Bulgaria	..	11	..	69	..	8	..	12
122 Czechoslovakia	18	15	72	68	1	2	9	15
123 German Dem. Rep.	..	..	..	..	..	..	..	..
124 Poland	..	32	..	51	..	2	..	16
125 Romania	..	25	..	45	..	2	..	29
126 USSR	..	39	..	46	..	3	..	12

a. Figures in italics are for 1982, not 1983.   b. Figures are for the South African Customs Union comprising South Africa, Namibia, Lesotho, Botswana, and Swaziland. Trade between the component territories is excluded.   c. Includes Luxembourg.

Table 13. Origin and destination of manufactured exports

| Origin | Destination of manufactured exports (percentage of total) | | | | | | | | Manufactured exports (millions of dollars) | |
| | Industrial market economies | | East European nonmarket economies | | High-income oil exporters | | Developing economies | | | |
	1965	1982a	1965	1982a	1965	1982a	1965	1982a	1965	1982a
Low-income economies	54 w	48 w	9 w	5 w	2 w	10 w	35 w	36 w		
China and India	..	..	..	..	..	..	..	..		
Other low-income	51 w	48 w	1 w	5 w	2 w	10 w	46 w	36 w		
Sub-Saharan Africa	69 w	29 w	1 w	(.) w	(.) w	3 w	29 w	68 w		
1 Ethiopia	67	76	(.)	9	20	2	13	13	(.)	3
2 Bangladesh	..	39	..	9	..	1	..	52	..	417
3 Mali	14	..	8	..	0	..	78	..	(.)	..
4 Nepal	..	50	..	(.)	..	(.)	..	50	..	39
5 Zaire	93	..	0	..	(.)	..	7	..	28	..
6 Burkina	2	19	0	0	0	0	98	81	1	11
7 Burma	73	..	1	..	(.)	..	26	..	1	..
8 Malawi	3	6	0	0	0	0	97	94	(.)	31
9 Uganda	7	..	(.)	..	0	..	93	..	1	..
10 Burundi	(.)	..	0	..	0	..	100	..	1	..
11 Niger	43	30	(.)	(.)	0	(.)	57	70	1	10
12 Tanzania	93	65	(.)	(.)	(.)	(.)	7	34	23	71
13 Somalia	21	54	(.)	0	2	6	77	39	4	1
14 India	55	..	12	..	2	..	31	..	828	4,476
15 Rwanda	95	..	0	..	0	..	5	..	(.)	..
16 Central African Rep.	..	..	..	..	..	..	..	..	..	..
17 Togo	37	9	(.)	1	0	0	62	90	1	32
18 Benin	15	..	0	..	0	..	85	..	1	..
19 China	..	..	..	..	..	..	..	..	..	12,225
20 Guinea	..	..	..	..	..	..	..	..	..	..
21 Haiti		..		..		..		..		..
22 Ghana	60	..	10	..	(.)	..	29	..	7	..
23 Madagascar	80	80	0	(.)	0	(.)	20	20	5	24
24 Sierra Leone	99	..	(.)	..	(.)	..	1	..	53	..
25 Sri Lanka	59	84	7	(.)	(.)	1	34	16	5	277
26 Kenya	23	9	2	(.)	2	5	73	86	13	138
27 Pakistan	40	49	1	6	3	17	57	28	190	1,417
28 Sudan	79	62	(.)	8	2	19	20	11	2	10
29 Afghanistan	98	..	(.)	..	0	..	2	..	11	..
30 Bhutan	..	..	..	..	..	..	..	..	..	..
31 Chad	6	..	0	..	25	..	69	..	1	..
32 Kampuchea, Dem.	28	..	1	..	0	..	71	..	1	..
33 Lao PDR	13	..	0	..	0	..	87	..	(.)	..
34 Mozambique	27	..	(.)	..	(.)	..	73	..	3	..
35 Viet Nam	..	..	..	..	..	..	..	..	..	..
Middle-income economies	52 w	48 w	9 w	5 w	2 w	5 w	37 w	42 w		
Oil exporters	43 w	60 w	10 w	2 w	4 w	3 w	44 w	34 w		
Oil importers	54 w	47 w	9 w	5 w	1 w	5 w	36 w	43 w		
Sub-Saharan Africa	23 w	..	(.) w	..	(.) w	..	77 w	..		
Lower middle-income	36 w	52 w	10 w	2 w	3 w	5 w	51 w	41 w		
36 Senegal	48	24	1	1	0	(.)	52	75	4	110
37 Lesotho b	..	..	..	..	..	..	..	..	..	..
38 Liberia	77	47	0	(.)	0	0	23	53	4	13
39 Mauritania	61	..	0	..	0	..	39	..	1	..
40 Bolivia	86	..	0	..	0	..	14	..	6	..
41 Yemen, PDR	32	..	(.)	..	6	..	62	..	11	..
42 Yemen Arab Rep.	..	..	..	..	..	..	..	..	..	..
43 Indonesia	25	42	1	(.)	(.)	7	74	51	27	868
44 Zambia	14	..	0	..	0	..	86	..	1	..
45 Honduras	2	33	0	0	0	0	98	67	6	58
46 Egypt, Arab Rep.	20	38	46	40	4	8	30	14	126	256
47 El Salvador	1	8	0	0	0	(.)	99	92	32	162
48 Ivory Coast	50	34	(.)	(.)	(.)	(.)	50	66	15	247
49 Zimbabwe	12	..	(.)	..	(.)	..	88	..	116	..
50 Morocco	63	56	2	3	(.)	3	35	37	23	707
51 Papua New Guinea	100	85	0	0	0	0	(.)	15	5	72
52 Philippines	93	75	0	(.)	(.)	1	7	23	43	2,492
53 Nigeria	85	..	(.)	..	(.)	..	15	..	17	90
54 Cameroon	46	39	0	0	(.)	(.)	54	61	6	78
55 Thailand	39	56	(.)	(.)	(.)	7	61	36	30	2,014
56 Nicaragua	4	3	0	(.)	0	0	96	97	8	30
57 Costa Rica	6	15	(.)	(.)	0	(.)	94	85	18	248
58 Peru	51	54	(.)	1	0	(.)	49	45	5	384
59 Guatemala	9	4	0	0	0	(.)	91	96	26	325
60 Congo, People's Rep.	..	..	..	..	..	..	..	..	..	..
61 Turkey	83	43	8	2	(.)	11	9	45	11	2,475
62 Tunisia	19	68	3	2	5	7	73	23	23	835
63 Jamaica	93	74	1	2	0	0	6	24	64	444
64 Dominican Rep.	95	77	0	0	0	0	5	23	3	102

Note: For data comparability and coverage see the technical notes.

	Destination of manufactured exports (percentage of total)								Manufactured exports (millions of dollars)	
	Industrial market economies		East European nonmarket economies		High-income oil exporters		Developing economies			
Origin	1965	1982[a]	1965	1982[a]	1965	1982[a]	1965	1982[a]	1965	1982[a]
65 Paraguay	93	..	0	..	0	..	7	..	5	..
66 Ecuador	25	7	0	(.)	0	0	75	93	3	69
67 Colombia	43	31	0	(.)	(.)	(.)	57	69	35	751
68 *Angola*	3	..	1	..	(.)	..	96	..	36	..
69 *Cuba*	27	..	70	..	0	..	3	..	27	..
70 *Korea, Dem. Rep.*	..	..	..	..	..	..	..	..	..	..
71 *Lebanon*	19	..	1	..	61	..	19	..	29	..
72 *Mongolia*	..	..	..	..	..	..	..	..	..	..
Upper middle-income	**55** *w*	**48** *w*	**9** *w*	**5** *w*	**1** *w*	**5** *w*	**34** *w*	**42** *w*		
73 Jordan	49	22	(.)	(.)	23	25	28	53	5	367
74 Syrian Arab Rep.	5	..	21	..	25	..	50	..	16	..
75 Malaysia	17	67	(.)	(.)	2	2	81	31	75	2,781
76 Chile	38	27	(.)	*(.)*	0	*0*	62	73	28	*301*
77 Brazil	40	50	1	1	(.)	2	59	47	134	7,9/1
78 Korea, Rep. of	68	62	0	0	(.)	11	32	27	104	19,237
79 Argentina	45	48	3	4	(.)	(.)	52	47	84	1,849
80 Panama	..	..	..	..	..	..	..	..	..	39
81 Portugal	59	83	(.)	2	(.)	1	41	14	355	3,138
82 Mexico	71	..	(.)	..	(.)	..	29	..	165	2,505
83 Algeria	50	59	1	18	1	(.)	48	23	24	89
84 South Africa[b]	94	0	0	0	(.)	0	6	100	443	13,081
85 Uruguay	71	46	6	7	0	0	23	48	10	332
86 Yugoslavia	24	22	52	53	1	3	24	22	617	8,393
87 Venezuela	59	59	(.)	*(.)*	(.)	*(.)*	41	41	51	417
88 Greece	56	56	8	5	9	16	27	23	44	2,154
89 Israel	67	63	4	1	0	0	29	37	281	4,246
90 Hong Kong	71	62	(.)	(.)	1	4	28	34	995	19,277
91 Singapore	9	49	(.)	1	3	6	88	44	338	11,834
92 Trinidad and Tobago	78	72	0	(.)	0	(.)	22	28	28	322
93 *Iran, Islamic Rep.*	61	..	1	..	17	..	21	..	58	..
94 *Iraq*	24	..	1	..	16	..	60	..	8	..
High-income oil exporters	**30** *w*	**21** *w*	**(.)** *w*	**(.)** *w*	**21** *w*	**29** *w*	**49** *w*	**49** *w*		
95 Oman	..	11	..	0	..	70	..	18	..	303
96 Libya	57	64	(.)	*(.)*	(.)	*1*	43	35	7	*62*
97 Saudi Arabia	31	10	0	(.)	18	16	52	73	19	824
98 Kuwait	18	*28*	(.)	*(.)*	33	*21*	49	*51*	17	*2,453*
99 United Arab Emirates	..	13	..	(.)	..	55		32	..	777
Industrial market economies	**67** *w*	**64** *w*	**3** *w*	**3** *w*	**1** *w*	**5** *w*	**29** *w*	**28** *w*		
100 Spain	57	53	1	2	(.)	5	42	39	382	14,525
101 Ireland	82	91	(.)	(.)	(.)	1	17	7	203	5,227
102 Italy	68	64	5	4	2	8	25	24	5,587	61,313
103 New Zealand	90	70	(.)	1	(.)	1	10	28	53	1,322
104 Belgium[c]	86	83	1	2	1	2	13	13	4,823	38,261
105 United Kingdom	61	62	2	2	2	8	35	29	11,346	65,448
106 Austria	67	68	18	12	(.)	3	15	17	1,204	13,333
107 Netherlands	81	81	2	2	1	3	16	14	3,586	32,734
108 Japan	47	48	2	3	2	8	49	41	7,704	134,209
109 France	64	63	3	3	1	4	33	30	7,139	68,618
110 Finland	63	56	26	33	(.)	2	11	9	815	10,066
111 Germany, Fed. Rep.	76	72	3	4	1	4	20	20	15,764	152,774
112 Australia	57	35	(.)	(.)	(.)	2	43	63	432	4,736
113 Denmark	79	75	4	2	(.)	3	16	20	967	8,458
114 Canada	88	88	(.)	(.)	(.)	1	12	10	2,973	36,065
115 Sweden	82	76	4	3	(.)	4	14	17	2,685	21,227
116 Norway	78	71	3	2	(.)	1	19	25	734	5,571
117 United States	58	53	(.)	1	1	6	40	40	17,833	147,831
118 Switzerland	75	68	3	3	1	5	21	23	2,646	23,770
East European nonmarket economies										
119 Hungary	11	20	74	56	(.)	2	15	22	1,053	5,603
120 *Albania*	..	..	..	..	..	..	..	..	..	..
121 *Bulgaria*	..	..	..	..	..	..	..	..	..	..
122 *Czechoslovakia*	..	13	..	70	..	1	..	16	..	13,760
123 *German Dem. Rep.*	..	..	..	..	..	..	..	..	..	..
124 *Poland*	..	17	..	56	..	2	..	26	..	9,983
125 *Romania*	..	..	..	..	..	..	..	..	..	..
126 *USSR*	..	..	..	..	..	..	..	..	..	..

a. Figures in italics are for 1981, not 1982.   b. Figures are for the South African Customs Union comprising South Africa, Namibia, Lesotho, Botswana and Swaziland. Trade between the component territories is excluded.   c. Includes Luxembourg.

Table 14. Balance of payments and reserves

		Current account balance (millions of dollars)		Receipts of workers' remittances (millions of dollars)		Net direct private investment (millions of dollars)		Gross international reserves		
								Millions of dollars		In months of import coverage
		1970	1983[a]	1970	1983[a]	1970	1983[a]	1970	1983[a]	1983[a]
	Low-income economies									6.4 *w*
	China and India									8.2 *w*
	Other low-income									3.0 *w*
	Sub-Saharan Africa									2.2 *w*
1	Ethiopia	−32	−171	..	..	4	..	72	206	2.5
2	Bangladesh	..	−77	..	629	..	(.)	..	546	2.6
3	Mali	−2	−103	6	36	..	2	1	23	0.6
4	Nepal	..	−143	..	..	..	..	94	191	4.1
5	Zaire	−64	−559	2	119	42	331	189	269	..
6	Burkina	9	..	18	..	(.)	..	36	89	..
7	Burma	−63	−343	..	..	..	..	98	185	2.6
8	Malawi	−35	−72	..	..	9	..	29	29	0.8
9	Uganda	20	−256	..	..	4	..	57	..	..
10	Burundi	..	..	..	..	..	..	15	34	..
11	Niger	(.)	..	..	..	1	..	19	57	..
12	Tanzania	−36	..	..	..	..	..	65	19	..
13	Somalia	−6	−150	..	22	5	(.)	21	16	0.4
14	India	−394	−2,780	113	2,617	6	..	1,023	8,242	5.4
15	Rwanda	7	−49	1	2	(.)	11	8	111	4.1
16	Central African Rep.	−12	−28	..	..	1	4	1	51	2.4
17	Togo	3	−32	..	..	1	..	35	178	7.1
18	Benin	−1	..	2	..	7	..	16	8	..
19	China	..	4,460	..	..	..	..	..	19,698	10.5
20	Guinea	..	..	..	..	..	..	..	..	..
21	Haiti	2	−100	17	89	3	15	4	16	0.4
22	Ghana	−68	−218	..	1	68	−6	58	291	4.3
23	Madagascar	10	−369	..	..	10	..	37	29	..
24	Sierra Leone	−16	−33	..	..	8	2	39	16	1.0
25	Sri Lanka	−59	−472	3	294	0	38	43	321	1.7
26	Kenya	−49	−174	..	..	14	50	220	406	2.8
27	Pakistan	−667	21	86	2,925	23	31	194	2,683	4.5
28	Sudan	−42	−213	..	275	..	..	22	17	0.2
29	*Afghanistan*	..	..	..	..	..	..	49	582	..
30	*Bhutan*	..	..	..	..	..	..	..	..	..
31	*Chad*	2	38	..	..	1	(.)	2	32	2.2
32	*Kampuchea, Dem.*	..	..	..	..	..	..	..	..	..
33	*Lao PDR*	..	..	..	..	..	..	6	..	..
34	*Mozambique*	..	..	..	..	..	..	..	..	..
35	*Viet Nam*	..	..	..	..	..	..	243	..	..
	Middle-income economies									2.8 *w*
	Oil exporters									3.3 *w*
	Oil importers									2.6 *w*
	Sub-Saharan Africa									1.0 *w*
	Lower middle-income									2.2 *w*
36	Senegal	−16	..	3	..	5	..	22	23	..
37	Lesotho	..	−14	..	..	..	4	..	67	1.4
38	Liberia	..	−135	..	..	..	3	..	20	0.4
39	Mauritania	−5	−196	1	1	1	1	3	110	2.1
40	Bolivia	4	−183	..	1	−76	43	46	509	5.2
41	Yemen, PDR	−4	−309	60	451	..	..	59	297	3.6
42	Yemen Arab Rep.	..	−558	..	1,161	..	8	..	369	2.1
43	Indonesia	−310	−6,294	..	..	83	289	160	4,902	2.2
44	Zambia	108	−252	..	..	−297	..	515	137	1.3
45	Honduras	−64	−225	..	..	8	21	20	120	1.3
46	Egypt, Arab Rep.	−148	−785	29	3,293	..	845	165	1,699	1.8
47	El Salvador	9	−152	..	41	4	−1	64	344	3.5
48	Ivory Coast	−38	−743	..	..	31	..	119	37	0.2
49	Zimbabwe	..	−459	..	2	..	−2	59	300	2.0
50	Morocco	−124	−889	63	916	20	46	141	376	0.9
51	Papua New Guinea	..	−372	..	..	..	137	..	474	3.8
52	Philippines	−48	−2,760	..	180	−29	104	255	896	0.9
53	Nigeria	−368	−4,752	..	..	205	354	223	1,252	1.0
54	Cameroon	−30	−289	..	23	16	156	81	170	1.1
55	Thailand	−250	−2,886	..	847	43	348	912	2,556	2.5
56	Nicaragua	−40	−451	..	..	15	8	49	*171*	2.1
57	Costa Rica	−74	−317	..	..	26	50	16	345	2.7
58	Peru	202	−871	..	..	−70	37	339	1,898	4.6
59	Guatemala	−8	−226	..	..	29	45	79	409	3.4
60	Congo, People's Rep.	..	−400	..	..	..	56	9	12	0.1
61	Turkey	−44	−1,880	273	1,514	58	72	440	2,710	2.8
62	Tunisia	−53	−561	29	359	16	186	60	639	2.1
63	Jamaica	−153	−355	29	42	161	−19	139	63	0.4
64	Dominican Rep.	−102	−442	25	190	72	−1	32	*171*	*1.1*

Note: For data comparability and coverage see the technical notes.

| | | Current account balance (millions of dollars) | | Receipts of workers' remittances (millions of dollars) | | Net direct private investment (millions of dollars) | | Gross international reserves | | |
| | | | | | | | | Millions of dollars | | In months of import coverage |
		1970	1983a	1970	1983a	1970	1983a	1970	1983a	1983a
65	Paraguay	−16	−247	..	(.)	4	5	18	694	10.1
66	Ecuador	−113	−104	..	..	89	50	76	802	3.4
67	Colombia	−293	−2,738	6	..	39	285	207	3,512	5.9
68	*Angola*	..	..	..	..	..	..	..	..	..
69	*Cuba*	..	..	..	..	..	..	..	..	..
70	*Korea, Dem. Rep.*	..	..	..	..	..	..	..	..	..
71	*Lebanon*	..	..	..	..	..	..	405	5,421	..
72	*Mongolia*	..	..	..	..	..	..	..	..	..
Upper middle-income										**3.2** *w*
73	Jordan	−20	−390	..	1,110	..	30	258	1,240	3.7
74	Syrian Arab Rep.	−69	−815	7	461	..	..	57	318	0.7
75	Malaysia	8	−3,350	..	..	94	1,370	667	4,673	2.9
76	Chile	−91	−1,068	..	..	−79	152	392	2,620	5.3
77	Brazil	−837	−6,799	..	2	407	1,374	1,190	4,561	1.8
78	Korea, Rep. of	−623	−1,578	33	..	66	−57	610	2,463	0.9
79	Argentina	−163	−2,439	..	..	11	182	682	2,840	2.8
80	Panama	−64	194	67	..	33	49	16	207	0.4
81	Portugal	..	−983	..	2,120	..	123	1,565	8,179	9.8
82	Mexico	−1,068	5,223	123	..	323	490	756	4,794	2.5
83	Algeria	−125	−86	211	383	45	−14	352	4,010	3.5
84	South Africa	−1,215	291	..	..	318	*349*	1,057	3,795	2.1
85	Uruguay	−45	−60	..	..	..	6	186	1,200	9.3
86	Yugoslavia	−372	275	441	3,427	..	..	143	1,686	1.2
87	Venezuela	−104	3,707	..	..	−23	−62	1,047	12,015	10.7
88	Greece	−422	−1,868	333	914	50	439	318	2,381	2.6
89	Israel	−562	−2,240	..	..	40	49	452	4,038	3.2
90	Hong Kong	..	..	21	..	..	..	..	..	..
91	Singapore	−572	−956	..	..	93	1,389	1,012	9,264	3.5
92	Trinidad and Tobago	−109	−909	3	*1*	83	*341*	43	*3,105*	9.6
93	*Iran, Islamic Rep.*	−507	..	..	..	25	..	217	..	..
94	*Iraq*	105	..	..	..	24	..	472	..	..
High-income oil exporters										**4.6** *w*
95	Oman	..	572	..	44	..	154	13	872	3.1
96	Libya	645	−1,682	..	..	139	−335	1,596	6,584	6.1
97	Saudi Arabia	71	−18,433	..	..	20	3,653	670	29,040	4.4
98	Kuwait	..	4,590	..	..	..	−241	209	6,161	6.5
99	United Arab Emirates	..	4,550	..	..	..	..	..	2,384	3.2
Industrial market economies										**3.9** *w*
100	Spain	79	−2,428	469	930	179	1,382	1,851	12,974	4.2
101	Ireland	−198	−1,867	..	..	32	242	698	2,786	2.7
102	Italy	902	647	446	1,136	498	−943	5,547	45,540	5.6
103	New Zealand	−232	−1,074	40	218	137	114	258	787	1.1
104	Belgium	717	−747	154	390	140	489	2,947	17,754	2.8
105	United Kingdom	1,975	3,429	..	..	−439	−167	2,919	18,592	1.7
106	Austria	−75	161	13	188	104	106	1,806	12,575	5.5
107	Netherlands	−483	3,747	..	..	−15	−862	3,362	26,934	4.1
108	Japan	1,980	20,942	..	..	−260	−3,196	4,877	33,845	2.5
109	France	50	−4,801	130	337	248	34	5,199	51,077	4.2
110	Finland	−239	−949	..	..	−41	−243	455	1,722	1.3
111	Germany, Fed. Rep.	850	3,998	350	..	−290	−1,561	13,879	78,986	4.9
112	Australia	−837	−5,774	..	..	785	2,235	1,709	11,895	4.8
113	Denmark	−544	−1,177	..	..	75	−96	488	4,242	2.2
114	Canada	821	1,380	..	..	566	−3,480	4,733	11,160	1.5
115	Sweden	−265	−929	..	..	−104	−1,006	775	6,349	2.1
116	Norway	−242	2,221	..	10	32	−93	813	7,081	3.5
117	United States	2,320	−41,915	..	..	−6,130	6,382	15,237	123,110	4.0
118	Switzerland	72	3,526	23	81	..	−220	5,317	46,805	14.2
East European nonmarket economies										**..**
119	Hungary	−25	46	..	..	..	..	..	2,148	2.5
120	*Albania*	..	..	..	..	..	..	..	..	..
121	*Bulgaria*	..	..	..	..	..	..	..	..	..
122	*Czechoslovakia*	..	..	..	..	..	..	..	..	..
123	*German Dem. Rep.*	..	..	..	..	..	..	..	..	..
124	*Poland*	..	..	..	..	..	..	..	..	..
125	*Romania*	..	1,160	..	..	..	..	..	1,906	2.0
126	*USSR*	..	..	..	..	..	..	..	..	..

a. Figures in italics are for 1982, not 1983.

Table 15. Flow of public and publicly guaranteed external capital

	Public and publicly guaranteed medium- and long-term loans (millions of dollars)					
	Gross inflow		Repayment of principal		Net inflow[a]	
	1970	1983	1970	1983	1970	1983
Low-income economies						
China and India						
Other low-income						
Sub-Saharan Africa						
1 Ethiopia	27	242	15	42	13	200
2 Bangladesh	..	568	..	80	..	488
3 Mali	21	109	(.)	6	21	103
4 Nepal	1	70	2	5	−2	66
5 Zaire	31	210	28	39	3	171
6 Burkina	2	89	2	7	(.)	83
7 Burma	16	333	18	86	−2	247
8 Malawi	38	66	3	29	36	38
9 Uganda	26	93	4	65	22	29
10 Burundi	1	98	(.)	4	1	93
11 Niger	12	127	1	36	10	91
12 Tanzania	50	303	10	30	40	274
13 Somalia	4	95	(.)	13	4	82
14 India	890	2,765	307	770	583	1,995
15 Rwanda	(.)	38	(.)	2	(.)	37
16 Central African Rep.	2	32	2	11	−1	22
17 Togo	5	76	2	17	3	60
18 Benin	2	121	1	13	1	108
19 China	..	..	..	..	..	..
20 Guinea	90	79	10	48	79	31
21 Haiti	4	45	4	8	1	37
22 Ghana	40	72	12	42	28	30
23 Madagascar	10	216	5	77	5	139
24 Sierra Leone	8	21	10	7	−2	14
25 Sri Lanka	61	373	27	81	34	292
26 Kenya	32	258	16	178	17	80
27 Pakistan	485	985	114	759	371	226
28 Sudan	52	439	22	54	30	385
29 *Afghanistan*	34	..	15	..	19	..
30 *Bhutan*	..	..	..	..	..	..
31 *Chad*	6	3	2	(.)	3	2
32 *Kampuchea, Dem.*	..	..	..	..	..	..
33 *Lao PDR*	..	..	..	..	..	..
34 *Mozambique*	..	..	..	..	..	..
35 *Viet Nam*	..	..	..	..	..	..
Middle-income economies						
Oil exporters						
Oil importers						
Sub-Saharan Africa						
Lower middle-income						
36 Senegal	15	429	5	17	10	412
37 Lesotho	(.)	38	(.)	6	(.)	32
38 Liberia	7	66	12	10	−4	56
39 Mauritania	4	195	3	14	1	181
40 Bolivia	54	86	17	102	37	−16
41 Yemen, PDR	1	306	(.)	32	1	274
42 Yemen Arab Rep.	..	326	..	29	..	297
43 Indonesia	441	4,965	59	1,295	382	3,670
44 Zambia	351	176	33	48	318	128
45 Honduras	29	236	3	38	26	199
46 Egypt, Arab Rep.	394	2,221	297	1,456	97	765
47 El Salvador	8	287	6	29	2	258
48 Ivory Coast	77	667	27	378	50	289
49 Zimbabwe	(.)	710	5	330	−5	381
50 Morocco	163	840	36	610	127	229
51 Papua New Guinea	25	225	0	44	25	181
52 Philippines	128	2,224	72	602	56	1,623
53 Nigeria	62	4,845	36	1,066	26	3,779
54 Cameroon	28	162	4	112	24	50
55 Thailand	51	1,315	23	419	27	896
56 Nicaragua	44	322	17	46	28	276
57 Costa Rica	30	418	21	92	9	326
58 Peru	148	1,622	101	347	47	1,275
59 Guatemala	37	314	20	65	17	249
60 Congo, People's Rep.	21	244	6	161	15	83
61 Turkey	328	1,598	128	1,175	200	423
62 Tunisia	87	555	45	403	42	151
63 Jamaica	15	224	6	104	9	120
64 Dominican Rep.	45	248	7	121	38	127

Note: For data comparability and coverage see the technical notes.

		Public and publicly guaranteed medium- and long-term loans (millions of dollars)					
		Gross inflow		Repayment of principal		Net inflow[a]	
		1970	1983	1970	1983	1970	1983
65	Paraguay	15	288	7	40	7	248
66	Ecuador	42	745	16	508	26	237
67	Colombia	252	1,357	78	388	174	970
68	*Angola*	..	..	..	..	..	..
69	*Cuba*	..	..	..	..	..	..
70	*Korea, Dem. Rep.*						
71	*Lebanon*	12	22	2	35	9	−13
72	*Mongolia*	..	..	..	..	..	..

Upper middle-income

		1970	1983	1970	1983	1970	1983
73	Jordan	14	450	3	125	12	325
74	Syrian Arab Rep.	59	325	30	232	30	94
75	Malaysia	43	3,026	45	286	−1	2,741
76	Chile	397	1,808	163	328	234	1,480
77	Brazil	884	7,095	255	1,979	629	5,117
78	Korea, Rep. of	441	3,634	198	1,999	242	1,635
79	Argentina	487	2,390	342	1,000	146	1,390
80	Panama	67	358	24	188	44	170
81	Portugal	18	2,238	63	1,010	−45	1,228
82	Mexico	772	6,908	476	3,104	297	3,804
83	Algeria	292	2,921	33	3,292	259	−371
84	South Africa	..	..	..	..	..	..
85	Uruguay	38	500	47	94	−9	406
86	Yugoslavia	180	1,307	168	526	12	781
87	Venezuela	224	1,825	42	937	183	889
88	Greece	164	2,255	61	562	102	1,692
89	Israel	410	1,236	25	840	385	396
90	Hong Kong	..	6	0	28	..	−22
91	Singapore	58	152	6	278	52	−126
92	Trinidad and Tobago	8	256	10	123	−2	132
93	*Iran, Islamic Rep.*	940	..	235	..	705	..
94	*Iraq*	63	..	18	..	46	..

High-income oil exporters

		1970	1983	1970	1983	1970	1983
95	Oman	..	506	..	91	..	416
96	Libya						
97	Saudi Arabia						
98	Kuwait						
99	United Arab Emirates						

Industrial market economies

100	Spain
101	Ireland
102	Italy
103	New Zealand
104	Belgium
105	United Kingdom
106	Austria
107	Netherlands
108	Japan
109	France
110	Finland
111	Germany, Fed. Rep.
112	Australia
113	Denmark
114	Canada
115	Sweden
116	Norway
117	United States
118	Switzerland

East European nonmarket economies

		1970	1983	1970	1983	1970	1983
119	Hungary	..	1,429	..	1,272		156
120	*Albania*						
121	*Bulgaria*						
122	*Czechoslovakia*						
123	*German Dem. Rep.*						
124	*Poland*						
125	Romania	..	1,345	..	1,141	..	204
126	*USSR*						

a. Gross inflow less repayment of principal may not equal net inflow because of rounding.

Table 16. External public debt and debt service ratios

		External public debt outstanding and disbursed				Interest payments on external public debt (millions of dollars)		Debt service as percentage of:			
		Millions of dollars		As percentage of GNP				GNP		Exports of goods and services	
		1970	1983	1970	1983[a]	1970	1983	1970	1983[a]	1970	1983[a]
Low-income economies				17.4 w	22.5 w			1.2 w	1.4 w	12.8 w	14.4 w
China and India				..	..			..	..	..	..
Other low-income				21.3 w	42.3 w			1.5 w	2.6 w	8.9 w	18.7 w
Sub-Saharan Africa				18.0 w	52.3 w			1.3 w	2.5 w	5.4 w	14.5 w
1	Ethiopia	169	1,223	9.5	25.9	6	24	1.2	1.4	11.4	11.5
2	Bangladesh	..	4,185	..	37.7	..	63	..	1.3	..	14.7
3	Mali	238	881	88.1	89.3	(.)	6	0.2	1.3	1.3	6.1
4	Nepal	3	346	0.3	14.1	(.)	4	0.3	0.3	..	3.0
5	Zaire	311	4,022	17.6	91.5	9	87	2.1	2.9	4.4	..
6	Burkina	21	398	6.4	38.2	(.)	7	0.6	1.3	6.3	..
7	Burma	101	2,226	4.7	36.3	3	64	0.9	2.4	15.8	33.8
8	Malawi	122	719	43.2	55.2	3	30	2.1	4.5	7.1	20.3
9	Uganda	138	623	7.5	17.9	4	17	0.4	1.9	2.7	..
10	Burundi	7	284	3.1	26.2	(.)	3	0.3	0.7	..	..
11	Niger	32	631	8.7	48.7	1	36	0.6	5.6	3.8	..
12	Tanzania	250	2,584	19.5	58.9	6	36	1.2	1.5	4.9	..
13	Somalia	77	1,149	24.4	62.0	(.)	10	0.3	1.2	2.1	13.1
14	India	7,940	21,277	14.9	11.2	189	553	0.9	0.7	22.0	10.3
15	Rwanda	2	220	0.9	13.9	(.)	2	0.2	0.3	1.3	2.6
16	Central African Rep.	24	215	13.3	33.1	1	7	1.6	2.7	4.8	11.3
17	Togo	40	805	16.0	113.9	1	28	0.9	6.3	2.9	16.8
18	Benin	41	615	16.0	59.2	(.)	13	0.7	2.5	2.3	..
19	China	..	..	..	..	..	..	..	..	..	..
20	Guinea	314	1,216	47.4	69.2	4	22	2.2	4.0	..	..
21	Haiti	40	433	10.3	26.8	(.)	7	1.0	0.9	7.7	5.0
22	Ghana	489	1,095	24.2	28.3	12	30	1.2	1.9	5.0	14.2
23	Madagascar	93	1,490	10.8	52.3	2	64	0.8	4.9	3.5	..
24	Sierra Leone	59	359	14.3	34.5	2	3	2.9	0.9	9.9	7.2
25	Sri Lanka	317	2,205	16.1	43.7	12	86	2.0	3.3	10.3	11.9
26	Kenya	319	2,384	20.6	43.1	12	127	1.8	5.5	5.4	20.6
27	Pakistan	3,060	9,755	30.5	31.3	76	309	1.9	3.4	23.6	28.1
28	Sudan	306	5,726	15.2	77.8	13	37	1.7	1.2	10.7	11.2
29	*Afghanistan*	547	..	58.1	..	9	..	2.5	..	..	..
30	*Bhutan*	..	..	..	..	..	..	..	..	..	..
31	*Chad*	32	129	11.9	43.5	(.)	(.)	1.0	0.1	3.9	0.6
32	*Kampuchea, Dem.*	..	..	..	..	..	..	..	..	..	..
33	*Lao PDR*	..	..	..	..	..	..	..	..	..	..
34	*Mozambique*	..	..	..	..	..	..	..	..	..	..
35	*Viet Nam*	..	..	..	..	..	..	..	..	..	..
Middle-income economies				12.7 w	34.2 w			1.6 w	4.5 w	10.5 w	18.1 w
Oil exporters				13.4 w	34.1 w			1.8 w	5.4 w	10.7 w	21.1 w
Oil importers				12.3 w	31.3 w			1.5 w	4.0 w	10.4 w	16.1 w
Sub-Saharan Africa				12.4 w	29.0 w			1.2 w	4.2 w	..	19.7 w
Lower middle-income				15.3 w	33.6 w			1.6 w	4.2 w	9.9 w	19.7 w
36	Senegal	100	1,496	11.9	61.2	2	31	0.8	1.9	2.8	..
37	Lesotho	8	145	7.8	23.0	(.)	6	0.4	1.9	..	2.5
38	Liberia	158	699	49.6	72.1	6	21	5.5	3.2	..	6.6
39	Mauritania	27	1,171	13.9	158.2	(.)	23	1.7	5.0	3.2	10.0
40	Bolivia	479	2,969	33.8	77.7	6	165	1.6	7.0	11.3	30.5
41	Yemen, PDR	1	1,263	..	118.5	..	14	..	4.3	..	25.1
42	Yemen Arab Rep.	..	1,574	..	38.4	..	13	..	1.0	..	13.9
43	Indonesia	2,443	21,685	27.1	28.9	24	1,256	0.9	3.4	6.9	12.8
44	Zambia	623	2,638	37.0	83.9	26	78	3.5	4.0	5.9	12.6
45	Honduras	90	1,570	12.9	56.3	3	83	0.8	4.3	2.8	14.9
46	Egypt, Arab Rep.	1,750	15,229	23.2	49.4	54	540	4.6	6.5	36.4	27.5
47	El Salvador	88	1,065	8.6	29.2	4	37	0.9	1.8	3.6	6.4
48	Ivory Coast	256	4,824	18.3	78.8	11	413	2.7	12.9	6.8	31.0
49	Zimbabwe	233	1,497	15.7	27.9	5	105	0.6	8.1	..	31.6
50	Morocco	711	9,445	18.0	69.6	23	510	1.5	8.3	8.4	38.2
51	Papua New Guinea	36	911	5.8	40.4	1	63	0.1	4.7	..	11.2
52	Philippines	572	10,385	8.1	30.4	23	650	1.4	3.7	7.2	15.4
53	Nigeria	480	11,757	4.8	17.7	20	974	0.6	3.1	4.2	18.6
54	Cameroon	131	1,883	12.1	26.7	4	107	0.8	3.1	3.1	13.9
55	Thailand	324	7,060	4.9	18.0	16	531	0.6	2.4	3.4	11.3
56	Nicaragua	156	3,417	15.7	133.3	7	37	2.4	3.2	11.1	18.3
57	Costa Rica	134	3,315	13.8	126.3	7	504	2.9	22.7	10.0	50.6
58	Peru	856	7,932	12.6	48.1	44	406	2.1	4.6	11.6	19.6
59	Guatemala	106	1,405	5.7	15.8	6	76	1.4	1.6	7.4	11.7
60	Congo, People's Rep.	144	1,487	53.9	76.1	3	77	3.3	12.2	..	20.5
61	Turkey	1,854	15,396	14.4	30.2	42	1,169	1.3	4.6	22.0	28.9
62	Tunisia	541	3,427	38.2	42.4	18	195	4.5	7.4	19.0	22.3
63	Jamaica	160	1,950	11.8	65.2	9	101	1.1	6.9	2.7	15.4
64	Dominican Republic	226	2,202	15.5	26.7	5	110	0.8	2.8	4.7	22.7

Note: For data comparability and coverage see the technical notes.

	External public debt outstanding and disbursed				Interest payments on external public debt (millions of dollars)		Debt service as percentage of:			
	Millions of dollars		As percentage of GNP				GNP		Exports of goods and services	
	1970	1983	1970	1983[a]	1970	1983	1970	1983[a]	1970	1983[a]
65 Paraguay	112	1,161	13.1	28.6	4	45	1.2	2.1	11.9	14.9
66 Ecuador	217	6,239	13.2	63.0	7	365	1.4	8.8	9.1	32.5
67 Colombia	1,293	6,899	18.4	18.3	44	516	1.7	2.4	12.0	21.3
68 *Angola*	..	..	..	..	..	..	..	..	..	..
69 *Cuba*	..	..	..	..	..	..	..	..	..	..
70 *Korea, Dem. Rep.*	..	..	..	..	..	..	..	..	..	..
71 *Lebanon*	64	182	4.2	..	1	15	0.2	..	..	..
72 *Mongolia*	..	..	..	..	..	..	..	..	..	..
Upper middle-income			11.5 *w*	31.7 *w*			1.7 *w*	4.7 *w*	10.8 *w*	17.4 *w*
73 Jordan	118	1,940	23.5	47.9	2	88	0.9	5.2	3.6	11.3
74 Syrian Arab Rep.	232	2,305	10.6	13.7	6	73	1.6	1.8	11.0	11.2
75 Malaysia	390	10,665	10.0	38.6	21	669	1.7	3.5	3.6	5.9
76 Chile	2,066	6,827	25.8	39.2	78	557	3.0	5.1	18.9	18.3
77 Brazil	3,234	58,068	7.7	29.3	133	5,004	0.9	3.5	12.5	28.7
78 Korea, Rep. of	1,797	21,472	..	..	70	1,744	..	..	19.4	12.3
79 Argentina	1,878	24,593	8.6	32.1	121	1,343	2.1	3.1	21.5	24.0
80 Panama	194	2,986	19.5	73.6	7	283	3.1	11.6	7.7	6.8
81 Portugal	485	9,951	7.8	50.8	29	843	1.5	9.5	..	26.7
82 Mexico	3,206	66,732	9.1	49.1	216	6,850	2.0	7.3	23.6	35.9
83 Algeria	937	12,942	19.3	28.0	10	1,212	0.9	9.8	3.8	33.1
84 South Africa	..	..	..	..	..	..	..	..	..	..
85 Uruguay	269	2,523	11.1	48.4	16	198	2.6	5.6	21.6	19.8
86 Yugoslavia	1,198	9,077	8.8	19.9	72	483	1.8	2.2	9.9	7.6
87 Venezuela	728	12,911	6.6	19.8	40	1,658	0.7	4.0	2.9	15.0
88 Greece	905	8,193	8.9	23.5	41	755	1.0	3.8	9.3	18.3
89 Israel	2,274	15,149	41.3	70.4	13	1,109	0.7	9.1	2.7	19.6
90 Hong Kong	2	224	0.1	0.8	..	18	..	0.2	..	..
91 Singapore	152	1,244	7.9	7.6	6	116	0.6	2.4	0.6	1.3
92 Trinidad and Tobago	101	887	12.2	10.7	6	101	1.9	2.7	4.4	*2.8*
93 *Iran, Islamic Rep.*	2,193	..	20.8	..	85	..	3.0	..	12.2	..
94 *Iraq*	274	..	8.8	..	9	..	0.9	..	2.2	..
High-income oil exporters										
95 Oman	..	1,125	..	16.1	..	52	..	2.1	..	3.2
96 Libya										
97 Saudi Arabia										
98 Kuwait										
99 United Arab Emirates										
Industrial market economies										
100 Spain										
101 Ireland										
102 Italy										
103 New Zealand										
104 Belgium										
105 United Kingdom										
106 Austria										
107 Netherlands										
108 Japan										
109 France										
110 Finland										
111 Germany, Fed. Rep.										
112 Australia										
113 Denmark										
114 Canada										
115 Sweden										
116 Norway										
117 United States										
118 Switzerland										
East European nonmarket economies										
119 Hungary	..	6,573	..	30.1	..	655	..	9.3	..	18.5
120 *Albania*										
121 *Bulgaria*										
122 *Czechoslovakia*										
123 *German Dem. Rep.*										
124 *Poland*										
125 *Romania*	..	7,576	..	..	473	..	..	9.0		
126 *USSR*										

a. Figures in italics are for 1982, not for 1983.

Table 17. Terms of public borrowing

	Commitments (millions of dollars)		Average interest rate (percent)		Average maturity (years)		Average grace period (years)	
	1970	1983	1970	1983	1970	1983	1970	1983
Low-income economies	3,035 *t*	7,978 *t*	2.8 *w*	3.9 *w*	31 *w*	30 *w*	9 *w*	7 *w*
China and India	..	..	..	..	..	..	..	..
Other low-income	2,102 *t*	6,093 *t*	3.0 *w*	3.5 *w*	29 *w*	30 *w*	9 *w*	7 *w*
Sub-Saharan Africa	983 *t*	3,036 *t*	3.1 *w*	3.4 *w*	27 *w*	29 *w*	8 *w*	7 *w*
1 Ethiopia	21	505	4.3	2.1	32	25	7	6
2 Bangladesh	..	593	..	1.7	..	39	..	9
3 Mali	30	72	0.3	3.1	27	26	11	7
4 Nepal	17	183	2.8	1.2	27	40	6	10
5 Zaire	257	144	6.5	1.6	13	42	4	9
6 Burkina	9	89	2.3	3.0	37	31	8	7
7 Burma	57	218	4.3	1.4	16	40	4	10
8 Malawi	13	103	3.8	2.4	30	28	6	9
9 Uganda	12	204	3.7	3.9	28	34	7	7
10 Burundi	1	69	2.9	4.3	5	26	2	7
11 Niger	18	107	1.2	5.4	40	28	8	7
12 Tanzania	283	307	1.2	3.9	40	24	11	5
13 Somalia	2	81	(.)	2.7	3	32	3	5
14 India	933	1,885	2.4	5.0	35	30	8	6
15 Rwanda	9	56	0.8	1.6	50	37	11	8
16 Central African Rep.	7	75	2.0	1.9	36	29	8	8
17 Togo	3	152	4.6	2.7	17	36	4	8
18 Benin	7	71	1.8	2.3	32	38	7	9
19 China	..	..	..	..	..	..	..	..
20 Guinea	66	122	2.9	4.6	13	24	5	6
21 Haiti	5	91	6.7	1.3	9	46	1	10
22 Ghana	50	72	2.4	0.7	39	50	10	10
23 Madagascar	23	283	2.3	3.7	40	27	9	7
24 Sierra Leone	24	22	3.5	0.8	27	47	6	10
25 Sri Lanka	79	281	3.0	1.9	27	40	5	10
26 Kenya	49	147	2.6	5.5	37	31	8	7
27 Pakistan	942	1,691	2.7	5.4	32	26	12	7
28 Sudan	95	349	1.8	5.5	17	21	9	5
29 *Afghanistan*	19	..	1.7	..	33	..	8	..
30 *Bhutan*	..	..	..	..	..	..	..	..
31 *Chad*	4	6	4.8	3.0	7	23	2	7
32 *Kampuchea, Dem.*	..	..	..	..	..	..	..	..
33 *Lao PDR*	..	..	..	..	..	..	..	..
34 *Mozambique*	..	..	..	..	..	..	..	..
35 *Viet Nam*	..	..	..	..	..	..	..	..
Middle-income economies	10,684 *t*	71,716 *t*	6.2 *w*	10.2 *w*	17 *w*	12 *w*	4 *w*	4 *w*
Oil exporters	4,232 *t*	33,867 *t*	6.3 *w*	10.2 *w*	16 *w*	11 *w*	4 *w*	3 *w*
Oil importers	6,452 *t*	37,849 *t*	6.2 *w*	10.2 *w*	17 *w*	12 *w*	5 *w*	4 *w*
Sub-Saharan Africa	790 *t*	7,305 *t*	4.5 *w*	10.3 *w*	25 *w*	10 *w*	8 *w*	3 *w*
Lower middle-income	3,768 *t*	31,119 *t*	5.0 *w*	8.9 *w*	23 *w*	15 *w*	6 *w*	4 *w*
36 Senegal	6	271	3.7	5.3	25	22	7	6
37 Lesotho	(.)	33	5.1	5.9	25	24	2	6
38 Liberia	11	36	5.4	8.7	19	14	5	5
39 Mauritania	7	154	6.6	5.6	11	16	3	4
40 Bolivia	24	439	3.7	4.9	26	28	6	7
41 Yemen, PDR	62	287	(.)	2.5	21	22	11	5
42 Yemen Arab Rep.	9	101	5.2	1.6	5	36	3	8
43 Indonesia	518	5,597	2.7	8.8	34	15	9	5
44 Zambia	555	120	4.2	4.8	27	26	9	7
45 Honduras	23	340	4.1	5.9	30	25	7	6
46 Egypt, Arab Rep.	448	2,698	7.7	8.8	17	22	2	4
47 El Salvador	12	121	4.7	2.9	23	34	6	8
48 Ivory Coast	71	634	5.8	10.8	19	16	6	4
49 Zimbabwe	..	477	..	9.7	..	13	..	4
50 Morocco	182	1,786	4.6	7.4	20	16	4	5
51 Papua New Guinea	58	284	6.0	7.5	24	14	8	4
52 Philippines	158	1,814	7.4	9.1	11	16	2	5
53 Nigeria	65	4,994	6.0	11.0	14	7	4	2
54 Cameroon	41	201	4.7	8.9	29	18	8	5
55 Thailand	106	1,189	6.8	8.3	19	20	4	7
56 Nicaragua	23	371	7.1	6.8	18	14	4	4
57 Costa Rica	58	413	5.6	8.3	28	11	6	5
58 Peru	125	1,782	7.4	9.9	13	12	4	3
59 Guatemala	50	350	5.2	8.4	26	13	6	4
60 Congo, People's Rep.	33	386	2.6	10.0	18	10	7	3
61 Turkey	487	2,454	3.6	8.3	19	14	5	4
62 Tunisia	141	614	3.4	8.5	27	12	6	5
63 Jamaica	24	294	6.0	7.0	16	24	3	8
64 Dominican Rep.	20	318	2.5	5.8	28	22	5	7

Note: For data comparability and coverage see the technical notes.

	Commitments (millions of dollars)		Average interest rate (percent)		Average maturity (years)		Average grace period (years)	
	1970	1983	1970	1983	1970	1983	1970	1983
65 Paraguay	14	195	5.7	7.7	25	21	6	6
66 Ecuador	78	975	6.1	10.6	20	10	4	3
67 Colombia	362	1,391	5.9	10.8	21	14	5	4
68 *Angola*	..	..	..	..	..	..	..	..
69 *Cuba*	..	..	..	..	..	..	..	..
70 *Korea, Dem. Rep.*	..	..	..	..	..	..	..	..
71 *Lebanon*	7	..	2.7	..	21	..	1	..
72 *Mongolia*	..	..	..	..	..	..	..	..
Upper middle-income	6,916 *t*	40,598 *t*	6.9 *w*	11.0 *w*	13 *w*	10 *w*	4 *w*	3 *w*
73 Jordan	33	532	3.9	7.3	12	14	5	3
74 Syrian Arab Rep.	14	443	4.4	6.0	9	20	2	2
75 Malaysia	83	3,101	6.1	9.5	19	11	5	6
76 Chile	343	2,132	6.9	11.9	12	9	3	4
77 Brazil	1,400	7,640	7.1	11.4	14	9	3	3
78 Korea, Rep. of	677	3,320	6.0	9.8	19	12	5	4
79 Argentina	489	1,854	7.4	12.5	12	5	3	2
80 Panama	111	689	6.9	11.3	15	10	4	3
81 Portugal	59	2,103	4.3	10.4	17	9	4	4
82 Mexico	826	7,517	8.0	11.9	12	9	3	3
83 Algeria	288	3,705	6.5	9.8	10	7	2	1
84 South Africa	..	..	..	..	..	..	..	..
85 Uruguay	72	501	7.9	12.0	12	7	3	2
86 Yugoslavia	198	1,953	7.1	10.9	17	11	6	3
87 Venezuela	198	1,600	8.2	11.6	8	7	2	3
88 Greece	242	2,169	7.2	10.2	9	9	4	4
89 Israel	439	1,000	7.3	12.8	13	29	5	10
90 Hong Kong	(.)	(.)	(.)	7.5	(.)	13	(.)	4
91 Singapore	69	82	6.8	9.7	17	9	4	2
92 Trinidad and Tobago	3	226	7.5	10.8	10	8	1	3
93 *Iran, Islamic Rep.*	1,342	..	6.2	..	12	..	3	..
94 *Iraq*	28	..	3.3	..	11	..	2	..
High-income oil exporters								
95 Oman	..	415	..	10.6	..	8	..	3
96 Libya								
97 Saudi Arabia								
98 Kuwait								
99 United Arab Emirates								
Industrial market economies								
100 Spain								
101 Ireland								
102 Italy								
103 New Zealand								
104 Belgium								
105 United Kingdom								
106 Austria								
107 Netherlands								
108 Japan								
109 France								
110 Finland								
111 Germany, Fed. Rep.								
112 Australia								
113 Denmark								
114 Canada								
115 Sweden								
116 Norway								
117 United States								
118 Switzerland								
East European nonmarket economies								
119 Hungary[a]	..	1,434	..	10.1	..	7	..	3
120 *Albania*								
121 *Bulgaria*								
122 *Czechoslovakia*								
123 *German Dem. Rep.*								
124 *Poland*								
125 *Romania*	..	750	..	..	..	..	..	..
126 *USSR*								

a. Includes only debt in convertible currencies.

Table 18. Official development assistance from OECD & OPEC members

	Amount									
	1965	1970	1975	1978	1979	1980	1981	1982	1983	1984[a]
OECD					**Millions of US dollars**					
102 Italy	60	147	182	376	273	683	666	811	827	1,105
103 New Zealand	..	14	66	55	68	72	68	65	61	59
104 Belgium	102	120	378	536	643	595	575	499	480	410
105 United Kingdom	472	500	904	1,465	2,156	1,854	2,192	1,800	1,605	1,432
106 Austria	10	11	79	154	131	178	220	236	158	181
107 Netherlands	70	196	608	1,074	1,472	1,630	1,510	1,472	1,195	1,268
108 Japan	244	458	1,148	2,215	2,685	3,353	3,171	3,023	3,761	4,319
109 France	752	971	2,093	2,705	3,449	4,162	4,177	4,034	3,815	3,790
110 Finland	2	7	48	55	90	111	135	144	153	178
111 Germany, Fed. Rep.	456	599	1,689	2,347	3,393	3,567	3,181	3,152	3,176	2,767
112 Australia	119	212	552	588	629	667	650	882	753	773
113 Denmark	13	59	205	388	461	481	403	415	395	449
114 Canada	96	337	880	1,060	1,056	1,075	1,189	1,197	1,429	1,535
115 Sweden	38	117	566	783	988	962	919	987	754	737
116 Norway	11	37	184	355	429	486	467	559	584	526
117 United States	4,023	3,153	4,161	5,663	4,684	7,138	5,782	8,202	7,992	8,698
118 Switzerland	12	30	104	173	213	253	237	252	320	286
Total	6,480	6,968	13,847	19,992	22,820	27,267	25,542	27,730	27,458	28,513
OECD					**As percentage of donor GNP**					
102 Italy	.10	.16	.11	.14	.08	.17	.19	.24	.24	.32
103 New Zealand	..	.23	.52	.34	.33	.33	.29	.28	.28	.28
104 Belgium	.60	.46	.59	.55	.57	.50	.59	.59	.59	.59
105 United Kingdom	.47	.41	.39	.46	.52	.35	.43	.37	.35	.33
106 Austria	.11	.07	.21	.27	.19	.23	.33	.35	.23	.28
107 Netherlands	.36	.61	.75	.82	.98	1.03	1.08	1.08	.91	1.02
108 Japan	.27	.23	.23	.23	.27	.32	.28	.28	.33	.35
109 France	.76	.66	.62	.57	.60	.64	.73	.75	.74	.77
110 Finland	.02	.06	.18	.16	.22	.22	.28	.30	.33	.36
111 Germany, Fed. Rep.	.40	.32	.40	.37	.45	.44	.47	.48	.49	.45
112 Australia	.53	.59	.65	.55	.53	.48	.41	.57	.49	.45
113 Denmark	.13	.38	.58	.75	.77	.74	.73	.76	.73	.85
114 Canada	.19	.41	.54	.52	.48	.43	.43	.41	.45	.47
115 Sweden	.19	.38	.82	.90	.97	.79	.83	1.02	.85	.80
116 Norway	.16	.32	.66	.90	.93	.85	.82	.99	1.06	.99
117 United States	.58	.32	.27	.27	.20	.27	.20	.27	.24	.23
118 Switzerland	.09	.15	.19	.20	.21	.24	.24	.25	.32	.30
OECD					**National currencies**					
102 Italy (billions of lire)	38	92	119	319	227	585	757	1,097	1,256	1,941
103 New Zealand (millions of dollars)	..	13	54	53	66	74	78	86	91	102
104 Belgium (millions of francs)	5,100	6,000	13,902	16,880	18,852	17,400	21,350	22,800	24,543	23,700
105 United Kingdom (millions of pounds)	169	208	407	763	1,016	797	1,081	1,028	1,058	1,072
106 Austria (millions of schillings)	260	286	1,376	2,236	1,751	2,303	3,504	4,026	2,838	3,622
107 Netherlands (millions of guilders)	253	710	1,538	2,324	2,953	3,241	3,768	3,931	3,411	4,069
108 Japan (billions of yen)	88	165	341	466	588	760	699	753	893	1,026
109 France (millions of francs)	3,713	5,393	8,971	12,207	14,674	17,589	22,700	26,513	29,075	33,125
110 Finland (millions of markkaa)	6	29	177	226	351	414	583	694	852	1,070
111 Germany, Fed. Rep. (millions of deutsche marks)	1,824	2,192	4,155	4,714	6,219	6,484	7,189	7,649	8,109	7,875
112 Australia (millions of dollars)	106	189	421	514	563	585	566	867	834	879
113 Denmark (millions of kroner)	90	443	1,178	2,140	2,425	2,711	2,871	3,458	3,612	4,650
114 Canada (millions of dollars)	104	353	895	1,209	1,237	1,257	1,425	1,477	1,761	1,988
115 Sweden (millions of kronor)	197	605	2,350	3,538	4,236	4,069	4,653	6,201	5,781	6,096
116 Norway (millions of kroner)	79	264	962	1,861	2,172	2,400	2,680	3,608	4,261	4,293
117 United States (millions of dollars)	4,023	3,153	4,161	5,663	4,684	7,138	5,782	8,202	7,992	8,698
118 Switzerland (millions of francs)	52	131	268	309	354	424	466	512	672	672
OECD					**Summary**					
ODA (billions of US dollars, nominal prices)	6.48	6.97	13.85	19.99	22.82	27.27	25.54	27.73	27.46	28.51
ODA as percentage of GNP	.48	.34	.35	.35	.35	.38	.35	.38	.36	.36
ODA (billions of US dollars, constant 1980 prices)	20.41	18.21	21.73	24.11	24.89	27.27	25.63	27.94	27.46	28.70
GNP (trillions of US dollars, nominal prices)	1.35	2.04	3.92	5.75	6.56	7.25	7.38	7.31	7.58	7.91
GDP deflator[b]	.32	.38	.64	.83	.92	1.00	1.00	.99	1.00	.99

Note: For data comparability and coverage see the technical notes.

208

		Amount								
		1975	1976	1977	1978	1979	1980	1981	1982	1983[c]
OPEC		**Millions of US dollars**								
53	Nigeria	14	83	50	26	29	33	141	58	35
83	Algeria	41	54	42	41	281	103	97	128	44
87	Venezuela	31	108	24	87	107	125	67	126	141
93	*Iran, Islamic Rep.*	593	753	169	240	−34	−83	−93	−121	139
94	*Iraq*	215	231	62	174	659	768	140	9	−3
96	Libya	259	94	101	131	140	382	293	43	85
97	Saudi Arabia	2,756	3,028	3,086	5,464	4,238	5,943	5,664	4,028	3,916
98	Kuwait	946	531	1,292	978	971	1,140	1,154	1,168	995
99	United Arab Emirates	1,046	1,021	1,052	885	970	909	811	402	100
	Qatar	338	195	189	105	291	270	250	50	22
	Total OAPEC[d]	5,601	5,154	5,824	7,778	7,550	9,515	8,409	5,828	5,159
	Total OPEC	6,239	6,098	6,067	8,131	7,652	9,590	8,524	5,891	5,474
OPEC		**As percentage of donor GNP**								
53	Nigeria	.04	.19	.10	.05	.04	.04	.18	.08	.05
83	Algeria	.28	.33	.21	.16	.88	.25	.23	.29	.09
87	Venezuela	.11	.34	.07	.22	.22	.21	.10	.18	.20
93	*Iran, Islamic Rep.*	1.12	1.16	.22	.33	. .	. .	. .	. .	.13
94	*Iraq*	1.62	1.44	.33	.77	1.97	2.09	.47	.03	. .
96	Libya	2.29	.63	.57	.77	.58	1.18	1.11	.18	.35
97	Saudi Arabia	7.76	6.46	5.24	8.39	5.55	5.09	3.54	2.61	3.53
98	Kuwait	7.18	3.63	8.13	5.40	3.52	3.52	3.60	4.49	4.46
99	United Arab Emirates	11.68	8.88	7.23	6.23	5.09	3.30	2.72	1.46	.42
	Qatar	15.58	7.95	7.56	3.62	6.26	4.05	3.77	.89	.42
	Total OAPEC[d]	5.73	4.23	3.95	4.69	3.49	3.73	2.82	2.02	2.10
	Total OPEC	2.92	2.32	1.96	2.48	1.83	2.41	1.94	1.37	1.45

		Net bilateral flow to low-income countries								
		1965	1970	1975	1978	1979	1980	1981	1982	1983
OECD		**As percentage of donor GNP**								
102	Italy	.04	.06	.01	.01	.01	.01	.02	.04	.05
103	New Zealand	. .	. .	.14	.01	.01	.01	.01	(.)	(.)
104	Belgium	.56	.30	.31	.23	.27	.24	.25	.21	.21
105	United Kingdom	.23	.15	.11	.14	.16	.11	.13	.07	.10
106	Austria	.06	.05	.02	.01	.03	.03	.03	.01	.02
107	Netherlands	.08	.24	.24	.28	.26	.30	.37	.31	.26
108	Japan	.13	.11	.08	.05	.09	.08	.06	.11	.09
109	France	.12	.09	.10	.07	.07	.08	.11	.10	.09
110	Finland	. .	. .	.06	.04	.06	.08	.09	.09	.12
111	Germany, Fed. Rep.	.14	.10	.12	.09	.10	.08	.11	.12	.13
112	Australia	.08	.09	.10	.04	.06	.04	.06	.07	.05
113	Denmark	.02	.10	.20	.29	.28	.28	.21	.26	.31
114	Canada	.10	.22	.24	.17	.13	.11	.13	.14	.13
115	Sweden	.07	.12	.41	.36	.41	.36	.32	.38	.33
116	Norway	.04	.12	.25	.34	.37	.31	.28	.37	.39
117	United States	.26	.14	.08	.03	.02	.03	.03	.02	.03
118	Switzerland	.02	.05	.10	.07	.06	.08	.07	.09	.10
	Total	.20	.13	.11	.07	.08	.07	.08	.08	.08

a. Preliminary estimates.   b. See the technical notes.   c. Provisional.   d. Organization of Arab Petroleum Exporting Countries.

Table 19. Population growth and projections

	Average annual growth of population (percent)			Population (millions)			Hypothetical size of stationary population (millions)	Assumed year of reaching net reproduction rate of 1	Population momentum 1985
	1965–73	1973–83	1980–2000	1983	1990ᵃ	2000ᵃ			
Low-income economies	2.6 w	2.0 w	1.8 w	2,342 t	2,663 t	3,154 t			
China and India	2.5 w	1.8 w	1.5 w	1,752 t	1,950 t	2,236 t			
Other low-income	2.6 w	2.6 w	2.6 w	590 t	713 t	918 t			
Sub-Saharan Africa	2.6 w	2.8 w	3.0 w	245 t	304 t	408 t			
1 Ethiopia	2.6	2.7	2.6	41	48	64	181	2035	1.9
2 Bangladesh	2.6	2.4	2.3	95	114	141	310	2025	1.9
3 Mali	2.6	2.5	2.5	7	9	11	37	2035	1.9
4 Nepal	2.0	2.6	2.6	16	19	24	74	2040	1.8
5 Zaire	2.1	2.5	3.1	30	37	50	145	2030	1.9
6 Burkina	2.0	1.9	2.0	6	7	9	32	2040	1.8
7 Burma	2.3	2.0	2.3	35	43	53	115	2025	1.9
8 Malawi	2.8	3.0	3.1	7	8	11	38	2040	2.0
9 Uganda	3.4	2.8	3.3	14	18	25	83	2035	2.0
10 Burundi	1.4	2.2	2.9	4	5	7	24	2035	1.9
11 Niger	2.6	3.0	3.2	6	8	11	40	2040	2.0
12 Tanzania	3.1	3.3	3.4	21	27	37	125	2035	2.0
13 Somalia	3.5	2.8	3.0	5	6	8	31	2040	1.9
14 India	2.3	2.3	1.8	733	844	994	1,700	2010	1.8
15 Rwanda	3.1	3.4	3.4	6	7	10	40	2040	2.0
16 Central African Rep.	1.6	2.3	2.7	2	3	4	12	2035	1.9
17 Togo	2.8	2.6	3.2	3	4	5	16	2035	2.0
18 Benin	2.6	2.8	3.1	4	5	6	21	2035	2.0
19 China	2.7	1.5	1.2	1,019	1,106	1,242	1,571	2010	1.6
20 Guinea	1.8	2.0	2.1	6	7	8	25	2045	1.8
21 Haiti	1.5	1.8	1.8	5	6	7	14	2025	1.9
22 Ghana	2.2	3.1	3.5	13	17	23	64	2025	2.0
23 Madagascar	2.4	2.6	3.1	9	12	16	55	2035	1.9
24 Sierra Leone	1.7	2.1	2.3	4	4	5	17	2045	1.8
25 Sri Lanka	2.0	1.7	1.8	15	18	21	32	2005	1.7
26 Kenya	3.7	4.0	3.9	19	25	36	120	2030	2.1
27 Pakistan	3.1	3.0	2.4	90	106	133	330	2035	1.9
28 Sudan	2.6	3.2	2.8	21	25	33	102	2035	1.9
29 *Afghanistan*	2.3	2.6	2.3	17	20	25	76	2045	1.9
30 *Bhutan*	1.3	1.9	2.2	1	1	2	4	2035	1.8
31 *Chad*	1.8	2.1	2.4	5	6	7	22	2040	1.8
32 *Kampuchea, Dem.*	1.8	. .	. .	. .	. .	. .	. .		
33 *Lao PDR*	1.4	2.2	2.5	4	4	6	18	2040	1.9
34 *Mozambique*	2.3	2.6	2.9	13	16	22	70	2035	2.0
35 *Viet Nam*	3.1	2.7	2.4	59	70	88	170	2015	1.9
Middle-income economies	2.5 w	2.4 w	2.2 w	1,166 t	1,374 t	1,690 t			
Oil exporters	2.6 w	2.7 w	2.5 w	543 t	652 t	830 t			
Oil importers	2.4 w	2.2 w	1.9 w	623 t	722 t	860 t			
Sub-Saharan Africa	2.6 w	2.9 w	3.1 w	148 t	178 t	256 t			
Lower middle-income	2.5 w	2.5 w	2.3 w	665 t	787 t	977 t			
36 Senegal	2.4	2.8	2.9	6	8	10	30	2035	1.9
37 Lesotho	2.1	2.5	2.6	1	2	2	6	2030	1.8
38 Liberia	2.8	3.3	3.1	2	3	3	11	2035	1.9
39 Mauritania	2.3	2.2	2.6	2	2	3	8	2035	1.8
40 Bolivia	2.4	2.6	2.4	6	7	9	22	2030	1.9
41 Yemen, PDR	2.1	2.2	2.4	2	2	3	8	2035	2.0
42 Yemen Arab Rep.	2.6	2.9	2.8	8	9	12	40	2040	2.0
43 Indonesia	2.1	2.3	1.9	156	179	212	368	2010	1.8
44 Zambia	3.0	3.2	3.3	6	8	11	33	2030	2.0
45 Honduras	2.9	3.5	3.0	4	5	7	15	2020	2.0
46 Egypt, Arab Rep.	2.3	2.5	2.0	45	52	63	113	2015	1.8
47 El Salvador	3.4	3.0	2.6	5	6	8	17	2015	1.9
48 Ivory Coast	4.6	4.6	3.6	9	13	17	47	2030	2.0
49 Zimbabwe	3.4	3.2	3.6	8	10	14	39	2025	2.1
50 Morocco	2.4	2.6	2.4	21	25	31	70	2025	2.0
51 Papua New Guinea	2.5	2.1	2.1	3	4	5	9	2025	1.9
52 Philippines	2.9	2.7	2.1	52	61	73	126	2010	1.9
53 Nigeria	2.5	2.7	3.3	94	118	163	532	2035	2.0
54 Cameroon	2.4	3.1	3.2	10	12	17	52	2030	1.9
55 Thailand	2.9	2.3	1.7	49	56	65	100	2000	1.8
56 Nicaragua	2.9	3.9	3.0	3	4	5	12	2025	2.0
57 Costa Rica	3.0	2.4	2.1	2	3	3	5	2005	1.8
58 Peru	2.8	2.4	2.2	18	21	26	49	2020	1.9
59 Guatemala	3.0	3.1	2.6	8	10	12	25	2020	1.9
60 Congo, People's Rep.	2.6	3.1	3.7	2	2	3	9	2020	1.9
61 Turkey	2.5	2.2	1.9	47	55	65	111	2010	1.8
62 Tunisia	2.0	2.5	2.2	7	8	10	19	2015	1.9
63 Jamaica	1.5	1.3	1.4	2	2	3	5	2005	1.6
64 Dominican Rep.	2.9	2.4	2.2	6	7	9	15	2010	1.9

Note: For data comparability and coverage see the technical notes.

		Average annual growth of population (percent)			Population (millions)			Hypothetical size of stationary population (millions)	Assumed year of reaching net reproduction rate of 1	Population momentum 1985
		1965–73	1973–83	1980–2000	1983	1990[a]	2000[a]			
65	Paraguay	2.7	2.5	2.2	3	4	5	8	2010	1.9
66	Ecuador	2.7	2.6	2.5	8	10	13	25	2015	1.9
67	Colombia	2.6	1.9	1.8	28	31	37	60	2010	1.8
68	*Angola*	2.2	2.6	2.8	8	10	13	44	2040	1.9
69	*Cuba*	1.8	0.8	1.0	10	11	12	15	2010	1.5
70	*Korea, Dem. Rep.*	2.8	2.5	2.1	19	22	27	46	2010	1.8
71	*Lebanon*	2.6	−0.3	1.2	3	3	3	6	2005	1.8
72	*Mongolia*	3.1	2.8	2.4	2	2	3	5	2015	1.9
Upper middle-income		**2.4** *w*	**2.3** *w*	**2.1** *w*	**501** *t*	**587** *t*	**713** *t*			
73	Jordan	3.0	2.7	3.8	3	4	6	17	2020	2.0
74	Syrian Arab Rep.	3.4	3.3	3.4	10	13	17	41	2020	2.0
75	Malaysia	2.6	2.4	2.0	15	17	21	33	2005	1.8
76	Chile	1.9	1.7	1.5	12	13	15	21	2005	1.6
77	Brazil	2.5	2.3	1.9	130	150	179	298	2010	1.8
78	Korea, Rep. of	2.2	1.6	1.4	40	45	50	70	2000	1.6
79	Argentina	1.5	1.6	1.3	30	33	37	54	2010	1.5
80	Panama	2.7	2.3	1.9	2	2	3	4	2005	1.8
81	Portugal	−0.2	1.1	0.5	10	10	11	13	2010	1.3
82	Mexico	3.3	2.9	2.3	75	89	109	199	2010	1.9
83	Algeria	2.9	3.1	3.5	21	27	38	107	2025	2.0
84	South Africa	2.6	2.4	2.7	32	39	49	104	2020	1.8
85	Uruguay	0.6	0.5	0.7	3	3	3	4	2005	1.3
86	Yugoslavia	0.9	0.8	0.6	23	24	25	30	2010	1.3
87	Venezuela	3.6	3.5	2.6	17	21	26	46	2010	1.9
88	Greece	0.5	1.1	0.4	10	10	10	12	2000	1.2
89	Israel	3.1	2.3	1.6	4	5	5	8	2005	1.6
90	Hong Kong	2.0	2.5	1.3	5	6	7	7	2010	1.4
91	Singapore	1.8	1.3	1.0	3	3	3	3	2010	1.4
92	Trinidad and Tobago	0.9	0.6	1.7	1	1	2	2	2010	1.7
93	*Iran, Islamic Rep.*	3.3	3.1	3.0	43	53	71	166	2020	1.9
94	*Iraq*	3.3	3.6	3.4	15	19	26	73	2025	2.0
High-income oil exporters		**4.5** *w*	**5.1** *w*	**3.6** *w*	**18** *t*	**24** *t*	**33** *t*			
95	Oman	2.9	4.8	2.9	1	1	2	4	2020	1.9
96	Libya	4.1	4.3	4.1	3	5	7	19	2025	2.0
97	Saudi Arabia	4.0	4.7	3.6	10	14	19	56	2030	1.9
98	Kuwait	8.3	6.4	3.5	2	2	3	5	2010	1.9
99	United Arab Emirates	11.8	11.3	3.7	1	2	2	4	2015	1.4
Industrial market economies		**1.0** *w*	**0.7** *w*	**0.4** *w*	**729** *t*	**752** *t*	**782** *t*			
100	Spain	1.0	1.0	0.6	38	40	42	49	2010	1.3
101	Ireland	0.8	1.3	1.0	4	4	4	6	2000	1.5
102	Italy	0.6	0.3	0.1	57	57	58	56	2010	1.1
103	New Zealand	1.4	0.6	0.7	3	3	4	4	2010	1.3
104	Belgium	0.4	0.1	0.1	10	10	10	10	2010	1.1
105	United Kingdom	0.4	(.)	(.)	56	56	57	58	2010	1.1
106	Austria	0.4	(.)	0.1	8	8	8	8	2010	1.1
107	Netherlands	1.1	0.7	0.4	14	15	15	15	2010	1.2
108	Japan	1.2	0.9	0.5	119	123	128	128	2010	1.2
109	France	0.8	0.4	0.4	55	56	59	63	2010	1.2
110	Finland	0.2	0.4	0.3	5	5	5	6	2010	1.2
111	Germany, Fed. Rep.	0.7	−0.1	−0.1	61	61	61	54	2010	1.0
112	Australia	2.1	1.3	1.0	15	17	18	21	2010	1.4
113	Denmark	0.7	0.2	(.)	5	5	5	5	2010	1.1
114	Canada	1.4	1.2	0.9	25	27	29	32	2010	1.4
115	Sweden	0.7	0.2	0.1	8	8	8	8	2010	1.1
116	Norway	0.8	0.4	0.3	4	4	4	4	2010	1.2
117	United States	1.1	1.0	0.7	234	247	261	289	2010	1.3
118	Switzerland	1.2	(.)	(.)	6	6	6	6	2010	1.0
East European nonmarket economies		**0.8** *w*	**0.8** *w*	**0.6** *w*	**386** *t*	**407** *t*	**429** *t*			
119	Hungary	0.3	0.3	(.)	11	11	11	11	2010	1.1
120	*Albania*	2.6	2.1	1.8	3	3	4	6	2000	1.8
121	*Bulgaria*	0.6	0.1	0.2	9	9	9	10	2010	1.2
122	*Czechoslovakia*	0.3	0.6	0.4	15	16	16	19	2000	1.3
123	*German Dem. Rep.*	(.)	−0.1	0.1	17	17	17	18	2010	1.1
124	*Poland*	0.7	0.9	0.7	37	39	41	50	2000	1.3
125	*Romania*	1.2	0.8	0.6	23	24	25	30	2000	1.3
126	*USSR*	0.9	0.9	0.7	273	288	306	377	2000	1.3
Total[b]					4,641	5,220	6,088			

a. For the assumptions used in the projections see the technical notes.   b. Excludes countries with populations of less than one million.

Table 20. Demographic and fertility-related indicators

	Crude birth rate per thousand population		Crude death rate per thousand population		Percentage change in: Crude birth rate	Percentage change in: Crude death rate	Total fertility rate		Percentage of married women of childbearing age using contraceptives[a]	
	1965	1983	1965	1983	1965–83	1965–83	1983	2000	1970[b]	1982[b]
Low-income economies	43 _w_	30 _w_	17 _w_	11 _w_	−30.3 _w_	−38.7 _w_	4.0 _w_	3.1 _w_	..	..
China and India	42 _w_	25 _w_	16 _w_	9 _w_	−39.3 _w_	−44.1 _w_	3.3 _w_	2.4 _w_	..	..
Other low-income	46 _w_	43 _w_	21 _w_	16 _w_	−7.3 _w_	−26.5 _w_	6.0 _w_	4.6 _w_	..	..
Sub-Saharan Africa	48 _w_	47 _w_	22 _w_	18 _w_	−2.0 _w_	−20.2 _w_	6.6 _w_	5.6 _w_	..	..
1 Ethiopia	44	41	19	20	−6.9	6.8	5.5	5.1	..	2
2 Bangladesh	47	42	22	16	−11.9	−27.0	6.0	3.7	..	25
3 Mali	50	48	27	21	−4.6	−22.2	6.5	5.9	..	1
4 Nepal	46	42	24	18	−9.0	−25.5	6.3	5.4	..	7
5 Zaire	48	46	23	16	−4.0	−32.6	6.3	5.3	..	3
6 Burkina	46	47	24	21	3.3	−12.5	6.5	6.0	..	1
7 Burma	42	38	19	13	−9.6	−33.5	5.3	3.6	..	5
8 Malawi	56	54	29	23	−3.6	−20.1	7.6	6.4	..	1
9 Uganda	49	50	19	17	2.2	−12.4	7.0	5.8	..	1
10 Burundi	47	47	24	19	−1.1	−22.6	6.5	5.9	..	1
11 Niger	48	52	25	20	7.3	−22.4	7.0	6.4	..	1
12 Tanzania	49	50	22	16	2.5	−27.3	7.0	5.8	..	1
13 Somalia	50	50	28	20	−0.4	−27.0	6.8	6.2	..	1
14 India	45	34	21	13	−25.0	−39.6	4.8	2.9	12	32
15 Rwanda	52	52	17	19	0.8	11.8	8.0	6.7	..	1
16 Central African Rep.	43	41	24	17	−4.7	−31.7	5.5	5.5	..	..
17 Togo	50	49	23	18	−1.2	−20.4	6.5	5.4	..	..
18 Benin	49	49	25	18	0.4	−26.8	6.5	5.4	..	18
19 China	39	19	13	7	−51.2	−50.8	2.3	2.0	..	71
20 Guinea	46	47	30	27	2.2	−9.8	6.0	5.6	..	1
21 Haiti	38	32	18	13	−16.2	−26.8	4.6	3.4	..	20
22 Ghana	50	49	16	10	−1.8	−35.9	7.0	4.8	..	10
23 Madagascar	44	47	21	18	6.9	−17.0	6.5	5.9	..	..
24 Sierra Leone	48	49	33	27	2.3	−19.2	6.5	6.1	..	4
25 Sri Lanka	33	27	8	6	−20.2	−26.8	3.4	2.3	..	55
26 Kenya	51	55	17	12	7.3	−29.4	8.0	5.7	6	8
27 Pakistan	48	42	21	15	−12.7	−29.4	5.8	4.2	6	14
28 Sudan	47	46	24	17	−2.1	−27.2	6.6	5.5	..	5
29 _Afghanistan_	54	54	29	29	0.6	−2.7	8.0	5.6	2	..
30 _Bhutan_	43	43	32	21	−0.2	−34.6	6.2	5.3	..	..
31 _Chad_	40	42	26	21	5.2	−19.2	5.5	5.6	..	1
32 _Kampuchea, Dem._	44	..	20	..	..	..	..	..	..	..
33 _Lao PDR_	45	42	23	20	−5.5	−14.1	6.4	5.5	..	..
34 _Mozambique_	49	46	27	19	−6.1	−29.6	6.5	5.9	..	1
35 _Viet Nam_	45	35	17	8	−22.2	−53.5	4.9	3.1	..	21
Middle-income economies	42 _w_	34 _w_	15 _w_	10 _w_	−17.8 _w_	−33.1 _w_	4.6 _w_	3.4 _w_	..	..
Oil exporters	46 _w_	39 _w_	18 _w_	12 _w_	−15.4 _w_	−36.1 _w_	5.2 _w_	3.9 _w_	..	..
Oil importers	38 _w_	30 _w_	13 _w_	9 _w_	−20.7 _w_	−29.6 _w_	4.0 _w_	2.9 _w_	..	..
Sub-Saharan Africa	50 _w_	49 _w_	22 _w_	16 _w_	−1.8 _w_	−26.1 _w_	6.8 _w_	5.6 _w_	..	..
Lower middle-income	45 _w_	36 _w_	18 _w_	12 _w_	−18.4 _w_	−34.5 _w_	4.9 _w_	3.6 _w_	..	..
36 Senegal	47	46	23	19	1.7	−19.2	6.6	5.6	..	4
37 Lesotho	42	42	18	15	(.)	−17.0	5.8	4.8	..	5
38 Liberia	46	49	22	18	6.1	−18.2	6.9	5.7	..	..
39 Mauritania	44	43	25	19	−3.0	−26.2	6.0	5.9	..	1
40 Bolivia	46	44	21	16	−4.8	−23.8	6.2	4.2	..	24
41 Yemen, PDR	50	48	27	19	−4.0	−29.3	6.3	4.4	..	..
42 Yemen Arab Rep.	49	48	27	22	−1.6	−19.6	6.8	5.8	..	1
43 Indonesia	43	34	20	13	−20.9	−37.3	4.3	2.8	..	58
44 Zambia	49	50	20	16	1.7	−21.4	6.7	5.5	..	1
45 Honduras	51	44	17	10	−12.8	−41.7	6.5	3.8	..	27
46 Egypt, Arab Rep.	42	34	19	11	−18.9	−42.6	4.6	3.0	..	24
47 El Salvador	46	40	14	8	−14.3	−44.0	5.5	3.3	..	34
48 Ivory Coast	44	46	22	14	5.1	−34.9	6.6	4.9	..	3
49 Zimbabwe	55	53	14	13	−4.4	−9.3	7.0	4.8	..	22
50 Morocco	49	40	19	14	−19.3	−22.7	5.8	3.8	..	26
51 Papua New Guinea	43	35	20	14	−18.6	−30.7	5.0	3.5	..	5
52 Philippines	46	31	12	7	−32.6	−43.7	4.2	2.7	15	48
53 Nigeria	51	50	23	17	−3.5	−26.8	6.9	5.7	..	6
54 Cameroon	40	46	20	15	16.3	−25.0	6.5	5.6	..	11
55 Thailand	43	27	12	8	−37.2	−35.5	3.4	2.2	15	59
56 Nicaragua	49	45	16	11	−9.3	−32.1	6.3	4.0	..	9
57 Costa Rica	45	30	8	4	−33.9	−50.0	3.5	2.3	..	65
58 Peru	45	34	17	11	−25.6	−36.1	4.5	3.2	..	41
59 Guatemala	46	38	16	9	−18.0	−44.4	5.2	3.4	..	18
60 Congo, People's Rep.	41	43	14	8	5.6	−43.9	6.0	5.5	..	..
61 Turkey	41	31	14	9	−25.7	−40.3	4.1	2.7	32	38
62 Tunisia	46	33	18	9	−29.3	−48.6	4.9	3.1	..	41
63 Jamaica	38	28	9	7	−26.6	−22.8	3.5	2.3	..	51
64 Dominican Rep.	47	33	14	8	−29.2	−44.8	4.2	2.7	..	46

Note: For data comparability and coverage see the technical notes.

		Crude birth rate per thousand population		Crude death rate per thousand population		Percentage change in: Crude birth rate	Crude death rate	Total fertility rate		Percentage of married women of childbearing age using contraceptives[a]	
		1965	1983	1965	1983	1965–83	1965–83	1983	2000	1970[b]	1982[b]
65	Paraguay	41	31	11	7	−25.9	−37.3	4.2	2.7	..	35
66	Ecuador	45	37	15	8	−18.1	−45.3	5.4	3.2	..	40
67	Colombia	43	28	12	7	−34.9	−37.6	3.5	2.5	..	55
68	*Angola*	49	49	29	22	−1.6	−25.3	6.5	6.0	..	..
69	*Cuba*	34	17	8	6	−50.3	−26.3	2.0	2.0	..	79
70	*Korea, Dem. Rep.*	39	30	12	7	−22.7	−38.5	4.0	2.6	..	..
71	*Lebanon*	41	29	13	9	−28.8	−28.3	3.8	2.4	53	..
72	*Mongolia*	42	34	12	7	−18.2	−43.1	4.8	3.1	..	..
	Upper middle-income	**38** *w*	**31** *w*	**12** *w*	**8** *w*	**−16.8** *w*	**−29.9** *w*	**4.1** *w*	**3.1** *w*	..	..
73	Jordan	48	45	18	8	−6.7	−55.4	7.4	5.3	22	26
74	Syrian Arab Rep.	48	46	16	7	−3.4	−56.3	7.2	4.0	..	23
75	Malaysia	41	29	12	6	−29.4	−46.8	3.7	2.4	33	42
76	Chile	32	24	11	6	−25.7	−44.4	2.9	2.2	..	43
77	Brazil	39	30	12	8	−22.9	−28.7	3.8	2.6	..	50
78	Korea, Rep. of	36	23	12	6	−36.3	−46.1	2.7	2.1	25	58
79	Argentina	22	24	9	9	12.0	1.1	3.4	2.5	..	..
80	Panama	40	28	9	5	−30.0	−43.2	3.5	2.3	..	61
81	Portugal	23	15	10	9	−34.8	−13.5	2.0	2.0	..	66
82	Mexico	45	34	11	7	−23.7	−36.1	4.6	2.8	..	39
83	Algeria	50	47	18	13	−6.8	−32.1	7.0	5.4	..	7
84	South Africa	40	40	13	9	(.)	−30.8	5.1	3.5	..	..
85	Uruguay	21	18	10	9	−14.6	−4.2	2.6	2.2	..	..
86	Yugoslavia	21	17	9	10	−21.0	9.1	2.1	2.1	59	55
87	Venezuela	43	35	9	6	−19.7	−40.2	4.3	2.7	..	49
88	Greece	18	14	8	9	−23.2	15.2	2.1	2.1	..	..
89	Israel	26	24	6	7	−6.6	9.5	3.1	2.3	..	..
90	Hong Kong	28	17	6	5	−39.3	−13.8	1.8	2.0	42	80
91	Singapore	31	17	6	5	−44.6	−9.1	1.7	1.9	60	71
92	Trinidad and Tobago	33	29	7	7	−10.8	−1.4	3.3	2.4	44	52
93	*Iran, Islamic Rep.*	50	40	17	10	−19.5	−39.9	5.6	4.3	..	23
94	*Iraq*	49	45	18	11	−9.2	−38.9	6.7	5.2	14	..
	High-income oil exporters	**49** *w*	**42** *w*	**19** *w*	**11** *w*	**−13.8** *w*	**−45.0** *w*	**6.9** *w*	**5.2** *w*	..	..
95	Oman	50	47	24	15	−6.0	−37.5	7.1	4.0	..	..
96	Libya	49	45	18	11	−8.5	−39.8	7.2	5.5	..	..
97	Saudi Arabia	49	43	20	12	−11.1	−41.4	7.1	5.7	..	..
98	Kuwait	47	35	8	3	−25.5	−60.5	5.7	3.0	..	..
99	United Arab Emirates	41	27	15	4	34.1	−73.3	5.9	4.1	..	..
	Industrial market economies	**19** *w*	**14** *w*	**10** *w*	**9** *w*	**−28.6** *w*	**−7.3** *w*	**1.7** *w*	**1.9** *w*	..	..
100	Spain	21	13	8	7	−38.1	−16.7	2.0	2.0	..	51
101	Ireland	22	20	12	9	−9.1	−20.9	3.0	2.1	..	..
102	Italy	19	11	10	10	−44.5	1.0	1.5	1.9	..	78
103	New Zealand	23	16	9	8	−31.0	−6.9	2.0	2.0	..	..
104	Belgium	17	12	12	11	−27.9	−7.4	1.6	1.9	..	..
105	United Kingdom	18	13	12	12	−29.3	2.6	1.8	1.9	69	77
106	Austria	18	12	13	12	−33.5	−5.4	1.6	1.9	..	..
107	Netherlands	20	12	8	8	−40.7	2.5	1.5	1.8	..	56
108	Japan	19	13	7	6	−30.5	−15.5	1.7	1.9	56	56
109	France	18	14	11	10	−23.0	−8.9	1.8	2.0	64	79
110	Finland	17	14	10	9	−18.1	−7.2	1.8	2.0	77	80
111	Germany, Fed. Rep.	18	10	12	12	−45.2	1.7	1.4	1.8	..	..
112	Australia	20	16	9	7	−19.4	−17.0	2.0	2.0	..	..
113	Denmark	18	10	10	11	−45.0	10.9	1.4	1.8	67	..
114	Canada	21	15	8	7	−29.6	−7.9	1.7	1.9	..	..
115	Sweden	16	11	10	11	−30.8	7.9	1.7	1.9	..	78
116	Norway	18	12	10	10	−32.6	7.4	1.7	1.9	..	71
117	United States	19	16	9	9	−20.1	−8.5	1.8	2.0	65	76
118	Switzerland	19	11	10	9	−40.3	−2.1	1.9	2.0	..	..
	East European nonmarket economies	**18** *w*	**19** *w*	**8** *w*	**11** *w*	**7.3** *w*	**32.9** *w*	**2.3** *w*	**2.1** *w*	..	..
119	Hungary	13	12	11	14	−9.2	31.1	1.8	2.0	67	74
120	*Albania*	35	28	9	6	−21.0	−33.3	3.6	2.2	..	..
121	*Bulgaria*	15	14	8	11	−11.1	39.0	2.0	2.1	..	76
122	*Czechoslovakia*	16	15	10	12	−9.8	20.0	2.1	2.1	..	95
123	*German Dem. Rep.*	17	14	14	13	−15.2	−1.5	1.9	2.0	..	..
124	*Poland*	17	20	7	10	13.9	29.7	2.4	2.1	60	75
125	*Romania*	15	15	9	10	2.7	12.8	2.4	2.1	..	58
126	*USSR*	18	20	7	10	9.8	41.1	2.4	2.1	..	..

a. Figures include women whose husbands practice contraception. See the technical notes. b. Figures in italics are for years or periods other than those specified. See the technical notes.

Table 21. Labor force

		Percentage of population of working age (15–64 years)		Agriculture		Industry		Services		Average annual growth of labor force (percent)		
		1965	1983	1965	1981	1965	1981	1965	1981	1965–73	1973–83	1980–2000
	Low-income economies	54 w	59 w	77 w	73 w	9 w	13 w	14 w	15 w	2.2 w	2.1 w	2.0 w
	China and India	57 w	60 w	..	73 w	..	13 w	..	14 w	2.2 w	1.5 w	1.8 w
	Other low-income	48 w	53 w	81 w	72 w	7 w	11 w	12 w	16 w	2.1 w	4.1 w	2.8 w
	Sub-Saharan Africa	53 w	51 w	84 w	78 w	7 w	10 w	9 w	13 w	2.2 w	2.1 w	3.1 w
1	Ethiopia	53	52	86	80	6	7	8	13	2.2	1.4	2.2
2	Bangladesh	51	54	87	74	3	11	10	15	2.3	2.8	2.9
3	Mali	53	50	93	73	4	12	3	15	2.2	2.0	2.6
4	Nepal	56	54	95	93	2	2	3	5	1.6	2.3	2.5
5	Zaire	53	51	81	75	10	13	9	12	1.8	2.2	3.0
6	Burkina	54	52	90	82	6	13	4	5	1.6	1.5	2.1
7	Burma	57	55	..	67	..	10	..	23	1.3	1.4	2.2
8	Malawi	51	49	91	86	4	5	5	9	2.4	2.8	2.8
9	Uganda	53	50	88	83	5	6	7	11	3.0	1.7	3.4
10	Burundi	54	53	89	84	4	5	7	11	1.2	1.6	2.5
11	Niger	51	51	94	91	1	3	5	6	2.4	3.0	3.1
12	Tanzania	53	50	88	83	4	6	8	11	2.5	2.5	3.1
13	Somalia	49	53	87	82	5	8	8	10	3.8	2.0	1.7
14	India	54	57	74	71	11	13	15	16	1.8	2.1	2.1
15	Rwanda	52	51	94	91	1	2	5	7	2.7	3.0	3.2
16	Central African Rep.	57	55	93	88	3	4	4	8	1.1	1.6	2.4
17	Togo	53	50	81	67	10	15	9	18	2.2	1.9	2.9
18	Benin	53	50	52	46	10	16	38	38	2.1	2.0	2.7
19	China	55	63	..	74	..	13	..	13	2.4	1.2	1.8
20	Guinea	55	53	87	82	7	11	6	7	1.2	1.3	2.4
21	Haiti	54	55	77	74	7	7	16	19	0.7	1.5	2.0
22	Ghana	52	49	61	53	16	20	23	27	1.6	2.0	3.8
23	Madagascar	54	50	92	87	3	4	5	9	1.9	1.7	3.0
24	Sierra Leone	54	55	75	65	14	19	11	16	0.7	1.2	1.7
25	Sri Lanka	55	60	56	54	14	14	30	32	2.0	2.1	2.2
26	Kenya	49	46	84	78	6	10	10	12	3.2	2.9	4.0
27	Pakistan	50	53	60	57	19	20	21	23	2.3	3.2	2.7
28	Sudan	53	52	84	78	7	10	9	12	2.5	2.5	2.9
29	Afghanistan	55	53	84	79	7	8	9	13	1.9	2.3	2.4
30	Bhutan	56	56	95	93	2	2	3	5	1.0	1.9	2.1
31	Chad	56	56	93	85	3	7	4	8	1.6	2.3	2.3
32	Kampuchea, Dem.	52	..	80	..	4	..	16	..	1.3	..	..
33	Lao PDR	56	52	81	75	5	6	14	19	0.6	0.9	2.5
34	Mozambique	56	52	77	66	10	18	13	16	2.2	3.0	2.9
35	Viet Nam	..	55	79	71	6	10	15	19	..	..	2.9
	Middle-income economies	53 w	56 w	57 w	44 w	16 w	22 w	27 w	35 w	2.2 w	2.6 w	2.5 w
	Oil exporters	52 w	54 w	61 w	48 w	15 w	21 w	25 w	32 w	2.3 w	2.6 w	2.9 w
	Oil importers	55 w	58 w	53 w	41 w	18 w	22 w	29 w	37 w	2.1 w	2.6 w	2.2 w
	Sub-Saharan Africa	53 w	50 w	70 w	60 w	11 w	16 w	19 w	24 w	2.0 w	2.1 w	3.2 w
	Lower middle-income	53 w	55 w	66 w	54 w	13 w	17 w	22 w	29 w	2.1 w	2.5 w	2.5 w
36	Senegal	54	53	82	77	6	10	12	13	1.7	2.2	2.6
37	Lesotho	56	54	92	60	3	15	5	25	1.7	1.9	2.5
38	Liberia	51	53	78	70	11	14	11	16	2.0	3.9	2.8
39	Mauritania	52	53	90	69	4	8	6	23	1.9	2.4	2.0
40	Bolivia	54	53	58	50	20	24	22	26	1.8	2.5	2.8
41	Yemen, PDR	52	52	68	45	16	15	16	40	1.1	1.8	3.3
42	Yemen Arab Rep.	54	51	81	75	8	11	11	14	1.0	2.1	3.3
43	Indonesia	54	56	71	58	9	12	20	30	1.9	2.3	2.4
44	Zambia	52	49	76	67	8	11	16	22	2.3	2.1	3.3
45	Honduras	51	50	68	63	12	20	20	17	2.4	3.3	3.5
46	Egypt, Arab Rep.	55	57	56	50	15	30	29	20	2.2	2.4	2.3
47	El Salvador	51	52	59	50	18	22	23	28	3.2	2.8	3.4
48	Ivory Coast	55	53	87	79	3	4	10	17	4.2	3.8	3.3
49	Zimbabwe	51	46	67	60	12	15	21	25	2.7	1.4	4.4
50	Morocco	51	52	60	52	15	21	25	27	1.6	2.8	3.1
51	Papua New Guinea	56	54	88	82	5	8	7	10	1.9	1.4	2.2
52	Philippines	52	56	57	46	16	17	27	37	2.1	3.0	2.5
53	Nigeria	52	50	67	54	12	19	21	27	1.8	2.0	3.3
54	Cameroon	56	51	86	83	6	7	8	10	1.9	1.8	3.2
55	Thailand	51	59	82	76	5	9	13	15	2.4	3.1	2.1
56	Nicaragua	49	51	57	39	16	14	27	47	2.8	4.0	3.8
57	Costa Rica	49	59	47	29	20	23	33	48	3.6	3.6	2.8
58	Peru	52	56	50	40	19	19	31	41	2.4	2.9	3.0
59	Guatemala	51	54	64	55	16	21	20	24	2.9	3.0	2.9
60	Congo, People's Rep.	55	51	47	34	19	26	34	40	1.9	1.8	3.8
61	Turkey	54	58	74	54	11	13	15	33	1.8	2.0	2.1
62	Tunisia	50	56	53	35	20	32	27	33	1.4	2.9	2.9
63	Jamaica	51	56	34	35	25	18	41	47	0.7	2.6	2.6
64	Dominican Rep.	48	55	64	49	13	18	23	33	2.7	3.2	2.8

Note: For data comparability and coverage see the technical notes.

	Percentage of population of working age (15–64 years)		Percentage of labor force in:						Average annual growth of labor force (percent)		
			Agriculture		Industry		Services				
	1965	1983	1965	1981	1965	1981	1965	1981	1965–73	1973–83	1980–2000
65 Paraguay	50	55	55	49	19	19	26	32	2.6	3.3	3.0
66 Ecuador	51	53	54	52	21	17	25	31	2.6	2.6	3.3
67 Colombia	50	59	45	26	20	21	35	53	3.1	2.8	2.6
68 *Angola*	55	53	67	59	13	16	20	25	1.7	2.8	2.8
69 *Cuba*	59	64	35	23	24	31	41	46	1.0	2.1	1.7
70 *Korea, Dem. Rep.*	52	57	59	49	25	33	16	18	2.6	2.9	2.7
71 *Lebanon*	51	56	28	11	25	27	47	62	2.5	−0.1	2.1
72 *Mongolia*	54	55	66	55	15	22	19	23	2.2	2.6	2.9
Upper middle-income	**54** *w*	**58** *w*	**45** *w*	**30** *w*	**21** *w*	**28** *w*	**34** *w*	**42** *w*	**2.3** *w*	**2.7** *w*	**2.5** *w*
73 Jordan	51	48	41	20	16	20	43	60	2.6	1.4	4.6
74 Syrian Arab Rep.	47	49	53	33	20	31	27	36	3.1	3.5	4.0
75 Malaysia	50	58	60	50	13	16	27	34	2.9	3.2	2.7
76 Chile	56	63	26	19	21	19	53	62	1.3	2.6	2.0
77 Brazil	54	59	49	30	17	24	34	46	2.5	3.1	2.4
78 Korea, Rep. of	54	64	58	34	13	29	29	37	2.9	2.7	1.9
79 Argentina	64	61	18	13	34	28	48	59	1.4	1.0	1.4
80 Panama	52	57	46	33	15	18	39	49	3.1	2.6	2.4
81 Portugal	63	64	39	28	31	35	30	37	0.1	0.9	0.6
82 Mexico	50	53	50	36	21	26	29	38	3.1	3.1	3.2
83 Algeria	50	50	59	25	14	25	27	50	1.6	3.6	4.5
84 South Africa	54	56	32	30	30	29	38	41	2.7	3.2	2.9
85 Uruguay	63	63	18	11	30	32	52	57	0.3	0.5	0.9
86 Yugoslavia	64	67	57	29	21	35	22	36	0.7	0.5	0.6
87 Venezuela	50	56	30	18	24	27	46	55	3.7	4.1	3.4
88 Greece	66	64	51	37	22	28	27	35	0.1	0.9	0.5
89 Israel	59	59	12	7	35	36	53	57	3.2	2.3	2.2
90 Hong Kong	56	69	6	3	54	57	40	40	3.6	4.1	1.3
91 Singapore	54	67	6	2	26	39	68	59	3.4	2.3	1.1
92 Trinidad and Tobago	54	61	23	10	35	39	42	51	1.8	1.2	2.3
93 *Iran, Islamic Rep.*	51	53	50	39	26	34	24	27	3.1	3.0	3.5
94 *Iraq*	51	51	50	42	20	26	30	32	2.9	3.1	3.7
High-income oil exporters	**53** *w*	**55** *w*	**58** *w*	**46** *w*	**15** *w*	**19** *w*	**27** *w*	**35** *w*	**4.0** *w*	**5.7** *w*	**3.3** *w*
95 Oman	53	53	. .	. .	. .	. .	. .	. .	. .	. .	. .
96 Libya	53	52	42	19	20	28	38	53	3.6	4.3	4.3
97 Saudi Arabia	53	54	69	61	11	14	20	25	3.9	5.8	3.2
98 Kuwait	60	57	1	2	34	34	65	64	5.3	7.1	3.2
99 United Arab Emirates	. .	68	. .	. .	. .	. .	. .	. .	. .	. .	. .
Industrial market economies	**63** *w*	**67** *w*	**14** *w*	**6** *w*	**39** *w*	**38** *w*	**48** *w*	**56** *w*	**1.2** *w*	**1.2** *w*	**0.5** *w*
100 Spain	64	64	34	14	35	40	31	46	0.4	1.2	0.8
101 Ireland	58	59	31	18	28	37	41	45	0.5	1.5	1.5
102 Italy	66	66	24	11	42	45	34	44	0.0	0.6	0.2
103 New Zealand	59	65	13	10	36	35	51	55	2.0	1.2	1.0
104 Belgium	64	67	6	3	46	41	48	56	0.5	0.7	0.2
105 United Kingdom	65	65	3	2	46	42	51	56	0.2	0.4	0.2
106 Austria	64	66	19	9	45	37	36	54	−0.2	0.9	0.3
107 Netherlands	62	68	9	6	43	45	48	49	1.4	1.4	0.5
108 Japan	68	68	26	12	32	39	42	49	1.7	1.1	0.7
109 France	62	66	18	8	40	39	42	53	0.7	1.0	0.6
110 Finland	65	67	28	11	33	35	39	54	0.5	0.4	0.4
111 Germany, Fed. Rep.	66	69	10	4	48	46	42	50	0.3	0.8	−0.1
112 Australia	62	66	10	6	38	33	52	61	2.5	1.6	1.2
113 Denmark	65	66	14	7	37	35	49	58	0.8	0.6	0.4
114 Canada	59	68	11	5	33	29	56	66	2.7	2.0	1.1
115 Sweden	66	65	11	5	43	34	46	61	0.7	0.4	0.4
116 Norway	63	64	15	7	37	37	48	56	0.6	0.7	0.6
117 United States	60	67	5	2	36	32	59	66	1.9	1.7	0.9
118 Switzerland	65	67	10	5	50	46	40	49	1.5	0.4	0.1
East European nonmarket economies	**63** *w*	**66** *w*	**35** *w*	**17** *w*	**34** *w*	**44** *w*	**32** *w*	**39** *w*	**0.9** *w*	**1.0** *w*	**0.5** *w*
119 Hungary	66	65	32	21	39	43	29	36	0.5	(.)	0.1
120 *Albania*	52	59	69	61	19	25	12	14	2.4	2.6	2.4
121 *Bulgaria*	67	66	52	37	28	39	20	24	0.6	0.1	0.2
122 *Czechoslovakia*	65	64	21	11	48	48	31	41	0.8	0.6	0.6
123 *German Dem. Rep.*	62	66	15	10	49	50	36	40	0.4	0.8	0.3
124 *Poland*	62	66	44	31	32	39	24	30	1.7	1.2	0.8
125 *Romania*	66	64	58	29	19	36	23	35	0.8	0.5	0.7
126 *USSR*	62	66	33	14	33	45	34	41	0.8	1.1	0.6

Table 22. Urbanization

| | Urban population | | | | Percentage of urban population | | | | Number of cities of over 500,000 persons | |
| | As percentage of total population | | Average annual growth rate (percent) | | In largest city | | In cities of over 500,000 persons | | | |
	1965[a]	1983	1965–73	1973–83	1960	1980	1960	1980	1960	1980
Low-income economies	17 *w*	22 *w*	4.4 *w*	4.5 *w*	10 *w*	16 *w*	31 *w*	55 *w*	55 *t*	146 *t*
China and India	18 *w*	22 *w*	..	..	7 *w*	6 *w*	33 *w*	59 *w*	49 *t*	114 *t*
Other low-income	13 *w*	21 *w*	5.2 *w*	5.0 *w*	25 *w*	28 *w*	19 *w*	40 *w*	6 *t*	32 *t*
Sub-Saharan Africa	11 *w*	20 *w*	6.2 *w*	6.0 *w*	33 *w*	41 *w*	2 *w*	35 *w*	1 *t*	13 *t*
1 Ethiopia	8	15	7.4	6.0	30	37	0	37	0	1
2 Bangladesh	6	17	6.6	7.6	20	30	20	51	1	3
3 Mali	13	19	5.4	4.4	32	24	0	0	0	0
4 Nepal	4	7	4.3	8.2	41	27	0	0	0	0
5 Zaire	19	38	5.9	6.9	14	28	14	38	1	2
6 Burkina	6	11	6.5	4.8	..	41	0	0	0	0
7 Burma	21	29	4.0	3.9	23	23	23	23	1	2
8 Malawi	5	11	8.2	7.3	..	19	0	0	0	0
9 Uganda	6	7	8.3	0.3	38	52	0	52	0	1
10 Burundi	2	2	1.4	3.2	..	..	0	0	0	0
11 Niger	7	14	7.0	7.0	..	31	0	0	0	0
12 Tanzania	6	14	8.1	8.6	34	50	0	50	0	1
13 Somalia	20	33	6.4	5.5	..	34	0	0	0	0
14 India	18	24	4.0	4.2	7	6	26	39	11	36
15 Rwanda	3	5	6.0	6.6	..	0	0	0	0	0
16 Central African Rep.	27	44	4.4	4.6	40	36	0	0	0	0
17 Togo	11	22	6.4	6.6	..	60	0	0	0	0
18 Benin	11	16	4.5	4.7	..	63	0	63	0	1
19 China	18	21	..	..	6	6	42	45	38	78
20 Guinea	12	26	5.0	6.3	37	80	0	80	0	1
21 Haiti	18	27	3.8	4.2	42	56	0	56	0	1
22 Ghana	26	38	4.5	5.3	25	35	0	48	0	2
23 Madagascar	12	20	5.3	5.5	44	36	0	36	0	1
24 Sierra Leone	15	23	5.0	3.3	37	47	0	0	0	0
25 Sri Lanka	20	26	3.4	2.9	28	16	0	16	0	1
26 Kenya	9	17	7.3	8.0	40	57	0	57	0	1
27 Pakistan	24	29	4.3	4.3	20	21	33	51	2	7
28 Sudan	13	20	6.3	5.5	30	31	0	31	0	1
29 *Afghanistan*	10	17	5.6	6.2	33	17	0	17	0	1
30 *Bhutan*	4	4	−2.1	4.6	0	0	0	0	0	0
31 *Chad*	9	20	6.9	6.6	..	39	0	0	0	0
32 *Kampuchea, Dem.*	11	..	3.4	..	..	..	..	..	..	..
33 *Lao PDR*	8	15	4.6	5.7	69	48	0	0	0	0
34 *Mozambique*	5	17	8.2	10.2	75	83	0	83	0	1
35 *Viet Nam*	16	20	5.5	2.4	32	21	32	50	1	4
Middle-income	36 *w*	48 *w*	4.5 *w*	3.9 *w*	28 *w*	29 *w*	35 *w*	48 *w*	54 *t*	127 *t*
Oil exporters	30 *w*	41 *w*	4.4 *w*	4.4 *w*	27 *w*	30 *w*	32 *w*	48 *w*	15 *t*	42 *t*
Oil importers	41 *w*	54 *w*	4.5 *w*	3.6 *w*	28 *w*	28 *w*	36 *w*	48 *w*	39 *t*	85 *t*
Sub-Saharan Africa	16 *w*	27 *w*	6.4 *w*	5.9 *w*	21 *w*	26 *w*	14 *w*	51 *w*	2 *t*	15 *t*
Lower middle-income	26 *w*	36 *w*	5.1 *w*	4.1 *w*	27 *w*	32 *w*	28 *w*	47 *w*	22 *t*	57 *t*
36 Senegal	27	34	4.3	3.8	53	65	0	65	0	1
37 Lesotho	2	13	7.8	21.4	..	..	0	0	0	0
38 Liberia	23	38	5.3	6.1	..	..	0	0	0	0
39 Mauritania	7	25	16.0	4.6	..	39	0	0	0	0
40 Bolivia	26	43	8.9	3.3	47	44	0	44	0	1
41 Yemen, PDR	30	37	3.4	3.5	61	49	0	0	0	0
42 Yemen Arab Rep.	6	18	9.7	8.8	..	25	0	0	0	0
43 Indonesia	16	24	4.1	4.8	20	23	34	50	3	9
44 Zambia	24	47	7.6	6.5	..	35	0	35	0	1
45 Honduras	26	38	5.4	5.8	31	33	0	0	0	0
46 Egypt, Arab Rep.	41	45	3.0	2.9	38	39	53	53	2	2
47 El Salvador	39	42	3.6	3.6	26	22	0	0	0	0
48 Ivory Coast	23	44	8.2	8.5	27	34	0	34	0	1
49 Zimbabwe	14	24	6.8	6.0	40	50	0	50	0	1
50 Morocco	32	43	4.0	4.2	16	26	16	50	1	4
51 Papua New Guinea	5	14	14.3	5.1	..	25	0	0	0	0
52 Philippines	32	39	4.0	3.8	27	30	27	34	1	2
53 Nigeria	15	22	4.7	5.1	13	17	22	58	2	9
54 Cameroon	16	39	7.3	8.4	26	21	0	21	0	1
55 Thailand	13	18	4.8	3.6	65	69	65	69	1	1
56 Nicaragua	43	55	4.4	5.2	41	47	0	47	0	1
57 Costa Rica	38	45	3.8	3.2	67	64	0	64	0	1
58 Peru	52	67	4.7	3.6	38	39	38	44	1	2
59 Guatemala	34	40	3.8	4.1	41	36	41	36	1	1
60 Congo, People's Rep.	35	55	4.4	5.5	77	56	0	0	0	0
61 Turkey	31	45	4.9	3.7	18	24	32	42	3	4
62 Tunisia	40	54	4.1	3.7	40	30	40	30	1	1
63 Jamaica	36	52	4.3	2.7	77	66	0	66	0	1
64 Dominican Rep.	35	54	5.6	4.7	50	54	0	54	0	1

Note: For data comparability and coverage see the technical notes.

		As percentage of total population		Average annual growth rate (percent)		In largest city		In cities of over 500,000 persons		Number of cities of over 500,000 persons	
		1965[a]	1983	1965–73	1973–83	1960	1980	1960	1980	1960	1980
65	Paraguay	36	41	3.2	3.3	44	44	0	44	0	1
66	Ecuador	37	46	3.9	3.9	31	29	0	51	0	2
67	Colombia	54	66	4.4	2.9	17	26	28	51	3	4
68	*Angola*	13	23	5.9	6.0	44	64	0	64	0	1
69	*Cuba*	58	70	2.8	1.9	32	38	38	32	1	1
70	*Korea, Dem. Rep.*	45	62	4.9	4.2	15	12	15	19	1	2
71	*Lebanon*	50	78	6.2	1.6	64	79	64	79	1	1
72	*Mongolia*	42	54	4.6	4.2	53	52	0	0	0	0
Upper middle-income		**49** *w*	**64** *w*	**4.0** *w*	**3.8** *w*	**28** *w*	**29** *w*	**38** *w*	**51** *w*	**32** *t*	**70** *t*
73	Jordan	47	72	4.7	4.8	31	37	0	37	0	1
74	Syrian Arab Rep.	40	48	4.8	4.2	35	33	35	55	1	2
75	Malaysia	26	31	3.3	3.5	19	27	0	27	0	1
76	Chile	72	82	2.8	2.4	38	44	38	44	1	1
77	Brazil	51	71	4.5	4.1	14	15	35	52	6	14
78	Korea, Rep. of	32	62	6.5	4.8	35	41	61	77	3	7
79	Argentina	76	84	2.1	2.1	46	45	54	60	3	5
80	Panama	44	50	4.1	3.0	61	66	0	66	0	1
81	Portugal	24	30	1.2	2.5	47	44	47	44	1	1
82	Mexico	55	69	4.8	4.1	28	32	36	48	3	7
83	Algeria	38	46	2.5	5.4	27	12	27	12	1	1
84	South Africa	47	55	2.6	3.9	16	13	44	53	4	7
85	Uruguay	81	85	0.8	0.8	56	52	56	52	1	1
86	Yugoslavia	31	45	3.1	2.8	11	10	11	23	1	3
87	Venezuela	72	85	4.8	4.3	26	26	26	44	1	4
88	Greece	48	64	2.5	2.6	51	57	51	70	1	2
89	Israel	81	90	3.8	2.7	46	35	46	35	1	1
90	Hong Kong	89	92	2.1	2.7	100	100	100	100	1	1
91	Singapore	100	100	1.8	1.3	100	100	100	100	1	1
92	Trinidad and Tobago	22	22	0.6	1.0	..	..	0	0	0	0
93	*Iran, Islamic Rep.*	37	53	5.4	5.1	26	28	26	47	1	6
94	*Iraq*	50	69	5.7	5.3	35	55	35	70	1	3
High-income oil exporters		**37** *w*	**68** *w*	**8.9** *w*	**7.9** *w*	**29** *w*	**28** *w*	**0** *w*	**34** *w*	**0** *t*	**3** *t*
95	Oman	4	25	10.8	17.6	..	..	..	..	..	..
96	Libya	29	61	8.9	8.1	57	64	0	64	0	1
97	Saudi Arabia	39	71	8.4	7.4	15	18	0	33	0	2
98	Kuwait	75	92	9.3	7.8	75	30	0	0	0	0
99	United Arab Emirates	56	79	16.7	11.2	..	..	..	..	..	..
Industrial market economies		**71** *w*	**77** *w*	**1.7** *w*	**1.0** *w*	**18** *w*	**18** *w*	**48** *w*	**55** *w*	**104** *t*	**152** *t*
100	Spain	61	76	2.5	2.0	13	17	37	44	5	6
101	Ireland	49	56	2.0	2.2	51	48	51	48	1	1
102	Italy	62	71	1.4	1.1	13	17	46	52	7	9
103	New Zealand	79	83	1.9	0.8	25	30	0	30	0	1
104	Belgium	68	89	0.9	1.3	17	14	28	24	2	2
105	United Kingdom	87	91	0.7	0.3	24	20	61	55	15	17
106	Austria	51	56	0.8	0.6	51	39	51	39	1	1
107	Netherlands	79	52	0.8	−1.1	9	9	27	24	3	3
108	Japan	67	76	2.4	1.3	18	22	35	42	5	9
109	France	67	80	2.0	1.2	25	23	34	34	4	6
110	Finland	44	60	2.8	1.9	28	27	0	27	0	1
111	Germany, Fed. Rep.	79	86	1.2	0.3	20	18	48	45	11	11
112	Australia	83	86	2.6	1.5	26	24	62	68	4	5
113	Denmark	77	85	1.3	0.7	40	32	40	32	1	1
114	Canada	73	75	1.9	1.2	14	18	31	62	2	9
115	Sweden	77	85	1.6	0.7	15	15	15	35	1	3
116	Norway	37	55	3.4	2.4	50	32	50	32	1	1
117	United States	72	74	1.6	1.2	13	12	61	77	40	65
118	Switzerland	53	59	1.9	0.7	19	22	19	22	1	1
East European nonmarket economies		**51** *w*	**64** *w*	**48** *w*	**−2.2** *w*	**9** *w*	**7** *w*	**23** *w*	**32** *w*	**36** *t*	**65** *t*
119	Hungary	43	55	2.2	1.4	45	37	45	37	1	1
120	*Albania*	32	38	3.5	3.2	27	25	0	0	0	0
121	*Bulgaria*	46	67	3.2	2.1	23	18	23	18	1	1
122	*Czechoslovakia*	51	65	1.8	1.8	17	12	17	12	1	1
123	*German Dem. Rep.*	73	76	0.2	0.2	9	9	14	17	2	3
124	*Poland*	50	59	1.5	1.9	17	15	41	47	5	8
125	*Romania*	34	51	4.2	3.1	22	17	22	17	1	1
126	*USSR*	52	65	5.9	−3.4	6	4	21	33	25	50

a. Figures in italics are for years other than those specified.

Table 23. Indicators related to life expectancy

	Life expectancy at birth (years)				Infant mortality rate (aged under 1)		Child death rate (aged 1–4)	
	Male		Female					
	1965	1983	1965	1983	1965	1983	1965	1983
Low-income economies	49 _w_	58 _w_	51 _w_	60 _w_	122 _w_	75 _w_	19 _w_	9 _w_
China and India	51 _w_	61 _w_	53 _w_	63 _w_	115 _w_	61 _w_	16 _w_	6 _w_
Other low-income	44 _w_	50 _w_	45 _w_	52 _w_	147 _w_	115 _w_	27 _w_	18 _w_
Sub-Saharan Africa	42 _w_	46 _w_	45 _w_	49 _w_	156 _w_	119 _w_	35 _w_	23 _w_
1 Ethiopia	43	..	47	..	166	..	37	..
2 Bangladesh	45	49	44	50	153	132	24	19
3 Mali	37	43	39	47	184	148	47	31
4 Nepal	40	47	39	45	184	143	30	21
5 Zaire	43	49	46	52	142	106	30	20
6 Burkina	40	43	42	46	193	148	52	31
7 Burma	45	53	48	57	143	93	21	11
8 Malawi	37	43	40	45	201	164	55	38
9 Uganda	46	48	49	50	126	108	26	21
10 Burundi	42	45	45	48	169	123	38	25
11 Niger	40	43	42	47	181	139	46	28
12 Tanzania	41	49	44	52	138	97	29	18
13 Somalia	..	43	..	46	166	142	37	30
14 India	46	56	44	54	151	93	23	11
15 Rwanda	47	45	51	48	159	125	35	26
16 Central African Rep.	40	46	41	49	184	142	47	29
17 Togo	40	47	43	50	158	112	36	17
18 Benin	41	46	43	50	193	148	52	31
19 China	55	65	59	69	90	38	11	2
20 Guinea	34	37	36	38	197	158	53	36
21 Haiti	46	53	47	56	160	107	37	15
22 Ghana	49	57	52	61	132	97	25	12
23 Madagascar	41	49	44	50	99	66	18	10
24 Sierra Leone	32	37	33	38	230	198	69	54
25 Sri Lanka	63	67	64	71	63	37	6	2
26 Kenya	48	55	51	59	124	81	25	14
27 Pakistan	46	51	44	49	150	119	23	16
28 Sudan	39	47	41	49	161	117	37	19
29 _Afghanistan_	34	..	35	..	223	..	39	..
30 _Bhutan_	34	44	32	42	184	162	30	26
31 _Chad_	39	42	41	45	184	142	47	29
32 _Kampuchea, Dem._	43	..	45	..	135	..	19	..
33 _Lao PDR_	39	42	42	45	196	159	34	25
34 _Mozambique_	36	44	39	47	148	109	31	16
35 _Viet Nam_	47	62	50	66	89	53	8	4
Middle-income economies	51 _w_	59 _w_	55 _w_	63 _w_	112 _w_	75 _w_	18 _w_	9 _w_
Oil exporters	47 _w_	55 _w_	49 _w_	58 _w_	129 _w_	91 _w_	23 _w_	12 _w_
Oil importers	55 _w_	62 _w_	59 _w_	66 _w_	98 _w_	61 _w_	15 _w_	6 _w_
Sub-Saharan Africa	41 _w_	48 _w_	44 _w_	51 _w_	150 _w_	112 _w_	32 _w_	17 _w_
Lower middle-income	47 _w_	55 _w_	50 _w_	59 _w_	127 _w_	87 _w_	22 _w_	11 _w_
36 Senegal	40	44	42	47	172	140	42	28
37 Lesotho	47	51	50	55	138	109	20	14
38 Liberia	41	47	43	50	149	111	32	17
39 Mauritania	39	44	41	47	171	136	41	16
40 Bolivia	42	49	46	53	161	123	37	21
41 Yemen, PDR	38	45	39	47	194	137	52	27
42 Yemen Arab Rep.	37	43	38	45	200	152	55	33
43 Indonesia	43	52	45	55	138	101	20	13
44 Zambia	42	49	46	52	137	100	29	19
45 Honduras	48	58	51	62	131	81	24	8
46 Egypt, Arab Rep.	48	56	49	59	123	102	21	14
47 El Salvador	52	62	56	66	120	70	20	6
48 Ivory Coast	43	50	45	53	160	121	37	20
49 Zimbabwe	50	52	58	60	106	69	15	7
50 Morocco	48	51	51	54	149	98	32	12
51 Papua New Guinea	44	54	44	53	148	97	23	12
52 Philippines	55	63	58	66	90	49	11	4
53 Nigeria	40	47	43	50	152	113	33	17
54 Cameroon	44	52	47	55	155	116	34	19
55 Thailand	53	61	58	65	90	50	11	4
56 Nicaragua	49	56	51	60	129	84	24	9
57 Costa Rica	63	72	66	76	74	20	8	1
58 Peru	49	57	52	60	131	98	24	12
59 Guatemala	49	58	51	62	109	67	16	5
60 Congo, People's Rep.	52	62	56	65	116	82	19	8
61 Turkey	52	61	55	66	157	82	35	8
62 Tunisia	51	60	52	63	145	83	30	8
63 Jamaica	63	68	67	72	51	28	4	2
64 Dominican Rep.	52	61	56	65	103	63	14	5

Note: For data comparability and coverage see the technical notes.

		Life expectancy at birth (years)				Infant mortality rate (aged under 1)		Child death rate (aged 1–4)	
		Male		Female					
		1965	1983	1965	1983	1965	1983	1965	1983
65	Paraguay	56	63	60	67	74	45	7	3
66	Ecuador	52	61	55	65	124	76	22	7
67	Colombia	53	62	59	66	80	53	8	3
68	*Angola*	34	42	37	44	193	148	52	31
69	*Cuba*	65	73	69	77	54	20	4	1
70	*Korea, Dem. Rep.*	55	63	58	67	64	32	6	2
71	*Lebanon*	60	63	64	67	57	48	4	3
72	*Mongolia*	55	63	58	67	89	49	11	4
Upper middle-income		**57** *w*	**63** *w*	**60** *w*	**68** *w*	**92** *w*	**59** *w*	**13** *w*	**5** *w*
73	Jordan	49	63	51	65	117	62	19	5
74	Syrian Arab Rep.	52	66	54	69	116	56	19	4
75	Malaysia	56	65	59	69	57	29	5	2
76	Chile	56	68	62	72	103	40	14	2
77	Brazil	55	61	59	66	104	70	14	6
78	Korea, Rep. of	55	64	58	71	64	29	6	2
79	Argentina	63	66	69	73	59	36	4	1
80	Panama	62	69	65	73	59	26	4	1
81	Portugal	61	68	67	74	65	25	6	1
82	Mexico	58	64	61	68	82	52	9	3
83	Algeria	49	55	51	59	155	107	34	15
84	South Africa	54	62	57	65	124	91	22	10
85	Uruguay	66	71	72	75	47	38	3	2
86	Yugoslavia	64	66	68	72	72	32	7	2
87	Venezuela	58	65	63	71	71	38	6	2
88	Greece	69	73	72	77	34	15	2	1
89	Israel	70	72	74	76	27	14	2	1
90	Hong Kong	66	74	71	78	28	10	2	..
91	Singapore	63	70	68	75	26	11	1	..
92	Trinidad and Tobago	63	66	67	70	47	28	3	1
93	*Iran, Islamic Rep.*	52	60	52	60	150	100	32	13
94	*Iraq*	50	57	53	61	121	71	21	6
High-income oil exporters		**46** *w*	**57** *w*	**49** *w*	**60** *w*	**153** *w*	**90** *w*	**34** *w*	**11** *w*
95	Oman	40	51	42	54	175	121	43	21
96	Libya	48	56	51	59	143	91	29	10
97	Saudi Arabia	45	55	47	58	164	101	38	13
98	Kuwait	61	69	65	74	66	29	5	1
99	United Arab Emirates	57	68	61	73	104	44	14	2
Industrial market economies		**68** *w*	**72** *w*	**74** *w*	**79** *w*	**24** *w*	**10** *w*	**1** *w*	**(.)** *w*
100	Spain	68	73	73	78	38	10	3	..
101	Ireland	68	70	73	76	25	11	1	..
102	Italy	68	73	73	79	36	12	3	1
103	New Zealand	68	71	74	77	20	13	1	..
104	Belgium	68	70	74	77	24	11	1	..
105	United Kingdom	68	71	74	77	20	10	1	..
106	Austria	66	70	73	77	28	12	2	1
107	Netherlands	71	73	76	80	14	8	1	..
108	Japan	68	74	73	79	18	7	1	..
109	France	68	72	75	79	22	9	1	..
110	Finland	66	69	73	78	17	7	1	..
111	Germany, Fed. Rep.	67	72	73	78	24	11	2	..
112	Australia	68	73	74	79	19	10	1	..
113	Denmark	71	72	75	78	19	8	1	..
114	Canada	69	73	75	79	24	9	1	..
115	Sweden	72	75	76	80	13	8	1	..
116	Norway	71	74	76	80	17	8	1	..
117	United States	67	72	74	79	25	11	1	..
118	Switzerland	69	77	75	81	18	8	1	..
East European nonmarket economies		**66** *w*	**66** *w*	**73** *w*	**74** *w*	**31** *w*	**30** *w*	**2** *w*	**1** *w*
119	Hungary	67	66	72	74	39	19	3	1
120	*Albania*	65	69	67	73	87	42	10	3
121	*Bulgaria*	66	67	73	73	31	17	2	1
122	*Czechoslovakia*	64	66	73	74	26	16	1	1
123	*German Dem. Rep.*	67	68	74	74	25	11	2	..
124	*Poland*	66	67	72	75	42	19	3	..
125	*Romania*	66	69	70	74	44	28	3	2
126	*USSR*	65	65	74	74	28	..	2	..

Table 24. Health-related indicators

		Population per:			Daily calorie supply per capita	
	Physician		Nursing person		Total	As percentage of requirement
	1965[a]	1980[a]	1965[a]	1980[a]	1982	1982
Low-income economies	12,419 _w_	5,556 _w_	6,762 _w_	4,564 _w_	2,408 _w_	105 _w_
China and India	..	1,858 _w_	..	3,279 _w_	2,503 _w_	109 _w_
Other low-income	26,097 _w_	17,990 _w_	7,296 _w_	8,697 _w_	2,118 _w_	93 _w_
Sub-Saharan Africa	38,268 _w_	27,922 _w_	4,627 _w_	3,148 _w_	2,098 _w_	91 _w_
1 Ethiopia	70,190	69,390	5,970	5,910	2,162	93
2 Bangladesh	..	7,810	..	22,570	1,922	83
3 Mali	49,010	22,130	3,200	2,380	1,731	74
4 Nepal	46,180	30,060	..	33,420	2,018	86
5 Zaire	39,050	13,940	..	1,810	2,169	98
6 Burkina	74,110	48,510	4,170	4,950	1,879	79
7 Burma	11,660	4,680	11,410	4,770	2,483	115
8 Malawi	46,900	41,460	12,670	3,830	2,242	97
9 Uganda	11,080	26,810	3,130	4,180	1,807	78
10 Burundi	54,930	45,020	7,310	..	2,206	95
11 Niger	71,440	38,790	6,210	4,650	2,456	105
12 Tanzania	21,840	17,740	2,100	3,010	2,331	101
13 Somalia	35,060	15,630	3,630	2,550	2,102	91
14 India	4,860	3,690	6,500	5,460	2,047	93
15 Rwanda	74,170	31,340	7,450	9,790	2,202	95
16 Central African Rep.	44,490	26,750	3,000	1,740	2,194	97
17 Togo	24,980	18,100	4,990	1,430	2,167	94
18 Benin	28,790	16,980	2,540	1,660	2,154	101
19 China	..	1,740	..	1,710	2,562	109
20 Guinea	54,610	17,110	4,750	2,570	1,987	86
21 Haiti	12,580	8,200	3,460	2,490	1,903	84
22 Ghana	12,040	7,160	3,710	770	1,573	68
23 Madagascar	9,900	10,220	3,620	3,670	2,577	114
24 Sierra Leone	18,400	17,520	4,890	2,040	2,049	85
25 Sri Lanka	5,750	7,170	3,210	1,340	2,393	107
26 Kenya	12,840	7,890	1,780	550	2,056	88
27 Pakistan	3,160	3,480	9,900	5,820	2,277	99
28 Sudan	23,500	8,930	3,360	1,430	2,250	96
29 Afghanistan	15,770	16,730	24,450	26,000	2,285	94
30 Bhutan	3,310	18,160	..	7,960	..	..
31 Chad	73,040	47,640	13,620	3,860	1,620	68
32 Kampuchea, Dem.	22,490	..	3,670	..	1,792	81
33 Lao PDR	26,510	..	5,320	..	1,992	90
34 Mozambique	18,700	39,140	4,720	5,610	1,844	79
35 Viet Nam	..	4,190	..	2,930	2,017	93
Middle-income economies	11,388 _w_	5,995 _w_	3,651 _w_	1,945 _w_	2,661 _w_	114 _w_
Oil exporters	20,016 _w_	8,089 _w_	5,436 _w_	2,053 _w_	2,612 _w_	113 _w_
Oil importers	4,146 _w_	3,870 _w_	2,162 _w_	1,840 _w_	2,703 _w_	114 _w_
Sub-Saharan Africa	35,517 _w_	11,929 _w_	4,745 _w_	2,650 _w_	2,370 _w_	101 _w_
Lower middle-income	18,399 _w_	7,555 _w_	4,891 _w_	2,292 _w_	2,495 _w_	109 _w_
36 Senegal	21,130	13,780	2,640	1,390	2,392	101
37 Lesotho	22,930	18,640	4,700	..	2,285	100
38 Liberia	12,450	8,550	2,300	2,940	2,267	98
39 Mauritania	36,580	14,500	..	2,100	2,228	97
40 Bolivia	3,310	..	3,990	..	2,158	90
41 Yemen, PDR	12,870	7,120	1,850	820	2,329	97
42 Yemen Arab Rep.	58,240	11,670	..	4,580	2,346	97
43 Indonesia	31,820	11,530	9,500	2,300	2,393	111
44 Zambia	11,390	7,670	5,820	1,730	2,054	89
45 Honduras	5,450	3,120	15,40	700	2,156	95
46 Egypt, Arab Rep.	2,260	970	2,030	1,500	3,210	128
47 El Salvador	4,630	3,220	1,300	910	2,060	90
48 Ivory Coast	20,690	..	1,850	..	2,652	115
49 Zimbabwe	5,190	5,900	990	940	2,119	89
50 Morocco	12,120	10,750	2,290	1,830	2,671	110
51 Papua New Guinea	12,520	13,590	620	960	2,109	79
52 Philippines	1,310	7,970	1,130	6,000	2,393	106
53 Nigeria	44,990	12,550	5,780	3,010	2,443	104
54 Cameroon	29,720	13,990	1,970	1,950	2,102	91
55 Thailand	7,230	7,100	5,020	2,400	2,296	103
56 Nicaragua	2,490	1,800	1,390	550	2,268	101
57 Costa Rica	2,040	1,460	630	450	2,635	118
58 Peru	1,620	1,390	880	970	2,114	90
59 Guatemala	3,830	8,610	8,250	1,620	2,115	97
60 Congo, People's Rep.	14,210	5,510	950	790	2,504	113
61 Turkey	2,860	1,630	6,340	1,130	3,077	122
62 Tunisia	8,040	3,690	1,150	890	2,656	111
63 Jamaica	1,930	2,830	340	630	2,489	111
64 Dominican Rep.	1,720	2,410	1,640	..	2,179	96

Note: For data comparability and coverage see the technical notes.

		Population per:				Daily calorie supply per capita	
		Physician		Nursing person		Total	As percentage of requirement
		1965[a]	1980[a]	1965[a]	1980[a]	1982	1982
65	Paraguay	1,840	1,310	1,550	1,100	2,820	122
66	Ecuador	3,020	760	2,320	570	2,072	91
67	Colombia	2,530	1,710	890	800	2,551	110
68	Angola	12,000	..	3,820	..	2,041	87
69	Cuba	1,150	720	820	370	2,997	130
70	Korea, Dem. Rep.	..	430	..	..	3,051	130
71	Lebanon	1,240	540	2,500	730	3,000	121
72	Mongolia	710	450	310	240	2,798	115
Upper middle-income		**2,507** w	**2,018** w	**2,076** w	**995** w	**2,880** w	**119** w
73	Jordan	4,670	900	1,810	1,990	2,882	117
74	Syrian Arab Rep.	4,050	2,240	11,760	1,390	3,040	123
75	Malaysia	6,220	..	1,320	940	2,688	120
76	Chile	2,080	1,930	600	450	2,669	109
77	Brazil	2,180	..	1,550	..	2,623	110
78	Korea, Rep. of	2,740	1,440	2,990	350	2,936	125
79	Argentina	640	430	610	..	3,363	127
80	Panama	2,170	980	680	420	2,498	108
81	Portugal	1,170	540	1,320	660	3,176	130
82	Mexico	2,060	..	950	..	2,976	128
83	Algeria	8,400	2,630	11,770	740	2,639	110
84	South Africa	2,140	..	530	..	2,840	116
85	Uruguay	870	540	590	190	2,754	103
86	Yugoslavia	1,190	550	850	280	3,642	143
87	Venezuela	1,270	990	560	380	2,557	104
88	Greece	710	430	790	600	3,554	142
89	Israel	410	370	300	130	3,059	119
90	Hong Kong	2,400	1,210	1,220	790	2,774	121
91	Singapore	1,910	1,150	600	320	2,954	128
92	Trinidad and Tobago	3,820	1,360	560	380	3,083	127
93	Iran, Islamic Rep.	3,770	6,090	4,170	2,520	2,855	119
94	Iraq	4,970	1,800	2,910	2,160	2,840	118
High-income oil exporters		**8,774** w	**1,360** w	**4,582** w	**836** w	**3,271** w	**..**
95	Oman	23,790	1,900	6,380	500	..	..
96	Libya	3,970	730	850	400	3,581	152
97	Saudi Arabia	9,400	1,670	6,060	1,170	3,111	129
98	Kuwait	830	570	270	180	3,423	..
99	United Arab Emirates	..	910	..	340	3,591	..
Industrial market economies		**752** w	**554** w	**302** w	**180** w	**3,400** w	**133** w
100	Spain	810	450	1,770	330	3,341	136
101	Ireland	960	780	170	120	4,054	162
102	Italy	590	340	..	..	3,520	140
103	New Zealand	820	640	980	120	3,549	134
104	Belgium	690	400	590	120	3,743	142
105	United Kingdom	860	650	200	140	3,232	128
106	Austria	550	400	470	230	3,524	134
107	Netherlands	860	540	..	130	3,563	133
108	Japan	930	780	240	240	2,891	124
109	France	810	580	300	120	3,572	142
110	Finland	1,280	530	160	100	3,098	114
111	Germany, Fed. Rep.	630	450	350	170	3,382	127
112	Australia	720	560	110	120	3,189	120
113	Denmark	740	480	190	210	4,023	150
114	Canada	770	550	130	90	3,428	129
115	Sweden	910	490	90	60	3,224	120
116	Norway	790	520	340	90	3,184	119
117	United States	670	520	120	140	3,616	137
118	Switzerland	750	410	340	160	3,451	128
East European nonmarket economies		**564** w	**345** w	**300** w	**130** w	**3,419** w	**133** w
119	Hungary	630	400	240	150	3,520	134
120	Albania	2,100	..	550	..	2,907	121
121	Bulgaria	600	410	410	190	3,711	148
122	Czechoslovakia	540	360	200	130	3,613	146
123	German Dem. Rep.	870	520	..	..	3,787	145
124	Poland	800	570	410	240	3,288	126
125	Romania	740	680	400	270	3,348	126
126	USSR	480	270	280	100	3,400	132

a. Figures in italics are for years other than those specified. See the technical notes.

Table 25. Education

| | Number enrolled in primary school as percentage of age group | | | | | | Number enrolled in secondary school as percentage of age group | | Number enrolled in higher education as percentage of population aged 20–24 | |
| | Total | | Male | | Female | | | | | |
	1965	1982[a]	1965	1982[a]	1965	1982[a]	1965	1982[a]	1965	1982[a]
Low-income economies	62 w	85 w	77 w	103 w	47 w	77 w	20 w	30 w	3 w	4 w
China and India	..	98 w	..	111 w	..	83 w	..	33 w	..	4 w
Other low-income	45 w	70 w	59 w	80 w	31 w	58 w	9 w	19 w	1 w	2 w
Sub-Saharan Africa	40 w	69 w	52 w	79 w	28 w	56 w	4 w	14 w	(.) w	1 w
1 Ethiopia	11	46	16	60	6	33	2	12	(.)	1
2 Bangladesh	49	60	67	68	31	51	13	15	1	4
3 Mali	24	27	32	35	16	20	4	9	(.)	(.)
4 Nepal	20	73	36	102	4	42	5	21	1	3
5 Zaire	70	90	95	104	45	75	5	23	(.)	1
6 Burkina	12	28	16	28	8	16	1	3	(.)	1
7 Burma	71	84	76	87	65	81	15	20	1	4
8 Malawi	44	62	55	73	32	51	2	4	(.)	(.)
9 Uganda	67	60	83	69	50	51	4	8	(.)	1
10 Burundi	26	33	36	41	15	25	1	3	(.)	1
11 Niger	11	23	15	29	7	17	1	5	..	(.)
12 Tanzania	32	98	40	101	25	95	2	3	(.)	(.)
13 Somalia	10	30	16	38	4	21	2	11	(.)	1
14 India	74	79	89	93	57	64	27	30	5	9
15 Rwanda	53	70	64	72	43	67	2	2	(.)	(.)
16 Central African Rep.	56	70	84	92	28	50	2	14	..	1
17 Togo	55	106	78	129	32	84	5	27	(.)	2
18 Benin	34	65	48	87	21	42	3	21	(.)	2
19 China	..	110	..	123	..	97	..	35	..	1
20 Guinea	31	33	44	44	19	22	5	16	(.)	3
21 Haiti	50	69	56	74	44	64	5	13	(.)	1
22 Ghana	69	76	82	85	57	66	13	34	1	1
23 Madagascar	65	100	70	..	59	..	8	14	1	3
24 Sierra Leone	29	40	37	..	21	..	5	12	(.)	1
25 Sri Lanka	93	103	98	106	86	101	35	54	2	4
26 Kenya	54	104	69	114	40	94	4	20	(.)	1
27 Pakistan	40	44	59	57	20	31	12	14	2	2
28 Sudan	29	52	37	61	21	43	4	18	1	2
29 *Afghanistan*	16	35	26	56	5	13	1	12	(.)	1
30 *Bhutan*	7	23	13	30	1	16	..	3	..	(.)
31 *Chad*	34	..	56	..	13	..	1	3	..	(.)
32 *Kampuchea, Dem.*	77	..	98	..	56	..	9	..	1	..
33 *Lao PDR*	40	97	50	105	30	89	2	18	(.)	(.)
34 *Mozambique*	37	104	48	119	26	72	3	6	(.)	(.)
35 *Viet Nam*	..	113	..	120	..	105	..	48	..	3
Middle-income economies	84 w	102 w	90 w	109 w	77 w	99 w	20 w	42 w	4 w	12 w
Oil exporters	70 w	102 w	79 w	111 w	60 w	103 w	15 w	36 w	2 w	8 w
Oil importers	95 w	103 w	99 w	107 w	91 w	96 w	24 w	48 w	6 w	15 w
Sub-Saharan Africa	44 w	96 w	54 w	99 w	34 w	81 w	5 w	17 w	(.) w	3 w
Lower middle-income	74 w	103 w	82 w	109 w	65 w	98 w	16 w	35 w	4 w	10 w
36 Senegal	40	48	52	58	29	38	7	12	1	3
37 Lesotho	94	112	74	95	114	129	4	20	(.)	2
38 Liberia	41	66	59	82	23	50	5	20	1	2
39 Mauritania	13	33	19	43	6	23	1	10	..	..
40 Bolivia	73	86	86	93	60	78	18	34	5	16
41 Yemen, PDR	23	64	35	94	10	34	11	18	..	2
42 Yemen Arab Rep.	9	59	16	99	1	17	..	7	..	1
43 Indonesia	72	120	79	124	65	116	12	33	1	4
44 Zambia	53	96	59	102	46	90	7	16	..	2
45 Honduras	80	99	81	100	79	98	10	32	1	10
46 Egypt, Arab Rep.	75	78	90	90	60	65	26	54	7	15
47 El Salvador	82	61	85	61	79	61	17	20	2	6
48 Ivory Coast	60	76	80	92	41	60	6	17	(.)	3
49 Zimbabwe	110	130	128	134	92	125	6	23	(.)	1
50 Morocco	57	80	78	98	35	62	11	28	1	6
51 Papua New Guinea	44	65	53	73	35	58	4	13	..	2
52 Philippines	113	106	115	107	111	105	41	64	19	27
53 Nigeria	32	98	39	..	24	..	5	16	(.)	3
54 Cameroon	94	107	114	117	75	97	5	19	(.)	2
55 Thailand	78	96	82	98	74	94	14	29	2	22
56 Nicaragua	69	104	68	101	69	107	14	41	2	13
57 Costa Rica	106	106	107	105	105	108	24	48	6	27
58 Peru	99	114	108	119	90	109	25	59	8	21
59 Guatemala	50	73	55	78	45	67	8	16	2	7
60 Congo, People's Rep.	114	..	134	..	94	..	10	69	1	6
61 Turkey	101	102	118	110	83	95	16	39	4	6
·62 Tunisia	91	111	116	123	65	98	16	32	2	5
63 Jamaica	109	99	112	99	106	100	51	58	3	6
64 Dominican Rep.	87	103	87	98	87	108	12	41	2	10

Note: For data comparability and coverage see the technical notes.

		Number enrolled in primary school as percentage of age group						Number enrolled in secondary school as percentage of age group		Number enrolled in higher education as percentage of population aged 20–24	
		Total		Male		Female					
		1965	1982[a]	1965	1982[a]	1965	1982[a]	1965	1982[a]	1965	1982[a]
65	Paraguay	102	103	109	107	96	99	13	36	4	7
66	Ecuador	91	114	94	116	88	112	17	56	3	35
67	Colombia	84	125	83	*129*	86	*132*	17	46	3	12
68	*Angola*	39	..	53	..	26	..	5	..	(.)	(.)
69	*Cuba*	121	109	123	112	119	105	23	72	3	19
70	*Korea, Dem. Rep.*	..	..	..	..	..	..	..	..	..	..
71	*Lebanon*	106	*118*	118	*122*	93	*114*	26	*58*	14	*28*
72	*Mongolia*	98	106	98	105	97	108	66	89	8	26
Upper middle-income		**96** *w*	**102** *w*	**100** *w*	**108** *w*	**92** *w*	**100** *w*	**26** *w*	**51** *w*	**5** *w*	**14** *w*
73	Jordan	95	*103*	105	*105*	83	*100*	38	77	2	32
74	Syrian Arab Rep.	78	101	103	111	52	90	28	51	8	16
75	Malaysia	90	92	96	93	84	91	28	49	2	5
76	Chile	124	112	125	113	122	100	34	59	6	10
77	Brazil	108	96	109	98	108	93	16	32	2	12
78	Korea, Rep. of	101	100	103	102	99	99	35	89	6	24
79	Argentina	101	119	101	120	102	119	28	59	14	25
80	Panama	102	110	104	112	99	108	34	63	7	23
81	Portugal	84	*121*	84	*120*	83	*121*	42	*50*	5	*11*
82	Mexico	92	121	94	123	90	119	17	54	4	15
83	Algeria	68	93	81	105	53	81	7	36	1	5
84	South Africa	90	..	91	..	88	..	15	..	4	..
85	Uruguay	106	*122*	106	*124*	106	*120*	44	63	8	20
86	Yugoslavia	106	101	108	100	103	100	65	82	13	21
87	Venezuela	94	*105*	93	105	94	*104*	27	40	7	22
88	Greece	110	*106*	111	*106*	109	*105*	49	*81*	10	*17*
89	Israel	95	95	95	96	95	96	48	*74*	20	*30*
90	Hong Kong	103	105	106	107	99	103	29	67	5	11
91	Singapore	105	108	110	111	100	105	45	66	10	11
92	Trinidad and Tobago	93	99	97	98	90	99	36	61	2	5
93	*Iran, Islamic Rep.*	63	97	85	112	40	81	18	40	2	4
94	*Iraq*	74	109	102	114	45	103	28	*59*	4	10
High-income oil exporters		**43** *w*	**76** *w*	**60** *w*	**86** *w*	**25** *w*	**65** *w*	**10** *w*	**44** *w*	**1** *w*	**9** *w*
95	Oman	..	74	..	90	..	57	..	22	..	..
96	Libya	78	..	111	..	44	..	14	67	1	6
97	Saudi Arabia	24	67	36	79	11	*54*	4	*32*	1	9
98	Kuwait	116	91	129	92	103	91	52	77	..	15
99	United Arab Emirates	..	132	..	133	..	131	..	67	(.)	7
Industrial market economies		**110** *w*	**102** *w*	**107** *w*	**102** *w*	**110** *w*	**102** *w*	**71** *w*	**87** *w*	**21** *w*	**37** *w*
100	Spain	115	*110*	117	*110*	114	*109*	38	88	6	*24*
101	Ireland	108	*100*	107	*100*	108	*100*	51	95	12	*22*
102	Italy	112	101	113	*101*	110	*101*	47	74	11	25
103	New Zealand	106	101	107	102	104	100	75	81	15	26
104	Belgium	109	98	110	97	108	98	75	94	15	28
105	United Kingdom	92	*102*	92	*102*	92	*103*	66	83	12	19
106	Austria	106	99	106	99	105	98	52	74	9	24
107	Netherlands	104	98	104	97	104	99	61	98	17	31
108	Japan	100	100	100	100	100	100	82	92	13	30
109	France	134	*111*	135	*112*	133	*111*	56	87	18	27
110	Finland	92	98	95	99	89	98	76	98	11	32
111	Germany, Fed. Rep.	..	100	..	100	..	100	..	50	9	30
112	Australia	99	108	99	109	99	108	62	90	16	26
113	Denmark	98	*98*	97	*98*	99	*98*	83	105	14	*28*
114	Canada	105	104	106	105	104	103	56	95	26	39
115	Sweden	95	99	94	98	96	99	62	85	13	38
116	Norway	97	*99*	97	*99*	98	*100*	64	95	11	27
117	United States	118	100	..	100	..	100	86	97	40	58
118	Switzerland	87	100	87	100	87	100	37	..	8	19
East European nonmarket economies		**103** *w*	**104** *w*	**103** *w*	**98** *w*	**103** *w*	**98** *w*	**66** *w*	**90** *w*	**26** *w*	**20** *w*
119	Hungary	101	100	102	100	100	100	..	73	13	14
120	*Albania*	92	102	97	105	87	99	33	66	8	6
121	*Bulgaria*	103	100	104	101	102	100	54	82	17	15
122	*Czechoslovakia*	99	89	100	88	97	90	29	46	14	17
123	*German Dem. Rep.*	109	94	107	93	111	96	60	88	19	30
124	*Poland*	104	100	106	101	102	100	58	75	18	18
125	*Romania*	101	100	102	101	100	99	39	71	10	11
126	*USSR*	103	*106*	103	..	103	..	72	97	30	21

a. Figures in italics are for years other than those specified. See the technical notes.

Table 26. Central government expenditure

	Defense		Education		Health		Housing; amenities; social security and welfare[a]		Economic services		Other[a]		Total expenditure (percent of GNP)		Overall surplus/deficit (percent of GNP)	
	Percentage of total expenditure															
	1972	1982b	1972	1982b	1972	1982b	1972	1982b	1972	1982b	1972	1982b	1972	1982b	1972	1982b
Low-income economies	12.4 w	18.5 w	15.2 w	5.5 w	6.1 w	3.0 w	3.8 w	5.0 w	26.3 w	25.2 w	36.2 w	42.8 w	20.8 w	16.3 w	−4.0 w	−6.1 w
China and India	..	..	..	..	..	..	..	..	..	..	..	..	..	..	..	..
Other low-income	12.8 w	16.2 w	15.2 w	10.6 w	6.1 w	4.0 w	3.8 w	6.0 w	26.3 w	26.6 w	35.8 w	36.6 w	20.8 w	7.3 w	−4.0 w	−5.4 w
Sub-Saharan Africa	12.6 w	9.5 w	15.5 w	15.6 w	6.2 w	5.3 w	3.9 w	4.2 w	25.2 w	24.5 w	36.6 w	40.9 w	21.7 w	18.0 w	−4.3 w	−5.9 w
1 Ethiopia	14.3	..	14.4	..	5.7	..	4.4	..	22.9	..	38.3	..	13.8	..	−1.4	..
2 Bangladesh	..	..	..	..	..	..	..	..	..	..	..	..	..	..	..	..
3 Mali	..	8.4	..	10.4	..	2.8	..	5.0	..	8.1	..	65.3	..	33.7	..	−9.3
4 Nepal	7.2	5.4	7.2	9.9	4.7	4.5	0.7	4.3	57.2	53.1	23.0	22.7	8.5	17.2	−1.2	−5.2
5 Zaire	..	..	..	..	..	..	..	..	..	..	..	..	38.6	35.6	−7.5	−10.6
6 Burkina	..	17.1	..	15.7	..	6.6	..	5.9	..	16.4	..	38.2	..	16.2	..	−1.6
7 Burma	..	19.0	..	11.2	..	7.0	..	9.3	..	35.2	..	18.4	..	17.1	..	0.7
8 Malawi	3.1	7.7	15.8	14.3	5.5	5.2	5.8	2.3	33.1	33.5	36.8	37.1	22.1	27.0	−6.2	−7.1
9 Uganda	23.1	19.8	15.3	14.9	5.3	5.2	7.3	6.5	12.4	11.7	36.6	42.0	21.8	5.0	−8.1	−1.5
10 Burundi	..	..	..	..	..	..	..	..	..	..	..	..	..	23.9	..	−5.6
11 Niger	..	..	..	..	..	..	..	..	..	..	..	..	..	..	..	..
12 Tanzania	11.9	11.2	17.3	12.1	7.2	5.5	2.1	2.4	39.0	37.4	22.6	31.5	19.7	32.2	−5.0	..
13 Somalia	23.3	..	5.5	..	7.2	..	1.9	..	21.6	..	40.5	..	13.5	..	0.6	..
14 India	..	20.2	..	1.9	..	2.2	..	4.3	..	24.3	..	47.1	..	15.1	..	−6.6
15 Rwanda	..	..	..	..	..	..	..	..	..	..	..	..	..	..	..	..
16 Central African Rep.	..	9.7b	..	17.6	..	5.1	..	6.3	..	19.6	..	41.7	..	21.9	..	−3.5
17 Togo	..	7.1	..	22.9	..	6.1	..	11.0	..	22.2	..	30.8	..	32.8	..	−1.8
18 Benin	..	..	..	..	..	..	..	..	..	..	..	..	..	..	..	..
19 China	..	..	..	..	..	..	..	..	..	..	..	..	..	..	..	..
20 Guinea	..	..	..	..	..	..	..	..	..	..	..	..	..	..	..	..
21 Haiti	..	..	..	..	..	..	..	..	..	..	..	..	14.5	18.5	..	−3.2
22 Ghana	8.0	6.2	20.1	18.7	6.2	5.8	4.1	6.8	15.0	19.2	46.6	43.4	19.5	10.8	−5.8	−5.5
23 Madagascar	3.6	..	..	9.1	..	4.2	..	9.9	..	40.5	..	32.7	20.8	..	−2.5	..
24 Sierra Leone	..	..	..	..	..	..	..	..	..	..	..	..	..	22.7	..	−10.7
25 Sri Lanka	..	1.4	..	7.4	..	3.3	..	12.8	..	13.1	..	62.0	..	34.4	..	−14.4
26 Kenya	6.0	13.2	21.9	19.9	7.9	7.3	3.9	0.8	30.1	26.9	30.2	31.7	21.0	29.7	−3.9	−8.4
27 Pakistan	..	33.5	..	2.2	..	1.1	..	6.8	..	31.0	..	25.3	..	16.1	..	−4.5
28 Sudan	24.1	9.5	9.3	6.1	5.4	1.3	1.4	2.3	15.8	23.5	44.1	57.3	19.2	16.9	−0.8	−4.6
29 Afghanistan	..	..	..	..	..	..	..	..	..	..	..	..	..	..	..	..
30 Bhutan	..	..	..	..	..	..	..	..	..	..	..	..	..	..	..	..
31 Chad	24.6	..	14.8	..	4.4	..	1.7	..	21.8	..	32.7	..	18.1	..	−3.2	..
32 Kampuchea, Dem.	..	..	..	..	..	..	..	..	..	..	..	..	..	..	..	..
33 Lao PDR	..	..	..	..	..	..	..	..	..	..	..	..	..	..	..	..
34 Mozambique	..	..	..	..	..	..	..	..	..	..	..	..	..	..	..	..
35 Viet Nam	..	..	..	..	..	..	..	..	..	..	..	..	..	..	..	..
Middle-income economies	15.1 w	12.1 w	13.0 w	11.6 w	6.5 w	4.7 w	20.2 w	17.7 w	24.1 w	21.4 w	21.1 w	32.5 w	19.8 w	25.8 w	−3.0 w	−6.2 w
Oil exporters	16.3 w	9.0 w	15.5 w	12.6 w	5.7 w	3.6 w	11.2 w	10.5 w	29.0 w	23.5 w	22.3 w	40.8 w	17.5 w	30.4 w	−2.8 w	−9.5 w
Oil importers	14.6 w	15.0 w	11.1 w	10.4 w	7.0 w	6.2 w	24.3 w	24.1 w	22.0 w	19.1 w	21.0 w	25.2 w	21.0 w	23.5 w	−3.2 w	−4.6 w
Sub-Saharan Africa	..	12.4 w	..	16.2 w	..	5.8 w	..	4.9 w	..	20.7 w	..	40.0 w	13.3 w	33.1 w	−2.3 w	−10.2 w
Lower middle-income	16.9 w	14.2 w	17.9 w	13.7 w	4.5 w	3.7 w	4.9 w	6.8 w	28.8 w	23.5 w	27.0 w	38.1 w	16.5 w	23.7 w	−2.4 w	−5.2 w
36 Senegal	..	9.1	..	15.8	..	3.6	..	7.0	..	20.4	..	44.1	17.4	30.9	−0.8	−9.8
37 Lesotho	..	..	19.5	..	8.0	..	6.5	..	24.5	..	41.5	..	16.6	..	−0.9	..
38 Liberia	..	13.5	..	15.3	..	7.2	..	0.7	..	29.9	..	33.4	..	39.4	..	−12.4
39 Mauritania	..	..	..	..	..	..	..	..	..	..	..	..	..	..	..	..
40 Bolivia	16.2	7.4	30.6	13.6	8.6	2.0	2.9	1.0	12.4	6.2	29.3	69.8	9.2	25.1	−1.4	−19.6
41 Yemen, PDR	..	..	..	..	..	..	..	..	..	..	..	..	..	..	..	..
42 Yemen Arab Rep.	..	35.5	..	16.4	..	4.5	..	..	..	8.8	..	34.7	..	45.7	..	−29.1
43 Indonesia	..	13.9	..	8.4	..	2.5	..	1.1	..	31.3	..	42.8	16.2	23.5	−2.6	−2.1
44 Zambia	..	..	19.0	15.2	7.4	8.4	1.3	1.8	26.7	23.9	45.7	50.7	35.4	41.9	−14.4	−20.0
45 Honduras	12.4	..	22.3	..	10.2	..	8.7	..	28.3	..	18.1	..	15.4	..	−2.7	..
46 Egypt, Arab Rep.	..	12.7	..	9.2	..	2.4	..	14.2	..	6.6	..	54.8	..	48.2	..	−14.8
47 El Salvador	6.6	11.9	21.4	16.9	10.9	7.1	7.6	5.0	14.4	21.1	39.0	38.1	12.8	19.1	−1.0	−7.5
48 Ivory Coast	..	..	..	..	..	..	..	..	..	..	..	..	..	..	..	..
49 Zimbabwe	..	17.3	..	21.9	..	6.4	..	6.7	..	23.3	..	24.4	..	39.0	..	−11.3
50 Morocco	12.3	16.5	19.2	16.2	4.8	2.8	8.4	6.9	25.6	30.5	29.7	27.0	22.4	38.7	−3.8	−12.0
51 Papua New Guinea	..	3.9	..	17.9	..	9.2	..	2.7	..	19.7	..	46.6	..	38.7	..	−6.2
52 Philippines	10.9	13.6	16.3	16.0	3.2	5.3	4.3	4.2	17.6	53.7	47.7	7.2	13.4	12.2	−2.0	−4.3
53 Nigeria	40.2	..	4.5	..	3.6	..	0.8	..	19.6	..	31.4	..	10.2	..	−0.9	..
54 Cameroon	..	5.1	..	7.5	..	2.7	..	5.1	..	10.0	..	69.6	..	21.9	..	−3.4
55 Thailand	20.2	20.6	19.9	20.7	3.7	5.0	7.0	4.9	25.7	22.2	23.5	26.5	17.2	19.9	−4.3	−5.9
56 Nicaragua	12.3	..	16.6	..	4.0	..	16.4	..	27.1	..	23.6	..	15.5	49.2	−4.0	−20.2
57 Costa Rica	2.8	2.9	28.3	22.6	3.8	32.8	26.7	14.1	21.8	14.9	16.7	12.6	18.9	21.6	−4.5	−1.0
58 Peru	14.8	..	22.7	..	6.2	..	2.9	..	30.3	..	23.1	..	17.1	18.0	−1.1	−1.2
59 Guatemala	11.0	..	19.4	..	9.5	..	10.4	..	23.8	..	25.8	..	9.9	14.8	−2.2	−4.8
60 Congo, People's Rep.	..	..	..	..	..	..	..	..	..	..	..	..	..	..	..	..
61 Turkey	15.4	15.2	18.2	16.8	3.3	2.1	3.3	8.9	41.9	25.7	17.9	31.3	21.8	23.3	−2.1	−1.8
62 Tunisia	4.9	10.6	30.5	14.2	7.4	6.7	8.8	..	23.3	..	25.1	68.5	22.5	36.9	−0.9	−5.1
63 Jamaica	..	..	..	..	..	..	..	..	..	..	..	..	..	..	..	..
64 Dominican Rep.	..	9.8	..	15.9	..	10.7	..	14.3	..	29.9	..	19.5	18.5	14.1	−0.2	−3.2

Note: For data comparability and coverage see the technical notes.

		Percentage of total expenditure												Total expenditure (percent of GNP)		Overall surplus/deficit (percent of GNP)	
		Defense		Education		Health		Housing; amenities; social security and welfare[a]		Economic services		Other[a]					
		1972	1982[b]	1972	1982[b]	1972	1982[b]	1972	1982[b]	1972	1982[b]	1972	1982[b]	1972	1982[b]	1972	1982[b]
65	Paraguay	13.8	12.5	12.1	12.0	3.5	3.7	18.3	32.2	19.6	14.0	32.7	25.7	13.1	11.8	−1.7	0.4
66	Ecuador	..	10.7	..	26.5	..	7.7	..	1.0	..	17.7	..	36.4	..	16.7	..	−4.8
67	Colombia	..	..	..	..	..	..	..	..	..	..	..	..	13.0	14.0	−2.5	−3.0
68	*Angola*	..	..	..	..	..	..	..	..	..	..	..	..	..	..	..	..
69	*Cuba*	..	..	..	..	..	..	..	..	..	..	..	..	..	..	..	..
70	*Korea, Dem. Rep.*	..	..	..	..	..	..	..	..	..	..	..	..	..	..	..	..
71	*Lebanon*	..	..	..	..	..	..	..	..	..	..	..	..	..	..	..	..
72	*Mongolia*	..	..	..	..	..	..	..	..	..	..	..	..	..	..	..	..
	Upper middle-income	14.6 *w*	11.5 *w*	11.6 *w*	10.9 *w*	7.0 *w*	5.1 *w*	24.2 *w*	21.0 *w*	22.9 *w*	20.8 *w*	19.7 *w*	30.7 *w*	21.0 *w*	26.7 *w*	−3.3 *w*	−6.6 *w*
73	Jordan	..	24.8	..	10.4	..	3.8	..	17.8	..	28.6	..	14.7	..	46.8	..	−9.5
74	Syrian Arab Rep.	37.2	*37.7*	11.3	*7.1*	1.4	*1.1*	3.6	*11.4*	39.9	*30.9*	6.7	*11.8*	28.1	*37.8*	−3.4	−6.2
75	Malaysia	18.5	15.1	23.4	15.9	6.8	4.4	4.4	10.5	14.2	29.0	32.7	25.2	27.7	41.0	−9.8	−15.9
76	Chile	6.1	11.5	14.3	14.7	8.2	6.8	39.8	45.1	15.3	9.0	16.3	12.9	42.3	37.6	−13.0	−1.1
77	Brazil	8.3	4.3	6.8	4.6	6.4	7.8	36.0	35.6	24.6	21.9	17.9	25.7	17.8	21.8	−0.4	−2.7
78	Korea, Rep. of	25.8	31.3	15.9	19.5	1.2	1.4	5.8	10.5	25.6	13.3	25.7	24.0	18.1	19.5	−3.9	−3.2
79	Argentina	8.8	11.0	8.8	6.2	2.9	1.1	23.5	29.4	14.7	17.5	41.2	34.8	16.5	21.6	−3.4	−7.5
80	Panama	..	..	..	11.0	..	13.1	..	12.2	..	13.5	..	50.2	..	39.7	..	−11.9
81	Portugal	..	..	..	..	..	..	..	..	..	..	..	..	..	..	..	..
82	Mexico	4.2	1.6	16.6	13.1	5.1	1.3	24.9	12.9	34.3	24.9	15.0	46.2	12.1	31.7	−3.1	−16.3
83	Algeria	..	..	..	..	..	..	..	..	..	..	..	..	..	..	..	..
84	South Africa	..	..	..	..	..	..	..	..	..	..	..	..	21.9	23.5	−4.2	−3.9
85	Uruguay	5.6	13.6	9.5	7.7	1.6	3.3	52.3	54.3	9.8	9.4	21.2	11.8	25.0	30.1	−2.5	−9.2
86	Yugoslavia	20.5	*50.4*	..	..	24.8	..	35.6	*7.2*	12.0	*16.6*	7.0	*25.8*	21.1	*8.5*	−0.4	*−0.1*
87	Venezuela	10.3	5.8	18.6	15.7	11.7	7.6	9.2	9.4	25.4	24.0	24.8	37.4	21.3	29.6	−0.3	−5.4
88	Greece	14.9	*10.8*	9.0	9.6	7.3	*10.5*	30.2	*33.1*	26.4	*17.1*	12.3	*18.8*	27.5	*39.2*	−1.7	*−10.7*
89	Israel	39.8	30.3	9.0	8.3	3.5	4.3	7.8	21.1	16.3	6.3	23.5	29.9	44.0	79.0	−16.3	−22.3
90	Hong Kong	..	..	..	..	..	..	..	..	..	..	..	..	..	..	..	..
91	Singapore	35.3	22.9	15.7	19.2	7.8	6.4	3.9	8.2	9.9	14.2	27.3	29.1	16.8	22.6	1.3	2.7
92	Trinidad and Tobago	..	*2.0*	..	*11.2*	..	*5.9*	..	*17.3*	..	*31.1*	..	*32.4*	..	*31.0*	..	3.3
93	*Iran, Islamic Rep.*	24.1	10.2	10.4	13.6	3.6	5.5	6.1	12.3	30.6	24.3	25.2	34.2	30.8	..	−4.6	..
94	*Iraq*	..	..	..	..	..	..	..	..	..	..	..	..	..	..	..	..
	High-income oil exporters	13.0 *w*	24.8 *w*	13.6 *w*	8.2 *w*	5.6 *w*	5.5 *w*	12.6 *w*	9.1 *w*	17.7 *w*	20.9 *w*	37.5 *w*	31.5 *w*	36.6 *w*	31.1 *w*	..	..
95	Oman	39.3	49.4	3.7	7.7	5.9	3.1	3.0	1.7	24.4	23.9	23.6	14.1	62.1	49.2	−15.3	−9.3
96	Libyan Arab Rep.	..	..	..	..	..	..	..	..	..	..	..	..	..	..	..	..
97	Saudi Arabia	..	..	..	..	..	..	..	..	..	..	..	..	..	..	..	..
98	Kuwait	8.4	10.9	15.0	8.8	5.5	5.4	14.2	14.3	16.6	27.2	40.1	33.5	34.4	40.7	17.4	7.6
99	United Arab Emirates	24.5	36.4	16.2	7.5	4.5	7.1	6.4	3.7	18.2	7.0	30.2	38.4	..	18.4	..	..
	Industrial market economies	23.3 *w*	13.9 *w*	4.3 *w*	4.8 *w*	9.9 *w*	11.7 *w*	36.8 *w*	40.4 *w*	11.6 *w*	9.7 *w*	14.1 *w*	19.5 *w*	21.8 *w*	30.1 *w*	−1.0 *w*	−4.5 *w*
100	Spain	6.5	*3.9*	8.3	*7.1*	0.9	*0.6*	49.8	*62.3*	17.5	*11.3*	17.0	*14.8*	19.8	*29.1*	−0.5	*−7.1*
101	Ireland	..	..	..	..	..	..	..	..	..	..	..	..	33.0	61.1	−5.5	−17.3
102	Italy	..	3.6	..	8.9	..	10.6	..	33.6	..	10.4	..	32.9	..	49.8	..	−11.7
103	New Zealand	..	5.3	..	12.7	..	13.5	..	30.4	..	15.4	..	22.7	..	41.5	..	−7.7
104	Belgium	6.7	..	15.5	..	1.5	..	41.0	..	18.9	..	16.4	..	39.2	57.4	−4.3	−12.5
105	United Kingdom	16.7	..	2.6	..	12.2	..	26.5	..	11.1	..	30.8	..	32.7	42.4	−2.7	−4.4
106	Austria	3.2	2.9	10.2	9.6	10.1	12.2	53.7	48.7	11.2	12.2	11.5	14.4	29.7	39.6	−0.1	−4.5
107	Netherlands	..	5.4	..	11.9	..	11.6	..	40.9	..	11.0	..	19.1	..	58.0	..	−7.7
108	Japan	..	..	..	..	..	..	..	..	..	..	..	..	12.7	18.9	..	..
109	France	..	*7.4*	..	*8.3*	..	*14.7*	..	*47.1*	..	*7.4*	..	*15.0*	32.5	*42.1*	0.7	*−2.8*
110	Finland	6.1	5.2	15.3	14.0	10.6	10.9	28.4	30.7	27.9	26.2	11.6	13.0	24.8	31.5	1.3	−2.2
111	Germany, Fed. Rep.	12.4	9.1	1.5	0.8	17.5	19.3	46.9	50.0	11.3	7.4	10.4	13.4	24.2	31.5	0.7	−1.9
112	Australia	14.1	9.8	4.4	8.2	8.2	10.0	21.0	29.8	13.1	7.8	39.2	34.4	19.5	25.9	−0.3	−0.3
113	Denmark	7.2	..	15.9	..	10.0	..	41.3	..	11.8	..	13.8	..	32.9	45.6	2.7	−8.5
114	Canada	..	7.8	..	3.2	..	5.2	..	37.2	..	18.3	..	28.4	..	26.0	..	−6.0
115	Sweden	12.5	7.3	14.8	10.1	3.6	2.1	44.3	50.4	10.6	10.5	14.3	19.6	28.0	44.9	−1.2	−9.7
116	Norway	9.7	8.5	9.9	8.6	12.3	10.6	39.9	35.7	20.2	21.3	8.0	15.3	35.0	39.7	−1.5	0.8
117	United States	32.2	23.1	3.2	2.1	8.6	10.8	35.3	36.1	10.6	9.0	10.1	18.9	19.4	25.0	−1.6	−4.1
118	Switzerland	15.1	10.4	4.2	3.1	10.0	12.8	39.5	50.2	18.4	12.4	12.8	11.0	13.3	19.3	0.9	−0.2
	East European nonmarket economies	..	..	..	..	..	..	..	..	..	..	..	..	..	..	..	..
119	Hungary	..	..	..	..	..	..	..	..	..	..	..	..	..	..	..	..
120	*Albania*	..	..	..	..	..	..	..	..	..	..	..	..	..	..	..	..
121	*Bulgaria*	..	..	..	..	..	..	..	..	..	..	..	..	..	..	..	..
122	*Czechoslovakia*	..	..	..	..	..	..	..	..	..	..	..	..	..	..	..	..
123	*German Dem. Rep.*	..	..	..	..	..	..	..	..	..	..	..	..	..	..	..	..
124	*Poland*	..	..	..	..	..	..	..	..	..	..	..	..	..	..	..	..
125	*Romania*	6.2	4.9	3.2	3.2	0.5	0.8	16.5	20.3	..	54.3	73.5	16.5	..	..	..	..
126	*USSR*	..	..	..	..	..	..	..	..	..	..	..	..	..	..	..	..

a. See the technical notes.   b. Figures in italics are for 1981, not 1982.

Table 27. Central government current revenue

	Percentage of total current revenue													
	Tax revenue												Total current revenue (percent of GNP)	
	Taxes on income, profit, and capital gain		Social security contributions		Domestic taxes on goods and services		Taxes on international trade and transactions		Other taxes[a]		Current nontax revenue			
	1972	1982[b]	1972	1982[b]	1972	1982[b]	1972	1982[b]	1972	1982[b]	1972	1982[b]	1972	1982[b]
Low-income economies	21.5 _w_	19.5 _w_	..	..	23.8 _w_	36.9 _w_	38.9 _w_	25.3 _w_	3.6 _w_	1.3 _w_	12.2 _w_	17.0 _w_	16.4 _w_	13.2 _w_
China and India	..	..	..	..	..	..	..	..	..	..	..	..	..	..
Other low-income	21.5 _w_	20.8 _w_	..	..	23.8 _w_	33.6 _w_	38.9 _w_	28.1 _w_	3.6 _w_	2.5 _w_	12.2 _w_	15.0 _w_	16.4 _w_	12.7 _w_
Sub-Saharan Africa	21.9 _w_	26.3 _w_	..	..	23.8 _w_	33.2 _w_	38.9 _w_	25.9 _w_	3.2 _w_	3.5 _w_	12.2 _w_	11.1 _w_	17.1 _w_	11.2 _w_
1 Ethiopia	23.0	..	..	..	29.8	..	30.4	..	5.6	..	11.1	..	10.5	..
2 Bangladesh	..	..	..	..	..	..	..	..	..	..	..	..	..	..
3 Mali	..	15.4	..	4.3	..	38.9	..	18.7	..	14.5	..	8.2	..	15.5
4 Nepal	4.1	7.2	..	..	26.5	38.5	36.7	31.3	19.0	7.1	13.7	15.9	5.2	8.7
5 Zaire	22.2	32.5	2.2	1.4	12.7	22.3	57.9	25.0	1.4	6.5	3.7	12.3	27.9	21.6
6 Burkina	..	15.9	..	6.5	..	17.1	..	42.4	..	6.8	..	11.3	..	14.0
7 Burma	..	3.2	..	..	..	39.5	..	19.2	..	..	..	38.2	..	16.2
8 Malawi	31.4	34.3	..	..	24.2	31.9	20.0	22.7	0.5	0.8	23.8	10.4	16.0	17.4
9 Uganda	22.1	9.7	..	..	32.8	31.5	36.3	56.0	0.3	0.1	8.5	2.7	13.7	3.1
10 Burundi	..	22.4	..	2.9	..	28.7	..	24.0	..	11.2	..	10.8	..	13.4
11 Niger	..	..	..	..	..	..	..	..	..	..	..	..	..	..
12 Tanzania	29.9	_31.1_	..	..	29.1	_50.6_	21.7	_10.2_	0.5	_0.9_	18.8	_7.2_	15.8	_19.6_
13 Somalia	10.7	..	..	..	24.7	..	45.3	..	5.2	..	14.0	..	13.7	..
14 India	..	18.7	..	..	..	39.0	..	23.5	..	0.6	..	18.2	..	13.6
15 Rwanda	..	..	..	..	..	..	..	..	..	..	..	..	..	..
16 Central African Rep.	..	_16.1_	..	6.4	..	_20.8_	..	_39.8_	..	_7.8_	..	_9.1_	..	_16.4_
17 Togo	..	33.7	..	6.4	..	15.3	..	33.0	..	−1.0	..	12.7	..	29.1
18 Benin	..	..	..	..	..	..	..	..	..	..	..	..	..	..
19 China	..	..	..	..	..	..	..	..	..	..	..	..	..	..
20 Guinea	..	..	..	..	..	..	..	..	..	..	..	..	..	..
21 Haiti	..	17.9	..	0.3	..	19.1	..	26.2	..	27.8	..	8.7	..	13.9
22 Ghana	18.2	28.7	..	..	29.1	39.2	40.8	19.0	0.4	(.)	11.4	13.0	15.1	5.4
23 Madagascar	12.7	15.5	7.0	13.7	29.1	41.7	35.3	22.2	5.3	3.3	10.5	3.6	18.8	13.6
24 Sierra Leone	..	24.1	..	..	..	23.5	..	49.5	..	1.1	..	1.8	..	11.6
25 Sri Lanka	..	17.4	..	..	..	34.1	..	39.8	..	1.9	..	6.8	..	17.2
26 Kenya	35.6	26.8	..	..	19.9	37.8	24.3	25.4	1.4	0.6	18.8	9.3	18.0	22.8
27 Pakistan	..	16.5	..	..	..	33.4	..	31.4	..	0.3	..	18.4	..	14.6
28 Sudan	11.8	15.8	..	..	30.4	14.1	40.5	49.7	1.5	0.7	15.7	19.7	18.0	11.8
29 Afghanistan	..	..	..	..	..	..	..	..	..	..	..	..	..	..
30 Bhutan	..	..	..	..	..	..	..	..	..	..	..	..	..	..
31 _Chad_	16.7	..	..	..	12.3	..	45.2	..	20.5	..	5.3	..	13.1	..
32 _Kampuchea, Dem._	..	..	..	..	..	..	..	..	..	..	..	..	..	..
33 _Lao PDR_	..	..	..	..	..	..	..	..	..	..	..	..	..	..
34 _Mozambique_	..	..	..	..	..	..	..	..	..	..	..	..	..	..
35 _Viet Nam_	..	..	..	..	..	..	..	..	..	..	..	..	..	..
Middle-income economies	25.5 _w_	28.8 _w_	..	..	26.8 _w_	23.8 _w_	13.2 _w_	11.3 _w_	17.5 _w_	13.7 _w_	17.0 _w_	22.4 _w_	17.8 _w_	22.2 _w_
Oil exporters	30.4 _w_	35.3 _w_	..	..	19.8 _w_	13.1 _w_	14.5 _w_	16.1 _w_	8.2 _w_	6.2 _w_	27.1 _w_	29.3 _w_	15.8 _w_	22.9 _w_
Oil importers	23.1 _w_	24.2 _w_	..	..	29.8 _w_	32.0 _w_	12.6 _w_	8.0 _w_	21.9 _w_	18.1 _w_	12.6 _w_	17.7 _w_	18.8 _w_	21.8 _w_
Sub-Saharan Africa	41.2 _w_	39.2 _w_	..	..	25.3 _w_	29.7 _w_	18.6 _w_	17.8 _w_	2.3 _w_	4.6 _w_	12.6 _w_	8.7 _w_	13.3 _w_	24.3 _w_
Lower middle-income	27.8 _w_	39.5 _w_			29.8 _w_	22.2 _w_	19.3 _w_	14.7 _w_	10.4 _w_	8.2 _w_	12.7 _w_	15.4 _w_	14.8 _w_	19.8 _w_
36 Senegal	17.6	22.8	..	3.5	24.5	25.8	30.9	35.0	23.8	5.3	3.2	7.4	16.8	20.1
37 Lesotho	14.3	..	..	..	2.0	..	62.9	..	9.5	..	11.3	..	11.7	..
38 Liberia	..	35.3	..	..	..	29.6	..	31.3	..	1.9	..	1.9	..	25.2
39 Mauritania	..	..	..	..	..	..	..	..	..	..	..	..	..	..
40 Bolivia	14.5	17.3	..	..	28.4	40.8	46.0	25.3	5.3	5.7	5.7	11.0	7.8	5.6
41 Yemen, PDR	..	..	..	..	..	..	..	..	..	..	..	..	..	..
42 Yemen Arab Rep.	..	11.7	..	..	..	7.3	..	49.8	..	13.5	..	17.6	..	20.4
43 Indonesia	45.5	76.9	..	..	22.7	10.4	17.5	4.7	3.6	1.4	10.6	6.7	14.4	22.2
44 Zambia	49.7	32.9	..	..	20.2	48.3	14.3	8.8	0.1	3.2	15.6	6.6	24.2	24.9
45 Honduras	19.2	_24.2_	3.0	..	33.8	25.9	28.2	42.4	2.3	_1.9_	13.5	5.7	12.6	_14.8_
46 Egypt, Arab Rep.	..	17.1	..	11.5	..	10.8	..	18.7	..	6.9	..	35.0	..	37.9
47 El Salvador	15.2	20.4	..	..	25.6	35.7	36.1	25.7	17.2	6.0	6.0	12.1	11.6	12.0
48 Ivory Coast	..	..	..	..	..	..	..	..	..	..	..	..	..	..
49 Zimbabwe	..	46.7	..	..	..	31.4	..	11.1	..	1.0	..	9.8	..	31.3
50 Morocco	16.4	15.7	5.9	5.2	45.7	32.9	13.2	20.4	6.1	7.0	12.6	18.8	18.1	26.5
51 Papua New Guinea	..	49.2	..	..	..	13.9	..	22.7	..	1.2	..	12.9	..	21.8
52 Philippines	13.8	21.8	..	..	24.3	40.9	23.0	23.9	29.7	3.1	9.3	10.4	12.4	11.2
53 Nigeria	43.0	..	..	..	26.3	..	17.5	..	0.2	..	13.0	..	11.6	..
54 Cameroon	..	39.0	..	6.2	..	14.5	..	26.0	..	3.9	..	10.3	..	18.5
55 Thailand	12.1	21.4	..	..	46.3	47.7	28.7	18.9	1.8	1.9	11.2	10.1	12.9	13.9
56 Nicaragua	9.6	10.2	14.0	11.3	37.4	40.6	24.3	15.9	8.9	9.7	5.8	12.4	12.6	27.6
57 Costa Rica	17.7	17.4	13.4	23.2	38.1	25.3	18.1	29.4	1.6	0.6	11.1	4.2	15.8	20.4
58 Peru	17.5	15.1	..	..	32.2	45.9	15.7	25.7	22.1	4.3	12.4	9.0	16.0	16.8
59 Guatemala	12.7	11.8	..	11.7	36.1	33.1	26.2	15.0	15.6	13.7	9.4	14.8	8.9	10.2
60 Congo, People's Rep.	19.3	..	..	..	40.3	..	26.5	..	6.4	..	7.4	..	18.4	..
61 Turkey	30.8	_51.7_	..	..	31.1	_19.9_	14.5	_5.3_	6.1	_6.7_	17.6	_16.4_	19.7	_22.0_
62 Tunisia	15.9	14.7	7.1	8.9	31.6	21.0	21.8	27.3	7.8	4.4	15.7	23.6	23.0	33.9
63 Jamaica	..	..	..	..	..	..	..	..	..	..	..	..	..	..
64 Dominican Rep.	17.9	21.8	3.9	4.8	19.0	32.6	40.3	23.9	1.8	2.5	17.0	14.4	17.9	10.7

Note: For data comparability and coverage see the technical notes.

	Percentage of total current revenue													
	Tax revenue												Total current revenue (percent of GNP)	
	Taxes on income, profit, and capital gain		Social security contributions		Domestic taxes on goods and services		Taxes on international trade and transactions		Other taxes[a]		Current nontax revenue			
	1972	1982[b]	1972	1982[b]	1972	1982[b]	1972	1982[b]	1972	1982[b]	1972	1982[b]	1972	1982[b]
65 Paraguay	8.8	15.4	10.4	12.9	26.2	21.4	24.8	14.6	17.0	21.9	12.8	13.9	11.5	11.7
66 Ecuador	..	55.7	..	..	..	17.0	..	21.2	..	1.0	..	5.0	..	11.9
67 Colombia	37.2	23.1	13.9	11.6	16.0	25.8	20.3	17.8	7.2	6.8	5.5	14.9	10.6	11.7
68 Angola	..	..	..	..	..	..	..	..	..	..	..	..	..	..
69 Cuba	..	..	..	..	..	..	..	..	..	..	..	..	..	..
70 Korea, Dem. Rep.	..	..	..	..	..	..	..	..	..	..	..	..	..	..
71 Lebanon	..	..	..	..	..	..	..	..	..	..	..	..	..	..
72 Mongolia	..	..	..	..	..	..	..	..	..	..	..	..	..	..
Upper middle-income	24.7 w	25.2 w	19.8 w	14.6 w	25.8 w	24.4 w	11.4 w	10.2 w	(.) w	1.0 w	18.3 w	24.6 w	19.0 w	23.3 w
73 Jordan	..	12.4	..	..	..	8.8	..	40.9	..	10.7	..	27.3	..	25.4
74 Syrian Arab Rep.	6.8	12.5	..	..	10.4	6.2	17.3	14.6	12.1	6.1	53.4	60.7	24.5	22.1
75 Malaysia	25.2	36.9	0.1	0.5	24.2	15.4	27.9	28.3	1.4	1.8	21.2	17.0	21.2	29.2
76 Chile	12.9	19.6	27.1	8.7	28.6	43.8	10.0	3.6	4.3	3.8	17.1	20.5	30.2	32.0
77 Brazil	18.3	13.3	27.4	28.8	37.6	26.2	7.0	2.6	3.7	4.6	6.0	24.6	19.0	26.1
78 Korea, Rep. of	29.2	23.9	0.8	1.1	41.7	44.5	10.7	13.3	5.2	3.6	12.3	13.6	13.2	19.1
79 Argentina	7.4	5.5	25.9	13.6	14.8	44.7	18.5	11.9	-3.7	5.7	37.0	18.5	13.1	16.5
80 Panama	..	22.5	..	21.8	..	14.8	..	10.0	..	3.5	..	27.4	..	29.7
81 Portugal	..	..	..	..	..	..	..	..	..	..	..	..	..	..
82 Mexico	36.5	30.5	19.4	14.1	32.4	29.1	13.1	33.1	-9.9	-14.9	8.4	8.1	10.4	17.0
83 Algeria	..	..	..	..	..	..	..	..	..	..	..	..	..	..
84 South Africa	54.8	53.3	1.2	1.2	21.5	26.1	4.6	4.5	5.0	3.0	12.9	11.9	21.3	22.3
85 Uruguay	4.7	5.8	30.0	26.2	24.5	43.2	6.1	10.3	22.0	5.8	12.6	8.7	22.7	21.6
86 Yugoslavia	..	..	52.3	..	24.5	68.2	19.5	30.1	..	..	3.7	1.7	20.7	8.4
87 Venezuela	54.2	62.2	6.0	4.4	6.7	4.8	6.1	8.4	1.1	1.0	25.9	19.2	21.8	29.3
88 Greece	12.2	15.6	24.5	30.0	35.5	33.9	6.7	3.3	12.0	7.1	9.2	10.1	25.4	28.5
89 Israel	36.2	40.2	..	9.2	23.0	26.4	21.6	5.2	6.8	6.6	12.4	12.4	31.8	58.8
90 Hong Kong	..	..	..	..	..	..	..	..	..	..	..	..	..	..
91 Singapore	24.4	37.6	..	..	17.6	14.5	11.1	5.5	15.5	15.0	31.4	27.4	21.6	28.5
92 Trinidad and Tobago	..	70.0	..	2.0	..	4.1	..	6.5	..	0.6	..	16.8	..	44.1
93 Iran, Islamic Rep.	7.9	7.3	2.7	7.3	6.4	4.0	14.6	8.0	4.9	4.1	63.6	69.4	26.2	..
94 Iraq	..	..	..	..	..	..	..	..	..	..	..	..	..	..
High-income oil exporters														
95 Oman	71.1	27.9	..	..	..	0.5	3.0	1.5	2.3	0.4	23.6	69.8	47.4	41.2
96 Libyan Arab Rep.	..	..	..	..	..	..	..	..	..	..	..	..	..	..
97 Saudi Arabia	..	..	..	..	..	..	..	..	..	..	..	..	..	..
98 Kuwait	68.8	2.1	..	..	19.7	0.6	1.5	2.0	0.2	0.3	9.9	95.0	55.2	57.4
99 United Arab Emirates	..	..	..	..	..	..	..	..	..	..	..	..	..	0.2
Industrial market economies	41.1 w	37.5 w	28.0 w	33.3 w	20.4 w	18.3 w	1.9 w	1.2 w	2.2 w	0.9 w	6.4 w	8.8 w	22.7 w	28.1 w
100 Spain	15.9	20.7	38.9	47.7	23.4	18.3	10.0	5.9	0.7	-0.3	11.1	7.8	20.0	25.4
101 Ireland	28.1	32.2	8.9	13.8	32.6	26.6	16.6	13.7	3.2	2.3	10.5	11.4	30.6	46.6
102 Italy	..	34.6	..	34.4	..	23.1	..	0.2	..	2.6	..	5.2	..	39.4
103 New Zealand	..	66.5	..	..	..	19.2	..	3.4	..	1.2	..	9.7	..	36.1
104 Belgium	31.3	39.5	32.4	30.0	28.9	23.9	1.0	(.)	3.3	1.8	3.1	4.7	35.0	45.7
105 United Kingdom	39.4	38.7	15.1	16.6	27.1	28.0	1.7	(.)	5.6	5.0	11.2	11.7	33.5	38.4
106 Austria	20.6	20.2	30.3	35.9	28.2	25.3	5.3	1.3	10.1	8.6	5.5	8.7	29.8	35.4
107 Netherlands	..	27.5	..	38.9	..	18.4	..	..	..	2.1	..	13.1	..	51.7
108 Japan	..	..	..	..	..	..	..	..	..	..	..	..	..	..
109 France	16.9	17.9	37.1	42.9	37.9	30.0	0.3	(.)	2.9	3.4	4.9	5.7	33.6	41.1
110 Finland	30.0	29.1	7.8	9.8	47.7	48.6	3.1	1.5	5.8	3.0	5.5	8.1	27.1	28.6
111 Germany, Fed. Rep.	19.7	17.1	46.6	55.4	28.1	21.4	0.8	(.)	0.8	0.1	4.0	6.0	25.2	29.7
112 Australia	58.3	63.6	..	..	21.9	22.0	5.2	5.2	2.1	0.2	12.5	9.1	21.4	26.2
113 Denmark	40.0	35.4	5.1	3.6	42.0	45.7	3.1	0.8	3.0	2.3	6.8	12.2	35.5	35.9
114 Canada	..	48.4	..	11.3	..	21.9	..	4.4	..	(.)	..	14.0	..	20.6
115 Sweden	27.0	15.6	21.6	33.9	34.0	29.6	1.5	0.6	4.7	4.6	11.3	15.8	32.5	38.4
116 Norway	22.5	27.4	20.5	22.5	47.9	38.1	1.6	0.6	1.0	1.1	6.6	10.4	37.0	43.8
117 United States	59.4	52.7	23.6	29.9	7.1	5.5	1.6	1.4	2.5	1.2	5.7	9.4	18.0	21.3
118 Switzerland	13.9	15.6	37.3	48.0	21.5	19.2	16.7	8.4	2.6	2.5	8.0	6.3	14.5	18.9
East European nonmarket economies	..	..	..	..	..	..	..	..	..	..	..	..	..	..
119 Hungary	..	..	..	..	..	..	..	..	..	..	..	..	..	..
120 Albania	..	..	..	..	..	..	..	..	..	..	..	..	..	..
121 Bulgaria	..	..	..	..	..	..	..	..	..	..	..	..	..	..
122 Czechoslovakia	..	..	..	..	..	..	..	..	..	..	..	..	..	..
123 German Dem. Rep.	..	..	..	..	..	..	..	..	..	..	..	..	..	..
124 Poland	..	..	..	..	..	..	..	..	..	..	..	..	..	..
125 Romania	6.3	..	7.9	16.7	..	..	..	..	..	11.6	85.8	71.7	..	..
126 USSR	..	..	..	..	..	..	..	..	..	..	..	..	..	..

a. See the technical notes.   b. Figures in italics are for 1981, not 1982.

Table 28. Income distribution

| | | Year | Percentage share of household income, by percentile groups of households[a] | | | | | |
			Lowest 20 percent	Second quintile	Third quintile	Fourth quintile	Highest 20 percent	Highest 10 percent
Low-income economies								
China and India								
Other low-income								
Sub-Saharan Africa								
1	Ethiopia		..	..	..	..	..	..
2	Bangladesh	1976–77	6.2	10.9	15.0	21.0	46.9	32.0
3	Mali		..	..	..	..	..	..
4	Nepal	1976–77	4.6	8.0	11.7	16.5	59.2	46.5
5	Zaire		..	..	..	..	..	..
6	Burkina		..	..	..	..	..	..
7	Burma		..	..	..	..	..	..
8	Malawi	1967–68	10.4	11.1	13.1	14.8	50.6	40.1
9	Uganda		..	..	..	..	..	..
10	Burundi		..	..	..	..	..	..
11	Niger		..	..	..	..	..	..
12	Tanzania	1969	5.8	10.2	13.9	19.7	50.4	35.6
13	Somalia		..	..	..	..	..	..
14	India	1975–76	7.0	9.2	13.9	20.5	49.4	33.6
15	Rwanda		..	..	..	..	..	..
16	Central African Rep.		..	..	..	..	..	..
17	Togo		..	..	..	..	..	..
18	Benin		..	..	..	..	..	..
19	China		..	..	..	..	..	..
20	Guinea		..	..	..	..	..	..
21	Haiti		..	..	..	..	..	..
22	Ghana		..	..	..	..	..	..
23	Madagascar		..	..	..	..	..	..
24	Sierra Leone	1967–69	5.6	9.5	12.8	19.6	52.5	37.8
25	Sri Lanka	1969–70	7.5	11.7	15.7	21.7	43.4	28.2
26	Kenya	1976	2.6	6.3	11.5	19.2	60.4	45.8
27	Pakistan		..	..	..	..	..	..
28	Sudan	1967–68	4.0	8.9	16.6	20.7	49.8	34.6
29	*Afghanistan*		..	..	..	..	..	..
30	*Bhutan*		..	..	..	..	..	..
31	*Chad*		..	..	..	..	..	..
32	*Kampuchea, Dem.*		..	..	..	..	..	..
33	*Lao PDR*		..	..	..	..	..	..
34	*Mozambique*		..	..	..	..	..	..
35	*Viet Nam*		..	..	..	..	..	..
Middle-income economies								
Oil exporters								
Oil importers								
Sub-Saharan Africa								
Lower middle-income								
36	Senegal		..	..	..	..	..	..
37	Lesotho		..	..	..	..	..	..
38	Liberia		..	..	..	..	..	..
39	Mauritania		..	..	..	..	..	..
40	Bolivia		..	..	..	..	..	..
41	Yemen, PDR		..	..	..	..	..	..
42	Yemen Arab Rep.		..	..	..	..	..	..
43	Indonesia	1976	6.6	7.8	12.6	23.6	49.4	34.0
44	Zambia	1976	3.4	7.4	11.2	16.9	61.1	46.3
45	Honduras		..	..	..	..	..	..
46	Egypt, Arab Rep.	1974	5.8	10.7	14.7	20.8	48.0	33.2
47	El Salvador	1976–77	5.5	10.0	14.8	22.4	47.3	29.5
48	Ivory Coast		..	..	..	..	..	..
49	Zimbabwe		..	..	..	..	..	..
50	Morocco		..	..	..	..	..	..
51	Papua New Guinea		..	..	..	..	..	..
52	Philippines	1970–71	5.2	9.0	12.8	19.0	54.0	38.5
53	Nigeria		..	..	..	..	..	..
54	Cameroon		..	..	..	..	..	..
55	Thailand	1975–76	5.6	9.6	13.9	21.1	49.8	34.1
56	Nicaragua		..	..	..	..	..	..
57	Costa Rica	1971	3.3	8.7	13.3	19.9	54.8	39.5
58	Peru	1972	1.9	5.1	11.0	21.0	61.0	42.9
59	Guatemala		..	..	..	..	..	..
60	Congo, People's Rep.		..	..	..	..	..	..
61	Turkey	1973	3.5	8.0	12.5	19.5	56.5	40.7
62	Tunisia		..	..	..	..	..	..
63	Jamaica		..	..	..	..	..	..
64	Dominican Rep.		..	..	..	..	..	..

Note: For data comparability and coverage see the technical notes.

		Percentage share of household income, by percentile groups of households[a]					
	Year	Lowest 20 percent	Second quintile	Third quintile	Fourth quintile	Highest 20 percent	Highest 10 percent
65 Paraguay		..	..	..	..	..	..
66 Ecuador		..	..	..	..	..	..
67 Colombia		..	..	..	..	..	..
68 *Angola*		..	..	..	..	..	..
69 *Cuba*		..	..	..	..	..	..
70 *Korea, Dem. Rep.*		..	..	..	..	..	..
71 *Lebanon*		..	..	..	..	..	..
72 *Mongolia*		..	..	..	..	..	..
Upper middle-income							
73 Jordan		..	..	..	..	..	..
74 Syrian Arab Rep.		..	..	..	..	..	..
75 Malaysia	1973	3.5	7.7	12.4	20.3	56.1	39.8
76 Chile	1968	4.4	9.0	13.8	21.4	51.4	34.8
77 Brazil	1972	2.0	5.0	9.4	17.0	66.6	50.6
78 Korea, Rep. of	1976	5.7	11.2	15.4	22.4	45.3	27.5
79 Argentina	1970	4.4	9.7	14.1	21.5	50.3	35.2
80 Panama	1970	2.0	5.2	11.0	20.0	61.8	44.2
81 Portugal	1973–74	5.2	10.0	14.4	21.3	49.1	33.4
82 Mexico	1977	2.9	7.0	12.0	20.4	57.7	40.6
83 Algeria		..	..	..	..	..	..
84 South Africa		..	..	..	..	..	..
85 Uruguay		..	..	..	..	..	..
86 Yugoslavia	1978	6.6	12.1	18.7	23.9	38.7	22.9
87 Venezuela	1970	3.0	7.3	12.9	22.8	54.0	35.7
88 Greece		..	..	..	..	..	..
89 Israel	1979–80	6.0	12.0	17.7	24.4	39.9	22.6
90 Hong Kong	1980	5.4	10.8	15.2	21.6	47.0	31.3
91 Singapore		..	..	..	..	..	..
92 Trinidad and Tobago	1975–76	4.2	9.1	13.9	22.8	50.0	31.8
93 *Iran, Islamic Rep.*		..	..	..	..	..	..
94 *Iraq*		..	..	..	..	..	..
High-income oil exporters							
95 Oman		..	..	..	..	..	..
96 Libya		..	..	..	..	..	..
97 Saudi Arabia		..	..	..	..	..	..
98 Kuwait		..	..	..	..	..	..
99 United Arab Emirates		..	..	..	..	..	..
Industrial market economies							
100 Spain	1980–81	6.9	12.5	17.3	23.2	40.0	24.5
101 Ireland	1973	7.2	13.1	16.6	23.7	39.4	25.1
102 Italy	1977	6.2	11.3	15.9	22.7	43.9	28.1
103 New Zealand	1981–82	5.1	10.8	16.2	23.2	44.7	28.7
104 Belgium	1978–79	7.9	13.7	18.6	23.8	36.0	21.5
105 United Kingdom	1979	7.0	11.5	17.0	24.8	39.7	23.4
106 Austria		..	..	..	..	..	..
107 Netherlands	1981	8.3	14.1	18.2	23.2	36.2	21.5
108 Japan	1979	8.7	13.2	17.5	23.1	37.5	22.4
109 France	1975	5.3	11.1	16.0	21.8	45.8	30.5
110 Finland	1981	6.3	12.1	18.4	25.5	37.6	21.7
111 Germany, Fed. Rep.	1978	7.9	12.5	17.0	23.1	39.5	24.0
112 Australia	1975–76	5.4	10.0	15.0	22.5	47.1	30.5
113 Denmark	1981	5.4	12.0	18.4	25.6	38.6	22.3
114 Canada	1981	5.3	11.8	18.0	24.9	40.0	23.8
115 Sweden	1981	7.4	13.1	16.8	21.0	41.7	28.1
116 Norway	1982	6.0	12.9	18.3	24.6	38.2	22.8
117 United States	1980	5.3	11.9	17.9	25.0	39.9	23.3
118 Switzerland	1978	6.6	13.5	18.5	23.4	38.0	23.7
East European nonmarket economies							
119 Hungary	1982	6.9	13.6	19.2	24.5	35.8	20.5
120 *Albania*		..	..	..	..	..	..
121 *Bulgaria*		..	..	..	..	..	..
122 *Czechoslovakia*		..	..	..	..	..	..
123 *German Dem. Rep.*		..	..	..	..	..	..
124 *Poland*		..	..	..	..	..	..
125 *Romania*		..	..	..	..	..	..
126 *USSR*		..	..	..	..	..	..

a. These estimates should be treated with caution. See the technical notes.

Technical notes

This eighth edition of the World Development Indicators provides economic indicators and social indicators for periods of years or for selected years in a form suitable for comparing economies and groups of economies. The statistics and measures have been carefully chosen to give an extensive picture of development. Considerable effort has been made to standardize the data; nevertheless, statistical methods, coverage, practices, and definitions differ widely. In addition, the statistical systems in many developing economies are still weak, and this affects the availability and reliability of the data. Readers are urged to take these limitations into account in interpreting the indicators, particularly when making comparisons across economies.

All growth rates shown are in constant prices and, unless otherwise noted, have been computed by using the least-squares method. The least-squares growth rate, r, is estimated by fitting a least-squares linear trend line to the logarithmic annual values of the variable in the relevant period. More specifically, the regression equation takes the form of $\log X_t = a + bt + e_t$, where this is equivalent to the logarithmic transformation of the compound growth rate equation, $X_t = X_o (1 + r)^t$. In these equations, X_t is the variable, t is time, and $a = \log X_o$ and $b = \log (1 + r)$ are the parameters to be estimated; e_t is the error term. If b^* is the least-squares estimate of b, then the annual average growth rate, r, is obtained as $[\text{antilog} (b^*)] - 1$.

Table 1. Basic indicators

The estimates of *population* for mid-1983 are primarily based on data from the UN Population Division. In many cases the data take into account the results of recent population censuses. Refugees not permanently settled in the country of asylum are generally considered to be part of the population of their country of origin. The data on *area* are from the computer tape for the FAO *Production Yearbook, 1983.*

Gross national product (GNP) measures the total domestic and foreign output claimed by residents. It comprises gross domestic product (see the note for Table 2) adjusted by net factor income from abroad. That income comprises the income residents receive from abroad for factor services (labor, investment, and interest) less similar payments made to nonresidents who contributed to the domestic economy. It is calculated without making deductions for depreciation.

The *GNP per capita* figures were calculated according to the newly revised *World Bank Atlas* method. The Bank recognizes that perfect cross-country comparability of GNP per capita estimates cannot be achieved. Beyond the classic, strictly intractable "index number problem," two obstacles stand in the way of adequate comparability. One concerns GNP numbers themselves. There are differences in the national accounting systems of countries and in the coverage and reliability of underlying statistical information between various countries. The other relates to the conversion of GNP data, expressed in different national currencies, to a common numéraire, conventionally the US dollar, to compare them across countries. The Bank's procedure for converting GNP to US dollars is essentially based on the use of a three-year average of the official exchange rate. For a few countries, however, the prevailing official exchange rate does not fully reflect the rate effectively applied to actual foreign exchange transactions and in these cases an alternative conversion factor is used.

Recognizing that these shortcomings affect the comparability of the GNP per capita estimates, the World Bank has introduced several improvements in the estimation procedures. Through its regular review of national accounts of its member countries, the World Bank systematically evaluates the GNP estimates, focusing on the coverage and concepts employed, and where appropriate makes adjustments to improve comparability. The Bank also undertakes a systematic review to assess the appropriateness of the exchange rates as conversion factors. For a very small number of countries, an alternative conversion factor is used when the official exchange rate is judged to diverge by an exceptionally large margin from the rate effectively applied to foreign transactions.

In an effort to achieve greater comparability, the UN International Comparison Project (ICP) has developed measures of GDP using purchasing-power parities rather than exchange rates. So far the project covers only a limited set of countries, and some inherent methodological issues remain unresolved. Nevertheless, the Bank will publish summary findings of the fourth phase of the ICP, relating to the comparison of GDPs in 1980 when these data become available. Readers are referred to Irving Kravis, Alan Heston, and Robert Summers, *World Product and Income: International Comparisons of Real Gross Product* (Baltimore, Md.: Johns Hopkins University Press, 1982), which reported on phase three of the project.

The estimates of 1983 GNP and 1983 per capita GNP are calculated on the basis of the 1981–83 base period. With this method, the first step is to calculate the conversion factor. This is done by taking the simple arithmetic average of the actual exchange rate for 1983 and of deflated exchange rates for 1981 and 1982. To obtain the latter, the actual exchange rate for 1981 is multiplied by the relative rate of inflation for the country and for the United States between 1981 and 1983; the actual exchange rate for 1982 is multiplied by the relative rate of inflation for the country and the United States between 1982 and 1983.

This average of the actual and the deflated exchange rates is intended to smooth the impact of fluctuations in prices and exchange rates. The second step is to convert the GNP at current market prices and in national currencies of the year 1983 by means of the conversion factor as derived above. Then the resulting GNP in 1983 US dollars is divided by the midyear population to derive the 1983 per capita GNP in current US dollars. The preliminary estimates of GNP per capita for 1983 are shown in this table.

The following formulas describe the procedure for computing the conversion factor for year t:

$$(e^{\cdot}_{t-2,t}) = \frac{1}{3} \left[e_{t-2} \left(\frac{P_t}{P_{t-2}} \middle| \frac{P^{\$}_t}{P^{\$}_{t-2}} \right) + e_{t-1} \left(\frac{P_t}{P_{t-1}} \middle| \frac{P^{\$}_t}{P^{\$}_{t-1}} \right) + e_t \right]$$

and for calculating per capita GNP in US dollars for year t:

$$(Y^{\$}_t) = Y_t / N_t \div e^{\cdot}_{t-2,t}$$

where:

Y_t = current GNP (local currency) for year t
P_t = GNP deflator for year t
e_t = annual average exchange rate (local currency/US dollars) for year t
N_t = mid-year population for year t
$P^{\$}_t$ = US GNP deflator for year t

Because of problems associated with the availability of data and the determination of exchange rates, information on GNP per capita is not shown for most East European nonmarket economies.

The *average annual rate of inflation* is the least-squares growth rate of the implicit gross domestic product (GDP) deflator, for each of the periods shown. The GDP deflator is first calculated by dividing, for each year of the period, the value of GDP in current market prices by the value of GDP in constant market prices, both in national currency. The least-squares method is then used to calculate the growth rate of the GDP deflator for the period. This measure of inflation, like any other measure of inflation, has limitations. For some purposes, however, it is used as an indicator of inflation because it is the most broadly based deflator, showing annual price movements for all goods and services produced in an economy.

Life expectancy at birth indicates the number of years a newborn infant would live if patterns of mortality prevailing for all people at the time of its birth were to stay the same throughout its life. Data are from the UN Population Division, supplemented by World Bank estimates.

The summary measures for GNP per capita and life expectancy in this table are weighted by population. The summary measures for average annual rates of inflation are weighted by the share of country GDP for the entire period in the particular income group. This method differs from previous editions' averaging procedures for this indicator; previously median values were computed.

The following table shows basic indicators for 35 countries that have a population of less than a million and are members of the United Nations, the World Bank, or both.

Tables 2 and 3. Growth and structure of production

Most of the definitions used are those of the UN *System of National Accounts.*

Gross domestic product (GDP) measures the total final output of goods and services produced by an economy—that is, by residents and nonresidents—regardless of the allocation to domestic and foreign claims. It is calculated without making deductions for depreciation. For most countries, GDP by industrial origin is measured at factor cost; for some countries without complete national accounts series at factor cost, market price series were used. GDP at factor cost is equal to GDP at market prices, less indirect taxes net of subsidies. The figures for GDP are dollar values converted from domestic currency by using the single-year official exchange rates. For a few countries where the official exchange rate does not fully reflect the rate effectively applied to actual foreign exchange transactions, an alternative conversion factor is used. Note that this procedure does not use the three-year averaging computation used for calculating GNP per capita in Table 1.

The *agricultural sector* comprises agriculture, forestry, hunting, and fishing. In developing countries with high levels of subsistence farming, much of the agricultural production is either not exchanged or not exchanged for money. This increases the difficulty of measuring the contribution of agriculture to GNP. The *industrial sector* comprises mining, *manufacturing*, construction,

Basic indicators for UN/World Bank members with a population of less than 1 million

UN/World Bank member	Population (thousands) mid-1983	Area (thousands of square kilometers)	GNP per capita[a] Dollars 1983	Average annual growth rate (percent) 1965-83[b]	Average annual rate of inflation (percent) 1965-73	1973-83[c]	Life expectancy at birth (years) 1983
Guinea-Bissau	863	36	180	..	..	6.9	38
Gambia, The	697	11	290	1.4	3.0	10.4	36
Sao Tome and Principe	103	1	310	−1.3	..	8.8	65
Cape Verde	315	4	320	..	..	11.9	64
Guyana	802	215	520	0.5	4.3	7.7	69
Solomon Islands	254	28	640	..	4.8	10.4	57
Grenada	92	(.)	840	0.9	..	..	69
St. Vincent and the Grenadines	102	(.)	860	1.8	6.1	11.6	69
Swaziland	705	17	870	2.6	4.3	14.1	55
Botswana	998	600	920	8.5	4.4	9.8	61
St. Christopher and Nevis	46	(.)	950	2.4	6.4	10.0	63
Dominica	81	1	980	−0.4	6.1	15.1	..
St. Lucia	125	1	1,060	3.1	5.5	10.5	69
Belize	153	23	1,140	3.6	..	8.1	66
Mauritius	993	2	1,160	2.8	5.6	13.1	67
Antigua and Barbuda	78	(.)	1,710	−0.4	6.6	9.1	..
Fiji	670	18	1,790	3.4	5.6	9.2	68
Seychelles	65	(.)	2,400	3.4	..	..	..
Suriname	374	163	3,420	4.5	..	10.1	65
Malta	360	(.)	3,490	8.7	2.4	5.8	73
Cyprus	655	9	3,680	5.5	1.6	10.8	75
Gabon	695	268	3,950	3.2	5.8	18.5	50
Barbados	253	(.)	4,050	3.8	6.5	12.9	72
Bahamas	222	14	4,060	−1.8	..	..	69
Iceland	237	103	10,260	2.6	15.1	45.2	77
Bahrain	391	1	10,510	..	..	..	69
Luxembourg	365	3	14,650	3.9	5.0	6.6	73
Brunei	209	6	21,140	..	..	..	..
Qatar	281	11	21,210	−7.0	..	..	72
Comoros	368	2	..	−0.6	..	..	48
Djibouti	399	22	..	−3.6	..	..	50
Equatorial Guinea	359	28	..	..	3.6	..	44
Maldives	168	(.)	..	..	..	..	47
Vanuatu	127	15	..	..	..	..	55
Western Samoa	161	3	..	..	..	..	65

Note: Countries with italicized names are those for which no GNP per capita can be calculated.
a. See the technical notes. b. Because data for the entire period are not always available, figures in italics are for periods other than specified.
c. Figures in italics are for 1973-82, not 1973-83.

and electricity, water, and gas. All other branches of economic activity are categorized as *services*.

National accounts series in domestic currency units were used to compute the indicators in these tables. The growth rates in Table 2 were calculated from constant price series; the sectoral shares of GDP in Table 3, from current price series.

For each indicator, constant US dollar values are first calculated for the time periods covered. For each of the years covered by the period, the values are then aggregated. The least-squares growth rate procedure is then applied to compute the summary measure. Note that this differs from previous editions when single-year weights were used. The average sectoral shares in Table 3 are weighted by GDP for the years in question.

Tables 4 and 5. Growth of consumption and investment; Structure of demand

GDP is defined in the note for Table 2.

Public consumption (or general government consumption) includes all current expenditure for purchases of goods and services by all levels of government. Capital expenditure on national defense and security is regarded as consumption expenditure.

Private consumption is the market value of all goods and services purchased or received as income in kind by households and nonprofit institutions. It includes imputed rent for owner-occupied dwellings.

Gross domestic investment consists of the outlays for additions to the fixed assets of the economy, plus net changes in the value of inventories.

Gross domestic savings are calculated by deducting total consumption from gross domestic product.

Exports of goods and nonfactor services represent the value of all goods and nonfactor services sold to the rest of the world; they include merchandise, freight, insurance, travel, and other nonfactor services. The value of factor services, such as investment income, interest, and labor income, is excluded.

The *resource balance* is the difference between exports of goods and nonfactor services and imports of goods and nonfactor services.

National accounts series were used to compute the indicators in these tables. The growth rates in Table 4 were calculated from constant price series; the shares of GDP in Table 5, from current price series.

The average annual growth rates for the summary measures in Table 4 are weighted by GDP. The new weighting procedure for Table 2 is used here also. The average expenditure component shares in Table 5 are weighted by GDP for the years in question.

Table 6. Agriculture and food

The basic data for *value added in agriculture* are from the World Bank's national accounts series in national currencies. The 1980 value added in current prices in national currencies is converted to US dollars by applying the single-year conversion procedure, as described in the technical notes for Tables 2 and 3. The growth rates of the constant price series in national currencies are applied to the 1980 value added in US dollars to derive the values, in 1980 US dollars, for 1970 and 1983.

Cereal imports and *food aid in cereals* are measured in grain equivalents and defined as comprising all cereals under the Standard International Trade Classification (SITC), Revision 1, Groups 041–046. The figures are not directly comparable since cereal imports are based on calendar-year and recipient-country data, whereas food aid in cereals is based on crop-year and donor-country data.

Fertilizer consumption is measured in relation to arable land, defined as comprising arable land and land under permanent crops. This includes land under temporary crops (double-cropped areas are counted once), temporary meadows for mowing or pastures, land under market and kitchen gardens, land temporarily fallow or lying idle, as well as land under permanent crops.

The figures on food and fertilizer are from the Food and Agriculture Organization (FAO). In some instances data are for 1974 because they provide the earliest available information.

The *index of food production per capita* shows the average annual quantity of food produced per capita in 1981–83 in relation to that in 1974–76. The estimates were derived from those of the FAO, which are calculated by dividing indices of the quantity of food production by indices of total population. For this index, food is defined as comprising cereals, starchy roots, sugar cane, sugar beet, pulses, edible oils, nuts, fruits, vegetables, livestock, and livestock products. Quantities of food production are measured net of animal feed, seeds for use in agriculture, and food lost in processsing and distribution.

Table 7. Industry

The percentage *distribution of value added* among manufacturing industries was calculated from data obtained from the UN Industrial Development Organization (UNIDO), with the base values expressed in 1975 dollars.

The classification of manufacturing industries is in accord with the UN International Standard Industrial Classification of All Economic Activities (ISIC). *Food and agriculture* comprise ISIC Major Groups 311, 313, and 314; *textiles and clothing 321–24*; *machinery and transport equipment 382–84*; and *chemicals 351 and 352*. *Other manufacturing* generally comprises ISIC Major Division 3, less all of the above; however, for some economies for which complete data are not available, other categories are included as well.

The basic data for *value added in manufacturing* are from the World Bank's national accounts series in national currencies. The 1975 value added in current prices in national currencies is converted to US dollars by applying the conversion procedure described in technical notes for Tables 2 and 3. The growth rates of the constant price series in national currencies are applied to the 1975 value added in US dollars to derive the values, in 1975 US dollars, for 1970 and 1981.

Table 8. Commercial energy

The data on energy generally are from UN sources. They refer to commercial forms of primary energy: petroleum and natural gas liquids, natural gas, solid fuels (coal, lignite, and so on), and primary electricity (nuclear, geothermal, and hydroelectric power)—all converted into oil equivalents. Figures on liquid fuel consumption include petroleum derivatives that have been consumed in non-energy uses. For converting primary electricity into oil equivalents, a notional thermal efficiency of 34 percent has been assumed. The use of firewood and other traditional fuels, though substantial in some developing countries, is not taken into account because reliable and comprehensive data are not available.

The summary measures of *energy production* and *consumption* are computed by aggregating the respective volumes for each of the years covered by the time periods, and then applying the least-squares growth rate procedure. For *energy consumption per capita* population weights are used to

compute summary measures for the specified years.

Energy imports refer to the dollar value of energy imports—Section 3 in the Standard International Trade Classification (SITC), Revision 1,—and are expressed as a percentage of earnings from merchandise exports. The summary measures are weighted by merchandise exports in current dollars.

Because data on energy imports do not permit a distinction between petroleum imports for fuel and for use in the petrochemical industry, these percentages may overestimate the dependence on imported energy.

Table 9. Growth of merchandise trade

The statistics on merchandise trade, Tables 9 through 13, are from UN publications and the UN trade data system, supplemented by statistics from the UN Conference on Trade and Development (UNCTAD), the International Monetary Fund (IMF), and in a few cases World Bank country documentation. Values in these tables are in current US dollars converted at official exchange rates.

Merchandise exports and imports cover, with some exceptions, all international changes in ownership of goods passing across the customs borders. Exports are valued f.o.b. (free on board), imports c.i.f. (cost, insurance, and freight), unless otherwise specified in the foregoing sources. These values are in current dollars. Note that these values do not include trade in services.

The *growth rates of merchandise exports and imports* are in real terms and calculated from quantum (volume) indices of exports and imports. Quantum indices are the ratios of the export or import value index to the corresponding unit value index. For most developing economies these indices are from the UNCTAD *Handbook of International Trade and Development Statistics* and supplementary data. For industrial economies the indices are from the UN *Yearbook of International Trade Statistics* and UN *Monthly Bulletin of Statistics*. The summary measures are calculated by aggregating the 1980 constant US dollar price series for each year, and then applying the least-squares growth rate procedure for the time periods shown. Note again that these values do not include trade in services.

The *terms of trade*, or the net barter terms of trade, measure the relative level of export prices compared to import prices. Calculated as the ratio of a country's index of export unit value to the import unit value index, this indicator shows changes over a base year in the level of export prices as a percentage of import prices. The terms-of-trade index numbers are shown for 1981 and 1983, with 1980 = 100. The unit value indices are from the same sources cited above for the growth rates of exports and imports.

Tables 10 and 11. Structure of merchandise trade

The shares in these tables are derived from trade values in current dollars reported in the UN trade data system and the UN *Yearbook of International Trade Statistics*, supplemented by other regular statistical publications of the UN and the IMF.

Merchandise exports and imports are defined in the note for Table 9.

The categorization of exports and imports follows the Standard International Trade Classification (SITC), Revision 1.

In Table 10, *fuels, minerals, and metals* are the commodities in SITC Section 3, Divisions 27 and 28 (mineral fuels, minerals, crude fertilizers, and metalliferous ores) and Division 68 (nonferrous metals). *Other primary commodities* comprise SITC Sections 0, 1, 2, and 4 (food and live animals, beverages and tobacco, inedible crude materials, oils, fats, and waxes) less Divisions 27 and 28. *Textiles and clothing* represent SITC Divisions 65 and 84 (textiles, yarns, fabrics, and clothing). *Machinery and transport equipment* are the commodities in SITC Section 7. *Other manufactures*, calculated as the residual from the total value of manufactured exports, represent SITC Sections 5 through 9 less Section 7 and Divisions 65, 68, and 84.

In Table 11, *food* commodities are those in SITC Sections 0, 1, and 4 and in Division 22 (food and live animals, beverages and tobacco, oils and fats, and oilseeds and nuts). *Fuels* are the commodities in SITC Section 3 (mineral fuels, lubricants, and related materials). *Other primary commodities* comprise SITC Section 2 (crude materials excluding fuels), less Division 22 (oilseeds and nuts), plus Division 68 (nonferrous metals). *Machinery and transport equipment* are the commodities in SITC Section 7. *Other manufactures*, calculated as the residual from the total value of manufactured imports, represent SITC Sections 5 through 9 less Section 7 and Division 68.

The summary measures in Table 10 are weighted by merchandise exports in current dollars; those in Table 11, by merchandise imports in current dollars. (See note to Table 9.)

Table 12. Origin and destination of merchandise exports

Merchandise exports are defined in the note for Table 9. Trade shares in this table are based on statistics on the value of trade in current dollars from the UN and the IMF. *Industrial market economies* also include Gibraltar, Iceland, and Luxembourg; *high-income oil exporters* also include Bahrain, Brunei, and Qatar. The summary measures are weighted by the value of merchandise exports in current dollars.

Table 13. Origin and destination of manufactured exports

The data in this table are from the UN and are among those used to compute special Table B in the UN *Yearbook of International Trade Statistics*. *Manufactured goods* are the commodities in SITC, Revision 1, Sections 5 through 9 (chemicals and related products, basic manufactures, manufactured articles, machinery and transport equipment, and other manufactured articles and goods not elsewhere classified) excluding Division 68 (nonferrous metals).

The country groups are the same as those in Table 12. The summary measures are weighted by manufactured exports in current dollars.

Table 14. Balance of payments and reserves

Values in this table are in current US dollars converted at official exchange rates.

The *current account balance* is the difference between (1) exports of goods and services plus inflows of unrequited official and private transfers and (2) imports of goods and services plus unrequited transfers to the rest of the world. The current account estimates are primarily from IMF data files.

Workers' remittances cover remittances of income by migrants who are employed or expected to be employed for more than a year in their new place of residence.

Net direct private investment is the net amount invested or reinvested by nonresidents in enterprises in which they or other nonresidents exercise significant managerial control. Including equity capital, reinvested earnings, and other capital, these net figures also take into account the value of direct investment abroad by residents of the reporting country. These estimates were compiled primarily from IMF data files.

Gross international reserves comprise holdings of monetary gold, special drawing rights (SDRs), the reserve position of IMF members in the Fund, and holdings of foreign exchange under the control of monetary authorities. The data on holdings of international reserves are from IMF data files. The gold component of these reserves is valued throughout at year-end London prices: that is, $37.37 an ounce in 1970 and $381.50 an ounce in 1983. The reserve levels for 1970 and 1983 refer to the end of the year indicated and are in current dollars at prevailing exchange rates. Due to differences in the definition of international reserves, in the valuation of gold, and in reserve management practices, the levels of reserve holdings published in national sources do not have strictly comparable significance. Reserve holdings at the end of 1983 are also expressed in terms of the number of months of imports of goods and services they could pay for, with imports at the average level for 1982 or 1983. The summary measures are weighted by imports of goods and services in current dollars.

Table 15. Flow of public and publicly guaranteed external capital

The data on debt in this and successive tables are from the World Bank Debtor Reporting System. That system is concerned solely with developing economies and does not collect data on external debt for other groups of borrowers. Nor are comprehensive comparable data available from other sources. The dollar figures on debt shown in Tables 15 through 17 are in US dollars converted at official exchange rates.

Data on the *gross inflow* and *repayment of principal* (amortization) are for public and publicly guaranteed medium- and long-term loans. The *net inflow* is the gross inflow less the repayment of principal.

Public loans are external obligations of public debtors, including the national government, its agencies, and autonomous public bodies. Publicly guaranteed loans are external obligations of private debtors that are guaranteed for repayment by a public entity.

The data in this table and in successive tables on debt do not cover nonguaranteed private debt because comprehensive data are not available at the country level, even though for some borrowers such debt is substantial. Some countries do not report debt contracted for purchases of military equipment and it is therefore excluded from their data.

Table 16. External public debt and debt service ratio

External public debt outstanding and disbursed represents the amount of public and publicly guaranteed loans that has been disbursed, net of repayments of principal and write-offs at year-end. For estimating external public debt as a percentage of GNP, the debt figures were converted into US dollars from currencies of repayment at end-of-year official exchange rates. However, GNP was converted from national currencies to US dollars by applying the conversion procedure described in the technical notes for Tables 2 and 3. The summary measures are weighted by GNP in current dollars.

Interest payments are those on the disbursed and outstanding public and publicly guaranteed debt in foreign currencies, goods, or services; they include commitment charges on undisbursed debt if information on those charges was available.

Debt service is the sum of interest payments and repayments of principal on external public and publicly guaranteed debt. The ratio of debt service to exports of goods and services is one of several conventional measures used to assess the ability to service debt. The average ratios of debt service to GNP for the economy groups are weighted by GNP in current dollars. (See above for the GNP conversion.) The average ratios of debt service to exports of goods and services are weighted by exports of goods and services in current dollars.

Table 17. Terms of public borrowing

Commitments refer to the public and publicly guaranteed loans for which contracts were signed in the year specified. They are reported in currencies of repayment and converted into US dollars at average annual official exchange rates.

Figures for *interest rates*, *maturities*, and *grace periods* are averages weighted by the amounts of loans. Interest is the major charge levied on a loan and is usually computed on the amount of principal drawn and outstanding. The maturity of a loan is the interval between the agreement date, when a loan agreement is signed or bonds are issued, and the date of final repayment of principal. The grace period is the interval between the agreement date and the date of the first repayment of principal.

The summary measures in this table are weighted by the amounts of loans.

Table 18. Official development assistance from OECD and OPEC members

Official development assistance (ODA) consists of net disbursements of loans and grants made at concessional financial terms by official agencies of the members of the Development Assistance Committee (DAC) of the Organisation for Economic Co-operation and Development (OECD) and members of the Organization of Petroleum Exporting Countries (OPEC) with the objective of promoting economic development and welfare. It includes the value of technical cooperation and assistance. All data shown were supplied by the OECD, and all US dollar values converted at official exchange rates.

Amounts shown are net disbursements to developing countries and multilateral institutions. The disbursements to multilateral institutions are now reported for all DAC members on the basis of the date of issue of notes; some DAC members previously reported on the basis of the date of encashment. *Net bilateral flows to low-income countries* exclude unallocated bilateral flows and all disbursements to multilateral institutions.

The nominal values shown in the summary for ODA from OECD countries were converted into 1980 prices using the dollar GNP deflator. This deflator is based on price increases in OECD countries (excluding Greece, Portugal, and Turkey) measured in dollars. It takes into account the parity changes between the dollar and national currencies. For example, when the dollar appreciates, price changes measured in national currencies have to be adjusted downward by the amount of the appreciation to obtain price changes in dollars.

The table, in addition to showing totals for OPEC, shows totals for the Organization of Arab Petroleum Exporting Countries (OAPEC). The donor members of OAPEC are Algeria, Iraq, Kuwait, Libya, Qatar, Saudi Arabia, and United Arab Emirates. ODA data for OPEC and OAPEC were also obtained from the OECD.

Table 19. Population growth, past and projected, and population momentum

The *growth rates of population* are period averages calculated from midyear populations. The summary measures are weighted by population in 1970.

The estimates of *population* for mid-1983 are primarily based on data from the UN Population Division and from World Bank sources. In many cases the data take into account the results of recent population censuses. Note again that refugees not permanently settled in the country of asylum are generally considered to be part of the population of their country of origin.

The *projections of population* for 1990 and 2000, and to the year in which it will eventually become stationary, were made for each economy separately. Starting with information on total population by age and sex, fertility rates, mortality rates, and international migration in the base year 1980, these parameters were projected at five-year intervals on the basis of generalized assumptions until the population became stationary. The base-year estimates are from updated computer printouts of the UN *World Population Prospects as Assessed in 1982*, from the most recent issues of the UN *Population and Vital Statistics Report* and *International Migration: Levels and Trends*, and from the World Bank, the Population Council, the US Bureau of the Census, *Demographic Statistics* (Eurostat 1984), and national censuses.

The *net reproduction rate* (NRR) indicates the number of daughters a newborn girl will bear during her lifetime, assuming fixed age-specific fertility rates and a fixed set of mortality rates. The NRR thus measures the extent to which a cohort of newborn girls will reproduce themselves under given schedules of fertility and mortality. An NRR of 1 indicates that fertility is at replacement level: at this rate childbearing women, on the average, bear only enough daughters to replace themselves in the population.

A *stationary population* is one in which age- and sex-specific mortality rates have not changed over a long period, while age-specific fertilty rates have simultaneously remained at replacement level (NRR=1). In such a population, the birth rate is constant and equal to the death rate, the age structure also is constant, and the growth rate is zero.

Population Momentum is the tendency for population growth to continue beyond the time that replacement-level fertility has been achieved; that is, even after NRR has reached unity. The momentum of a population in the year *t* is measured as a ratio of the ultimate stationary population to the population in the year *t*, given the assumption that fertility remains at replacement level from the year *t* onward. In India, for example, in 1985 the population is 765 million, the ultimate stationary population assuming that NRR = 1 from 1985 onwards, is 1,349 million, and the population momentum is 1.76.

A population tends to grow even after fertility has declined to replacement level because past high growth rates will have produced an age distribution with a relatively high proportion of women in, or still to enter, the reproductive ages. Consequently, the birth rate will remain higher than the death rate and the growth rate will remain positive for several decades. A population takes 50–75 years, depending on the initial conditions, before its age distribution fully adjusts to the changed fertility rates.

To make the projections, assumptions about future mortality rates were made in terms of female life expectancy at birth (that is, the number of years a newborn girl would live if subject to the mortality risks prevailing for the cross-section of population at the time of her birth). Economies were first divided according to whether their primary-school enrollment ratio for females was above or below 70 percent. In each group a set of annual increments in female life expectancy was assumed, depending on the female life expectancy in 1980–85. For a given life expectancy at birth, the annual increments during the projection period are larger in economies having a higher primary-school enrollment ratio and a life expectancy of up to 62.5 years. At higher life expectancies, the increments are the same.

To project fertility rates, the first step was to estimate the year in which fertility would reach replacement level. These estimates are speculative and are based on information on trends in crude birth rates (defined in the note for Table 20), total fertility rates (also defined in the note for Table 20), female life expectancy at birth, and the performance of family planning programs. For most economies it was assumed that the total fertility rate would decline between 1980 and the year of reaching a net reproduction rate of 1, after which fertility would remain at replacement level. For most countries in sub-Saharan Africa, and for a few countries in Asia and the Middle East, total fertility rates were assumed to remain constant for some time and then to decline until replacement level was reached; for a few they were assumed to increase until 1990–95 and then to decline.

In some countries, fertility is already below replacement level or will decrease to below replacement level during the next 5 to 10 years. Because a population will not remain stationary if its net reproduction rate is other than 1, it was assumed that fertility rates in these economies would regain replacement levels in order to make estimates of the stationary population for them. For the sake of consistency with the other estimates, the total fertility rates in the industrial economies were assumed to remain constant until 1985–90 and then to increase to replacement level by 2010.

International migration rates are based on past and present trends in migration flow. The estimates of future net migration are speculative. For most economies the net migration rates were assumed to be zero by 2000, but for a few they were assumed to be zero by 2025.

The estimates of the hypothetical size of the stationary population and the assumed year of reaching replacement-level fertility are speculative. *They should not be regarded as predictions.* They are included to provide a summary indication of the long-run implications of recent fertility and mortality trends on the basis of highly stylized assumptions. A fuller description of the methods and assumptions used to calculate the estimates is available from the Bank publication: *World Population Projections 1984—Short- and Long-term Estimates by Age and Sex with Related Demographic Statistics.*

Table 20. Demographic and fertility-related indicators

The *crude birth and death rates* indicate the number of live births and deaths per thousand population in a year. They are from the same sources mentioned in the note for Table 19. Percentage changes are computed from unrounded data.

The *total fertility rate* represents the number of children that would be born per woman, if she were to live to the end of her childbearing years and bear children at each age in accord with prevailing age-specific fertility rates. The rates given are from the same sources mentioned in the note for Table 19.

The *percentage of married women of childbearing age using contraception* refers to women who are practicing, or whose husbands are practicing, any form of contraception. These generally comprise male and female sterilization, intrauterine device (IUD), condom, injectable and oral contraceptives, spermicides, diaphragm, rhythm, withdrawal, and abstinence. Women of childbearing age are generally women aged 15–49, although for some countries contraceptive usage is measured for other age groups.

Data are mainly derived from the World Fertility Survey, the Contraceptive Prevalence Survey, the World Bank, and the UN report: *Recent Levels and Trends of Contraceptive Use as Assessed in 1983.* For a few countries for which no survey data are available, program statistics are used; these include India, Bangladesh, Indonesia, and several African countries. Program statistics may understate contraceptive prevalence because they do not measure use of methods such as rhythm, withdrawal, or abstinence, or of contraceptives not obtained through the official family planning program. The data refer to a variety of years, generally not more than two years distant from those specified.

All summary measures are weighted by population.

Table 21. Labor force

The *population of working age* refers to the population aged 15–64. The estimates are based on the population estimates of the World Bank for 1983 and previous years. The summary measures are weighted by population.

The *labor force* comprises economically active persons aged 10 years and over, including the armed forces and the unemployed, but excluding housewives, students, and other economically inactive groups. *Agriculture, industry, and services* are defined in the same manner as in Table 2. The estimates of the sectoral distribution of the labor force are from International Labour Organisation (ILO), *Labour Force Estimates and Projections, 1950–2000,* and from the World Bank. The summary measures are weighted by labor force.

The *labor force growth rates* were derived from the Bank's population projections and from ILO data on age-specific activity rates in the source cited above. The summary measures for 1965–73 and 1973–83 are weighted by labor force in 1973; those for 1980–2000, by the labor force in 1980.

The application of ILO activity rates to the Bank's latest population estimates may be inappropriate for some economies in which there have been important changes in unemployment and underemployment, in international and internal migration, or in both. The labor force projections for 1980–2000 should thus be treated with caution.

Table 22. Urbanization

The data on *urban population as a percentage of total population* are from the UN *Estimates and Projections of Urban, Rural and City Populations 1950-2025: The*

1982 Assessment, 1985, supplemented by data from the World Bank, the US Bureau of Census, and from various issues of the UN *Demographic Yearbook.*

The *growth rates of urban population* were calculated from the World Bank's population estimates; the estimates of urban population shares were calculated from the sources cited above. Data on urban agglomeration are from the UN *Patterns of Urban and Rural Population Growth, 1980.*

Because the estimates in this table are based on different national definitions of what is "urban," cross-country comparisons should be interpreted with caution.

The summary measures for urban population as a percentage of total population are weighted by population; the other summary measures in this table are weighted by urban population.

Table 23. Indicators related to life expectancy

Life expectancy at birth is defined in the note for Table 1.

The *infant mortality rate* is the number of infants who die before reaching one year of age, per thousand live births in a given year. The data are from a variety of sources—including issues of UN *Demographic Yearbook*, and *Population and Vital Statistics Report*, and UN "Infant Mortality: World Estimates and Projections, 1950–2025" *Population Bulletin of the United Nations* (1983), and from the World Bank.

The *child death rate* is the number of deaths of children aged 1–4 per thousand children in the same age group in a given year. Estimates were based on the data on infant mortality and on the relation between the infant mortality rate and the child death rate implicit in the appropriate Coale-Demeny Model life tables; see Ansley J. Coale and Paul Demeny, *Regional Model Life Tables and Stable Populations* (Princeton, N.J.: Princeton University Press, 1966).

The summary measures in this table are weighted by population.

Table 24. Health-related indicators

The estimates of *population per physician and nursing person* were derived from World Health Organization (WHO) data, some of which have been revised to reflect new information. They also take into account revised estimates of population.

Nursing persons include graduate, practical, assistant, and auxiliary nurses; the inclusion of auxiliary nurses enables a better estimation of the availability of nursing care. Because definitions of nursing personnel vary—and because the data shown are for a variety of years, generally not more than two years distant from those specified— the data for these two indicators are not strictly comparable across countries.

The *daily calorie supply per capita* was calculated by dividing the calorie equivalent of the food supplies in an economy by the population. Food supplies comprise domestic production, imports less exports, and changes in stocks; they exclude animal feed, seeds for use in agriculture, and food lost in processing and distribution. The *daily calorie requirement per capita* refers to the calories needed to sustain a person at normal levels of activity and health, taking into account age and sex distributions, average body weights, and environmental temperatures. Both sets of estimates are from the Food and Agriculture Organization (FAO).

The summary measures in this table are weighted by population.

Table 25. Education

The data in this table refer to a variety of years, generally not more than two years distant from those specified, and are mostly from Unesco.

The data on *number enrolled in primary school* refer to estimates of total, male, and female enrollment of students of all ages in primary school; they are expressed as percentages of the total, male, or female populations of the primary school age to give gross primary enrollment ratios. While many countries consider primary-school age to be 6–11 years, others do not. The differences in country practices in the ages and duration of schooling are reflected in the ratios given. For some countries with universal primary education, the gross enrollment ratios may exceed 100 percent because some pupils are below or above the country's standard primary-school age.

The data on *number enrolled in secondary school* were calculated in the same manner, with secondary-school age considered to be 12–17 years.

The data on *number enrolled in higher education* are from Unesco.

The summary measures in this table are weighted by population.

Table 26. Central government expenditure

The data on central government finance in Tables 26 and 27 are from the IMF *Government Finance Statistics Yearbook*, IMF data files, and World Bank country documentation. The accounts of each country are reported using the system of common definitions and classifications found in the IMF *Draft Manual on Government Finance Statistics*. Due to differences in coverage of available data, the individual components of central government expenditure and current revenue shown in these tables may not be strictly comparable across all economies. The shares of total expenditure and revenue by category are calculated from national currencies.

The inadequate statistical coverage of state, provincial, and local governments has dictated the use of central government data only. This may seriously understate or distort the statistical portrayal of the allocation of resources for various purposes, especially in large countries where lower levels of government have considerable autonomy and are responsible for many social services.

It must be emphasized that the data presented, especially those for education and health, are not comparable for a number of reasons. In many economies private health and education services are substantial; in others public services represent the major component of total expenditure but may be financed by lower levels of government. Great caution should therefore be exercised in using the data for cross-country comparisons.

Central government expenditure comprises the expenditure by all government offices, departments, establishments, and other bodies that are agencies or instruments of the central authority of a country. It includes both current and capital (development) expenditure.

Defense comprises all expenditure, whether by defense or other departments, for the maintenance of military forces, including the purchase of military supplies and equipment, construction, recruiting, and training. Also falling into this category is expenditure for strengthening the public services to meet wartime emergencies, for training civil defense personnel, and for foreign military aid and contributions to military organizations and alliances.

Education comprises expenditure for the provision, management, inspection, and support of pre-primary, primary, and secondary schools; of universities and colleges; and of vocational, technical, and other training institutions by central governments. Also included is expenditure on the general administration and regulation of the education system; on research into its objectives, organization, administration, and methods; and on such subsidiary services as transport, school meals, and medical and dental services in schools.

Health covers public expenditure on hospitals, medical and dental centers, and clinics with a major medical component; on national health and medical insurance schemes; and on family planning and preventive care. Also included is expenditure on the general administration and regulation of relevant government departments, hospitals and clinics, health and sanitation, and national health and medical insurance schemes.

Housing and community amenities and social security and welfare covers (1) public expenditure on housing, such as income-related schemes; on provision and support of housing and slum clearance activities; on community development; and on sanitary services; and (2) public expenditure for compensation to the sick and temporarily disabled for loss of income; payments to the elderly, the permanently disabled, and the unemployed; and for family, maternity, and child allowances. The second category also includes the cost of welfare services such as care of the aged, the disabled, and children, as well as the cost of general administration, regulation, and research associated with social security and welfare services.

Economic services comprises public expenditure associated with the regulation, support, and more efficient operation of business, economic development, redress of regional imbalances, and creation of employment opportunities. Research, trade promotion, geological surveys, and inspection and regulation of particular industry groups are among the activities included. The five major categories of economic services are fuel and energy, agriculture, industry, transportation and communication, and other economic affairs and services.

Other covers expenditure for the general administration of government not included elsewhere; for a few economies it also includes amounts that could not be allocated to other components.

Overall surplus/deficit is defined as current and capital revenue and grants received less total expenditure less lending minus repayments.

The summary measures for the components of central government expenditure are weighted by central government expenditure in current dollars; those for total expenditure as a percentage of GNP

and for overall surplus/deficit as a percentage of GNP are weighted by GNP in current dollars.

Table 27. Central government current revenue

Information on data sources and comparability is given in the note for Table 26. Current revenue by source is expressed as a percentage of total current revenue, which is the sum of tax revenue and current nontax revenue, and is calculated from national currencies.

Tax revenue is defined as all government revenue from compulsory, unrequited, nonrepayable receipts for public purposes, including interest collected on tax arrears and penalties collected on nonpayment or late payment of taxes. Tax revenue is shown net of refunds and other corrective transactions. *Taxes on income, profit, and capital gain* are taxes levied on the actual or presumptive net income of individuals, on the profits of enterprises, and on capital gains, whether realized on land sales, securities, or other assets. *Social Security contributions* include employers' and employees' social security contributions as well as those of self-employed and unemployed persons. *Domestic taxes on goods and services* include general sales, turnover, or value added taxes, selective excises on goods, selective taxes on services, taxes on the use of goods or property, and profits of fiscal monopolies. *Taxes on international trade and transactions* include import duties, export duties, profits of export or import marketing boards, transfers to government, exchange profits, and exchange taxes. *Other taxes* include employers' payroll or manpower taxes, taxes on property, and other taxes not allocable to other categories.

Current nontax revenue comprises all government revenue that is not a compulsory nonrepayable payment for public purposes. Proceeds of grants and borrowing, funds arising from the repayment of previous lending by governments, incurrence of liabilities and proceeds from the sale of capital assets are not included.

The summary measures for the components of current revenue are weighted by total current revenue in current dollars; those for current revenue as a percentage of GNP are weighted by GNP in current dollars.

Table 28. Income distribution

The data in this table refer to the distribution of total disposable household income accruing to percentile groups of households ranked by total household income. The distributions cover rural and urban areas and refer to different years between 1967 and 1982.

The data for income distribution are drawn from a variety of sources including Economic and Social Commission for Asia and the Pacific (ESCAP), the Economic Commission for Latin America and the Caribbean (ECLAC), International Labour Organisation (ILO), the Organisation for Economic Co-operation and Development (OECD), the World Bank, national sources, the UN *Survey of National Sources of Income Distribution Statistics*, 1981, and more recent UN data.

Because the collection of data on income distribution has not been systematically organized and integrated with the official statistical system in many countries, estimates were typically derived from surveys designed for other purposes, most often consumer expenditure surveys, which also collect some information on income. These surveys use a variety of income concepts and sample designs. Furthermore, the coverage of many of these surveys is too limited to provide reliable nationwide estimates of income distribution. Thus, although the estimates shown are considered the best available, they do not avoid all these problems and should be interpreted with extreme caution.

The scope of the indicator is similarly limited. Because households vary in size, a distribution in which households are ranked according to per capita household income, rather than according to total household income is superior for many purposes. The distinction is important because households with low per capita incomes frequently are large households, whose total income may be relatively high. And conversely, many households with low household incomes may be small households with relatively high per capita incomes. Information on the distribution of per capita household income exists, however, for only a few countries. The World Bank's Living Standards Measurement Study is developing procedures and applications that can assist countries to improve their collection and analysis of data on income distribution.

Bibliography of data sources

National accounts and economic indicators

International Monetary Fund. 1974. *Draft Manual on Government Finance Statistics.* Washington, D.C.

———. 1983. *Government Finance Statistics Yearbook.* Vol. VII. Washington, D.C.

Sawyer, Malcolm. 1976. *Income Distribution in OECD Countries.* OECD Occasional Studies. Paris.

UN Department of International Economic and Social Affairs. Various years. *Statistical Yearbook.* New York.

———. 1968. *A System of National Accounts.* New York.

———. 1981. *A Survey of National Sources of Income Distribution Statistics.* Statistical Papers, Series M, no. 72. New York.

FAO, IMF, and UNIDO data files.

National sources. World Bank country documentation. World Bank data files.

Energy

UN Department of International Economic and Social Affairs. Various years. *World Energy Supplies.* Statistical Papers, Series J. New York.

World Bank data files.

Trade

International Monetary Fund. Various years. *Direction of Trade.* Washington, D.C.

———. Various years. *International Financial Statistics.* Washington, D.C.

UN Conference on Trade and Development. Various years. *Handbook of International Trade and Development Statistics.* Geneva.

UN Department of International Economic and Social Affairs. Various years. *Monthly Bulletin of Statistics.* New York.

———. Various years. *Yearbook of International Trade Statistics.* New York.

United Nations trade tapes. World Bank country documentation.

Balance of payments, capital flows, and debt

International Monetary Fund. 1977. *Balance of Payments Manual,* 4th ed. Washington, D.C.

The Organisation for Economic Co-operation and Development. Various years. *Development Co-operation.* Paris.

IMF balance of payments data files. World Bank Debtor Reporting System.

Labor force

International Labour Organisation. 1977. *Labour Force Estimates and Projections, 1950–2000,* 2nd ed. Geneva.

International Labour Organisation tapes. World Bank data files.

Population

Statistical Office of the European Communities (Eurostat). 1984. *Demographic Statistics.* Luxembourg.

UN Department of International Economic and Social Affairs. Various years. *Demographic Yearbook.* New York.

———. Various years. *Population and Vital Statistics Report.* New York.

———. 1980. *Patterns of Urban and Rural Population Growth.* New York.

———. 1982. "Infant Mortality: World Estimates and Projections, 1950–2025." *Population Bulletin of the United Nations,* no. 14. New York.

———. Updated printout. *World Population Prospects as Assessed in 1982.* New York.

———. 1983. *World Population Trends and Policies: 1983 Monitoring Report.* New York.

———.1984. *Recent Levels and Trends of Contraceptive Use as Assessed in 1983.* New York.

———.1985. *Estimates and Projection of Urban, Rural and City Populations, 1950-2025; The 1982 Assessment.* New York.

US Bureau of the Census. 1983. *World Population: 1983.* Washington, D.C.

World Bank data files.

Social indicators

Food and Agriculture Organization. October 1980; October 1984. *Food Aid Bulletin.* Rome.

———. 1983. *Fertilizer Yearbook.* Rome.

———. 1983. *Production Yearbook.* "Standard" Computer Tape.

———. 1983. *Trade Yearbook.* "Standard" Computer Tape.

UN Department of International Economic and Social Affairs. Various years. *Demographic Yearbook.* New York.

———. Various years. *Statistical Yearbook.* New York.

UN Educational Scientific and Cultural Organization. Various years. *Statistical Yearbook.* Paris.

World Health Organization. Various years. *World Health Statistics Annual.* Geneva.

———. 1976. *World Health Statistics Report,* vol. 29, no. 10. Geneva.

World Bank data files.